Travellers' Health

How to stay healthy abroad

Editor's Health Warning

We've done our best to make sure that the information in this book is accurate and up-to-date at time of going to press. You can find updates and further information on our web-site at ✆ www.travellershealth.com

Advice from books, and websites, has limitations—and can't take account of your own individual needs and circumstances. Advice offered here is not a substitute for skilled medical care when such care is available.

Travellers' Health

How to stay healthy abroad

FIFTH EDITION

Devised and edited by

Dr Richard Dawood

OXFORD
UNIVERSITY PRESS

OXFORD
UNIVERSITY PRESS

Great Clarendon Street, Oxford OX2 6DP

Oxford University Press is a department of the University of Oxford.
It furthers the University's objective of excellence in research, scholarship,
and education by publishing worldwide. Oxford is a registered trade mark of
Oxford University Press in the UK and in certain other countries

© Oxford University Press 2012

The moral rights of the authors have been asserted

Fourth Edition published 2002
Fifth Edition published 2012

Impression: 1

British Library Cataloguing in Publication Data
Data available

ISBN 978–0–19–921416–7

Printed in Great Britain by
Clays Ltd, St Ives plc

Oxford University Press makes no representation, express or implied, that the
drug dosages in this book are correct. Readers must therefore always check
the product information and clinical procedures with the most up-to-date
published product information and data sheets provided by the manufacturers
and the most recent codes of conduct and safety regulations. The authors and
the publishers do not accept responsibility or legal liability for any errors in the
text or for the misuse or misapplication of material in this work. Except where
otherwise stated, drug dosages and recommendations are for the non-pregnant
adult who is not breast-feeding.

Links to third party websites are provided by Oxford in good faith and for
information only. Oxford disclaims any responsibility for the materials contained
in any third party website referenced in this work.

Foreword

Travellers' Health remains the bible for all who want to understand the basic physical problems of travelling. This is important, in-depth information which covers every contingency and which, along with toilet paper, is one of the true indispensables in any adventurous traveller's bag.

Michael Palin
London
May 2012

Preface to the fifth edition

In 1986, the first edition of *Travellers' Health* threw down a gauntlet: 'Travellers' health has been a neglected corner of medicine for too long,' we proclaimed. For the first time, this book brought together a redoubtable team of experts in a wide range of medical fields, from entomology, virology, and parasitology to gynaecology, aviation, and military medicine, and defined the parameters for the thriving, modern discipline that Travel Medicine has since become.

The growth of interest in Travel Medicine has been more than matched by massive growth in international travel—from 340 million international arrivals in 1986 to over 980 million in 2011, with particular expansion in travel to developing countries. The world's most remote and inhospitable places are accessible as never before, and last-minute travel is now commonplace. The Internet has supplanted the traditional roles of the travel agent, tour operator, airport ground staff, and perhaps even the doctor or nurse: the riskiest of trips can now be undertaken with minimal opportunity for human interaction or outside advice.

Globally, disease patterns have changed somewhat, but health issues remain a huge challenge. Familiar diseases like TB have undergone resurgence and become harder to treat. More obscure ones, like chikungunya, a virus spread by mosquitoes, has changed its geography, appearing in India and the Indian Ocean where it caused a widespread outbreak in 2006. Cholera created havoc in Zimbabwe in 2009, and then in Haiti in 2010; collapse of the public health infrastructure was to blame in both instances, albeit with different causes. Meningitis outbreaks continue in the Sahel, Africa's 'meningitis belt.' Developed countries are by no means immune: an outbreak of animal rabies occurred in New York's Central Park during 2010, and norovirus—the vomiting bug—remains a continuing threat to the cruise ship industry. In southern Europe, a small number of locally acquired cases of malaria and dengue fever have recently occurred in Greece. Entirely new diseases and disease strains have emerged—like SARS in 2002, H5N1 avian flu (no longer making headlines, but still causing a steady trickle of cases in Asia and north Africa), and the pandemic strain of H1N1 flu in 2009, now established as a global, seasonal flu strain. The world is little healthier, and the health risks of travel are undiminished. For some destinations, health problems afflict 70% of travellers, perhaps more. Most of the problems are minor (although they are certainly able to dampen our enjoyment of travel, or reduce our work effectiveness); but some are serious, and some kill.

There are new weapons in our armoury: important new medicines, better vaccines against old foes, and new vaccines and vaccine technologies in the pipeline. There's a new, purified vaccine against Japanese encephalitis (another mosquito-borne virus that is present through much of rural Asia)—produced using modern cell culture methods rather than extracts of mouse brain: safer, but also much more expensive. (Healthcare costs remain a huge issue globally, not least in the UK where many Travel Medicine costs find their way back to the general taxpayer—an unsustainable situation.) New vaccines against dengue fever are close to completion, and there's the prospect of an effective vaccine against travellers' diarrhoea, in the form of a stick-on skin patch.

Travellers' Health is not just about infectious diseases. A new generation of long-range aircraft is entering service: what will the health impact be, of 20-hour, non-stop flights? The mysteries of the body clock are now more clearly understood, with new drugs and better strategies to combat the effects of jetlag. The number of young gap-year travellers has increased, many bound for poor, developing countries, quite unprepared for the risks to personal security. The number of older travellers has grown—and so has the probability that these travellers will need medical support or complex treatment whilst away. The number of people travelling abroad for the purpose of obtaining medical treatment—'health tourism'—has also increased, with all the attendant pitfalls. Accidents and injuries still take the heaviest toll, but with awareness and forethought can be prevented to a much greater degree than most people realize. Changing terrorist threats and the impact of a new era of economic uncertainty around the world bring unpredictability and new dangers.

Some things do not change. The best protection for travellers remains personal knowledge and understanding of the likely risks, and of the many options for preventing and controlling them. The aim of this book is to provide practical information and advice—from leading experts in every aspect of Travel Medicine—for travellers who want a deeper understanding of how to stay healthy abroad.

In keeping with the aim of making this information as accessible to travellers as possible, every effort has been made to reduce the size of this edition, which is available in electronic, as well as printed formats.

Dr Richard Dawood
London, 2012

From the Preface to previous editions

From the moment they leave the security of their accustomed environment, travellers are at risk. Hazards arise not just from strange diseases they encounter on their travels, but from other factors too: home comforts such as a safe water supply, sanitation and public hygiene controls, legal safety standards for motor vehicles and road maintenance, to give just a few examples, may not seem relevant, and are easily taken for granted when they are present, but simply do not exist in many popular travel destinations. Environmental factors such as arduous conditions, adverse climate and high altitude may constitute a hazard; and so may travellers' own behaviour while away—on holiday, free from the restraints of the daily routine, and determined to have a good time with scant regard for the consequences.

When illness or injury occurs abroad, travellers are again at a disadvantage—from inability to communicate with a doctor on account of language or cultural difficulties, inability to find a doctor owing to ignorance of the local medical system, inability perhaps to pay for skilled care in a sudden emergency. There may be a complete absence of skilled medical care, or of medical facilities of a standard acceptable to travellers from technologically more sophisticated countries.

When symptoms of an illness acquired abroad do not appear until *after* return home (up to a year later, for example, in certain cases of malaria) a final hazard becomes apparent: the symptoms may be unfamiliar, may pass unrecognized, and the correct diagnosis may not be considered until it is too late.

This book offers neither an exhaustive catalogue of obscure tropical diseases nor a course of training in first aid; it is an anthology of invited, specialist opinion on a wide range of problems of concern to travellers; concern, either because a genuine hazard exists that travellers should know about, and should take precautions to avoid, or because a disease or hazard that constitutes little threat has been a source of unwarranted anxiety.

Many people think of exotic infections as posing the principal risk to travellers' health; but accidents are the single most frequent cause of death in travellers abroad, causing 25 times as many deaths as infectious diseases. Some accidents and disasters are indiscriminate, raising issues of safety and security. Most accidents involving travellers, however, like the majority of travellers' health problems, are preventable or within the realm of individual control.

The scope of this book largely reflects the range of problems that I have come across during my own travels—often without having been able to deal with them to my own satisfaction at the time—and many subjects discussed here have not previously been given detailed attention in books for travellers. A specialist view is presented on each topic, because the range of subjects considered extends beyond the first-hand experience and expertise of any one individual.

Like the rest of medicine, however, travellers' health is not an exact science, and consensus is lacking on many crucial issues. A 1987 survey found visitors from different countries to the same part of East Africa following no fewer than *sixty eight* different antimalarial drug regimens. (Perhaps even more surprising, an update of the same study published in 2002 showed a fall in this number to only *sixty three*!) Some of the problems raised in this book have no satisfactory solution, or have solutions that remain a matter of opinion

Doctors in developed countries receive minimal training in, and remain largely unfamiliar with, hazards outside their own environment. Things are slowly changing: increasing numbers of doctors are taking an interest in travel medicine, and increasing numbers of travel clinics have appeared. Some of these clinics provide good service. A glance through this book will make it clear that vaccines and medication can only protect you against a limited number diseases, many of which are not common; judge your travel clinic by the attention it devotes to other precautions, which are just as important.

Deaths still occur in developed countries from malaria, and occur in previously fit, healthy young travellers; initial symptoms are all too easily confused with influenza and deterioration is often rapid without prompt treatment. In the past decade, some 50,000 cases of malaria have occurred in travellers entering Europe. Each year, there are now more than 2000 cases of malaria in travellers entering the UK, and around 1000 cases in travellers entering the USA. Most of the travellers either did not seek or receive appropriate advice, or did not follow it. The number of people coming home with malaria rises every year.

It is difficult for doctors to provide large numbers of departing travellers with detailed information and effective advice for their trip when the usual forum for doing so is a single, hurried consultation, just before departure. There are limits to what can be achieved in or should be expected from a medical consultation under the best of circumstances, even when the doctor is well motivated and well informed about the subject, and the traveller is receptive, has a perfect memory, and is good at doing what he or she is told.

What kind of advice should travellers receive? A list of rules and instructions given without explanation or justification implies that travellers are incapable of understanding the principles involved, are not interested, or do not 'need' to know. It is hardly surprising that advice offered on such condescending terms is seldom followed for long.

Throughout this book, we have studiously avoided giving blanket advice to consult a doctor without stating the reason for doing so. 'Consult your doctor' is a useful formula to enable advice-givers to evade difficult issues, but is a particularly unhelpful one when it relates to a problem that may arise abroad. It is not easy to find a doctor in a remote place, or to communicate with one in an alien land. Merely finding a doctor does not guarantee that correct advice or treatment will be given. Some 85 per cent of the world's population have never seen a doctor, and never will; advice for travellers must take account of the fact that travellers to many parts of the world will be in the same position.

Advice from doctors, travel agents, embassies, or immunization centres too often goes no further than to provide details of statutory vaccination certificate entry requirements. Few legal requirements now remain, and they are generally no more than public health measures, designed to protect countries from imported disease; they should not be confused with, and are no substitute for, clear advice and instruction on staying healthy abroad. All those who dispense 'advice' limited to information about statutory requirements have a responsibility to make it clear that additional precautions are almost always necessary for personal protection. Such further precautions need to be spelt out in detail: advice to 'take care with food hygiene' is practically meaningless to anyone who has never given serious thought to the problems of travelling or living in an environment where total absence of 'basic' sanitary measures is the norm; there is growing public awareness of food safety and hygiene issues, however, which can only help for the future.

In the time since this book first appeared, there has been undoubted growth in awareness of the health problems of travel, and it would be gratifying to think that this book might have made even a small contribution to the process. One group has failed to make any large scale contribution, however: the travel industry still views health information for travel as bad for business, often belittling concerns about health risks instead of pointing out the need for advice and directing travellers to suitable sources.

An American survey showed that only 28 per cent of travellers to malarial areas had received any kind of notification from their travel agent that malaria might be a possible hazard. A British victim of malaria, which was acquired on a holiday in the Gambia, was actually told by the travel agent who made the booking that there was no malaria in the Gambia. A Dutch survey showed that travellers who had used travel agents as their sole source of advice were in fact at even greater risk that those who had not troubled to seek advice from any source. There are cases on record where elderly people have been booked on tours to Peru, without any warning about the dangers of high altitude, and have died as a result. One third of British travel brochures made no reference to health whatsoever, according to another survey, while only 10 per cent gave any useful specific health information.

Tour operators are in a position to influence, monitor, and enforce hygiene and safety standards in hotels and resorts, but the opportunity to do so is largely ignored. The industry is less lukewarm about disclaiming legal liability for the consequences, thinly concealed in the fine print of the brochures. There are notable exceptions, and there are signs that things may improve in the future; in the meantime, judge your travel agent not just by his or her ability to get you a good deal, but also by the interest that is taken in the health aspects of your trip.

Destination countries are also concerned about discouraging tourism or harming their image, and under-report or play down statistics for diseases like malaria, yellow fever, HIV infection and reports of violence, making it more difficult for travellers to take steps to protect themselves; their embassies and tourist offices consistently supply misleading information, either deliberately or through sheer incompetence and lack of care. Surveys repeatedly show that embassies and tourist offices are not worth consulting for any kind of health information.

If the foregoing gives a rather gloomy view of the state of affairs confronting today's traveller—for whom it is tempting, though incorrect, to assume that advances in medical technology at home have been matched by like progress in combating disease abroad—it is because gloom is justified. Close to half of all international travellers experience some kind of adverse effect upon their health as a result of their trip. The majority of problems are inevitably minor ones, but Britons now take over 56 million trips abroad every year; there are 699 million international tourist, and 1647 million air travellers worldwide (figures for 2000). The scale on which international travel is now taking place lends perspective to the problem.

It is perhaps fitting that this discussion of the health risks of travel should conclude with a statistic on the health risks of staying at home. A 20-year investigation—the Framingham study—found a definite link between heart disease and not travelling: women who took vacations seldom or not at all were twice as likely to suffer a heart attack, or die from heart disease, as women who went on holiday at least twice each year. If you are a careful, responsible traveller, travel will be good for your health and well-being, and good for the people and places you visit. This book is by travellers, for travellers; it contains detailed, practical advice direct from specialists in every branch of travel medicine, and its sole purpose is to help you stay healthy wherever in the world you choose to go.

What unites all of the experts who have participated in this project, however, is deeply-rooted belief that nowhere on this planet is off limits—on health grounds at least—to travellers who are adequately prepared; that the health problems of travel are preventable, and that understanding the risks is the surest way to avoid them.

R.M.D.

Contents

Detailed contents

List of contributors

Lt Col Mark Bailey RAMC
Military Consultant Physician and Associate Professor in Infectious Diseases and Tropical Medicine at Birmingham Heartlands Hospital, Warwick Medical School and the Royal Centre for Defence Medicine, UK.

Dr Buddha Basnyat
Practices medicine in Nepal and does research on high altitude medicine and infectious diseases in collaboration with Oxford University/Patan Academy of Health Sciences. Loves to trek in the remote Himalayan regions and encourage young Nepali doctors to do the same.

Professor A. J. Batchelor CBE
A retired consultant physician with almost 40 years RAF service, including 10 as Whittingham Professor of Aviation Medicine. Now Director Aviation Medicine at King's College London and visiting consultant physician to the UK CAA.

Dr Ron H. Behrens
Consultant in Tropical and Travel Medicine, Hospital for Tropical Diseases and London School of Hygiene and Tropical Medicine, London, UK.

Dr Alan J. Benson
Formerly, Senior Medical Officer (Research) at the Royal Air Force Institute of Aviation Medicine, Farnborough. Currently, Visiting Consultant at the Royal Air Force Centre of Aviation Medicine, Henlow, UK.

Dr Delia B. Bethell
Clinical Trials Investigator based at AFRIMS in Bangkok and Honorary Consultant Paediatrician at the Oxford Childrens' Hospital, Oxford, UK.

Professor Robert Bor
Rob is a Chartered Clinical Psychologist and a specialist in aviation psychology. He is a Director of Dynamic Change Consultants (⌨ www.dcclinical.com), a psychology consultancy providing evidence based interventions to children and adults as well as within organizations.

Dr Michael Brown
Michael is a Consultant Physician at the Hospital for Tropical Diseases and Senior Lecturer at the London School of Hygiene and Tropical Medicine. He has research interests in helminths, tuberculosis and migrant health.

Dr Philip S. Brachman Sr.
Professor, in the Hubert Department of Global Health, Rollins School of Public Health, Emory University, USA.

Dr Ian F. Burgess

Ian is a parasitologist who has been working with arthropods of public health importance for over 25 years. His specialism is development, testing, and clinical studies on treatments for ectoparasite infestations.

Simon D. Butler

Simon is a practicing barrister at 9 Gough Square, London. His areas of expertise include holiday litigation, clinical negligence, personal injury, health care law, and litigation following overseas treatment.

Mr James Campbell

Public Health Officer, Directorate of Force Health Protection, Canadian Forces Health Services, Department of National Defence, Ottawa, Canada.

Dr Will Cave

GP and Travel Health Consultant at the Fleet Street Clinic, London, UK.

Dr Ping Chutema

Dr Chutema is Clinic Director with the Phnom Penh-based Reproductive Health Association of Cambodia (RHAC).

Dr Andrea Collins

Andrea graduated from Bristol University in 2002 and is now a final year respiratory registrar at the Liverpool School of Tropical Medicine, studying for a PhD in respiratory infection. Her specialist interests include pneumonia and tuberculosis.

Dr Elphis Christopher

Recently retired Consultant for Family Planning and Reproductive Care for Haringey Primary Healthcare Trust. Currently Locum Consultant Psychosexual Clinic University College London Hospital. Author *Sexuality and Birth Control in Community Work* 2nd Ed, 1987.

Professor Nick Day

Professor of Tropical Medicine, University of Oxford; Director, Wellcome Trust—Mahidol University—Oxford Tropical Medicine Research Programme, Bangkok, Thailand; and Honorary Consultant in Infectious Diseases and General Medicine, Oxford University Hospitals NHS Trust.

Dr Jon Dallimore

Jon is a GP and Specialty Doctor in Emergency Medicine. He has spent more than two years on mountain, jungle and desert expeditions and is Medical Director of Wilderness Medical Training.

Dr Robert N. Davidson

Ex-South Africa, he has worked in many parts of Africa; for more than twenty years has been Consultant in Infectious Diseases & Tropical Medicine at Northwick Park Hospital, Harrow, UK. Special interests are tropical diseases, leishmaniasis and TB.

Professor Peter Davies

Professor Davies trained in Medicine at Oxford and St Thomas's Hospital London, qualifying in 1973. While working at the Medical Research Council's TB Unit he developed an interest in TB. He was appointed Consultant Physician in Liverpool in 1988 where he continued to work on tuberculosis, publishing over 100 peer reviewed papers. He is the Editor of *Clinical Tuberculosis* of which the 5th edition is in preparation.

Dr Andrew Dawood

Andrew is a specialist in implant dentistry and prosthetics. He works in private practice in London, with honorary appointments at University College, St Bartholomew's, and the Royal London Hospitals.

Dr Richard Dawood

Richard is a specialist in Travel Medicine and Medical Director of the Fleet Street Clinic, London, where he looks after travellers to the world's most dangerous places. He has been involved in Travel Medicine for more than thirty years, has travelled in more than 100 countries around the world, and writes and broadcasts frequently on travel health issues.

Dr Arthur L. Diskin

Vice President and Global Chief Medical Officer for Royal Caribbean Cruise Lines, Ltd. and is responsible for all medical facilities on board 30+ ships, medical care for 50 000 crew and all public health issues.

Dr Matthew Dryden

Director of Infection and Consultant Microbiologist, Hampshire Hospitals, Winchester. Interest in travel medicine and medical director of Winchester Travel Health Clinic.

Paula Dudley

Formerly, Senior Lecturer in Podiatric Medicine at Westminster University (Chelsea School of Chiropody). Currently, Clinical Podiatrist at Fleet Street Clinic, London, UK.

Professor Herbert L. DuPont

Professor and Director, Center for Infectious Diseases, University of Texas School of Public Health; Chief of Internal Medicine, St. Luke's Episcopal Hospital and Vice Chairman, Department of Medicine, Baylor College of Medicine, USA.

Dr Michael Eddleston

Scottish Senior Research Fellow, Lister Prize Fellow, and Reader at the University of Edinburgh. My research interests are in tropical toxicology, in particular prevention of deaths from pesticide poisoning.

Dr Charles D. Ericsson

Dr Ericsson is past president of the International Society of Travel Medicine, and founding editor of *Journal of Travel Medicine*. His research interests include travellers' diarrhea.

Dr Susan P. Fisher-Hoch

Dr. Fisher-Hoch studied Viral Hemorrhagic Fever for more than 30 years, having lived and worked extensively in Africa and Asia for the Public Health Laboratory Service in London and for the CDC in Atlanta, Georgia.

Agnes Fletcher

Agnes is a disabled person and has worked to promote disability equality for 20 years, in the public and third sectors. A former Director of the Disability Rights Commission, Agnes is now a consultant.

Tifany Frazer

Tifany is the Medical College of Wisconsin's Global Health Program manager. She has worked with Peace Corps and United Nations in three different continents and received a master of public health from Tulane University.

Dr Andrew Freedman

Reader in Infectious Diseases, Cardiff University School of Medicine; Hon. Consultant Physician, University Hospital of Wales, Cardiff, UK; Hon. Secretary British HIV Association.

Professor Hemda Garelick

Professor of Environmental Science and Public Health Education at Middlesex University, London UK. Her research investigates both chemical and microbiological aspects of water pollution, its effect on human as well as environmental health. She also investigates a variety of low cost methods for water purification and pollution remediation.

Professor Larry Goodyer

Currently Head of the Leicester School of Pharmacy and also Director of Nomad Travel Stores. He is a Fellow of the Faculty of Travel Medicine and Deputy Chair of the British Travel and Global Health Association.

Paul Goodyer

Managing Director, Nomad Travellers Store and Medical Centre, London, UK.

Professor Stephen Hargarten

Professor and Chairman of Emergency Medicine, Director of the Injury Research Center, and the Associate Dean for Global Health at the Medical College of Wisconsin. He is a practicing emergency medicine physician for over 30 years. He has published numerous research studies over 25 years, with one focus on how US citizens die while travelling abroad.

Professor David L. Heymann

Head and Senior Fellow at the Centre on Global Health Security and Professor of Infectious Disease Epidemiology at the LSHTM. He spent 25 years as a medical epidemiologist with the CDC based in sub-Saharan Africa and Asia, and on assignment to WHO where he was assistant director general for communicable diseases and health security.

Dr Chris Johnson

Chris has researched the effects of cold on humans while working in Antarctica and has travelled extensively in both hot and cold climates. A consultant anaesthetist, he now leads the medical advisory panel of the Royal Geographical Society.

Dr John Kenafake

John is a General Practitioner on the Sunshine Coast, Queensland, Australia. He combines his passion for travel and aquatic activities with special interests in Travel Medicine and Diving Medicine.

Professor Roy Kennedy

Roy is a Professor of Microbial Science at the University of Worcester. The basis of his research on allergy and infection provides an understanding of the interactions between pathogenic spore populations and human health.

Dr Camille Nelson Kotton

Clinical director of Transplant Infectious Disease at the Massachusetts General Hospital, one of the teaching hospitals of Harvard Medical School. She has spearheaded national efforts to encourage patients to travel safely after transplant.

Dr Mike Langran

Mike is a GP and ski patrol doctor based in Aviemore. He maintains the ☞ www.ski-injury.com website and is currently President of the International Society for Skiing Safety.

Dr Jerker Liljestrand

Jerker is an obstetrician-gynecologist who has worked with international women's health for the past 35 years.

Professor Diana Lockwood

Consultant in Infectious Diseases and Tropical Medicine UCLH since 1995; Professor of Tropical Medicine, Clinical Research Department, London School of Hygiene and Tropical Medicine; Editor of the *Leprosy Review* since 1996, and elected member of the International Leprosy Federation (ILEP) Technical Forum

Professor David R. Matthews

David Matthews is a Professor of Diabetes Medicine, University of Oxford, Emeritus Founding Chairman of the Oxford Centre for Diabetes, Endocrinology and Metabolism (OCDEM), an NIHR senior research fellow and Vice Principal of Harris Manchester College, Oxford. In 2012 he chaired and published the European and USA consensus position statement on type-2 diabetes.

Professor John Macfarlane

John has had a long term clinical and research interest in lung infections, including Legionnaires' disease. Formally a respiratory physician at Nottingham University Hospitals, he is an honorary professor at Nottingham and Manchester Universities.

Charlie McGrath

Charlie is a director of Objective Travel Safety. Objective specializes in providing safety training to journalists, NGOs, Business and Gap Year students. Charlie backpacked around South America on leaving school and spent 15 years in the Army. He continues to travel extensively.

Dr Iain B. McIntosh

Former GP, hospital practitioner (Geriatrics), expedition leader, air repatriation physician, and President of the British Travel Health Association. Extensive travel over seven continents. Editor of the *BGTHA* journal and author of several books and many articles on travel related medicine.

Dr Nebojša Nikolić

Past President of the International Maritime Health Association. Published more than 80 scientific papers and two books on maritime medicine. Active sport sailor and member of the Medical Commission of The International Sailing Federation.

Professor John Oxford

Professor of Virology, St Bart's, The London, Queen Mary School of Medicine; Founder and President of Retroscreen Virology; an SME at QMC; Chairman of HygieneCouncil.org and co-founder of Oxford Media and Medicine. Published two textbooks and 250 scientific papers. Travels and lectures and contributes to TV widely.

Dr John Paul

John is currently based in Brighton and working for the HPA as Regional Microbiologist. Gained tropical experience when working with the Wellcome Trust programme in Kenya.

Dr Michael Phelan

Michael Phelan is a consultant psychiatrist with West London Mental Health Trust and an honorary senior lecturer at London's Imperial College, Faculty of Medicine. He is a general adult psychiatrist, who has an interest in physical health issues relating to mental illness and was a member of the recent Royal College of Psychiatrists' Scoping Group on Physical Health in Mental Health.

Dr Robin Philipp

Consultant Occupational and Public Health Physician, and Director, Centre for Health in Employment and the Environment (CHEE), Bristol Royal Infirmary; Member of Council and the Royal Society for Public Health (RSPH).

Professor Andrew J. Pollard

Professor of Paediatric Infection and Immunity at the University of Oxford and Director of the Oxford Vaccine Group. He trained in paediatrics and infectious disease in the UK and Canada and now works on vaccines to prevent serious infections in children with a special interest in meningitis.

Dr C. J. Schofield

Dr Chris Schofield has carried out research on Chagas disease and its control throughout Latin America for over 30 years. Since retiring from the World Health Organization in Geneva, he has been based at the London School of Hygiene and Tropical Medicine, working on trypanosomiasis control both in Latin America and in Africa.

Dr Steve Schofield

Dr Steve Schofield works in the Directorate of Force Health Protection within the Canadian Forces Health Services. He has been the medical entomologist for the Canadian military for 10 years.

Dr Owen Seddon

Specialty Trainee in the Infectious Diseases department of University Hospital of Wales, Cardiff, UK.

Professor David Snashall

David Snashall is Professor of Occupational Medicine, Kings College London and Honorary Consultant and Clinical Director Occupational Health and Safety Services, Guy's and St Thomas' NHS Foundation Trust. Previously Chief Medical Adviser, Foreign and Commonwealth Office.

Professor Tom Solomon

Chair of Neurological Science, University of Liverpool Head, Liverpool Brain Infections Group Director, Brain Infections UK Director, Liverpool Institute of Infection and Global Health, UK.

Professor S. Bertel ("Bertie") Squire

Professionally trained in internal medicine, infectious diseases and respiratory medicine at the Royal London Hospital and the Royal Free Hospital. From 1992 to 1995 he was Head of the Department of Medicine, Kamuzu Central Hosptial, and Lilongwe, Malawi. He continues to look after patients with this disease and lectures on schistosomiasis on LSTM's postgraduate courses.

Dr J. R. Rollin Stott

Dr Stott has been involved in aviation medicine research since 1979 with particular interest in motion sickness, vibration and spatial disorientation in flight. He is a CAA aeromedical examiner and honorary senior lecturer at King's College, London, UK.

Dr Martin Tepper

Dr Martin Tepper of the Directorate of Force Health Protection in the Canadian Forces Health Services has been a public health physician for the Canadian military for 20 years, principally in communicable disease control.

Colonel Michael J. G. Thomas

Clinical Director, Blood Care Foundation. Colonel Thomas served 34 years in the British Army, the last eight of which as Director of the Army Blood Transfusion Service.

Pamela Thorne
Research Psychologist Centre for Health in Employment and the Environment (CHEE), Bristol Royal Infirmary, UK.

Dr C. Louise Thwaites
Louise has worked in Ho Chi Minh City investigating and treating patients with tetanus.

Rochelle Turner
Rochelle works for *Which?* as the Head of Research for *Which? Travel* and looks after travel content in the magazine and online. She is also a regular spokesperson in the media on consumer travel issues.

Professor Francisco Vega-Lopez
Francisco Vega-Lopez is a Consultant since 1982 who has worked in Internal Medicine and Dermatology in London, Mexico and Nepal. He has clinics in General Dermatology and also in Tropical Dermatology and Skin in the Traveller at University College London Hospitals—NHS.

Professor David A. Warrell
Emeritus Professor of Tropical Medicine and Honorary Fellow, St Cross College, University of Oxford. Physician, teacher, traveller and researcher in many tropical countries. Founded Oxford Tropical Medicine Research Network in 1979. Author of papers on tropical diseases, envenoming and expedition medicine. Senior editor of the *Oxford Textbook of Medicine* (5th edition).

Dr Tony Waterston
Retired consultant paediatrician and clinical senior lecturer whose working life was spent mainly in community paediatrics in Newcastle upon Tyne, after two spells working in Africa. His chief clinical interests are in child mental health, child public health and global health. He has been active in teaching and training and has edited a student textbook on paediatrics and a postgraduate text on child public health.

Gillian Whitby
Gillian Whitby trained in Glasgow and has been an Optometrist and contact lens practitioner in London since 1981. Her practice, Whitby & Co, has a close working relationship with the Fleet Street Clinic, where she looks after large numbers of travellers, before travel as well as on their return.

Dr David J. M. Wright
Retired Director of National Lyme Reference Laboratory, and Head of Microbiology, Charing Cross and Chelsea Westminster Hospitals, Emeritus Reader in Medical Microbiology, Imperial College, London, UK.

Professor Antony R. Young
Professor Young has over 30 years' experience of research on the effects of solar ultraviolet radiation on the skin.

Professor Arie Zuckerman

Professor of Medical Microbiology. Formerly Principal and Dean of the Royal Free School of Medicine and later the Royal Free and University College Medical School of UCL. Director of the WHO Collaborating Centre for Reference and Research on Viral Diseases and formerly of the WHO Centre for Viral Hepatitis. Honorary Consultant to the Royal Free Hospital, University College Hospital, Charing Cross Hospital, and the North East London Regional Blood Transfusion Centre.

Dr Jane N. Zuckerman

Director of the Academic Centre for Travel Medicine and Vaccines, a WHO Collaborating Centre for Reference, Research and Training in Travel Medicine. She also holds the posts of Senior Lecturer and Honorary Consultant, University College London Medical School and the Royal Free Hampstead NHS Trust. She is also the Medical Director of the Royal Free Travel Health Centre.

About using this book

This book contains more information than other health books for travellers: is all this information really necessary? For example, all most travellers really *need* to know about rabies is that it is a serious disease, spread by animal bites. If you are unlucky enough to be bitten abroad, however, your life may suddenly depend upon having detailed information you would probably not want to carry in your head: how to treat the bite, what kind of vaccine to insist on, and what to do. 'Ten top tips' won't always help. The main objective of this book is to draw together all the health information you might need, direct from the experts who really know. You may not want to read all of it in advance, and you may choose not to follow all of the precautions we suggest, but having the information available at least allows *you* to make that choice.

- This book is mainly about prevention, so to get the most from it you should become familiar with it before you travel. It will also help you deal with problems that may occur while you are travelling, although diagnosis of infectious diseases may be difficult even with skilled medical care and laboratory facilities
- Don't be put off by the names of strange diseases you have not come across before, or by some of the more technical information this book provides. You do not have to know everything, but it is there if you need it
- *If you are travelling only within North America, northern Europe, and Australasia*, most of the infectious and parasitic diseases referred to in the first half of this book will not be a significant hazard. Some basic vaccines are needed for everyone, however, and the sections on diarrhoea (Chapter 2.1), rabies (Chapter 6), and Chapter 5 on diseases spread by insects (particularly Chapter 5.12 on personal protection) may also be relevant to you. There is much more to the subject of health problems in travellers than infectious diseases, as you will see from the second half of the book
- If you are travelling elsewhere, especially to *Africa, Asia,* or *Latin America*, the sections on diseases of poor hygiene and diseases spread by insects will be particularly important
- Remember that accidents are the commonest cause of death in travellers, and that most accidents are preventable (see Chapter 8.1)
- Malaria is the most serious tropical disease hazard that travellers are likely to come across (see Chapter 5.1)
- Hepatitis A is common and serious, but is preventable with a safe and effective vaccine (see Chapter 2.4)
- Diarrhoea and sunburn are the two 'minor' problems that most often interfere with travel plans, and they too are preventable
- Depending on the nature of your trip, the risk of other diseases is probably small anyway, but simple precautions can often dramatically reduce or eliminate the risks altogether; this book is for travellers whose health abroad is too important to be left to chance

- There's no substitute for understanding the basics, when it comes to protecting your health abroad. But for additional information, and to keep you up-to-date with news of outbreaks and other developments, you can find a detailed listing of specialist sources and websites in Appendix 2. Links to all of these sites can be found on the book's own website at ⌘ www.travellershealth.com.

Dedication

To my parents.

Acknowledgements

I should like to thank all of the contributors to this edition of *Travellers' Health*. This book owes an enormous debt to contributors to previous editions, and to the many colleagues, friends and erstwhile travelling companions who have contributed to my own knowledge of travel medicine, or who have provided advice and practical help with this project since work began on the first edition of this book in the early 1980s.

Special thanks to all my colleagues at the Fleet Street Clinic, my family, and everyone at Oxford University Press who has worked tirelessly on this project over the years.

Introduction: staying healthy abroad

1.1 Introduction: Staying healthy abroad prevention is the best strategy

Richard Dawood

Staying healthy abroad is too important to leave to chance. Health precautions really work, and the time you invest in understanding and applying them will be well rewarded. Knowledge is power—the purpose of this book is to give you the information you need to *prevent* health problems when you travel.

Why prevention?

Of all the hazards and infectious diseases to which travellers are exposed, some are lethal, many are dangerous, and several have long-term effects on health and well-being. Some may be passed on to family and friends on return home.

Most problems are relatively 'minor' in their health impact. This is just as well, given the large numbers of travellers who experience illness abroad, but also helps explain the meagre attention such problems receive.

A problem does not have to be serious, however, to have a devastating effect upon the success or enjoyment of a trip. A bout of travellers' diarrhoea can be all it takes to mar a much anticipated holiday, force a major change of plans, abort a business trip, or halt the trek of a lifetime up Kilimanjaro.

Health problems in travellers are common. The risks are not decreasing and we are all susceptible. Healthcare abroad is costly, travel is expensive, our leisure time is precious, and some business travellers have much at stake; if only for economic reasons, prevention is a strategy for health that no traveller can afford to neglect.

Prevention: who is responsible?

Can travel health issues be legislated away? Many of the world's most interesting travel destinations are developing countries with limited resources and unreliable infrastructure. On matters of health, local legislation is largely meaningless.

By contrast, in more developed countries, extensive health and safety legislation is now the norm, and travellers can and do benefit. Lower your guard at your peril, however. There may still be serious lapses.

The travel industry is perilously vulnerable to circumstance: wars, terrorism, volcanic eruptions, tsunamis, hurricanes, economic recession, and our changing travel habits. We need the travel industry to be strong, so that it can do more. Best practice needs to be universally applied, particularly at hotels and resorts that are under the virtual control of Western operators or that use their name (such as hotels belonging to international chains, even though they may be locally owned and run)—good fire safety, food hygiene, pool safety, and vehicle safety ought to be the norm wherever Western tour operators regularly send their clients. So should adequate information about health risks—something that European Union directives now provide for. Too often, however, litigation *after* failure proves to offer a more potent incentive to good practice than a proactive, industry-led approach to health promotion.

Devising a strategy

Do not delegate responsibility for your health abroad to anyone else, however busy or preoccupied you may be with more pressing concerns—take personal charge. Business travellers are consistently at fault in this regard. Many people are surprised to discover that such regular travellers are often *less* well informed on health matters than the average package tourist! Even when they have made efforts in the past to find out about health precautions, they fail to update their knowledge and become complacent.

Intelligence, good health, an extensive general knowledge, being a celebrity or a VIP do not absolve you from the need to obtain careful advice and up-to-date information about the risks that apply to your circumstances and travel plans. This book will help you do that. Even if you are well informed about health issues that apply to your home environment, don't assume that this will help you abroad. Many of the precautions that are necessary are neither logical nor intuitive.

Not all medical sources are equally able to provide the information you need. Not all clinics that provide vaccines have staff with adequate knowledge and experience of travel medicine. Doctors are not the sole source of reliable health advice; nurses and other staff at immunization centres, travel clinics, and university health centres frequently have considerable experience, and more time to talk to you. Listen carefully to them. If you travel frequently, develop a relationship with a local, specialist clinic that will look after all your travel health needs and might be able to help you if you become ill abroad.

Be cautious when using the Internet as a source—it is possible to find information to validate almost *any* viewpoint on health issues. There's no substitute for skilled, personal care, and a professional risk assessment (Chapter 13.1).

Specific prevention measures

Immunization offers protection from several important diseases, and should not be neglected (see Chapter 13.2). Current vaccines, the product of years of research, are effective and safe. There are new, improved vaccines against meningitis and Japanese encephalitis. Others in the pipeline include new vaccines against dengue fever, and possibly even against norovirus and other causes of travellers' diarrhoea. There is even the tantalizing prospect of a malaria vaccine at some point in the future, but don't forget that the commonest vaccine-preventable disease is ordinary 'flu' (Chapter 4.12).

The only remaining formal vaccination certificate requirements for travel relate to yellow fever. Do not let this fool you—diminishing regulations are not the same as diminishing risk, so always check on *recommendations*, not just *requirements* for your trip.

Immunizations don't work if they have not been given or are allowed to lapse, and their timing requires some thought—not all offer 100% protection. For frequent travellers, a strategy of continuous protection is an attractive option that offers many advantages over the conventional 'trip-by-trip' approach.

Some people think travel medicine is only about vaccines, but this is untrue: *only a small minority of disease risks can be prevented by immunization*. Never assume that just because you may have had some vaccines, no further precautions will be necessary.

Prevention (prophylaxis) with drugs

This is an essential protective measure for travellers to malarial areas (see Chapter 5.1)—malaria is a potential killer that should never be underestimated. However, anti-malarial drugs are never enough on their own, and measures to avoid mosquito bites remain of the utmost importance.

Drug treatment can sometimes also be used to prevent certain diarrhoeal diseases, and may be an appropriate option in special circumstances, but the issue is a controversial one (p.26); the desired results are more likely to be achieved by careful precautions with food, water, and hygiene.

Preventing specific diseases by taking medication may seem an attractive concept, but unfortunately it is not a precaution on which travellers may rely.

General precautions

In most cases, each disease of concern to the traveller does not have its own unique preventive measure. There is a limit to the number of possible ways in which diseases can spread. Whether you are in Kathmandu, Kabul, or Corfu, and whether the problem you are trying to avoid is amoebic dysentery, giardiasis, or simply travellers' diarrhoea, the principles of food hygiene are the same. Anti-insect precautions, assiduously followed, will protect you from dengue fever in the Caribbean just as surely as from filariasis in West Africa and other unpleasant diseases elsewhere.

Although detailed information in this book about a large number of diseases and hazards may appear frightening, the important point is that prevention is not only feasible in virtually every case, but is usually not difficult; it follows logical principles that relate directly to how the disease is spread. This book presents further details, too—for interest, perspective, and to give purpose to precautions that might otherwise seem obscure or not really necessary.

Food hygiene

One of my favourite surveys of visitors to East Africa found that only 2% of them were taking adequate dietary precautions. Are dietary precautions a lost cause? Many people think they don't work. Unfortunately, nothing less than a process of education/re-education in the fundamental principles of food hygiene will protect travellers to most countries outside northern Europe, North America, or Australasia. Appetite is a poor guide to food safety—food should never be assumed to be safe unless you know that it has been freshly and thoroughly cooked (heat sterilized)—in the case of meat, until no red colour remains. If it is important for you to avoid illness, this rule must dictate your choice from even the most tempting menu. Satisfy yourself that today's lunch is not yesterday's evening meal, re-heated, and re-arranged. Intricate delicacies that have received much handling during preparation and cold platters left out in the open are highly likely to have been contaminated. Prawns, oysters, and other seafood, feed by filtering the water around them; they are rapidly able to accumulate dangerous levels of bacteria and viruses. Shellfish should be boiled vigorously for at least 10 min or preferably avoided altogether. Even within the USA, the risk of gastrointestinal illnesses is estimated to be 18 000 greater from eating shellfish than from eating fish. Fruit and vegetables need careful preparation—they should be freshly cooked or freshly peeled. In Western countries, we are so used to thinking of foods such as salad vegetables as 'healthy' that many of the necessary precautions seem counter-intuitive.

Observing food precautions means that you won't always be able to eat what you want or what is on offer when you are hungry. The principles of food hygiene are of crucial importance to travellers, and are discussed again at length in the next chapter and elsewhere throughout the book (see also Appendix 3).

Expensive hotels

Many travellers draw comfort from the fact that they will be staying in multi-starred or 'luxurious' establishments, but these offer no guarantee of safety from diseases of poor hygiene. Surveys have frequently found appalling examples of poor hygiene standards and contaminated food in hotel kitchens at popular European resorts. The UK consumer publication *Which?* has repeatedly concluded that a hotel's star rating bears little relation to its standard of food hygiene. Look at the kitchen yourself and check for flies. Do you see food lying around, exposed? Flies cannot discriminate between the plate of a wealthy tourist and any of their other preferred habitats. African flies carry African diseases and you can acquire dysentery from the foot of a single fly. (Avoiding flies can sometimes be hard—in Africa's Rift Valley, 'fly counts' in a typical home reach 30 000–40 000 per 24 hour period.)

Low-budget travellers

Low-budget travellers are at no greater risk of illness than those who stay in luxury hotels. Whether you eat in a street market or anywhere else, you can rely on the same principles of food hygiene to protect you. Do you enjoy eating bread fresh from the oven, food that you have selected and watched cooking, and fresh fruit, peeled carefully yourself? (I always travel with a small spoon and a sharp knife for just this purpose.) Food like this is easy to find, is cheap and appetizing, and almost always safe to eat.

Clean hands

It is all very well washing your hands before a meal, but if you then proceed to wipe your hands on a towel contaminated by others, touch a grubby bathroom door handle, and then handle food, you are asking for trouble. Hand sanitizers are convenient, and often more reliable. I often observe travellers—including my own supposedly well-trained children—

who believe themselves to be taking careful precautions, yet repeatedly bring contaminated fingers, pencils, or other objects to their mouths or faces. Studies have shown that banknotes (especially lower denominations!) are often heavily contaminated with faecal organisms. In developing countries, regard your hands as an 'unclean' surface and avoid eating food that you have handled directly.

Water

Water safety and purification are discussed in detail on Chapter 3. In most countries outside northern Europe, North America, and Australia, water from the public drinking supply is likely to be just a very dilute solution of sewage, and should be regarded as such, unless known to be safe.

Ice

Ice is only as pure as the water from which it is made (p.49). However, even when the water supply is safe, chilling happens to be an excellent way of preserving bacteria and viruses. Ice machines readily become contaminated—it takes a careful programme of maintenance and de-contamination to ensure their continuing safety—even, for example, in British hospitals, where such programmes are understood and in place, but where a survey found 75% of ice machines to be visibly dirty and most to be heavily contaminated.

Hospitality

This is a dangerous pitfall for the unwary. It takes diplomacy and determination to refuse food prepared (unhygienically) by someone who has clearly gone to great lengths to please an honoured visitor. This can be an extremely delicate problem in rural areas of developing countries, where food is scarce. My personal advice is not to relax your standards of food hygiene under any circumstances—plead illness, use any excuse and, if necessary, even permit the food to be put on your plate and toy with it, but *do not eat food you consider to be suspect.* The possible embarrassment of such a situation and reluctance to offend one's host (genuine offence is rarely taken) must be balanced against the risk of illness that may put you out of action for several days.

Faecal aerosols

Fascinating work by Jeff Siegel and his colleagues at the University of Texas shows that toilets have the ability to aerosolize faecal matter when they flush. At busy locations, like airports, each toilet may flush up to 200 times per day—once every 7 min. A seldom-recognized mode of spread for travellers' diarrhoea, perhaps, and one that may also apply in other dirty, dusty environments.

Insects

Insects transmit a multitude of diseases, not all of which can be prevented individually, and their bites can be a painful nuisance. Personal protection against them is an essential precaution for travellers (Chapter 5.12). One of the most notable advances in recent years has been the introduction of insecticide-treated bed nets (pioneered by a contributor to previous editions of this book, the late Professor Chris Curtis). These are over 30 times more effective than untreated nets, now used globally to combat malaria. Travellers to some infected areas can expect to be bitten by malaria-bearing mosquitoes at least once a day; my own preferred method of fighting back is with an electric mosquito bat, bulky to carry, but satisfying, and often cheaply available at your destination.

Sex

Sex abroad has always been a risky business and the penalties are undiminished. Infection rates of HIV and other sexually-transmitted diseases in many countries are rising. It has been estimated that there are perhaps 2.8 million prostitutes in Thailand alone, most of whom have had 5000 sexual partners by the age of 19. One-third of male visitors to Thailand have sex with prostitutes, more than 70% of whom are thought to be infected with sexually-transmitted diseases at any one time. Meanwhile, a recent study has found that more than one in three British travellers has had unprotected sex with a new partner while abroad; the same study found that people in their 50s were least likely to use contraception with a new lover.

Sun

In men, the UK death rate for malignant melanoma, the deadliest form of skin cancer, has more than doubled in the past 30 years. It is no coincidence that the same 30-year period has seen an explosion in overseas travel. In older age groups, the death rate is very much higher: 15.2 per 100 000 in men aged over 65, compared with 4.5 per 100 000 in the 1970s. Meanwhile, the number of new cases of melanoma has grown five-fold. More women are diagnosed with melanoma, but more men are dying from it—men are less likely to seek treatment in time. Other, more treatable skin cancers are also on the rise, with an estimated 100 000 cases every year. These cancers commonly occur on the nose, eyelids, face, scalp, ears, and front of the chest; they may not be lethal, but there's nothing pleasant about having a chunk of tissue removed from your nose (see Chapter 8.5). Cancer Research UK fears that the recession will fuel growth in the indoor tanning industry, as travellers swap holidays for sun beds, a cheaper although not a safer option.

Exposure to ultraviolet light also causes cataract formation and retinal damage. Protect your eyes with good quality sunglasses that filter out the harmful rays.

The environment

The environment holds many hazards, including heat, cold, the effects of high altitude, the bites of wild animals, and accidents—the biggest hazard of all. A large part of this book is devoted to such subjects, and it is often the simplest precautions that are most important. For example, if you have children and you rent a car abroad, remember that child seats cut their risk of dying in a car crash by 70%. According to one analysis of 100 000 accidents, the risk of dying in the front seat in a car crash is five times higher when passengers in the back are not wearing seat belts. If you are planning to use a moped or motorcycle, your risk of injury is at least 40 times greater than if you use a car. A bicycle helmet reduces the risk of head injury by 70%. These dangers don't just mysteriously vanish when you go abroad; in fact, they may be amplified by reduced access to good emergency care.

Many accidents abroad relate to alcohol (at least 20% of drownings, for example). Remember that drinks may not come in standard measures or even in standard strengths. Many countries have lower blood alcohol limits for drivers than you may be used to and in many countries there is also a high likelihood of being tested. Pedestrians involved in accidents may also be tested and penalties may be high. Travel insurance policies often exclude cover for accidents, injuries, and losses that take place while under the influence of alcohol.

A recent study found that we are 5.5 times more likely to drown abroad than at home. Most people lower their guard when they go on holiday, which is a huge mistake.

Remember to travel unobtrusively, be discreet with your possessions, and avoid flourishing large sums of money in poor areas. As the late Dr Alistair Reid, an expert on hazards from wild animals, enjoyed pointing out, the greatest animal danger to travellers is man. Issues surrounding personal security are discussed in detail in Chapter 8.2.

Illness abroad

When prevention fails or the unavoidable occurs, coping with illness abroad, and if necessary getting yourself or someone else home again quickly, demands resourcefulness and judgement. It helps if a doctor can be found, and knowledge of the local language is a valuable asset. Mobile phones, e-mail, and the ability to obtain medical advice from home have made things much easier for travellers to remote places—nowhere is quite as remote as it used to be. Often, though, self-help is everything.

Medical treatment abroad may itself be dangerous. Public awareness of HIV has helped draw attention to some of the hazards—screened and unscreened blood transfusions; non-sterile needles, syringes, and medical and dental instruments; acupuncture; and surgery may all spread the virus (see Chapter 10.2).

A carefully constructed personal medical kit can be a valuable aid (see Chapter 13.5).

Hepatitis B, however, is more common and is spread by the same routes. Not all medical attention is undertaken voluntarily—you may be required to produce a blood sample following a car accident, for example, and the sterility of the needle that is used will depend on where you are unfortunate enough to have your accident.

Other hazards include drugs and vaccines that may be ineffective or dangerous. In some poor countries, where the likelihood of being bitten by a dog and the frequency of rabies are both high, locally-produced rabies vaccine may be almost as dangerous as the disease itself.

Medical skills, approaches, and standards of practice also vary. Women should always make sure that a chaperone is present when they are examined. In some countries, there may be an over-enthusiasm for surgical treatment— undoubtedly the case in many ski resorts, where local surgeons may be eager to exercise their undoubted skills, but will not be around to assist with follow-up care or rehabilitation. Other than in a clear emergency, repatriation is usually possible prior to surgery and is sometimes prefer- able, although the choice can be very hard.

The most usual problems, however, are inadequacy of emergency ser- vices, and scarcity or inaccessibility of skilled medical facilities when they are needed. Places with quite reasonable facilities for local people may not be capable of dealing with emergencies in foreigners, and this remains a problem at resorts—particularly island resorts—all over the world. Each year, there is a distressing toll of injuries in young tourists who are injured in moped accidents on islands that have no or only limited facilities for neuro-surgical care. On the relatively well-developed island of Crete, for example, visitors who are injured on the south side of the island face a 3-hour ambulance journey to the main hospital. With head injuries in particular, survival may well hinge on the proximity to medical care.

Adequate insurance may remove anxiety about expense and should provide for emergency repatriation if necessary, but it is also important to have enough cash to cover immediate costs. A general awareness of the likely health risks will be invaluable. Specific advice for coping with individual diseases is given in each of the chapters on the main diseases.

In my view, *all* travellers to remote areas with limited medical facilities should also have a knowledge of basic first aid and should attend a course of instruction if necessary.

Coming home

The value of post-tropical screening is discussed in Appendix 5. All travellers should realize, however, that it is possible for symptoms of infectious diseases—especially malaria—not to appear until several weeks, or even longer, after return home. When symptoms do appear, their significance may not be recognized immediately. Roughly half of all fatal malaria cases are initially misdiagnosed as flu and the worst place for diagnosis is a country that sees few cases. If illness does develop after a trip, make sure that your doctor knows that you have been travelling.

Attitude

A positive attitude to health and perception of one's health as a vital element in the success of a trip, rather than as an inconvenient obstacle to enjoyment, are powerful weapons for any traveller.

Finally

The message of this book is not that you should worry about each and every disease or problem that is mentioned here whenever you go abroad. Worse still, that you would be better off staying at home. It is simply this—by informing yourself of the nature of the hazards and how they can be overcome, you will learn healthy travel habits that will open new horizons and protect you wherever you go. You could, of course, learn them the hard way, as I have had to do on my own travels, in which case you need read no further . . .

Food, drink, and hygiene-related diseases

2.1 Diarrhoea and intestinal infections

Herbert DuPont and Charles Ericsson

"Travel broadens the mind and loosens the bowels."

Sherwood Gorbach

Millions of people know how true this can be, but travellers' diarrhoea is both preventable and readily treatable:

- For help with symptoms, see 'What to do about diarrhoea' (p.20)
- For simple preventive advice see 'Prevention' (p.26), 'How diarrhoeal diseases are spread' (p.10) and Appendix 3
- To understand why these measures may or may not work, read on.

What are the risks?

Any kind of travel increases the likelihood of travellers' diarrhoea. Where you come from and where you are going are the main factors determining your risk.

Regarding diarrhoeal risk, the world can be broadly divided into:

- *High risk:* Latin America, Africa, southern Asia
- *Low risk:* United States, Canada, north-west Europe, Australia, New Zealand, and Japan
- *Intermediate risk:* northern Mediterranean, Jamaica, China, Eastern Europe, and the former Soviet Union.

When a person from a low-risk region travels to a high-risk region, the likelihood of a diarrhoeal illness is about 40%. When the same individual travels to an intermediate risk area, the likelihood is approximately 10%. For a traveller who goes from one low risk region to another, the risk is between 2 and 5%—higher than the rate of illness in people who just stay at home. Naturally, the longer the trip, the more likely it is that illness will occur.

The 2–5% background rate of diarrhoea among low-risk travellers arises from such things as:

- The stress of travel itself
- The fact that many more meals are prepared by others, with greater opportunity for contamination than when food is prepared at home
- Increased alcohol consumption
- The presence of poorly-absorbed salts and other non-infective diarrhoea-producing substances found in unfamiliar food and water sources.

Some travellers are at higher risk, so should take much more careful precautions:
- The elderly, or very young
- Travellers living under conditions of reduced hygiene, in close contact with the local community
- Travellers who have little or no opportunity to choose what they consume
- Travellers with an important underlying disease, including diabetes requiring insulin, heart disease requiring regular medication, chronic liver disease, and reduced immunity
- Travellers taking medication to reduce gastric acid secretion—especially potent drugs like proton pump inhibitors (PPIs), e.g. omeprazole).

Diarrhoea: not just a problem for travellers

For healthy western travellers, a diarrhoeal episode may be at worst debilitating. For malnourished children, diarrhoeal illnesses are life-threatening. At a rough estimate, there are 1.3 billion episodes, leading to death in at least 5 million children each year. Such episodes also contribute to chronic ill health, increased susceptibility to other diseases and poor economic performance, so are a compelling public health priority.

How diarrhoeal diseases are spread: the cornerstone of prevention

Many different bacteria, viruses, and protozoa may be responsible and all are transmitted in the same manner. You must actually swallow contaminated material to contract the disease.

This has two practical consequences. First, take pains to avoid food, drink, or anything else you might swallow that has a high risk of being contaminated. Secondly, ensure that you do not touch the food you eat, or if you do that your hands are scrupulously clean and as dry as possible (if necessary, use clean paper tissues to handle food while eating). Plates and cutlery should also be clean and dry.

If your appetite is for aromatic alien delicacies, then you must either accept the risks involved or establish whether the food is safe. Eat something else if it isn't.

Food poisoning is common in all countries. In most outbreaks, a breakdown in recommended food preparation or storage practices is responsible.

Thus, even in a country where organisms that cause diarrhoea are not common, the diseases they cause remain inadequately controlled despite widely-disseminated knowledge of hygienic practices.

Unfortunately, the micro-organisms responsible for diarrhoeal disease do not reveal their presence by making food look rotten. Instead, the reverse may occasionally be true, since organisms that cause food spoilage can prevent growth of diarrhoea-causing organisms. In practice, food whose temperature has reached the boiling point of water for at least 15 min is nearly always safe from the most common bacteria causing illness.

If not eaten straight away, cooked food should be protected from contamination and refrigerated immediately. The pre-refrigeration period is often where contamination occurs. Contact by hands, flies, cutlery, or the cutting board onto which uncooked food has been placed leads to contamination. Small numbers of surviving bacteria may grow at phenomenal rates if left in a slowly cooling medium. In addition, room temperature in tropical countries is much closer to that required for optimal bacterial growth, so safe storage times without refrigeration are much shorter.

Specific food hazards

Bacteria need moisture to survive and so dry foods (e.g. breads) are safer than those that are moist (e.g. salads, sauces). Other factors include the acid content of the item (citrus is generally safe because of its citric and ascorbic acid content), and salt or sugar content—syrups and jams, for example, should also be safe. The following foods can be particularly risky:

Shellfish and seafood

This arises from their mode of feeding, which involves filtering large volumes of seawater with accumulation of micro-organisms, such as vibrios, *Plesiomonas*, *Aeromonas*, and hepatitis viruses. This is only a problem where seawater is contaminated, but it is not unusual for untreated human excreta to be deposited close to areas where shellfish are collected. With poor handling, they may also become contaminated after harvesting.

Vegetables, salads, and fruit

The use of human faeces as fertilizer (night soil)—widespread in the tropics—and substandard hygiene practices, make salads and uncooked vegetables risky unless they have been carefully washed with clean water to remove all surface contamination. Even where night soil is not used, salads and fresh fruit are still quite common sources of infection because they frequently become contaminated during transit, storage, or preparation.

Travellers to remoter areas who peel fruit themselves without contaminating the contents and eat it immediately, and wash their own vegetables are at little risk of infection.

Rice

Freshly cooked rice is generally safe. However, leftovers are sometimes reheated at the next meal. *Bacillus cereus*, a bacterium that often contaminates rice even in the UK, can survive the initial cooking process by producing heat-resistant spores. In the interval between meals, these spores germinate and bacterial growth converts the surrounding rice into a deadly emetic cocktail. By this stage, the emetic toxin is so robust that even pressure-cooking will not destroy it.

Drinks

For water purification, see Chapter 3.2. However, water contamination is not a matter that can be ignored: ice, ices, and anything else prepared from suspect water supplies should be considered contaminated, since freezing will kill only a fraction of any organisms present. Remember, that even the most stylish swimmers swallow small quantities of water.

Milk products

Unpasteurized milk (and products made from it) should always be avoided. Diarrhoeal diseases and others such as brucellosis (Box 2.1.1) and tuberculosis are a real problem in some regions. Listeriosis is a disease that has received much publicity and has also been linked to certain dairy products.

Eggs

This is mainly a problem in countries with intensive farming methods. *Salmonella* infection predominates in growing chickens, but falls in the egg-laying population. Tests on individual eggs show infection rates no greater than one in 1000 eggs.

Bulk catering, where large numbers of pooled eggs are used, poses the greatest risk. Uncooked or lightly cooked eggs, and foods made with them, such as mayonnaise, sauces, milk shakes, ice cream, and sandwiches, are frequently incriminated.

Travellers are at no greater risk of acquiring salmonella from eggs. Thorough cooking kills the organisms.

Box 2.1.1 **Brucellosis and listeriosis**

Brucellosis is a bacterial disease acquired from animals. It occurs with varying, but moderate frequency in most areas of the world outside northern Europe, Australia, New Zealand, the USA, and Canada. Symptoms are non-specific, with fever, headache, profuse sweating, chills, weight loss, depression, joint pains, and generalized aching.

The risk to travellers arises from eating unpasteurized dairy products, particularly goat cheese. Every year, cases are reported in recent travellers to southern Europe, Africa, the Middle East, and South America. Most cases respond to several weeks' treatment with a combination of antibiotics, although delay in diagnosis and initiation of therapy may lead to prolonged disability. Because the time interval between consuming the contaminated food item and onset of illness is typically a month or more, the diagnostic clue of having eaten an unpasteurized dairy product may have been forgotten.

A variety of other infections can be acquired from eating unpasteurized goat cheese. Bacterial infections are most common and include bovine tuberculosis, listeriosis, salmonellosis, and a variety of diarrhoeal agents. Listeriosis presents a particular hazard for pregnant women (see p.371). The mother may have no symptoms, but the mother's infection may result in foetal infection. This can lead to miscarriage, stillbirth, or meningitis and septicaemia in the newborn.

Alcohol

Alcoholic drinks should not be assumed to be self-sterilizing. Excessive alcohol intake may itself cause diarrhoea by an irritant action. Alcohol within a drink has a dehydrating effect, and reduces the amount of water available for rehydration. For these reasons, alcoholic drinks are not recommended as a source of water intake in hot countries.

Food from buffets

Buffets are a way to try many local dishes, but the food is easily contaminated and they are best avoided. If it is not possible to have something prepared freshly for you, the principles of food safety discussed in this chapter should be followed closely. If there is a flame under the dish and the food is steaming, take a portion from directly over the flame: this is more likely to be at a safe temperature.

Aeroplane food

Food served on aeroplanes can be a source of intestinal infection. This is not surprising considering flight delays and the time in the air before some meals are served. Meals on flights originating in tropical or semi-tropical developing countries are even more likely to be contaminated. Take careful precautions or, better still, don't eat it.

Cruise ships

Food and water can be considered safe on most cruise ships, where rigid hygiene controls exist. The greatest risk usually arises when consuming meals on shore excursions. Precautions should be taken and also be followed if there is any suspicion that food or water is being taken on board in a high-risk area or during a known outbreak of gastroenteritis.

Flies

Flies live with equal happiness on dung and food. If you allow flies to walk on your food, for all practical purposes you are eating excreta. Flies are vectors in the 'faecal–oral' transmission of infection. Avoid food that has not been protected by fly screens.

Hands

Micro-organisms sticking to your hands easily contaminate food. A conscious effort not to bring your hands up to your mouth unless they are clean is therefore worthwhile. Proper hand drying after washing is an equally important part of the cleansing process. Alcohol gel is useful under extreme conditions.

Other modes of transmission

Several diarrhoea-causing organisms can be transmitted directly from person to person or from animals. However, in most cases, transmission will involve swallowing contaminated material, so the precautions outlined previously will remain effective. Transmission via fine droplets produced by coughing or sneezing is a possible route for the viral agents of diarrhoea. Rotaviruses and noroviruses may also be transmitted in this way, and remain largely uncontrolled worldwide. They are notorious for evading even the most careful cross-infection precautions in modern hospitals.

Organisms responsible for travellers' diarrhoea

The main causes of travellers' diarrhoea are listed in Fig. 2.1.1 and described here. Details of treatment are given in pp.20–5 and summarized in Fig. 2.1.2.

Enterotoxigenic Escherichia coli (ETEC)

ETEC bacteria multiply in the small intestine and make toxins that cause most of the symptoms. They are responsible for about a third of cases of travellers' diarrhoea in all high-risk areas other than Southeast Asia (e.g. Thailand).

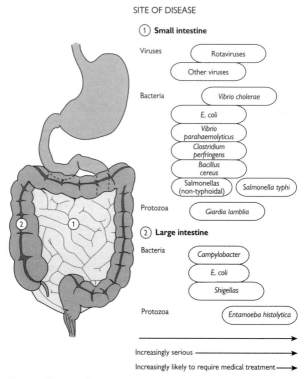

SITE OF DISEASE

1 **Small intestine**

Viruses
- Rotaviruses
- Other viruses

Bacteria
- Vibrio cholerae
- E. coli
- Vibrio parahaemolyticus
- Clostridium perfringens
- Bacillus cereus
- Salmonellas (non-typhoidal)
- Salmonella typhi

Protozoa
- Giardia lamblia

2 **Large intestine**

Bacteria
- Campylobacter
- E. coli
- Shigellas

Protozoa
- Entamoeba histolytica

Increasingly serious ⟶

Increasingly likely to require medical treatment ⟶

Fig. 2.1.1 The main infectious causes of diarrhoea.

The toxins interact with cells on the lining of the small intestine and cause an uncontrolled activation of the mechanisms that normally move water across the gut wall. The result is a dramatic net flow of salt and water into the gut.

The large intestine normally absorbs 1–2L of water passing down from the small intestine daily. It has a reserve absorption capacity of a further 2–3L that must be exceeded before diarrhoea appears. Given that, in severe cases, several litres of fluids may be lost in the stools, the level of disturbance is impressive.

ETEC diarrhoea is self-limiting and rarely lasts more than 48 hours The cholera vaccine Dukoral may provide some protection.

Another type of E.coli—E.coli O157:H7—has been responsible for outbreaks in the UK, the USA, and Germany that have received much publicity, particularly on account of the kidney failure that can sometimes be a complication in children and the elderly. This type of E. coli is seldom associated with travel.

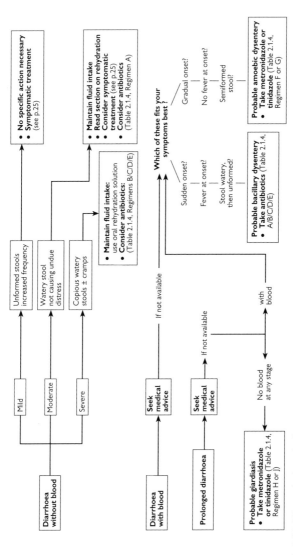

Fig. 2.1.2 What to do about diarrhoea.

Shigella and Campylobacter

These organisms together explain up to 20% of diarrhoea (highest among travellers to India). Both of them can produce bloody diarrhoea and fever, with illness lasting up to a week.

Salmonella (non-typhoid)

Salmonella infections (salmonellosis) may account for up to 10% of cases of travellers' diarrhoea. They predominantly affect the lower end of the small intestine.

The organisms penetrate deeper than the shigellas and can produce blood poisoning (bacteraemia) in susceptible people. Surprisingly, they seem to produce less damage to the lining of the intestine than *Shigella*, and affected people pass grossly bloody stools less frequently. Infection with no bowel symptoms, just fever and rigors, or shivering with fever, is common.

Noroviruses

These account for about 10% of cases. Very small numbers of viral particles can initiate an illness, which is one reason why noroviruses remain largely uncontrolled worldwide. Most cruise-associated diarrhoea and vomiting is caused by this class of viruses (see also p.225).

The mechanism of immunity to noroviruses is unclear. Infections continue to occur in adult life, probably because of the number of different noroviruses responsible.

Other viruses

Rotavirus is a pathogen that mainly affects babies and small children, and is increasingly being controlled by immunization (see Chapter 13.2).

Giardia lamblia

This protozoan parasite occurs throughout the world (see p.30) and is able to stick firmly to the wall of the small intestine. It probably accounts for less than 3% of cases of travellers' diarrhoea, though it accounts for a much larger proportion of cases of diarrhoea persisting after return home.

In prolonged infections it destroys the inward projections of the gut (called villi), which are responsible for absorbing digested food. Untreated, this can lead to a state of malnutrition.

Cryptosporidium

This organism (a distant relative of the malarial parasite) lives in the small intestine and stimulates an outflow of water that normally lasts up to 10 days, but can persist for weeks. None of the treatments described here apart from rehydration therapy can affect the course of cryptosporidiosis. Moreover, the organism is resistant to all chemical means of water decontamination available to the traveller (including iodine) unless used in higher concentrations than usually employed. For travellers, likely sources of cryptosporidiosis include contaminated water supplies and faecal–oral transmission via food handlers or close contact with an infected individual. The reservoir (where the organism lives normally) of the parasite is in people (*Cryptosporidium hominis*) or cattle (*Cryptosporidium parvum*).

Boiled water and well-cooked food provide the only guarantees against this cause of diarrhoea.

Cyclospora

A recently recognized organism causing persistent diarrhoea in travellers through Nepal and Peru, as well as an outbreak in the USA that was linked to raspberries imported from Guatemala (contaminated water used for crop-spraying is believed to have been the cause).

Entamoeba histolytica

E. histolytica is another protozoan parasite. It accounts for less than 3% of cases of travellers' diarrhoea. It occurs in most tropical countries and may cause amoebic dysentery (see p.31).

The active disease-producing stage of this organism's lifecycle, the 'trophozoites', invade the intestinal wall, causing bleeding and mucus production. Tissue destruction may be extensive and lead to ulcers in the large intestine. Trophozoites may spread to the liver (in about one in five cases) and occasionally (in about one in 1000 cases) produce liver abscesses. Spread to other parts of the body, notably the lungs and the brain, rarely occurs, but usually has fatal consequences.

Bacillary and amoebic dysentery are very difficult to distinguish. The presence of blood or mucus in the stool always requires medical attention and if one cannot, by microscopic examination, separate the cause, medical advice on treatment should be sought.

Giardia and *Entamoeba* are discussed further in the next chapter.

Unidentified causes

In surveys attempting to establish the cause of diarrhoeal illness, no clearly defined infecting agent may be found in more than 40% of cases.

Patterns of illness

The main patterns of illness in travellers with intestinal infection are summarized in Table 2.1.1.

Enteropathogens

Several other agents of diarrhoeal disease (enteropathogens) are known to be important, although their significance to travellers is not established. They are all considered to be causes of 'food-poisoning', a loose term denoting any acute illness from recent consumption of food—see Table 2.1.2. They can to an extent be differentiated by the sufferer on the basis of the interval between eating contaminated food and the onset of the symptoms, and the nature of the symptoms themselves.

There are many non-infectious causes of diarrhoea and blood in the stool (e.g. anxiety and haemorrhoids respectively). *Blood in the stool* (other than small amounts of blood on toilet paper from external haemorrhoids) *always warrants investigation by a doctor.*

In typhoid fever, diarrhoea may occur, but the high fever and headache are important in considering the diagnosis (see Chapter 9.1).

Two other enteropathogens that can cause a severe illness if not appropriately treated are those that cause typhoid and cholera.

Table 2.1.1 Patterns of illness

Vomiting only	Most likely to be caused by toxins produced by bacteria such as *Staphylococcus aureus* and *Bacillus cereus*: vomiting typically occurs 1–5 hours after eating contaminated food.
Vomiting and diarrhoea (gastroenteritis)	Usually due to a toxin (from *S. aureus* or *B. cereus*) or a virus (norovirus or rotavirus); the incubation period (24–48 hours versus 1–7 hours for food poisoning due to pre-formed toxins) is helpful in identifying the likely cause.
Watery diarrhoea	Most people with travellers' diarrhoea have a non-specific syndrome of watery diarrhoea without excessive vomiting, fever, or blood or mucus in the stools. Between 3 and 40 unformed stools are passed over a 3–5 day period, often with abdominal cramps and pain. Cholera can cause an extreme form of this syndrome, with profound fluid loss.
Diarrhoea with fever or blood	When fever or bloody mucoid stools (dysentery) occur, the traveller usually has an infection caused by a bacterium that invades the intestinal lining and produces inflammation. Anti-microbial treatment is necessary. The two major causes of this syndrome in travellers are *Shigella* spp. and *Campylobacter jejuni*. Other less common causes are *Aeromonas* spp., *Vibrio parahemolyticus*, *Entamoeba histolytica*, and non-infectious inflammatory bowel disease.
Persistent diarrhoea	Diarrhoea lasting over 2 weeks is usually due to: *Giardia*; lactose malabsorption; bacterial overgrowth syndrome; persistent infection by a bacterial agent; or non-specific injury pattern of the gut.
Typhoid fever	The person with typhoid will have high fever, headache, abdominal pain, and either constipation or diarrhoea.

Typhoid or enteric fever

The bacteria responsible for enteric fever are *Salmonella typhi* and *Salmonella paratyphi*. After localizing in the lymph glands of the large intestine and terminal small intestine, they spread into the blood. Symptoms generally take about 7 days to appear after exposure (but may range from 3 to 60 days) and include fever, headache, abdominal pain, constipation, and less frequently, diarrhoea. Typhoid is a serious illness and a fatal outcome is common without treatment.

Cholera

Cholera continues to break out in parts of Africa, Asia, South America, and the Pacific, particularly in relation to natural disasters, conflict, and poverty. A serious outbreak began in the refugee camps of Haiti 10 months after the 2010 earthquake, which killed more than 200 000 people and displaced 2 million; more than 360 000 people were infected, with more than 6000 deaths occuring; it could persist in the region for some years.

The fear associated with cholera is out of proportion to the severity of the disease in its modern context. During the 19th century, the disease caused death in most of those infected. However, the *Vibrio cholerae*

Table 2.1.2 Types of bacterial food-poisoning

Causal agent	Incubation period	Symptoms	Comments
Salmonellas (non-typhoid)	6–72 hours (usually 12–36 hours)	Diarrhoea, abdominal pain, vomiting, and fever	See text
Clostridium perfringens	8–22 hours (usually 12–18 hours)	Diarrhoea, abdominal pain (vomiting is rare)	Toxin formed in small intestine
Staphylococcus aureus	1–7 hours (usually 2–4 hours)	Nausea, vomiting, abdominal pain, prostration, dehydration, low temperature, sometimes diarrhoea	Preformed toxin in the food (hence rapid onset)
Campylobacter	1–11 days (usually 2–5 days)	Abdominal pain, diarrhoea, sometimes with blood, fever	Similar to shigellosis; probably very common
Bacillus cereus	1–5 hours or 8–16 hours	Predominantly vomiting Predominantly diarrhoea	Preformed toxins made in small intestine
Vibrio parahaemolyticus	2–48 hours (usually 12–24 hours)	Abdominal pain, diarrhoea, sometimes nausea, vomiting, fever, and headaches	Toxins made in small intestine; classically caught from uncooked seafood

bacteria that caused classic cholera (prior to 1961) were different and more dangerous than those that cause the disease today.

Throughout history, cholera has always tended to occur in pandemics (global epidemics) lasting decades or longer. The current (seventh) pandemic started in Indonesia in 1961. It reached Latin America in 1992 (after an absence from the continent of more than a century) causing much panic, but ultimately resulting in greatly improved sanitation. The strain involved is the El Tor 01 biotype—after infection, severe diarrhoea develops in only 2–5% of those infected, while over 75% have no symptoms at all.

How it is spread

The bacteria that cause the disease survive mainly in estuarine waters and semi-saline coastal lagoons. It has been suggested that some algae act as an environmental reservoir.

Cholera is spread by contamination of food and water by faeces or raw sewage. Shellfish and seafood have been a major source of infection in South America, unwashed vegetables being another.

Like all diarrhoeal illnesses, the likelihood of infection depends on the weakest link in the food and water hygiene chain. Even if water is decontaminated by boiling, contamination of ice cubes in a glass will cause infection.

Children and people with blood group O are at greater risk of infection.

The illness

Diarrhoea caused by the El Tor strain is a mild illness. Its onset is quite sudden, vomiting is frequent and is thought to reflect dehydration; it improves as fluid replacement progresses. Hospital management is not necessary unless sufficient oral fluid intake proves difficult. The illness lasts between 3 and 5 days, leaving no disability when properly treated.

Non-infectious causes of diarrhoea

Some non-infectious causes of diarrhoea are listed in Table 2.1.3.

Table 2.1.3 Non-infectious causes of diarrhoea

Agent	Incubation	Signs and symptoms	Food
Ciguatera fish poisoning (ciguatera toxin)	2–6 hours	Abdominal pain, nausea, vomiting, diarrhoea	A variety of large reef fish, including grouper, red snapper, amberjack, and barracuda
Shellfish toxins (diarrhoeic, neurotoxic, amnesic)	30 mins–2 hours	Nausea, vomiting, diarrhoea, and abdominal pain accompanied by chills, headache, and fever	Shellfish, primarily mussels, oysters, scallops, and shellfish from Florida
Nitrite poisoning Pesticides (organo-phosphates) Mushroom toxin Drugs, including proguanil and chloroquine			

What to do about diarrhoea

Practical help for diarrhoea starts with a description of stool quality and pattern of onset of symptoms. A simple approach based on such descriptions is presented in Fig. 2.1.2. The various courses of action—oral rehydration, seeking medical advice, antibiotics and antidiarrhoeal medicines—are discussed in further detail herein.

Keep in mind that:

1. Most cases resolve within 48–72 hours without any treatment
2. Complications following diarrhoea are commoner in children, the elderly, or those with underlying medical problems
3. Fluid replacement or rehydration by mouth is an effective and safe treatment
4. Diarrhoea containing blood or lasting more than 4 days warrants medical attention.

In rare instances where diarrhoea is severe enough to be life-threatening, it is adequate fluid replacement, not drugs, that will prove life saving.

Rehydration

Travellers' diarrhoea in hot climates may cause dehydration even if mild. Fluid requirements are difficult to predict. Thirst is a reminder that the body needs fluid, but is not always present. Young children cannot communicate their thirst other than by crying or becoming drowsy, which makes them especially susceptible to dehydration.

Rehydration salts are widely available, sold in sachets containing a mixture of salt and glucose (e.g. Dioralyte, Electrolade) to be added to clean water. You can make your own, either using a special measuring spoon, or by combining:

- 8 level or 4 heaped teaspoons of sugar (white, brown, or honey)
- half a teaspoon of salt
- 1L of clean water.

Other carbohydrates produce the same effect as glucose or sucrose. These include 50g (10–15 teaspoons) per L of powdered rice (and other cereals), which needs to be added to a small volume of boiling water before diluting to 1L.

Oral rehydration should be started early, rather than later. Vomiting is often a major feature of dehydration—as you replace fluids vomiting will decrease.

For healthy adults with mild to moderate attacks, an adequate intake of most non-alcoholic drinks will normally suffice, but rehydration fluids should always be prepared for infants.

When ministering to others, look for evidence of significant dehydration, such as dry tongue, dark, concentrated, smelly urine in small quantities, or no urine at all, and a weak, rapid pulse. If such evidence is found, particularly in children, the sufferer should be coerced to take as much rehydration solution as possible until he or she starts to pass urine of normal appearance and volume. A simple regimen for adults is to insist on a glass of oral rehydration solution for every bowel movement, plus a further glass every hour.

For children, careful fluid replacement is necessary. As a guide, 1.5 times the normal feed volume as rehydration solution, while continuing the normal feed would be necessary. For children who are breast feeding, this should continue, with additional rehydration solution also provided, although breast-fed infants can obtain all they need from the breast alone (see Chapter 11.2).

Anyone showing signs of worsening dehydration should receive immediate medical attention, since intravenous rehydration may be necessary.

Antibiotics

Most forms of diarrhoeal disease will resolve without the use of antibiotics. Antibiotics have *no* effect when the cause is a virus or parasite.

There are a number of fairly clear circumstances where antibiotics are needed for gut problems, ideally, always under medical supervision. However, in an emergency the following regimens may be considered after consultation with Table 2.1.4.

- *'Quinolones'*: the antibiotic group that includes ciprofloxacin, norfloxacin, and ofloxacin are an effective treatment for most cases of diarrhoea. They must not be used in children before puberty, or in pregnant or breast-feeding women. Because there have been reports of visual disturbance, you should find out how you react to the drug before driving or operating machinery. Table 2.1.4 (regimens A and B) gives recommendations for the use of ciprofloxacin. The simplest regimen is a single dose taken at the first sign of diarrhoea. Drug resistance can be a problem in some parts of the world, especially *Campylobacter* infections in Southeast Asia. Achilles tendon rupture is a rare complication of therapy

- *Azithromycin (Zithromax):* a possible alternative to these drugs, with the added advantage of being suitable for use in children. Resistance is less widespread and this drug may be preferred for persons passing bloody stools with fever
- *Metronidazole (Flagyl):* an effective and safe drug that can be used in the treatment of suspected amoebiasis and giardiasis. Minor side effects are an unpleasant metallic taste, nausea, and a furry tongue. Do not drink alcohol during treatment. The regimens for use of metronidazole for giardiasis are shown in Table 2.1.4 (regimens F and H)
- *Tinidazole (Fasigyn):* in a single dose this is an alternative that is slightly more pleasant to take. It is important to take a second drug in amoebiasis that treats the cysts to prevent recurrence
- *Sulphamethoxazole with trimethoprim (Bactrim, Septrin):* this is now of limited use for the treatment of diarrhoea and bacillary dysentery (shigellosis). Resistance is widespread and side effects can be a problem. Signs of toxicity are rashes, blood in the urine, and jaundice
- If, after starting ciprofloxacin for dysentery, there is no improvement after 36 hr, it is quite reasonable to take a course of metronidazole at the same time
- *New antibiotics:* these include rifaximin, one of a new generation of antibiotics that is not absorbed and acts locally on the intestine. The dose of rifaximin for treatment is 200mg three times a day for three days.

Typhoid

Typhoid often begins like flu, with severe headache, sore throat, and a gradually increasing fever over several days. Signs of a serious infection are usually obvious and the sufferer is confined to bed. A pulse of only 80 bpm or less, in the presence of an obviously high fever, makes typhoid a likely cause. The illness is more severe in the second week and the victim may become delirious. Medical help should always be sought. In an emergency, antibiotic treatment with ciprofloxacin in the doses shown in Table 2.1.4 regimen J should be used.

Cholera

Oral antibiotics such as doxycyline, ciprofloxacin or erythromycin can reduce the length of infection, if taken early in the illness. As with other types of travellers' diarrhoea, treatment with abundant quantities of oral rehydration solution is the most effective measure. Since fluid loss is the most important complication of severe cholera, oral rehydration therapy has completely disarmed the disease, reducing the death rate from over 80% to less than 1%.

Symptomatic treatment

'Anti-motility' agents

'Anti-motility' or antidiarrhoeal agents inhibit intestinal movement, and can reduce diarrhoea by 80%. Their use is recommended mainly when sanitary arrangements are difficult, and then limited to two to four doses. They should never be used when the sufferer has bloody diarrhoea or fever—they can occasionally make the illness worse unless antibiotics are also given. They should be stopped as soon as diarrhoea improves.

With the above warnings in mind, the two antidiarrhoeal agents that might be considered are loperamide hydrochloride (Imodium) and codeine phosphate. These should not be used in children without medical advice. The WHO advises that anti-secretory or binding agents should not be used in infants or children.

'Anti-secretory drugs'

The best known drug of this type is bismuth subsalicylate (Pepto-Bismol); it can reduce diarrhoea by 50% (see p.27). It should not be used in infants and children. Bismuth subsalicylate turns stools and tongues black due to harmless bismuth salts.

Racecadotril (Hidrasec) has a powerful effect on reducing water secretion into the gut. It is available in several countries, although not the UK or USA, and is considered safe and effective; it has been widely used in children in combination with oral rehydration therapy.

Adsorptive agents

Adsorbents such as attapulgite (Diasorb or Kaopectate) are very safe since they are not absorbed from the intestine, making them useful in children and pregnant women. However, relapse is common as soon as treatment stops.

What to eat if you are ill

It is important to alter your diet during a bout of diarrhoea, because food absorption is often impaired. Don't try to starve yourself! The gut needs energy for repair.

With watery diarrhoea, take only liquids such as soups and broths, and easily digestible foods, such as saltine crackers. As stools assume some soft form, move on to foods like toast, potatoes, bananas, tortillas, and baked fish or chicken. Once stools become formed again, move back to a normal diet. Milk and dairy products should be avoided during the early stages of diarrhoea since lactose malabsorption may occur.

When to see a doctor

The major reasons for seeing a physician include:
- Temperature above 38°C
- Significant fever lasting longer than 48 hours
- Diarrhoea lasting longer than 4 days
- Severe diarrhoea with difficulty keeping up with fluid and salt replacement
- Diarrhoea with blood.

Table 2.1.4 Antibiotic regimens for treatment of various suspected causes of diarrhoea

Suspected cause	Regimen	Antibiotic	Age	Amount per dose	Doses per day and duration
	A	Ciprofloxacin	Adult	500–750mg	Single dose (may be sufficient in 80–90% of cases)
Suspected bacillary dysentery (shigellosis), ETEC	B	Ciprofloxacin	Adult	500mg	One dose twice a day for three days; opt for 3-day course in presence of fever blood.
	C	Norfloxacin	Adult	400mg	One dose twice a day for three days
	D	Ofloxacin	Adult	400mg	One dose twice a day for three days
	E	Azithromycin	Adult	1000mg	One single dose
			Child over 6 months (only with fever and bloody diarrhoea)	Initial dose: 10mg per kg of body weight; thereafter 5mg per kg	Once daily for 3 days
Suspected amoebiasis (see also p.31)	F	Metronidazole (Flagyl)	Adult	750–800mg	One dose three times per day for 5 days followed by diloxanide furoate (p.31)
			8–12 years	400–500mg	
			4–7 years	375–400mg	
			2–3 years	200–120mg	
			Under 2 years	80–120mg	
	G	Tinidazole (Fasigyn)	Adult	2g (4 tablets)	Daily for 5 days
			Child	50–60mg per kilo of body weight	Daily for 3 days

		Drug	Age	Dose	Regimen
Suspected giardiasis	H	Metronidazole (Flagyl)	Adult	200–250mg	One dose three times per day for 5 days
			8–12 years	200–250mg	
			3–7 years	100–125mg	
			Under 3 years	50–62mg	
	I	Tinidazole (Fasigyn)	Adult	2g (4 tablets)	Single dose, repeated once if necessary
			Child	50–75mg per kg of body weight	
Suspected typhoid	J	Ciprofloxacin	Adult	500mg	One dose twice a day for 14 days
	K	Chloramphenicol (Chloromycetin)	12 years–adult	500mg–1g	One dose four times per day
			8–12 years	250mg	
			3–7 years	125mg	

Notes:

1. Any antibiotic treatment should preferably be prescribed by a doctor. The above regimens are for emergency use only

2. Use of the above regimens should be considered only after reading the accompanying text on antibiotics and consulting Fig. 2.1.2.

3. For regimens F and H, the choice of dose given allows for the fact that tablets sometimes come in different strengths.

When you've got to go...

To relieve urgency if you have a sudden bout of diarrhoea, but can't find a lavatory, try lying on your left side; this may allow gas to pass through the otherwise impenetrable obstacle of liquid stool in the rectum, and provide temporary relief.

RD

Prevention

The most important preventive measures are outlined in the section on transmission.

Antibiotics

Antibiotics are occasionally advocated for prevention in some circumstances. The main arguments against this practice are:
1. Some of the rare side effects of antibiotics are worse than the diseases they prevent
2. Widespread antibiotic use promotes development of antibiotic-resistant bacteria, which may make other infections more difficult to treat
3. Antibiotics make diagnosis difficult when infection does occur.

The main arguments in favour of the prophylactic use of antibiotics are:
1. Several regimens are known to be effective
2. The personal cost of being out of action may outweigh the risks involved.

Our feeling is that antibiotics should be taken as a preventive only when important plans are at risk or when the traveller is already weakened from long-standing illness (e.g. heart disease).

Travellers taking proton pump inhibitors (PPI) for gastric or duodenal ulcers to reduce gastric acidity may be at increased risk, and should consider taking antibiotics for prevention. Rifaximin 400mg once a day with the major daily meal, for trips up to two weeks, is one regimen that may be considered.

Vaccination

Typhoid

Two vaccines are currently available (see p.448) and immunization is recommended when travelling to areas of poor sanitation.

The injected Vi antigen vaccine causes very little reaction, and only a single dose is necessary. The oral typhoid vaccine is based ingeniously on freeze-dried bacteria that 'come to life' briefly in the small intestine and then 'commit suicide'.

Both vaccines are roughly 50–90% effective.

Cholera

The original injected cholera vaccine is no longer used, and provided very little protection. New, effective oral vaccines generate surface immunity at the intestine—the natural site of infection. The Dukoral vaccine contains a combination of killed cholera vibrios and recombinant B subunit toxin and has been shown to also partially cross-protect against diarrhoea caused by *Escherichia coli*, the bacteria responsible for most of travellers' diarrhoea, which produce a similar toxin. Two doses are given, 1 week apart. (Children aged 2–6 years receive three doses.)

CVD 103-HgR (Mutachol) is licensed in Canada and is effective against the cholera 01 serogroup. The vaccine is administered as a single dose, and is approved for adults and children over 2 years of age.

Health professionals working in endemic areas, aid workers, and travellers to remote cholera areas without access to safe water supplies should certainly consider receiving the vaccine. Travellers should seek an individual risk assessment to determine their need for vaccination.

Other medicines for prevention

Rifaximin 400mg once a day with the major daily meal, for trips up to two weeks.

Bismuth subsalicylate (Pepto-Bismol), taken in a dose of two tablets four times a day, for up to 3 weeks, will prevent 65% of the illnesses that would occur without prophylaxis. The only side effects are harmless blackening of stools and tongue; other salicylate-containing drugs should not be taken at the same time (notably aspirin), because this can lead to excessive salicylate blood levels.

Lactobacilli are available in various preparations. The concept is that the organisms displace the dangerous organisms and improve the symptoms. There is not much evidence to suggest they work either in the treatment or prevention of diarrhoea.

The traveller will find a host of tempting preparations for the current or potential sufferer in any pharmacy. Many of these are useless or actually damaging. For example, clioquinol (Entero-Vioform) is still a popular remedy in some countries—despite being toxic and ineffective.

Persisting symptoms

Most episodes in travellers last 48–72 hours, but 10% of people have illnesses that last longer than a week, 2% have diarrhoea that lasts over a month, and a small proportion have diarrhoea lasting 2–12 months.

In travellers with persistent diarrhoea, a different set of conditions is usually the cause—parasites like *Giardia*, for example; another common cause is lactose intolerance—reduced digestion and absorption of milk sugars following damage to the intestinal lining.

In 1–5% of people with travellers' diarrhoea, a chronic functional bowel disease will occur. Some of those affected will be later diagnosed with post-infectious irritable bowel syndrome (IBS). IBS has a better prognosis when it follows a bout of diarrhoea than when there is no antecedent bout of intestinal infection and most will be well within the next 5 years.

Several even rarer illnesses also became relatively more important in this context. These include tropical sprue, a poorly understood condition in which the small intestine contains large numbers of bacteria and several of the parasitic worms dealt with in the next chapter. These illnesses are rarely life threatening, but warrant careful investigation.

Other, non-infective disorders may also cause diarrhoea, bleeding, and abdominal symptoms. Careful medical investigation is extremely important. Box 2.1.2 gives a summary of advice for travellers.

Box 2.1.2 **Summary of advice for travellers**

- Most travellers' diarrhoea is the result of swallowing contaminated material
- The contaminating bacterial micro-organisms are rendered harmless by cooking (by bringing temperatures to 60°C) all the way through
- Cooked food remains safe only if eaten immediately or if sealed and refrigerated without delay
- Precautions with food are summarized in Appendix 3
- Diarrhoeal episodes are usually self-limiting, get better after 1–3 days, and require no specific treatment
- Replacement of fluid losses is the first consideration of treatment, especially with children (see p.382)
- Guidelines for use of antibiotics and other drugs are given in pp.21–5
- Diarrhoeal illnesses are not always avoidable.

2.2 Parasites from infected food and drink

Bertie Squire

Intestinal parasitic and protozoan infections are amongst the most common infections worldwide. The risk to travellers from these infections varies greatly according to geographic location visited, the food eaten, and local hygiene.

The mouth is a major portal of entry for human parasites. The infective stage may be ingested as microscopic protozoan cysts, worm eggs, or larvae that contaminate food or drink. Alternatively, food consumed may be tissue from an animal that is itself infected by a parasite such as *Toxoplasma* or a tapeworm; or fluke larvae from aquatic snail hosts may encyst in fish, crustaceans, or water plants.

Human parasites fall into two groups:
- those that remain in the gut throughout most of their cycle in man— *resident intestinal parasites* (see Table 2.2.1)
- those that leave the intestine soon after infection and disperse to other organs—*transient intestinal parasites* (see Table 2.2.2).

The latter may manifest themselves as disease weeks, months, or even years later. The number of potential species transmitted in these ways exceeds 50, but some are rare or very local in their distribution. Nevertheless, there is a significant chance that visitors might pick up one or more of them.

Travellers to rural areas are generally at greater risk, especially those who share in cultural experiences, such as wedding or hunting feasts, and local food specialities.

Table 2.2.1 Resident intestinal parasites acquired from food and drink

	Location	Source of infection	Distribution
Protozoa			
Giardia	Small intestine	Cysts on food or in water	C
Cryptosporidium	Small intestine	Cysts on food or in water	C
Amoebiasis (*Entamoeba*)	Large intestine	Cysts on food or in water	PT
Helminths (worms)			
Herring worm (*Anisakis*)	Stomach and duodenum	Larval worm in fish	L
Roundworm (*Ascaris*)	Small intestine	Eggs on food	PT
Tapeworm (*Taenia*)	Small intestine	Larval cysts in meat	L
Intestinal flukes	Small intestine	Larval cysts in fish or on water plants	L
Abdominal angiostrongyliasis	Caecum	Larvae from molluscs on salads	L
Whipworm (*Trichuris*)	Large intestine	Eggs on food	PT

Key: C = cosmopolitan (worldwide); PT = pantropical (throughout the tropics); L = localized.

Resident intestinal parasites

Some major symptoms and clinical features caused by the parasites listed in Table 2.2.1 are:

- Colicky abdominal pains—all species
- Upper abdominal pain, sometimes severe—*Ascaris, Anisakis*
- Simple diarrhoea—*Cryptosporidium*
- Diarrhoea with malabsorption (bulky, pale, offensive and difficult to flush away)—*Giardia*
- Dysentery (diarrhoea with blood)—amoebiasis
- Worms seen in stool—*Ascaris*, tapeworms, threadworms
- Skin wheals (urticaria) and wheezing—*Ascaris*, intestinal flukes
- Itchy bottom—*Enterobius* and *Taenia saginata* (beef tapeworm)
- Retarded growth and malnutrition among children in heavily infected populations—*Ascaris, Trichuris*, and *Giardia*.

These infections are diagnosed by examining stool samples under the microscope. Most can be effectively treated with anti-parasitic drugs and self-treatment is sometimes appropriate.

Table 2.2.2 Transient intestinal infections derived from food and drink

	Final location	Source of infection	Distribution
Protozoa			
Amoebiasis (*Entamoeba*)	Liver, rarely lung	Cysts on contaminated food or drink	PT
Toxoplasma	Most tissues including eye	Cysts in meat or from cat faeces	C
Helminths (worms)			
Trichinosis (*Trichinella*)	Muscle and elsewhere	Larval worm in meat	L
Cysticercosis (*Taenia solium*)	Brain, eye, and elsewhere	Eggs contaminate food	L
Hydatid (*Echinococcus*)	Liver, lung, and elsewhere	Eggs contaminate food and fingers	L
Liver flukes	Liver and biliary system	Larval cysts in fish or on vegetables	L
Lung flukes	Lung	Larval cysts in crayfish	L
Angiostrongylus cantonenis	Meninges of brain	Larvae from molluscs on salads	L
Toxocara	Liver, lung, eye, and brain	Eggs contaminate food and fingers	C

Key: C = cosmopolitan (worldwide); PT = pantropical (throughout the tropics); L = localized.

Protozoan infections

Giardasis

Giardia is a common cosmopolitan species. Most infections in the tropics are derived from infected children, but animals, especially dogs, are also important. In Canadian mountain resorts, mountain beavers can contaminate water supplies. The parasite adheres to the epithelial cells lining the gut by means of a sucking disc, affecting cell function with reduced absorption of nutrients. Symptoms start within a few days with abdominal bloating, flatulence, poor appetite, and loose, pale, fatty stools. Morning diarrhoea is characteristic. The illness may subside after a week or so, but in some persons it is prolonged.

Stool specimens show cysts or the swimming flagellate. Treatment is with metronidazole (400mg, three times a day for 5 days) or tinidazole (2g as a single dose). Self-treatment on clinical suspicion is justified. Some people have very persistent infections that are difficult to eradicate.

Cryptosporidium and other small gut protozoa

Cryptosporidium is common and cosmopolitan; infection is often waterborne. Farm and some domestic animals are a common source. The parasites invade epithelial cells and undergo repeated cycles of multiplication, causing local damage and inflammation. The illness is often quite acute with watery diarrhoea, cramps, and fever; most infections are self-limiting after a week or so. Drug treatment is ineffective.

Two related parasites are widespread but local. *Isospora* is reported especially from tropical Africa and the West Indies, while *Cyclospora* is common in Nepal and Latin America. Their life cycle is similar to *Cryptosporidium*. The illness they cause is often more severe than *Cryptosporidium*, more prolonged, and may resemble giardiasis with fatty stools. Both can be treated with co-trimoxazole (Septrin, Bactrim).

While the cysts of these three parasites are present in faecal specimens, they are commonly overlooked. These infections are of major importance in persons with HIV, in whom they are the major secondary cause of the wasting, diarrhoeal AIDS-related illness that is so common in tropical countries. Other gut protozoa, called microspora, cause similar problems in HIV patients. These organisms require electron microscopy (EM) of gut biopsies to identify them; the commonest is *Enterocytozoon*.

Amoebiasis (amoebic dysentery)
Entamoeba histolytica once had a worldwide distribution, but is now common only in the tropics; Nepal has a bad reputation for this parasite.

Swallowed cysts reach the large intestine. These 'hatch' to produce amoebae that live on the mucosal surface and usually invade it, resulting in ulcers that can severely damage the bowel wall. Invading amoebae are actively motile, killing host cells and feeding on cell debris and red blood cells. Invading amoebae may enter local blood vessels and be carried to the liver to cause liver abscess (see p.34).

Symptoms start 2 weeks to a month or so after infection. Colicky pains and loose blood-stained stools may persist for weeks or even months, often with a relapsing course. Severe infections cause dysentery with bloody diarrhoea and, untreated, this may be a significant danger to life. More chronic infections can cause tumour-like masses called amoebomas.

Early diagnosis is essential and is best made by microscopic examination of fresh faeces or exudate taken from the rectal wall. Living invasive amoebae are actively motile and contain red blood cells. Finding amoebic cysts in stool specimens by light microscopy is of little value as they are indistinguishable, without additional genetic testing, from those of a harmless species called *Entamoeba dispar*. Even in the tropics this second species is much more common than *E. histolytica*. Travellers should beware of laboratories that use unreliable methods and practitioners who offer unnecessary and sometimes toxic medications.

The standard course of treatment consists of metronidazole 750–800mg, three times a day for 5 days, followed by diloxanide 500mg, three times a day for 10 days. Unless the second drug is given, relapses from infection can occur. An alternative is metronidazole, taken alone for 8 days, but this will give a lower rate of parasite elimination. There is a dilemma here for the traveller since amoebiasis is potentially dangerous, and it is better to know whether one is really infected or not. Empirical treatment, even self-treatment, is sometimes justified, but when symptoms recur there will be the temptation to repeat it, when it is possible that the illness was not amoebiasis at all. Side-effects of metronidazole in short courses may be unpleasant, but are unlikely to be serious and alcohol should not be taken with it. Tinidazole (more expensive) is an alternative to metronidazole; it has the advantage of being taken as a single daily dose, but is probably less effective.

Worm infections

Roundworm, whipworm, and threadworm infections

These are all common; they are nematode worms, whitish in colour, cylindrical in cross-section and pointed at both ends.

- *The roundworm* (*Ascaris*) is usually about 30cm in length and 4mm in diameter. Infection occurs when eggs, usually on food and vegetables, are swallowed; after hatching in the intestine, larvae migrate through the lungs to be swallowed again and so back to the small intestine. Worms live free in the gut lumen and mature in about 9 weeks, when eggs appear in the faeces; they live for about a year. During the lung migration phase, wheezing and rashes can occur; later the main symptoms are colicky abdominal pains and loss of appetite. Worms may be passed per rectum. Illness is serious in heavily-infected children, in whom bowel obstruction or migration into the bile and pancreatic duct may require surgical treatment. More than a billion people worldwide harbour this parasite

- *The whipworm* (*Trichuris*) is much smaller, up to 4cm in length. It lives in the lower colon and rectum, where it is attached to the mucosa. There is no lung migration phase. Sources of infection are similar to *Ascaris*. Light infection may cause no symptoms, but lower left abdominal pains and loose bowel habit with some blood can occur. Heavy infections in children can cause dysentery, constant straining at stool and rectal prolapse

- *Threadworms* (*Enterobius*) are a familiar problem in children throughout the world. Contrary to some opinions, they are common in the tropics and quite often picked up by travellers. The worms measure up to 1cm and live in the large intestine; female worms migrate to the rectum and emerge from the anus at night to lay eggs on the skin. This leads to scratching; eggs are then transferred to fingers, toys, food, etc. Self-infection is common and prolongs the problem. Parents commonly notice worms in children's underpants. Children become irritable and sleep poorly.

Mebendazole is effective for all the parasites described above, but is not recommended for children under 2 years. For *Ascaris* and *Trichuris*, 100mg is given twice a day for 3 days. For threadworms, a single 100mg dose, repeated after 2 weeks is sufficient. This infection often spreads to close contacts and it is wise to treat all the family simultaneously to prevent reinfection. Piperazine should be used for children under 2 years.

Tapeworms

Larval cysts of the beef tapeworm (*Taenia saginata*) occur in undercooked beef. The swallowed worm attaches to the gut wall, grows to maturity in 3 months, and may live for many years. Most are solitary. The worm is creamy white, flat, and segmented; it can grow to 4m. Mature segments containing eggs are shed at its posterior end, while new segments form at the anterior end. Colicky pains and impaired or increased appetite are typical symptoms, but often the problem becomes apparent only when segments are seen in the stool or are found in underpants. The life cycle of this parasite involves only humans and cattle; cattle become infected from eggs in human faeces.

Infection with the related pork tapeworm (*Taenia solium*) occurs when undercooked pig meat is eaten. Symptoms are similar except that worm segments are not motile and do not migrate through the anus. The importance of the pork tapeworm is that under conditions of poor hygiene, eggs can be swallowed by other people and can develop into cystic larval worms. The result is a serious condition—cysticercosis (see p.34).

Several other tapeworms infect man, including the fish tapeworm, found mainly in Canada, northern Europe, Scandinavia, and Russia, and the cosmopolitan dwarf tapeworm (*Hymenolepis*), which requires no animal host in its cycle.

Tapeworm infections are treated with Praziquantel, usually as a single dose. The recommended dosages are slightly different for each species so seek specialist advice.

Rarities

Symptoms occur within 24 hours of eating raw seafish or squid containing the herring worm (*Anisakis*), which burrows into the wall of the stomach or duodenum. There is upper abdominal pain and vomiting, and emergency endoscopy may reveal the worm and enable its extraction. It occurs especially in the Pacific, where whales and other cetaceans are the hosts. To infect man, seafood must be eaten partly raw or lightly pickled. The Japanese delicacy sushi is particularly risky.

Intestinal flukes come in many sizes and include the giant *Fasciolopsis* of Southeast Asia, acquired by eating water chestnuts; others are acquired from cysts in undercooked fish.

Abdominal angiostrongyliasis due to *Angiostrongylus costaricensis* was first described in Costa Rica in 1971. It is now recognized as being quite common, especially in children, in Latin America and the Caribbean. Worms live in the arteries of the appendix area of the gut and set up local inflammation. The normal hosts are cotton rats and other rodents; transmission occurs via slugs that contain the larval stage. While humans are unlikely to eat slugs, their mucus trails containing larvae can easily contaminate salads and fallen fruit. Diagnosis is usually made at surgery for suspected appendicitis. There is no drug treatment.

Transient intestinal parasites

Major symptoms and clinical features of the parasites listed in Table 2.2.1 are:

- *Muscle pain and stiffness:* trichinosis
- *Raised blood eosinophil count:* most worm infections in tissue
- *Liver enlargement and pain:* liver flukes, amoebic liver abscess, hydatid cysts, *Toxocara*
- *Lung disease with cough and shortness of breath:* lung fluke, hydatid cyst
- *Fever and generalised illness:* amoebic liver abscess, toxoplasmosis, trichinosis
- *Allergic features (wheals, facial swelling and wheezing):* most worm parasites

- *Brain disease with fits, meningitis or brain tumour simulation:* cysticercosis, Angiostrongylus, hydatid cyst, and toxoplasmosis
- *Eye disease with visual impairment:* Toxoplasma, Toxocara.

The diagnosis may require blood tests for specific antibody, imaging with ultrasound, and X-rays. Anti-parasitic drugs may not be sufficient and surgery may be necessary.

Amoebic liver abscess

This serious condition can occur during an attack of amoebic dysentery, but more commonly weeks or even years later. It usually presents with fever, rigors (shivers), and pain in the liver region, back, or right shoulder tip, but may present as an undifferentiated fever. The abscess contains dead liver tissue and can reach many centimetres in diameter. Untreated, abscesses enlarge progressively and rupture into adjacent structures. Ultrasound scans and antibody tests establish diagnosis. Metronidazole is used for treatment, but to prevent relapse, gut infection must be eliminated with diloxanide. Drainage of the abscess is sometimes needed.

Toxoplasmosis

Although the risk from cat boxes is well known, infection also follows eating undercooked meat containing tissue cysts. Burgers have a bad reputation and epidemic outbreaks can occur. A febrile illness with enlarged lymph nodes results and sometimes the retina is affected. Pregnant women are at special risk because the foetus may be infected. Latent infections can be reactivated in persons with late HIV infection. The resulting brain lesions can mimic a tumour; the retina may also be affected.

Trichinosis

Infection follows eating poorly cooked pork, but wild boar, bush pig, or even hippopotamus are other sources. After a short diarrhoeal illness patients develop generalized muscle pains, weakness, fever, prostration, and swelling of the face and eyelids. The initial gut infection can be treated with mebendazole, but once muscle is invaded by larval worms the steroid prednisolone must be used to control symptoms and limit damage to the heart.

Larval tapeworms causing cysticercosis and hydatid disease

In environments contaminated by human faeces of persons infected by the pork tapeworm, eggs may be ingested on food and man becomes an accidental intermediate host. Larval cysts, up to 2 cm, develop in any tissue but especially the brain, muscle, heart or beneath the skin. Brain lesions can cause epilepsy or serious pressure effects. Drug treatment is available, but difficult and surgery may be necessary. High-risk areas for travellers are Latin America (especially Mexico), central and southern Africa, and the Indian subcontinent.

Hydatid cysts are the larval cysts of the dog tapeworm *Echinococcus granulosus*. They may reach 10cm or more in size, and occur especially in the liver, lung, or brain. Symptoms result from pressure or from leakage, leading to severe allergic reactions that may be fatal. Leakage may occur after trauma or during surgical procedures. Travellers are at risk especially in the Middle East, North and East Africa, and Latin America.

Infection is derived from eggs in dog faeces that contaminate food and fingers; stroking infected dogs is a risk.

Fluke infections of liver and lung

Liver flukes cause painful liver enlargement and sometimes jaundice following ingestion of pickled or undercooked fish. Species of liver fluke occur in East and Southeast Asia. The sheep liver fluke (*Fasciola*) has a cosmopolitan distribution that includes Europe and South America. Infection follows ingestion of watercress and other water plants on which there are larval cysts.

Lung fluke infections occur in the Far East, South America, and West Africa after eating crayfish and other freshwater crustaceans. Larval flukes penetrate the gut, diaphragm, and lung to reach the bronchial airways, where pairs of worms live for many years. Symptoms include breathlessness, coughing, and blood-stained sputum. Drug treatments for these fluke infections are available, but some are toxic.

Eosinophilic meningitis due to Angiostrongylus cantonensis

This occurs in the Pacific area and follows ingestion of salads containing snails or their slime. The larval worm migrates to the meninges, where a chronic infection occurs; the diagnostic clue is numerous eosinophil cells in the cerebrospinal fluid and blood. The illness lasts several weeks and no specific treatment is yet available.

Toxocariasis

Infection rates for this dog roundworm are often high in the tropics and children are vulnerable to ingesting eggs from sand and soil contaminated by dog faeces. Heavy infections cause coughing and wheezing, or painful liver enlargement. A few children, even with light infections, develop retinal lesions that resemble eye tumours and epilepsy.

Box 2.2.1 **Summary of advice for travellers**

- Particular hazards are: contaminated water that has not been boiled or sterilized; raw, pickled or undercooked meat, fish and shellfish, salads and raw vegetables; fruit that cannot be peeled; cold drinks, ice, and cooked foods sold by street vendors
- Understanding how parasites are transmitted is the key to reducing the risk
- Self-treatment is appropriate for some protozoan and worm infections of the gut, and it may be helpful to take medication (such as metronidazole and mebendazole) as part of your medical kit. Many of the intestinal parasites, however, need more specialist therapy
- Seek medical advice on returning home if you develop symptoms or feel you have been at risk. Tell your doctor where you have been and what you have eaten. Delays in diagnosis are often due to failure to take travel history into account
- Keep in mind that stool samples often need a specialist laboratory for correct diagnosis and may need to be repeated a number of times before infection can be ruled out.

2.3 Poliomyelitis

Tom Solomon

As the result of a global immunization campaign, the final eradication of polio now seems close. For the time being, however, polio remains a risk in some parts of the world, and travellers should ensure that they don't miss out on protection.

The remarkable story of poliomyelitis encompasses some of the landmark achievements and successes of medical science in the 20th century, in terms of diagnosis, prevention, and eradication.

Poliomyelitis (often known just as polio) has been around since antiquity. The earliest record of a withered, shortened leg with the characteristic appearances is an Egyptian stele of the 18th dynasty (1580–1350 BC). The name (derived from the Greek 'polio', meaning grey, and 'myelos' meaning marrow or spinal cord) is descriptive of the pathological lesions that affect the grey matter in the anterior horn of the spinal cord, where lower motor nerves originate. The infectious nature of the disease was proved in the early 1900s by injecting spinal cord material from fatal polio cases into monkeys to reproduce the symptoms and the pathological lesions of the disease. The poliovirus was subsequently shown to be a small enterovirus (intestinal virus), transmitted between humans via the faecal–oral route, which occurs as three strains.

Before the late 19th century, polio was predominantly a sporadic disease that mostly affected children under 5 years. Epidemiological evidence supports the idea that the virus was ubiquitous. Almost all under-fives became infected, but in most there was no obvious illness, and they simply developed immunity; only the unlucky few developed the disease. Then, during the 20th century, the disease pattern changed. It is speculated that because of improved hygiene, younger children avoided infection, and large populations of uninfected and non-immune older children became vulnerable to infection, succumbing in mass epidemics.

Immunization

In the 1950s, two vaccines were produced. In the first (developed by Salk and others) formalin-inactivated (i.e. killed) poliovirus was injected into the skin; in the second (developed by Sabin and others) live virus that had been attenuated (i.e. changed to a mild form that does not cause disease) was used orally. There was a dramatic decline in polio epidemics in countries where the vaccines were used.

In 1988 the World Health Organization (WHO) resolved to eradicate polio by the year 2000. Like smallpox before it, polio is a suitable target for global eradication because the virus is found only in humans (there is no animal reservoir to contend with), and cheap effective vaccines are available. The campaign consisted, in essence, of mass vaccination with the live oral polio vaccine and disease surveillance for clinically suspected cases of polio. Although there was initially some controversy, the campaign has undoubtedly been a success.

By 1998 the Americas were free from polio, and transmission had been interrupted in the WHO Western Pacific Region (including China) and in the European Region (except for a small focus in Southeast Turkey). A total of 5000 cases were reported in 1999, compared with more than 350 000 cases in 1988. Although cases were reported from 30 countries in 1999, these mostly came from one of three large foci of transmission— South Asia (India, Pakistan, and Afghanistan), West Africa (mainly Nigeria), and Central Africa.

By 2006 polio was endemic in only four countries (Nigeria, India, Pakistan, and Afghanistan), although it continued to cause epidemics in nearby countries, and transmission subsequently became re-established in Angola, Chad, and the Democratic Republic of Congo. A Global Polio Eradication Initiative strategic plan 2010–2012 galvanized renewed efforts, and since January 2010 the number of cases decreased by 95% in the main reservoirs of northern India and northern Nigeria. For the latest update, visit ℘ http://www.polioeradication.org/

Clinical features
Infection with polioviruses can cause one of five clinical presentations:
- Asymptomatic infection
- 'Abortive poliomyelitis' (a mild non-specific febrile illness)
- 'Non-paralytic poliomyelitis' (essentially a viral meningitis syndrome)
- 'Paralytic poliomyelitis' (which may be spinal or bulbar)
- 'Polio encephalitis' (which is rare).

Of these, paralytic poliomyelitis affecting the spinal cord is the most frequently recognized syndrome. Typically, the illness is biphasic: a couple of days of a non-specific fever is followed by a brief asymptomatic period before the central nervous system infection begins. This is heralded by more fever, headache, nausea, vomiting, neck stiffness, and limb paralysis. The paralysis is flaccid (floppy), progresses rapidly, and is usually asymmetrical, involving the legs more frequently than the arms. Paralysis is more likely in a limb that has been the site of an intramuscular injection or injury within 2–4 weeks before the onset of infection. There may be muscle pains early in the illness and, although these may be relieved by gentle exercise, this increases the severity of the paralysis that follows.

Recommendations for travellers
Inactivated polio vaccine is usually combined with diphtheria and tetanus vaccine. A booster dose is recommended for travellers to areas where polio is still endemic, unless they have received a dose within the previous 10 years. Individuals who have never been vaccinated should receive a primary immunization course of three doses at 1-month intervals.

Box 2.3.1 **Summary of advice for travellers**
- Polio remains a threat to travellers despite the success of the WHO polio eradication campaign
- Travellers to endemic areas should receive a booster vaccine dose (unless they have received one in the last 10 years) or a primary course if they have never been vaccinated).

2.4 Viral hepatitis

Jane Zuckerman and Arie Zuckerman

Hepatitis is an important risk for travellers to areas outside North America, northern Europe, and Australia, and may result in an unpleasant prolonged illness. All travellers should understand how the different types of hepatitis are spread.

Viral hepatitis is common, occurs worldwide, and is a major public health problem. At least six different viruses are capable of causing infection, resulting in the following similar illnesses:

- Hepatitis A (previously called infectious hepatitis or epidemic jaundice)
- Hepatitis B
- Hepatitis C (previously called non-A, non-B hepatitis)
- Hepatitis D (delta hepatitis)
- Hepatitis E.

The viruses responsible for hepatitis A, B, C, D, and E have been 'characterized': much is known about their size, structure, and biology. Sensitive laboratory tests are available for detecting components of the viruses (viral antigens) and antibodies against them in blood or tissues of people who have been infected—so a diagnosis can be made with precision. This is not the case with non-A, non-E hepatitis; the diagnosis is therefore made only in cases of hepatitis where hepatitis A, B, C, D, and E, and other viruses known to cause liver damage have been excluded.

The illness

The illness of all forms of hepatitis is similar, and results from acute inflammation of the liver. It is heralded frequently by symptoms such as fever, chills, headache, fatigue, generalized weakness, and aches and pains. A few days later, there is often loss of appetite, nausea, vomiting, right upper abdominal pain or tenderness, followed closely by dark urine, light-coloured faeces, and jaundice of the skin or the sclerae (outer coating of the eyeballs). Many infections, particularly in children, are without specific symptoms or without jaundice. In others, jaundice may be severe and prolonged; liver failure may occur, and the patient may lapse into a coma.

Hepatitis A

Hepatitis A is common in all parts of the world, but the exact incidence is difficult to estimate because of the high proportion of non-symptomatic cases and infections without jaundice. Antibody surveys have shown that while the prevalence of hepatitis A in industrialized countries (particularly North America, Europe, and Australia) has decreased significantly, the infection is virtually universal elsewhere, particularly in countries with warm climates.

Only one form of hepatitis A has been identified, and the antibody that develops against it persists for many years, but immunity may decline in advanced age.

The highest risk areas for hepatitis A include central and Eastern Europe, the Mediterranean countries, the Middle East, and developing countries in Africa, Asia, and Central and South America.

How it is spread

Hepatitis A virus is spread by the faecal–oral route, usually by person-to-person contact, particularly in conditions of poor sanitation and over-crowding. Outbreaks result most frequently from faecal contamination of drinking water and food (although water-borne transmission is less often a factor in countries where the piped water supply has been adequately treated and chlorinated).

Food-borne outbreaks, which have become more important and fre-quent in developed countries, are due to shedding of the virus in the faeces of infected food handlers during the incubation period of the illness. Raw or inadequately cooked shellfish cultivated in sewage-contaminated tidal or coastal water, and raw vegetables grown in soil fertilized with untreated human faeces and excreta are associated with a high risk of infection. Non-immune travellers from areas of low to areas of high prev-alence contract hepatitis A infection frequently. Hepatitis A virus is very rarely transmitted by blood transfusion or by inoculation.

The incubation period of the virus is between 3 and 5 weeks, with an average of 28 days.

Age incidence and seasonal patterns

All age groups are susceptible. In North America and Western Europe, most cases occur in adults, frequently after travel abroad, but elsewhere, the highest incidence is in children of school age. In temperate zones, the peak incidence often tends to be in autumn and early winter. In many tropical countries, infection peaks during the rainy season with low inci-dence in the dry months.

Consequences of infection

Although the disease has a low mortality, patients may be incapacitated for many weeks. There is no evidence of persistence of infection with hepatitis A virus, nor of progression to chronic liver disease.

Control

Control of the infection is difficult. Since faecal shedding of the virus and therefore infectivity is at its highest during the incubation period, strict isolation of cases is not a useful measure. Spread of infection is reduced by simple hygienic measures and the sanitary disposal of excreta.

Hepatitis A and the traveller

There are several vaccines against hepatitis A (alone or in combination with hepatitis B or typhoid), and immunization is strongly recommended for travellers who are not already immune (if necessary, this can be checked with a blood test), who are travelling to endemic areas. One recent study demonstrated that the relative risk of contracting hepatitis A in unprotected travellers was 1 in 300 per month of travel in tourist/resort areas, increasing to a risk of 1 in 50 if the traveller is backpacking or trekking. (These vaccines are an important advance: previously, the only protection was by repeated, painful injections of immunoglobulin—a blood product providing only short-term immunity.)

Other preventive measures include strict personal hygiene, avoiding raw or inadequately cooked shellfish and raw vegetables, and not drinking untreated water or unpasteurized milk.

Hepatitis B

Hepatitis B also occurs worldwide, and its continued survival is assured by the large number of individuals who carry the virus, estimated to be at least 350 million. It can be spread either from carriers or from people with inapparent infection, or during the incubation period, illness, or early convalescence.

A person is defined as a carrier if hepatitis B surface antigen—a marker of the virus—persists in their circulation for more than 6 months following infection. A person may be a lifelong carrier and remain apparently healthy, although variable degrees of liver damage can occur with progression to chronic liver disease, cirrhosis, and liver cancer.

The highest risk areas include Southeast Asia, China, the Pacific Islands, sub-Saharan Africa, and a number of countries in central Asia and South America. Rates of infection are especially high among homosexual men, prostitutes, and drug addicts; these also tend to be higher among adults living in urban communities and in poor conditions. Infection may become established in closed institutions, such as for the mentally handicapped and those in prisons.

In North America, northern Europe, and Australia, less than 0.1% of the population are carriers (at least among blood donors); in central and eastern Europe, up to 5%; in southern Europe, countries bordering the Mediterranean, and parts of Central and South America, a higher frequency; and in parts of Africa, Asia, and the Pacific area, 20% or more of the apparently healthy population may be carriers.

Certain groups of people—recipients of unscreened blood transfusions and blood products, healthcare, and laboratory personnel, staff in institutions for the mentally handicapped, male homosexuals, prostitutes, and abusers of injectable drugs and narcotics—are at considerably increased risk of contracting hepatitis B. Travellers or expatriates belonging to any of these groups are at higher risk in countries where the carrier rate is high. The incidence of symptomatic and asymptomatic hepatitis B infection in long-term travellers, including expatriates, is 0.8–2.4 per 100 per month of travel. This figure falls up to 10 times lower in short-term travellers (travelling for less than 1 month) to endemic areas. The incubation period is about 60–180 days.

How it is spread

Transmission may result from accidental inoculation with minute amounts of blood, which may occur:

- during medical, surgical, or dental procedures
- during immunization with inadequately sterilized syringes and needles
- with sharing of needles during intravenous drug abuse
- tattooing, ear piercing, and nose piercing
- acupuncture
- laboratory accidents and accidental inoculation with razors and similar objects that have been contaminated with blood.

Hepatitis B surface antigen and other markers of hepatitis B virus have also been found in other body fluids such as saliva, menstrual and vaginal discharges, and seminal fluid, also implicated in transmission. In certain defined circumstances, the virus may be infective by mouth, and there is much evidence for the transmission of hepatitis B by sexual contact. Persons who change sexual partners frequently are at high risk of hepatitis B.

In the tropics and in warm climates, additional factors may be important for transmission, including traditional tattooing and scarification, bloodletting, ritual circumcision, and possibly by repeated biting by bloodsucking insects. Hepatitis B surface antigen has been detected in several species of mosquito and in bed-bugs that have either been trapped in the wild or fed experimentally on infected blood, but no convincing evidence of multiplication of the virus in insects has been obtained. Mechanical transmission of the infection via an insect's biting parts is a theoretical possibility, but appears to be rare.

Hepatitis B also tends to occur within family groups, although the precise mechanism of intrafamilial spread is not known.

Viral transmission from carrier mothers to their babies can occur around the time of birth and is an important factor in determining the prevalence of the infection in some regions, particularly China and Southeast Asia.

The carrier state

Progression to the carrier state is more common in males, following infections acquired in childhood, and in people with natural or acquired immune deficiencies. The carrier state becomes established in approximately 5–10% of infected adults. In countries where hepatitis B infection is common the highest prevalence of surface antigen is found in children aged 4–8 years, with steadily declining rates among older age groups.

Consequences of infection

The symptoms and clinical manifestations of hepatitis B are similar to those of the other types of viral hepatitis, although complicated by the carrier state and by chronic liver disease, which may follow the infection. Chronic liver disease may be severe and may progress to primary liver cancer. In many parts of the world, primary liver cancer is one of the commonest human cancers, particularly in men.

Prevention and control

Immunization against hepatitis B can be carried out in two ways.

Active immunization

- Hepatitis B vaccines have been developed using recombinant DNA technology
- They are safe and highly effective
- They contain hepatitis B surface antigen, and 'prime' the body's immune system to produce its own antibodies.

Among the high-risk groups who might benefit from the vaccine are homosexual men, drug addicts, prostitutes, people who require multiple transfusions, people with immune deficiencies or malignant disease, healthcare personnel, and others at occupational risk. Immunization should also be considered by non-immune persons living in areas where the prevalence of hepatitis B infection is high. Hepatitis B has been added to childhood immunization schedules in most countries (including the USA, Canada, and Australia), where universal immunization against hepatitis B has been introduced. A few countries in Northern Europe, including the UK use only selective immunization for defined groups.

Vaccination of travellers is advisable if:

- They belong to a high-risk group
- They will remain in an endemic area for longer than about 6 months
- They will reside in rural areas, or engage in sporting or other activities that carry an increased risk of accidents, injury, or occupational exposure to blood
- They are likely to need medical treatment abroad—such as kidney dialysis or blood transfusion.

Passive immunization

Hepatitis B immunoglobulin contains antibody against hepatitis B. It is not used for prevention in travellers, but for protection after accidental exposure, such as when blood or other material containing hepatitis B surface antigen is inoculated, swallowed, or splashed in the eyes. Two doses administered 30 days apart are required: the first dose should preferably be administered within 48 hours, but not later than 7 days following exposure. A course of active immunization should be started at the same time.

Hepatitis B and the traveller

Travellers should take common-sense precautions to reduce the risk. They should employ great caution in any intimate or sexual contact (particularly male homosexual contact) with possible hepatitis B carriers. They should, where possible, avoid any procedure involving penetration of the skin: tattooing, ear piercing, any sort of injections, blood transfusions, and medical, surgical, and dental procedures carried out under dubious sanitary conditions.

Hepatitis C

The hepatitis C virus—considered responsible for the majority of cases of non-A, non-B hepatitis—was identified by molecular biology techniques in 1989. Although, in general the illness is mild and often without jaundice, severe hepatitis does occur and in many patients the infection is followed by a persistent carrier state. Chronic liver damage may occur in over 80% of patients, and there is evidence of an association between hepatitis C virus and primary liver cancer.

The virus is transmitted by blood and blood products, and by other routes, as yet undefined apart from intravenous (IV) drug abuse. There is a very high prevalence of infection with hepatitis C virus among intravenous narcotic drug abusers. Some evidence indicates transmission by the sexual route and during childbirth, but the route of infection has not been established in as many as 50% of cases.

Vaccines against hepatitis C are being developed. Methods of prevention are at present identical to those that apply to hepatitis B.

Hepatitis D

The delta virus is a defective infectious agent that can infect actively only in the presence of hepatitis B. The infection is common in parts of southern Europe, the Middle East, parts of tropical Africa, and in parts of South America. The virus is spread in the same way as hepatitis B and precautions against it are identical. Immunization against hepatitis B will also protect against delta hepatitis.

Hepatitis E

An epidemic illness similar to that caused by hepatitis A and transmitted commonly by contaminated water has been observed in India, Burma, eastern states of the former Soviet Union, parts of the Middle East, East Africa, North Africa and parts of West Africa, and in Central America and elsewhere. The virus responsible for this type of hepatitis has been identified and characterized as hepatitis E. There is evidence that this virus is prevalent in many non-industrialized countries and where a safe piped water supply is not available.

It should be noted that, although infection does not lead to chronic liver damage, it is extremely serious during late pregnancy, causing a high mortality and dictating an urgent need for a vaccine.

Methods of prevention include strict personal hygiene, not drinking untreated water, and not eating raw food, particularly raw or undercooked meat. Immunoglobulin does not afford any protection.

Treatment of viral hepatitis

No specific treatment is available for any of the types of acute viral hepatitis. A number of potent antiviral substances are available for the management of chronic liver disease associated with hepatitis B and C. Bed rest is required, and a low-fat diet is preferred during the acute phase of the disease. Alcohol should not be consumed for 6 months after recovery.

Women using oral contraceptives (the pill or progestogen-only pill) can continue with taking them during convalescence and recovery. Evacuation of a patient with acute hepatitis is not usually necessary unless serious complications develop, when special facilities may be required.

The different types of hepatitis virus

The five hepatitis viruses—A, B, C, D, and E—are distinct infectious agents and infection with one virus does not confer immunity against infection with a different virus. Similarly, vaccination against hepatitis A or hepatitis B does not protect against another hepatitis virus. The only exception is immunization against hepatitis B, which will afford protection against infection with the defective interfering delta virus (hepatitis D). It should be emphasized that the hepatitis viruses are common in all countries. See Box 2.4.1 for a summary of advice.

Box 2.4.1 **Summary of advice for travellers**

- Hepatitis A and E occur where hygienic and sanitary conditions are poor. Strict personal hygiene, and avoiding untreated water and raw or inadequately cooked food, particularly raw vegetables, shellfish, and milk, can help prevent infection. Hepatitis A immunization must be considered for non-immune travellers anywhere outside the USA, Canada, northern Europe, Australia, and New Zealand
- Hepatitis B is a risk to healthcare personnel, male homosexuals, those who change sexual partners frequently, and other 'high-risk' groups. The risk increases in developing countries, where there are generally more carriers, so extra caution is needed, especially with intimate or sexual contact with local people. Immunization is advisable for healthcare personnel, members of other risk categories working in the subtropics or tropics, and frequent or long-term travellers to endemic areas
- Penetration of the skin by any object that may have come in contact with someone else's blood or other body fluids—tattooing, ear piercing, sharing of razors, acupuncture, needle-sharing by drug abusers, any medical, dental, or surgical procedure, including blood transfusion/donation under dubious hygiene conditions should be avoided
- Hepatitis C is transmitted in the same manner as hepatitis B, and avoidance measures are also similar. It is particularly associated with IV narcotic drug use. No preventive immunization is available
- Travellers who develop a general malaise and symptoms such as right upper abdominal pain, jaundice, and dark-coloured urine either abroad or after their return should suspect viral hepatitis. Seek medical advice immediately.

2.5 Poisons and contaminants in food

Michael Eddleston

Foods that carry a substantial danger should be avoided or eaten with great caution; in the tropics, fish and shellfish pose a particular hazard.

Acute poisoning

Plant toxins

Local customs have developed to allow consumption of poisonous plants following careful preparation. Travellers should be wary of preparing unusual foods for themselves, but may be reasonably confident, except in times of drought or famine, that food prepared by local people will be innocuous.

Cassava (manioc)

A food staple in sub-Saharan Africa and South America that contains cyanogens. Bitter varieties produce a lot of cyanide and must be processed before consumption; sweet varieties can be eaten fresh. Consumption of unprocessed roots may cause acute cyanide poisoning. Acute features include abdominal pain and vomiting, progressing to confusion and neurological problems. These syndromes include spastic paraparesis (*Konzo* in East Africa), blindness, deafness, and loss of sensation (tropical ataxic neuropathy). Epidemics occur during drought years, when other food is scarce and cassava processing is less thorough than usual. There is no specific treatment.

Lathyrism

A disease similar to *Konzo*, characterized by the acute onset of paralysis. It is caused by consumption of the drought-resistant chickling pea (*Lathyrus* spp.).

Ackee

Toxins in unripe or poorly-prepared ackee fruit (*Blighia sapida*) in the Caribbean or West Africa cause hypoglycaemia. Patients develop vomiting, convulsions, coma, and in many cases die. Treatment involves supportive care and treatment of hypoglycaemia and seizures.

Cycads

These plants are used for food throughout the tropical areas of the Far East and Southeast Asia. However, in western Pacific islands, acute ingestion may cause seizures and chronic ingestion may cause fatal neurodegenerative disease (amyotrophic lateral sclerosis, Parkinsonism).

Honey poisoning

Honey made from the flowers of mountain laurel, rhododendron, or azaleas may contain grayanotoxin. Common in Turkey, poisoning causes life-threatening bradycardia (slowing of the heart rate), hypotension, respiratory depression, and altered mental status.

Seed poisoning

The two most toxic flowering plants are the castor bean (*Ricinus communis*) and rosary pea (*Abrus precatorius*). Their seeds are often used for necklaces but contain highly potent toxins that inhibit protein synthesis. Seeds that are not damaged pass through the GI tract without causing problems. However, ingestion of damaged seeds may cause severe bloody diarrhoea and then multi-organ failure. Early replacement of fluids and supportive care may be effective at preventing death.

Mushroom poisoning

Many mushrooms are toxic, but generally produce self-limiting gastrointestinal symptoms. Other mushroom syndromes include an alcohol-sensitizing (disulfiram) effect, seizures and coma, hallucinations, rhabdomyolysis (breakdown of muscle cells) and renal failure. However, only *Amanita phalloides* and similar hepatotoxic mushrooms are likely to be fatal.

Animal toxins

Most poisoning results from eating fish or other forms of sea food (1200 marine species are known to be poisonous or venomous). Because most toxins are heat-stable, cooking offers no protection.

Puffer fish poisoning

This fish contains tetrodotoxin in ovaries, roe, gall bladder, liver, and skin. The toxin blocks sodium channels. The first effects after ingestion are often a tingling sensation of the lips; systemic poisoning will result in respiratory arrest and a need for mechanical ventilation. Cooks remove the toxic organs from the fish, but mistakes are made. Many other marine animals also contain this toxin, including porcupine fish, triggerfish, and blue-ringed octopus.

Shellfish poisoning
Paralysis occurs after eating shellfish (particularly mussels, cockles, clams, and scallops) or sometimes fish contaminated with plankton containing saxitoxin or brevetoxin. These toxins block sodium channels leading to paralysis and respiratory arrest, or open sodium channels causing gastroenteritis and paraesthesia. Amnesia and seizures occur after ingesting mussels contaminated with domoic acid, a neuroexcitatory amino acid derived from plankton.

Ciguatera poisoning
Worldwide this is the most common food-borne illness caused by a toxin. It follows the ingestion of a wide variety of coral reef fishes, particularly in tropical Pacific and Caribbean, which have accumulated one of several ciguatoxins via the marine food web. Ciguatoxin opens sodium channels; symptoms appear a few hours after the meal and range from mild gastroenteritis to death. Following gastroenteritis, cardiovascular and neurological complications occur, such as paraesthesias, ataxia, myalgia, and respiratory paralysis. Deaths may occur from paralysis and respiratory failure, poorly-controlled seizures, or severe dehydration due to vomiting and diarrhoea.

Scombroid poisoning
Results from ingestion of a variety of dark meat fish that have been poorly stored. During storage, histidine is converted to histamine; ingestion of large amounts causes vomiting, diarrhoea, facial flushing, dysphagia (difficulty swallowing) and urticaria. Features settle over several hours.

Pesticides
Pesticides, particularly organophosphorus and organochlorine insecticides, regularly contaminate food in rural areas of the developing world, causing acute severe poisoning.

Chronic poisoning
The long-term effects of food toxins are of less importance to travellers than acute poisons.

Mycotoxins
Toxins produced by moulds cause outbreaks of encephalopathy in China (sugar cane mould), Balkan nephropathy in Southeast Europe (a maize mould) and liver disease in Africa (aflatoxin from *Aspergillus flavus*, which grows on nuts, seeds, and grains).

Metals
Lead from cooking pots is found in high levels in home-brewed beers in Africa. Mercury present in seed dressing has caused poisoning where people ate grain intended for planting. High arsenic content of tube well water is currently a serious problem in Bangladesh and Northeast India. See Box 2.5.1 for a summary of advice.

Box 2.5.1 **Summary of advice for travellers**

• Food toxins and contaminants are so diverse that there are no really hard-and-fast rules to follow. Generally, where food is known to be hazardous, traditional local methods of preparation have evolved to minimize the risk. Most have a basis in fact and are best observed
• Decayed or mouldy foods, either plant or animal, are likely to cause toxic effects
• Problems are more likely to arise in areas of drought and famine.

Chapter 3

Water-related diseases

3.1 Safe water

Hemda Garelick

Careful choice or treatment of water—whether for drinking, washing, preparing food, or swimming in—is one of the most important health precautions a traveller can take.

Water is essential for our survival: according to our size, activity, culture, health status, climate, and choice of clothing, we require between 2 and 5L of water every day.

In the developed world, the availability of safe water in more or less unlimited quantities is taken for granted. This does not apply in the developing world: in many countries, easy access to a safe water supply is not always available. Access to sanitary facilities lags behind access to water, so it is hardly surprising that water-related diseases remain a major problem in the developing world, where they kill at least five million people every day. Travellers to developing countries are obviously also at risk.

Water and disease

Water-related infections can be considered in four groups, according to how they are transmitted:
- Those spread by drinking contaminated water
- Those spread through lack of hygiene and sanitary facilities (lack of water)
- Those spread through *direct* contact with contaminated water (e.g. swimming) or *indirect* contact (e.g. eating fish that carry infection from contaminated water)
- Those spread by insects that need water to breed (e.g. malaria, Chapter 5.1).

In the first two categories, the infections of greatest importance to the traveller are those transmitted by the faecal-oral route that is from one person's faeces to another person's mouth. These include diarrhoeal diseases, dysenteries, typhoid, hepatitis A, and worm infections (see earlier chapters). In the third category, diseases transmitted through direct or indirect contact with water include leptospirosis (see Chapter 4.11), schistosomiasis (see Chapter 4.4), fish tapeworms (see Chapter 2.2) and liver flukes (see Chapter 2.2).

Chemical contamination (unless substantial) is likely to affect travellers far less than the local population—harmful effects tend to be cumulative and related to duration of exposure. In contrast, biological contamination (e.g. pathogenic micro-organisms) has a more acute effect on travellers than on local people, who may have acquired partial or full immunity to locally prevalent infections.

Chemical contamination has caused serious problems in Bangladesh, where water from tube wells—widely used to reduce the hazards of microbial contamination—has a high natural arsenic content; many local people have suffered chronic arsenic poisoning. Excessive fluoride in groundwater can be a hazard in large areas of India and the African Rift Valley.

Water and the traveller

Contamination of water supplies is usually due to poor sanitation close to water sources, sewage disposal into the sources themselves, leakage of sewage into distribution systems, or contamination with industrial or farm waste. Even if a piped water supply is safe at its source, it is not always safe by the time it reaches the tap. Intermittent tap water supplies should be regarded as suspect.

On short trips to areas with water supplies of uncertain quality, avoid drinking tap water or untreated water from any other source. Keep to hot, bottled, or canned drinks of well-known brand names. In some countries, bottled water may be counterfeited and simply replaced with tap water. Carbonated drinks are acidic, slightly safer, and less likely to have been counterfeited. Make sure all bottles have unbroken seals when you buy them and that they are opened in your presence.

Boiling is always a good way of treating water. Some hotels supply boiled water on request and this can be used for drinking or for brushing teeth. Refuse politely any cold drink from an unknown source.

Ice is only as safe as the water from which it is made and should not be put in drinks unless it is known to be safe. Drinks can be cooled by placing them on ice, rather than by adding ice to them.

Alcohol may be a medical disinfectant, but should not be relied upon to sterilize water. Ethanol is most effective at a concentration of 50–70%; below 20% its bactericidal action is negligible. Spirits labelled 95% proof contain only about 47% alcohol. Beware of methyl alcohol, which is poisonous and should never be added to drinking water.

If no other safe water supply can be obtained, tap water that is too hot to touch can be left to cool and is generally safe to drink.

Travellers should understand the various possible methods for making water safe.

Water treatment

The choice of processes used in a public water treatment plant depends on the physical, chemical, and microbiological characteristics of the water, but the main steps generally necessary are:

1. Removal of suspended solids by precipitation, sedimentation or filtration
2. Chemical disinfection—usually by chlorination or iodination—to inactivate and kill the possible pathogens (disease-causing infective agents).

Treating small quantities of water is based on similar principles, but is rather easier, and a wider range of processes is possible.

Begin by choosing the purest possible source, such as tap water, well water, spring water, or collected rainwater, all of which are preferable to surface water, e.g. rivers, streams, or pond water, which tend to be polluted. Rainwater can be collected from roofs, which should be clean and made of tiles or sheeting, not of lead or thatch.

Boiling

Boiling is the most effective way of sterilizing water. It kills all infective agents, including amoebic cysts, which are resistant to chlorine, and is unaffected by the turbidity or chemical characteristics of the water. Its only limitation is that it is not always practical and is generally suitable only for small quantities. Water should be boiled vigorously for five min (sufficient even at high altitude).

Portable boiling elements and travel kettles may be useful for small quantities of water.

Boiling tends to make water taste flat, because it reduces the amount of dissolved gases. To improve the taste, drinking water should be allowed to cool for a few hours in a covered, partially filled, clean container, preferably in the same container in which it has been boiled.

Filtration

Filtration is a process that should be used when boiling is not practicable. It is either an initial step or can produce safe water in a single step when the right equipment is used.

Removal of suspended solids

In order to make disinfection (with chlorine or iodine) as effective as possible, suspended solids and organic matter must be removed. Organic matter interferes with the process of chemical disinfection, and pathogens adsorbed to suspended solid are less susceptible to disinfection.

Filtration through a closely woven cloth is adequate, and filtration bags such as the Millbank bag are available commercially. These can take from 5 to 25L. However, it is important to remember that although the water may look clear it has not yet been made safe, and requires further treatment.

Removal of pathogens

Ceramic filter 'candles' of a very fine pore size (under 0.5 microns) are available commercially, and some units can be attached to piped water supplies. They remove most pathogens found in water (bacteria, amoebic cysts, and some viruses). Some types are impregnated with silver, which acts as a limited bactericide.

Manufacturers' instructions on operation and maintenance should be followed: they should be examined regularly for cracks and leaks, cleaned by scrubbing, and boiled (unless impregnated with silver) when clogged and at weekly intervals.

Disposable paper cartridge filters are also available. They should be kept wet when in use, or the paper filter may shrink or crack.

Activated carbon filters are not recommended for making water safe: they can improve the taste, but may shed adsorbed pathogens when overloaded.

Some ceramic filter candles have the option of adding activated carbon to improve the taste, but the carbon should not be relied upon to remove pathogens. Only in cases of high chemical contamination will addition of activated carbon to a filter be advantageous to health.

Filtered water should always be boiled or disinfected before being given to babies and small children.

Many convenient-looking purification devices are based on filtration, and are often recommended to travellers (see Chapter 3.2). Manufacturers often exaggerate the effectiveness and safety of their products. Without objective and convincing evidence to support their claims—such as precise details of how and by whom microbiological tests were performed—such gadgets must always be regarded with suspicion. The safest purification methods are boiling and chemical disinfection.

Chemical disinfection

Chemical disinfection is recommended when boiling or fine-pore filtration is not possible, or when extra safety is required. Cysts from protozoa tend to be more difficult to remove by chemical means, although diarrhoeas caused by these organisms represent only about 5% of cases.

The two most widely used chemicals are the halogens iodine and chlorine. Their ability to sterilize water will depend upon how long the water is left in contact with the disinfectant before drinking, the temperature of the water, and the concentration of the disinfecting solution. These factors can be 'traded-off' against one another: for instance, a weaker solution could be used if left in contact for longer at higher temperatures. Treated water should generally be left for 20–30min before drinking or longer if the water is very cold (a few hours if possible). Some organisms are harder to remove, particularly amoebic cysts and *Giardia*—longer contact times and/or higher concentrations may be required.

Halogens also react with any other organic matter that may be present in the water, which reduces the amount of halogen available to kill pathogens. Water should therefore be filtered to remove suspended solids before disinfection (see 'Removal of pathogens', p.50). Chlorine, in particular, is less active if the water is alkaline, which is one possible reason for preferring iodine.

Chlorine

Chlorine kills living organisms by inactivating biologically active compounds. It is effective against bacteria and some viruses at reasonably low concentrations and with short contact times, but are less effective against amoebic cysts: the amount of chlorine needed for inactivation of amoebic cysts is 10 times that needed for inactivation of bacteria.

Chlorine-based purification tablets are available commercially (see p.57), in a variety of formulations, including chlorine dioxide.

Liquid chlorine laundry bleach can be used, but the exact constituents and concentration of the solutions should be determined. Liquid chlorine laundry bleach usually contains 4–6% available chlorine; and one to two drops of such a solution (or alternatively four to eight drops of a 1% solution) should be added to each litre of water. Water treated in this way should be left for 20–30min before drinking.

Chlorine in a concentrated form (e.g. bleach solution) is toxic, should be handled with care, never mixed with other chemicals, and kept away from children.

Iodine

The concentration of free iodine most widely recommended is 8mg/L, which should allow sterilization of water containing *Giardia* within about 20min, providing the water is clear and above 5°C. However, always follow manufacturers' instructions since iodine concentrations, and therefore contact times at different water temperatures, may vary.

Iodine-based disinfection tablets are sold in the USA (although no longer in Europe); they take time to dissolve and lose potency once the bottle is opened. Tincture of iodine is more economical and usually contains 2% iodine; five drops should be added to 1L of water, increasing to 12 drops if *Giardia* is suspected. Adding ascorbic acid (vitamin C) may remove the taste and the red colour imparted by iodine, but also neutralizes its disinfectant properties. It should therefore only be added *after* the water has been left to stand for the correct time, not to a storage container, but ideally to a cup just before drinking.

Long-term, large-volume use of iodine-treated water is not recommended as it may cause thyroid problems. Use in pregnancy has not been associated with harmful effects, but is best avoided on theoretical grounds; anyone with a thyroid problem should consult their doctor first.

Silver

Silver tablets and solutions are available (e.g. Katadyn, Micropur); although less effective than halogens, particularly against viruses and protozoa, they are free of unpleasant tastes and are claimed to prevent recontamination of stored water. Follow manufacturers' instructions carefully.

Solar and ultraviolet (UV) disinfection

If other options are not available, a good measure of disinfection can sometimes be obtained by filling clear, plastic, soft drink bottles with water and leaving them exposed to sunlight—a method known as SODIS (see http://www.sodis.ch/index_EN). The combination of warmth and UV radiation kills most micro-organisms. The required exposure time ranges from 6 hours under bright conditions to 2 days under cloudy conditions. A number of devices are also marketed that claim to rely on UV disinfection.

Storage of treated water

Consume treated water within 24 hours. To prevent recontamination, keep it in the same container in which it was treated, or ensure storage containers are sterile, disinfected, and covered. They should have a tap at the bottom or a narrow opening, to minimize the risk of contamination when drawing off the treated water. Store treated water in a cool place, away from children. Keep sanitary facilities as far from water and food as possible, and always ensure hands are clean.

Food hygiene

Food, especially local produce where sanitary conditions are poor, should always be regarded as contaminated.

Fruit and vegetables should be washed thoroughly in clean soapy water, and then rinsed with treated water. Rinsing alone is not enough—sterilizing chemicals in treated water will not kill pathogens on fruit and vegetables because contact time is insufficient.

Soaking in chlorine (e.g. using Milton tablets) or iodine—at roughly three times the concentration used for drinking water purification—is usually effective, though the contact time necessary depends on how much contamination is present.

Soaking in potassium permanganate, traditionally recommended for this purpose, is less reliable; permanganate has few medical uses these days.

Dipping in boiling water is a simple and effective alternative.

Avoid eating any raw vegetables or cold food prepared by others—especially in restaurants and hotels, and particularly salads. (If you really must eat a salad that looks suspect, plenty of lemon juice or strong vinegar in the dressing will slightly reduce the risk.)

Seafood, fish, and meat should always be well-cooked, and unpasteurized milk should be boiled or avoided.

Swimming

From the point of view of infection, swimming in the sea, away from human habitation, is usually safe. Avoid uncontrolled beaches close to highly populated areas with no proper sanitary facilities, or near sewage outfalls. Swimming in fresh surface water is inadvisable, especially in areas where schistosomiasis (bilharzia) (see Chapter 4.4) is found or leptospirosis is a possible hazard (Chapter 4.11).

Further information

🕭 http://www.cdc.gov/safewater/

3.2 Water purification devices

Paul Goodyer

A large number of water filters and purification devices are now on the market, and claims are sometimes made for them that are difficult to assess. This chapter gives a brief personal review of some of the units currently available to travellers.

Ensuring a safe water supply to enable adequate fluid intake, especially under arduous field conditions such as tropical jungle or desert terrain, is an immensely important requirement. A supply of pure bottled water is hardly practical in such a setting, if only because of the huge amount required. The same applies to boiling, limiting factors being the difficulty of carrying sufficient fuel and the time and effort of frequent boil-ups.

A more practicable approach would be some form of treatment for contaminated water; chemical purification, and the general principles involved have been considered in detail in Chapter 3.1; this Section gives a brief survey of specific filtration and purification products that can be used as an adjunct or an alternative, their effectiveness, and factors such as cost and weight.

Criteria to be met

Units intended to filter water should be dependable, easily maintained, and give some strong indication of when their useful life has ended.

Bear in mind that nothing lasts a lifetime, and be wary of units that are claimed to be able to cope with thousands of litres. While it may be true that thousands of litres can be run through, the amount that will be treated effectively may be a different matter. Using a commonly recognized technique of 'methyl-blue' dye extraction, testing has shown that for most activated carbon units (see pp.50–1) 'breakthrough' usually occurs after less than 200L.

Don't be misled

It is pertinent to clarify some of the terms used in manufacturers' literature that may sometimes mislead. A 'filter' removes suspended solids by mechanical straining; further purification is almost always required. However, a 'purifier' both filters and sterilizes, giving safe potable water, and obviating the need for further treatment. Product literature sometimes makes much play of a filter unit being 'bacteriostatic'—particularly in relation to activated carbon units. This merely means that bacterial growth is inhibited, *not* that bacteria are actually killed. Only a 'bactericide', defined as being lethal to bacteria, will do this.

Furthermore, virus removal test results are not always given, even though a unit may be quite effective. Such tests may require a high degree of skill, and can be expensive.

Bear in mind that no uniform, objective, agreed standards exist for such devices, and that external safeguards on quality control are generally lacking. Look, therefore, for test data from a good university department or approval by a well-known independent organization.

Iodine in water purification

For many years Iodine has been the treatment of choice for the purification of water for the individual both as a tablet and tincture. In addition to this it has also been used, in resin form as the main component for sterilizing water within purification pumps.

Due to EU biocides regulations iodine can no longer be used in this way, throughout Europe, so many of the purifiers that previously were available can no longer be found. This has severely reduced the amount of choice in this field.

Selecting a unit

The current devices on offer to travellers can generally be classified as follows:

Simple gravity filters

These are trickle filtration units, fine for pre-filtering and some removal of larger micro-organisms by adsorption. Their main advantage is aesthetic, whereby bad odours and tastes are eliminated. Heavy microbiological loading would require further chemical treatment; indeed, this underscores their primary function of pre-filtration prior to adding chemical purification tablets. Be quite clear that these are filters, not purifiers.

Drinking bottle filters

These are bottles with filters attached to the top, the best-known of which is the Aqua Pure traveller (£35, 108g, and 750mL). The bottle is filled with the water to be treated, and then squeezed into a drinking cup for purification. Their appearance is slightly misleading as they look as though you should be able to drink safe water straight from the bottle.

Pump-action filters

Of all the units currently available, the First Need Portable Water Purification Device (£99.99, 425g; canister 7 × 10cm, pump 14cm) is the most effective against chemical contamination. The First Need comprises a pump, purifying cartridge, and a pre-filter to prevent inadvertent clogging of the purification cartridge. With 10 microns retention, the pre-filter is back-washable and cheap.

Inside the purification cartridge, three functions take place simultaneously. Ultra-filtration with 0.4 microns retention (absolute) extracts larger micro-organisms and other particles. A system of absorption materials is integrated into the matrix, scrubbing out a wide range of chemical contaminants and removing smells and tastes. Electrostatic charges remove colloidal and other ultra-small particles, binding them to the matrix without affecting the 'pass through' of water.

Although only filtering 400L or so before self-clogging, the First Need avoids potentially hazardous exposure to micro-organisms; these remain sealed inside the cartridge, which is then replaced when the flow rate drops to an unacceptable level. It needs to be protected from freezing and dropping, to prevent breakage of the structured matrix. If a rattle or 'thump' is heard when holding the unit up to the ear and shaking it gently, it is broken and should not be used; replacement cartridges (£50) are available.

Pumping the First Need can be quite stiff, and the little rubber stoppers on the inlet and outlet tubing can get mislaid in three seconds flat. The First Need is registered by the US Environmental Protection Agency as a 'purification device', one of very few to have this verification.

Another unit, that has been standard issue to the International Red Cross for over 50 years, is the Swiss-made Katadyn Pocket Filter (£300, 650g, 25–155cm), which filters raw water through a 0.2-micron microporous ceramic filter element. A built-in pump draws water up through a pipe, filtering it at a rate of 3/4L/min. All pathogenic bacteria, protozoa, cysts, and helminths are extracted, including those that cause amoebic and bacillary dysentery, giardia, typhoid, cholera, and schistosomiasis. The pocket filter is much larger than the name implies, its little brother the Mini Filter is recommended for back packing (£115, 218g).

While the Katadyn will treat heavily silted and algae-laden water, it may clog quickly. However, the ceramic 'candle' can be lightly brushed up to 300 times to restore full flow. This is best done using an old soft toothbrush, since the brush supplied is too abrasive.

A silver lining inside the ceramic candle prevents bacterial growth, so, in particular, one should not try to desalinate sea or brackish water with it. Salt would react with the silver lining and destroy its effectiveness. In freezing temperatures, the unit should be kept well insulated to prevent residual water turning to ice and cracking the candle. Likewise it should not be dropped. Furthermore, it must be stressed that brushing off the ceramic candle should be done upwind, and with care, to prevent potential exposure to disease organisms by aerosol effect.

Although viruses are far smaller than the 0.2micron pore size of the Katadyn's ceramic candle, some viruses will be arrested during filtration by being contained in host cells, or by adsorption on to the filter medium itself. However, further chemical treatment against viral contamination is advisable.

The Katadyn should give years of continuous use, with replacement candles available (rather expensive, at £180). A larger stirrup-pump version for base-camp needs, the Katadyn Expedition Pump (£750) comes in a canvas carrying bag, and has a flow rate of up to 3L/min.

Purifiers

A purifier is usually defined as a filter that also employs a chemical disinfectant thus removing all organic matter and all but the smallest microorganisms through the filtering system and being 'finished off' with the chemical disinfectant. Iodine was the chemical that was most suitable to be employed in this manner but as this is no longer a permitted chemical, within the EU, 'purifiers' in the true sense, have ceased to be available. There are, however a few products that are supplied with chemicals as a package.

The best of these is probably the MSR Sweetwater purifier system (£85, 194g, 20 × 5cm). The Sweet Water combines a 0.2micron filter with a carbon filter in a two-way pump and is supplied with sweet water purifier solution for post filtration treatment. The solution is sodium hypochlorite (chlorine) add 5 drops to a litre of filtered water, wait 5min and the water is safe to drink. The dual action pump makes the Sweet water efficient and easy to use and the filter has a 750L life span.

The sweet water filter is also available without the treatment (£70) allowing the user to use the water sterilizer of their choice.

UV water purifiers

UV water treatment for personal water purification is a relatively new concept and has proved to be an effective way to produce safe drinking water. The disadvantages of these systems are that they will not remove turbidity, improve odour or taste, and the water must be drunk within 24 hours to guarantee purity. These units are battery powered so it is essential to carry a good supply of these.

At the time of writing the only product on the market is the Steripen made by Hydro-photon. There are two versions available and both will treat ½ or 1L at a time. The principle and mechanism is simple: push the button on the hilt once for 1L or twice for 2L. A small light will flash green showing the unit is armed. Place the light stick end into the water allowing two electrodes on the bottom of the hilt to come into contact with the water and agitate the wand, when the water is safe to drink the light will go out. If at any time a red light appears the process has failed, usually due to battery life.

The Steripen Classic (£56, 204g, including 4 AA batteries 19 × 4cm) is supplied with a 4-micron filter to fit a wide mouth Nalgene bottle.

The Steripen Adventurer (£72, 102g, including 2 CR123 batteries. 16 × 2 × 4cm) is probably one of the smallest, lightest means of purifying water available and is both robust and slick.

Choose carefully

Remember that none of the units reviewed here is designed for desalination. Above all, be sure to exercise healthy scepticism when assessing manufacturers' claims.

Suppliers

- Purification tablets;
  - Lifemarque Ltd—℘ www.lifemarque.co.uk. Tel: 01189811433
  - Nomad Ltd—℘ www.nomadtravel.co.uk. Tel 08452600044
  - Scotmas—℘ www.scotmas.com. Tel: 01573226901
- Filtration bags (Millbank):
  - Nomad Ltd—℘ www.nomadtravel.co.uk. Tel: 08452600044
- Filtration units, pumps, and purification units:
  - Aqua Pure Traveller—℘ www.thirstpoint.com Abbey Business Park, Monks Walk, Farnham, Surrey GU9 8HT, UK. Tel: 01252 722 022
  - Katadyn: Ark Group—℘ www.arkconsultants.co.uk. Tel: 01524824417
  - First Need filter—℘ www.travelwithcare.com. Tel: 01980626360
  - MSR Sweet Water: First Ascent—℘ www.firstascent.co.uk. Tel: 01629580484.
- Retail stockists:
  - Cotswold—℘ www.cotswoldoutdoor.com. Tel. 01285 643434
  - Nomad—℘ www.nomadtravel.co.uk. Tel: 08452600044
  - Safariquip—℘ www.safariquip.co.uk. Tel. 01433 620320

For further advice

Departments of Medical Microbiology and Tropical Hygiene, London School of Hygiene and Tropical Medicine, Keppel Street, London, WC1E 7HT, UK.

3.3 Recreational water and beaches

Robin Philipp and Pam Thorne

Beaches and the coastal environment attract travellers, but rapid development and mass tourism have led to deterioration in recreational water quality and beach cleanliness. Much of the pollution comes from municipal sewage and waste, and from litter left by visitors or thrown from boats. These, and the growth in popularity of watersports, have increased the risks inherent in a recreational water environment.

In response, the World Health Organization and other organizations encourage standards that enable travellers to select a *clean* and *safe* beach.

Water pollution

Coastal waters or fresh waters may be polluted by local discharges of municipal sewage or industrial effluent, or by agricultural fertilizers and pesticides carried to the coast by rivers.

The risk of bacterial infections from bathing in seawater is generally low, but there is an increased risk of intestinal symptoms if swimming in the proximity of a sewage outfall pipe. Viruses are a greater risk as they survive longer than other pathogens.

The risk of serious illness is low, but the following are associated with bathing in contaminated waters:

- Gastroenteritis
- Hepatitis A
- Eye, ear, nose and throat infections
- Pneumonia
- Skin infections

- Salmonellosis and poliomyelitis
- Shigellosis
- Meningitis
- Acute neurotoxicity.

See also: Freshwater swimming risks from schistosomiasis (Chapter 4.4), leptospirosis (Chapter 4.11); toxic algal blooms (Chapter 3.4); dangerous and/or venomous sea creatures (Chapter 6).

Human hygiene and environmental safety

Other disease sources in beach areas include food, drinking water, toilet facilities, air/water temperature, human contact, and poor sand cleanliness. Beach surveys report increasing medical waste, and syringes and needles left by drug users. The latter have been found in secluded sand dunes or rocks, as well as known drug-user sites such as at the backs of toilet blocks.

Judging the safety of a beach

Water quality

Most countries have legislation requiring recreational water quality monitoring to at least the minimal standards laid down by international convention. Some areas include fungal examination of sand. In principle, if water is below standard on successive samplings, local authorities will warn users or ban bathing until the source of pollution is controlled. On a beach that is well managed water quality parameters should be displayed, but visual evidence of pollution should also be checked. Storms and heavy rainfall can overwhelm drainage systems, raising pollution temporarily.

Beach award schemes make annual assessments to stringent standards. The Foundation for Environmental Education in Europe (FEE)'s 'Blue Flag' award scheme is widely used internationally. It covers the following aspects.

Water quality

Including compliance with microbiological parameters of current EEC standards; no industrial or sewage discharges affecting the beach area.

Environmental education and information

Including information about water quality displayed; information on award scheme displayed.

Environmental management

Including a clean beach with adequate, well-maintained facilities for waste disposal; adequate, clean toilet facilities; properly maintained buildings/ equipment.

Safety and services

Including safe access to the beach; first-aid equipment; adequate number of lifeguards, and/or life-saving equipment.

Other awards
An example is the rural category of the UK's 'Seaside Award', which assesses standards at more isolated beaches that are not actively managed or developed.

Sample criteria for rural beaches
Include:
- Compliance with European water quality standards
- Adequate cleansing of beach and surrounding area
- Any toilets/buildings clean and well maintained
- Safe, well maintained access
- Appropriate safety and general information for visitors.

A beach *not* displaying an award is *not* necessarily *un*clean or *un*safe. A personal visual assessment should be made. If information about local conditions such as tides and currents is not provided, advice should be sought before bathing. Estuaries can be particularly dangerous.

Warning flags
Many countries worldwide have adopted flag systems on bathing beaches to advise the public about sea conditions.
- Yellow = Caution
- Red = Danger
- Orange cone shape = offshore winds, no inflatables.

Zoning
Flags may define zones for different water-based activities, for example:
1. The area between red over yellow rectangular flags is a lifeguard-patrolled safe area for swimming
2. The area between black and white quartered flags is for surfboards and other watercraft only.

Beach and water safety risks
Drowning and swimming accidents are often caused by ignorance, disregard, or misjudgement of danger. Currents and tides, vegetation, and the activities of other water users are all potentially hazardous.

Alcohol consumption
Alcohol consumption is a factor in 50% of drowning accidents. It can lead to rapid heat loss if a person should fall into water, or to sudden exhaustion in swimmers. Even small amounts, if taken with insufficient food, can cause hypoglycaemia on a long-distance swim.

Water temperature
Even strong swimmers may succumb in cold water and life jackets should be worn in small craft when the water is cold. Exercise in water increases loss of body heat, so remaining close to a sunken craft may increase the chances of survival. Prolonged immersion in water warmer than 34–35°C is hazardous.

Diving or tombstoning
Diving or tombstoning (jumping from a height) in unfamiliar water of uncertain depth is not advisable. This applies particularly in freshwater rivers, lakes, and estuaries.

Injuries

Injuries from broken glass, metal objects or needles are best avoided by wearing beach footwear.

Additional risks

- Sunburn (see Chapter 8.5)
- Contaminated seafood (see Chapter 2.2)
- Watersports hazards (see Chapter 8.8).

3.4 Algal blooms

Robin Philipp

Pollution of seawater, lakes, and rivers with fertilizers, sewage, and organic material has caused sudden increases in the growth of microscopic plants or algae—algal blooms. The phenomenon is on the increase, with recent dramatic blooms along the Adriatic and elsewhere. The algae can be toxic or merely a slimy nuisance, interfering with swimming, windsurfing, and other watersports. This chapter explains the background to the problem.

Blue-green algae (BGA) are microscopic plants found in fresh and brackish waters. They have some characteristics of bacteria and are therefore described as photosynthetic bacteria, also called cyanobacteria. They are particularly common in lowland, nutrient-laden waters in the warm, sunny summer months. Mountain reservoirs generally have low numbers, except where contributory water sources drain forested areas on which phosphate or nitrogenous fertilizers have been used.

Some free-floating forms contain gas bubbles that regulate buoyancy in response to the light intensity. Normally this keeps them away from the surface, but in windy conditions that mix the water, the cells may become too buoyant and rise rapidly to the surface if the wind subsides abruptly. They accumulate downwind and at the water's edge to form scums that look like blue-green paint or jelly. In high density within the water, they can also form a visible blue-green bloom; they may also be coloured purple or red. They are an increasing problem due to nutrient enrichment of natural waters, agricultural fertilizer run-off, domestic, and industrial effluents, and possibly global warming. Scums and blooms can also encourage other bacterial growth and colonization by insects.

Toxins

Toxins produced by some BGA have caused deaths in agricultural livestock, pets, wild animals, and fish. Toxicity can fluctuate daily in that BGA can be toxic one day and not the next. Blooms can also appear one day, disappear suddenly, and reappear at any time. The toxins are of three main types—those that affect the nervous system, those that damage the liver, and those that irritate the skin.

Clinical effects relating to wildlife and man

Deaths have occurred in animals venturing into thick concentrations of algae to bathe and drink the water, or licking scum and deposits off their fur when coming ashore. Inhalation of aerosols containing desiccated algal material can also occur. In the UK, this has recently affected pets belonging to holidaymakers to the Lake District, and in 2010, the UK's biggest swimming competition (the Great North Swim) was cancelled due to the presence of BGA in Lake Windermere.

℘ http://www.lakedistrict.gov.uk/caringfor/policies/algae

℘ http://www.telegraph.co.uk/health/petshealth/8735638/Dog-dies-after-swallowing-algae-in-Lake-Windermere.html

No deaths have been reported in humans although harmful effects of BGA on human health have been widely reported, most commonly in developed countries with hot climates such as Australia and parts of the USA, but also from the UK, Canada, China, Scandinavia, the Baltic States, the former USSR, South Africa, Zimbabwe, India, New Zealand, Israel, Venezuela, and Argentina.

In humans, ingestion of toxic algae or body immersion in scum-containing water has been associated with dizziness, headaches, muscle cramps, runny nose, sore eyes, hay fever, asthma, pneumonia, nausea, vomiting, gastroenteritis, and liver damage; skin contact has been associated with burning, itching, and inflammation of the skin, eyes, and lips, hand, and sore throat, and also dizziness. Outbreaks of gastroenteritis affecting travellers to countries such as Nepal have also been attributed to BGA-like organisms (p.17).

The main exposure situations and associated risks

Drinking water

BGA can give a 'musty', 'geranium', or 'vegetable' taste and odour to drinking water. Dense blooms of blue-green algae in drinking water reservoirs have occasionally resulted in inflammation of the liver and gastroenteritis in people who have been drinking affected water.

Eating contaminated fish or meat

Some BGA toxins can accumulate in fresh-water shellfish such as the swan mussel (*Anadonta cygnea*). BGA toxins can also accumulate in some fish organs, particularly the liver. In the 1920s and 1930s, for example, outbreaks of a condition called Haff disease were common around the Baltic Coast and were linked with eating fish, in particular, fish liver from fresh waters affected by algal blooms: the livers were regarded as a delicacy if tasting of musty blue-green-algal-type flavour compounds. Haff disease was occasionally fatal and was characterized by muscular pain, vomiting, respiratory distress, and the passage of brownish-black urine. Elsewhere, there do not seem to have been any such outbreaks, even when fresh-water algal blooms have been prominent. There is no evidence at present that algal toxins can affect the flesh of fish. Fish are therefore considered safe to eat provided they are properly gutted and cleaned. The flesh of animals which have been drinking water that is affected by an algal bloom is also safe to eat.

Contact with sea-water algae and eating shellfish

Sea-water algal blooms are caused by increased nutrient loads and low oxygen levels in the water. They cause 'red algal tides' and mucilage formation. Mucilage is an amorphous, messy, viscous substance suspended in the water. It can be deposited on beaches.

The commonest toxic algae to be found in marine waters are called dinoflagellates (they are single-celled, motile algae). Their toxins are mainly a problem when they become concentrated by fish and shellfish that are subsequently eaten by humans. Toxic marine dinoflagellates can cause several illnesses.

Paralytic shellfish poisoning (PSP)

This occurs in several parts of the world. It begins with numbness and tingling around the mouth and in the hands and fingers within 5–30min of eating affected shellfish, followed by numbness and weakness of the arms and legs. Usually, the illness is mild and self-limiting, but in severe cases when large amounts of toxin have been eaten, paralysis of the diaphragm leads to respiratory failure, which may be fatal. There is no evidence that PSP can be caused by skin exposure, drinking seawater, or from inhaling sea-water droplets.

Diarrhoeic shellfish poisoning

Algae associated with diarrhoeic shellfish poisoning (DSP) are *Dinophysis* and *Prorocentrum* (okadaic acid). The symptoms and signs of DSP are mainly diarrhoea, nausea, vomiting, abdominal pain, and chills coming on within 30min to 12 hours of eating shellfish.

Neurotoxic shellfish poisoning (NSP)

This resembles PSP, but is non-fatal and paralysis does not occur. So far, blooms causing it have been reported only in the Gulf of Mexico. Sea spray containing the same algae (*Ptychodiscus brevis*) or their toxins cause an irritant aerosol that leads to inflammation of the eyes and nose, with cough and tingling lips; in windy conditions, the effects can be observed up to a few kilometres inland.

Amnesic shellfish poisoning

This is a rare illness first recognized in 1987 when a mysterious outbreak in Canada was traced to a bloom of the diatom *Nitzschia pungens*. (Diatoms are unicellular plankton with a silicified cell wall, and are widely distributed.) The illness was associated with a shellfish toxin (domoic acid) which had become concentrated in mussels. Severe headache, vomiting, abdominal cramps, and diarrhoea were followed by confusion, memory loss, disorientation, and coma. *Nitzschia pungens* is widely distributed in the coastal waters of the Atlantic, Pacific, and Indian Oceans.

Ciguatera and puffer-fish poisoning (see also pp.45–6)

This resembles PSP, and the term 'pelagic paralysis' has been proposed to cover all three because their neurotoxins are believed to act in the same way. Ciguatera is mainly a hazard in Pacific and Caribbean waters: the dinoflagellates involved are benthic (found at the bottom of an ocean) and therefore probably not related to blooms. It is, however, the most common form of fish poisoning and the most frequently reported food-borne disease of a chemical nature in south-east Florida and Hawaii. Puffer-fish poisoning is still a public health hazard in Japan. Both types of poisoning may occur in Europe from imported fish.

Marine cyanophyte dermatitis

This is a severe contact dermatitis known as swimmers' itch or seaweed dermatitis. It may occur after swimming or handling fishing nets in seas containing blooms of the filamentous marine cyanophyte *Lynbya majuscula*. Two of the toxic agents are known to be potent tumour-producing compounds. Outbreaks have been reported from countries such as Japan and Hawaii. A toxic dermatitis known as Dogger Bank itch or weed rash also occurs in European trawler fishermen from the handling of trawl nets. It is caused by moss animals called sea chervils found in the North Sea, and not by algae.

Skin irritation in bathers can also be caused by jelly-fish fragments or by small crustacea in the bloom which become trapped inside bathing suits. The bloom may also dry on the skin after bathing and irritate or sensitize it if it is not washed off. Hay fever or asthma may also be provoked by bloom material drying on the shore, becoming airborne, and affecting sunbathers and others exposed to on-shore winds.

Hints for personal health

The risk of harmful effects from different patterns of exposure to BGA is not fully understood. Unfortunately, the potential toxicity of a bloom or scum cannot be determined by its appearance, odour, texture, or any other simple feature. If treated with reasonable care, there is little hazard to human health: although algal scums and blooms are not always harmful, it is sensible to regard them as such. The following points will help minimize possible risks associated with drinking water and recreational exposures.

Drinking water

Standard water treatment does not remove algal toxins from water. The toxins are heat stable and unlikely to be destroyed by boiling. There is also no evidence that water purification tablets either destroy the toxins or encourage their release from algal cells. Although an extremely uncommon and temporary phenomenon, any drinking-water supply that is obviously discoloured blue-green should be avoided. Nevertheless, there is little present evidence of particular risks from public supplies.

Shellfish are best avoided if there is doubt about the purity of the waters they came from.

In rural or wilderness areas where raw water is consumed, take the following precautions to reduce the risk of exposure:

- Where possible, take drinking water from flowing rather than still water
- In still water, scums and decaying cells accumulate downwind on the surface, and are more likely to be associated with the release of toxins. Water should therefore be taken away from any visible scum, out from the water's edge, from below the surface, and on the windward side of a lake or reservoir
- Brownish, peaty upland waters are less likely to be contaminated with BGA than lowland nutrient-enriched waters
- If drinking water has been taken in the presence of a scum or algal bloom, the water should be filtered to remove particles of algal material
- Affected water is generally safe for irrigation, but if in doubt, avoid eating leafy vegetables, or at least wash them carefully in clean, treated water.

Freshwater recreational activities

Studies have not yet identified any particular illnesses that could be linked to BGA exposure through recreation. As a precaution though, the following guidance is recommended:

- If the water is clear there is little danger of ill-effects as a result of recreational contact
- Toxins are more concentrated where there are visible algal scums. These areas should always be avoided. Direct contact with a visible scum, or swallowing appreciable amounts, are associated with the highest chances of a health risk
- On a lee shore and windy day, algae and scum can be found at some distance from the water's edge—keep away from these areas
- If sailing, windsurfing, or undertaking any other activity likely to involve accidental water immersion in the presence of scums or algal blooms, wear clothing that is close-fitting at the wrists and neck, and also boots and sailing suits that fit into the boot tops
- Spend as little time as possible in shallow water launching and recovering boats; launching and recovery should be undertaken in areas away from thick aggregations of algae or scum
- After coming ashore, hose, shower, or wash yourself down to remove any scum or algae
- All clothing and bathing costumes should be washed and thoroughly dried after any contact with scums or blooms. Do not store wet clothes
- During sailing or boating activities when scums or blooms are present, keep capsize drills to a minimum, ensure rescue boats are on hand to take crews out of the water as soon as possible, and wash boats and wet gear down immediately on coming ashore. Races should be staged away from affected areas
- When fishing, keep away from algal scums and clean your hands after handling fish or fishing tackle
- If any health effects are experienced subsequently, whatever the nature of the exposure, seek prompt medical attention.

Seawater bathing

- As far as exposure to algae is concerned, seawater is generally safe to bathe in provided there is no red algal tide or mucilage, and the water is not otherwise obviously polluted
- Avoid floating clumps of seaweed or aggregations along the shoreline.
- On the beach, do not sit downwind of any bloom material drying on the shore which could form an aerosol and be inhaled
- If available, use beach showers after bathing, and rinse bathing costumes thoroughly in fresh water to remove salt, crustaceans, algae, or jellyfish fragments that can cause skin irritation.

Diseases of 'contact'

4.1 Tuberculosis

Peter Davies and Andrea Collins

Tuberculosis (TB) is the infectious disease that causes the most deaths in the world today—it is 'the disease that never really went away'. Despite the worsening global situation and the limited options for prevention, however, it is a disease that is often straightforward to detect and treat.

Background

A new era in the history of TB began in the mid-1980s when it was realized that the disease had not only ceased to decline in many developed countries, notably the USA, but was actually increasing. A reappraisal showed that the disease was out of control across many of the poorest regions of the world, especially Central Africa and South Asia. More than 90% of TB cases and deaths occur in the developing world. One-third of the world's population are infected with the tubercle bacillus—known as latent infection, *not* the same as disease. Deaths from TB are expected to increase from the current 3 million a year to 5 million by 2050.

The global rise of tuberculosis

There are several main factors responsible for the massive upsurge in the spread of TB.

Population explosion

The highest incidence of TB across the globe is in central Africa, where annual death rates exceed 200 per 100 000 population, and in southern Asia, particularly India, where annual death rates are 100–200 per 100 000. These are the areas in which the population increases most rapidly: in the next 20–30 years, the population of India is expected to rise by 75% and that of central African countries, such as Malawi, by 150%.

The menace of HIV/AIDS

It is known that co-infection with HIV increases the risk of TB infection (latent TB) developing into disease, approximately 100-fold. The lifetime risk of about 10% of infection developing into disease in a person infected with TB alone becomes an *annual* risk of 10% in a HIV-positive individual. The epidemic of co-infection has overwhelmed the health services in all sub-Saharan African countries.

Poverty increase

The association between poverty and TB is well established. Even within the developed world the highest rates of disease are seen in the poorest sections of the community. In the last 10–15 years the number of people living on less than a dollar a day (the definition of absolute poverty) has increased from 0.75 to 1.3 billion.

Multidrug-resistant TB

Multidrug-resistant TB (MDRTB) is defined as the presence of bacteria resistant to at least isoniazid and rifampicin (the two most effective drugs in the treatment of TB), and is an increasing problem. Drug treatment may need to be prolonged from the usual 6 months to as long as 2 years. Using second-line (reserve) drugs is difficult and expensive, and adverse effects are common. Some parts of the world (Russia and the Baltic states) have rates of drug resistance of up to 50%.

Immigration

This is the main factor contributing to the increase within the developed world. In England, 60% of cases are in ethnic minority groups (mostly from the Indian subcontinent) that comprise only 5% of the population.

The course of tuberculosis

TB is spread in the same way as the common cold. It is usually caught by inhaling airborne bacilli (rod-shaped bacteria), *Mycobacterium tuberculosis*, coughed into the air by an individual with infectious disease. TB tends to be less infectious than the cold virus, and contact usually has to be prolonged for a serious risk to be present. This is why TB tends to be transmitted mainly within households, and in poor (small/cramped living conditions) and over-populated areas.

The primary infection of TB occurs in the lungs and usually goes unnoticed. A short period of malaise and non-specific respiratory tract symptoms may develop. The great majority (probably 90%) of people infected will never go on to develop the disease; it may take anywhere between a few months and many years for 'post-primary' disease to develop in those that do. This long incubation explains why the highest incidence in the Caucasian UK population is among the over-65s: these people acquired infection in early adult life, when TB was highly prevalent, with TB disease only appearing much later in life, when their immune system is thought to become weaker.

Symptoms

TB may cause disease in any part of the body, but the lung is the most usual site. If detected early enough, such as by contact screening, there may be no symptoms. The commonest early symptom is cough, continuing for weeks or months, becoming progressively worse—blood may be coughed up. Malaise and weight loss are also common, appearing gradually over weeks or months. A raised temperature often occurs at night, causing the patient to sweat profusely. In severe cases, where much of the lung has been destroyed, breathlessness occurs.

Confirming the diagnosis

TB of the lung usually causes characteristic changes on a chest X-ray that will suggest the presence of disease. The diagnosis must be confirmed by obtaining sputum (or some other sample) for bacteriological analysis. Because the bacterium is difficult to grow (culture), this process can take weeks, though molecular technology is being developed to provide more rapid confirmation of disease.

Tuberculin skin test (Mantoux test)

Skin testing is often used for screening. A small quantity of protein from the TB bacillus (PPD) is injected into the skin; a reaction (swelling) will occur in someone previously infected. The test is read 48–72 hours later by measuring the area of swelling at the injection site. A weakly positive test may be caused by mycobacteria other than TB, including the BCG vaccination. A strongly positive test usually indicates infection (though not necessarily disease) caused by *M. tuberculosis*.

Interferon gamma release assay (IGRA)

This new blood test can also be used to screen for latent TB, and is better at differentiating TB infection from previous BCG vaccination than the skin test.

Treatment

Once TB is suspected, treatment should be started. This involves four specific antibiotics—isoniazid, rifampicin, pyrazinamide, and ethambutol. Treatment must continue for at least 6 months, although the number of antibiotics can be reduced once tests have confirmed the bacterium's sensitivity to the antibiotics being used.

Contact screening

Individuals who are in close and frequent contact with a patient, such as family members, are at risk of disease, and need to be screened by carrying out a Mantoux or IGRA, and a chest X-ray. Those with 8 hours of exposure to a known case of smear-positive TB (e.g. during a long-haul air flight) are at increased risk.

BCG vaccination

At the beginning of the 20th century, BCG vaccine was developed by repeatedly subculturing *M. bovis* (the bacteria responsible for TB in cattle) to result in an attenuated (weakened, less virulent) strain.

Efficacy of BCG

Vaccine trials show variable results. About a third have shown no protective effect, while the remainder have shown protection of up to 80% at best, lasting a maximum of 15 years. (Protective efficacy for most vaccines exceeds 95%.) There is not much hope that a better vaccine can be developed in the future.

BCG in the UK

BCG is given at birth to those at high risk of disease, born in an area with a high TB rate, those with a family history of TB, and those with close family born in an area of high-incidence.

Most UK citizens aged over 13 will have had BCG. About 1% of those who have had BCG remain tuberculin negative (negative skin test) and there is no correlation between protective efficacy of the BCG and the presence of tuberculin positivity. Even 15 years or longer after receiving BCG, there is no need for further vaccination.

Children under the age of 13 who have not had BCG should be advised to have a vaccination if they are travelling for a prolonged period to an area with high endemic TB (Africa, South, and Southeast Asia, parts of Eastern Europe, and Central and South America). Children who have had BCG at birth do not require further testing or vaccination.

BCG takes at least 6 weeks to give protection and it is generally not necessary for short holidays. Adults who have not had BCG and who are travelling to a high-incidence area may wish to be tested for tuberculin sensitivity and, if negative, have BCG. However, there is little evidence that vaccination in adults provides protection. Skin testing is usually needed before BCG vaccination: giving BCG to a tuberculin-positive individual may result in abscess formation. (Skin testing is not usually needed for children under 6 years, unless they have previously lived in a country with a high rate of TB.)

BCG policy in other countries

Most countries give BCG at birth to provide protection in the early years when infection can often lead to devastating widespread disease such as *miliary tuberculosis* (of the lung) or *tuberculous meningitis* (of the brain). This is particularly important where the chance of being infected in very early life is high.

Effect of BCG on the tuberculin test

BCG vaccine leads to a positive Mantoux test, as does infection with *M. tuberculosis*. In the UK, we believe it is possible to tell the difference between skin test positivity caused by BCG and by TB. In some cases, an IGRA test is performed.

Adverse effects of BCG

Lymph node swelling and abscess formation (at the site of BCG injection) may occur. Very rarely indeed, BCG may cause disseminated infection in immunocompromised infants. This is usually fatal. For this reason, BCG should not be given to symptomatic HIV-positive individuals as it is a live vaccine (see also Chapter 10.2).

Preventive therapy

This involves giving a specific course of antibiotics to people with latent TB infection—people with a positive skin test/IGRA, but in the *absence* of disease. Anti-TB antibiotics can cause adverse effects, particularly on the liver. The risk to benefit ratio of treating latent TB infection increases with age. Treatment does not prevent future TB infection (approximately 10% of TB occurs in previously treated individuals); nor does previous infection or disease provide protection for the future. BCG is offered to all healthcare workers in the UK with a negative skin test or IGRA.

Avoiding infection

Travellers from developed countries travelling to endemic areas incur a measurable risk of being infected. In practice, there is probably little one can do to be sure of avoiding TB, since most infections occur from unsuspected cases. Once patients start treatment they are rapidly rendered non-infectious (usually within 2 weeks), with the exception of drug-resistant TB cases. Medical staff working with these patients should take specific precautions (e.g. special face masks). Avoid milk unless you know it has been properly treated/pasteurized. HIV-positive individuals should avoid risk of contact with TB. If this is unavoidable, preventive medication may be considered while in the high-risk area to prevent initial infection.

Box 4.1.1 Summary of advice for travellers going to an area of high TB endemicity

- Children who have not had previous BCG should be tuberculin/IGRA tested and be given BCG if negative
- Adults who have not previously received BCG may wish to be tuberculin tested and given BCG, but there is little evidence for efficacy in this situation
- Anyone who has had a BCG vaccination need not have further testing or BCG vaccination
- In special situations, such as those going to work amongst people likely to have TB (healthcare workers), individual advice should be sought.

Further information

Davies PDO. (ed.) (2008) *Clinical Tuberculosis*, 4th edn. London: Chapman and Hall.
TB Focus. ℘ www.priory.com/cmol/TBpapers.htm
TB Alert. ℘ www.tbalert.org
National Institute for Health and Clinical Excellence. ℘ www.nice.org.uk

4.2 Tetanus

Louise Thwaites

All travellers need to be immunized against tetanus because the risks are widespread and correct treatment following injury may be difficult to obtain overseas.

Tetanus (from the Greek word 'tetanos', meaning to contract) is a disease of muscle stiffness and spasms. It occurs throughout the world and, untreated, is often fatal. It is preventable by immunization, so is rarely seen in the Western world, but remains a major problem where immunization programmes are inadequate, killing over half a million newborn babies every year, as well as many children and young adults.

In the UK, around 10 cases occur each year, with two or three deaths. A small number of cases have occurred following travel.

Travellers are at higher risk because they are more vulnerable to injury and may not find appropriate treatment. All travellers should therefore be immunized before leaving home.

How do you get tetanus?

Tetanus is caused by *Clostridium tetani* bacteria that lie dormant as spores in the soil. The spores are resistant to heat, light, drying, and chemicals. They have been found in human and animal faeces, on unsterile surgical instruments, toothpicks, acupuncture needles, and needles used by intravenous (IV) drug abusers.

Spores enter the body through soil contamination of wounds or via unclean surgical instruments and needles. In newborn babies, soil contamination of the umbilical stump is often the source of infection. Once inside the wound, the spores germinate, and the bacteria grow and multiply. Environments with low oxygen concentrations, such as deep wounds with a poor blood supply and/or lots of residual dead tissue, are especially favourable for bacterial growth.

What are the symptoms of tetanus?

Clostridium tetani produces a powerful toxin that spreads through the body in the blood, and is taken up into nerves, where it exerts its effects. Days or weeks after the initial infection, symptoms begin to occur, especially stiffness of the jaw muscles causing 'lock-jaw' and difficulty in swallowing. Neck and back stiffness usually follow. As the disease progresses, more and more muscles are affected. In very mild forms of tetanus, this may be all that the patient experiences. However, most patients will go on to experience muscle spasms. They are excruciatingly painful. Spasm of facial muscles gives rise to the ironic yet characteristic facial appearance of tetanus—an apparent smile. Involvement of chest muscles interferes with breathing, leading to death by asphyxiation if artificial ventilation is not available.

In severe cases, the nerves that regulate the heart may be involved, resulting in dangerously high or low blood pressure.

Treatment

Once the tetanus toxin is bound within the nerves there is nothing to be done, except to support the patient, usually with intensive care expertise, until its effects wear off.

Prevention

Tetanus is easily preventable by immunization and careful cleaning of wounds. In the UK, the primary immunization course consists of three doses of tetanus toxoid at 2, 3, and 4 months of age, usually in combination with the diphtheria toxoid and pertussis vaccine. Two boosters of diphtheria and tetanus toxoids are given at 3–5 years of age and at 13–18 years of age.

In some countries, obtaining vaccine may be difficult or the vaccine may be of poor quality. *Travellers should therefore have a booster before setting out if they have not had one within the last 10 years* (see also Chapter 13.2). UK schedules recommend a Td/IPV booster (tetanus, diphtheria, and polio combination vaccine).

The next precaution is to avoid sustaining tetanus-prone wounds. These include puncture wounds, burns (especially those with devitalized tissue), animal and human bites, wounds contaminated with soil or faeces, fractures with broken over-lying skin, and any wound where treatment is delayed for more than 6 hr. Avoid going barefoot, ear piercing, tattooing, and acupuncture. IV drug users are at particular risk.

Following injury, a wound should be thoroughly cleansed with clean water and a mild detergent. Splinters, foreign material, or dead tissue should be removed. Skilled medical attention may be needed, especially with tetanus-prone wounds. Revaccination should be considered. If a person has received a full course or a booster of tetanus toxoid within the previous 10 years, no further dose is required. Otherwise, a booster should be given. If there is any doubt about immunization history, a full primary course should be given. Immunosuppressed people should be treated as 'incompletely immunized' (Chapter 11.5).

In addition, tetanus antitoxin (human tetanus immunoglobulin (HTIG), 250U) should be given to people sustaining tetanus-prone wounds (see p.70). Even if the person has had a recent booster, anti-toxin may still be given if it is thought that the risk of tetanus is very high.

In parts of the world where HTIG is not available, the older horse serum preparation, SAT (1500U) may be substituted. Unfortunately, this preparation causes more allergic reactions.

Box 4.2.1 Summary of advice for travellers

- Tetanus is a potentially fatal disease that can be acquired throughout the world. It can be prevented by immunization and careful wound care
- All travellers should check that they have received a primary immunization course against tetanus and that they have had a booster injection within the last 10 years. If a wound is sustained and there is any doubt about the vaccination history a booster should be given
- Any wounds should be thoroughly cleaned. Travellers should seek medical advice about large or contaminated wounds as they may require specific medical treatment.

4.3 Diphtheria

Delia Bethell

Diphtheria is a serious bacterial infection of the respiratory tract or skin, with potentially life-threatening complications. It remains a small but significant risk for anyone travelling outside Western Europe, North America, and Australasia. Immunization provides complete protection, but needs to be updated during adult life.

In the UK, between one and three cases are reported each year. In the USA the last reported case was in 2005, in a traveller returning from Haiti. Diphtheria is much more prevalent in poorer regions of the world, particularly Haiti, Eastern Europe, Central and Southeast Asia, the Indian subcontinent, and South and Central America, where it remains endemic. The 1990s saw a major epidemic in countries of the former Soviet Union, now largely under control after voluntary mass vaccination. In 2009, there were 857 cases reported worldwide by WHO, whereas in 2007 there were 4190.

Diphtheria is spread by respiratory droplets or secretions, and by contact with broken skin. Humans are the only reservoirs of the disease; carriers may harbour the organism for prolonged periods. In non-immune individuals the bacteria multiply in the upper respiratory tract, most commonly the throat and nostrils, causing intense inflammation and formation of the typical greyish 'pseudomembrane'. At this stage the patient has a high fever, sore throat, and feels very unwell. In severe cases, complete obstruction of the airways can occur. The multiplying bacteria release a potent toxin, which travels through the bloodstream to affect many organs in the body, most notably the heart, kidneys, and nerves. Death from toxin damage can occur several weeks after the patient appears to have made an uneventful recovery.

The diphtheria bacilli may also colonize pre-existing skin injuries to cause cutaneous diphtheria, often on the lower legs, feet and hands. These infections are usually mild but chronic and represent the major reservoir of diphtheria in tropical countries.

Diagnosis of diphtheria depends on recognising clinical signs together with cultures and more specialized tests (modified Elek plate test to detect toxin, PCR for *tox* gene). Treatment consists of antibiotics (such as penicillin or erythromycin) to eradicate the organism and prevent further toxin production, and anti-toxin. The efficacy of anti-toxin is reduced if administration is delayed more than 48 hr after the onset of symptoms, so in a person who is unwell, treatment needs to be started before a diagnosis of diphtheria has been confirmed.

Diphtheria and the traveller

Because of wide disease prevalence, all individuals travelling outside Western Europe, North America, and Australasia should be immunized. Serological studies from several countries, including the UK, have shown that up to 50% of adults aged over 20 years are susceptible to diphtheria, with significant decreasing immunity with increasing age. Older women are least likely to be immune.

All non-immune individuals should receive a primary course of three injections at 1–2-monthly intervals. In children under 8 years, this should be with vaccines containing standard doses of diphtheria toxoid, but above this age, a lower dose is considered safer, although less is known about its duration of protection.

Following primary immunization, immunity that is not reinforced by constant natural exposure wanes relatively quickly, but single booster doses usually stimulate a strong response. Adults should receive booster doses at least every 10 years. One study showed response rates to single booster doses in adults aged 20–60 years of 45%, if no history of immunization was given, 80% if prior immunization was unknown, and 86% if they were definitely previously immunized. At least 70% of adults who receive a booster dose respond with a protective level of diphtheria antibodies.

4.4 Schistosomiasis (bilharzia)

Bertie Squire

Schistosomiasis, or bilharzia as it is also called, is present in many tropical countries. It is a grave problem in countries where it is common, because, although not a 'killer' disease in the usual sense, it gnaws insidiously at the general health of entire populations. The geographical distribution of the disease is shown in Map 4.4.1.

At least 200 million people around the world are infected. Although some control successes have been achieved in Asia, the Americas, North Africa, and the Middle East, in other areas numbers of infections are rising. Ironically, the dams, irrigation schemes, and agricultural projects so necessary for the fight against world poverty and hunger, themselves create conditions in which the disease thrives. Schistosomiasis is a special problem in young children—it hinders development and reduces life expectancy. It remains a problem in China despite a nationwide attempt at eradication.

How infection is spread

Schistosomiasis is an infection with one of several kinds of worm (see Table 4.4.1): *Schistosoma haematobium* (urinary schistosomiasis), *Schistosoma mansoni* (intestinal schistosomiasis) and *Schistosoma japonicum* (Far Eastern schistosomiasis) are the most commonly acquired, so the emphasis of this chapter is on these.

The fully grown worms live in the veins around the urinary bladder and genitals (*S. haematobium*), or the veins around the intestine (*S. mansoni* and *S. japonicum*). The worms produce large numbers of eggs that leave the body through the lining of the bladder or intestines. On contact with freshwater, larvae hatch from the eggs and infect certain varieties of snail, in which they develop further and multiply. More larvae are produced (called *cercariae*), which swim freely in freshwater, actively seeking out and penetrating the skin of a human host.

After burrowing through the skin, the young worms find their way (via the lungs) to the veins of the bowel or bladder once again. The adult worms lay eggs for the rest of their lives, which may be as long as 15 years. So many eggs and larvae are produced that a single infected person passing eggs daily can infect a whole river if the appropriate snails abound.

Water is necessary for drinking and washing, and in rural communities around the world, daily exposure to infection is inevitable from an early age. In the Nile valley, East Africa (especially the coastal regions), West Africa (especially the savannah), along the Euphrates and the Tigris rivers in the Middle East, and in parts of Brazil, the majority of the population may be infected from childhood. Almost all children of school age pass large numbers of eggs in the urine or stool daily. Later in life, some immunity builds up so that the worst effects of infection may be avoided.

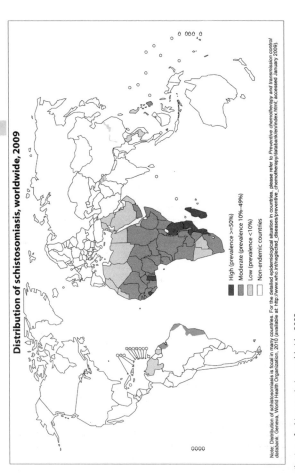

Map 4.4.1 Distribution of schistosomiasis, worldwide, 2009.

Reproduced from *Weekly Epidemiological Record*, No. 9, 2011, **86**, p.74, with permission of the World Health Organization.

Table 4.4.1 Parasite species and geographical distribution of schistosomiasis

	Species	**Geographical distribution**
Intestinal schistosomiasis	Schistosoma mansoni	Africa, the Middle East, the Caribbean, Brazil, Venezuela, Suriname
	Schistosoma japonicum	China, Indonesia, the Philippines
	Schistosoma mekongi	Several districts of Cambodia and the Lao People's Democratic Republic
	Schistosoma intercalatum and related S. guineansis	Rainforest areas of Central Africa
Urogenital schistosomiasis	Schistosoma haematobium	Africa, the Middle East

Most of the harmful effects of the disease are due to the eggs; these cause bleeding, ulceration, and the formation of small tumours as they lodge in the tissues around the kidneys, bladder and genitals, or the intestine, or become trapped in the liver and other tissues. Long-term effects include severe liver damage (the eggs cause liver fibrosis), kidney failure, and cancer of the bladder.

Disease in travellers

Expatriates and travellers with no previous exposure to schistosomiasis may become seriously ill in the early stages of an infection, although it is unusual for them to suffer in the same way as local people, who are exposed to the disease over a long period.

A few hours after contact with infected water, there is sometimes tingling of the skin and a slight rash where the larvae enter the body (cercarial dermatitis or 'swimmers' itch, see Box 4.4.1). These symptoms subside, but weeks later, once the worms begin producing eggs, a high fever may develop. This may be severe, and may be confused with typhoid or malaria. An increased number of white blood cells (especially of a type called *eosinophils*) may appear in the blood and give a clue to the true diagnosis, although not many doctors outside the tropics are aware of this. Travellers should always tell their doctor if they have been in contact (swimming or washing) with fresh, untreated water in endemic countries. This acute schistosomiasis, sometimes called 'Katayama fever', does not always occur, and symptoms may be completely absent, or may be no more than a general feeling of lassitude and ill health.

Once the infection becomes established, the vast majority of people report very few or even no symptoms. In those who do develop symptoms, abdominal pain, and blood in the urine or faeces are commonly reported. Genital symptoms caused by S. haematobium have also received increasing attention. Some female travellers have presented with small tumours on the vulva or cervix, and some infected males report changes

Box 4.4.1 **Swimmers' itch**

This is an intensified variety of cercarial dermatitis caused by schistosome larvae that die in the skin and do not develop further. This condition can occur in temperate, as well as in tropical countries. Some hours after exposure to the water, an itching sensation develops on the exposed skin surfaces, followed by a rash composed of small, red, intensely irritant papules, which fade after 24 hours. Provided the infecting cercariae are not from a species of schistosome that infects humans (i.e. in a schistosomiasis-free country), no further symptoms occur and no harm results. Anti-histamine tablets or ointment are all that is necessary for treatment (see also pp.62–3).

in semen consistency or blood in the ejaculate. Severe disease, such as kidney obstruction due to obstruction of the ureters or liver fibrosis due to lodging of eggs in the liver, may develop several years after the initial infection. Occasionally, eggs may lodge in the brain, causing epilepsy, or in the spinal cord, causing limb paralysis.

Safe and effective treatment

A safe drug is now available that is effective against all species of schistosomes. Praziquantel tablets are given, usually as a single dose of between 40 and 60mg/kg, and side effects are rare. The limitations of this drug are that it will only clear worms that have reached maturity and that it will not heal established scarring (for example, in the liver or bladder) when heavy infection has been established for several years. Early recognition and treatment of infection are therefore very important.

Travellers at risk

Travellers to all countries listed in Table 4.4.1 may be in danger of infection. Especially at risk are those who swim in streams, rivers, or lakes, or who take part in water sports such as water-skiing, wind-surfing, and scuba-diving in freshwater areas; water sports are particularly dangerous because they may involve exposure to surface water over a large area and water contact is prolonged. Activities such as snipe- and duck-shooting, and cross-country walking safaris, where streams have to be crossed, are also hazardous.

Some areas are especially risky—the Nile valley, Lake Victoria, the Tigris and Euphrates river systems, and artificial lakes, such as Lake Kariba in Zimbabwe and Lake Volta in Ghana (which are both notorious). Even small collections of water, far from human habitation, can give rise to serious infections, since both wild and domestic animals can harbour some schistosome species.

Lake Malawi, which for many years was advertised as schistosomiasis-free, is acknowledged to be a significant source of infection with both *S. mansoni* and *S. haematobium*, despite the fact that many tour operators and diving centres claim that it is safe (see Box 4.4.2). It is true that diving from boats in deep water carries less risk than swimming or snorkelling

Box 4.4.2 **Lakes and waterfalls: look, don't swim**

Lake Malawi is a popular tourist destination in Africa. Scuba-diving, snor-kelling and wind-surfing are among the main attractions. The risk to visitors can be made worse if the people who run these activities insist that the water is safe—a false reassurance that has quickly found its way into guide books and magazines around the world. Alternatively, some destinations acknowledge the risk, but offer patients praziquantel as preventive therapy. Some travellers will take this medication and then live with a false sense of security, either because the tablets were not quality-assured, were the incorrect dose, or because they were taken before the worms had matured.

Cape Maclear, one of the most popular points on the lake, and one that is often claimed to be especially safe, is known to carry a risk that is nearly three times higher than the risk in other parts of the lake. Between half and three-quarters of people who spend a single day swimming or diving at Cape Maclear can expect to end up testing posi-tive for schistosomiasis.

One well-documented case involved a 30-year-old Peace Corps volunteer who developed headaches, convulsions, and blindness in one eye; a brain tumour seemed the most likely cause. Only after neuro-surgery did tests confirm that he was suffering from schistosomiasis. Three months earlier he had snorkelled for 2 days at Cape Maclear. In another case, a 26-year-old Peace Corps volunteer developed gradual paraplegia, and a spinal tumour was suspected. At surgery she, too, was found to be suffering from schistosomiasis and she, too, had been snor-kelling at Cape Maclear.

Elsewhere in Africa, other examples of cases include a research biolo-gist who began passing blood in her urine, 6 months after a trip to Mali. She had bathed just once during the trip, at a remote waterfall, miles from anywhere. It took a month for her to recognize the symptoms—even though schistosomiasis happened to be the very subject of her own research. An entire group of 43 Spanish tourists to Mali also came down with schistosomiasis.

in shallow coastal water near vegetation with high snail populations. However, *no freshwater exposure in an endemic area is entirely free of* the risk of schistosome infection.

Personal protection

No vaccine is available and none is likely to be in the near future.

Never assume freshwater to be free from bilharzia in any endemic area. Infection can occur on contact with infected water from streams, rivers, and lakes. Deep water, far offshore, carries less risk, but it can still be dan-gerous to swim from boats in infected lakes. Salt water and brackish water are, however, safe from schistosomiasis.

Since the larvae die quickly on removal from water and cannot survive drying, quick drying of exposed skin and clothing does offer some protection, provided contact time in the water has been less than 5 min.

Water that has been chlorinated or stored in a snail-free environment for 48 hr is safe, since any cercariae present will have died off.

Swimming pools that are snail-free are safe, but care must be taken that any water entering the pool has been treated. Neglected swimming pools can rapidly become colonized with snails. Dams are especially dangerous and invariably become infected within 10 years of construction in endemic countries.

If contact with water cannot be avoided, always observe the following precautions:

- Keep contact time with water to a minimum
- Do not cross streams at points where there is much human contact, such as village river crossings; always cross upstream of a village
- Wear waterproof footwear when possible
- Always take particular care to avoid contact with water and remember the risks of animal-contaminated water. Resist the temptation to strip off and swim after a long hot hike. If you cannot resist, choose a stretch of clear water with a sandy bottom, as little vegetation as possible, and plenty of wave action. Swimming in the early morning and late evening, although still not risk-free, carries less risk of infection than swimming when the sun is at its zenith.

Check-up on return home

It is advisable to have a check-up on return home (see Appendix 5) whether or not suggestive symptoms are present.

In the absence of symptoms

If, after possible or unavoidable exposure in freshwater (such as during canoeing or rafting), there are no symptoms of the kind described previously, a check-up 3 months after the last possible freshwater exposure is worthwhile. In these cases, the simplest and most sensitive screening test is a blood test—enzyme-linked immunoabsorbent assay (ELISA) detecting antibodies. Such antibodies are present in patients who have been infected, but they are not reliably detectable until 3 months have elapsed from the last possible time of infection. Also, the test does not reliably revert to negative following adequate treatment.

A positive antibody test, therefore, does not necessarily indicate a currently active infection. This can be established only through demonstration of viable eggs in the urine or faeces, or semen. Modern egg-concentration methods should specifically be used if there is doubt about the current activity of an infection (for example, in travellers with previous infections). Not all infected travellers, however, will harbour sufficient numbers of worms to produce enough eggs for these to be detected in stool or urine samples.

A white blood cell count is advisable to look for the presence of eosinophilia, which may be a further indicator of infection.

If any of these tests indicate an infection in a person who does not have symptoms, a single course of praziquantel is advised to eradicate the infection and reduce the risks of tissue damage developing in future years.

There is some debate about whether tests to confirm infection are really necessary—why not just have treatment if you think you have been exposed? Unfortunately praziquantel is not always easily available.

For example, in the UK it is not licensed and can be provided only on a named-patient basis, in which case evidence of infection is usually required. The alternative practice of swallowing some praziquantel tablets that have been obtained in the country where there has been some risk of exposure is advocated by some. The problems with this approach are:

- The drug quality and effectiveness may not be reliable
- The dose given may be incorrect
- Praziquantel will clear only mature worms. If it is taken while worms are still maturing (i.e. within 40 days of the last possible exposure), some worms may survive to reach maturity.

If there are symptoms
Acute schistosomiasis ('Katayama fever') can be diagnosed only when other likely causes of fever (e.g. malaria or typhoid) have been excluded. There is no specifically reliable test for detecting schistosomes at this stage of infection. As most acute schistosomiasis is self-resolving and very unlikely to lead to death there will be very few occasions when presumptive self-treatment with praziquantel is necessary. It will be more important to treat for malaria and typhoid, and praziquantel can usually wait until skilled medical advice is at hand.

If there are suggestive symptoms of established infection (such as blood in the urine or stool, or a change in semen consistency), then a combination of available blood, urine, stool, and semen tests should be carried out in order to establish if schistosomiasis is the cause. If schistosomiasis is confirmed, then follow-up about 3 months after treatment, to document resolution of symptoms and clearance of eggs from samples, is advised. Once again, established schistosomiasis very rarely poses an immediate threat to life and definitive treatment can wait for authoritative diagnosis.

Research and future prospects for those in endemic regions

Although understanding of the pathology and immunology of schistosomiasis has advanced considerably through research, prospects for a vaccine in the short to medium term are bleak. In the meantime, controlling morbidity with targeted or mass drug treatment (especially in school-age children) is a feasible and effective strategy. Health education and provision of safe water are invaluable and carry benefits beyond those specific to schistosomiasis.

Further information

A range of relevant publications, maps, and information on countries affected is available through the WHO website ℘ http://www.who.int/topics/schistosomiasis/en/ and its links.

4.5 Meningococcal disease

Andrew Pollard

Meningococcal disease (meningitis and septicaemia) is rare amongst travellers, but can be devastating—up to 10% of those affected die. The risk is highest for travellers to regions affected by epidemics, those attending mass gatherings or working in crowded refugee camps. Vaccines cover the most important strains.

Meningococcal disease is caused by *Neisseria meningitidis* bacteria ('the meningococcus') that lives naturally in the human throat, only rarely causing disease. Five different types (serogroups) cause most of the disease: serogroups A, B, C, Y, and W. Ten per cent of adults and up to one-third of adolescents and young adults have the meningococcus residing harmlessly in their throat at any one time and most will never suffer any symptoms. Bacteria spread via respiratory droplets, and require very close contact to transmit from one person to another. Very rarely, soon after a person acquires a new strain, it may enter the bloodstream; it can then multiply there (meningococcal septicaemia or blood-poisoning) or 'seed' to the covering of the brain (meninges), causing meningococcal meningitis. After exposure in these rare susceptible individuals, disease usually develops within about 4 days.

The following are known risk factors for developing the disease:
• Young age (under 2 years)
• Adolescence and young adulthood
• Close contact with an individual suffering from the disease
• Exposure to cigarette smoke
• Winter season (or the dry season in Sub-Saharan Africa)
• Recent respiratory infection
• Crowded conditions (bars and nightclubs, the Hajj pilgrimage to Mecca, refugee camps)
• Rare genetic conditions affecting the immune system (e.g. complement deficiency).

Where it occurs

Meningococcal disease is found worldwide but the rate of disease varies enormously. In most developed countries, disease is rare and occurs as sporadic cases or in small clusters (often associated with institutions such as schools or universities). Less than 0.3 cases per 100 000 population are currently reported in North America (mostly serogroups B, C, and Y), but a 10 times higher rate occurs in Europe (mostly serogroup B and C).

The situation is very different in developing countries, with some epidemics affecting more than 1000 per 100 000 people (predominantly serogroup A, but epidemics of W and X strains have occurred). The most frequently-affected area is the 'meningitis belt' of Sub-Saharan Africa, extending from the Sudan in the east to the eastern part of the Gambia to the west, and from the Sahara in the north to the forested areas of West Africa in the south (see Map 4.5.1). These epidemics occur in the dry season (January–April) and come in explosive cycles every few years. A new vaccine (for serogroup A meningococcal disease) has been introduced in the meningitis belt that has the potential to halt many of these epidemics.

Whilst most of the epidemics in the past decade have been in Africa, the first ever description of the disease came from an epidemic in Geneva in 1805, and similar epidemics occurred across Europe during and after the 20th-century military conflicts, and more recently in Russia and Poland. We don't know why epidemics in Europe have subsided in recent history.

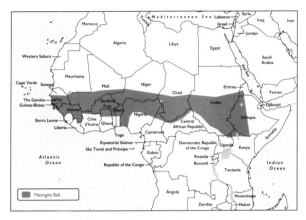

Map 4.5.1 Areas with frequent epidemics of meningococcal meningitis.

Adapted from CDC and edited by Gary W. Burnette, *CDC Health Information for International Travel 2012*, 2012, p.251 with permission from Oxford University Press Inc.

In the past 30 years epidemics in India, Nepal, Kenya, Tanzania, and Brazil have also occurred, and several outbreaks have been associated with the annual Hajj pilgrimage to Mecca in Saudi Arabia.

Symptoms of meningococcal disease

Meningococcal disease is a medical emergency. Some patients die within hours of the onset of symptoms, so recognizing them and taking prompt action can be life-saving. The most distinctive feature of meningococcal disease is the rash, which is typically non-blanching (does not fade under pressure) and occurs in 80% of cases (see Fig. 4.5.1). Pressing a glass against the skin to see if the rash disappears can be a helpful way of recognizing the rash. Two main forms of the disease occur—meninigitis and septicaemia, although some patients will have a mixture of the two:

Meningitis

Symptoms of meningococcal meningitis include some or all of the following:
• Non-blanching rash
• Non-specific symptoms (vomiting and irritability especially in young children)
• Headache
• Fever
• Stiff neck
• Bulging fontanelle (the soft spot on the head) in infants
• Photophobia (fear of bright lights)
• Decreased level of consciousness
• Seizures or fits.

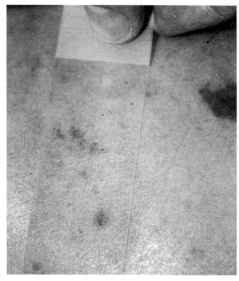

Fig. 4.5.1 Meningococcal disease.

Patients with meningitis need urgent assessment by a doctor (including a lumbar puncture to collect some of the infected fluid from around the spinal cord) and treatment.

Septicaemia

Symptoms of meningococcal septicaemia (meningococcaemia) include some or all of the following:
- Initial flu-like symptoms (fever, headache, sore muscles, vomiting, abdominal pain)
- Non-blanching rash, which may extend to large areas that look like bruises
- Pain in arms and legs
- A mottled appearance of the skin
- Cold hands and feet
- Confusion, agitation, loss of consciousness.

Patients with meningococcal septicaemia are often seriously ill and need urgent medical treatment.

Treatment

Meningococcal disease is best treated in a hospital urgently, with antibiotics and, in septicaemia cases, IV fluids for resuscitation. Often, support for the heart and breathing is used. When medical assistance is not available, antibiotics should be given as soon as possible. Most antibiotics will kill the meningococcus (e.g. penicillins, cephalosporins, and chloramphenicol) and should ideally be given by IV or intramuscular (IM) injection (or by mouth if nothing else available) until the patient reaches medical attention. Patients often become dehydrated, so should be encouraged to drink, and may take ordinary painkillers for headache.

Prevention

The risk of acquiring meningococcal meningitis during a short visit to the African meningitis belt, even if an epidemic is in progress, is small. The risk is probably a little higher in long-term visitors. However, because meningococcal disease can be fatal and because meningococcal vaccines are safe, vaccination is recommended, even when the risk of infection is only small.

Vaccination is advisable for:

- All visitors to the African meningitis belt during the dry season
- Visitors to other areas where an epidemic is occurring (check before travel)
- Visitors to the Holy Places in Saudi Arabia (proof required for admission to the country)
- All travellers who have had their spleen surgically removed (e.g. after trauma to the abdomen) or have been born without a spleen
- All travellers with complement deficiency.

The meningococcal ACYW conjugate vaccines (e.g. Menactra, Menveo, Nimenrix—depending on local availability) are recommended as a single dose and can be administered from early infancy (6 weeks–2 months of age). The older meningococcal vaccines should be used only where conjugate vaccines are unavailable. Children or young adults who have previously received the meningococcal C conjugate vaccine (Menjugate, Meningitec, or Neisvac-C) should still have the ACYW conjugate vaccine if travelling to a risk area, as most epidemics are caused by A and not C. There is no vaccine for serogroup X as yet.

Close contacts of cases (e.g. household or kissing contacts, healthcare workers exposed to respiratory secretions) should receive preventive antibiotics to reduce their own risk of disease, ideally on specialist advice:

- Rifampicin (10mg/kg by mouth twice daily for 2 days; 600mg in an adult)
- Ciprofloxacin (one oral dose of 500mg >12 years; 250mg for ages 5–12 years; 125mg for 2–4 years of age)
- Cetriaxone (one IM dose of 125mg from 1 month to 12 years; 250mg >12 years).

Protection against meningococcal disease with the new meningococcal ACYW conjugate vaccines should be considered for travellers to epidemic areas, including the meningitis belt of Africa and to the Hajj pilgrimage; and by travellers with no spleen or with complement deficiency.

4.6 Legionnaires' disease

John Macfarlane

What is legionellosis and Legionnaires' disease?

Legionellosis describes illnesses caused by *Legionella* bacteria, most commonly *Legionella pneumophila*. These include Legionnaires' disease (pneumonia—named after the defining outbreak that affected over 200 members of the American legion in Philadelphia in 1976, of whom 34 died) and Pontiac fever (a self-limiting influenza-like illness).

How do you catch it?

Legionella bacteria thrive in many natural and man-made water systems, multiplying in the presence of warmth, sludge, and stagnation. Infection is caused by inhaling contaminated water aerosols.

Common sources include:
- Drift from wet cooling towers (often linked to large outbreaks)
- Showers, whirlpool spas, and fountains (causing single cases and small outbreaks).

Less common sources include:
- Cooler cabinets
- Car washes and windscreen sprayers
- Moist soil and compost.

How common is it?

Legionnaires' disease causes 2–3% of pneumonias, more in warmer countries including the Mediterranean. Cases are commoner in summer months and up to half are linked to travel, e.g. from hotel stays.

How does it present?

Men, the middle aged, smokers, and excess alcohol drinkers are at increased risk. After an incubation period of 2–10 days, there is typically high fever, chills, headache, aches and pains, increasing breathlessness, and (often minimal) cough. Confusion and diarrhoea can predominate, and some patients become very unsteady and appear 'drunk'.

How is it diagnosed and treated?

The chest X-ray, and routine blood and sputum tests are non-specific; a rapid urine *Legionella* antigen test has revolutionized prompt, early diagnosis. The first choice antibiotics are macrolides (erythromycin and clarithromycin) and fluoroquinolones (examples include levofloxacin and ciprofloxacin). Penicillin and amoxicillin are ineffective. Many who develop pneumonia become ill enough to require hospital admission. Some patients can deteriorate rapidly and require critical care support. The mortality is 5–15%, but higher in those with underlying ill health.

How is it prevented?

Person-to-person spread does not occur. Cases should be reported to health authorities to trigger a source search. Good design and mainte-nance of building water systems is essential. Some sufferers or relatives initiate legal action against those alleged to be responsible for not maintaining a *Legionella* infection-free water system. Infection risk has been linked to those who shower first in the morning, if water has stagnated in pipes overnight.

Travellers should consider dribble-running showers and spray taps to flush out stagnant water without producing a water mist, if the appliance has not been used for some time.

Key points: Legionnaires' disease and the traveller

- Uncommon cause of pneumonia and an influenza-like illness
- Linked to inhaling infected water mist from poorly maintained wet cooling towers, showers, whirlpool baths, particularly in holiday hotels and large buildings
- Can result in severe pneumonia
- Responds to specific antibiotics, but not penicillin.

Further information

⅋ http://ecdc.europa.eu/en/activities/surveillance/ELDSNet. European information on the incidence, source and outcome from the European Legionnaires' Disease Surveillance Network (ELDSNet).

⅋ http://www.hpa.org.uk/Topics/InfectiousDiseases/InfectionsAZ/LegionnairesDisease. Useful and readable source of information from the UK Health Protection Agency.

⅋ http://www.brit-thoracic.org.uk/guidelines/pneumonia-guidelines.aspx. Provides a good medical overview on the presentation, management and outcome of Legionnaires' disease pneumonia.

⅋ http://www.patient.co.uk/health/Legionnaires'-Disease.htm. Useful information for patients and their relatives.

4.7 Worm infections from soil contact

Michael Brown

Skin contact with soil contaminated by infective worm larvae can lead to localized skin problems or important gut infections. Travellers become infected through skin contact, usually the feet or lower limbs. Larvae, derived from the faeces of infected people, migrate through the skin and enter the circulation to be carried to the lungs, where they ascend the airways to be swallowed and take up residence in the small intestine. The two important human infections acquired in this way are hookworm and strongyloidiasis—as many as a billion people worldwide may be infected. Non-human hookworm larvae deposited in the soil in cat and dog faeces can also infect man; these infections are confined to the skin, producing cutaneous *larva migrans*.

Hookworm

Two species of human hookworm are found in the tropics: *Necator americanus* and *Ancylostoma duodenale*. Adult worms are 1 cm long and live attached to the lining of the small intestine by their powerful jaws; they feed on blood and can live for 5–10 years. Tourists may acquire infection when visiting villages, urban slums, or beaches—anywhere with soil contaminated by human faeces. Adequate footwear will prevent most infections, but may be insufficient under wet conditions.

During lung migration there may be coughing and wheezing; when worms reach the gut there is sometimes upper abdominal pain and diarrhoea, but usually the infection is asymptomatic. If enough worms are present, the blood-sucking activity of the worms can cause anaemia. Diagnosis is made by finding eggs in stool specimens. Effective treatments include mebendazole, albendazole, or pyrantel.

Strongyloidiasis

This is rarer than hookworm, but may have more serious, delayed consequences. Infection is acquired in the same way; adult *Strongyloides stercoralis* measure only 4mm and live within the epithelium of the upper small intestine.

Diagnosis is by finding larvae, not eggs, in stool specimens, or by finding antibodies to Strongyloides in the blood (serology). Most larvae develop in the soil through one generation of free-living adult worms that produce infective larvae, which then infect exposed human skin. Uniquely, however, freshly passed larvae can also directly penetrate the skin, either around the anus or within the intestine before defecation; this self-infection can be perpetuated for many years. Some Burma railway prisoners of war infected in 1945 were found still infected 40 years later.

Symptoms include episodic wheezing, upper abdominal pains, and a rapidly moving form of larval skin migration known as *larva currens,* occurring around the buttocks, lower trunk, and thighs. An abnormal white blood cell count (eosinophilia) is a common finding and should prompt a physician to look for Strongyloides and other worm infections in someone who has been in the tropics. Many infections are apparently symptomless. More severe infections cause abdominal bloating, malabsorption, diarrhoea, and even bowel obstruction.

A unique feature of Strongyloides in contrast to other worm infections is the 'hyperinfection' that can occur in persons with compromised immune systems, and those given steroid and other immunosuppressive treatment. Numerous larvae in many body tissues can cause very heavy, even fatal, infection.

Most experts use ivermectin for treatment. A 3-day course of albendazole is a less effective alternative, if this is not available.

Larva migrans

Itchy, red, wavy lines appear on the skin and may move several millimetres each day. Blistering and secondary bacterial sepsis are common. Untreated, it may persist for many weeks. Common sites are the soles and other parts of the feet, legs, buttocks, or even the trunk or arms—anywhere that comes into contact with infected soil or sand. Beaches above a high water mark, which have been fouled by dogs, are the greatest risk to travellers. Cases occur from all over the tropics, including the Caribbean and Gulf coasts of North America. At least one dog hookworm, *Ancylostoma caninum*, can reach the human gut and cause eosinophilic enteritis—a serious condition presenting with abdominal pain and vomiting severe enough to warrant exploratory surgery.

Treatment is by albendazole or ivermectin tablets. Alternatively, thiabendazole ointment, made up by a pharmacist to contain 0.5g of the drug in 10g of petroleum jelly, can be used.

Box 4.7.1 **Summary of advice to travellers**

- Proper footwear and care on beaches polluted with human or dog faeces will minimize risks
- Returning travellers found to be anaemic or to have a blood eosinophilia should have stool and blood examined for hookworm and strongyloidiasis
- Strongyloidiasis must be excluded in former travellers who develop immune defects or receive drugs affecting the immune system.

4.8 Leprosy

Diana Lockwood

The mythology surrounding leprosy has made it a feared disease. However, although once associated with limb loss and social exclusion, leprosy is treatable, and considerable progress has been made towards controlling it. Travellers almost never catch leprosy and there is nothing to fear from treated leprosy patients.

Key facts about leprosy

- It does not develop after short visits to the tropics
- It is not spread by touching, kissing, or sex
- It is curable with antibiotics
- It may cause permanent nerve damage in sufferers
- It does not eat away at one's fingers and toes.

What causes leprosy and where does it occur?

Leprosy is caused by the bacterium *Mycobacterium leprae*, an organism similar to the tuberculosis germ. A minority of untreated leprosy patients cough and sneeze the germ into the environment, where it can survive for weeks before entering another human. The only animals susceptible to leprosy are nine-banded armadillos in Central America—these have been associated with some cases in the Southern USA.

Leprosy is found throughout the tropics and subtropics; it was common in Britain in medieval times. Now, most patients are found in Asia, parts of Africa, and South America. India has 60% of the world's leprosy patients, followed by Brazil (11%). At the beginning of 2009, the number of confirmed leprosy cases detected each year was 250 000.

Who gets leprosy?

Most people living in endemic regions have probably met the leprosy germ at some point and mounted a good immune response to it. Only a very small number go on to develop the disease. There are no tests that reliably identify people at risk. Touching, sharing meals or having sex with leprosy patients does not spread the disease. All recent cases of leprosy in the UK have occurred in people who have lived in endemic regions for more than 8 years.

What are the effects of the disease?

Leprosy has a very long incubation—2–15 years. The germ lives in the skin and nerves of the arms, legs, and face. One of the first signs of disease are skin patches that are usually pale and numb. Skin nodules and infiltration may also develop. The skin lesions may be disfiguring, but it is the damage to the nerves that causes long-term problems. Patients may be left with weak muscles, so that they cannot close their eyes or walk properly. They also lose sensation in their eyes, hands, and feet. So, a woman cooking will not feel her hand burning and a farmer ploughing will be unaware of a piece of bamboo lodging in his foot. These injuries can rapidly become infected. It is repeated episodes of infection that cause the loss of fingers and toes that one sees in leprosy patients.

How is leprosy treated?

Fortunately, there are antibiotics that kill the germs very rapidly. Patients are treated with either two or three antibiotics, for 6 or 12 months, and become non-infectious within 3 days of starting them. Relapse after treatment is rare. With this treatment, over 16 million patients worldwide have been cured of leprosy. However, nerve damage may never recover.

Sadly, the stigmatization associated with leprosy also continues, and many patients will conceal their disease even from close family. It will take decades yet to remove old prejudices.

No vaccine specific for leprosy exists, although several trials have shown that BCG vaccine protects against leprosy, as well as tuberculosis.

> Leprosy is a curable disease with a very low infectivity, and the chances of catching it are negligible. Beggars and other people with overt signs of the disease are not contagious and pose no threat to the traveller.

4.9 Anthrax

Philip Brachman

Anthrax is a lethal bacterial disease of livestock that is occasionally transmitted to humans. It occurs or has occurred in virtually every country. It is currently only a minor public health problem due to the wide use of animal anthrax vaccines. Lapses in local control programmes, however, can have serious consequences, such as the epidemic in the 1990s of almost 10 000 human cases in Zimbabwe. The most frequent victims are those closely associated with raising livestock or processing animal bones, hair, and hides.

How it is spread

Anthrax is caused by *Bacillus anthracis*, a bacterium normally present in soil. The bacillus grows rapidly when environmental conditions are optimal, then forms spores to survive adverse periods. These spores can remain viable for many years. Animals become infected by grazing when the anthrax bacillus is in its active growth phase.

Human anthrax results from handling the products from infected animals. When an animal dies of anthrax, the carcass should be burned or buried. Poverty, however, frequently leads animal owners to salvage anything of value. The meat may be eaten, and bones, skin, and hair sold or used. Spore contamination of these by-products can therefore become a hazard to people far away.

Forms of anthrax

Cutaneous anthrax

The commonest type results when the bacillus is introduced beneath the skin (e.g. by a puncture or through a pre-existing break). A red, raised area develops, progressing to a large blister, then an ulcer covered with a dark scab. This form can be treated effectively with antibiotics such as penicillin and tetracycline.

Gastrointestinal anthrax

This results from eating raw or undercooked meat from infected animals, and causes severe abdominal symptoms.

Inhalational anthrax

This is almost exclusively an occupational respiratory disease, associated with industrial processing of goat hair from western Asia.

These last two forms of the disease are difficult to diagnose and are often fatal; however, both are rare.

A new presentation of anthrax is called *injectional anthrax*, which has been reported in IV drug users. It is hypothesized that the drug or cutting agent has been contaminated with *B. anthracis*. Fifty-one cases and 16 deaths from injectional anthrax have been reported in the United Kingdom since 2010.

Anthrax and terrorism

In 2001, the anthrax bacillus was employed by terrorists in the USA. A powder form of the bacillus was placed into envelopes that were then mailed. Victims developed either cutaneous or inhalational anthrax. This development does not present a specific threat to travellers. Public health advice will be issued if the situation changes, and can be found at ℘ www.bt.cdc.gov. Anthrax vaccine is available for individuals at high risk.

Anthrax and commercial products

Several cases of anthrax have resulted from contact with contaminated animal skins that have been processed into the heads of small drums.

A summary of advice for travellers is given in Box 4.9.1.

Box 4.9.1 **Summary of advice for travellers**

- Although cutaneous anthrax may cause severe illness, the disease presents little risk. Only one travel-associated case has occurred in a US citizen in the past 40 years. This patient acquired her infection from a goat skin handicraft purchased in Haiti
- Studies revealed that Haitian handicrafts incorporating goat skins were commonly contaminated with anthrax spores. As a result, handicrafts containing goat skin with attached hair are not permitted to be brought into the USA. Another case, not in a traveller, was traced to a coarse goat-hair yarn produced in Pakistan
- Travellers should not buy any item made of coarse goat hair or goat skin with attached hair in any developing country
- General precautions of eating only well-cooked meat and avoiding unnecessary handling of dead animals also apply. Otherwise, no special precautions or immunizations are necessary.

4.10 Viral haemorrhagic fevers

Sue Fisher-Hoch

Lassa fever and other viral haemorrhagic fevers periodically hit the headlines. Except in special circumstances, however, the risk to travellers is extremely small.

What are viral hemorrhagic fevers (VHFs)?

- VHFs are 'zoonoses'—infections of animals that only occasionally affect humans
- VHFs are caused by viruses naturally carried by rodents, ticks, bats, mosquitoes
- VHFs are found mostly in the remotest parts of the developing world
- Risk of infection is confined to more adventurous travellers engaged in projects such as healthcare, agriculture, peace-keeping, or mining
- Infections in visitors to endemic areas are extremely rare
- Most fevers in short-term visitors to endemic areas are due to common diseases, such as typhoid or malaria, all eminently treatable so vital to exclude first.

Haemorrhagic fevers are diseases of poverty, and most sufferers are local people with poor housing, and little or no access to medical care. Four VHFs—Lassa fever, Ebola, Marburg, and Crimean-Congo haemorrhagic fever (CCHF)—are capable of spreading from person to person, especially in hospitals with poor hygiene, particularly where needles or other equipment is re-used without sterilization. Indeed, it was the high mortality in early hospital outbreaks that led to their fearsome reputation as 'killer' diseases. We now know that many infections are mild or symptomless.

How to avoid viral haemorrhagic fevers

- Use simple, basic hygiene
- In healthcare settings, use good techniques with emphasis on gloves, disinfection/decontamination and sharps disposal
- Avoid direct contact with animals, animal excreta, or blood or other fluids from animals or humans
- Use repellents for mosquitoes and ticks, and avoid exposure to both
- Use special care if visiting locations such as bat-infested caves, rodent-infested housing, etc., to avoid contamination with animal excreta or fluids.

Effective treatment is now available for some VHFs. Visitors to endemic areas who are likely to put themselves at risk by, for example, living in primitive rural conditions or working in medical facilities, should always inform themselves before travel about viruses they might encounter. Hopefully, they will then be able to avoid infection, but if not they will at least know what immediate steps to take if they do fall ill. Physicians treating such travellers need to pay particular attention to exposure history, and be well informed about the endemicity of viruses, and the treatment and management procedures they need to follow.

Lassa fever

Lassa fever is found in West Africa, from southern Senegal to Cameroon. It is by far the most important VHF transmissible from human to human with more than 100 000 infections and 3000–5000 deaths annually. Humans are infected from the urine of a local rodent, *Mastomys natalensis*— the multimammate rat—which is larger than a mouse, but smaller than the common rat. It infests village homes throughout Africa, although only in West Africa does it appear to carry Lassa virus, most commonly in secondary bush areas. The rat is peridomestic and nocturnal, and feeds on unprotected food and refuse in the house, on which it may deposit the virus. Infection can be prevented by enclosing all food in rat-proof containers, and ridding the house of rats. Person-to-person spread is from contact with blood and body fluids. Lassa fever is not spread by the respiratory route, so entering a patient's room carries no risk. It can be spread, however, by sexual contact, while the patient is sick or just recovering. Avoiding intimate contact with blood or other fluids from people with fevers is the most important method of avoiding infection. There is no risk of infection from recovered persons.

The disease has an incubation period of 1–2 weeks, and the illness lasts about 2 weeks. Fever, headache, and other general symptoms develop slowly, and make the illness very difficult to distinguish from a number of common diseases. A severe sore throat is common, and combined with high fever and protein in the urine is a strong indication of Lassa fever in the endemic area. Many people then recover and may not even know they have been infected; others develop further symptoms, such as vomiting, diarrhoea, and in severe cases, bleeding and circulatory collapse, neurological, or cardiovascular complications. Many cases are mild or asymptomatic, however.

Lassa fever can be treated with IV ribavirin, started as soon as possible after the onset of symptoms. Ribavirin tablets may also be used to prevent illness in individuals with a known history of exposure to the virus (500mg every 6hr for 7 days). The risk to women during the last 3 months of pregnancy is very high. The baby is usually lost, and the mother may also die. Children, on the other hand, appear to have milder infections. Recovery in survivors is usually complete except for the risk of deafness, measurable in about 25% of cases; most deafness resolves.

There continue to be devastating Lassa fever outbreaks and deaths in hospitals in endemic areas, as the result of failure to employ careful disinfection techniques and take measures to prevent blood-to-blood contact, or where surgical facilities are poor. Local wars and civil unrest also promote outbreaks. Since 1970 there have been two importations of Lassa fever to the USA; more than 10 cases to the UK; and several to other countries, none of whom died. Unfortunately, a patient who died of Lassa fever in the USA in 1989 visited four emergency rooms before he saw anyone who was aware that he had recently returned from Nigeria or who knew that Lassa fever was endemic there, and that it could be treated. It is essential for travellers who fall sick to make sure their physicians have all details of travel and possible exposure to viruses. Simple infectious disease precautions for the care of patients in regular isolation rooms are recommended, using gloves, gowns, masks and strict disinfection. Patient isolators ('bubbles') are not necessary or desirable.

South American haemorrhagic fevers

At least four haemorrhagic fevers are recognized in South America: Junin in Argentina, Machupo in Bolivia, Guanarito in Venezuela, and Sabia in Brazil. Recently, there have been reports of two possible cases of haemorrhagic fever due to a related arenavirus in North America. These diseases are caused by rodent arenaviruses (which are related to and closely resemble Lassa virus). Outbreaks are local, and mostly involve farmers in clearly defined areas coming into contact with field rodents. Little or no person-to-person spread has been reported, and none in travellers. Treatment with immune plasma and ribavirin is recommended for Junin virus infection. A Junin vaccine for human use has been shown to be effective.

Marburg and Ebola viruses

Marburg and Ebola viruses are related to each other. Primary human cases are extremely rare, and the reservoirs are a number of bats in Africa and Asia. Marburg disease was first recognized in 1967 in people handling imported monkeys in Marburg, Germany. In 1976, simultaneous outbreaks of a similar haemorrhagic fever, Ebola, occurred among humans in Zaire and Sudan. These outbreaks were associated with needle-sharing, and poor hygiene in remote clinics and hospitals. In the 1990s, a large outbreak in the Republic of Congo (in the town of Kikwit) and two outbreaks in Gabon demonstrated the ongoing hazard of this virus. Isolated cases have also been reported in the Ivory Coast. Outbreaks of Marburg disease in the Democratic Republic of Congo were associated with disused gold mines. Transmission in these recent and current outbreaks has been in hospitals and in villages. As with Lassa fever, unstable political conditions and rebel activities are heavily implicated in the spread of disease. In 1989, monkeys infected with a virus related to Ebola were imported into the USA; many of them became sick and died. The source of this virus has also not been found, but it is clear that this Asian strain does not cause disease in humans.

Both Ebola and Marburg disease have an incubation period of less than 1 week and a very sudden, violent onset with rapid deterioration, bleeding, and shock. Like Lassa fever, patients may have a severe sore throat. No imported cases have ever been seen outside Africa. Unfortunately, there is currently no specific treatment. Recovery, in survivors, is complete.

Crimean–Congo haemorrhagic fever

CCHF is widely distributed throughout Africa, parts of Southern and Eastern Europe, the Middle East, and Asia. Human cases are uncommon, and associated with close contact with animal blood, infected humans, or with tick bites. Thus, animal herders in dry areas, farmers, slaughterhouse workers, butchers, and people sleeping or working on tick-infested ground may be infected. Hospital outbreaks have been associated with high mortality, but were again invariably associated with unhygienic practices particularly ill-advised surgery on a febrile patient. Good nursing techniques, and care with blood and needles is sufficient to prevent transmission. Cases continue to be reported, particularly from areas of Pakistan bordering Afghanistan, where it is clear that outbreaks are not uncommon.

CCHF has a very short incubation period, as little as 3 days, and a very sudden onset with violent headache, fever, and body pains. Patients may then bleed, and a small number may die. CCHF may be successfully treated with ribavirin. Vaccines have been made in China and in Bulgaria, but these are not generally available, and there are no data on efficacy or safety of these mouse-brain vaccines. Prevention is best assured by avoiding ticks and intimate contact with blood from animals or infected people. Oral ribavirin may be used to prevent illness in people who have been exposed.

Hantaviruses

Hantaviruses are very common in parts of Asia, particularly China, where thousands of infections each year were recorded in the late 1980s, with major economic impact, and they also occur in Europe and the Americas. Disease is caused by a family of viruses of small field rodents, voles, and rats, which excrete the virus in the urine. Mortality in the rural disease may be as high as 15%, but death is rare in the urban and European settings. This is the same disease as Korean haemorrhagic fever, which affected 3000 United Nations troops during the war in Korea in the 1950s, and is closely related to an old disease in Scandinavia called nephropathia epidemica. Infections are therefore most common in people travelling, living, or working in rural areas with poor housing.

The incubation period may be 2–3 weeks and onset is slow. Some patients may experience brief kidney failure, and a very few bleed and may die. The American hantaviruses cause a pulmonary syndrome, however, with severe pulmonary oedema. An outbreak of hantavirus pulmonary syndrome occurred among visitors to Yosemite National Park in August 2012. Most patients make a complete recovery. Treatment with ribavirin may be effective, but must be started early in disease.

Avoidance of contact with rodent urine, directly or in dust, is the most important preventive measure. Person-to-person spread has not been reported except with the South American virus. Vaccines are under development in China and in the USA, and have been applied in China, but satisfactory efficacy and safety data are not available.

Rift Valley fever

Rift valley fever (RVF) is spread by mosquitoes and is mainly confined to animals, although there have been large human outbreaks in Egypt, Mauritania, and Saudi Arabia. The disease is usually mild, but occasional severe cases do occur. There is an animal vaccine. Humans should avoid mosquito bites.

Conclusion

With some basic knowledge it is normally possible to avoid infection. Despite their reputation, recovery is often rapid and complete within a month or two of infection, and fully effective treatment may be available. Medical and veterinary staff may be at special risk. They should seek additional, thorough briefing before arrival and understand appropriate protective measures and therapy.

4.11 Leptospirosis

Matthew Dryden

Leptospirosis (also called Weil's disease) may follow contact with fresh or brackish water. Swimming, canoeing, mountain biking, jungle trekking, canyoning, kayaking, freshwater fishing, and caving may bring travellers into contact. It is a zoonosis—an infection that spreads naturally between vertebrate animals and man. It occurs worldwide, most frequently in tropical and sub-tropical regions (including popular destinations such as the Caribbean). Leptospires—the spiral-shaped bacteria responsible—survive best in a warm and moist environment.

Leptospires are carried in the kidneys of many animal species, especially rodents, and in Central America and the Caribbean, amphibians and reptiles. These 'maintenance hosts' form a reservoir of infection, shedding leptospires into the environment in their urine. They gain entry through small cuts or abrasions of the skin, or through the intact mucous membranes of the eye and mouth. Outbreaks can follow heavy rains and flooding.

Symptoms appear 7–12 days after exposure. Most often, the illness is mild. Early symptoms resemble an influenza-like illness with headache, fever, muscle pains, particularly in the lower back and thighs, usually with conjunctival redness, nausea, and vomiting. Most cases improve without treatment and without significant liver or kidney involvement. Severe disease, with jaundice and kidney failure, is rare—a few patients need supportive hospital treatment including temporary dialysis, whilst their kidneys and liver recover. Provided adequate medical care is available, the mortality associated with leptospirosis is less than 5%. Confirmation of the diagnosis requires a blood test—not universally available. Antibiotics may aid recovery if given within 72 hours of onset. Penicillin by injection is the drug of choice (benzylpenicillin, 1.2g IV or IM every 4–6 hours) for severe cases, or amoxicillin or doxycycline orally in mild cases.

Simple measures significantly reduce the risk of infection—cover cuts and abrasions with waterproof plasters, wear footwear and swimming goggles, and avoid swallowing water (see Box 4.11.1).

If you become unwell, make sure that any doctor looking after you knows you may have been exposed (see Box 4.11.2).

Prophylaxis with doxycycline may help in high-risk situations (e.g. for extreme sportsmen or military personnel)—seek expert medical advice first. (A dose of 200mg of doxycycline taken once a week prevents infection if you can.) Those taking doxycycline for malaria prophylaxis are also protected against leptospirosis.

Box 4.11.1 **Summary**

Leptospirosis is a generalized bacterial infection acquired from water or moist vegetation contaminated with the urine of rats and other animals. Frogs and reptiles can also carry it.

- *Incubation:* about 10 days
- *Symptoms:* variable from mild flu-like symptoms to severe organ failure. Fever, headache, red eyes, muscle aches. Sometimes meningitis, confusion, jaundice
- *Occurrence:* worldwide except in the polar regions, usually associated with contact with rivers, canals and lakes
- *Diagnosis:* blood test for antibodies
- *Treatment:* supportive, if there is organ failure; antibiotics such as doxycycline or penicillins
- *Prevention:* avoid contact with contaminated water, especially in mouth and eyes; cover cuts and abrasions. No effective human vaccine. Antibiotic prophylaxis not usually recommended.

Box 4.11.2 **Case study**

A 45-year-old man developed fever, sore throat, sore eyes, muscle aches, and severe headaches 2 weeks after a trip to Tobago. His wife and two children had just had a flu-like illness, but were not sick enough to come to hospital.

Blood tests showed abnormal liver and kidney function.

The family had stayed in a beach hotel, fished in mangrove swamps and swam in jungle waterfalls (where there were lots of mating frogs). They'd had appropriate vaccinations prior to travel.

Blood tests ruled out malaria, bacterial septicaemia, dengue, and hepatitis, but showed positive antibodies to leptospirosis. The rest of the family was also positive. He recovered fully on treatment with doxycycline.

Top tip: don't swim with mating frogs!

4.12 Influenza A and B

John Oxford

Influenza A is Mother Nature's most consummate handmaiden and can inflict instant devastation. Most notably, in the 6 months spanning late autumn 1918 and early winter 1919, when more than 50 million citizens of every country in the world died. Subsequent pandemics occurred in 1957, 1968 and 2009 (Table 4.12.1).

Table 4.12.1 History of recent global outbreaks (pandemics) of influenza A

Year	Colloquial name and subtype	Origin	Impact
1889	Russian pandemic (H2N?)	Emerged in eastern Russia and spread westward	Less than Spanish pandemic
1918	Spanish pandemic (H1N1)	Possible emergence from birds in Europe	At least 50 million deaths
1957	Asian pandemic flu (H2N2)	Mixed infection of an animal with human N1N1 and avian H2N2 virus strains in Asia	5 million deaths; the 1918 H1N1 virus disappeared
1968	Hong Kong pandemic (H3N2)	Mixed infection of an animal with human H2N2 and avian H3 virus strains in Asia	2 million deaths; the H2N2 virus disappeared
2009–2011	Swine flu (H1N1)	Possible emergence from Mexico/USA	18 000 deaths and 2 million years of life lost to date

Influenza A and B

Influenza A occurs in two distinct patterns—epidemic and pandemic. The epidemic pattern threatens year-on-year, and kills more people in total than the rare pandemics. Epidemic influenzas A and B are the last diseases most travellers think about as they leave the northern hemisphere in summer, and travel southwards to Australasia and South America, where winter epidemic influenza is on the move.

Tropical equatorial regions are the epicentre of new epidemic influenza viruses, with constant, year-round genetic change. New genetic variants move northwards and southwards at wintertime for each hemisphere. In winter, congregating indoors enhances person-to-person spread.

Epidemic influenza does not kill many young people, but rather, seeks out over 65s, diabetics and persons with chronic conditions of the airways, heart, and kidney of all ages. Together with obese persons, these form an 'at risk' group calling for special attention. For travellers of any age, however, a bout of influenza illness can remove a week from the best-planned trip. These groups can and should be protected by vaccination and judicious use of antiviral drugs plus sensible practice of hand hygiene and social distancing (see p.98).

Bird influenza A (H5N1): still a threat

Vietnam, China, Indonesia (Bali), Turkey, and Egypt remain favourite tourist destinations. There is a consistent, but low chance of a visitor becoming infected with avian influenza A H5N1 virus. Human infections are restricted to those in close physical contact with chickens, ducks, and geese, usually keepers of small domestic flocks that have themselves become infected from migrating birds. The most important risk to travellers is a visit to a live avian market where birds are de-feathered and butchered on the spot.

Highly pathogenic influenza A virus causes a disease in chickens or turkeys that is entirely different from influenza in a human: in birds, the illness is 'pantropic'—the virus infects most organs of the body. Heavy infestation of spleen and intestines of the bird means that a butcher immediately contacts around 100 million influenza virions. Virus is present in high numbers in bird droppings. Birds spend considerable time preening their feathers, transferring virus from the cloaca to the entire plumage. Feathers are therefore an important source of infection.

Influenza A viruses have a high mutation rate: perhaps 10% of the 100 million viruses infecting a single bird might be mutants. If one of these 10 million mutant viruses has an amino acid change in the receptor-binding site of its haemagglutinin spike (HA) protein that allows it to attach to a human cell as well as, or even in preference to, an avian cell, the crucial protective 'species barrier' between avians and humans is broken. At this stage, the virus is still 'avianized'. In a human, it could cause pantropic disease, affecting the nervous system, gut and lungs, soon causing a dangerous pneumonia (although without the tendency to spread to others via the upper airways). The case fatality of those unfortunates is 50% higher than for any other known human virus, with the exception of Lassa, Marburg, and rabies.

Symptomless domestic ducks or geese may act as an undetected reservoir of H5N1, excreting virus, but showing no clinical signs whatsoever: this is the "Trojan Duck" scenario, enabling the virus to evade 'zone protection' controls based on slaughtering birds with overt symptoms. The virus can be present in duck blood, sometimes ingested as uncooked paté. On the other hand, cooking completely destroys influenza viruses.

In summary, the traveller can at present rest assured of a minimal chance of infection, unless staying on a farm or village in Southeast Asia, Egypt, or Turkey, visiting a live bird market, attending the a hospital where infected patients might be treated, or eating uncooked poultry products. See also p.450.

Using hygiene principles to prevent infection

Hygiene is a key factor in reducing the chance of infection. Many respiratory viruses are spread by fingers that touch the eye, mouth or nose many times each day. Influenza viruses from coughs and sneezes contaminate hands or surfaces, such as tabletops, but are easily destroyed by hot water and soap or detergent, proprietary germicides, alcohol hand wipes and sanitizers (⊗ www.hygienecouncil.com). The new etiquette of shielding coughs and sneezes using the inside arm and elbow, rather than hands is also important.

Social distancing

Keeping at least a metre away from a person with influenza symptoms has a definite protective effect (and is the rationale for preventing large gatherings during a pandemic).

Airports and taxis may be important centres of virus spread

Influenza virus infection by airborne aerosols (very small droplets) is unlikely. On an aeroplane the most likely source of contamination is a shared facility, such as the doorknob of the toilet, where virus droplets have settled, or other surfaces. An infected person in an adjacent seat could spread infection by coughing, but probably not from several rows away. Most modern planes incorporate HEPA filters that filter off bacteria and viruses (Chapter 7.1). Paradoxically, a higher infection hazard may be present in the taxi to the airport.

Medicines for treatment and prevention: the neuraminidase inhibitors (NIs)

Tamiflu, Relenza, and the newer drug Peramivir combat flu viruses by targeting the viral enzyme neuraminidase. Early treatment reduces the severity and duration of fever and other symptoms, as well as the risk of secondary complications.

In my view, it would be a sensible precaution for a traveller to Southeast Asia and Egypt to pack a course of one of the NI inhibitors, and be prepared to use it to abort symptoms of influenza (shivering, fever, cough, and headache) within hours of onset.

Alternatively, the NIs can be used preventively, or to block infection after contact with a suspect case. (Studies of household contacts showed protective efficacy over 86% for Tamiflu and a 69% reduction in cases with Relenza).

Influenza vaccination for travellers

Travellers should consider being vaccinated against flu. In particular, over-60s travel widely, and should always be immunized with the current epidemic vaccine. World production capacity of vaccine has now increased to 900 million doses and enough should be available throughout the year. Travellers should appreciate that, in tropical regions, influenza outbreaks occur throughout the year.

Conclusions and a look forward

Influenza circles the globe continually and is always causing outbreaks somewhere. The 2009 pandemic also demonstrated the ability of the virus to disrupt travel on a massive scale, with advisories, local restrictions, and even quarantine in some countries.

Armed with our current knowledge of influenza, the 21st-century traveller can have better protection than ever before, including hand sanitizers, possibly face masks, NIs, and an epidemic vaccine (and possibly very soon, pre-pandemic vaccines against H5N1, H3N2, and H9N1 viruses).

The scientific message is clear—apply hygiene principles, such as hand and surface disinfection, and use Tamiflu and Relenza, and vaccines, all of which have been shown to be effective.

Chapter 5

Diseases spread by insects

5.1 Malaria

David A. Warrell

Malaria remains the tropical disease most likely to cause severe illness or death in travellers visiting large areas of tropical Africa, Asia, Latin America, and Oceania. Malaria, respiratory infections, diarrhoeal diseases, HIV, and tuberculosis are the major causes of infectious disease mortality, each responsible for more than one million deaths per year. However, travellers can virtually eliminate the risk of malaria by protecting themselves against nocturnal mosquito bites and using anti-malarial drugs appropriately.

Malaria parasites

Malaria parasites belong to the genus *Plasmodium*. Five species infect humans: *Plasmodium falciparum, P. vivax, P. ovale, P. malariae* and *P. knowlesi*. All these species except *P. knowlesi* are widely distributed exclusively human parasites that are transmitted by *Anopheles* mosquitoes. *Plasmodium knowlesi* is a zoonotic infection primarily of long-tailed macaque monkeys in Borneo and other Southeast Asian countries. It is transmitted by *Anopheles* mosquitoes that occasionally infect humans including travellers.

The global problem

Malaria occurs throughout the tropics except in the Pacific Islands east of Vanuatu (Map 5.1.1). There are an estimated 515 million clinical cases of *P. falciparum* malaria each year causing more than a million deaths, 75% of which occur in Africa and 25% in Southeast Asia. More than 3 billion people are at risk, more than half of the world's population, living in 100 countries.

After the abandonment of World Health Organization's (WHO's) global malaria eradication program in 1969, there was a resurgence of malaria in Asia and Africa, but more recently, despite the increase in multiple drug-resistant malaria, there has been a decline in morbidity and mortality, attributable partly to increased funding for insecticide treated mosquito nets and improved treatment and diagnostics.

Importance of malaria in travellers

According to the HPA Malaria Reference Laboratory at the London School of Hygiene and Tropical Medicine, 1761 cases of malaria were reported in the UK in returned travellers in 2010, 1263 (72%) of which were caused by *Plasmodium falciparum*. There were 7 deaths. 806 (46%) of the cases had acquired the infection in West Africa. Similar patterns but lower numbers are reported in travellers returning to France, Germany, USA, and Australia.

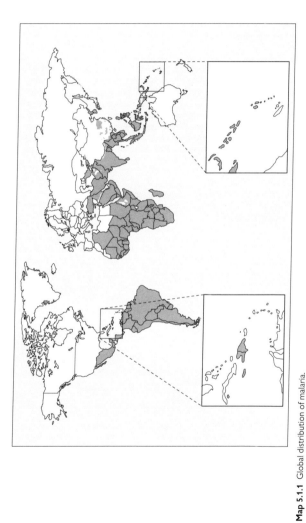

Map 5.1.1 Global distribution of malaria.
Reproduced and adapted from Johnson et al., *Oxford Handbook of Expedition and Wilderness Medicine*, 2008, p.475, with permission of Oxford University Press.

Malarial immunity

The frequency and severity of infection in different age groups varies greatly from one malarial region to another. In endemic areas, fragile immunity is acquired through infective mosquito bites, so that after childhood, infection causes negligible or no symptoms. However, young children may develop severe, fatal malaria before this immunity has been established, which explains why, in parts of sub-Saharan Africa, malaria accounts for 25–50% of all deaths in children under 5 years old. A million children may die of this infection each year. In other parts of the tropics, such as Madagascar, Rajasthan, and Northeastern Kenya, infections may be too infrequent to create and sustain immunity. In these areas, climatic or other changes may precipitate epidemics of malaria in vulnerable, non-immune populations, with devastating effects. Those who have acquired immunity by being brought up in malaria endemic countries may lose it if they move to western countries for even a few years. This explains why West African or Indian migrants who have settled in Britain may develop severe malaria when they return to visit friends and relations back home. There are typically 500 such cases every year in the UK, accounting for the majority of deaths from imported malaria.

For travellers from temperate Western countries, however, there can be no question of immunity to malaria, even after a few attacks of the disease. Vulnerability to severe, life-threatening malaria is increased in travellers who have had their spleens removed or whose spleens are not functioning normally.

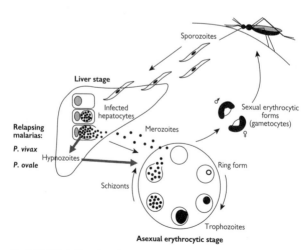

Fig. 5.1.1 Malaria life cycle and transmission.

During the malaria parasite's complicated life cycle (Box 5.1.1, Fig. 5.1.1), each 'stage' differs in its susceptibility to drugs and in its immunological identity (antigenicity). For travellers at risk of malaria, the life cycle has some key practical implications:

1. The shortest period between an infective mosquito bite and the onset of symptoms of malaria is 7 days for *P. falciparum* and longer for other species. This means that a fever developing less than 7 days after arrival in a malarious region cannot be caused by malaria acquired there

2. The delay between an infective mosquito bite and the emergence of parasites from the liver into the bloodstream is up to 4 weeks; most prophylactic anti-malarial drugs act only on blood-stage parasites, so these drugs must be continued for at least 4 weeks after the last possible exposure to malaria if they are to be effective (Malarone is an exception—see p.104)

3. To eradicate hypnozoites of *P. vivax* and *P. ovale* from the liver and so prevent malaria relapses, a different drug (primaquine) must be taken

4. When malaria is acquired by blood transfusion, the incubation period is shorter because meroites are introduced which can immediately invade erythrocytes without an initial liver cycle.

Box 5.1.1 **Malaria life cycle and transmission (Fig. 5.1.1)**

When an infected female *Anopheles* mosquito bites a human to take a blood meal she injects sporozoites into the bloodstream. These travel rapidly to the liver, and in the liver cells (hepatocytes) the parasites divide and mature. In the case of *P. vivax* and *P. ovale*, some of the sporozoites remain dormant in the liver cells as hypnozoites. These are not vulnerable to the drugs usually used for prevention, and are capable of causing relapsing attacks of malaria, months or even years later. *Plasmodium falciparum*, *P. malariae* and *P. knowlesi* have no resting phase in the liver, but in the case of *P. malariae*, merozoites may persist in the bloodstream in undetectably small numbers for long periods to give rise to recrudescent attacks of malaria up to many years later.

After 1–3 weeks (depending on the species), merozoites of all five species are released into the bloodstream and invade red blood corpuscles (erythrocytes) in which they develop from early 'ring' forms to fatter trophozoites containing black pigment (digested haemoglobin) and finally multinucleated schizonts. The erythrocyte ruptures, releasing a new generation of merozoites which can infect more erythrocytes, but cannot reinvade the liver.

At the moment of schizont rupture (schizogony or merogony), a malarial pyrogen or toxin is released that sets in train a series of reactions responsible for the violent fevers, chills, and shivering attacks that characterize a classic attack of malaria. Towards the end of the infection, some intra-erythrocytic parasites develop into sexual forms, male and female gametocytes, which are taken up by mosquitoes during a blood meal. Inside the mosquito's gut, a sexual cycle of fusion is completed, resulting in the sporozoites which will infect a new human host when the mosquito feeds again.

Malaria mosquitoes

The females of many different species of *Anopheles* mosquitoes can transmit malaria. They are distinguished from other mosquitoes by the way the body is angled up from the surface of the skin when they are taking their blood meal (Fig. 5.1.2). *Anopheles* mosquitoes lay their eggs on fresh or brackish water, where the larvae develop. Malaria-transmitting mosquitoes bite between dusk and dawn, indoors or outdoors. This is the time when protection against bites is crucial (see Box 5.1.1 and Chapter 5.12).

Malaria was eliminated from Europe in the twentieth century, but several species of *Anopheles* mosquitoes capable of transmitting the infection exist in UK and other European countries, allowing the possibility of reintroduction of malaria as is happening currently in Greece (*Plasmodium vivax*).

Malaria transmission

Malaria almost always results from bites by infected mosquitoes in malaria endemic areas of the world. However, infected mosquitoes can be transported, for example by aircraft, to temperate countries where they may survive long enough to bite and infect local people. This explains the occasional cases of 'airport malaria' affecting people who work in or live around busy international airports such as Schipol, Amsterdam, or Gatwick. If the climate is right and appropriate species of Anopheles mosquitoes are available, small outbreaks of locally transmitted malaria may result. This has happened in New York and California and in 2011, when *P. vivax* became re-established in two locations in Greece (this is termed autochthonous malaria). Aircraft travelling from one non-malarious country to another may stop for a while, en route, in a malaria endemic area. On the tarmac, the aircraft's doors may be open for long enough to allow a local mosquito to enter the cabin and infect a passenger. This has been called 'runway malaria'. Aircraft spraying or 'disinsection' is intended to prevent this. The phenomenon of 'suitcase malaria', following accidental transportation of mosquitoes in luggage, has also been reported.

Non-mosquito transmission

Blood forms of malaria can be transmitted directly, without mosquito bites, in transfusions of blood and blood products and transplants of bone marrow and other organs or tissues. Malaria has also been transmitted by needle among drug addicts. This has been a problem in some large North American cities and continues in countries such as Vietnam. In malarious regions, blood donors, and donated blood may need to be screened and treated (see p.470). Transmission of malaria among patients

(a)   (b)

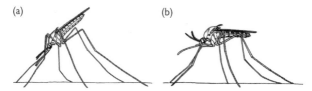

Fig. 5.1.2 Resting position of malaria-transmitting *Anopheles* mosquito, (a) compared with that of a *Culex* mosquito (b).

in hospital (nosocomial malaria) has resulted from non-sterile technique with intravenous lines and catheters.

Malaria—the disease

Except in those who have acquired immunity, infection with any of the five species of *Plasmodium* will cause fever, aches and pains, and other generalized symptoms, sometimes in particular patterns. Falciparum malaria, caused by *P. falciparum*, used to be known as 'malignant tertian malaria'— malignant because it was potentially fatal; tertian because spikes of fever might occur every third day (the asexual erythrocytic cycle takes about 48 hours). *P. vivax* and *P. ovale* malarias, caused by *P. vivax* and *P. ovale* were called 'benign tertian malaria'—benign because they rarely kill anyone; tertian for the same reason as in falciparum malaria. However, vivax malaria has lost its benign image. *Plasmodium malariae* infection has been known as 'quartan malaria' because the spikes of fever might occur every fourth day (the asexual erythrocytic cycle takes about 72 hours). *Plasmodium knowlesi* causes daily spikes of fever (quotidian periodicity) because the asexual erythrocytic cycle takes 24 hours.

All five species of malaria cause similar symptoms initially. However, *P. falciparum* multiplies much more rapidly than the other species, producing high densities of parasites in the blood stream (parasitaemia). Small blood vessels in the brain may become blocked by parasitized erythrocytes, reducing their blood supply and causing 'cerebral malaria'. The placenta and other vital organs may be similarly affected. As a result, *P. falciparum* can cause a very severe disease, rapidly involving a number of vital organs. *Plasmodium vivax* can, on rare occasions, cause severe disease. *Plasmodium knowlesi* is also capable of producing high parasitaemias and human fatalities.

The attack of malaria

Most travellers with falciparum malaria become ill within 1 month after leaving a malarious area but, exceptionally, the illness may be delayed for a year or longer. 10% of *P. vivax* infections do not appear until more than a year after the person has returned home.

Symptoms usually start suddenly. Patients feel unwell and feverish with headache (often severe), aches and pains (including backache and pain in the muscles), mild nausea, and loss of appetite. Symptoms often mimic those of 'flu', but without the running nose and sore throat of true influenza. Severe teeth-rattling, bed-shaking chills, followed over the space of a few hours by high fever, profuse sweating, and exhaustion, are classic features of the malarial paroxysm. Other symptoms include dry cough, dizziness, or faintness when standing up, nausea, vomiting, stomach ache, and diarrhoea. Most travellers are too ill, weak and exhausted to get out of bed while the attack is on.

Signs of the infection are a fluctuating temperature (sometimes exceeding 40°C, 104°F); paleness of the skin, nail beds, tongue, and eyes, resulting from the destruction of infected erythrocytes (anaemia); jaundice (yellowness of the whites of the eyes), resulting from the breakdown of excessive amounts of blood pigment (haemoglobin) released from the destroyed erythrocytes; and an enlarged, tender spleen (felt under the left side of the rib cage).

Severe disease

In the case of falciparum malaria, severe complications can start within 24 hours of the first symptom, though usually a few days later. Cerebral malaria may begin dramatically with a generalized seizure or convulsion (like an epileptic fit), after which the victim remains deeply unconscious. In other cases, the patient sinks slowly into a coma. Even with effective treatment, patients may not wake up for several days. Other severe complications of falciparum malaria are: profound anaemia, bleeding, deep jaundice (partly the result of liver damage), low blood sugar (hypoglycaemia), and low blood pressure with shock, acute kidney injury, fluid leaking into the lungs (pulmonary oedema), and a complicating additional infection with bacteria (septicaemia). Blackwater fever is a rare complication of falciparum malaria, in which blood pigment (haemoglobin), released after massive destruction of erythrocytes, is passed in the urine which becomes 'coca-cola' coloured or black. *Plasmodium vivax* generally produces a benign, non-fatal disease but in areas such as Rajasthan, cerebral malaria, pulmonary oedema, acute kidney injury and fatalities have been described. *Plasmodium knowlesi* can cause severe gastrointestinal, respiratory, and other symptoms that are fatal in about 2% of victims.

Survival and long-term complications

Even with the best modern medical care, about *1 out of 10 people who develop severe forms of falciparum malaria will die*. Most of the survivors will recover completely, even if they have been unconscious with cerebral malaria for several days, but as many as 1 in 20 of the African children who survive an attack of cerebral malaria will be left with permanent brain damage.

Rare complications of an attack of *P. falciparum* malaria are transient psychiatric disturbances ('malarial psychosis'), often attributable to medication, and a transient disturbance of balance associated with jerky movements of the eyes (post-malarial cerebellar ataxia). In rare cases, especially in Africa and New Guinea, there can be long-term immunological damage to the kidney (*P. malariae*) or massive enlargement of the spleen (tropical splenomegaly syndrome). Repeated attacks of falciparum malaria in combination with Epstein–Barr virus (the virus causing infectious mononucleosis, or glandular fever) can result in a cancer, Burkitt's lymphoma.

How to recognize a malaria attack

Since no symptom or sign is diagnostic of malaria, it must be considered, excluded, or treated presumptively in any traveller who develops an acute feverish illness after visiting a malarious country, especially if the illness develops within 3 months of return. Many different infections can start with headache, shivering, chills, and fevers—especially pneumonia, viral hepatitis, and ascending infections of the bile ducts in the liver (cholangitis) and urinary tract (pyelonephritis). If malaria is not considered as a possible cause of a feverish illness in a traveller, the symptoms may be mistakenly attributed to another infection and valuable time may be lost in confirming the diagnosis and starting life-saving treatment.

Confirming the diagnosis of malaria

Confirming the diagnosis requires medical and technical skills that may not be readily available. The most reliable method is microscopic examination of a film or smear of blood made on a glass slide, dried, fixed with strong methyl alcohol, and treated with a special stain (such as Giemsa or Wright's stains). When parasites are scanty, as in most *P. vivax*, *P. ovale*, or *P. malariae* infections, a thick blood film must be examined. Experienced microscopists can detect as few as 5 parasites per mL (0.0001% parasitaemia) in a thick film and 200 per mL (0.004% parasitaemia) in a thin film.

Rapid malarial antigen detection dipsticks are a convenient addition or alternative to microscopy. They are quick (taking about 20min), sensitive (detecting >100 parasites/μL or 0.002% parasitaemia), and species specific. NOW malaria tests (Inverness Medical), ParaSight F (Becton-Dickinson), ICT Malaria Pf (ICT Diagnostics), and OptiMAL (Flow Laboratories) are available in the UK. If these tests are initially negative, they should be repeated at least three times over 72 hours before the diagnosis of malaria is excluded.

Dangerous misdiagnoses

- Fever and jaundice misdiagnosed as viral hepatitis
- Fever with severe headache and a stiff neck might suggest meningitis
- Fever and headache followed by loss of consciousness misdiagnosed as viral encephalitis or heatstroke
- Fever, stomach ache, and bowel disturbances misdiagnosed as typhoid
- Fever with bleeding misdiagnosed as a viral haemorrhagic fever (e.g. yellow fever, Lassa fever, Ebola/Marburg disease)
- Fever, stomach pains, and profuse diarrhoea misdiagnosed as travellers' diarrhoea, cholera, or dysentery.

None of the tests or treatments for these conditions will detect or cure malaria. Many deaths in travellers have resulted from a mistaken diagnosis. The common piitfalls are listed below.

Box 5.1.2 **Beware! Some common medical pitfalls**

- Do not rule out the possibility of malaria just because the traveller was taking anti-malarial drugs—no drug is 100% effective
- Do not be put off the diagnosis of malaria by misleading symptoms, such as stomach pains and diarrhoea, or a normal temperature on one occasion
- Beware of unusual types of exposure such as 'runway malaria', 'transfusion malaria', and 'needlestick malaria'
- Do not be discouraged from diagnosing malaria because the traveller was born or brought up in a malarious country and believes that they are immune
- If one person develops malaria after a family/group holiday, check on the other members in case they are also harbouring infection
- Always regard malaria in a non-immune traveller as a *medical emergency*; the interval between the first symptom and death may be less than 24 hours
- If the symptoms or signs are consistent with severe malaria, start treatment immediately, even if laboratory confirmation is not possible or tests are initially negative.

Laboratory tests

A routine full blood count may show a reduced haemoglobin concentration or haematocrit, a reduced platelet count (thrombocytopenia), and a normal, low, or increased white blood cell count. The serum bilirubin concentration and levels of serum enzymes (such as lactic dehydrogenase, and alanine and aspartate amino-transferases) may be moderately raised. The erythrocyte sedimentation rate (ESR) and C-reactive protein (CRP) concentration may be grossly elevated.

If you develop malaria while abroad, you should bring home the results of any tests and, ideally, the blood film on which the diagnosis as made; these might be helpful if you develop further symptoms.

Special dangers of malaria in pregnancy

Pregnant women are particularly vulnerable to severe falciparum malaria. Severe anaemia, miscarriage, and delivery of a still born or low birth weight baby are common complications. Pregnant travellers should be strongly discouraged from entering a malarious area, especially during the last 3 months of the pregnancy. If travel is unavoidable, chemoprophylaxis with a safe drug combination such as proguanil and chloroquine should be considered (together with meticulous anti-mosquito precautions), and any feverish illnesses should be investigated and treated very promptly. Tetracyclines and primaquine should not be given to pregnant women.

Treatment of malaria

Treatment with anti-malarial drugs should be started as soon as possible. Patients who are not vomiting and can swallow and retain tablets can be given anti-malarial tablets by mouth (Table 5.1.1). Otherwise, treatment must be given by injection or IV infusion (drip). Chloroquine is the drug of

Table 5.1.1 Anti-malarial drugs for treating uncomplicated disease

Drug	Adult dose*	Comment
Riamet	4 tablets (each containing 20mg artemether + 120mg lumefantrine) twice daily for 3 days	For resistant *P. falciparum* infection
Malarone	4 tablets (each containing 250mg atovaquone + 100mg proguanil) once daily for 3 days	For resistant *P. falciparum* infection
Chloroquine	2 tablets (each containing 300mg chloroquine base) on days 1 and 2; 1 tablet on day 3	For chloroquine-sensitive *P. falciparum* and all other malarias
Primaquine	1 tablet (containing 15mg primaquine base) each day for 14 days	To eradicate *P. vivax* and *P. ovale* hypnozoites. *Not* for pregnant/lactating women or G6PD-deficient people

*For more details and doses for children see Lalloo *et al.* (2006) and WHO (2010), on p.505.

choice for malarias caused by *P. vivax*, *P. ovale*, *P. malariae*, *P. knowlesi*, and also for *P. falciparum* definitely acquired in Central America or Hispaniola (Haiti and Dominican Republic), where it remains fully sensitive to chloroquine. Chloroquine-resistant *P. vivax* malaria has been reported from New Guinea and adjacent islands, but a higher dose of chloroquine will cure these infections.

If malaria is being treated 'blind' or if, despite a positive blood smear, the species is uncertain or a mixed infection is possible, the infection should be treated as for presumed resistant falciparum malaria, with tablets of Co-artemether/Co-artem/Riamet (artemether-lumefantrine) or Malarone (atovaquone + proguanil). Artekin (dihydroartemisinin-piperaquine), not yet licensed in UK, is also suitable. In cases of severe malaria (when the patient is unable to swallow tablets or is jaundiced, unconscious, bleeding, or has any of the other severe features already described), the treatment of choice is artesunate, given by intravenous or intramuscular injection, or artemether (by intramuscular injection) (Table 5.1.2). Quinine (by slow intravenous infusion or intramuscular injection) is less effective and more likely to cause side-effects.

Advice for health care professionals about treatment and provision of artesunate

In UK, call Hospital for Tropical Diseases, London (0845 1555000) or Liverpool School of Tropical Medicine (0151 7053100 working hours/ Royal Liverpool Hospital 0151 7062000 out of hours) or Oxford (01865 225430).

In USA, for treatment advice and supply of artesunate, call CDC Malaria Branch (+1 770-488-7788 working hours/+1 770-488-7100 out of hours) ☏ http://www.cdc.gov/malaria/diagnosis_treatment/treatment.html

Table 5.1.2 Anti-malarial drugs for initial treatment of severe disease

Drug	Adult dose*	Comment
Artesunate	2.4mg/kg body weight (loading dose) by intravenous injection, followed by 1.2mg/kg daily for at least 3 days until patient can take drugs by mouth	
Artemether	3.2mg/kg body weight (loading dose) by intramuscular injection, followed by 1.6mg/kg daily for at least 3 days until patient can take drugs by mouth	
Quinine	20mg quinine salt/kg body weight (loading dose) diluted in 10mL/kg isotonic fluid by intravenous infusion over 4 hours, followed by 10mg/kg over 4 hours until patient can take drugs by mouth	BEWARE of too rapid infusion, monitor patient's electrocardiogram, blood pressure and blood sugar

*For more details and doses for children, see Lalloo *et al.* (2006) and WHO (2010), on p.505.

Anti-malarial drugs recommended for treatment of malaria (Tables 5.1.1 and 5.1.2)

Artemisinin (qinghaosu) derivatives

These are the most effective anti-malarial drugs, acting against highly resistant strains of *P. falciparum* and clearing parasites from the bloodstream very quickly. They have proved more effective, safer, and easier to administer than quinine in treating severe falciparum malaria. Artemisinins should be given as combinations (ACTs): Artemether + lumefantrine (Riamet, Co-artemether, Co-artem) and dihydroartemisinin + piperaquine (Artekin). For treating severe falciparum malaria, parenteral (given by injection) artesunate is the drug of choice (available from contacts on p.109 in UK and USA). Unfortunately, there are early signs of emergence of resistance to these drugs in Cambodia.

Malarone (proguanil hydrochloride plus atovaquone)

This has proved effective in the treatment of uncomplicated multi-drug-resistant falciparum malaria in Thailand and elsewhere. It is relatively free from side effects.

Chloroquine

The use of this safe, synthetic anti-malarial drug is greatly restricted by the emergence of highly resistant strains of *P. falciparum*, but it remains the treatment of choice for all the other malarias.

Quinine

Resistance to this drug is emerging in Southeast Asia, requiring addition of tetracycline or clindamycin to achieve complete cure. Even when given by mouth for uncomplicated *P. falciparum* malaria, it causes unpleasant side effects such as ringing in the ears, deafness, dizziness, nausea, trembling, and blurred vision. When used for severe *P. falciparum* malaria, it must be diluted and given by IV infusion (drip) over several hours. Important side effects are hypoglycaemia (a fall in blood sugar), a fall in blood pressure, and electrocardiographic abnormalities.

Primaquine

This drug is used to eliminate hypnozoites of *P. vivax* and *P. ovale* from the liver to prevent relapses. Resistant strains of *P. vivax* in Southeast Asia and Oceania required prolonged treatment. Primaquine can cause severe breakdown of erythrocytes (intravascular haemolysis) in patients of Mediterranean, African, or Asian origin who have inherited erythrocyte glucose-6-phosphate dehydrogenase deficiency. They should be screened with a blood test before being given primaquine.

Prevention of malaria in travellers

Travellers can take the following steps to prevent malaria:

- Avoiding mosquito bites (dusk to dawn) by all means (repellents, insecticide/repellent-treated clothing (long sleeves, long trousers), insecticide-treated bed net, insect-proof bedroom, knock-down insecticide, air-conditioning, etc.
- Taking medicine for prevention (chemoprophylaxis): e.g. 'Malarone', mefloquine ('Lariam') or doxycycline OR Standby Emergency Treatment depending on geographical area, season or duration of stay

- In case of feverish illness during the weeks after return, *SEE A DOCTOR, AND MENTION MALARIA!*

Awareness and assessment of risk

Risky places

Even within a single country regarded as malarious, the risk of infection may vary greatly depending on environmental factors (temperature, rainfall, altitude, vegetation, effectiveness of local mosquito control measures). In Africa, some large cities are free from malaria transmission because of their high altitude and cool climate (e.g. Addis Ababa and Nairobi), and in some areas, such as the Gambia, malaria transmission occurs only during a brief rainy season.

Ideally, reliable local advice should be obtained about the status of malaria transmission, not only at the destination but also along the route. A visitor to Peru may be safe from malaria while climbing in the High Andes, but could be infected during the overnight coach trip back to Lima. The risk of being bitten by an infected mosquito varies from less than once per year to more than once per night. The chances of catching malaria during a 2 week visit, without any attempt at protection, are estimated to be 0.2% in Kenya and 1% in West Africa.

Risky activities

Night-time military exercises or zoological studies have an especially high risk, while people back-packing, camping, and on safari run a greater risk than conventional tourists.

Risky people

Pregnant women, infants, and young children, and people who have had their spleen removed or whose immune system has been suppressed in any other way, are especially vulnerable to malaria and should avoid entering a malarious area.

Anti-mosquito measures

Sleeping in an air-conditioned, insect-proofed bedroom or under a mosquito net reduces substantially the risk of being bitten. Insecticide-treated mosquito nets (ITNs) which are soaked in pyrethroid insecticide such as permethrin ($0.2g/m^2$ of material) or deltamethrin, every 6 months, afford excellent protection against mosquitoes and other biting arthropods (e.g. sandflies, lice, fleas, bed-bugs, mites, ticks). More expensive longer-lasting insecticide nets (LLINs) ('PermaNet', 'Olyset', 'DAWA Plus') are effective for 5 years. At dusk, bedrooms should be sprayed with a knock-down insecticide to kill mosquitoes that have entered the room during the day. Electrical heating plates ('No Bite' and 'Buzz Off') will vaporize synthetic pyrethroids such as bioallethrin from tablets. A methylated spirit burner can be used where there is no electricity. Burning cones or coils of mosquito repellent ('incense') may also be effective but electronic buzzers are useless.

After dusk high-necked, light-coloured, long-sleeved shirts and long trousers should be worn. Exposed areas of skin should be rubbed or sprayed with repellents containing N-N-diethyl-m-toluamide (DEET), icaridin (picaridin) or lemon eucalyptus. Soaps and suntan oils containing insecticide are also available, and clothes, head, and wrist bands can be soaked in DEET- or permethrin-based solutions (see p.166).

Fake prophylaxis

Many alternative methods for preventing malaria have been advocated, including garlic, other herbs, vitamins and homeopathic concoctions. All are useless and dangerously misleading (see ℬ http://www.hpa.org.uk/ Topics/InfectiousDiseases/InfectionsAZ/Malaria/Guidelines/mala40guide-lineshomeopathicstatement/).

Use of anti-malarial drugs for prevention: two strategies

Two different strategies have been proposed for the use of anti-malarial drugs to protect travellers against malaria. In areas of high incidence (more than 10 cases of malaria per 1000 of the local population per year) such as West Africa, the risk of infection outweighs the risk of taking anti-malarial drugs (side-effects) and so chemoprophylaxis is justified. However, in areas of low incidence (less than 10 cases of malaria per 1000 of the local population per year) such as Central America and Southeast Asia, the risk of adverse effects from taking anti-malarial drugs outweighs the risk of infection and so reliance is placed on anti-mosquito measures and carrying a course of standby emergency treatment (SBET) to be taken if the traveller develops symptoms suggestive of malaria while out of reach of medical care (Table 5.1.3).

Anti-malarial drugs recommended for prevention (chemoprophylaxis)

In most malarious regions *P. falciparum* is resistant to chloroquine, pyrimethamine and, increasingly to other antimalarial drugs such as mefloquine. Failure to take anti-malarial tablets regularly and to continue taking them for 4 weeks after leaving the malarious area (7 days in the case of Malarone) is a major cause of breakthrough infections. ('Not being bitten' should never be a reason for stopping tablets early). During bouts of vomiting and travellers' diarrhoea, the drugs may not be properly absorbed.

The following drugs are recommended for prevention of malaria. Details of dosage are given in Table 5.1.4.

Malarone

Atovaquone with proguanil (Malarone) is recommended both for treatment and prevention of multi-resistant falciparum malaria. Since it affects both the pre-erythrocytic and erythrocytic stages of *P. falciparum*, it is not necessary to continue taking it for more than a short period after leaving the malarious area. Malarone is expensive. It has few side effects.

Proguanil plus chloroquine

The safe and well-tried combination of proguanil (Paludrine) and chloroquine is recommended for pregnant women for whom travel to a malarious area is absolutely unavoidable. It is also recommended for some areas of South America, the Middle East, and the Indian subcontinent.

Table 5.1.3 Chemoprophylaxis and standby emergency treatment (SBET)

Country	Strategy	Drug
Central America + Hispaniola	SBET	Chloroquine
South America: Brazil—Rondônia, Roraima, Acre; Guyana, Suriname, French Guiana—interior	Chemoprophylaxis	Malarone, mefloquine or doxycycline
South America: other malarious areas	SBET	Riamet or Malarone
Africa (including Madagascar): malarious areas	Chemoprophylaxis	Malarone, mefloquine or doxycycline
Middle East: malarious areas	SBET	Riamet or Malarone
Central India, Assam, SE Bangladesh*	Chemoprophylaxis	Chloroquine-proguanil/ Malarone, mefloquine or doxycycline*
Some parts of Burma, Laos, Cambodia, Vietnam*	Chemoprophylaxis	Malarone or doxycycline
Rest of Indian subcontinent and Southeast Asia + China: malarious areas*	SBET	Riamet or Malarone
Lombok, Eastern Indonesia, New Guinea, Solomon Islands	Chemoprophylaxis	Malarone, mefloquine or doxycycline
Vanuatu	SBET	Riamet or Malarone

*For more details see Chiodini et al. (2007), on p.505. Available at: ℘ http://www.hpa.org.uk/Publications/InfectiousDiseases/TravelHealth/0701MalariapreventionfortravellersfromtheUK/

Also Schlagenhauf and Petersen (2008) and ℘ http://www.dtg.org/uploads/media/Malariakarte_2011_02.pdf

Caution:

Chloroquine may cause itching in dark-skinned races and can exacerbate epilepsy and photosensitive psoriasis. Although no prescription is necessary to obtain these drugs in the UK, specialist advice is strongly recommended before using this combination of drugs in any part of the world with drug-resistant malaria.

After continuous prophylactic use for 5 or 6 years, sufficient chloroquine may accumulate in the eye to damage the retina.

Table 5.1.4 Anti-malarial drugs for prevention (chemoprophylaxis)

Drug	Adult dose*	Comment
Malarone (Atovaquone-proguanil)	1 tablet daily (250mg atovaquone + 100mg proguanil)	Start 1 day before travel and continue for 7 days after returning
Mefloquine	1 tablet weekly 250mg	Start 4 weeks before travel (to detect side-effects) and continue for 4 weeks after returning
Doxycycline	1 tablet/capsule daily 100mg	Start 1 week before travel and continue for 4 weeks after returning **NOT** for pregnant women or children
Proguanil + chloroquine	Proguanil 2 × 100mg tablets daily plus chloroquine 2 × 150mg (base) tablets weekly	Start 1 week before travel and continue for 4 weeks after returning
Chloroquine	2 × 150mg (base) tablets weekly	Start 1 week before travel and continue for 4 weeks after returning

*For more details including doses for children see Chiodini *et al.* (2007) on p.505.

Mefloquine (Lariam)

Mefloquine is approximately 90% effective against *P. falciparum* infection in Africa, but unpleasant neuropsychiatric side effects are experienced by between 0.1 and 1% of those who take the drug prophylactically. Side effects are more common in women than men. They include anxiety, insomnia, nightmares, depression, delusions, convulsions (fits), and dizziness. See also p.337. More than 75% of these reactions come on by the time the third weekly dose has been taken. Travellers taking mefloquine for the first time should start 4 weeks before they are due to travel so that there is time to change to another drug if serious side effects develop. It is necessary to start taking the drug at least 2 weeks prior to departure in order to build up a sufficiently protective blood level, and to continue taking one tablet weekly until 4 weeks afterwards.

Caution:

Mefloquine should not be taken by people who have suffered from epilepsy or psychiatric disease in the past, and those taking certain kinds of heart tablets.

Doxycycline

Doxycycline is a tetracycline antibiotic. In Africa, its effectiveness is considered to be similar to that of mefloquine—in the region of 90–95%. Its main side effects are indigestion, a tendency to cause vaginal thrush in women, and the possibility of a photosensitive rash—an exaggerated sunburn-like reaction that can follow exposure to bright light. (The rash occurs in roughly 3% of users.)

Caution:

Doxycycline and other tetracyclines must not be taken by pregnant women or children under 8 years old.

For women travellers actively trying to conceive

The best advice would be to take chloroquine and proguanil, plus maximum anti-mosquito precautions. These are the best-tried and safest drugs in pregnancy, but it is better to avoid all drugs during the first trimester!

Illness after travel

All the discussed measures may fail to prevent malaria. In cases of feverish illness within a few months of return from a malarious area, it is vital to see a doctor immediately and to mention the possible exposure to malaria.

Expatriates and long-term visitors

Long-term expatriates in malarious countries are 'a law unto themselves' as far as malaria prevention and treatment are concerned. They often refuse chemoprophylaxis and other anti-malarial precautions and not only hold wrong beliefs about malaria but promulgate them to short-term travellers. Immunity is not easily acquired and expatriates who have spent decades living in malarious areas may continue to contract malaria and even die of it!

Long-term prophylaxis with chloroquine and proguanil is limited by the risk of retinal damage (p.113)—periodic ophthalmological assessments are needed. Very long-term use of other anti-malarials has not been well documented; for example, with mefloquine in elderly expatriates there is an increasing risk of drug interactions (such as with beta-blockers used to control high blood pressure).

The best advice is to reduce the risk of infection through strict anti-mosquito measures, combined with judicious use of chemoprophylaxis during seasons of high transmission (usually during and after the raining season). Fevers should be treated seriously. An attempt should be made always to confirm the diagnosis of malaria by microscopy or rapid antigen ('dipstick') tests.

Many expatriates wrongly attribute all fevers to malaria and then dismiss the use of anti-malarial drugs because they fail to cure them. Confirmed attacks should be treated promptly and appropriately. Artemisinin drugs are increasingly available, often 'across the counter' in tropical countries. They should be used only in combination (e.g. as 'Riamet' or 'Co-artem') and in full dosage.

Short-term visitors should be wary of health advice from 'wise locals'. They are better guided by pre-travel advice from qualified advisers.

Visiting friends and relations

Members of ethnic minorities in Western countries who return to their malarious countries of origin to see friends and relations are at special risk of contracting malaria and other diseases, and are less likely to seek or receive sound travel medical advice. Many wrongly assume that they are immune to malaria, having grown up in the country. However, immunity can be lost in as little as 2–3 years away from the malarious area, or may never have been acquired at all if, for example, they lived in the Indian subcontinent in the days of near elimination of malaria. More recently, many parts of the subcontinent have become malarious. This group of patients poses a real challenge to travel medicine practitioners.

Malaria vaccines

Progress has been slow and, despite some promising results of trials of the Glaxo RTS,S/AS02(A) vaccine in Mozambican children, there is no vaccine for travellers anywhere near the horizon.

Advice for healthcare professionals about prophylaxis

In UK, fax a completed risk assessment template ✎ http://www.hpa.org.uk/web/HPAwebFile/ HPAweb_C/1244763931077 to National Travel Health Network and Centre (NaTHNaC) on 020 7637 0248. For urgent advice for health professionals, call 0845 602 6712.

In USA, access CDC Travelers' Health website: ✎ http://wwwnc.cdc.gov/travel/default.aspx

5.2 Arboviruses: dengue, Japanese encephalitis, yellow fever, and others

Tom Solomon

Arboviruses are a group of infections confined mainly to the tropics. Vaccination can be given against some of them; otherwise prevention depends mainly on avoiding insect or tick bites.

Introduction

Most medical students will tell you that the classification of viruses is something of a nightmare. They can be categorized according to shape, size, capsule, and whether they contain RNA or DNA. The official approach—the phylogenetic system—classifies viruses according to their genetic relatedness: closely related viruses are grouped into a 'genus', and closely related 'genera' into a family. However, because this tells you nothing about the illnesses they cause, or the means of transmission, alternative ways of classifying viruses are often used.

Viruses that are transmitted from one animal host to the next by insects, midges, and ticks (arthropods) are known as 'arboviruses' (arthropod-borne viruses). They have evolved from a variety of backgrounds, belong to different families and cause a wide spectrum of diseases. Some arboviruses were named after the disease they cause, for example, yellow fever or o'nyong nyong ('joint weakening' in a Ugandan dialect). Some were named after their insect vector, e.g. phleboviruses named after the phlebotomus sandfly. For many, the name includes a geographical location, either where the disease first occurred or where the virus was first isolated. However, such geographical associations are often now irrelevant: there is currently very little Japanese encephalitis in Japan.

Although there are more than 500 arboviruses contained in five viral families (the Flaviviridae, Togaviridae, Bunyaviridae, Orbiviridae and Rhabdoviridae), the number of viruses of medical importance is around 25 (Table 5.2.1). Many of them are rapidly evolving to fill new ecological niches. They have a disarming ability to spread to new geographical locations, and cause massive outbreaks with devastating results. Collectively, the arboviruses constitute some of the most important emerging and re-emerging pathogens, and some of the greatest challenges to biomedical research. The Medscape programme for monitoring emerging diseases (Pro-MED, found at ✍ www.promedmail.org) is a noticeboard with regular bulletins giving details of the latest outbreaks.

Here, some general principles will be considered before some of the most important arboviruses are looked at in more detail.

Life as an arbovirus

Viruses comprise small pieces of genetic material (nucleic acid) whose sole purpose in life is to self-replicate. Because they don't have all the enzymes they need to do this, they have to muscle into 'host' cells and borrow bits of their machinery. The host develops an immune response to fight off this unwanted invasion, and the rest follows as a consequence of this eternal struggle. To avoid the host immune response, viruses have a choice of hiding within the host or jumping to a new host. 'Hiding' viruses include HIV (which enters and damages immune cells) and hepatitis viruses (which sit deep in the liver). 'Jumping' viruses need a safe means of travelling from one host to the next. Respiratory viruses achieve this by jumping inside a droplet of mucus or spit; enteric viruses use the faecal-oral route; and arboviruses hitch a ride in the belly of insects that feed on the blood of host animals.

Vectors and hosts

Each arbovirus evolved to use whichever animal hosts and insect vectors were present in that particular area. In warm, tropical climates mosquitoes are the most important vectors, whereas in cooler, northern climates many arboviruses have evolved to use ticks. After infection, an animal develops life-long immunity to that arbovirus, so a constant supply of new, unexposed, non-immune hosts is needed. Although humans are the natural hosts for a few arboviruses (dengue, chikungunya, o'nyong nyong), for the vast majority the natural hosts are birds or small mammals (often rodents) that have a high reproduction rate, providing a ready supply of non-immune hosts. For these 'enzootic' arboviruses, humans become infected only accidentally because they live or travel in close proximity to the animal-insect-animal cycle. Sometimes an 'amplifying host', such as a farm animal, is infected first, and by increasing the total circulating viral load this leads to human infection.

In general, infection does not cause severe disease in the natural host. You are not a very successful arbovirus if you have killed your host before you have had chance to move on to a new one!

Table 5.2.1 Medically important arboviruses*

Flavivirus, Flaviviridae		
Dengue virus	}	*mosquito-borne, FAR/VHF*
Yellow fever virus		
Japanese encephalitis virus		
West Nile virus	}	*mosquito-borne, CNS*
St Louis encephalitis virus		
Murray Valley encephalitis virus		
Omsk haemorrhagic fever virus	}	*tick-borne, FAR/VHF*
Kyasanur forest disease virus		
Tick-borne encephalitis virus		
Louping ill virus	}	*tick-borne, CNS*
Powassan virus		
Alphavirus, Togaviridae		
Venezuelan equine encephalitis virus		
Eastern equine encephalitis virus	}	*mosquito-borne, CNS*
Western equine encephalitis virus		
Chikungunya virus		
O'nyong nyong virus		
Ross River Virus	}	*mosquito-borne, FAR*
Sindbis virus		
Nairovirus, Bunyaviridae		
Crimean-Congo haemorrhagic fever virus		*tick-borne, VHF*
Phlebovirus, Bunyaviridae		
Rift Valley fever virus		*mosquito-borne, VHF/CNS*
Sandfly fever virus		*sandfly-borne, FAR*
Tosacana virus		*sandfly-borne, CNS*
Bunyavirus, Bunyaviridae		
La Crosse virus		*mosquito-borne, CNS*
California encephalitis virus		*mosquito-borne, CNS*
Oropouche		*mosquito-borne, FAR*
Coltivirus, Rheoviridae		
Colorado tick fever virus		*tick-borne, FAR/CNS*

*Viruses are listed by genus and family.

Key: FAR = fever arthralgia rash syndrome, VHF = viral haemorrhagic fever, CNS = central nervous system infection.

Human disease

Human infection with arboviruses can result in one of four clinical syndromes.

Mild febrile illness

The commonest outcome is asymptomatic infection, or a mild non-specific febrile illness indistinguishable from any 'flu-like illness. This is especially true for children in areas endemic for the particular virus. Following infection the child will develop immunity to that virus and will never be troubled by it again.

The 'fever-arthralgia-rash' triad

There is a sudden onset of high fever, chills, headache, nausea, vomiting, and a combination of joint pains (arthralgia), muscle pains (myalgia), backache, pain behind the eyes (retro-orbital pain) and sensitivity to light (photophobia). These symptoms are often accompanied by conjunctivitis, lymph node swelling (lymphadenopathy) and a variety of rashes (exanthemas) or mouth eruptions (enanthemas). Depending on the virus, rashes may be transient blanching, erythematous, itchy maculopapular, petechial, vesicular, morbilliform (like measles), or scarlatiniform (like scarlatina). There may also be papular or vesicular changes in the mouth, especially on the palate. The fever is often biphasic, and there maybe a leukopenia (reduction in the number of white blood cells), but the fever-arthralgia-rash syndrome is usually self-limiting.

Viral haemorrhagic fever

Following an initial fever-arthralgia-rash syndrome, some arboviruses cause bleeding manifestations (sometimes after an interval of a few days). Petechiae (tiny spots of blood in the skin) may coalesce to form larger areas of purpura. There may be bruising, prolonged bleeding at injection sites, gum and nose bleeding, and in more severe disease, gastrointestinal bleeding. A variety of factors may contribute to the bleeding tendency, including derangement in clotting factors (secondary to liver damage), a reduced number of platelets that function abnormally, and damage to the blood vessels. Shock (low blood pressure) may develop leading to acidosis, further clotting, biochemical derangement, and a high mortality if untreated.

The virus may attack the liver causing hepatitis (liver inflammation) and hepatomegaly (liver enlargement); deep jaundice is a sign of severe liver damage. In some infections (notably dengue haemorrhagic fever) leakage of fluid from the vessels can cause a drop in blood pressure without frank bleeding. As well as flaviviruses, phleboviruses, and nairoviruses there are many non-arboviral causes of haemorrhagic fevers (see Chapter 4.10).

Central nervous system infection

Following a non-specific febrile prodrome some arboviruses invade the central nervous system. Infection and inflammation of the meningeal membranes that cover the brain and spinal cord is called 'meningitis'. It is characterized by headache and vomiting, photophobia, neck stiffness, and pain on extension of the knee when the hip is flexed (Kernig's signs). Examination of the cerebrospinal fluid reveals an increased number of white blood cells (usually lymphocytes).

In encephalitis, the virus invades and destroys the brain substance with accompanying inflammation. The clinical features range from mild confusion or behavioural changes (which may be mistaken for hysteria), to focal neurological signs, convulsions, and deep coma. There are usually, though not always, increased lymphocytes in the spinal fluid. Where facilities are available, computed tomography (CT) or magnetic resonance imaging (MRI) scans may aid diagnosis by revealing characteristic areas of focal damage within the brain.

In myelitis, viruses attack the spinal cord to give weakness in one or more limbs, which are usually flaccid and areflexic.

The term 'meningoencephalomyelitis' is used to reflect the fact that many viruses attack all three components of the central nervous system. The differential diagnosis for arboviral encephalitis includes members of the *Alphavirus*, *Flavivirus*, *Bunyavirus*, and *Phlebovirus* genera as well as many other causes. Most arboviruses are known by just one or two of these four syndromes, but it is becoming apparent that some arboviruses have a disarming ability to cause different clinical presentations in different settings.

Diagnosis

Broadly speaking, viral infections are diagnosed by either demonstrating that the virus is present, or that it was present and the host now has an immune response against it. Culturing virus from clinical samples (the traditional 'gold standard') requires a sophisticated laboratory, highly trained personnel and the maintenance of cell lines (or a supply of small mammals) in which to isolate the virus—not very practical in most rural tropical settings.

Newer methods for detecting minute amounts of viral nucleic acid using the polymerase chain reaction have been developed for many arboviruses. Although frequently used in specialized research laboratories, many have yet to prove their worth in a routine diagnostic service. The older sero-logical techniques for demonstrating anti-viral antibodies, such as the hae-maglutination inhibition test, are technically fiddly, and since they require both acute and convalescent sera, are not useful for making an early diag-nosis or for diagnosing patients that die soon after admission.

The development of new IgM- and IgG-capture ELISAs to allow early detection of anti-viral antibody in single serum or cerebrospinal fluid samples has been a major advance. These tests have become the accepted standard for diagnosis of many arboviral infections. Some have recently been adapted into simple bedside kits requiring no specialized laboratory equipment, making them even more appropriate for rapid diagnosis in the field. Additional new tests include antigen-capture ELISAs that measure viral proteins in the serum.

Treatment and prevention

For a few arbovirus infections (Crimean-Congo haemorrhagic fever, Rift Valley fever) specific antiviral treatment is available, but for the majority there is none. In these cases, current management consists of treating the complications of the disease, such as high fever and aches, low blood pres-sure, blood loss, convulsions, or raised intracranial pressure.

Vaccines are available against some arboviral infections (yellow fever, Japanese encephalitis, tick-borne encephalitis) and are being developed against others. However, the simplest preventive measure is to avoid bites from the insects that carry the viruses (see Chapter 5.12). Although this might be practical for the short-term visitor, it is rarely possible for residents.

In the following sections, arboviruses are classified according to their most important clinical presentation, though to some extent these divi-sions are artificial because of the considerable overlap.

Haemorrhagic arboviruses

Dengue

Dengue (genus *Flavivirus*, family Flaviviridae) is now numerically the most important arbovirus worldwide, with an estimated 100 million cases per year and 2.5 billion people at risk. The virus has spread dramatically since the end of the Second World War, in what has been described as a global pandemic. Virtually every country between the tropics of Capricorn and Cancer is affected (Map 5.2.1), and it is the arbovirus that travellers are most likely to encounter, though thankfully usually in its mildest form.

Dengue is unusual among arboviruses in that humans are the natural host. There are four slightly different types of dengue virus (distinguished serologically). The expansion of dengue has been linked to a world-wide resurgence of the main mosquito vector *Aedes aegypti* (Fig. 5.2.1), overcrowding of human populations and increasing human travel. Intercontinental transport of used car tyres containing eggs of *Aedes albopictus* has also been implicated in dengue resurgence.

Dengue tends to occur in cities—particularly poor, overcrowded areas on the edge of cities—rather than in the countryside, where the human population maybe widely dispersed. The mosquito breeds in clean water, for example, in water storage jars and in rainwater accidentally collected in tyres and other rubbish.

In endemic areas, most of the population is infected by dengue viruses during early childhood, when most infections are asymptomatic or cause a non-specific 'flu-like illness. When the virus spreads to new areas, adults and children are both affected, since neither group has pre-existing immunity. Infection with dengue viruses can cause one of two diseases: dengue fever and dengue haemorrhagic fever.

Dengue fever

Named 'breakbone fever' by Benjamin Rush, 200 years ago, this is a classic fever-arthralgia-rash syndrome. In young children it is often an undifferentiated febrile illness. In older children and adults there is an abrupt onset of high fever, muscle, and joint aches (which may be severe), often with pain behind the eyes, photophobia, and lymphadenopathy. There may be a transient mottling rash or sometimes petechiae (spotty bleeding into the skin). Occasionally, there is frank bleeding in dengue fever, but in most cases the disease is self-limiting and hospital admission is not necessary.

Patients should be encouraged to drink and given paracetamol for symptomatic relief. Aspirin should be avoided because of the risk of Reye's syndrome (a severe liver complication). A fine maculopapular 'recovery rash' on the limbs during convalescence, or skin peeling on the extremities is not infrequent, and sometimes may be the only clue that a febrile illness was dengue. Although the fever usually resolves within a few days, many patients feel prolonged lethargy and depression.

Dengue haemorrhagic fever

In the 1950s, an apparently new haemorrhagic disease in Southeast Asia was shown to be due to dengue virus, and named dengue haemorrhagic fever. It is believed to occur when infection with one dengue virus serotype is followed by infection with a different serotype (usually in a subsequent season), perhaps because falling levels of antibody to the first

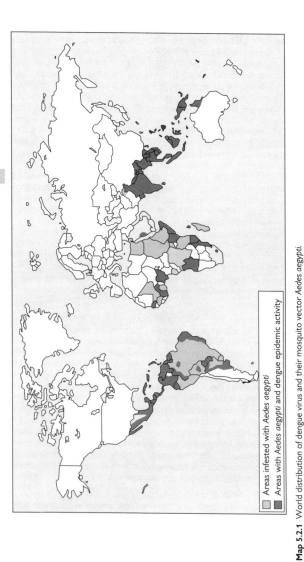

Map 5.2.1 World distribution of dengue virus and their mosquito vector *Aedes aegypti.*

Reproduced and adapted from Johnson et al., *Oxford Handbook of Expedition and Wilderness Medicine*, 2008, p.462, with permission of Oxford University Press ; with data from the WHO ℗© http://apps.who.int/ithmap/.

Areas infested with *Aedes aegypti*
Areas with *Aedes aegypti* and dengue epidemic activity

Fig. 5.2.1 Female *Aedes aegypti* mosquito (4–6mm long).

virus serotype enhance the entry of the second into macrophage blood cells (antibody-dependent enhancement). It thus tends to occur in areas where two or more serotypes co-circulate, such as in Southeast Asia and the Western Pacific region, the Indian subcontinent, and southern China, Cuba, the Caribbean, the Pacific Islands, Venezuela, and Brazil; it is rare in travellers.

The disease is characterized by increased vascular permeability allowing fluid to leak from the blood vessels into the tissue, a low platelet count (thrombocytopenia), leukopenia with atypical lymphocytes, and haemorrhagic manifestations (which are often very mild). Further features are shown in Fig. 5.2.2.

Patients with mild disease are encouraged to drink and need to be monitored closely for deterioration with repeated haematocrit measurements as well as observation of vital signs. For severe disease, the WHO recommends initial IV crystalloid (e.g. Ringer's lactate solution) followed by a colloid solution (e.g. dextran 40) if shock persists. Only rarely are blood products needed. If possible, oxygen should be given. Fluid infusion needs to be carefully tailored: even cautious treatment may precipitate peripheral and facial oedema, ascites, pleural effusions, and pulmonary oedema; diuretics and ventilatory support are sometimes needed.

Although there are no anti-viral drugs against dengue, in expert hands the mortality of dengue haemorrhagic fever has dropped from around 10% untreated to less than 1%.

Diagnosis of dengue infection is possible by virus isolation polymerase chain reaction (PCR) detection, or antigen detection in the first few days of the illness. After this, viral titres are low, but anti-dengue antibodies can be measured in serum by ELISAs.

Prevention
Vaccines have proved hard to produce because of concern that antibodies raised against one virus serotype might enhance infection with a different serotype. Vaccines equally effective against all four serotypes are being developed and several are in trial; it is likely that one will be available soon.

Preventive measures against dengue include steps to limit the breeding of *Aedes* mosquitoes around the house (e.g. removing stagnant pools

DENGUE ± WARNING SIGNS

SEVERE DENGUE

1. Severe plasma leakage
2. Severe haemorrhage
3. Severe organ impairment

CRITERIA FOR DENGUE ± WARNING SIGNS

Probable dengue

live in/travel to dengue endemic area.
Fever and 2 of the following criteria:

- Nausea, vomiting
- Rash
- Aches and pains
- Tourniquet test positive
- Leukopenia
- Any warning sign

Warning signs*

- Abdominal pain or tenderness
- Persistent vomiting
- Clinical fluid accumulation
- Mucosal bleed
- Lethargy, restlessness
- Liver enlargment > 2cm
- Laboratory: increase in HCT
  concurrent with rapid decrease
  in platelet count

*(requiring stict observation and
medical intervention)

Laboratory-confirmed dengue

[important when no sign of plasma
leakage]

CRITERIA FOR SEVERE DENGUE

Severe plasma leakage

leading to:

- Shock (DSS)
- Fluid accumulation with respiratory
  distress

Severe bleeding

as evaluated by clinician

Severe organ involvement

- Liver: AST or ALT >= 1000
- CNS: Impaired consciousness
- Heart and other organs

Fig. 5.2.2 Suggested dengue case classification and levels of severity.

of water collected in tyres and other rubbish), and steps to avoid being bitten. However, given that *Aedes* mosquitoes bite during daylight hours, this is almost impossible for those living in endemic areas. Some comfort may come from the fact that although most of the European staff I have known working in tropical units in Asia have been infected with dengue at some time, none has come to serious harm.

Yellow fever

In the early 1900s, American efforts to link the Atlantic and Pacific Oceans with the Panama Canal were severely hampered as hundreds of labourers succumbed to yellow fever. A local physician, Dr Carlos Finlay, suggested that the disease was transmitted by mosquito bites (a revolutionary idea at the time), and a team of USA Army physicians, headed by Dr Walter Reed, was sent to investigate. To prove the point, one of the team, Dr Jesse Lazaer, allowed a mosquito that had just fed on a yellow fever patient to bite him: he subsequently developed the disease and died. The vigorous mosquito-control efforts that followed enabled the Panama Canal to be completed; and subsequent virological studies established that yellow fever was caused by a virus. It was the first arbovirus identified, and gave its name to the flaviviruses (in Latin, flavus = yellow).

Yellow fever occurs in jungle and urban cycles in West Africa and South America (Map 5.3). In South American 'jungle yellow fever', *Haemagogus* mosquitoes transmit the virus between monkeys. Humans become infected by entering this cycle, and carry the disease to populated areas. Here, *Aedes* mosquitoes are responsible for transmission between humans to give 'urban yellow fever'. In West Africa, *Aedes* mosquitoes are responsible for both jungle and urban transmission.

Yellow fever is characterized by abrupt onset of high fever, headache, back and muscle aches, nausea and vomiting. Most infections are mild, but in more severe disease there is liver failure, causing the mild jaundice by which the disease is known. Bleeding into the stomach produces characteristic black vomit and darkened stool (melaena). There may also be bleeding from the eyes, nose, bladder, and rectum, and renal failure, and, occasionally, nervous system involvement. Faget's sign (failure of the heart rate to rise with a rising temperature) indicates damage to heart muscle. Laboratory tests confirm elevated liver enzymes, leukopenia, thrombocytopenia, and clotting abnormalities. The diagnosis is confirmed by virus isolation in the first few days, or ELISA after that. Councilman bodies, found in the liver at autopsy, were thought to be pathognomic (i.e. unique to yellow fever), but they also occur in Crimean-Congo haemorrhagic fever and Rift Valley fever (Map 5.2.2).

The vaccine against yellow fever was one of the first live attenuated vaccines, and is essential for visitors to all endemic areas—even if no cases have recently been reported. A single 0.5mL dose of 17D yellow fever vaccine confers immunity for 10 years or more (see also Chapter 13.2). Be sure to obtain an International Certificate of Vaccination, because travel to and from certain countries may be restricted without it. In addition, travellers should take standard measures to limit mosquito bites (see Chapter 5.12). In recent years, a small number of cases of adverse events following immunization with this vaccine have occurred in the elderly or those with thymomas, but for most people the benefits outweigh the risks.

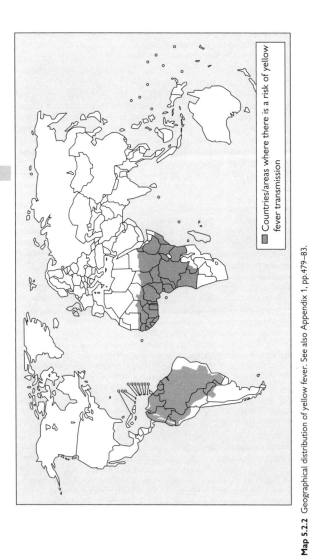

Map 5.2.2 Geographical distribution of yellow fever. See also Appendix 1, pp.479–83.

Reproduced and adapted from Johnson et al., *Oxford Handbook of Expedition and Wilderness Medicine*, 2008, p.44 with permission of Oxford University Press; with data from CDC and edited by Gary W. Burnette, *CDC Health Information for International Travel 2012*, 2012, pp.343–344 with permission from Oxford University Press Inc.

Countries/areas where there is a risk of yellow fever transmission

Crimean-Congo haemorrhagic fever (CCHF)

Crimean-Congo haemorrhagic fever (genus *Nairovirus*, family Bunyaviridae) is unusual among arboviruses in that direct human-to-human transmission can occur without the need of an insect vector. The name reflects the fact that 'Congo virus', isolated from a febrile child in the Belgian Congo (now Zaire) in 1956, proved to be identical to the filterable agent identified in 1944 as the cause of 'Crimean haemorrhagic fever'.

The virus is transmitted naturally between mammals by *Ixodes* ticks, and is widely distributed through Africa, Asia, the former USSR, Eastern Europe and the Middle East. Humans become infected when bitten by an infected tick, but secondary cases can occur in healthcare workers and others in direct contact with blood from infected patients (see also Chapter 13.6).

Rift Valley fever

As its name implies, Rift Valley fever (genus *Phlebovirus*, family Bunyaviridae) is endemic in the Rift Valley and much of eastern Africa. Although genetically close to the viruses transmitted by sandflies (and hence a member of the phlebovirus genus), the virus is principally mosquito-borne. *Aedes* and *Culex* mosquitoes are the most important vectors. Epidemics are associated with the explosive increases in mosquito populations that follow heavy rainfalls and new irrigation projects.

Rift Valley fever virus causes disease in sheep, cattle (causing abortions) and other farm animals, as well as humans. There were 200 000 human cases during an epidemic in Egypt in the late 1970s. The illness is indistinguishable from other arboviral fevers, but 5–10% have haemorrhagic manifestations, meningoencephalitis or ocular complications (reduced visual acuity due to exudates). This triad of symptoms during an epidemic of a febrile illness may provide a clue that Rift Valley fever is the cause, especially if there is concurrent disease in animals. Intravenous ribavirin is effective treatment for severe disease.

Omsk haemorrhagic fever

Omsk haemorrhagic fever is a flavivirus of rodents (particularly musk rats) in the Omsk area of Siberia, transmitted to humans by *Dermacentor* ticks. The disease can also be contracted by direct contact with infected carcasses. Most infections are asymptomatic, but there may be a papulovesicular eruption on the soft palate, and mucosal and gastrointestinal bleeding. Kyasanur forest disease is caused by a closely related tick-borne flavivirus found in forest rodents in western India. Most cases consist of a febrile illness, but haemorrhagic disease and even meningoencephalitis can occur.

Central nervous system arboviruses

Japanese encephalitis

Can there be anything more devastating than watching a previously well child deteriorate from a mild 'flu-like illness to severe coma and death within the space of a few days? Although considered by many in the West to be a rare and exotic infection, Japanese encephalitis is probably the most important viral encephalitis worldwide. Around 50 000 cases and 15 000 deaths are reported every year, but the true numbers may be much higher.

Japanese encephalitis virus (genus *Flavivirus*, family Flaviviridae) is transmitted between birds, chickens, pigs, and other animals by *Culex* mosquitoes. The most important, *Culex tritaeniorhynchus*, breeds in rice paddy fields. The geographical area affected by the virus has expanded in the last 50 years and now includes all of Southeast Asia, most of the Indian subcontinent, and much of China and the Pacific Rim (Map 5.2.3). In addition, there have recently been epidemics in the Kathmandu Valley of Nepal and, in 1998, Japanese encephalitis was reported for the first time in northern Australia. The reasons for this expansion are incompletely understood, but probably include increased irrigation facilitating mosquito breeding and changing farming habits (e.g. more animal husbandry). The situation would probably be far worse were it not for the use of Japanese encephalitis vaccine in some countries (see below).

In northern temperate regions (China, Nepal, and northern parts of India, Thailand, and Vietnam) Japanese encephalitis occurs in summer epidemics. In southern tropical climates (Indonesia, Malaysia, Southern India, Thailand, and Vietnam) the virus is endemic, with sporadic cases occurring throughout the year. These two patterns probably relate to mosquito numbers, rainfall, and temperature, though different viral strains are also a possible explanation.

In many parts of rural Asia, Japanese encephalitis virus is so abundant that it is almost impossible to avoid. Serological studies (looking for antibody to the virus in the blood) show that by early adulthood almost all people living in rural Asia have already been infected. Thankfully, the majority of infections do not cause disease. Only about one in 30 to one in 300 infected people develop symptoms. These may range from a mild 'flu-like illness to a severe meningoencephalitis leading to death. Patients typically present with a few days of fever, headache, nausea, and vomiting, followed by a reduced level of consciousness (often heralded by convulsions). In addition, a new variant of the disease has recently been described in which the predominant lesion is in the spinal cord (myelitis), causing an acute flaccid paralysis that looks very similar to polio. Whether viral or host factors determine which symptoms develop following infection remains to be determined.

In endemic areas, most new cases of Japanese encephalitis occur in children, because the majority of adults have already been infected. However, adults who have not previously been exposed to the virus (including travellers) are equally susceptible. This was amply demonstrated by the many Western troops who succumbed to Japanese encephalitis during conflicts in Asia. Although there is no anti-viral treatment, some of the complications of infection (convulsions, brain swelling, and pneumonia) are treatable.

The risk of infection with Japanese encephalitis virus can be reduced by avoiding the bites of *Culex* mosquitoes (which bite from dusk to dawn) and by vaccination.

Vaccines

The original vaccines, produced over 30 years ago, contained mouse-brain proteins, and occasionally caused immune reactions, giving the vaccine a bad name. However, newer, safer inactivated (killed) vaccines grown in tissue culture, are available; the most widely used, Ixiaro, is given as

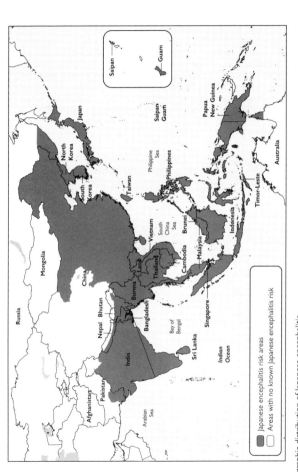

Map 5.2.3 Geographic distribution of Japanese encephalitis.

Reproduced from CDC and edited by Gary W. Burnette, *CDC Health Information for International Travel 2012*, 2012, p.207 with permission from Oxford University Press Inc.

an intramuscular injection, in two doses 4 weeks apart. Only about one per million people given the inactivated vaccine will develop serious neurological side-effects—comparable to conventional childhood vaccines in the West. Allergic-type reactions (itching and swelling, probably related to gelatin in the vaccine) may occur, and very occasionally require treatment with steroids. Previously, Japanese encephalitis vaccine was recommended only for those spending 1 month or more in affected areas, or for those on shorter trips to a known epidemic area, or engaging in extensive outdoor activity. However, considering the devastating nature of the disease and the paucity of good epidemiological data, it has been argued that all visitors to endemic areas should be vaccinated. A newer, cheaper, live-attenuated vaccine has been developed and tested in China. Preliminary data suggest it is highly effective and related vaccines may be available worldwide in the future. Another new live vaccine has been developed by modifying yellow fever 17D vaccine to carry some of the Japanese encephalitis virus's proteins.

> West Nile fever virus, St Louis encephalitis virus, Murray Valley encephalitis virus, and Kunjin virus are four flaviviruses closely related to Japanese encephalitis virus, with clinical and epidemiological similarities.

West Nile fever virus

This virus (genus *Flavivirus*, family Flaviviridae) was first isolated from the blood of a febrile Ugandan in 1937. It was subsequently shown to have a very wide area of distribution that included most of Africa, southern Europe, the Middle East and even parts of the Far East. In its natural cycle, the virus is transmitted primarily between pigeons and crows by *Culex* mosquitoes.

Classically, West Nile fever virus causes a non-specific febrile illness, and until recently nervous system manifestations were considered a rarity. However, in recent years the epidemiology has changed, with the virus spreading to new areas and causing different disease patterns. In 1996, an epidemic of West Nile encephalitis affected several hundred people in Romania and, in 1999; the virus caused an epidemic in New York. Since then the virus has spread across much of America and continues to cause sporadic disease. There are no vaccines. Travellers are advised to avoid mosquito bites, especially if there is known to be West Nile virus activity. Detailed surveys of mosquitoes and birds mean that good information is usually available.

St Louis encephalitis

St Louis encephalitis (genus *Flavivirus*, family Flaviviridae) is the most important arboviral encephalitis in the USA. The arbovirus branch of America's Center for Disease Control was founded following outbreaks of the disease in the 1930s in St Louis, Missouri. The virus occurs naturally in many birds and is transmitted by *Culex* mosquitoes. Up to 3000 cases have been reported during epidemics in some years. However, the continuing surveillance for St Louis encephalitis virus and intensive mosquito spraying in affected areas reduce the chances of such epidemics in the future. In the United States the annual number of cases fluctuates widely with large epidemics followed by quiet years; the average number of cases has been approximately 100, mostly in Florida and Texas.

Murray Valley encephalitis virus

This flavivirus causes sporadic cases of encephalitis every year in Australia, and occasionally causes small outbreaks (up to 20 cases). The disease is transmitted between wild birds by *Culex* mosquitoes, but the means of over-wintering is uncertain. The virus has also been found in New Guinea.

Tick-borne encephalitis (TBE)

In cooler climates flaviviruses evolved to use the more abundant tick vector as their means of transmission. Tick-borne encephalitis virus circulates in small wild animals, mostly rodents, and is transmitted by *Ixodes* ticks. Humans may also become infected by drinking goat's milk. It has a wide area of distribution across Europe and the former Soviet Union, and its seasonal incidence is reflected in one of the many pseudonyms, 'Russian spring-summer encephalitis' (Map 5.2.4).

Genetic sequencing has allowed Western tick-borne encephalitis virus, which is endemic in Germany, Austria and much of Europe, to be distinguished from Far-Eastern tick-borne encephalitis virus, found across the former Soviet Union. The number of cases is rising; 40% of victims have no recollection of having been bitten by a tick. Austria vaccinates its entire population against the disease.

After 1–2 weeks' incubation the virus causes a sudden onset of fever, headache, nausea, and photophobia. In mild cases this resolves after a week, but in more severe cases there is a second phase of illness with meningoencephalitis or myelitis. The latter tends to cause flaccid paralysis of the upper limb and shoulder girdle. Respiratory muscle and bulbar (brainstem) involvement lead to respiratory failure and death.

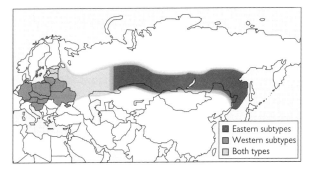

Eastern subtypes
Western subtypes
Both types

Map 5.2.4 Distribution of Western and Eastern subtypes of tick-borne encephalitis.

Reproduced from Johnson et al., *Oxford Handbook of Expedition and Wilderness Medicine*, 2008, p.44, with permission of Oxford University Press.

Far-Eastern tick-borne encephalitis has a higher case fatality rate; the Western form is often associated with neurological damage. Overall, there is a 10% risk of death or disability.

An inactivated vaccine is available, and recommended for those likely to be exposed in the endemic forested areas of Europe and the former Soviet Union (this includes walkers, campers and hikers) (see p.450).

Other central nervous system arboviruses

Other central nervous system (CNS) arboviruses include: louping ill, the equine encephalitis viruses, bunyaviruses, and Colorado tick fever virus.

Louping ill

This virus is a closely related tick-borne virus, notable for being the only flavivirus found naturally in the British Isles (as well as Scandinavia). It occurs among small mammals (hares, wood-mice, and shrews), but is also transmitted to highland sheep, which develop encephalitis. The disease is named after the leaping (or louping) demonstrated by the encephalitic sheep. Very occasionally the virus infects humans, causing meningoen-cephalitis, which can be severe. Powassan virus is a distantly related tick-borne flavivirus found principally among small mammals in Canada that has occasionally caused meningoencephalitis in humans.

Equine encephalitis viruses

These mosquito-borne alphaviruses (genus *Alphavirus*, family Rubellaviridae) cause epidemics of encephalitis in horses and humans in the Americas. Venezuelan equine encephalitis virus is normally trans-mitted in an enzootic cycle involving small mammals and *Aedes* and *Culex* mosquitoes. Following high rainfalls, the number of circulating mosquitoes increases and horses become infected. They act as amplifying hosts, and human infection follows. Massive outbreaks of human and equine disease occur every few years in Venezuela and neighbouring central and southern American countries. In 1995, there were up to 100 000 human cases, most of which had a mild, non-specific febrile illness; but 300 of these were fatal. Recent work has shown subtle genetic differences between enzootic and epidemic strains of the virus.

Eastern equine encephalitis virus is found along the eastern coast of North America, Central America, and northern countries of South America. It is transmitted between wild birds by *Culiseta* and *Aedes* mos-quitoes. Although it currently only causes a handful of cases each year, large epidemics have occurred. Western equine encephalitis virus is trans-mitted between wild birds by *Culex* and *Culiseta* mosquitoes. It has a wide area of distribution across much of the USA, but only rarely gives human disease.

Bunyaviruses

These viruses (genus *Bunyavirus*, family Bunyaviridae) are widely distrib-uted mosquito-borne, tick-borne, and biting fly-borne viruses, named after Bunyamwera, the village in Uganda where the first one was isolated. Most cause non-specific febrile illnesses, but the mosquito-borne American bun-yaviruses of the California serogroup also cause encephalitis. The most important, La Crosse virus, is transmitted between chipmunks and squirrels principally by *Aedes* mosquitoes. It causes up to 200 cases of encephalitis in the USA annually, but the fatality rate is low. Other members of the same serogroup include California encephalitis virus and viruses with such unlikely names as Jamestown Canyon and Snowshoe hare. Toscana virus (genus *Phlebovirus*, family Bunyaviridae) is transmitted by sandflies, and is an important cause of viral meningitis and encephalitis in children in Italy.

Colorado tick fever virus
This virus (genus *Coltivirus*, family Rheoviridae) is transmitted among small mammals (chipmunks and ground squirrels) by *Dermacentor* ticks in the Rocky Mountain States of the USA. Because of its geographical distribution, vector, and symptoms it is often confused with the rickettsial disease, Rocky Mountain spotted fever. Infection presents with a non-specific fever, myalgia, and maculopapular rash, and up to 10% of children may develop neurological features (from mild meningitis to severe encephalitis). A haemorrhagic disease is also occasionally reported.

Fever-arthralgia-rash arboviruses
Many of the viruses described previously as 'haemorrhagic' can also cause a febrile syndrome, with arthralgia and rash. However, for other arboviruses, the triad of fever, arthralgia, and rash is the *only* significant clinical presentation. The 'old world' alphaviruses (genus *Alphavirus*, family Togaviridae) are the most important of these. Chikungunya virus ('that which bends up' in a Tanzanian dialect) is very widely distributed across Africa, India, and Southeast Asia, and is transmitted by *Aedes* and *Anopheles* mosquitoes. Humans and non-human primates are the only hosts. The virus causes massive epidemics of an illness very similar to dengue fever, some of which can last for years. O'nyong nyong virus is a closely related alphavirus that causes severe arthritis, often with conjunctivitis; epidemics are far less frequent. *Anopheles* mosquitoes are the vectors and humans are the only natural host.

Ross River fever virus (genus *Alphavirus*, family Togaviridae) is numerically the most important arbovirus in Australia, and is responsible for 'epidemic polyarthritis'. There are approximately 5000 cases per year in adults, but when the virus spread to the Pacific in 1979 there was a massive

---

Box 5.2.1 **Summary of advice for travellers**

- Minimize the risk of mosquito, tick, and sandfly bites by wearing appropriate clothing and using DEET insect repellent and impregnated bed-nets
- Where vaccines are available (yellow fever, Japanese encephalitis, tick-borne encephalitis), the benefits of vaccination usually outweigh the possible risks
- Anti-viral treatment is available for a few arboviruses (Rift Valley fever and Crimean-Congo haemorrhagic fever), but for most the treatment is symptomatic
- Dengue is the arbovirus infection you are most likely to encounter, but it is usually no worse than a very nasty bout of flu.

epidemic of 50 000 cases. Ross River fever is characterized by arthralgia (joint pain) and myalgia (muscle pain), with fever and rash apparent in only 50% of cases. Occasionally, the disease progresses to give chronic arthritis (joint inflammation). *Aedes* and *Culex* mosquitoes are the main vectors, and the natural hosts are thought to include kangaroos and wallabies.

Other fever-arthralgia-rash arboviruses include Sindbis (an alphavirus found in South Africa) and Oropouche (a bunyavirus from Brazil). Sandfly fever viruses (genus *Phlebovirus*, family Bunyaviridae) are transmitted by sandflies across Africa, Asia, and Europe. They cause a non-specific febrile illness with myalgia, retro-orbital pain and marked conjunctival infection; 'dog disease' was an early description because of the resemblance to the eyes of a bloodhound.

Further information

The USA Centers for Disease Control Division of Vector-Borne Infectious Diseases website has lots of up-to-date information on arboviral infections: ₰ http://www.cdc.gov/ncezid/dvbd/

5.3 Filarial infections

Michael Brown

This group of worm infections is transmitted by biting insects.

Filarial worms live in the tissues and can survive for several years. They reach up to 30cm in length and live in the lymphatic system or in the deeper layers of skin; they are acquired only in the tropics.

The female releases numerous embryos called microfilariae that either circulate in the bloodstream or persist in the skin. The transmission cycle begins when insects bite the skin to ingest a blood meal. Larval worms develop in the insect, which at a later bite are released into a new host, where they mature over a period of about a year.

Nearly all cases of disease occur in local residents living in high transmission areas over long periods of time. However, travellers occasionally develop symptoms, sometimes long after exposure. Special diagnostic methods are needed; self-treatment may be dangerous and is not recommended.

Lymphatic filariasis

Two parasites are involved, infecting over 120 million people: *Wuchereria bancrofti* is responsible for 90% of cases and occurs throughout the tropics; *Brugia malayi* occurs on the Indian subcontinent and in Southeast Asia (Map 5.3.1). Adult worms live in the lymphatic vessels and nodes, particularly those of the legs and male genitalia. Microfilariae circulate in the bloodstream, usually at night.

Transmission is by several species of mosquito, including *Anopheles* (which also transmit malaria), *Culex* and *Aedes*, that breed mostly in stagnant water collections (including pit latrines) around dwellings and in urban areas.

In the early stages of infection, sometimes after only 3 months, there is recurrent painful swelling of lymph nodes and lymph vessels, especially in the groin, with fever, malaise, and sometimes transient limb swelling.

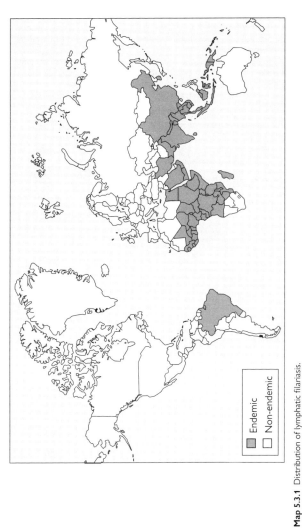

Map 5.3.1 Distribution of lymphatic filariasis.

Adapted from Johnson et al., *Oxford Handbook of Expedition and Wilderness Medicine*, 2008. p.487, with permission of Oxford University Press.

Endemic

Non-endemic

After many such episodes, usually over years, permanent limb swelling (lymphoedema) may result, which in severe cases earns the condition the name 'elephantiasis'. Fluid collecting around the testis (hydrocele) and passing cloudy urine containing lymphatic fluid (chyluria) may also occur. Diagnosis is by blood films but, in the early stages, antibody tests are used. Treatment is with diethylcarbamazine. Other drugs (e.g. ivermectin, albendazole, and doxycycline) are also used as part of control programmes, but they are less active against the adult worms than against the microfilariae.

Some patients, who usually have few lymphatic features and no microfilariae in the blood, develop a lung problem called *tropical pulmonary eosinophilia* with cough, breathlessness, and wheezing. Diagnosis is made by an antibody test and an abnormally high white blood cell count; response to treatment is good.

River blindness (Onchocerciasis)

Onchocerca volvulus is a filarial infection of the skin and eyes that affects people in West and Central Africa and some parts of South America. In Africa it occurs both in dry savannah and forested areas.

Adult worms live in the deeper skin and connective tissue, mostly within smooth, non-tender nodules, up to 4cm in diameter, often over bony prominences such as the hips, knees, and skull. Several pairs of worms live in each nodule. Microfilariae live in the upper skin layers, where they are taken up by small biting *Simulium* blackflies (see Fig. 5.3.1), which breed in swift-flowing, well-oxygenated streams and rivers. *Simulium* bites during the daytime or at dusk; bites are painful and often numerous.

Heavily infected people develop a disfiguring skin condition called onchodermatitis, with skin thickening, then atrophy and depigmentation. Microfilariae in the eye cause damage to the cornea and also choroidoretinitis at the back of the eye, leading to blindness. Diagnosis is by finding microfilariae in snips of skin. Treatment is with ivermectin, but this must be repeated every 6 months until the worms produce no more microfilariae; nodules containing adult worms can be removed surgically.

Following successful control programmes, infections in travellers are now rare. Itchy rashes on the trunk or limbs may occur a year or more after exposure, and some will experience eye irritation and minute snowflake opacities in the cornea. With proper treatment, lightly infected persons suffer no permanent eye damage. Control measures require regular insecticidal treatment of river breeding sites together with annual iverm-ectin treatment to kill microfilariae. Since adult worms live for up to 15 years, vector control without mass chemotherapy must continue for this long.

African eye worm (Loiasis)

This occurs in the rainforest areas of West and Central Africa. Adult *Loa loa* worms live under the skin. The microfilariae occur in the bloodstream during the daytime to coincide with the biting of the vector *Chrysops*, which resembles a very large, brown horsefly, and inflicts a painful bite. *Chrysops* breeds in the mud of forest pools and is attracted to wood smoke.

The commonest manifestations of infection are *Calabar swellings*—painful red lumps, often several centimetres in diameter, usually on the forearms and wrists. Adult or maturing worms can sometimes be seen migrating across the white of the eye beneath the conjunctiva. This produces severe itching, lacrimation, and transient swelling of the eyelids without permanent eye damage. Diagnosis is made by finding microfilariae in daytime blood films. Treatment is with diethylcarbamazine under supervision as severe allergic complications can occur.

Fig. 5.3.1 Simulium fly (1.5–4mm long).

Box 5.3.1 **Summary of advice to travellers**

- Use insect repellents and bed-nets to reduce the risk
- Symptoms can appear long after leaving endemic areas
- Eosinophilia (p.494) and unusual skin manifestations or tender lymphatic tissues should raise suspicion of filariasis. Early male genital lesions may be wrongly attributed to a sexually transmitted infection
- Diagnosis and treatment require specialist attention.

5.4 Lyme disease

David Wright

The characteristic feature of Lyme disease is an expanding skin rash (erythema migrans), which is often accompanied by headache, muscle pains, joint aches, and low-grade fever. There are sometimes more serious complications involving the nervous system, heart, or joints.

Most cases occur in summer or early autumn. The disease is acquired through the bites of hard ticks. Female ticks bite to obtain blood from man or other mammals to undergo their next phase in development. A few ticks survive the winter and then bite in spring. The causative bacteria, *Borrelia burgdorferi*, reside in the tick's salivary glands, and are transmitted to the victim when the tick bites. To ensure transmission, the tick should remain attached to the host for at least 24 hours. In Europe, and especially in Sweden, an early skin recurrence may appear as a reddish-blue swelling or plaque, called lymphadenosis cutis. These nodules tend to occur over areas of loose skin such as ear lobes, nipples, and scrotum. There are also recurrences many years after the initial rash. Unlike the early skin changes, this late manifestation, termed acrodermatitis chronica atrophicans, tends to result in occlusion of the blood vessels and nerve damage in the locality of the bite. Both these recurrences are found in about 1% of those affected with Lyme disease.

Distribution

There have been more than 200 000 documented cases in the USA since 1980, from almost every state, but the true number of cases is perhaps 10 times that (Map 5.4.1). In the UK there are up to 3000 cases of Lyme disease each year, with about a fifth occurring in travellers from abroad.

Lyme disease is found throughout the northern hemisphere; cases have even been reported from coastal areas of Australia though not Latin America or southern Africa.

The species of tick able to transmit the disease differs slightly with geography: *Ixodes pacificus* being found on the western USA seaboard, while *Ixodes scapularis* (formerly *dammini*) is found in the Atlantic coastal areas of America. The main vector in Europe is *Ixodes ricinus* and in Asia, *Ixodes persulcatus*. Other ticks implicated are *Ixodes hexagonus* (the hedgehog tick), the sheep tick, and *Amblyomma americanum* (the Lone Star tick). Small mammals (such as field mice, voles, and badgers) or birds, particularly or ground-feeding birds, tend to be the repository of the infecting organism. Ticks that usually feed on these species may accidentally bite man or his pets, dogs much more often than cats. Wild deer, whilst carrying large numbers of ticks, tend not to suffer from the disease but, being 'nomadic' animals, tend to, disperse the ticks, and hence the disease, more widely than other animals (see Box 5.4.1). Although mosquitoes and other insects can spread the disease by biting, their role tends to be minimal as disease transmission depends on their mouth parts being transiently infected (like a contaminated needle), unlike ticks where *Borrelia* survive inside their bodies.

The illness

Mercifully, subclinical infections are the rule. Symptoms can begin between three and 32 days after the tick bite (typically after 14 days), but only about 15% of patients remember having been bitten. This is partly because the tick may be too small to be noticed or because with each tick bite, anti-inflammatory, and anaesthetic substances are injected into the victim, so that there is little or no reaction. The ticks are often first observed following their blood meal, when they enlarge, sometimes to the size of a small thumbnail.

The first sign to appear is a red area on the skin surrounding the tick bite. Over the next few days the rash may expand in a circular fashion, the centre of the ring returning to normal skin colour. The rash is usually painless and non-irritating. If left untreated, the rash may resolve in a few

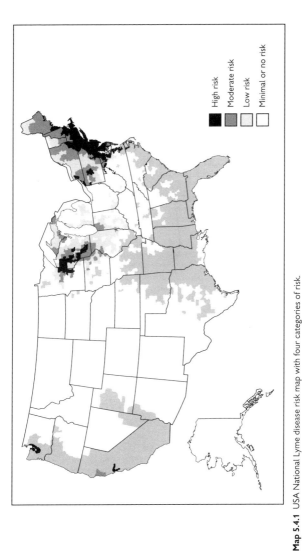

Map 5.4.1 USA National Lyme disease risk map with four categories of risk.
Reproduced from *Morbidity and Mortality Weekly Report (MMWR)*, Issue 48, pp.21–4, published by the Centers for Disease Control and Prevention (CDC).

High risk
Moderate risk
Low risk
Minimal or no risk

Box 5.4.1 **Tick bites and nudity**

In a study published in the *Journal of the American Medical Association*, Dr Henry M. Feder reported unexpectedly low levels of tick bites at a nudist camp in Connecticut. The camp had abundant deer, woods, rocks, and grass, and was deep in the heart of Lyme disease territory. Were there truly not many ticks around? Do deer ticks not like nudists?

Dr Feder went on to probe the undergrowth around the camp: his quest for ticks was successful, lending weight to his theory that ticks prefer to bite under the shelter of clothing. His advice to non-nudists is never to wear shoes without socks, to wear long trousers tucked into socks, and to use plenty of repellent.

weeks or spread for up to a year, with the ring approaching a metre in diameter. Multiple tick bites can cause multiple, often small red circles on the skin—a finding more common in the USA.

In less than a fifth of patients, the rash may be accompanied by mild 'flu-like symptoms, muscle paralysis, particularly on one side of the face (a Bell's-like palsy), and nerve pain in specific areas supplied by the nerves either in the head or body. Rarely, the patient complains of an insidiously developing stiff neck—a sign of chronic meningitis. This may be associated with a degree of unsteadiness brought about by the involvement of the nerves from the brain passing to the cerebellum. In children and the over 60s, attacks of delirium have been recorded. In a smaller number of patients, inflammation of the tendons and joints occurs, particularly of the lower limb, although no joint or tendon is immune. Occasionally, arthritis may persist. In fewer than 1 in 30 patients with a rash, irregularity of the heartbeat may be detected. This may require urgent antibiotic treatment as well as the insertion of a temporary pacemaker. There are many patients who do not have, or fail to notice, any rash and may present with just one complication of Lyme disease. Blood tests like ELISA and immunoblot tests may confirm the diagnosis. These tests may not become positive for 6 weeks from the time that the initial skin signs appear, while supervening antibiotic treatment may prevent these blood tests from ever becoming positive. In endemic areas of Lyme disease, a positive blood test may occur in patients who do not remember exposure to tick bites, or remember having suffered symptoms that could be ascribed to Lyme disease, or who have had the disease many years previously, or who have had a subclinical exposure. Tests employing the cultivation of borrelia or the polymerase chain reaction are not routinely available but can be done on difficult cases in specialist reference laboratories. Other, non-standardized tests are unreliable and may give either false positive or false negative results.

On the Baltic Island of Wisby, some 80% of the population have a positive blood test for Lyme disease, whereas less than 3% give a history of having had the infection. This makes the diagnosis of Lyme disease somewhat questionable without the hallmark of the initial specific rash.

Unfortunately, there are an increasing number of residents in Lyme endemic areas with non-diagnostic general symptoms of Lyme disease like fatigue, fibromyalgia, loss of concentration, and a feeling of 'pins and needles'—all of whom have a positive blood test for Lyme disease but in whom the relationship to the clinical manifestation remains doubtful. In fact, labelling them as suffering from Lyme disease may lead to more appropriate psychiatric or physical treatments being withheld. In early cases of Lyme disease, when the standard blood test may be negative, the polymerase chain reaction on tissue taken from the specific rash or body fluids, other than blood, may sometimes prove helpful in establishing the diagnosis.

Prevention and treatment

In most cases Lyme disease is a self-limiting infection, the condition usually resolving within 3 months. Even when subject to a tick bite, there is less than a one in 50 chance of developing overt disease. The risk can be further reduced if, when entering Lyme disease territory, the traveller tucks trouser legs into socks or wears Wellington boots and long-sleeved shirts. Insect repellents can be used (see Chapter 5.12). Or clothes impregnated with insect repellent can be worn.

Following a visit to a tick-infested area, examine your skin, including above the hairline, as well as your pet's coat for ticks. Removal by application of lighted cigarette stubs is frowned upon by 'Health and Safety', who prefer removal with tweezers. Take care not to leave the head of the tick embedded in the skin.

If antibiotics are required, a course of doxycycline, 100mg twice daily for 10 days, is usually adequate for treatment. Some physicians claim that a prolonged course of 21 days is more effective in preventing long-term complications. There is certainly no reason to give antibiotics for a longer period of time. In children under 12, amoxicillin, 500mg, three times a day for 10 days, is a useful alternative, and in the occasional complicated refractory case a course of ceftriaxone maybe tried. In Scandinavia, a course of penicillin is often preferred. Sometimes, within 4 hr of commencement of treatment, a fever with headache and a rise in temperature is seen, which lasts no longer than a day, occasionally, at the same time, the rash may become more florid (the Jarisch–Herxheimer reaction). The reaction does not usually have any long term consequences and paracetamol 500mg taken by mouth, once only is often adequate in controlling symptoms. If there is a history of tick bite, yet the clinical signs are atypical, it should be remembered that ticks transmit a variety of other diseases that may occur either together with Lyme disease or separately, such as Q fever, babesiosis, ehrlichiosis, or tick-borne virus encephalitis which, being a virus, is resistant to antibiotics. Failure to cure the disease with antibiotics always merits specialist advice.

It is not advisable for people going into Lyme disease areas to take preventive antibiotics. If a prolonged stay in Central Europe is intended, it may be worthwhile to be immunized against tick-borne encephalitis (p.131, p.450), and preventive antibiotics are not normally advised for people who have been bitten by a tick, but have no other symptoms.

5.5 Leishmaniasis

Robert Davidson

Leishmaniasis occurs in Mediterranean countries, the Middle East, India, Nepal, east Africa, and Central and South America. The internal (visceral) form is fatal if untreated; the skin (cutaneous) form is a persistent nuisance; the rare mucocutaneous form is disfiguring. Fortunately, all forms of leishmaniasis are uncommon in travellers.

Deforestation, irrigation, war, and famine have all led to an increase in leishmaniasis, which occurs widely (Maps 5.5.1–5.5.4). Each year, there are about 2 million cases of cutaneous leishmaniasis and about 250 000 cases of visceral leishmaniasis (also called kala-azar). Mucocutaneous leishmaniasis is rare.

What is leishmaniasis?

Leishmania are single-celled microbes that infect macrophage cells in skin, spleen, liver, bone marrow, and lymph glands. They are carried in the salivary glands of sandflies (Fig. 5.5.1), which have themselves become infected when feeding on an infected animal or human. Sandflies do not live on the beach, as one might suppose, but in scrubland, forests, cracks in walls, animal burrows, or termite mounds. They are small (2–3 mm) and beige-coloured, and scarcely noticeable. They fly silently, and their bites may itch but are not painful. They usually bite at night, sometimes indoors, but more often outdoors.

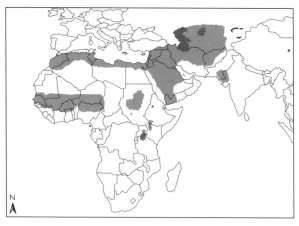

Map 5.5.1 Geographical distribution of Old World cutaneous leishmaniasis due to *L. major*.

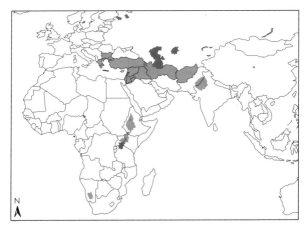

Map 5.5.2 Geographical distribution of Old World cutaneous leishmaniasis due to *L. tropica* and related species and *L. aethiopica*.

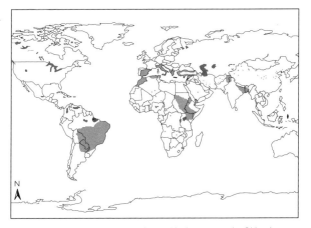

Map 5.5.3 Geographical distribution of visceral leishmaniasis in the Old and New world.

Map 5.5.4 Geographical distribution of cutaneous and mucocutaneous leishmaniasis in the New World.

Fig. 5.5.1 *Phlebotomus* sandfly (2–5mm long).

Wild or domestic animals are carriers of certain species of *Leishmania*, with which man is 'accidentally' infected. Other species affect mainly humans, and are transmitted from man to man in towns or rural areas.

Cutaneous leishmaniasis (European, African, and Asian forms)

This consists of one or several persistent nodules or ulcers, commonly on the face or limbs. They gradually form about 2–8 weeks after being bitten. Ulcers are relatively painless and not particularly pus-producing. Without treatment, lesions usually heal in about 3–12 months, leaving a scar.

An urban species (*Leishmania tropica*) is common in cities such as Kabul, Aleppo, Baghdad, Damascus, and Tehran. Protection against this is by sleeping in an air-conditioned room or under an impregnated mosquito net, and using repellents in the evenings. A rural species (*Leishmania major*) is common in Israel, Jordan, Libya, Tunisia, Algeria, Morocco, Iran, Iraq, and some parts of Saudi Arabia. When camping in the desert, keep your tent away from gerbil burrows.

The transmission season in Europe and the Middle East is the summer. Rarely, the disease is acquired in regions bordering the Mediterranean, including the islands.

Small ulcers may heal naturally, but some types require injections of an antimonial drug; an oral drug, miltefosine, is an alternative.

Visceral leishmaniasis (kala-azar)

This is widespread in north-eastern India, especially Bihar state, and in Bangladesh and Nepal. There have been epidemics in India and Sudan, and it remains common in parts of Sudan, Ethiopia, western Kenya, eastern Uganda, and southern Somalia. In all these areas, the *Leishmania donovani* parasite is transmitted from person to person by sandflies.

In Brazil, and countries bordering the Mediterranean, dogs are commonly infected with *Leishmania infantum* (called *Leishmania chagasi* in the Americas). Visceral leishmaniasis is spread by the bite of an infected sandfly—close contact with pets does not spread *Leishmania*. Canine cases outnumber human cases by thousands to one.

In visceral leishmaniasis, the parasites spread internally, to the spleen, bone marrow, liver, and lymph glands. The symptoms start weeks to months after being bitten: fever, weight loss, abdominal discomfort, weakness, and anaemia. The spleen, liver and, sometimes, lymph glands become enlarged. *When it occurs in travellers, it is usually suspected as being lymphoma or leukaemia, which it mimics.*

Fortunately, bone-marrow examination shows *Leishmania* parasites, not malignancy. There is also a fairly reliable blood test (serology). Visceral leishmaniasis in Europe and South America chiefly affects those with HIV or young children and is uncommon in travellers. *The illness may begin up to two years after visiting the endemic area*—unwell travellers should remind their doctors of this.

Treatment is effective: the best modern drug is liposomal amphotericin B (AmBisome). In Africa, Brazil, and India, older pentavalent antimony drugs, sodium stibogluconate (Pentostam) and meglumine antimoniate (Glucantime), are still used. In India, miltefosine is an alternative.

Occasionally, the disease has been spread by needles shared between HIV-infected drug users; very rarely by blood transfusion; and even more rarely from mother to unborn child.

American cutaneous leishmaniasis and mucocutaneous leishmaniasis

Travellers to Belize, and other parts of rural Central and South America, may contract cutaneous leishmaniasis from a sandfly bite. The parasites here are *Leishmania mexicana* and *Leishmania braziliensis*. Lesions will usually heal spontaneously over several months. The disease caused by *Leishmania braziliensis* can progress to, or recur as, mucocutaneous leishmaniasis. In this disfiguring disease the nose and lips become swollen and over the course of months or years the lesions spread along the cartilage of the nose. For this reason only, cutaneous leishmaniasis from the Americas needs specialist attention and careful treatment. Fortunately, mucocutaneous leishmaniasis is rare.

Box 5.5.1 **Summary of advice for travellers**

- Awareness of leishmaniasis is very low outside the regions where the disease is a problem. However, the disease is unpleasant and efforts to prevent it are worthwhile
- The key precaution is to try to avoid sandfly bites by using an impregnated mosquito net, indoors or outdoors. Sandflies bite in darkness, and although small enough to pass through the mesh of a net, they will not do so if it is impregnated with permethrin, deltamethrin, or lambda cyhalothrin. Permethrin can also be impregnated into clothing
- Repellents containing DEET (see Chapter 5.12) should be applied liberally.

5.6 Sleeping sickness (African trypanosomiasis)

Richard Dawood

Sleeping sickness (or human African trypanosomiasis) occurs in some 36 countries in sub-Saharan Africa (Map 5.6.1). It is transmitted by tsetse flies (Fig. 5.6.1). It declined greatly during the 1960s, but in recent years large epidemics have recurred in Central Africa, largely as the result of instability and unrest, there are few surveillance programmes in place, and the current scale of the problem is not accurately known. In East and southern Africa, travellers to game parks are potentially at risk from this infection, which is both difficult to diagnose and complicated to treat. A small number of recent cases have been recorded in European travellers (on average, about one case per year in travellers returning to the UK,

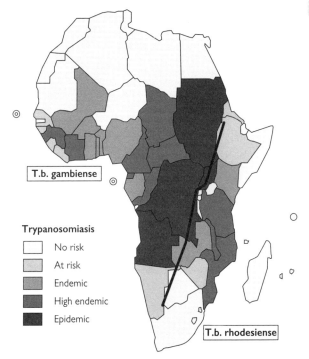

Map 5.6.1 Distribution of Gambiense and Rhodesians sleeping sickness in sub-Saharan Africa.

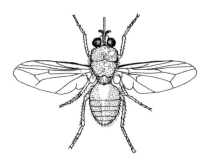

Fig. 5.6.1 Tsetse fly (female, 6–15mm long).

and the same rate in travellers returning to the USA). Trypanosomiasis is also an economically important infection of cattle in much of Africa.

The disease

What causes it?

Sleeping sickness is caused by a motile, single-celled organism. Infection is acquired from the bite of a tsetse fly. There may be redness and swelling at the site of the bite, followed by illness with fever, and eventually the organisms enter the central nervous system where they cause fatal encephalitis. The disease gets its name from the characteristic sleep disorder where individuals fall asleep at inappropriate times.

How is it spread?

Sleeping sickness is spread by tsetse flies infected with trypanosomes. The flies are sturdy, about the size of a housefly, and the bite is painful. Characteristically, they rest with the wings folded across their back. Tsetse flies require shade and humidity and tend to occur in association with game animals in East Africa and along rivers and lake shores in Central and West Africa. They are attracted to moving vehicles, the scent of animals, and contrasting colours.

What are the features of the disease?

There are two forms of the disease: one type occurs in rural areas of West and Central Africa, and the other in East and southern Africa. The infection is fatal if not treated.

West and Central Africa (Gambian trypanosomiasis)

In Central and West Africa sleeping sickness is initially a chronic disease, with mild early symptoms, but leading to extensive brain disease after months or years. It may be difficult to diagnose. People are infected in rural areas, close to water, and all age groups and both sexes are affected. Over the past decade there has been a dramatic increase in this infection especially in rural areas of Central African countries including Congo–Zaire, southern Sudan, northern Uganda, and Angola, partly as a result of civil disturbance. There are believed to be several hundred thousand people currently infected. Longer-term visitors to rural areas and aid workers are more at risk than tourists or short-term visitors.

East and southern Africa (Rhodesian trypanosomiasis)

The infection in East and southern Africa is much more acute and presents as a severe febrile illness, often with a lesion at the site of the tsetse bite (a chancre), severe fever, and early onset of central nervous system abnormalities. This form of trypanosomiasis occurs in game animals and tourists are at special risk visiting game parks and game lodges. Recent epidemics of this form of the infection have occurred in Busoga, in south-eastern Uganda.

The diagnosis

Sleeping sickness should be considered in travellers who have recently visited game parks in East or southern Africa (including Kenya, Tanzania, Zambia, and Zimbabwe) and who have a severe fever. A characteristic inflamed lesion at the site of the tsetse bite (the chancre) may be present. They will give a history of tsetse bites whilst viewing game and may have a skin rash.

Sleeping sickness should also be considered in travellers from rural parts of Central or West Africa, who may present with a more chronic febrile illness or symptoms suggestive of an infection of the central nervous system, including the typical sleep disorders, behavioural changes, or neurological abnormalities. This form of infection may not present for months or even years after periods of travel. Among travellers, it is more common in those working for extended periods in endemic areas.

The parasite can be detected in the blood, though often only in small numbers. A range of concentration techniques may be required to establish the diagnosis, especially with the Gambian form. Progression of the infection to involve the brain can be confirmed by examining the cerebrospinal fluid.

Treatment

The treatment options for trypanosomiasis are limited to the drugs suramin, melarsoprol, pentamidine, and eflornithine (a drug used in some western countries for its effects against unwanted facial hair!). All need careful specialist prescription and monitoring, and have high side effects profiles.

Prevention

The main preventive measure is to avoid being bitten by tsetse flies. Use plenty of DEET-based repellents, treat clothing with insecticide (permethrin), and carry a knock-down insecticide when travelling in safari vehicles.

5.7 Chagas disease (South American trypanosomiasis)

Chris Schofield

Chagas disease is widespread in Latin America and parts of the southern USA (Map 5.7.1). About 8 million people may be infected. Infection can be serious, but large-scale control campaigns have greatly reduced the risk of transmission. Travellers to rural areas may be at risk if they sleep in huts

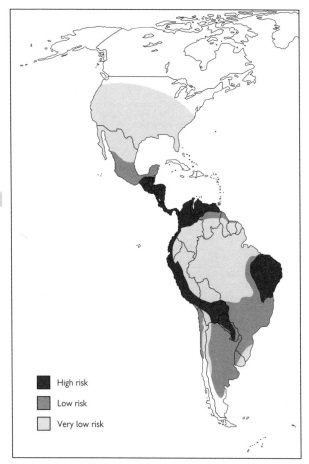

Map 5.7.1 Approximate distribution of the insect vectors of Chagas disease, shaded to indicate relative risk of Chagas disease transmission.

infested with the insect transmitters. Less often, transmission can follow blood transfusion from infected donors or eating raw or undercooked small mammals, especially opossums, infected with the parasite.

What is Chagas disease and how is it spread?

Named after the Brazilian clinician Carlos Chagas, who first described it in 1909, it is caused by a microscopic protozoan parasite, *Trypanosoma cruzi*,

Fig. 5.7.1 Triatoma (average size of adult is 2.4cm long; species range from 5mm to 4.5cm).

which is mainly transmitted by blood-sucking insects known as cone-nosed bugs or kissing bugs. These have a variety of local names (e.g. 'vinchucas' in the southern cone countries, 'barbeiros' in Brazil, 'chirima-chas' in Peru, 'chinchorros' in Ecuador, 'pitos' or 'chipos' in Colombia and Venezuela). Most bug species live in sylvatic habitats, associated with small nest-building mammals or birds, but a few have adapted to live in rural dwellings. These domestic species emerge from crevices at night to suck blood from sleeping occupants. Their bite is painless and often unremarked. All developmental stages of kissing bugs, including small wing-less nymphs, will feed on vertebrate blood and can transmit *T. cruzi* (see Fig. 5.7.1).

T. cruzi is not transmitted by the bite of the insects, but instead by their faeces, which are often deposited while feeding. Transmission is inefficient: on average, more than 1000 contacts with infected bugs are required to produce one new human infection.

The parasite is readily transmitted by blood transfusion from infected donors (see also Chapter 13.6). Most Latin American countries now have strict screening procedures, but transfusions are still a risk. Transmission has also been reported from drinking local fruit or cane juices contaminated by bugs falling into the crushing machines.

Symptoms

The infection proceeds through two phases. The initial acute phase lasts up to 8 weeks. There may be no obvious symptoms, but fever and lymph node swellings are common. The acute phase declines as parasites move from the bloodstream to cells of most of the vital organs—particularly heart muscle. The parasites reproduce inside the cells, eventually producing chronic tissue destruction. The infection may remain without symptoms, but about 30% of infected people develop serious cardiac lesions, particularly arrhythmias and conduction difficulties, often 10–20 years after the initial infection. Some parasite strains can also cause important intestinal problems (e.g. megaoesophagus, megacolon).

Prevention and personal protection

In general, Chagas disease represents a very low risk to travellers. At highest risk are those who sleep in infested rural dwellings. Ask locals if kissing bugs are present: if in doubt, sleep in the middle of the room away from the walls and check the bed for insects. Most importantly, check in the morning for any dark deposits that may be bug faeces, and wash these away with alcohol or soap and water.

Unscreened blood transfusions should be avoided (Chapter 13.6).

Check-up

During the early acute phase, parasites can usually be detected microscopically in the blood, but may not remain apparent during the chronic phase. Instead, serological tests are needed—they are highly accurate and advisable for anyone who has received a blood transfusion in Latin America. These tests are also important if you are considering becoming a blood donor, and also for pregnant women, because there is a small risk that the parasite can be passed to the foetus. In such cases, the newborn baby can be treated, with a high chance of eliminating any infection.

After treatment, serological tests should be carried out annually to check that the level of seropositivity is declining. Seronegativity may take decades to return.

5.8 Plague

Tom Solomon

Perhaps remarkably, the ancient scourge of plague is still with us, though the risk to travellers is extremely small.

Few diseases strike more fear into the hearts of men, and few organisms have affected the globe with such devastating consequences. Although a disease comparable with plague was described in the eleventh century BC, the first of three pandemics occurred in the sixth century AD. The second, known as the 'Black Death', wiped out between a third and a quarter of the European population during the fourteenth century. By now, the communicable nature of the disease was known, as was the importance of overcrowding and poor sanitation, but not the cause. The third pandemic began in China in the mid-nineteenth century.

By 1894 it reached Hong Kong, where the causative organism, a gram-negative cocco-bacillus, was first identified. Who deserves the credit for this has been one of the most prolonged controversies in medical history. Although Kitasato, a Japanese investigator, laid claim to the discovery for many years, the taxonomic name of the bacillus, *Yersinia pestis*, reflects that ultimately a Frenchman, Alexandre Yersin, was credited with it. It was subsequently shown that the disease spread to man from infected rats, via the bites of fleas. The flea's proventriculus (gullet) becomes blocked by the replicating bacterium, and it thus regurgitates the organism whilst feeding on mammals.

Epidemiology

During the third plague pandemic the disease reached South America, Africa, and Asia. Although urban plague was largely controlled by sanitary measures, plague spread to forest rodents (rats, rabbits, squirrels, chipmunks) and has persisted as a rural disease ever since. In its natural cycle, the bacterium is transmitted between these rodents, which remain relatively free from symptoms. Sporadic human cases occur when individuals encroach on this cycle and are bitten by infected fleas.

Perhaps because of climate and availability of host animals, the flea population can suddenly grow and the bacterium is spread to urban rats, particularly the black rat (*Rattus rattus*) and the brown sewer rat (*Rattus norvegicus*), which act as *amplifying* hosts. In these rats infection causes severe illness, and as they die, the fleas jump to new hosts, including humans. Thus, urban plague epidemics are associated with large dead rats, and 'rat fall' is been recognized as an indicator of impending plague.

Typically, the number of cases reported to the WHO each year is 1000–3000. Areas affected include China, Southeast Asia (especially Vietnam), much of Africa, South America (especially Peru), and India, where there was a large outbreak in 1994 (see Map 5.8.1). There were also a handful of cases in Eastern Europe and North America.

Clinical features

Three main clinical syndromes are recognized: *bubonic plague*, *septicaemic plague*, and *pneumonic plague*. Two to seven days after the bite of an infected flea, patients develop a high fever, rigors, headache, and muscle aches. In bubonic plague, the bacterium moves through the bloodstream to the lymph nodes (usually in the groin), where it causes a painful swelling known as a 'bubo'. Occasional bleeding into the skin causes a patchy dark discolouration (purpura), giving rise to the name 'Black Death'.

In some patients, the bacterium spreads into the rest of the bloodstream, causing septicaemic plague. Patients have fever, malaise, and headaches, and, if untreated, rapidly deteriorate into shock (low blood pressure), dying in a few days.

In other plague patients, the bacteria spread into the lungs to give pneumonic plague. A severe pneumonia develops, with shortness of breath and a cough productive of blood-stained sputum. It is this cough, and in particular droplets infected with bacteria, that are responsible for the direct spread of pneumonic plague between humans. Untreated, pneumonic plague can be rapidly fatal. Persons seemingly fit and well, may be dead within a day—hence the nursery rhyme: 'Ring o' ring o' roses, a pocket full of poses, atishoo, atishoo, we all fall down.'

Diagnosis, treatment, and prevention

Plague is diagnosed by identifying the bacillus in bubo aspirate or sputum and by culturing the organism from these samples and blood cultures.

Surprisingly, given the panic associated with the disease, it is easily treated with antibiotics, so long as they are started early enough. In suspected cases treatment should therefore be started as soon as diagnostic samples have been taken, without waiting for the results. Streptomycin, tetracycline, and

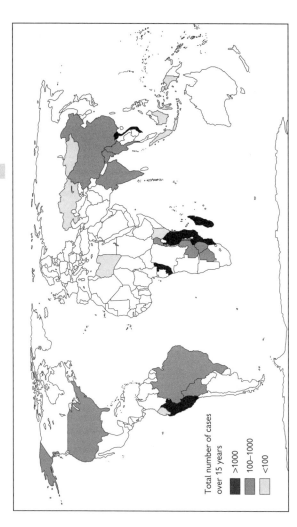

Map 5.8.1 Countries reporting human plague 1983–97.

Total number of cases
over 15 years

>1000
100–1000
<100

chloramphenicol are all effective treatments; streptomycin is not always readily available, so gentamicin is sometimes used. Doxycycline is easily given orally, achieving high serum concentrations. Chloramphenicol is especially useful if high tissue penetration is needed, e.g. in plague meningitis or endocarditis. Treatment is typically 7–10 days. Patients with pneumonic plague should be nursed in isolation, if possible, and prophylaxis with tetracycline is recommended for their close contacts.

Although there is a formalin-inactivated vaccine, this is only given to individuals at an especially high risk of exposure, e.g. laboratory personnel working on the bacterium, or field-workers who come into regular contact with rodent fleas in affected areas. In endemic areas regular insecticide and rodenticide use around the dwelling is recommended. Flea powder should be used on dogs, cats, and other pets that might come into contact with infected rodents. During epidemics, flea and rodent control measures are used to limit the spread of the disease. It is important that the fleas are killed before the rats, so they don't simply jump onto humans.

Box 5.8.1 **Summary of advice for travellers**

Despite the fear associated with it, plague is a relatively rare disease that is easily treatable if caught early. Those going to endemic areas should minimize exposure to fleas from rats, use an insect repellent containing DEET, and seek medical advice early if they develop fever or other symptoms of the disease.

5.9 Typhus: the rickettsial infections

Nick Day

'Typhus' encompasses a range of febrile illnesses caused by arthropod-borne intracellular bacteria grouped in the family *Rickettsiaceae*. They can occasionally be a risk to travellers on walking holidays or to medical aid workers in refugee camps.

Epidemic typhus

Epidemic typhus is a serious illness caused by *Rickettsia prowazeckii*, and is spread by the faeces of the human body louse (inhaled or rubbed into the louse bite). It especially occurs in time of war and social upheaval, in prisons and refugee camps. Huge epidemics occurred in the past, notably decimating Napoleon's army during his invasion of Russia. Hundreds of thousands died of epidemic typhus in Nazi concentration camps during the Second World War. It remains a major public health risk in cooler mountainous areas of the tropics, particularly in crowded refugee camps. An epidemic in Burundi in 1995, at altitudes over 1500m, caused more than 45 000 cases in prisons before spreading to the general population, in which it remains a problem. Other countries recently affected have been Ethiopia, Nigeria, and Peru. Recently, cases have occurred in North America transmitted by ectoparasites of flying squirrels.

Untreated mortality is 10–60%, but early treatment with doxycycline (200mg daily for 3–7 days) will rapidly cure nearly all cases. Control consists of mass treatment with doxycycline (100mg single dose) and vigorous delousing of the populations at risk (e.g. all refugees in a camp) by the provision of clean clothing and the use of dusting with 10% DDT, 1% malathion, or 1% permethrin powder. Potentially exposed aid workers can take doxycycline prophylaxis (100mg daily).

Scrub typhus

Scrub typhus, caused by *Orientia tsutsugamushi* and transmitted by the larval stage of tiny trombiculid mites ('chiggers'), is the world's most common rickettsiosis. Over a billion people are exposed and at least one million cases occur per annum. It is a hazard for travellers to rural Japan, Southeast Asia, the Indian subcontinent and Indian Ocean islands, Papua New Guinea, and North Queensland, particularly to those who spend time in areas of secondary forest. The mites usually feed on rodents, with humans as accidental hosts. Mite bites occur painlessly in the armpits, groins and trouser belt areas, with symptoms arising six to 10 days later with fever, headache, a skin rash and commonly a small painless black necrotic scab (eschar) at the bite site. Regional lymphadenopathy is common. Complications include central nervous system involvement, interstitial pneumonia, jaundice, and renal failure.

Diagnosis is by indirect immunofluorescence assay (IFA) or PCR (neither of which is widely available). Treatment is usually given empirically in suspected cases; doxycycline 200mg daily for 3–7 days, or azithromycin and chloramphenicol as alternatives.

Prevention is helped by clothing impregnation with permethrin, the use of DEET repellents and by wearing jungle boots and gaiters with long trousers. People who have to pass through known infected areas (e.g. soldiers) can also take prophylactic doxycycline, 200mg once weekly.

Murine typhus

Murine or endemic typhus is caused by *Rickettsia typhi* and spread by the bites of rat fleas. It is endemic worldwide, occuring in urban as well as rural settings. Usually a mild illness, it can become severe if untreated. Rash is present in less than half of patients, and unlike in scrub typhus eschars (scabs at the site of the bite) do not occur. Treatment is with doxycycline 100mg twice daily, or in pregnant women chloramphenicol or azithromycin.

Rickettsial spotted fevers (tick typhus)

These febrile illnesses are caused by a large and diverse group of rickettsial species, all of which are transmitted by ticks (with the exception of rickettsialpox, caused by *R. akari*, which is mite-borne, and infection with *R. felis*, which is flea-borne).

Important spotted fever group infections include Mediterranean spotted fever (caused by *R. conorii*, occurs in southern Europe, Africa and parts of Asia); African tick-bite fever (*R. africae*, occurrs in sub-Saharan Africa); and Rocky Mountain spotted fever (*R. rickettsii*, prevalent in the Americas. More than 10 other rickettsial species are known to cause disease in man.

The clinical picture differs between species in terms of severity and features, such as the presence of one or more eschars, but all present with fever, myalgia, and headache 6–10 days after the arthropod bite. Despite the name, the presence of a rash is variable, with some spotted fevers being 'spotless'. Treatment is with doxycycline 200mg/day for 3–7 days. Macrolides and chloramphenicol are suitable alternatives in children and pregnant women.

Box 5.9.1 Summary of advice for travellers

- There are no commercially available vaccines against any variety of typhus
- Anyone walking through tropical bush should inspect their skin carefully at the end of the day. Remove any attached ticks (see Chapter 5.12). Repellents give useful protection
- Seek prompt medical attention for any fever acquired in the tropics.

5.10 Myiasis (maggot infestation)

John Paul

Myiasis is infestation of the body by larvae (maggots) of Diptera (flies). Common causes in travellers are *Dermatobia hominis* (human botfly) and *Cordylobia anthropophaga* (tumbu fly). Both invade healthy skin to cause dermal myiasis.

The human botfly occurs in tropical Latin America. The fly lays her eggs on mosquitoes that transmit the botfly larvae when they bite humans. Mosquito repellents help to prevent botfly infestation. Larvae grow over the course of about 8 weeks. Travellers become aware as the spiny larva develops inside a boil.

After applying petroleum jelly, larvae can be squeezed out through the larva's small breathing hole. Snake venom extractor syringes are reported to serve as useful tools for this purpose. Failure to remove the whole larva can result in bacterial infection or, later, in unsightly skin reaction. Hence, it may be better to remove the larva through a small incision.

The tumbu fly frequents sub-Saharan Africa. Flies lay their eggs on damp sand (or damp clothing). After skin contact, larvae grow over the course of a few weeks to form boils. Larvae may be removed through a simple excision or with care by squeezing after applying petroleum jelly. A hazard of dermal myiasis is secondary bacterial infection.

A more serious threat is wound myiasis. Numerous species of maggot may infest wounds. While some are harmless, others, such as *Cochliomyia hominivorax* (New-World screw-worm), invade living tissues and may be life-threatening. Such cases require urgent surgical removal. Travellers should keep wounds clean and covered.

In sheep-rearing areas, *Oestrus ovis* (sheep nasal botfly) may drop its larvae accidentally into human eyes (ocular myiasis). Patients describe being buzzed by the fly and then a gritty sensation of the tiny larva on the eye surface. The larvae do not develop but cause conjunctivitis and can be removed by an ophthalmologist.

Caution:

In the tropics, laundered clothes should always be ironed.

5.11 Fleas, lice, bugs, scabies, and other creatures

Ian Burgess

Insects and related creatures that feed on humans can be divided into two groups. The first are micro-predators, such as mosquitoes, that may also bite other creatures. The second are totally dependent upon us for food and shelter. Some of these may be encountered in any country, while others may be met only in more tropical climates.

In general, few problems relate directly to hygiene. Insects cause greater problems in developing countries because the environment provides optimal conditions for their survival, while lack of money prevents employment of anything beyond rudimentary pest-control measures.

Fleas

Most flea species are highly host-specific and never bite humans; others bite with varying degrees of avidity. The majority are found only in and around the nests of their preferred hosts so exposure is unlikely unless you sit nearby, disturb the nest, or else the fleas have jumped off a sick animal.

Fleas are mostly small (2–4mm long), brownish, wingless insects that are flattened from side to side. They jump using their powerful hind legs (Fig. 5.11.1). All species have larvae, like caterpillars, that forage on the detritus in the host nest. Some species (e.g. cat fleas) emerge from their pupae when stimulated by vibration.

Tropical rat fleas, and a few other species, are able to transmit bubonic plague (see Chapter 5.8). This disease is common in rural parts of Africa and Asia and parts of North and South America. Most infections occur when people work or play near infected rats' holes (ground squirrels in North America). Epidemic plague only occurs in urban areas when rural rat populations spill over and accidentally infect town rats that are susceptible to the disease.

In some heavily populated urban areas, urban rat fleas may transmit 'murine' (endemic) typhus (see Chapter 5.9). This infection is usually associated either with urban squalor or working in infested warehouses.

Most fleas just cause irritating bites, but the Chigoe fleas (*Tunga penetrans*) are true parasites. These normal-looking fleas are found in dry sandy places in sub-Saharan Africa and Central and South America. After attaching to the skin, the female burrows beneath it and then swells up with eggs to form a sac up to 10mm across. If left untreated, secondary infections, including

Fig. 5.11.1 *Pulex irritans* flea (male, 20.1–50.3mm long).

gangrene, may result in loss of toes. The best protection is to wear fully enclosed shoes or boots at all times when visiting rural communities.

Lice

All lice are highly host-specific and never transfer from animals to humans or *vice versa*, so a puppy crawling with lice is not a risk for anyone touching it. The three kinds of lice found on humans are of worldwide distribution and all feed on blood. All three are spread by direct contact between people. In the case of head lice this requires head to head contact, with crab lice (see pp.309 and 344), which live amongst the hairs on the body, the contact is usually rather more intimate. Clothing, or body lice, live in the seams of clothing and only visit the skin of the body to feed. In the main, lice are harmless and only produce irritant reactions.

Lice are wingless insects that are flattened from top to bottom (Fig. 5.11.2). Those found on humans are all pale in colour, which helps camouflage them. Head and clothing lice are 2–3 mm long and cigar-shaped, but crab lice are triangular with large claws on the rear two pairs of legs.

Clothing lice are the most important because they can spread classic (epidemic) typhus and louse-borne relapsing fever (LBRF). These diseases are currently restricted mainly to tropical upland areas (e.g. Ethiopia, Rwanda, Burundi) and also to parts of southern Sudan. The Himalayas, Atlas, and Andes may also be affected. These are all areas where for economic or cultural reasons people do not completely change their clothing regularly or else do not launder them at high enough temperatures to kill the insects.

Typhus is spread by inhalation or exposure to infected louse droppings that have accumulated in folds of clothing. So it is possible to contract the disease without having lice. LBRF is often only caught by people with lice, because the infective spirochaetes that cause the disease are mostly found in the blood of the louse and only released if the insect is crushed. However, recent research has also found the bacteria in louse faeces.

Quintana fever (trench fever), a major problem in World War I, has reappeared since the 1980s and cases may occur worldwide. The infective organism, related to typhus, produces milder symptoms and is also transmitted in louse faeces.

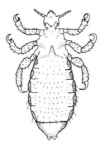

Fig. 5.11.2 *Pediculus humanus*, the human body (or clothing) louse (2–3mm long).

Clothing lice are mainly passed between fully clothed people sleeping huddled together for warmth. It is most unlikely that clothing lice could be contracted simply by sleeping in a bed in which someone else has previously slept.

True bugs

Bugs are flattened insects with a proboscis that is held beneath the front of the body. Most bugs feed on plant sap, but a few suck blood, most notable of which are the bed-bugs and the triatomine or cone-nosed bugs. They feed on a wide range of hosts.

Bed-bugs

Bed-bugs (Fig. 5.11.3) are oval, brown, wingless, and 4–6mm long when fully grown. They live in crevices in furniture and walls and the architrave of doors and windows. They mainly feed at night, although in some cinemas in tropical countries they may bite at any time.

Fig. 5.11.3 *Cimex* bed-bug (male, 4–6mm long).

They are found world-wide and have increased considerably in distribution since about 1990. They are often found in hostels and hotels, and it is not uncommon for insects to hitch a ride in luggage. They are not known to carry disease, but they can be a severe nuisance. The best protection is to use an insecticide-impregnated mosquito net.

Triatomine bugs

These bugs are mainly found in Central and South America. They are common in rural areas and some have adapted to urban life. The insects are relatively large (adult size 15–40mm, depending upon the species). They have narrow heads, brown or black bodies, often ornamented with red or orange at the edges, and large wings. The bugs shelter in crevices in thatch, adobe or broken plaster during the day and bite at night.

Some triatomines are capable of transmitting South American trypanosomiasis (Chagas' disease, see Chapter 5.7). These bugs produce liquid faeces while feeding, and any parasites in the gut are excreted too. The parasites can then enter any scratch in the skin.

Scabies

Scabies is an immune reaction to a parasitic mite (*Sarcoptes scabiei*) that burrows in the skin. It is passed from one person to another by moderately prolonged physical contact. The infection is long-lasting and the intensely itchy symptoms appear only after about 4–8 weeks in most people. Scabies is widespread in developing countries. It is not highly infectious and it is unlikely that travellers will contract the infection from chance contacts. Scabies mites cannot survive away from their host and so the infection is not contracted from bedding.

Biting mites

Several species of mites that normally parasitize animals can bite humans. The most common of these are the red poultry mites that affect birds and rodents (*Dermanyssus* and *Ornithonyssus*). These animals crawl around the host nest and bite anything suitable. They do not live on the body.

In several parts of the world, the larvae of 'harvest' or trombiculid mites can be picked up off long grasses and other vegetation. They do not suck blood but feed off dissolved tissue causing highly itchy lesions that may last for weeks. The biting season is usually limited to the late summer/ early autumn period. In parts of Asia, these mites can carry 'scrub' typhus (see Chapter 5.9) and are sometimes known as 'jiggers'.

Ticks

Ticks of several species can be both biting nuisances and vectors of disease. There are two main groups.

Soft ticks

These mostly feed off birds, but some will attack any suitable host. They usually hide in crevices in buildings or in thatch and crawl out at night to feed. They feed rapidly and leave the host before it rises in the morning. They transmit tick-borne relapsing fever in the Americas, Africa, and Asia.

Hard ticks (Fig. 5.11.4)

Hard ticks are usually picked up from tall grasses or other undergrowth. You may pick up tiny larvae not much bigger than 'full stops on legs',

Fig. 5.11.4 Hard tick (about 3–8mm long, but up to 20mm when engorged with blood).

though as adults they may be 6–8 mm before engorgement. It usually takes about a week for an adult to complete feeding, by which time the tick may have increased in size by three- to five-fold.

Disease transmission by hard ticks happens at any time during feeding. Lyme disease is one of the most widely distributed tick-borne infections, being found in Europe, North America, and parts of Asia (see Chapter 5.4). More serious infections, such as Rocky Mountain spotted fever (see p.133) and the Russian and European tick-borne encephalitides (see p.131) are more restricted in distribution. Ticks also transmit malaria-like organisms between cattle and occasionally these can be transferred to humans.

Some species of tick may release a toxin that affects the central nervous system, resulting in 'tick paralysis'. This occurs most usually when ticks attach to the neck or head. The problem often resolves when the tick is removed.

Any tick attached to the skin should be removed as soon as possible. The most effective way is to grasp the animal close to the skin with fingertips or tweezers, and then lift it away. The animal or wound should be examined to see if any of the mouthparts have been left behind. Any fragments left in the wound should be removed. It is a good idea to flush the wound with hydrogen peroxide or an iodine-based antiseptic. Keep the tick in a sealed container, with a note of the date, for future reference and identification if any disease symptoms appear.

Bites

It is virtually impossible to examine an isolated bite and decide what type of arthropod delivered it. But, it may be possible to make an educated guess about the cause of an itchy reaction from its location on the body and the circumstances in which you acquired it. However, you may not show any reaction to bites for up to 3–4 days after being bitten. It may therefore be impossible to pinpoint what actually bit you.

Fleas

Fleas do not bite humans except in the total absence of their normal host. Consequently, if cats live in the house there will be fleas at some time.

Similarly, if there are rat holes near where you sit for your lunch, there will be some rat fleas. Most fleas do not jump high nor crawl upwards very far, so bites are likely to be around the lower legs. The only exception to this is bird fleas entering rooms from nests in roof voids, when they bite the head and shoulders as they fall onto sleeping persons.

Fleas do not usually hide in fabrics. It is, therefore, normally possible to see them hopping about if you disturb them by banging around along the junctions of walls and floor in a room.

Bed-bugs and triatomine bugs

These usually bite whilst you sleep. The most likely places to be bitten are the face, shoulders, arms and legs, where these protrude from the bed clothes. These bugs all defecate whilst feeding, or soon after. This black liquid material may be found dried onto the skin, bedding, or around the entrance to the cracks where the insects shelter.

Lice

Contrary to popular opinion, the bites of lice often do not itch much. Clothing lice cause more irritation and are difficult to find but, since they congregate in the seams of clothing, most bites are likely to be in the vicinity of these clusters and louse eggs will also be found there.

None of the human lice is able to survive away from its host for more than a few hours. So it is unlikely that any of them can be acquired other than through close physical contact with an infested person. Despite much popular anecdote that lice can be transmitted via objects such as combs, bed linen, and toilet seats, there is no scientific evidence to support it.

Scabies

Scabies is characterized by an intense itch that is worse at night or after clothing has been removed. The first physical symptom is a rash that appears around the midriff and down the insides of the thighs. This is away from where any mites may be found, which is often on the hands and arms. If scabies is contracted in a tropical climate it is more likely that the mites may also spread to the head than would be the case in cooler conditions.

Biting mites and soft ticks

These are virtually never seen and identifying them as a source of irritation is often largely circumstantial, except in the case of the trombiculids, which leave a characteristic dark scar (eschar) at the bite site. Similarly, soft ticks may come and go without leaving a sign.

Hard ticks

These are usually discovered by their hosts only a short time before they are due to drop off, when fully engorged. Subsequent to dropping off there is usually little to see apart from a reddish area with a small puncture in the middle. It is good practice, therefore, in an area known to have ticks, to use a repellent product, to wear long trousers, and to tuck them into socks to prevent the animals climbing up the legs. See also Chapter 5.4.

Treatment

Recommended treatments for the various types of bites are summarized in Table 5.11.1.

Table 5.11.1 Treatment for insect bites and parasitic arthropods

Problem	Treatment	Method of application
Insect bites: fleas, bed-bugs, mites; also mosquitoes, midges etc.	Topical creams or lotions: dilute ammonia (Afterbite), antihistamines, hydrocortisone 1%.	Dab or spread on affected parts as soon as symptoms are experienced. Repeat application once or twice only. If symptoms persist seek medical advice.
Head lice	Topical lotion: [dimeticone 4%, Hedrin (EU, AU, Tk, Is]; [malathion 0.5%, Ovide (USA)]; crème rinse [permethrin 1%, Nix (worldwide)]	Apply lotion to dry hair, leave minimum 8 hours, then wash. Apply créme rinse to damp hair, leave 10mins, rinse. Apply pyrethrum shampoo to dry hair, leave 10mins, add water, lather, rinse. In all cases repeat treatment after 7 days
Crab lice	Topical cream: [permethrin 5%, Lyclear dermal cream (UK), Elimite (USA), other brand names elsewhere].	Apply to whole body below neck.
Clothing lice	Hot laundering or drying of clothes. Hot pressing of seams. Dry cleaning	Wash clothes in hot 55°C water (too hot to keep hands in) for at least 15mins. Alternatively tumble dry on hottest setting for 15mins or dry in full tropical sun. Rotate complete sets of clothing so no cross-contamination at 1–2 week intervals. Do not use insecticides on the person
Scabies	Topical cream: [permethrin 5% cream, Lyclear dermal cream (UK), Elimite (USA), other brand names elsewhere]; lotion [malathion 0.5% aqueous liquid Derbac-M (UK), Filvit (Sp)]; or suspension [benzyl benzoate, Ascabiol (EU)].	Apply to whole body below neck. Benzyl benzoate requires 3 applications over 3 days. Repeat other preparations after 7 days
Ticks	Physical removal (keep the tick for reference in case of disease).	Hold the tick firmly close to the skin, press, twist slightly and then remove with a twisting action. Treat the wound with a topical antiseptic e.g. iodine. If inflammation occurs or other disease symptoms follow seek medical advice

5.12 Personal protection against insect pests

Ian Burgess

Many serious diseases in the tropics and elsewhere are spread by insects. Personal protection against insect bites is thus an important health precaution for travellers. Remember, though, that insects are not just a problem in hot countries: the nuisance of biting insects can be at least as great, or even greater, in the arctic summer as it is in the tropics.

Several types of insect—as well as related creatures like ticks and mites—obtain all their food by sucking blood from humans or animals, i.e. 'biting'. In the flying insects that bite, including mosquitoes, the females require a blood meal in order to produce each batch of eggs. (See Fig. 5.12.1 for method of distinguishing male and female mosquitoes.)

The irritation and discomfort that insect bites cause is due to a sensitization reaction to saliva introduced by the insect during blood-sucking. Bites in order to feed should be distinguished from the stings of bees, wasps, or ants, whose function is to drive away intruders approaching their nests (see Chapter 6); and the bites of spiders or centipedes, which are for immobilizing prey. The severity of skin reaction in different people to bites and stings varies greatly, and people also differ widely in their apparent attraction to biting insects. (For treatment, see pp.164 and 465).

Biting insects are attracted to warmth at close range. At longer range, different species of insect are attracted to different degrees by carbon dioxide in the breath, and by components of body odour. The dangerous African mosquito, *Anopheles gambiae*, and the tropical house mosquito, *Culex quinquefasciatus*, are both attracted by foot odour caused by bacterial action on sweat. If this is washed off with anti-bacterial soap, the mosquitoes simply bite any exposed warm skin.

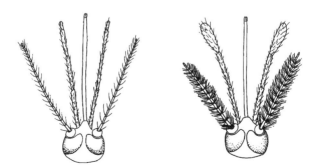

Fig. 5.12.1 Heads of female (left) and male (right) *Anopheles* mosquitoes. Unlike the females, male mosquitoes do not bite and can be recognized by their bushy antennae.

Diseases spread by insects

Insect-borne diseases are important health hazards that are mostly found in the tropics. However, people in Europe and North America have recently become more aware of diseases transmitted by ticks and mosquitoes, partly because of the spread of tick-borne infections such as Lyme disease (Chapter 5.4), and tick-borne encephalitis (Chapter 5.2) over wider areas and into regions where more people may be exposed, and partly because two mosquito-borne infections—West Nile fever (Chapter 5.2) in North America and chikungunya virus in Italy—have made headlines due to the numbers of people affected. It is because insects and ticks have the habit of feeding on blood that the viruses, bacteria, protozoa, or worms responsible for causing the different diseases can be transported from the bloodstream of one victim to another.

Some ticks and insects hatch from their eggs already infected with viruses or the larger organisms called *Rickettsiae* (see Chapter 5.9), which can cause human disease, but this is the exception rather than the rule. Most insects become infected when biting an infected individual. The infection then develops inside the insect and is passed on to someone else during a subsequent feed or, with some diseases, by defecation on to the skin.

Table 5.12.1 gives a summary of the commoner biting insects and the diseases they may carry. The list of diseases may appear daunting, but the only ones commonly contracted by visitors to the tropics are malaria (see Chapter 5.1) and, in certain places, dengue (see Chapter 5.2), chikungunya virus (Chapter 5.2), and cutaneous leishmaniasis (see Chapter 5.5). Of these, malaria presents by far the most serious risk. The other diseases need be considered mainly by travellers who may be living under local conditions, and may spend time in tropical villages, urban slums, or refugee camps. In such cases it would be wise to take local advice about the particular risks and possible counter-measures.

Insects spread many diseases for which drug treatment is difficult, dangerous, or non-existent, and for which we do not yet have vaccines. Prevention of insect bites is therefore the single most sensible and effective precaution a traveller can take to avoid these diseases.

Protection from insect bites outdoors

Quite apart from the hazard of disease, insect bites themselves can be more than a trivial nuisance in some places—in Howrah, near Kolkata, and parts of Dhaka, 500 bites by *Culex* mosquitoes per person per night (about one a minute throughout the night) are usual—and in such situations few visitors would need encouragement to take measures for personal protection.

Repellents

A chemical repellent is the best, and perhaps *only* suitable personal protection against outdoor biting insects. As far as is known, repellents act by making you taste unpleasant and possibly by interfering with the sense organs with which insects locate their victims. Most of the commercially available insect repellent preparations contain diethyltoluamide (commonly known as 'DEET' or DET), p-menthane-3,8-diol (present in oil

Table 5.12.1 Insects, mites, and ticks that bite or burrow in the skin, and risk of disease transmission in different tropical and subtropical areas (also some parts of Europe and N. America in the case of two tick-borne and one Culex-borne diseases). Risk of disease transmission: x = slight risk; xx = moderate risk; xxx = high risk

Pest	Rough guide to identification of adult	Time and place of biting or burrowing	Disease	Africa	Asia	Americas	Western Pacific
Mosquitoes: Anopheles	Head and body in straight line and at an angle to surface (Figure 5.1.2)	Night; indoors or out; mainly rural	Malaria	xxxx	xx	x	xx
			Filariasis	x			x
Culex	Body parallel to surface, head bent down, whining flight; dull brown (Figure 5.1.2)	Evening and night; indoors or out; urban or rural	Filariasis	x	x	x	x
			Encephalitis		x	x	
			West Nile fever		xx	x	
			Chikungunya virus		xx		
Aedes	Body shape as for Culex; but tropical species are black and white (Figure 5.2.1)	Day; indoors or out; urban or rural	Dengue	x	xx	x	x
			Yellow fever	x		x	
			Filariasis	x			
			Chikungunya virus				
Mansonia	As Culex; but patterned wings and legs	Night; outdoors; rural	Filariasis		x		
Tsetse flies	Brown fly with proboscis projecting in front of head (Figure 5.6.1)	Day; outdoors; rural; tropical Africa only	Sleeping sickness	x			

(Continued)

Table 5.12.1 (Contd.)

Pest	Rough guide to identification of adult	Time and place of biting or burrowing	Disease	Africa	Asia	Americas	Western Pacific
Blackflies	1.5–4 mm; stout and black with humped body (Figure 5.3.1)	Day; outdoors; rural	Onchocerciasis	×		×	
Phlebotomine sandflies	Tiny hairy flies (Figure 5.5.1)	Evening; indoors or out; rural or urban	Leishmaniasis	×	×	×	
			Sandfly fever	×	×	×	
			Bartonellosis			×	
Biting midges	Tiny flies with spotted wings	Evening; outdoors; rural	No significant human disease—only nuisance				
Gadflies, horseflies, stable-flies	As large or larger than house-fly; fast flying	Day; outdoors; rural	Loiasis	×			
Ticks	Eight-legged creatures which attach tightly to the skin and swell up with blood to pea size (Figure 5.11.4)	Day or night; cling to long grass or hide on cave floors and attach to passers-by or sleepers	Relapsing fever	×		×	×
			Typhus	×		×	×
			Lyme disease[1]				
			Encephalitis[2]				
Bed-bugs	1 cm; brown beetle-like; but wingless (Figure 5.11.3)	Night; in beds	No proven disease transmission—only a nuisance				

Triatomine bugs	1–4cm; cone-like head; long legs (Figure 5.7.1)	Night; in beds	Chagas disease			X	
Fleas	2–3mm; brown; flattened sideways; run and jump (Figure 5.11.1)	Night or day; indoors or out	Bubonic plague	X	X		
Lice	2–3mm; cream or brown; claws often visible; flattened top to bottom; crawl (Figure 5.11.2)	Night or day; on body hair or clothes for their whole life cycle	Typhus		X		
			Relapsing fever	X	X	X	
Tumbu fly	9–12mm; robust; yellow-brown; non-biting fly	Larvae attach to clothing while it is being dried on the ground and burrow into skin (p.385)	Larva creates a large boil	X			
Mites	Tiny eight-legged creatures	Climb on to skin from undergrowth or from other people and cling to or burrow in skin	Typhus	X	X		X
			Scabies	X	X		X

Notes: 1. Northeast USA and Europe, 2. East and Central Europe.

of lemon eucalyptus), or hydroxymethyl isobutyl piperidine (picaridin or icaridin). These preparations come as lotions, sticks, gels, creams, or in aerosol cans or pump-action dispensers.

DEET is harmful to some hard plastics and paint, causes a stinging sensation if it gets into the eyes, and tastes unpleasant: it should be applied with care. Conventional toxicity tests when DEET first came on to the market in the 1950s were reassuring, and DEET has been used without harm by millions of people. More recently, however, occasional reports have appeared of serious reactions in a few individuals. Anyone who suspects an adverse reaction to DEET should stop using it immediately and seek medical advice.

DEET is reputed to be effective against most free-flying biting insects, although the dose required may depend on the species of insect.

Clothing treatment

When applied to the skin, DEET remains effective for only a few hours. However, when impregnated into cotton (not synthetic) material it remains effective for several weeks, if the material is kept in a plastic bag or tin when not in use. The chances of an adverse skin reaction are presumably much reduced if DEET is impregnated into clothing rather than applied direct to the skin.

Clothing can be impregnated with the pyrethroid insecticide, permethrin, by the same method as treatment of bed-nets (see p.172). Studies in the USA showed that such treated clothing, plus DEET-treated skin, reduced mosquito biting more than either method on its own. Data are also available from the Colombian army using permethrin-treated uniforms and from Afghanistan using permethrin-treated Islamic shawls (chaddurs) and bed-sheets. These data show significant reductions in the risk of both malaria and cutaneous leishmaniasis when universal usage of these materials was backed up by military discipline or strong religious traditions.

When one is sitting on a chair, most mosquito bites occur on the ankles or feet. Cotton anklets (ankle bands), 10 cm wide and each impregnated with 4mL DEET, have been found to give 80–85% reduction in biting by several species of tropical night-biting mosquitoes. One impregnation remains effective for several weeks if the anklets are kept sealed up when not in use. One can make anklets for oneself or purchase ready-impregnated sets.

Alternative repellents

Citronella oil is distilled from a tropical grass and is used as a soap perfume. It has long been sold as an insect repellent but does not remain effective for as long as DEET and is no longer approved as a repellent in the European Union. However, p-methane-3,8-diol—an extract of lemon eucalyptus—appears to be as long-lasting a repellent as DEET; unlike DEET, it does not attack plastics, and some people prefer its lemony smell to the less agreeable smell of DEET.

Mosquitoes tend to be diverted away from a person wearing a repellent (or naturally unattractive to mosquitoes) towards a nearby person not using repellent (or naturally more attractive to mosquitoes). This might suggest that the best protection would be to sleep with someone more attractive to mosquitoes than yourself! (See Box 5.12.1.)

Box 5.12.1 **Methods that don't work: buzzers and vitamins**

'Repellents' that don't repel are dangerous, because they not only fail to give protection, but they also promote a false sense of security.

- Buzzers which are advertised as repelling mosquitoes have been repeatedly shown to be completely useless because female mosquitoes, the ones that bite, are unable to detect sound
- Taking large doses of B vitamins is believed by some to make one repellent to mosquitoes, but two separate studies have failed to confirm this. High doses of some vitamins can result in toxic effects
- Eating garlic has also been claimed to offer protection, but there is no evidence to support this, and it must be remembered that in many countries where mosquitoes are a nuisance and transmit disease, garlic is used extensively in the diet of the local people, who still get bitten!

Clothing

Long sleeves and long trousers have for many years been recommended to be worn after dark to minimize the risk of mosquito bites. Canvas mosquito boots can be purchased that make it impossible for mosquitoes to bite the ankles. Denim jeans are thick enough to be impenetrable to the proboscis of blackflies, which prefer to attack the lower legs. Blue clothing is said to be very attractive to tsetse flies and should be avoided in the tsetse-infested areas of Africa.

However, the frequently-given advice to avoid dark-coloured clothing to prevent mosquito bites is not well-founded, since mosquitoes respond more to olfactory than to visual stimuli, and most bite at night when colouring is obscured.

Protection from insect bites indoors

In addition to the repellents already described, several other useful counter-measures can be employed when the 'target area' is confined to a house or hotel room.

Tight closure of well-fitting windows keeps out most mosquitoes but would be an uncomfortable proposition in a hot climate unless the room is air-conditioned. Ceiling fans help to distract the blood-seeking flight of weak fliers such as phlebotomine sandflies but do not deter mosquitoes.

Screens

Windows kept open for ventilation should be screened: fibreglass netting coated with PVC is more durable, more easily fitted, and less expensive than wire netting. The netting should have six or seven threads per centimetre width to keep out mosquitoes and should be closed before sunset, when *Culex* and *Anopheles* mosquitoes become active. Similar netting should be used to keep mosquitoes from laying eggs in domestic water containers, in which their larvae could flourish. In cities such as Mumbai the screening of roof water tanks, etc. has been a strictly enforced legal requirement to prevent the breeding of the urban malaria mosquito *Anopheles stephensi* and the dengue-carrying mosquito *Aedes aegypti*. The screening of vent pipes and other apertures to cesspits, septic tanks, and pit latrines helps to prevent the mosquito *Culex quinquefasciatus* from breeding in these collections of polluted water, to which it is attracted. A 1cm thick floating layer of expanded polystyrene beads (as used in the manufacture of packing material) is highly effective in preventing mosquito breeding and lasts for years in such sites.

Sprays, coils, and vaporizing mats

Screening windows is seldom completely effective in keeping mosquitoes out of rooms, so other lines of defence may also be needed. Aerosol spray cans of insecticide are available in many tropical countries. They usually contain pyrethroids, which are synthetic near-relations of the natural product pyrethrum and are very safe, although they should not be used over uncovered food. They do not harm pets or domestic animals.

Air passengers from the tropics may notice the aircraft being sprayed after take-off. This is a reasonable precaution as almost every year there are malaria cases near European airports that are attributed to infected mosquitoes arriving from the tropics on improperly sprayed aircraft. (A summary of disinsection policies for various countries can be found at ℜ http://ostpxweb.dot.gov/policy/safetyenergyenv/disinsection.htm)

Aerosols are good for clearing out mosquitoes that are lurking in a room before one goes to bed, but they have no residual effect on mosquitoes that enter later on during the night. The old-fashioned, but often still effective, way of dealing with these insects is to light a slow-burning 'mosquito coil' which smokes gently, giving off a vapour of pyrethrum or pyrethroid insecticide for 6–8 hours. Coils are available cheaply in many tropical countries. Local advice should be sought about which brands to buy because some have been shown to contain no insecticide. Always check to see if the coils you have bought actually work against the mosquitoes invading your room.

A more modern version of the same idea is a small mains-operated heating plate that slowly vaporizes insecticide from a mat (or tablet). They are probably more effective than mosquito coils, but a reliable electricity supply and a supply of the mats may not be available in some parts of the tropics. It is also possible to heat the mats by placing them a few centimetres above an oil lamp, although this could constitute a fire hazard.

The smoke emitted by coils kills mosquitoes in unventilated rooms, but in comfortably ventilated rooms the smoke may do no more than irritate or stun insects so that they do not bite. Care may be needed to achieve even this—for example, on a porch or veranda one should always place the source of vapour upwind of those to be protected and perhaps at floor level, to deter mosquitoes heading for the ankles.

The pyrethroid vapour from vaporizing mats is more effective in draughty conditions and less offensive to the user than the smoke from coils. The mats are manufactured and used on a very large scale in India.

Mosquito nets

The use of a mosquito bed-net is strongly recommended wherever there is any risk of bites from *Anopheles* mosquitoes that carry malaria and bite at night, or the nuisance of *Culex* mosquitoes. It is well worth buying a good-quality net, because slippage of the weave can allow mosquitoes to enter. Tears should be repaired or blocked with cotton wool, and the net should always be tucked in carefully under the mattress.

The net should be checked after getting into bed, using an electric torch to make sure that no gaps are left and that no mosquitoes have entered along with you. Take care not to sleep with any part of the body resting against the net—mosquitoes feed through nets and never miss an opportunity. Rectangular nets are safer in this respect than the 'tent' type. Increased security can be achieved by impregnating nets with a pyrethroid insecticide such as permethrin or deltamethrin, which are effective for several months in killing or repelling mosquitoes that come into contact with it. A dose of $0.2g/m^2$ is usually sufficient, which can be achieved by dipping the net in a 1% emulsion made by diluting in water an emulsifiable concentrate of permethrin. The net is wrung out and laid to dry on a plastic sheet. It used to be the case that, because many of the mosquitoes making contact with a permethrin-treated net are killed, one person using such a net provided some degree of protection to a companion in the same room, but not using the net. However, the now widespread use of treated nets has resulted in more mosquitoes becoming resistant to the insecticide. Resistance to pyrethroid insecticides has been detected in malaria vectors in various parts of the world but the evidence is still equivocal about whether this resistance is at a sufficient level to nullify the effect of net treatment on malaria. It appears that resistant insects are irritated by landing on treated bed nets, don't want to remain in contact with the treated surface and fly away. This is possibly likely to increase the risk of them attacking anyone without a net. Nevertheless it is much better than the situation where only one person uses a repellent (see above) or an untreated net and overall there is a communal benefit when almost all the inhabitants of a village are using permethrin-impregnated nets—the risk of a malaria infective bite to those in the village, but temporarily or permanently not using nets, has been found to be greatly reduced in experiments in Tanzania.

Many hotels in the tropics provide mosquito nets. If in doubt it may be worth taking your own, and if suitable anchorage points are not available you should ask the management to provide some or to provide poles of sufficient height that can be lashed to the bed legs.

Other methods

Containers around houses that can hold water but are not used for storage should be disposed of, flattened and buried, or punctured so that they cannot hold water and become breeding sites for *Aedes* mosquitoes. Longer term measures can include stocking ornamental ponds with small fish to eat any mosquito larvae that may start to develop there.

It almost goes without saying that residents should always co-operate with any community-wide insect control measures run by local authorities, e.g. house spraying against malaria vectors in parts of India and South America, or elimination of *Aedes* breeding sites in Cuba and Singapore.

Traps

Very effective traps have been developed for tsetse flies based on visual and/or olfactory stimulants. They are used to prevent tsetse invading places where people come to collect water or where cattle are vulnerable.

Various types of baited trap for mass killing of houseflies have been developed including a very cheap one based on discarded bottles (details available from TALC, see ℘ http://www.talcuk.org/accessories/talc-fly-trap.htm). As yet, there are no cheap traps for effective elimination of mosquitoes, although traps using a light or carbon dioxide as attractants are used to monitor control campaigns.

Control of domestic non-biting pests

Although they do not bite, houseflies, cockroaches, ants, and termites are often worrying pests in the tropics and some may be a serious health hazard. Flies, for example, are able to carry more than 100 different types of harmful disease-producing organisms, and may transfer them directly from excreta to food and children's faces. There is now evidence that community-wide fly control operations reduce the risk of diarrhoea and the blinding disease, trachoma. In the kitchen, exposed food, unwashed plates, crumbs, and rubbish are an open invitation to flies, cockroaches, and ants. Very attractive foods such as sugar and jam should be kept in the refrigerator and others, such as breakfast cereals, biscuits, or bread, should be kept in screw-topped containers.

Flies, ants, and cockroaches

Houseflies breed in rotting rubbish, and if refuse is not regularly collected by the local authorities it should be buried under a thick layer of soil. Screening of the vent pipes of pit-latrines and cesspits is a most effective measure against houseflies and *Chrysomya* blowflies, because light filtering in attracts them into the pipes, and they are unable to escape. Mothballs (no longer available in the European Union) placed on bathroom drain grilles may discourage cockroaches from emerging from the drain. Tramp ants such as Pharoah's ant and its relatives (*Monomorium* spp.) do not form permanent nests. They can often be found forming long trails across walls and floors onto cracks in walls and furniture. Treatment with insecticides only results in fragmentation of the colonies, creating a bigger problem in the long term. Consequently, it is better to leave them alone and to minimize their access to food and water.

Old-fashioned sticky fly paper can help to limit the numbers of flies' casually entering food preparation areas but, in the event of a persistent fly problem, periodic use of insecticide aerosol spray cans may be necessary, although screening of windows and removal of any breeding sites is the best long term option for minimizing fly problems. Pyrethroid insecticides may also be effective in irritating cockroaches and driving them out of the crevices in which they hide. However, the most effective treatments against cockroaches are sold for professional use only, although some may be available for purchase in some developing countries.

Termites

In the many tropical areas where there is a serious termite problem, houses should be protected by pouring a persistent insecticide into a trench around the foundations and impregnating timber with insecticide. In most countries this is a procedure controlled and limited to professional application. Before starting long-term occupation of a house, it is wise to enquire whether such precautions have been taken. For the short-term resident, termite infestation will be revealed by sinuous earth-covered tunnels adhering to the walls.

Termites can completely destroy books and other objects from within and, as a precaution, bookcases can be stood on bricks placed in basins of water covered in an oil film to reduce evaporation and prevent them becoming breeding places for *Aedes aegypti* and *Aedes albopictus* mosquitoes.

Chapter 6

Animal attacks, rabies, venomous bites and stings

David A. Warrell

Many travellers worry about snake bites or scorpion stings, but dog bites are a much more likely problem, which can carry a terrifying risk of rabies.

Attacks by land animals

Each year, an estimated 800–1600 people are killed by tigers, 60–200 by lions, 30–125 by leopards, 200–500 by elephants, 200–300 by hippo-potamuses, 20–100 by African buffaloes, 10–50 by hyenas, and 20–50 by wolves. Many other large animals, even ostriches, have killed people.

Bears

In North America, black bears attack humans about six times each year, leading to one death every 3 years. Brown bears (e.g. grizzlies and Kodiaks) are responsible for about two attacks and one death every year. Brown bears in Romania and Scandinavia, and sloth bears in India are also a danger. Polar bears are the most predatory and dangerous of all bears. Attacks occur every few years in Canada, Alaska, and Svalbard. Close encounters are becoming more frequent as climate change increases contact between humans and starving bears.

Prevention

Travel in groups making plenty of noise (wear bells), avoid disturbing bears scavenging carcasses or garbage tips. Never approach bears to photograph them, especially those with cubs. In camp, store food more than 100 yards away in a tree more than 14 feet above ground and more than 4 feet away from the trunk. In polar bear country, camps should be protected by perimeter trip wires activating explosive flares, watch dogs and round-the-clock armed guards (see ℘ http://kho.unis.no/doc/Polar_bears_Svalbard.pdf).

Irritated bears stand up, hiss, growl, yawn, and swing their heads. If you are approached or charged by a bear, stand your ground avoiding eye contact. In the case of polar bears, make a loud noise, fire flares or shots and, if all else has failed, shoot the bear in its heart. For black and brown bears, at 30 feet, squirt capsicum spray at their eyes. If a black bear attacks, growl, shout, and fight back with any available weapon. If a grizzly attacks, play dead by rolling into a ball, protecting your back with a backpack, the back of your neck with interlocked hands and your throat with your elbows. Remain in this position until the bear has left the scene.

Big cats

Tigers and pumas (mountain lions) usually attack by day. Lions and leopards attack by night and may enter dwellings. In Tanzania, most attacks occur between 18:00 and 21:00 hours during the first 10 days after the full moon.

Prevention

Protect long-term camps by fencing and burning camp fires all night. Observe big cats only from a vehicle, hide, or the back of an elephant. High calibre firearm protection may be necessary in dangerous areas. If attacked, fight for your life, using any available weapon and making as much noise as possible.

Elephants

Despite their popular 'jumbo' image, elephants, whether wild or captive in safari parks, circuses, or timber works, are immensely powerful, unpredictable, and dangerous animals that can throw, trample, or impale human victims.

Prevention

Always treat elephants with great respect, even if they are 'domesticated'. In the wild, unless accompanied by an armed ranger, stay in your vehicle or down wind, and avoid cows with calves and bulls obviously in musth (a phase of hypervirilization indicated by black oily discharge from temporal glands, urinary incontinence, priapism, green algal staining of the penis, and extreme aggression). Warning signs before a charge include spread ears, raised swaying head and tail, lowered trunk, and trumpeting. Retreat to your vehicle or other refuge immediately!

Domestic dogs

The USA has 65 million dogs and 312 million humans. Each year, 2% of the population is bitten. About 800 000 victims require medical attention. In 2010, 34 people were killed by dogs.

Prevention

Avoid packs of strays and guard dogs. In dangerous areas, carry a heavy stick or club, and fill your pockets with stones. If approached by an aggressive dog, avoid eye contact and do not run away. Shout, protect yourself with your backpack and fight back with sticks and stones. The nape of a dog's neck and its nose are most vulnerable.

Attacks by aquatic animals

Crocodiles, alligators, and caimans

Nile crocodiles (*Crocodilus niloticus*) kill about 1000 people each year in Africa. Saltwater crocodiles are responsible for several reported attacks each year in northern Australia resulting in one or two deaths. This species also causes many deaths in India, Philippines, Borneo, and New Guinea. In the USA there have been an average of six attacks by alligators (*Alligator mississippiensis*) each year with a fatality every 3 years. Bite wounds are inevitably infected with a range of bacteria.

Prevention

Avoid walking too close to lakes, rivers, and waterfalls. If camping near water, do not discard food into the water as this attracts crocodilians. It is foolhardy to wade, bathe, or swim in rivers or lakes in the tropics unless they are known to be safe from crocodilians. Do not bathe between dusk and dawn. Canoeing is hazardous in crocodile-infested waters. If attacked on land, run. If attacked in the water, hit the animal on the nose and eyes with any available weapon.

Sharks

Each year, about 60–80 unprovoked attacks by sharks are reported with four or five fatalities. Most attacks occur between latitudes 30°N and 30°S off North America, Australia, and South Africa.

Prevention of shark attacks

Do not bathe between sandbars and the ocean, where dead fish or sewage effluent are discharged, or flocks of birds are feeding, or if you're injured, bleeding, wearing jewellery or brightly coloured/patterned clothing, or are with a pet dog. Do not splash on a surfboard. Take local advice, and bathe in groups, close to shore, during daylight. Chemical and electrical-field repellents and chainmail protective suits have been developed. If attacked, fight back, hitting the shark on its nose, and clawing at its eyes and gills.

First aid of animal wounds

Secure the casualty out of danger and out of the water then resuscitate them (ABCDE), starting intravenous (IV) fluid volume repletion if possible. Control bleeding with local pressure or tourniquet. Close perforating injuries with pressure dressings. If delay in reaching medical care is likely, clean and irrigate wounds using soap and water or 1% povidone iodine. Start broad-spectrum antibiotics, such as amoxicillin clavulanate, or azithromycin or ciprofloxacin. Evacuate to hospital as soon as is practicable.

Hospital treatment

Replace blood loss, assess and treat fractures, tension pneumothorax, damage to large blood vessels, bowel perforation, visceral lacerations, and intraperitoneal bleeding. Débride/amputate dead tissue, removing animals' teeth, etc. In the case of head and neck wounds, suture immediately. For other wounds, delay suturing for 48–72 hours. Irrigate and drain wounds. Give tetanus prophylaxis. Consider rabies risk (see below). Give appropriate antibiotics, being in marine pathogens.

Rabies

Human rabies encephalomyelitis is a fatal zoonosis caused by classic rabies virus (genotype 1) and four rabies-related bat lyssaviruses (genotypes 4–7). Rabies circulates among domestic dogs and cats, and wild mammal reservoir species. These include foxes in the Arctic; insectivorous bats, skunks, raccoons, foxes and other carnivores in North America; mongooses and vampire bats in the Caribbean; vampire bats in Central and South America;

foxes, wolves, raccoon dogs, and insectivorous bats in Europe; wolves, jackals, and small carnivores, such as mongooses and civets throughout most of Africa and Asia; and flying foxes (fruit bats) in Australia. Humans can contract rabies from any rabid mammal, domestic or wild, but the intimate association between humans and dogs, and the prevalence of canine rabies explains why dogs are the most common source of human rabies, accounting for an estimated 60 000 deaths each year. In the USA, where canine rabies has been eliminated, humans are still at risk of transmission from wild mammals, notably insectivorous bats. Rodent bites carry little or no risk of transmitting rabies.

In the UK, the last human death from indigenous canine rabies virus occurred in 1902, but in 2003 a man died of a rabies-like illness in Scotland. It was caused by a rabies-related European bat lyssavirus, now known to be enzootic in Daubenton's bats in UK and in insectivorous bats in mainland Europe. Since 1902, 24 cases of imported human rabies have died in the UK. Fifteen of these exposures had occurred in the Indian Sub-Continent, all but two from dog bites.

Geographical distribution
Rabies occurs in most parts of the world (Map 6.1). The continuing recognition of bat lyssaviruses in new areas makes the concept of rabies-free countries misleading. Human rabies is most common where canine rabies is most prevalent—the Indian subcontinent, Southeast Asia, China and most parts of Africa.

How infection occurs
Rabies is transmitted to humans when a bite or scratch from a mammal is infected with saliva containing the virus. The virus can penetrate mucosae and broken skin. On several occasions, recipients of corneal and other organ transplants from patients dying of unsuspected rabies have been infected.

Unless virus deposited in the wound is killed, it soon invades the nerves in which it travels to the spinal cord and brain. It then multiplies and causes a severe infection of the central nervous system (encephalomyelitis). The incubation period (between bite and first symptoms of rabies) is usually 2–3 months, but can vary from 4 days to many years. Itching, irritation, tingling, or pain of the healed bite wound is an early (prodromal) symptom. Soon, headache, fever, paralysis and episodic confusion, aggression, and hallucinations develop. The most characteristic symptom is hydrophobia (literally, fear of water)—attempts to drink induce powerful contractions of the neck muscles and the muscles involved in swallowing and breathing associated with indescribable terror. The patient dies within a few days.

Although human rabies is untreatable it is readily preventable.

Prevention of rabies
In rabies-endemic areas, travellers should avoid close contact with domestic or wild mammals. They should be particularly wary of wild animals that appear unusually tame as this change in behaviour is a common effect of rabies.

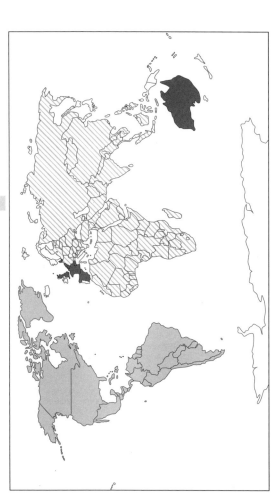

Map 6.1 Global distribution of rabies and rabies-related lyssaviruses. *Cross-hatched* rabies in terrestrial mammal species (lyssavirus genotype 1) and bat infections by other lyssavirus genotypes. *Light grey* terrestrial and bat rabies are all genotype 1. *Dark grey* bat lyssaviruses, genotypes 5, 6, or 7 only. *White:* no lyssaviruses detected.

Pre-exposure prophylaxis

This is strongly recommended for inhabitants of and travellers in dog rabies enzootic countries. It confers long lasting recall of neutralizing antibody in response to boosting after a subsequent exposure. There have been no reported failures of pre-exposure prophylaxis with post-exposure boosting. Intradermal pre-exposure vaccination must not be given concurrently with chloroquine (malaria prophylaxis).

Action following a bite

Irrespective of the risk of rabies, all mammal bites, scratches, and licks on mucous membranes or broken skin should be cleaned immediately and vigorously (Box 6.1). Mammal bites (including human) are usually contaminated by a variety of bacteria, some of which can cause serious infections.

Box 6.1 **Treatment of mammal bites, licks, and scratches**

First-aid

- Scrub with soap or detergent, preferably under a running tap, for at least 5 min
- Remove foreign material (e.g. dirt, broken teeth)
- Rinse with plain water
- Irrigate with a virucidal agent, such as povidone-iodine (Betadine), 0.01% aqueous iodine, or 40–70% alcohol (gin and whisky contain 40%).

Note: hydrogen peroxide, mercurochrome, and quaternary ammonium compounds (e.g. Cetrimide) are *not* ideal for this purpose.

At the hospital or dispensary

A medical attendant should:

- Check that first-aid measures (above) have been carried out
- Explore and irrigate deep wounds (if necessary, under anaesthesia). Dead tissue should be cut away, but wound excision is rarely necessary
- Avoid immediate suturing (stitches) and occlusive dressings
- Consider tetanus risk and treat accordingly—booster dose of tetanus formol toxoid (0.5mL by intramuscular (IM) injection) for those fully immunized in the past and boosted within the last 10 years; human tetanus immunoglobulin (250mg by IM injection) for severe or grossly contaminated wounds that have been left untreated for more than 4 hours in a previously unimmunized person. In the case of serious or neglected wounds, antibiotics such as penicillin or metronidazole should be given to kill tetanus bacteria
- Consider risk of infection with other bacteria, viruses, and fungi particularly associated with mammal bites. Preventive antibiotic treatment is advisable for severely contaminated wounds, e.g. a broad-spectrum antibiotic, such as amoxicillin (500mg, three times a day for 5 days)
- If the mammal bite, lick, or scratch occurred in a rabies-endemic area, consider full post-exposure rabies prophylaxis.

Post-exposure prophylaxis

If rabies post-exposure prophylaxis is indicated (Box 6.2), thorough wound cleaning is followed by a combination of active immunization with rabies vaccine and passive immunization with rabies immune globulin (RIG) raised either in humans (HRIG) or horses (ERIG) (Box 6.3). The aim is to kill any rabies virus introduced by the bite before it can enter the nervous system. Active immunization stimulates the body to produce rabies neutralizing antibodies, which takes about a week, whereas passive immunization provides 'ready-made' neutralizing antibodies to give immediate protection before the response to active vaccination kicks in. Travellers who are exposed to the risk of rabies (Box 6.2) should seek post-exposure treatment immediately, rather than waiting for days. Only orthodox/ Western medical practitioners should be consulted about rabies, not herbalists, homeopaths, traditional practitioners, or other purveyors of 'fringe medicine'. In some countries, even Western-style practitioners may not give adequate treatment. Those who have received a complete pre- or post-exposure course of vaccine previously require only post-exposure booster injections of vaccine without RIG (Box 6.3). Although the chances of preventing rabies decrease with delay, full post-exposure prophylaxis should be given even if the person exposed presents late— weeks or months after the bite.

Box 6.2 Indications for rabies post-exposure prophylaxis

Intact skin is a barrier to infection

Minor exposure

Nibbling (tooth contact) with uncovered skin, or minor scratches, or abrasions without bleeding:
- Start vaccine immediately
- Stop treatment if the animal remains healthy for 10 days
- Stop treatment if animal's brain proves negative for rabies by appropriate investigation.

Major exposure

Single or multiple bites or scratches that break the skin, or licks on broken skin, or licks or saliva on mucosae, or physical contact with bats:
- Immediate rabies immunoglobulin and vaccine
- Stop treatment if animal remains healthy for 10 days
- Stop treatment if the animal's brain proves negative for rabies by appropriate investigation.

In the UK, expert advice and materials for post-exposure treatment are available from the Health Protection Agency (HPA) (Tel: 020 8200 4400 or 020 8200 6868), or in the USA, from local or state health departments, or from the Division of Viral Diseases at the Centers for Disease Control and Prevention (Tel: 800-CDC-INFO (800-232-4636) TTY: (888) 232-6348—24 hour service), (see also Appendix 2) or may also be obtained via the Blood Care Foundation (Chapter 13.6).

Box 6.3 **Rabies immunization schedules**

Tissue culture vaccines
Verorab (Sanofi-Pasteur) is reconstituted to 0.5mL IM dose; Rabipur/
Rabavert (Novartis) is reconstituted to 1.0mL IM dose.

Pre-exposure prophylaxis
Regimen
Days 0, 7, 28: single site 0.1mL ID of any vaccine or whole ampoule IM.

Post-exposure prophylaxis
Do not forget wound cleaning! (Box 6.1)

*1. Post-exposure boosting in those who have already had
pre-exposure rabies vaccine*
No passive immunization (HRIG or ERIG) is needed.

Regimens
• *Days 0 and 3:* single site whole ampoule IM **or**
• *Day 0:* 0.1mL of any vaccine at 4 ID sites (2x deltoids and 2x
  suprascapular or thighs).

*2. Post-exposure prophylaxis in those who have not had
pre-exposure rabies vaccine*
Regimens
• *Standard 5 dose IM method:* Days 0, 3, 7, 14, 28—whole ampoule (0.5
  or 1.0mL) into 1 site (deltoid)
or
• *4-site ID method:*
  • *Day 0*—divide whole ampoule (0.5 or 1.0mL) between 4 sites
    (×2 deltoids and ×2 suprascapular or thighs)
  • *Day 7*—0.1 (for 0.5mL vials) or 0.2mL (for 1mL vials) ID into
    2 sites (×2 deltoids)
  • *Day 28*—0.1 (for 0.5mL vials) or 0.2mL (for 1mL vials) ID into
    1 site (deltoid)
or
• *2-site ID method:* Days 0, 3, 7 and 28—0.1 or 0.2mL ID at each of
  2 sites (deltoids).

This regimen should be given only by experienced staff together with
RIG. ID regimens require the use of 1mL syringes and must raise a
papule (*peau d'orange*) immediately, as with BCG vaccination. If given
too deep, withdraw needle and repeat at an adjacent site.
and
Rabies immunoglobulin, either HRIG 20IU/kg or ERIG 40IU/kg. If
possible, infiltrate the whole dose into and around all the bite wounds,
diluting with saline if there are multiple bites. Inject any residue IM
distant from vaccination sites.

Useful websites
USA *advice*
🕉 http://www.cdc.gov/rabies/

UK *advice*
🕉 http://www.hpa.org.uk/Topics/InfectiousDiseases/InfectionsAZ/Rabies/
European epidemiology. Available at: 🕉 http://www.rbe.fli.bund.de/
WHO advice. Available at: 🕉 http://www.who.int/rabies/en/

Venomous bites and stings

Travellers to tropical countries should find out about the venomous fauna
well in advance. Those visiting remote, snake-infested areas should learn
first-aid techniques. For more advice, Toxbase in UK (for health professionals 🕉 http://www.toxbase.org/ Tel: 0844 892 0111) or American
Association of Poison Control Centers (Tel: 1-800-222-1222).

Snake bites
Venomous snakes have one or more pairs of enlarged teeth, the fangs, in
the upper jaw. Venom passes from the venom gland just behind the eye,
through a duct to the base of the fang, and then through a channel or
groove to its tip.

Dangerous species
Medically-important venomous snakes belong to four families:
- Elapidae, which include cobras (Figs 6.1 and 6.7), kraits (Fig. 6.8),
  mambas (Fig. 6.9), coral snakes, Australasian snakes, and sea snakes.
  The South African ringkhals, and African and Asian spitting cobras
  can eject venom from the tips of their fangs towards the eyes of an
  aggressor as a defensive strategy
- Viperidae, the largest family of venomous snakes, including the
  subfamilies Viperinae, the Old World or typical vipers and adders
  (Figs 6.2 and 6.10); and Crotalinae, the New World rattlesnakes,
  moccasins and lance-headed vipers (Fig. 6.3), and Asian pit vipers
  (Fig. 6.6) all of which possess a heat-sensitive pit organ situated
  between the eye and the nostril
- Atractaspidinae (burrowing asps or stiletto snakes) are found in
  Africa and the Middle East. They strike sideways, with one long fang
  protruding from the corner of their mouth (Fig. 6.4)
- Colubridae have fangs at the back of their mouth (Fig. 6.5). Effective
  bites in humans are uncommon but African boomslangs, bird, twig,
  tree, or vine snakes and Asian keel-backs (Fig. 6.5) have caused some
  fatalities.

Dangerously venomous snakes do not occur at altitudes above 5000m
(16 000 feet), in the Antarctic, nor in many islands such as Ireland, Iceland,
Crete, New Zealand, Madagascar, and most Caribbean and Pacific islands
(Map 6.2). Sea snakes inhabit the warmer oceans within latitudes 40°N
and 40°S, but not the Atlantic (Map 6.3).

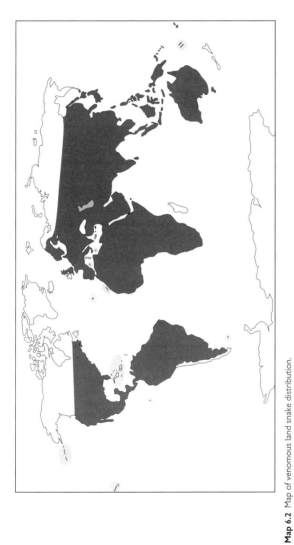

Map 6.2 Map of venomous land snake distribution.

Reproduced from Johnson et al. *Oxford Handbook of Expedition and Wilderness Medicine*, 2008, p.525 with permission of Oxford University Press.

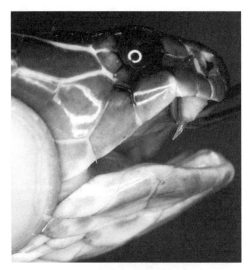

Fig. 6.1 Profile of fangs of the Indian cobra (*Naja naja*), Sri Lanka.
© David A. Warrell.

Fig. 6.2 Profile of West African Gaboon viper fangs (*Bitis rhinoceros*).
© David A. Warrell.

Fig. 6.3 Profile of Brazilian jaracuçu fangs and venom (*Bothrops*).
© David A. Warrell.

Fig. 6.4 Profile of burrowing asp (*Atractaspis aterrima*) fangs, Nigeria.
© David A. Warrell.

Fig. 6.5 Profile of red-necked keelback (*Rhabdophis subminiatus*) fangs, Thailand. © David A. Warrell.

Fig. 6.6 Chinese habu (*Protobothrops mucrosquamatus*) showing pit organ between eye and nostril. © David A. Warrell.

Fig. 6.7 Indochinese spitting cobra (*Naja siamensis*). © David A. Warrell.

Fig. 6.8 Chinese many banded krait (*Bungarus multicinctus*). © David A. Warrell.

Importance

In India, 46 000 people are killed by snakes each year. Worldwide, snakes kill more than 100 000 people and permanently disable many more. Most bites are inflicted on the legs, ankles, and feet of impoverished agricultural workers, herdsmen, and their children. In the USA, Australia, and most parts of Europe, there are few deaths each year. In the UK, the last death was in 1975. Western travellers have been severely envenomed while abroad and a few have been killed. Although a rare occurrence, snake bite induces disproportionate fear among travellers. Reassurance, based on sound preventive strategies, is important (p.194).

Fig. 6.9 Black mamba (*Dendroaspis polylepis*). © David A. Warrell.

Fig. 6.10 Common European adder or viper (*Vipera berus*). © David A. Warrell.

Clinical effects

About half of bites by venomous snakes (with puncture marks, confirming penetration of the skin) are so called 'dry bites'. Negligible amounts of venom are injected. However, bites by any snake may cause symptoms of anxiety—rapid pulse, excessive breathing, pins-and-needles, stiffness of hands and feet, lightheadedness, and fainting. Symptoms of local envenoming are pain, tenderness, swelling, and bruising spreading from the site of bite with tender enlargement of local lymph nodes (in the groin after leg bites, in the arm pit after arm bites). Nausea, vomiting, and fainting are early signs of systemic envenoming.

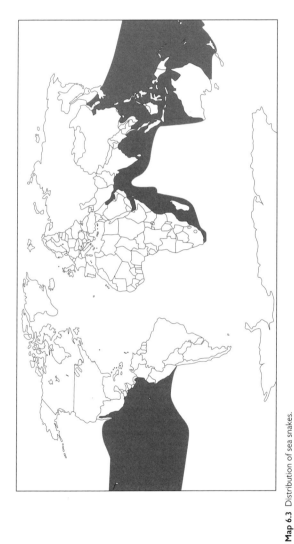

Map 6.3 Distribution of sea snakes.

Reproduced from Johnson et al. (2008). *Oxford Handbook of Expedition and Wilderness Medicine*, p.542, with permission of Oxford University Press.

Elapids

Bites by African spitting cobras cause painful local swelling, blistering, and tissue damage (necrosis or gangrene). Most other elapid venoms cause paralysis, first detectable as drooping of both upper eyelids (ptosis) and paralysis of the eyeballs (external ophthalmoplegia), producing double vision (diplopia) from 15min to 10 hours after the bite. Pupils, face, palate, jaws, tongue, vocal cords, neck muscles, and muscles of swallowing and breathing are affected in succession over the next few hours. Asian cobras cause paralysis and local tissue damage. As well as paralysis, terrestrial Australasian elapids can cause bleeding, blood-clotting disturbances, generalized break down of muscles (rhabdomyolysis) and acute kidney injury (AKI). Sea snake bites cause generalized muscle damage, lock jaw (trismus), brown muscle pigment (myoglobin) in urine, and generalized paralysis.

Spitting elapids eject their venom into the eyes of perceived enemies, provoking intense pain, spasm, and swelling of the eyelids, and profuse whitish conjunctival secretions. Corneal ulcers, pus in the anterior chamber of the eye, inflammation of the iris, secondary infections, and blindness may develop.

Vipers and pit-vipers

Local swelling may affect the entire bitten limb, adjacent areas of trunk and, in children, the whole body. Bruising and blistering appear within hours, tissue necrosis in days. Low blood pressure, shock, bleeding and blood clotting abnormalities are common. Patients may bleed from their gums, nose, gut, urinary tract, vagina, lungs and into their skin, conjunctivae and brain. Some viper venoms cause paralysis and rhabdomyolysis. AKI is an important complication.

Colubrids (back-fanged snakes)

Colubrids can cause bleeding, blood-clotting problems, and AKI. Burrowing asps may cause local necrosis, and rarely, shock and sudden death.

Management of snake bite

First-aid for snake bite, either by the victim or a person on the spot, is summarized in Box 6.4.

Medical treatment by health professionals

The only specific remedy for snake bite is antivenom (antivenin, antivenene, or anti-snake venom, ASV), which is made by immunizing horses or sheep with increasing doses of snake venom. Antivenoms may cause anaphylactic reactions, which are not predicted by skin tests. To be effective, antivenom must be given by IV infusion. It is indicated if there is evidence of envenoming: low blood pressure, failure of the blood to clot in a glass vessel within 20min, bleeding from the nose, gums, gut, or elsewhere, generalized pain and stiffness in the muscles, paralysis, or rapidly extending local swelling that involves more than half the bitten limb.

Prevention of antivenom reactions

Adrenaline (epinephrine) in an adult dose of 0.25mL of 0.1% solution given subcutaneously (SC) before the start of antivenom infusion reduces the risk of serious early (anaphylactic) antivenom reactions

Box 6.4 **Snake bite: first-aid**

1. Reassure the patient
2. Immobilize the victim and especially the bitten part, using a splint or sling
3. Unless a neurotoxic elapid can be excluded, consider pressure-immobilization or pressure-pad methods (Box 6.5)
4. Move the patient to hospital or a dispensary as quickly as possible
5. Avoid traditional first-aid methods (tight tourniquets, incisions, suction, ice packs, chemicals, herbs, snake stones, electric shocks etc.)
6. Treat pain with paracetamol, codeine, or dihydrocodeine, not aspirin or non-steroidal anti-inflammatory agents, such as ibuprofen
7. If you have your own supply of antivenom, take it with you to the hospital
8. Do not attempt to pursue or kill the snake, but if it has been killed take it along with you to the hospital or dispensary; do not handle it with your bare hands, even if it appears dead.

Box 6.5 **Pressure-immobilization and pressure-pad**

Both methods delay systemic absorption of lethal venom toxins by compressing lymphatics and veins draining the bite site, using a pressure below arterial (50–70mmHg) to avoid the unacceptable dangers of an arterial tourniquet.

Pressure immobilization
Several elasticated (not crepe) bandages, approximately 10–15cm wide and 4.5m long are bound firmly around the entire bitten limb (but not so tightly as to obliterate pulses at the wrist or ankle) incorporating a splint, starting around the fingers or toes, and extending proximally, up to the armpit or groin.

Pressure pad
A rubber and/or folded material pad approximately 5cm square and 2–3cm thick is bound firmly directly over the bite site using a non-elastic bandage.

Antivenom administration
Reconstituted freeze-dried antivenom or neat liquid antivenom is diluted in approximately 5mL of isotonic fluid/kg body weight and infused intravenously over 30–60min. The same dose should be given to children as to adults.

Early anaphylactic antivenom reactions

Itching and nettle rash (urticaria) are followed by coughing, vomiting, wheezing, swelling of the lips, gums, tongue and throat (angioedema) and shock. Adrenaline (epinephrine) [0.5–1.0mL (children 0.01mL/kg) of 0.1% (1 in 1000, 1mg/mL] must be readily available to be given by IM injection at the first sign of a reaction.

Antihistamines, such as chlorphenamine maleate (Piriton, Chlor-Trimeton; adults 10mg) by IV injection, can also be given.

Do not rely on hospitals in developing countries having antivenom in stock. You may have to supply your own.

Patients should be given a booster dose of tetanus toxoid, but prophylactic antibiotics are not justified unless the wound has been interfered with (e.g. incised with an unsterile instrument).

Prevention

Avoid snakes as far as possible or enjoy them from a safe distance. Do not disturb, corner, attack, or touch snakes, even if they are said to be a harmless species or appear to be dead. *Some snakes sham death and even a severed head can bite!*

In snake country, wear boots, socks, and long trousers. Always carry a light at night. Paths are especially dangerous at night after rainstorms or floods. Never collect firewood, or move logs and boulders with your bare hands, and never push your hands or sticks into burrows, holes, or crevices. Avoid climbing trees and rocks that are covered with thick foliage, and never swim in overgrown rivers or lakes (there are a good many other reasons for not swimming in tropical lakes and rivers).

When sleeping in the open or under canvas, use a hammock, camp bed, sewn-in ground-sheet, or tucked-in mosquito net.

Useful websites

Clinical guidelines

Africa: ℜ http://www.afro.who.int/en/clusters-a-programmes/hss/essential-medicines/ highlights/2358-whoafro-issues-guidelines-for-the-prevention-and-clinical-management-of-snakebite-in-africa.html

South Asia: ℜ http://www.searo.who.int/LinkFiles/BCT_snake_bite_guidelines.pdf

Australia: ℜ http://www.toxinology.com/

Global VAPAGuide: ℜ http://www.vapaguide.info/cgi-bin/WebObjects/vapaGuide.woa/wa/ getContent?type=page&id=1

Antivenoms

WHO 'Antivenoms website': Venomous Snakes Distribution and Species Risk Categories and 'WHO Guidelines' for the Production, Control and Regulation of Snake Antivenom Immunoglobulins. ℜ http://www.who.int/bloodproducts/snake_antivenoms/en/

Munich AntiVenomINdex (MAVIN): ℜ http://toxinfo.org/antivenoms/

CSL Australian antivenoms: ℜ http://www.toxinology.com/generic_static_files/cslb_index.html

Global crisis solutions center: ℜ http://globalcrisis.info/latestantivenom.htm

For poison centers' prescribers only: ℜ https://www.pharmacy.arizona.edu/avi/verify.pl#top

Fish stings

Venomous spines are situated in dorsal and pectoral fins, and gill covers or, in stingrays, at the base of the tail. Tropical coral reefs, especially of the Indo-Pacific region, harbour the greatest number of venomous fish. Stings by weeverfish can also occur in temperate waters, such as along the Adriatic and Cornish coasts.

Dangerous species

Very rarely, stinging dogfish, stingrays and mantas, catfish, weeverfish, scorpionfish, and stargazers have caused fatalities.

Stingrays cause many stings around the coasts of North America, the Pacific, and in the rivers in South America when they are trodden on. The tail, armed with a sting spine, is lashed against the victim's ankle. Spines of large rays may penetrate swimmers' chests or abdomens, causing fatal trauma.

Scorpionfish (Scorpaenidae) include stonefish (which lie motionless and well camouflaged on the bottom) and attractive zebra or lionfish (Fig. 6.11) of the Indo-Pacific region.

Clinical effects

Fish stings cause excruciating pain, local swelling, necrosis with secondary infection, vomiting, diarrhoea, sweating, a fall in blood pressure, and irregularities of the heartbeat.

Treatment

To relieve pain, immerse the stung part in hot (just under 45°C, 113°F) but not scalding water. Infiltration with local anaesthetic, such as procaine (Novocain) or lignocaine, is much less effective. The stinging spine and membranes should be removed to prevent secondary infection.

Antivenom for Scorpaenidae is manufactured in Australia.

Prevention

Waders and bathers should adopt a shuffling gait in sand or mud and prod in front of them with a stick to avoid stepping on fish. Rubber footwear and wetsuits are protective against all but stingray spines.

Jellyfish stings

Jellyfish, sea wasps, Portuguese men-o'-war ('bluebottles'), polyps, hydroids, sea anemones, sea nettles, and corals are Cnidarians (formerly Coelenterates). Their tentacles are armed with millions of stinging capsules (nematocysts) that discharge when touched. Stings cause painful lines of blisters and surrounding inflammation, sometimes with severe systemic envenoming. Box jellyfish or sea wasps (Chironex fleckeri) of the north coast of Australia and related Indo-Pacific species are the most dangerous, producing violent shivering, vomiting, and diarrhoea with a fall in blood pressure, paralysis of breathing muscles, and fits. People who have been sensitized by previous stings may suffer acute life-threatening anaphylaxis (see Appendix 7).

Coral cuts are common injuries in snorkelers and scuba divers. They are part mechanical, caused by the calcareous exoskeleton, part envenoming and part infective caused by marine bacteria.

Treatment

For box jellyfish stings, inactivate nematocysts by dousing with vinegar or dilute acetic acid. For Atlantic sea nettles (Chrysaora quinquecirra), use a wet compress of baking powder (sodium bicarbonate). Hot water treatment is effective in controlling pain from stings of Portuguese men o' war and box jellyfish. Pressure-immobilization is not recommended.

Coral cuts must be thoroughly cleaned, explored for coral fragments, debrided of dead tissue and dressed with antiseptic. Systemic antibiotics may be needed.

Prevention
Swimmers should stay out of the sea during seasons when large numbers of jellyfish are washed ashore and when warning notices are posted.

Other venomous marine animals

Starfish and sea urchins (Echinodermata) have long sharp stinging spines and grapples that should be removed from the wound, usually on the sole of the foot, after softening the skin with 2% salicylic acid ointment.

Fig. 6.11 Zebra or lion fish (*Pterois volitans*). © David A. Warrell.

Fig. 6.12 Geography cone (*Conus geographus*). © David A. Warrell.

Fig. 6.13 Southern or lesser blue-ringed octopus (*Hapalochlaena maculosa*). © David A. Warrell.

Cone shell (Fig. 6.12) stings and blue-ringed octopus (Fig. 6.13) bites (Mollusca) have caused fatal envenoming. No specific treatment is available.

Bee, wasp, hornet, and ant stings

Stings by Hymenoptera (bees, wasps, hornets, yellow jackets, and ants) are common almost everywhere, but they usually cause only transient focal pain, swelling, and redness. Mass attacks are rare except during the Africanized 'killer bee' sting epidemic that claimed hundreds of lives. It started in Brazil in 1956 and spread north to Nevada, USA, and south to Argentina by the 1990s, but is now dying out.

Allergy

Many people become so hypersensitive to bee, wasp, or ant venoms, that a single sting can cause fatal anaphylaxis. Venom allergy is confirmed by skin or blood tests, or by live sting challenge.

Prevention

People who know they are allergic to stings should carry an identifying tag, as provided by Medic-Alert Foundation International (In the UK: 1 Bridge Wharf, 156 Caledonian Road, London NI 9UU; Tel: 0800 581420 within the UK or 1800 581420 in Ireland; www.medicalert.co.uk; in the USA: 2323 Colorado Avenue, Turlock, CA 95382; Tel: 888-633-4298; www.medicalert.org) in case they are found unconscious. They should always carry self-injectable epinephrine (adrenaline; e.g. 'Epi-Pen', 'Ana-Kit', 'Min-i-Jet'). Desensitization using purified specific venoms is safe and effective.

Treatment
Bee stings must be removed immediately. Aspirin is an effective painkiller. Insect-sting anaphylaxis is a medical emergency (see Appendix 7).

Spider bites
Spiders possess a pair of venom jaws (chelicerae).

Dangerous species
- Black and brown widows (*Latrodectus* spp.) of the Mediterranean region, the Americas, and South Africa
- Brown recluse spiders (*Loxosceles* spp.) of the Americas and elsewhere
- Banana, wandering, or armed spiders of South America (*Phoneutria* spp.; Fig. 6.14)
- Funnel web spiders of Australia (e.g. Sydney funnel web *Atrax robustus*).

Fig. 6.14 Brazilian armed, wandering, or banana spider (*Phoneutria nigriventer*). © David A. Warrell.

Clinical features
Neurotoxic spiders (*Latrodectus*, *Phoneutria*, and *Atrax*) cause painful muscle spasms, local sweating, and goose flesh.

Necrotic spiders (*Loxosceles*) cause local necrosis, fever, rash, haemolysis, and AKI.

Treatment
Local infiltration of lignocaine (1–2%) is effective for painful bites (e.g. *Phoneutria*). Pressure-immobilization (see Box 6.5) is recommended for Sydney funnel web spider bites. Spider bite antivenoms are manufactured in a number of countries. Benzodiazepines help to relieve painful muscle spasms caused by *Latrodectus* envenoming.

Scorpion stings

Dangerously venomous scorpions are found in South Africa (Fig. 6.15), North Africa, the Middle East (notably Iran), India, North, Central and South America, and the Caribbean. In Mexico, there are an estimated 250 000 scorpions stings each year with 50 deaths. Case fatality is higher in young children. In Arizona, 15 000 stings (mainly *Centruroides exilicauda*) are reported each year but there have been no deaths since 1968.

Fig. 6.15 Granulated thick-tailed scorpion (*Parabuthus granulatus*).
© David A. Warrell.

Clinical features

Stings are excruciatingly painful, and may cause sweating, tachycardia, hypotension, vomiting, and diarrhoea. Damage to the heart muscle may cause a fall in blood pressure, irregular heartbeat, and development of heart failure.

Treatment

Local anaesthetic, given as a ring block in the case of stings on fingers or toes, provides the most effective pain relief. If this does not work, a powerful analgesic such as pethidine (50–100mg by IM injection for an adult) or even morphine. For systemic envenoming, antivenoms are made in Mexico, South America, the Middle East, North and South Africa, and India.

Millipede and centipede stings

Millipedes can secrete an irritant liquid that may produce blistering of the skin or more severe effects if it gets into the eyes. Centipedes can produce painful venomous stings that are rarely, if ever, dangerous.

Moth, caterpillar, and beetle stings

Some moths, hairy caterpillars, and beetles can produce irritation of the skin and conjunctiva through contact, causing pain, inflammation, and blistering. Serious effects caused by the fibrinolytic venom of atlas moth caterpillars (*Lonomia* spp.) are common in some South American countries. In 2008, a tourist who trod on some of these caterpillars in Peru developed severe bleeding and AKI after her return to Canada. Unfortunately, she did not receive *Lonomia* antivenom manufactured in Brazil until 10 days after envenoming, too late to save her life. Blister beetles (*Meloidae*) secrete the vesicant substance, cantharidin, which is emitted in defence or if the insects are crushed. Beetles may be trapped inadvertently in body crevices and skin creases, such as under the arm or in front of the elbow. Painful blisters are produced. The most famous species is *Lytta vesicatoria*, misleadingly known as 'Spanish fly'.

Tick bites

Rocky mountain wood ticks and American dog ticks (*Dermacentor* species) in northwestern and eastern North America and bush or dog ticks in eastern Australia (*Ixodes holocyclus*) are venomous, causing paralysis especially in children. The tick may be hidden in a hairy area or even inside the ear. The victim may vomit and eventually die when ascending paralysis reaches the breathing muscles unless the tick is found and removed or mechanical ventilation is instituted. Ticks should be detached without being squeezed: either painted with ether, chloroform, paraffin, gasoline or turpentine or prised out between partially separated tips of curved forceps. No antivenom is available.

Leech bites

Leeches are a severe nuisance to travellers in damp rainforest regions of Southeast Asia. Land leeches wait in low vegetation near tracks or paths until a large, warm-blooded animal approaches. They sense their victim and quickly attach themselves. In humans, they usually suck blood from the lower legs or ankles, easily penetrating long trousers, socks, and lace-up boots. An anticoagulant is secreted so that even after the leech has been removed or has fallen off engorged with blood, there is persistent bleeding.

Aquatic leeches attack swimmers and crawl into the mouth, nostrils, eyes, vagina, or urethra.

Treatment

Leeches are best removed by application of salt, alcohol, vinegar, or a lighted match or cigarette. If they are pulled off forcibly their mouth-parts may remain in the wound, causing infection.

Prevention

Smother your boots, socks and trouser-legs with 50% dibutylphthalate or *n,n*-diethylmetatoluamide (DEET, see Chapter 5.12). Avoid aquatic leeches by not swimming or bathing in forest streams and pools.

Useful web sites (venomous animals in general)

Global, especially Australia: http://www.toxinology.com/
Global VAPAGuide: http://www.vapaguide.info/cgi-bin/WebObjects/vapaGuide.woa/wa/
    getContent?type=page&id=1
Antivenoms: see under 'Snakes' in p.193.

Chapter 7

Air and sea travel

7.1 Air travel

Anthony Batchelor

Air transport today offers the traveller a remarkably safe and rapid way in which to cover great distances but, balanced against the convenience of this, some compromises have to be expected. To begin with, airports can be confusing environments for those not used to such adventures and tiring for even the fittest, but especially so for the elderly, those with health or disability issues, and for those travelling with young children. Security checks, while essential, are time consuming and tedious, and can involve removing items of clothing, unpacking hand luggage, undergoing body searches and passing through scanners.

Once aboard the aircraft, space is at a premium, with limited opportunities to move about, and the noise is at a moderate and persistent level. The modern airliner maintains a highly controlled environment within the cabin as it ascends to altitude, avoiding the perils experienced by early pioneers who lost consciousness as the air became too thin to provide adequate oxygen for normal metabolism. By limiting the fall in atmospheric pressure in the aircraft cabin to the equivalent of that found at 6000–8000 feet above sea level, the tension of oxygen in the air is sufficient to maintain entirely normal biological functions in healthy individuals, although it may have some impact on those with chronic respiratory and cardiac disorders.

The cabin air is derived from the external environment and at altitude is extremely dry. A proportion of this cabin air is recycled, a process that has led some in the past to express concerns that the potential for transmission of infections is thereby enhanced. However, in most aircraft the re-circulated air is passed through high efficiency particulate air (HEPA) filters of the type found in surgical operating theatres, designed to minimize such risks. Furthermore, the total air volume of the cabin is completely replaced every 2–3 min.

As the aircraft ascends and descends, gases contained in closed spaces within the body will expand and contract and this can have physiological consequences. In order to limit such effects, commercial aircraft flights normally maintain fairly slow rates of change in the cabin altitude. Finally, ascent to altitude is associated with an increased exposure to the natural radiation that strikes the earth from outer space—cosmic radiation. As the aircraft gains altitude, so the thickness of the protective blanket of atmosphere overhead is reduced, and thus the radiation dose increases. However, this is considered highly unlikely to attain biologically meaningful levels or to be associated with any long-term health impacts apart from, perhaps, on the foetuses of pregnant women who undertake very frequent long-haul journeys.

Fear of flying

Mile for mile, travel by commercial air transport is safer than any other form of transport, but anxiety about flying is nevertheless common. For some people this anxiety verges on the unbearable. There are some excellent books available to help manage symptoms and a few airlines run helpful 'fear of flying' courses, during which the sounds and sensations experienced in the aircraft are explained and coping strategies introduced. Consuming alcohol before a flight to allay anxiety is not to be recommended, but some passengers may want to discuss the use of a mild tranquillizer with their own doctors.

The aircraft cabin environment and the human body

Gas expansion

All will have experienced the 'popping' sensation that occurs in the ears as the altitude increases, even when climbing high hills in cars. This is caused by expansion of the air in the middle ear and leads to venting through a tube connecting to the nasopharynx (the eustachian tube). However, the flap valve that protects the opening of this tube does not so readily allow the reverse to occur when descending. Most people quickly learn to 'clear' their ears by swallowing or yawning, while others need to pinch their noses and swallow. What starts as an uncomfortable sensation can rapidly become painful, however, if the ears cannot be cleared. This is more likely when the lining of the upper respiratory tract is inflamed in the presence of a viral infection, or allergy such as hay-fever. Under those circumstances passengers should seriously consider postponing their trips but, if they do decide to fly, a nasal decongestant aerosol can be valuable if used early in anticipation of descent, rather than delayed until the ear is painful. Clearing the ears for sleeping infants can be a problem, but fortunately crying often corrects the situation! Alternatively, infants can be given a dummy or pacifier to suck to promote swallowing movements. Older children can usually be instructed in effective manoeuvres (but in case of difficulties the Editor's modification of a technique first described by the Austrian, Adam Politzer, is to be commended! See Box 7.1.1).

Box 7.1.1 **Children**

A method of relieving ear pain that I have found to work well with my own children is to gently pinch the child's nose, placing your lips around the child's mouth as if to give artificial ventilation; now blow gently! This may need to be repeated a number of times during a descent, but the relief is immediate.

RD

The process of gas expansion affects all organs in the body that contain gas and water vapour. Hence, the mild abdominal discomfort often apparent during ascent is directly related to gas in the gut obeying that same physical law, a matter to be borne in mind when selecting one's diet the day before a flight! More serious can be the effects of expanding gas remaining in closed body compartments after surgery (Table 7.1.1). Following eye surgery, for example, tiny collections of air can persist for a few days and expansion of such gas could have disastrous effects on the circulation of blood through the eye. As for most significant illnesses, disabilities or recent surgery, advice from the patient's general practitioner should be sought, or the medical department of the airline contacted.

Hypoxia

The systems that carry oxygen in the red cells of the blood and distribute it throughout the body have evolved to compensate for the moderate reductions in atmospheric oxygen breathed by people living in the higher regions of the earth, many of whom live comfortably at 5000–6000 feet or more. Mexico City, for example, is over 7000 feet above sea level, the same sort of altitude that is simulated in the cabin of an airliner. At levels above 8000 feet, however, the availability of useable oxygen in the blood stream does start to fall and have physiological consequences even for healthy individuals. Such effects, however, may be apparent at even lower altitudes in those with chronic lung disease and other ailments, including heart disease and anaemia (Table 7.1.1). A good test of whether such an individual might be vulnerable at cabin altitude is to consider their exercise tolerance at ground level: anyone who can walk 50–100 yards at a good pace, or climb a flight of stairs without inducing symptoms, is likely to be able to tolerate the cabin environment.

Reduced humidity

Although the opposite has been stated, even long-haul flights do not cause significant whole body dehydration. The dry air in the cabin does, however, have an effect on the mucous membranes of the eyes, mouth and nose, and can lead to local discomfort. Contact lens wearers may feel more comfortable wearing their glasses, a lip salve and frequent small soft drinks may ease the mouth and a moisturising cream may help the skin. However, the extra body water lost in such circumstances is extremely small. Sitting immobile for long periods does, though, encourage fluid to collect in the lower legs and this can have a small influence on the circulating blood volume. This latter process is responsible for the common experience of shoes being rather more difficult to put on at the end of a flight. A sensible intake of fluids throughout the flight is to be encouraged, but preferably limiting the alcohol content, which tends to promote extra urinary fluid loss and also to encourage immobility.

Disability and immobility

There is little spare space on aircraft and airlines must ensure that passengers can move quickly and without any obstruction in an emergency. People who have a problem with mobility therefore need to contact airlines in advance for special arrangements to be made. Airlines will not take responsibility for helping disabled passengers with the toilet, so those who require assistance may need to travel with an able-bodied companion. Nor should such disabled individuals consciously restrict their fluid intake in the hope of avoiding the need to use toilet facilities, as this might enhance their already increased risk of venous thrombosis. However, with planning, most people will be able to travel satisfactorily and all airlines have experience of handling wheelchair bound patients.

Time zones and circadian rhythms

This is discussed in more detail in Chapter 7.2. However, travellers by air should bear in mind that the 'body clock' will take several days, depending on the time zones crossed, to adapt to a new day/night cycle. This is of relevance for those planning to contribute to a conference or business meeting soon after a long transmeridian flight, or who plan to drive for any distance after landing. Allowance must be made for the state of alertness that will exist at the point of arrival, as this will be related more to the time of day at the point of departure, with the consequent potential for adverse effects on mental functions and psychomotor performance.

Passenger fitness to fly

For all those with chronic health impairment, fitness to undertake a commercial flight should be reflected upon well in advance of departure. Table 7.1.1 outlines some of the health problems for which it may be sensible to seek advice, either from general practitioners, hospital specialists or airline medical departments, which have experience in dealing with the practical aspects of such issues. Some additional health problems are discussed in the subsequent text. In general, do not plan a long flight after an illness or major surgery until you feel you have fully recovered, wounds are healed, normal bodily functions are restored and reasonable mobility has been achieved.

Table 7.1.1 Pre-existing medical conditions unsuited to or requiring special consideration for air travel

Disease or disorder	Explanation and advice
Chronic chest disease (e.g. chronic obstructive pulmonary disease (COPD))	Exercise capacity is a good guide and for those who are breathless at rest or on minor exertion, advice is required before flying. Supplementary oxygen is *not* available as standard on commercial aircraft and, if required, arrangements will need to be made in advance and a cost is likely to be involved.
Asthma	In a 1997 BA survey, asthma was responsible for 1 in 5 emergency aircraft diversions for health reasons, and the third commonest emergency drug used in flight was the asthma 'rescue' medication—salbutamol. Dry air in the aircraft cabin may aggravate asthma and sufferers should therefore carry their 'rescue' inhaler with them and show it at the airport security checks.
Collapsed lung (pneumothorax)	Flying should not be contemplated until the lung is fully re-expanded and preferably not for 6 weeks after that. There is a high risk of recurrence in early months.
Heart disease (including angina, a recent heart attack or heart failure for any reason)	Those who get chest pain on minimal exertion, and who could not manage the 50-yard test or a flight of stairs without symptoms, should seek advice in advance of flying. Individuals should avoid flying for a minimum of 2 weeks after an uncomplicated heart attack. Those with heart failure and symptoms at rest or on minor exertion should consider alternative modes of travel.

(Continued)

Table 7.1.1 Pre-existing medical conditions unsuited to or requiring special consideration for air travel

Disease or disorder	Explanation and advice
Anaemia	Those with significant anaemia of relatively sudden onset, for example, due to bleeding, should avoid flying until both the anaemia and the cause are corrected. For those with a more chronic form of anaemia, advice should be sought before making travel arrangements.
Recent surgery	During the recovery period from surgery there may be an enhanced risk of venous thrombosis. Other concerns relate to the trapping of air in closed body cavities and the need to avoid flying until it is all reabsorbed. Advice should be sought, particularly after procedures involving the eyes, ears and chest, or after abdominal or neurosurgery. Where surgery involves the intestines, some time needs to pass in order to restore normal bowel function and to ensure that the healing gut is not exposed to pressure from expanding gas.
Cancer	Many cancer patients will be fit to travel if sensible thought is given to the risks involved, but obtaining appropriate health insurance is an issue to be borne in mind. Management of the additional thrombosis risk needs to be considered in advance.
Epilepsy	Individuals with stable and well-controlled epilepsy should be fit to fly, but travel by air should be avoided by those prone to frequent convulsions. It should be remembered that anxiety, fatigue and alcohol can all lower the threshold for convulsions and all medications should be taken on time, preferably using home time on long flights.
Pregnancy	The aircraft cabin will not provide a comfortable environment for prolonged sitting in advanced pregnancy and is far from ideal for childbirth. Those with an uncomplicated single pregnancy should be fit to fly up to 36 weeks—but perhaps avoiding long-haul flights after 34 weeks. Those with twin pregnancies should avoid flying beyond 30–32 weeks and any complications should prompt professional advice in advance. Particular attention should be paid to anti-thrombosis advice.
Babies	Babies should not be taken by air until they are at least 7 days old and their lungs have had a chance to fully expand and establish normal function

Diabetes

Management of insulin-dependent diabetes does require some planning before a long-haul flight (Chapter 11.4). The same is true of other disorders in which the timing of medication is critical, and where dietary needs are important. Seeking advice from medical specialists should be part of the planning process, the airline should be alerted in advance to ensure dietary needs are catered for, and arrangements should be made to carry spare insulin in case of accidents. While insulin is usually kept in the refrigerator at home, it will remain perfectly stable for the duration of a long-haul flight at room temperature. Modern short-acting insulin regimes offer much greater flexibility to manage changes in daily routine. On transmeridian flights—those crossing time zones—adjustments for the shortening or lengthening of the day will need to be made. On long east-bound flights, where the day is compressed, those taking once daily long-acting insulins combined with short-acting insulin before food (basal bolus regime) should decrease the dose of the former and continue to use the latter in the normal way. If in doubt, one way in which to manage diabetes (and other conditions requiring strictly regular medication) is to stick to home times for meals and insulin throughout the flight, and then to make adjustments once safely at the destination.

Infectious disease

Sitting in close proximity to someone with an active respiratory infection, who is coughing and sneezing, presents an obvious risk of contracting the same infection in any environment. This remains true when flying and if such infections spread from one person, it is usually to those in the immediate vicinity of their seat. Those in the rest of the aircraft cabin, however, are not exposed to the same level of risk, as is commonly feared, despite the fact that approximately half of the air is re-circulated. This is because in all but the oldest airliners, the re-circulated air is passed through HEPA filters, which remove bacteria and viruses. Nevertheless, those with acute infectious illnesses, such as measles, influenza, and chickenpox, should not fly until recovered and no longer infectious. Equally, those with diarrhoeal illnesses should avoid flying—aircraft toilets are at a premium at the best of times.

Passengers' medical aids, drugs, dressings and equipment

Those passengers who have implanted metal components should carry a doctor's note to that effect. This includes those with pacemakers and automated defibrillators in particular, who may need to avoid some types of body scanners. A doctor's letter is also advisable for those carrying drugs for use during the journey, but is mandatory for those carrying syringes and needles, which should be declared at security. In order to avoid embarrassment, passengers with colostomies need to understand that the gas in the bowel and the bag will expand as the aircraft climbs to altitude, whilst patients with leg plasters should discuss the need to 'split' the plaster in advance of the flight. Increased swelling of the leg during the journey may require some room for expansion.

The use of portable oxygen concentrators is becoming common. However, those considering using them in flight need to discuss their plans with airline medical departments well in advance of departure—battery life is a factor to reflect on, as are the clinical details of the underlying condition.

Venous thrombosis

Deep venous thrombosis (DVT) describes a process whereby blood in the deep veins (usually starting in the legs) clots spontaneously, causing local disturbance of blood flow, swelling, inflammation, and discomfort. In the worst cases, pieces of the clot can break off and travel to the lungs causing pulmonary embolism—an occasionally fatal complication. DVT becomes more common with age and is encouraged by immobility, but by other factors too.

During World War II there seemed to be an epidemic of the problem, thought to be related to sleeping in deckchairs in underground stations to shelter from the bombing. It is now appreciated that sitting still for long periods with the legs bent and with pressure behind the knees predisposes to this problem and it has been described in travellers covering lengthy distances in cars, trains and aircraft, but also in theatregoers!

For most healthy people the risk of such a development is extremely small, but it can be enhanced by the presence of health issues, ranging from the use of oral contraceptives to recent abdominal surgery, from lower limb trauma to a history of thrombosis, and particularly by various forms of cancer. There are also small groups within the population who unknowingly inherit minor variants of the factors that control blood clotting, which make them slightly more susceptible to thromboses. One of the best recognized of these is known as Factor V Leiden, which is present in about 5% of white Europeans. The adverse influence of such an abnormality may then be further enhanced by some of the other circumstances already mentioned. So a 40-year-old woman who is unknowingly positive for Factor V Leiden might also be using the contraceptive pill, then suffer an injury to a leg while skiing in Canada, and finally make a long flight home. Her risk of thrombosis was already a little higher because of her inherited Factor V abnormality; it is higher at 40 years of age than it was when she was 20; and she has further increased it by being on the contraceptive pill. Then she injures her leg, so the risk goes up even further, before she boards a 9 hour overnight flight, when she tries to sleep with the aid of a sleeping tablet. The scene is set! For most of us, however, that risk is extremely small and can be reduced further by sensible precautions.

Appropriate advice is provided by most airlines in their passenger information sheets and includes maintaining a sensible fluid intake, undertaking regular lower leg exercises and avoiding long periods of total immobility by getting out of the seat from time to time. Sadly, though, this last piece of advice could create havoc if obeyed by all passengers! Another important tip is to avoid stowing large bags under the seat in front, causing the knees to be even more bent and the room for leg movement even more restricted. For those at increased risk, a restless sleep is preferable to the lack of any body movement that might accompany the deep slumber induced by sleeping tablets. These agents are best avoided in such circumstances and alcohol intake minimized. Table 7.1.2 outlines some of the factors that are known to be associated with an increased risk of thrombosis.

For those in the mildly increased risk group, performing leg exercises, maintaining a reasonable fluid intake and moderating alcohol consumption should be adequate, but well-fitting support socks can aid comfort. For those at medium extra risk, graduated support stockings should be considered in order to discourage blood pooling in the leg veins, together with leg exercises and moving around the aircraft cabin. The high-risk group should seek medical advice well before departure. In addition to the precautions already described, this group may benefit from injections of an anticoagulant prior to the flight.

Table 7.1.2 Factors associated with an increased risk of thrombosis

Risk level	Cause
Mildly increased risk	• Age over 40 years • Recent minor surgery (within 3 days) • Obesity • Active inflammatory diseases such as arthritis
Moderately increased risk	• Pregnancy, oral contraception • Recent leg injuries (within 6 weeks) • Recent heart attack; heart failure • Paraplegia
High risk	• Previous episodes of thrombosis; family history of thrombosis and know abnormalities of blood clotting (thrombophilia) • Malignant disease (cancer) • Recent major surgery (within 6 weeks) • Combinations of other risks—each of which may not be high in itself, but which have a cumulative effect

Diving

SCUBA diving enthusiasts are well aware of the potential for decompression illness or 'the bends' and manage the timings and ascents of their dives to avoid such problems. However, climbing to altitude in an aircraft after diving can accentuate such a risk and divers should avoid diving for a minimum of 12 hours before a flight and for 24 hours if they have been undertaking deeper or more frequent dives.

Illness on board

Cabin crews are trained in first aid to deal with minor accidents and injuries and some may be trained in resuscitation. All airlines carry emergency medical kits containing common requirements for first aid, resuscitation equipment, simple analgesics and usually a range of drugs that could be made available if a suitably qualified medical professional was available on the flight. A number of long-haul airlines also have facilities for telemetry links to ground-based emergency medical centres, enabling information to be transmitted and expert advice to be received. These arrangements are in place to ensure that medical emergencies can be dealt with as effectively as possible under difficult circumstances. However, the aircraft cabin is not the ideal environment in which to be acutely ill and many emergencies occur in those with known conditions who could have been appropriately guided beforehand had they declared their health problems. So the message must be—if in doubt, ask!

Box 7.1.2 **Air rage**

Rob Bor

Recent media reports suggest that incidents of disruptive passenger behaviour are becoming more frequent and more violent. Our own research confirms increasing concern within the airline industry and a move towards formulating policies and procedures for dealing with incidents.

The earliest recorded incident of passenger disruption occurred in 1947, on a flight from Havana to Miami. Three crew members who intervened were injured, one of which was bitten; the passenger was able to walk away from any charges because jurisdiction aboard aircraft flying international routes had not yet been established.

Between 1994 and 1995, American Airlines reported a 200% increase in passenger interference with flight attendants' duties, and there were 450 similar cases on board United Airlines flights during 1997. Tempers can also run high on the ground. A fracas in Newark, New Jersey, left a Continental Airlines employee with a broken neck.

Results of our own survey of the **causes of 'air rage'**, based on responses from the airlines, are shown below. More than a third of airline staffs have no training in dealing with air rage. A third of airlines had no policy on whether or not crews were permitted to leave the flight deck to deal with incidents.

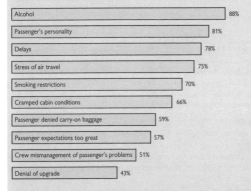

Alcohol	88%
Passenger's personality	81%
Delays	78%
Stress of air travel	75%
Smoking restrictions	70%
Cramped cabin conditions	66%
Passenger denied carry-on baggage	59%
Passenger expectations too great	57%
Crew mismanagement of passenger's problems	51%
Denial of upgrade	43%

'Air rage' is not just a passenger problem: airlines need to train their staff to manage violent passengers; to make clear the airline's policy on disruptive behaviour at the start of the flight; and to do more to prevent such situations arising in the first place.

Conclusion

Travel by air can be safely undertaken by the great majority of people, even those with health problems. For the latter group, the provisos must be that advice is sought in advance, that relevant issues are discussed with airline medical departments and that enough time is given to planning and

Box 7.1.3 **Fear of flying**

Rob Bor

Ten to thirty per cent of people suffer from a fear of flying: for some, it is solely unpleasant while for others it is incapacitating. The good news is that there are effective techniques to reduce the anxiety associated with flying.

What causes your fear of flying?

Some people feel claustrophobic in an aircraft. Others fear heights. Many have a horror of turbulence and fear that they might die as a consequence of it. Some passengers have difficulty coping with a separation from their loved ones or baggage. Heightened anxiety about not being in control is common. Others worry about coping with their own feelings if they become distressed, or other people's reactions to them. Yet others find the prospect of being abroad difficult to contend with. In fact, there are probably as many causes of fear of flying as there are people who dislike flying!

How do psychological techniques overcome a fear of flying?

Cognitive behavioural therapy is highly successful in treating fear of flying. Techniques focus on how people cope with their irrational fears and present ways in which they can manage feared situations more positively. The therapy includes:

- *Education:* covering factual information about anxiety, fears, and phobias that will aid an understanding of the problem
- *Understanding your specific fear:* so that treatment can be targeted
- *Challenging ideas and beliefs:* the person is helped to view their problem differently
- *Addressing your worst fears:* exercises gradually expose you to some aspects of them to improve your confidence and coping skills
- *Challenging your safety behaviours:* for example, avoiding flying. They may be preventing you from making progress in life
- *Homework:* a lot of change comes from working on the issues outside therapy sessions.

preparation. The airline cabin is a busy and crowded environment and it must be recognized that the main responsibility of cabin crew is passenger safety and that they are not there primarily to act as health care workers.

7.2 Jet lag

Richard Dawood

Jet lag is a difficult problem for large numbers of air travellers. Understanding the factors that control the human 'body clock' is the key to helping travellers develop a personal strategy for overcoming or reducing its effects.

While many strategies can help alleviate some symptoms of jet lag, there are only two known factors with a proven ability to speed adjustment to a new time zone: exposure to bright light, and small doses of melatonin, but the problem is to know when and how to use them effectively. With correct timing and dosage, it is possible to manipulate and adjust the body clock, and to eliminate much of the discomfort and inconvenience that have come to be an almost inseparable part of the experience of modern air travel.

The body clock

Almost every living creature exhibits circadian rhythms. In humans, every natural process within the body shows some variation in pattern between night and day. The most obvious patterns are sleep and wakefulness, but an internal body clock (located in a portion of the brain known as the suprachiasmatic nuclei) also controls alertness, hunger, digestion, bowel habits, urine production, body temperature, secretion of hormones, and even blood pressure.

These rhythms differ in their ability to be altered by external factors (such as light and darkness, social cues like mealtimes, and the ambient temperature and apparent time of day—known as *zeitgebers*). Rapid air travel across several time zones outstrips the ability of the body to re-synchronize these rhythms. The resulting physiological desynchronization causes symptoms such as malaise, gastrointestinal disturbance, loss of appetite, tiredness during the day, disorientation, memory impairment, and reduced mental performance that every air traveller recognizes as 'jet lag'.

In turn, these external factors differ in their ability to influence the body clock and draw it back into line—some are much more powerful than others. Experiments confirm that the two most powerful factors are exposure to light and the hormone melatonin.

Light exposure

Exposure to light during the mid-portion of the day, not surprisingly, has no effect on the body clock. Experiments show that light exposure earlier in the day will shorten (i.e. bring forward or advance) the normal circadian cycle, whereas light exposure occurring later in the day has the effect of lengthening (delaying) it. By experimenting with the timing and duration of the light exposure, it becomes possible to determine the times when light exposure reaches its maximum 're-setting' effect. This effect turns out to be greatest during the night: during the first half of the night, light causes a delay; during the second half, light causes an advance. The same experiments show that prolonged exposure is not necessary—relatively short pulses of bright light (as short as 30min) are all that is needed.

Melatonin

Melatonin is the so-called 'hormone of darkness'—a naturally occurring substance secreted in the brain by the pineal gland during the hours of night. The pineal gland was once believed to be a functionless evolutionary remnant, like the appendix; but in a primitive creature called the lamprey, the pineal is actually a third eye, and is directly responsive to light. In the human body, melatonin levels in the blood rise as darkness descends, reaching a peak around 4am, and falling again as morning approaches.

Melatonin is known to be a major regulator of circadian rhythms. Thirty years ago, experiments demonstrated that bright light suppresses human melatonin production. Experiments with the timing of a dose of synthetic melatonin show a pattern that is an exact mirror image of the re-setting power of light. A dose of melatonin taken during the night has little effect on the body clock. By experimenting with bringing the dose forward, or delaying it, it is possible to advance or delay the circadian cycle, and to calculate the most effective timing. The effect is greatest during the day (Fig. 7.2.1). With correct timing, only tiny doses of melatonin are needed to achieve a powerful effect.

Melatonin has been available in the USA for many years, where it is sold as an over-the-counter nutritional supplement. More recently, a slow-release version of melatonin in 2mg dosage (Circadin) has become fully licensed in the UK, where it can be prescribed as a remedy for sleep disturbances. Although used widely in the USA with no safety concerns, very little is known of its effects in children or pregnant woman, in whom it should therefore not be used.

A simple, practical way to use melatonin is to take a small dose (2–5mg) before going to bed. A more complex but more effective approach to using both light exposure and melatonin can be found at: ⌖http://www.fleetstreetclinic.com/travel-clinic/air-travel-and-flying/jet-lag-calculator

Overcoming jet lag

Most people who fly across time zones can expect to adjust naturally to their new 'local time' at a rate of approximately 1 hr/day. For example, a traveller flying between Portland, Oregon, and Amsterdam (a difference of nine time zones), would probably take around 9 days to adjust fully, and another 9 days to adjust back at the end of the trip. For most people, such a trip therefore represents an 18-day commitment to jet lag.

To achieve phase advances:

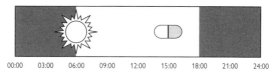

| 00:00 | 03:00 | 06:00 | 09:00 | 12:00 | 15:00 | 18:00 | 21:00 | 24:00 |

To achieve phase delays:

| 00:00 | 03:00 | 06:00 | 09:00 | 12:00 | 15:00 | 18:00 | 21:00 | 24:00 |

Fig. 7.2.1 Phase-shifting effects of light and melatonin. In order to cause a phase advance light should be scheduled in the morning and melatonin administered in the afternoon. In order to cause a phase delay, light should be scheduled in the evening and melatonin should be administered in the morning.

Reproduced with permission of Dr A Lewy.

Two additional factors can make the situation slightly better than this, or substantially worse. The first is that, left to their own resources, our bodies have a natural tendency towards operating on a cycle that is 25 hours long, not 24 hours. (If you are a 'late-night' person, your natural cycle may be even longer.) This makes it easier to adapt to a longer day (as in westward travel) than to a shorter one (as in eastward travel). The second is that inappropriately timed light exposure following arrival can reset the body clock in the wrong direction, making jet lag considerably worse.

Travellers who use **either** correctly timed light exposure **or** correctly timed low-dose melatonin can generally adjust to their new local time at a rate of approximately 2 hours/day—twice as fast as by nature alone. By combining both methods, a rate of 3 hours/day can be accomplished.

Instructions for overcoming jet lag can be followed to different levels of complexity.

Other remedies

A vast range of treatments and remedies have been claimed to offer relief, including:

- Aromatherapy
- Homeopathy
- Diet
- Stimulation of energy meridians
- Kinesiotherapy
- Magnetic therapy/use of rare earth magnets
- Pendants with mysterious properties
- Pressure-point massage.

While some of the above may go part way to helping the traveller feel better, melatonin and light are the only two methods of speeding adaptation to a new time zone that have attained any level of scientific proof.

Sleeping medication at your destination

Sleeping medication *does not* speed up adaptation to a new time zone, and is therefore not a treatment for jet lag, though it may reduce some of its effects. Studies show that medication can help reduce fatigue, with better next-day performance. Modern sleeping medications have a much-reduced potential for becoming habit-forming, especially when used infrequently.

Following eastbound travel, most people have difficulty initiating sleep at a normal local time; there is a tendency to stay up late, followed by difficulty waking at a normal time. A short-acting drug like zolpidem (e.g. Ambien) may help—it works quickly and is then rapidly eliminated from the body.

For westbound travel, the tendency is towards early waking. One option would be to use short-acting medication during the night, as long as you have time for another 4 hr sleep; another option would be to use a longer-lasting sleeping tablet (such as temazepam) to help you sleep through with less chance of waking.

These medicines require a prescription and should of course be discussed carefully with your doctor. Sleeping medicines should not be used in-flight under cramped seating conditions, because of a possible increased risk of DVT (see Table 7.2.1).

Staying awake

A drug called modafinil (Provigil) can help improve alertness in a new time zone. (Its main intended use is to help people suffering from narcolepsy—a condition in which they fall asleep suddenly during the day.) A closely related drug, armodafinil (Nuvigil), is also available in the USA: a formal study of air travellers crossing six time zones demonstrated improved wakefulness in those taking Nuvigil, though neither drug is currently licensed for this purpose.

Similar effects can be achieved by drinking large amounts of coffee.

Other jet lag tips

- Adjust your itinerary to minimize sleep loss and fatigue
- Avoid night-time flights when possible, and if you can't, build a rest period on arrival into your schedule
- Travel in the highest class that you can afford
- Avoid eating inappropriately timed large meals during your journey
- Give your body as many 'clues' to your new time zone as you can—adjust your wristwatch, observe local meal times and bed times, and so on
- Accept that your performance may be reduced through jet lag, and avoid important business activities for at least the first 24 hours following arrival
- If you need to arrange activities on arrival that require you to be mentally alert, pick a time corresponding to daylight hours in your home time-zone
- For very short trips, consider staying on home time.

Table 7.2.1 Sleeping medications and their duration

Medication	Standard dose	Duration of effect	Notes
Zolpidem (Ambien)	5mg	3–4 hours	If you wake during the night, take a further dose if you'll be able to stay in bed for 4 more hours
Zopiclone (Zimovane)	3.75mg	4–6 hours	Leaves a bitter taste that indicates when the drug is present.
Temazepam	10mg	6–8 hours	

7.3 Motion sickness

Alan Benson and Rollin Stott

Motion sickness is one of the commonest and most familiar problems relating to travel, and it is helpful for sufferers to understand the underlying mechanisms and treatment.

About half the adult population admits to having felt travel sick at some time in their lives. Most commonly this will have been car or coach sickness, or seasickness in rough weather. Air sickness on passenger aircraft is nowadays relatively infrequent as cruising altitudes tend to remain well above the weather, but it can still occur if the aircraft encounters high-level turbulence or in rough weather conditions during the climb and descent phase of the flight. Less familiar forms of travel sickness are associated with riding on camels and elephants (though not horses). Those contemplating a trip into space should be aware that 50% of trained astronauts suffer the effects of space sickness, another form of motion sickness. It is not for nothing that the aircraft designed to fly manoeuvres that give the occupants experience of weightlessness is known as the 'Vomit Comet'. While for some, travel sickness is a minor, but dispiriting experience, for more susceptible individuals it has the potential to ruin a holiday or discourage them from travel or continuing with leisure activities such as gliding or sailing.

Despite the diversity of possible causal situations and environments, all provoke what is termed sensory conflict, either between the eyes and the balance organ of the inner ear or between the functional components within the balance organ itself. Pedestrian man has the expectation that his movements will be against a background of a predominantly fixed visual world, and a sensation of gravity that remains fixed in direction and intensity. Motion sickness tends to occur when the combined signals from the body's sensors of motion—the eyes and inner ear—fail to reflect these expectations.

Virtually everybody can be made motion sick given a sufficiently provocative environment, and only those rare individuals who have lost all function in the balance organs of the inner ear are totally immune. A further feature of motion sickness is that, with repeated exposure to a stimulus that initially provokes nausea; an individual will gradually adapt and become less susceptible to its effects.

Signs and symptoms

It is worth being aware of the early symptoms of motion sickness, since at this stage, preventive measures may still be effective. In circumstances where the onset of motion sickness is gradual, the first indication may be an increasing lethargy and loss of interest often accompanied by a tendency to repeated yawning and a need for fresh air. Stomach awareness is usually the next symptom, and this progresses to nausea of increasing severity. The face becomes pale and the individual begins to sweat. There may also be a feeling of light-headedness, dizziness, or headache. The increasing sense of depression and apathy may have significant consequences if, as a result, an individual fails to carry out some essential task.

With continued provocative motion, vomiting is generally not long delayed, though some individuals can remain severely nauseated for long periods without vomiting. Having vomited the sufferer may feel better for a time, before the cycle of nausea and vomiting begins again. The increasing nausea sometimes provokes hyperventilation (over-breathing) and this can contribute to the light-headedness and sometimes to numbness and tingling in the hands and feet and around the mouth.

Prevention

Behavioural measures

There are a number of things an individual can do that may prevent the development of symptoms. The passenger aboard ship should seek out a position in the vessel where the motion is least, usually near the middle of the ship, and on a low deck if there is much roll motion. The driver of a car should take bends gently and avoid frequent and powerful braking and acceleration. The captain of a boat may be able, by regulating its speed and heading, to provide a more comfortable passage.

Restriction of head movement by pressing the head firmly against the seat or other available support is likely to be beneficial; adopting a recumbent position can also reduce head movements. It is a common observation that those suffering from seasickness have less malaise when made to lie down with their eyes closed.

Procedures to reduce conflict between vision and sensation arising from the balance organs of the inner ear can also be helpful. When below deck in a boat or in the enclosed cabin of an aircraft, it is better to close the eyes than to keep them open. On the other hand, when able to see out, one should fixate on the horizon or some other stable external visual reference. Passengers in a car should, like the driver, look at the road ahead. Susceptible coach passengers should likewise choose a seat with a good forward view. For children confined to the back seat of a car the use of a booster cushion may improve their view of the road ahead, and on winding roads they could usefully be encouraged to lean into the corners as a means of getting them to anticipate the motion of the vehicle. Reading in a car is well known to precipitate motion sickness, so tasks involving visual search and scanning within the vehicle should be avoided.

The person in control of a car, boat, or plane is less likely to suffer from motion sickness than other passengers, presumably because of a greater ability to anticipate the motion and to make appropriate postural adjustments so that sensory conflict is reduced. A further benefit of being in control may derive from the mental distraction that it provides. There is experimental and anecdotal evidence that symptoms are reduced by mental activity that directs the subject's attention away from features of the provocative motion and introspection about lack of well-being.

Dietary factors

Dietary factors do not play an important part in the prevention of motion sickness and the avoidance of food before a rough sea crossing makes little difference to the likelihood of seasickness. Motion sickness sufferers tend, however, to avoid alcohol before and during a voyage, and are probably correct in assuming that alcohol would increase their susceptibility.

Root ginger, a traditional oriental remedy for sickness, has been shown in sea trials to reduce the incidence of vomiting, but to have little effect on the degree of nausea.

Adaptation

In addition to the behavioural measures outlined on p.217, a further important factor in reducing susceptibility is adaptation to the provocative motion. Adaptation is 'nature's own cure' and in many respects is the ideal prophylaxis, although adaptation gained in one environment does not necessarily transfer to a different motion environment.

Aboard ship the process of 'getting one's sea legs' usually takes 2 or 3 days and involves not only an improved sense of balance but also a reduced susceptibility to sea sickness. However, a minority of the population (estimated at about 5%) are 'non-adapters' and continue to have problems as long as the rough weather persists. Having adapted to the motion of the ship, symptoms may recur on return to dry land—the so called 'mal de débarquement'. Although any nausea is rarely severe, transient illusory sensations of motion may persist for a day or more.

Acupressure

Claims have been made that pressure applied to a point above the wrist, known to acupuncturists as the P6 or Nei-Kuan point, is effective in preventing motion sickness and elasticated bands, sold as 'Sea bands®' or 'Acubands', are available for this purpose. However, controlled laboratory trials have failed to show any significant efficacy. Nevertheless, the placebo effect of any form of treatment, prescribed with conviction, can be beneficial to some individuals.

Drugs

Drugs that are of value in the prevention of motion sickness are listed in Table 7.3.1. They vary in the time they take to be effective and the length of time for which they act. All effective drugs for motion sickness act within the brain and all have central side effects, notably drowsiness. In addition, hyoscine may cause light-headedness, a dry mouth and, with prolonged use, blurring of vision. It has the advantage of a rapid onset of action but a relatively short duration of action. This can be extended by administering the drug through a skin patch when, after a slow onset of action (which can be covered by a single oral dose), it remains effective for 2–3 days. Hyoscine is not recommended for use in children and should be used with caution in the elderly. The remaining drugs listed are earlier generation antihistamines and in appropriate dose are more suitable for these age groups. Modern antihistamines are designed not to cross the blood brain barrier so as to avoid causing drowsiness. However, for this reason they are not effective in motion sickness. Similarly, drugs used in nausea and vomiting from chemotherapy are ineffective since they act on a different vomiting mechanism.

When vomiting from motion sickness persists, drugs taken by mouth are not absorbed. In these circumstances the doctor on a cruise ship may prescribe an injection of promethazine or possibly hyoscine.

Table 7.3.1 Anti-motion sickness drugs

Drug	Route	Adult dose	Time to take effect	Duration of action (hours)
Hyoscine hydrobromide (Joyrides, Kwells) (ScopodermTTS)	Oral	0.3–0.6mg	30min	4
	Patch	Content 1.5mg	6–8 hours	72
	Injection	0.2mg	15min	4
Cinnarizine (Stugeron)	Oral	15–30mg	4 hours	8
Promethazine teoclate (Avomine)	Oral	25mg	2 hours	24
Promethazine hydrochloride (Phenergan)	Oral	25–50mg	2 hours	18
	Injection	25–50mg	15min	18
Cyclizine hydrochloride (Valoid)	Oral	50mg	2 hours	12
Meclozine hydrochloride (Sea-legs)	Oral	12.5–25mg	2 hours	8

Box 7.3.1 **Summary of advice for travellers**

• If you suffer from motion sickness, always carry a suitable remedy at times when you will be at risk, and start using it before symptoms appear

• Don't drive when taking a remedy that causes drowsiness

• Read leaflets carefully before deciding on the suitability of any drugs, particularly during pregnancy.

7.4 Cruise ship medicine

Arthur L. Diskin

The cruise industry has expanded rapidly in recent years—both in the number and size of ships, some now exceeding 8000 guests and crew. This growth has been accompanied by substantial improvements in the medical facilities on the major cruise lines.

The small ships and elegant ocean liners of the past have been replaced by modern fleets, offering a myriad of activities, including ice skating, rock climbing, surfing, and sports courts. Shore excursions now include eco- and adventure tourism with hiking, zip lines, 4-wheel drive, and various water sports, to name a few. All of these present more than enough opportunity for the traveller to sustain significant injuries. The days of cruises being only for retirees and newlyweds are long gone.

Cruise passengers, like any other travellers, should assess the risks and availability of health care services at the locations where they will be travelling and consider their own health in relation to these risks, as well as taking responsibility for following up promptly with their medical provider upon their return home, should they become ill. Travelling the world with a ship's doctor by your side is very tempting but should be done wisely and the ship, length of cruise and itinerary should be appropriately selected. Potential shore excursions available should also be carefully considered.

The World Health Organization (WHO) advises travellers to consult a travel medicine clinic or practitioner as early as possible before travel to any destination where significant health risks may be foreseen, particularly developing countries, and preferably 4–8 weeks before departure (though even up to the day before departure if necessary).

The WHO recommends travellers be aware of any particular hazards to personal safety and security presented by the destination and suggests appropriate precautions be taken. All travellers should take out comprehensive travellers' health insurance from a reputable provider (Chapter 13.3) and be aware of the specific features and exclusions of the policies. Your cruise operator or travel agent may directly offer a policy.

The traveller should also be aware of any mandatory vaccination requirements, such as yellow fever; the need for precautions against malaria or other health hazards at the travel destination; and the presence or absence of good-quality medical facilities on the ship or ashore.

Holidaymakers should also carefully pack their own medical kit and carry it with them, as well as a summary of their medical records (see Box 7.4.1). Bear in mind that the ship's dispensary may not stock your medications, nor may supplies be available in the ports. Any necessary equipment, such as oxygen tanks or continuous positive airway pressure (CPAP) machines, should be carefully arranged before travel. The cruise line should be informed of any special medical needs and be given the opportunity to discuss the capabilities of the ship and the ports in relation to those needs.

Preparation and planning

Travel insurance and medical assistance

As most domestic land-based health insurance policies do not cover illness or injury at sea or abroad, all guests should strongly consider purchasing travel insurance. The insurance should be examined to understand the terms and exclusions, such as pre-existing illnesses.

Most illnesses and injuries can be treated on board, but patients with serious problems must be disembarked for specialist care, hospitalization or repatriation. An experienced medical assistance company will select, plan, and co-ordinate all of the shore-side care while their agents resolve language problems, financial difficulties, and provide accommodation and support for travelling companions. These arrangements can be very costly and difficult to make. Treatment on board normally carries a cost, which can also be quite high in critical cases. Passengers should be prepared to pay at time of service or have charges added to their bill. Those planning to participate in activities such as scuba diving may need special insurance policies.

Box 7.4.1 **Essential information and items for the traveller**

Medical history
- List of all medications, including non-prescription—dose, frequency, and indication
- Allergies
- Medical summary letter from primary provider, including recent hospital summaries
- Copy of recent ECG/EKG if appropriate
- Copy of recent laboratory results if appropriate
- Vaccination certificates.

Other things to bring
- Travel medical and primary insurance company information
- Policy number and 24 hour contact number
- Telephone numbers of your primary doctor and all consultants/specialists
- Contact information for any special suppliers, such as oxygen or wheelchairs
- Advanced Directives and Powers of Attorney considered and signed prior to travel (leave copy at home with emergency contacts), where appropriate.

Travel medicine check-up
Travellers are advised to contact their doctor or a travel medicine clinic or physician for appropriate advice. The initial consultation should ideally be 6–8 weeks before the scheduled date of departure. You should take with you your complete itinerary, as well as your medical history and all your medications.

Vaccinations, medicines, and health precautions
Most cruise lines will advise their passengers of any vaccination certificates that are *required* by the International Health Regulations and, in particular, whether a yellow fever vaccination certificate is *required* for some itineraries to South America and Africa (Appendix 1). Cruise lines do not routinely provide information on *recommended* immunizations, or on prophylactic medications (such as for malaria). More exotic itineraries require careful consideration of needs. All guests should consider updating all immunizations including those against tetanus, diphtheria, pneumococcal infection (pneumonia), shingles, and seasonal influenza.

Pre-existing medical conditions
Access to quality medical care is not always easy and what starts as a minor complication can escalate into a major medical problem. Anyone with a known health issue that may require medical care on board (including pregnancy) should first:
- Consult their doctor and ensure that they are in a stable condition
- Complete any scheduled medical or dental treatment

- Recuperate from any major illness or surgery (unless your doctor approves your plans)
- Understand that specialist medical care might not be readily available
- Advise cruise line medical departments of any conditions that may require medical care or equipment on board.

Usually cruise lines can provide prospective travellers or their health care providers with information including special embarkation procedures, policies regarding infants and pregnancy, medical device resources and safety requirements, e.g. maintenance certificates/CE mark, medical device compatibility with shipboard electrical systems, oxygen resources for international travellers, cylinders and connections, medical gas safety in the shipboard environment, peritoneal and haemodialysis capabilities, and referrals and procedures for individuals with a history of food allergies and/or anaphylaxis.

Travellers with any dental problems should consult their dentist before the cruise (Chapter 9.2). Most cruise ships do not carry dentists and shore-side dentists with appropriate facilities are not always readily available in port.

Cruise ship medical staff and facilities

There are no international standards of care for cruise ships, but many, including most Cruise Lines International Association (CLIA) member lines who are also members of the European Cruise Council (ECC), have medical facilities that are staffed and equipped in accordance with guidance provided by the American College of Emergency Physicians Health Care Guidelines for Cruise Ship Medical Facilities (which can be found at ℘ http://www.acep.org/Content.aspx?id=29980).

A ship's medical facility is not a hospital—there are no operating rooms, CT or MRI scanners. The small, usually well-equipped clinics are usually staffed by one to three doctors and two to five nurses. A typical medical facility has one or two consulting rooms, a simple laboratory, X-ray machine, and wards for the treatment and isolation of passengers and crew. At least one of the wards will have an intensive care bed for the initial treatment of life-threatening illnesses.

The ACEP guidelines recommend that the ship's medical facilities be equipped with cardiac defibrillators, external pacemakers, electrocardiogram (ECG) machines, cardiac monitors, infusion pumps, respirators, pulse oximeters, and a comprehensive range of medications including thrombolytics. Small or older ships may not have these capabilities.

The staff can begin treatment for conditions such as heart attacks and chest infections in the intensive care ward and when necessary will consider obtaining advice from specialist shore-side colleagues via Internet or telephone. Depending on the illness, the ship and the itinerary, the guest may often be able to receive better medical care on the ship than at the next port. If medical evacuation to a port is needed for additional care, it should be the next most appropriate port able to deliver a higher level of care than aboard the ship. Sometimes, it is better for the patient to remain in the ship's medical facility until the end of the cruise.

Telemedicine

On some of the newer ships, shore-side specialists can review a patient's X-rays, interpret ECGs, and provide real time audio-video consultations via satellite links or Internet. Many ships' digital X-ray capabilities yield easily transmissible images. One line has instituted a Teledermatology program.

Emergency medical disembarkation/evacuation

Helicopter evacuations by the USA Coast Guard, Royal Navy, or other provider are dramatic but they are often impractical and rarely improve the medical outcome. If a ship is within the rescue helicopter's range, the weather and lighting are adequate, and the patient can be efficiently transferred to an appropriate hospital, the ship's doctor has to decide whether or not an immediate evacuation will benefit their patient. Does the time factor justify the risks? Is the helicopter safe? How will the patient respond as they are winched aboard? Will the noise or vibration cause any problems? Are there any doctors or nurses on board? Do they have enough space and equipment to provide treatment during the transfer? Are the services available superior to those onboard the ship?

Usually, the only time helicopter evacuation should be considered is in the event surgical intervention or blood transfusion is needed. In all but a few cases, the patient is much better off being managed in the ship's medical facility until they can be disembarked at the next port. The ship is often the best possible ambulance.

Seasickness

La maladie de la mer is the body's natural reaction to the motions that often accompany sea travel. Previous experience predicts future susceptibility. Small boats are more provocative than mega-liners and the roughest seas can affect everyone.

Modern passengers are rarely bothered by the ship's motion but anyone planning a cruise should have a 'seasickness prevention strategy' based on the itinerary, the season and the ship's size. Fresh air and a distant horizon may be all that a seasoned seafarer needs but herbal medicines, tablets, and patches may be required by some.

Scopolamine patches may cause confusion in the elderly, blurry vision, and urinary retention but are very effective for those that don't mind feeling a little sleepy. The patches work for 72 hours, so carry enough for the entire trip. Wash your hands after removing. If you rub your eyes after touching the scopolamine, your pupil might dilate and someone may think you have had a stroke. Always tell the doctor if you have been using scopolamine. Never cut the patch before applying. Apply behind the ear.

Divers and anyone else who needs to remain alert may want to experiment with ginger or stimulation of the acupuncture point at the wrist, subject to variable reports of success. If you are on any medications, especially blood thinners, or are pregnant, check with your doctor before taking ginger.

The most common seasickness pills are often misused. When taken as a last resort, they have no effect. The first dose should be taken at least 4–6 hours before embarkation in those very prone to seasickness. A doctor may prescribe other oral medications or an injection once severe symptoms have started. Seasickness is discussed further in Chapter 7.3.

Mal de débarquement
This is a rare condition, but if you continue to experience a rocking motion for more than a week after disembarkation, you should consult a neurologist or otolaryngologist.

Infectious diseases

If joining guests are already infected with a contagious illness, this can spread rapidly to other passengers, resulting in severe disease in the frail and elderly or immunocompromised.

On-board concerns include food poisoning, norovirus, chickenpox (*Varicella*), German measles (*Rubella*), and influenza A & B. Vaccination programmes and additional hygiene strategies have been implemented to decrease the risk of outbreaks.

In spite of these precautions, cruise ship travellers may be exposed to a variety of infectious diseases. Most of these infections can be prevented or mitigated by vaccinations, prophylactic medication, hygiene awareness or timely treatment.

Food and water-related problems

The United Kingdom's Health Protection Agency (HPA), the European Union's SHIPSAN, and the USA Centers for Disease Control and Prevention (CDC) Vessel Sanitation Program (VSP) have successfully worked with the cruise industry to minimize food and waterborne illness and disease aboard cruise ships.

Ships undergo regular health and hygiene inspections and the CDC and Health Canada publish each ship's scores on their web sites:
- CDC VSP ℘ www.cdc.gov/nceh/vsp/
- Health Canada ℘ www.hc-sc.gc.ca/hl-vs/travel-voyage/general/ship-navire-eng.php

HACCP (Hazard Analysis Critical Control Point) and similar programmes designed to monitor food and water from source to consumption have been effectively used on ships to ensure food and beverage safety. However, eating and drinking in ports of call increases the risk of gastrointestinal disease. Advice on food, hand washing, and hygiene precautions given elsewhere should be followed carefully. Certain locations, such as the Nile River in Egypt, have presented particular problems and extra precautions should be taken. Traveller's diarrhoea (see Chapter 2.1) is common in many areas of the world. Guests with underlying medical problems or who are immunocompromised may want to consider prophylactic antibiotics, such as rifaximin (p.26).

If you will spend time eating on shore, especially in underdeveloped locations, avoid ice, tap water, salads, mayonnaise-containing products, fruits, and vegetables you have not washed and peeled yourself and food transported from a location other than where it is being served. Make sure bottled water is sealed before opening. All cases of gastrointestinal illness after eating on shore should be reported to the ship's physician.

Quarantine regulations require all cases of gastrointestinal disease (diarrhoea and/or vomiting) and all on-board sales of anti-diarrhoeal medications to be documented. To ensure full compliance, most cruise lines do not sell anti-diarrhoeal medications without a medical consultation.

Norovirus and related infections

Norovirus is a highly infectious form of gastroenteritis characterized by vomiting, diarrhoea, fever, and often body aches (Chapter 2.1).

Some cruise ship outbreaks of Norovirus—like gastroenteritis have been caused by contaminated ice, shrimp, and fresh cut fruit. Infected boarding passengers, and crew, and environmental contamination may have contributed to outbreaks in which no food or water source could be identified. Even if the source is unknown, secondary spread can usually be halted if the index cases are identified and a rapid response programme initiated.

If intensive cleaning reduces but does not eliminate new cases, environmental contamination, person-to-person contact and airborne transmission can still infect each new group of passengers and crew within a short period of (24–36 hours) joining the vessel. In this way, the outbreak can be extended. If back-to-back cruises have been infected, health authorities may delay ships for one or more days to allow time for total sanitation.

Most, if not all, cases of Norovirus are first brought aboard by infected guests who have not reported illness prior to boarding or who become sick after boarding. Most cases are spread through public vomiting episodes. The virus is very small, travels far, and is highly contagious. It is also possible for guests who practice poor personal hygiene and do not wash their hands thoroughly after bowel movements to spread the illness by touching surfaces such as hand rails or elevator buttons. This is why you see such frequent cleaning of these surfaces by crew. Outbreaks have also been reported from contaminated ice machines.

Noroviruses are responsible for most cases of gastroenteritis worldwide and are estimated to cause about 60% of all cases in the USA—with more than 5 million cases estimated during 2011. The peak season is December through March, especially in cold climates where it is sometimes referred to as winter vomiting disease.

Cases have been increasing worldwide in recent years, but fewer outbreaks on cruise ships reflect greatly increased knowledge and enhanced sanitation and isolation procedures. The current circulating strain is very virulent with high transmission rates, but illness is usually limited to 24–36 hours. Alcohol-based hand-washing lotions, very effective for bacteria such as staphylococci, are less effective against Norovirus and frequent thorough hand washing is preferred. Guests should immediately report any vomiting or diarrhoea to the ship's physician. You can expect to be isolated for 24 hours after your last vomiting episode.

Airborne disease/droplet spread

Legionnaires' disease

Legionella pneumophila can cause severe pneumonia and death especially in the elderly, the immunocompromised and those with underlying lung diseases, including smokers (see Chapter 4.5). Legionella species are found in many rivers, lakes, and streams, and they can find their way into a ship's potable and recreation water systems. The ship's systems are normally designed to provide adequate cold and hot temperature controls, proper chlorination, and precise water management to prevent Legionella growth. Outbreaks on several vessels have shown that a ship's whirlpools and showers can generate the aerosols necessary to spread this disease. The availability of the *Legionella pneumophila sero-group 1* urinary antigen rapid test helps with diagnosis and initiation of proper treatment. All travellers returning home who develop severe respiratory infections should be tested for Legionella.

Influenza

Influenza can cause severe illness or even death in the very young, the frail, and the immunocompromised (Chapter 4.12). However, flu can also cause severe disease in children and young adults. Pregnant women can be especially affected with high morbidity and mortality rates.

Passengers can contract influenza before leaving home or on the way to the ship, arrive feeling well and develop symptoms after boarding. All guests should consult their physicians regarding seasonal influenza vaccine. Immunization is the best prevention. All those who are elderly or with underlying medical problems should be vaccinated and the CDC has recently recommended all persons be vaccinated each year.

Influenza is caused by strains of the Influenza A or the Influenza B virus. Typical symptoms include high fever, cough, body aches, and malaise. Pneumonia is the most critical complication and respiratory distress of any degree should prompt a visit to the medical facility.

Hand washing and cough-etiquette practices can markedly decrease the spread of infection. Flu viruses are more easily killed on surfaces than norovirus, so the actions that cruise ships take against norovirus are usually effective against influenza virus.

Effective crew vaccination programs shorten outbreaks by reducing the ship's pool of susceptible individuals (herd immunity). Many cruise lines have very aggressive crew vaccination programmes for influenza.

Other vaccine-preventable diseases

Any passenger with a fever and a rash should call the medical facility for the doctor to come to the cabin, so he or she does not walk through the ship.

Varicella (chickenpox)

Varicella is highly infectious and travellers may be exposed at home or abroad. The incubation period for varicella is quite long—up to 21 days before someone may become ill.

Guests are often notified when there has been a case on board in case they are pregnant or immune-compromised. Chickenpox in adults can cause pneumonia.

Varicella vaccine can help protect susceptible individuals who have been exposed. International travellers (passengers and crew) who are not immune should consult their doctor for advice. Chickenpox vaccine is available and is split into two doses, given several weeks apart (p.445).

Rubella (German measles)

Travellers may be exposed to rubella virus at home or abroad. Shipboard outbreaks have occurred amongst crew. Infection during the first 20 weeks of pregnancy can cause congenital rubella syndrome—a group of birth defects including deafness, cataracts, heart defects, and mental retardation. Female travellers of childbearing age who do not have documented immunity should consult their physician and strongly consider immunization.

Vector-borne diseases

Yellow fever

A valid International Certificate of Vaccination is *required* for entry to some ports. A certificate's validity begins 10 days after the date of vaccination and extends for a period of 10 years (see p.446). Travellers lacking the appropriate documentation may not be allowed ashore, if so determined by local authorities.

Malaria

Malaria is an acute illness causing high fevers caused by transmission of one of four species of the protozoan parasite *Plasmodium* through the bite of the female *Anopheles* mosquito, usually between dusk and dawn (Chapter 5.1). Symptoms include fever, chills, headache, muscular aching and weakness, vomiting, cough, diarrhoea, and abdominal pain. Some patients can become critically ill in a matter of hours after symptoms begin. The minimum incubation period is 7 days, so a fever starting less than 7 days after arrival in a malaria endemic zone is not malaria. Symptoms can start up to 3 months or even years later.

Malaria poses significant risk to infants and young children, the elderly, pregnant women, and the immune-compromised. Choices of prophylactic medications depend on the malaria endemic region, the length of time there, and the prevalent species in that area, resistance patterns and the underlying medical condition of the traveller. Some medications must be started well before leaving on your trip and continued after your return. Strict adherence to the scheduled treatment as prescribed is critical. Protective clothing and insect repellent containing DEET are also very important.

Cruise guests are usually at lower risk of malaria since most cruise ships generally dock after dawn and leave before dusk, and malaria is not a common problem in most areas that cruise ships visit. However, with more exotic itineraries, overnight stays and pre- and post-trip land extensions, malaria prophylaxis and yellow fever immunization must be given. Any traveller who has been to a malaria endemic region and experiences a fever should immediately consult their health care provider and mention their travel history.

Surgery and blood transfusions

Cruise ships do not carry blood products and the ships' medical staffs do not have the resources to perform endoscopy or surgery to investigate or arrest internal bleeding. Patients with uncontrolled bleeding need to be disembarked for definitive treatment.

Kits that enable the bedside typing of blood (O, A, B, or AB) have been used for type-specific blood transfusions from passenger or crew donors. Ships with the proper testing kits and supplies may call out for guests or crews who have been previous donors. HIV antibody tests are available for screening but the ship's medical staff cannot perform the other screening tests that would be performed in a blood bank. Therefore, receiving a transfusion on ship carries a higher risk, but is often life saving. See also Chapter 13.6.

Accessibility

Accessibility may be an issue. On many ships, 'scooters' may be available to use on board and/or ashore. Consult your cruise line. Advance arrangements are usually required.

When a ship anchors in a port and uses tenders (small boats) to get the guests ashore, transfers can be difficult. Guests with mobility concerns should consider the itineraries of their ships, as well as facilities at ports. (See also Chapter 11.6)

Dietary restrictions

Food and Beverage Departments are becoming more familiar with managing special dietary concerns. Those guests on complex diets should contact the cruise lines in advance. All guests with a history of significant food allergies should carry injectable epinephrine (EpiPen) at all times. Your servers should be made aware of all food allergies or intolerances you have, at every meal.

Safety

Millions of passengers enjoy cruises each year without incident, and accidents and injuries are very unusual. However, never be complacent. On ships, always observe the following simple safety measures:

- Pay careful attention to safety drills, and ask questions if anything is unclear
- Know the location of your lifejacket, the emergency exits, and your muster station for the lifeboats
- Understand what signals will be used in an emergency
- Exercise caution when getting on/off tenders, lifeboats or walking u/down ramps to get on/off the ship
- Be careful when going up and down stairs
- Pay careful attention to any safety recommendations given by the ship regarding safety precautions in ports of call
- Ensure someone at home knows of your travel plans.

Minor injuries from rough seas are by far the most likely hazard. Remain seated, make sure you are clear of any loose fittings that may crash around, or lie down in your cabin. Watch out for wet floors and slip hazards. Like professional sailors, always use both hands on steep stairways. And be safety-conscious at all times.

Environmental and recreational hazards

8.1 Accidents

Stephen Hargarten and Tifany Frazer

Accidents are the leading cause of death and injury in travellers, but they are predictable and preventable. Travellers can take steps to avoid accidents and reduce risk of injury.

Many travellers think of tropical infections as the biggest danger to their health, but these represent only a small proportion of medical problems they encounter. Infectious diseases are important and preventable, and a proper programme of vaccination, together with the general precautions described elsewhere in this book, are vital. However, travellers need to employ similar strategies to protect themselves against injury, the foremost of these being simply to avoid circumstances in which there is an increased risk of injury. It is believed that tourists tend to be more at risk of injury because they find themselves in unfamiliar environments participating in unfamiliar activities.

Everyday risks for the traveller

The language of risk analysis is rich with value-laden words. Whether the risk is avoidable or unavoidable very much depends on your perspective. There may be many opportunities to try new things and, in the absence of the usual constraints of home, family, and work, travellers may behave differently, sometimes in a reckless, uncharacteristic manner, exposing themselves to risks they would not take at home. There is a certain amount of risk when travelling, but to avoid accident and injury, you must think carefully about them and decide if they are worthwhile.

Travellers should realize that they face at least the same probability of everyday accidents abroad as they do at home. Travel does not suddenly remove these dangers and the carefree feeling that travel engenders can increase the hazards.

As a general rule, you should continue to apply your usual safety standards even if the legal requirements do not require you to. For example, travellers from higher income countries mostly comply with seatbelt and helmet laws in the knowledge that this markedly reduces the risk of serious injury. To stop wearing seatbelts or helmets abroad, just because there may be no legal requirement to do so, increases the risk of injury. Such dangers are no less common abroad. Be alert and apply a strict safety code to anything you do.

The possibility of robbery and assault is another risk for travellers. Tourists are prime targets, yet travellers who will not walk through their own city centre for fear of attack are often happy to stroll unaccompanied through the more dangerous areas of the world. These risks are under your own control, and are considered in detail in Chapter 8.2.

Transport risks

All forms of transport pose some risk to the traveller—with road transport at the top of the list. However, most hazards can be minimized with safety precautions and attention to detail.

Road transport

Globally, motoring is by far the most dangerous form of transport. Over 90% of deaths on the roads occur in low- and middle-income countries, which have less than half of the world's registered vehicles. Road traffic injuries are predicted to become the fifth leading cause of death by 2030, resulting in 2.4 million deaths a year (Table 8.1.1). This projected ranking is the result of an increase in road traffic deaths, coupled with reductions in deaths due to other health conditions. Pedestrians, cyclists, and riders of motorized two-wheelers and their passengers account for almost half of all global road traffic accident (RTA) deaths. This proportion is greatest in low-income countries. Speed control is an important factor in reducing road traffic injuries, particularly among pedestrians, cyclists, and motorcyclists. Less than one-third of countries have taken measures to reduce speed in urban areas.

Table 8.1.1 Top 10 leading causes of death: 2004 (actual) and 2030 (predicted)

Total 2004		Total 2030	
Rank	Leading cause	Rank	Leading cause
1	Heart disease	1	Heart disease
2	Cerebrovascular disease	2	Cerebrovascular disease
3	Lower respiratory disease	3	Lower respiratory disease
4	Chronic pulmonary disease	4	Chronic pulmonary disease
5	Diarrhoeal disease	5	Road traffic injuries
6	HIV/AIDS	6	Lung cancers
7	Tuberculosis	7	Diabetes
8	Lung cancers	8	Hypertensive heart disease
9	Road traffic injuries	9	Stomach cancer
10	Prematurity and low birth rate	10	HIV/AIDS

Adapted from World Health Statistics 2008, p.30, with permission of the World Health Organization (℞ http://www.who.int/whosis/whostat/2008/en/index.html).

While seatbelt laws are much more widespread, often the law does not pertain to all car occupants (Map 8.1.1). The use of child restraints can reduce deaths by over half in the event of a crash (Map 8.1.2). Consider bringing your child's car or booster seat from home for travel abroad when visiting countries where laws are not enacted or enforced. Wearing a seatbelt significantly reduces the risk of death among front-seat passengers and can reduce deaths among rear-seat car occupants considerably.

Less than half of all countries have a helmet law and require helmets to meet a specific standard (Map 8.1.3). Even fewer enforce helmet use. Wearing a good-quality helmet can reduce the risk of death from a road crash by almost half, and the risk of severe injury by over 70%. Consider bringing a helmet from home if you know you will be renting a motorcycle or bicycle. Additionally, when you rent a vehicle, always insist on being provided with one that has both front and rear seatbelts.

Other risks to avoid are driving at night on unfamiliar roads or when you are tired. Insist on proper child restraints if you are travelling with children. Above all, do not to consume alcohol and drive. Table 8.1.2 provides some road traffic safety recommendations.

Table 8.1.2 Road traffic safety recommendations for travellers

1. Wear a seatbelt no matter where you are seated in any vehicle. Bring appropriate car seats or arrange with the vehicle rental agency about availability. Guidelines about use of car seats are as follows:
   - *Children—birth to age 1 and at least 20lbs (9kg):* a rear-facing child safety seat in the rear of the vehicle
   - *Children ages 1 and 20lbs (9kg) until age 4 and 40lbs (18kg):* a front-facing car seat in the rear of the vehicle
   - *Children ages 4–8 years:* should be placed in a booster seat in the rear of the vehicle unless taller than 4'9" (1.45m)
   - *Children older than 8 years and taller than 4'9":* should use a seatbelt and sit in the rear of the vehicle
   - *Children 12 and younger:* should always ride in the rear of the vehicle.

2. Avoid driving abroad if possible.

3. Use a driver. Look for a reputable company through your embassy, hotel concierge, or other reliable source that employs certified, trained drivers, familiar with local driving culture, laws, and roads. Avoid journeys at night, or drivers under the influence of drugs or alcohol.

4. Avoid driving under the influence of alcohol, when fatigued, or with jet lag; avoid all-night driving; learn local road signs, roads, driving customs, and laws. Understand local licensing requirements, road permits, car insurance, and road conditions (your embassy may be able to advise).

5. Rent a vehicle (with or without driver) equipped with seatbelts for all seats (rear and front), air bags, and the lower anchors and tethers for children (LATCH) system if travelling with small children who require child safety seats.

6. Choose commonly available cars when renting (with or without driver), ask for any obvious rental car markings to be removed. Request a map, directions, list of local traffic signs and laws pertaining to road travel, and a full familiarization of the rental vehicle from staff of the rental agency prior to their departure. Take time to inspect the tyres, breaks, lights, airbags, and seatbelts.

7. Carry a cell phone and know how to obtain emergency help should a crash occur. Do not use the phone while driving.

8. Avoid riding on or driving a moped or motorbike while travelling. If travellers rent mopeds, motorbikes, or bicycles, helmets should always be worn by adults and children. Bring appropriately fitting helmets, especially for children.

9. Be aware of possible car-jacking hotspots and keep vehicle doors locked.

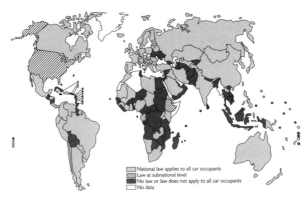

Map 8.1.1 Seatbelt laws by country.

Reproduced from *Global Status Report on Road Safety: Time for Action*, 2009, p.25, with permission from the World Health Organization.

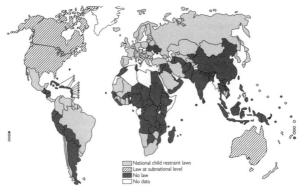

Map 8.1.2 Child restraint laws by country.

Reproduced from *Global Status Report on Road Safety: Time for Action*, 2009, p. 27, with permission from the World Health Organization.

Air transport

The risk of injury on a scheduled airline is very small. The threat of hijacking is discussed briefly in Chapter 7.1. Of course, certain airlines and airports have poor safety records. The website for *Flight Global* (℅ www.flightglobal.com) regularly publishes data on these risks and provides plane safety updates. This kind of information can lead to a potentially safer routing for your trip.

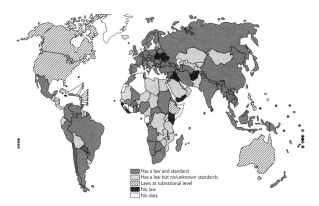

Map 8.1.3 Motorcycle helmet laws and regulations by country.

Reproduced from *Global Status Report on Road Safety: Time for Action*, 2009, p.23, with permission from the World Health Organization.

Another factor that may influence your choice of airline is the type of on-board medical equipment and the training of cabin staff in its use. Medical kits vary considerably between airlines. Defibrillators are the only way of treating fatal complications of heart attacks; automated electrical defibrillators (AEDs) are compact, safe, and simple to use with minimal training. For years, a lot of airlines refused to carry them, but now many have introduced defibrillators. They have become a legal requirement in the USA.

Part of your safety strategy should start at the airport. There have been several terrorist attacks in airport buildings—check in promptly and go through customs and immigration to the much more secure 'air-side' terminals.

Airlines are required by their regulating bodies to provide safety briefings on every flight. Listen carefully to the briefing and read the safety instruction card. Even though you may have travelled by air several times before, a particular airliner might have a different configuration and different safety equipment. Not all oxygen masks fall out of the cabin roof on depressurization (on DC10 aircraft they are in the head rest of the seat in front of you); and as a direct result of the British Midland M1 crash the 'brace position' has been changed to minimize injuries to the lower limbs. On flights with only short over-water periods, the crew may not brief you on the location of life-vests; make sure you know where they are.

Turbulence occasionally causes injury and death, so move around the cabin as carefully as possible, and when seated keep your seatbelt fastened at all times. Be particularly careful when hot drinks and meals are being served, because sudden movement can spill scalding liquids into your lap.

Baggage poses an additional hazard, both on and off the plane. Avoid travelling with more baggage than you can carry comfortably and beware of other travellers who cannot keep their luggage trolleys under control—this is a frequent cause of injury. On boarding the plane, try to restrict your hand luggage to one small item: the more cluttered the cabin, the greater the risk in an accident. Overhead racks are getting larger, but resist the temptation to put heavy items in these racks; in an accident they may fall on top of you and may even prevent your escape.

The risks of accidents increase greatly with unscheduled aircraft travel. If you are thinking of travelling in a private aircraft, try to form an impression of whether the operation is being run professionally. If it is not, it is probably dangerous and you should find another way of getting to your destination.

Water sports and water transport

Each year about 450 000 people drown worldwide. The exact number of travellers who drown or experience a near-drowning is not known, but certainly drowning accounts for 14% of deaths of US citizens abroad.

Many popular travel destinations are situated in warmer climates, near oceans and lakes, and feature activities such as surfing, scuba diving, snorkelling, boating, parasailing, and water-skiing (see also Chapter 8.8). Visitors to Central America, Southeast Asia, the Caribbean, and Mexico have significantly higher proportions of death from drowning than native citizens. In low- to middle-income countries in Central and South America, drowning accounts for 13% of injury deaths to US tourists, but only 5% to native citizens.

Drowning is consistently reported as a leading cause of death among tourists, while near-drowning or submersion commonly appears as a cause of injury in non-fatal data. The risk factors have not been clearly defined, but are most likely related to unfamiliarity with local water currents and marine life.

Accidents and injuries at sea to passengers on Western-owned carriers are unusual, although not uncommon. There have been several horrific accidents in the Far East, mostly due to overloading. If a ferry is full, wait and catch the next one. On ships, always observe simple safety measures. Make sure you know how all the safety devices work, and where they are located. Ask the captain the following questions:

- Where is your life-jacket?
- Where is your muster station for the life-boats?
- Where are the emergency exits?
- What signals will be used in case of an emergency?
- Does someone at home know of your travel plans?

See Table 8.1.3 for water safety and drowning prevention recommendations for travellers.

In rough seas, the risks of injury are greater on-board than from the vessel foundering. Remain seated, make sure you are clear of any loose fittings that may crash around, or if possible lie in your bunk. If you have to move around, be very careful of wet floors, and always use both hands on steep stairways.

Rail travel

Rail travel is remarkably safe in Europe, but a succession of accidents in the United Kingdom and Spain demonstrates that there is risk. Rail safety standards in high-income countries are currently under close scrutiny, with attention focusing on signalling technology, escape systems, and the safety and structural strength of older railway carriages. Safety standards in middle- and low-resourced countries are unlikely to be better.

In a number of incidents, many injuries have been caused simply by the impact of one human upon another—the time when we will see safety belts and closed luggage bins in trains may not be far away. When travelling by train, sit down—passengers who are standing at the moment of impact are much more likely to be seriously hurt than passengers who are seated. In one crash that involved a commuter train travelling at a speed of just 10mph, 50 out of 59 passengers who were standing received injuries to the head and face; only 13 of 32 seated passengers who were taken to hospital had head injuries.

Most injuries are the result of being hit by a carriage door or falling under the train upon getting off. So keep well away from your train as it approaches the station and, at the end of your journey, refrain from opening the door and stepping off until the train has stopped.

Finally, in low-income countries it is common to ride on the train's carriage roofs. This habit and that of walking on the outside of carriages, while picturesque and tempting in the heat, are extremely unsafe and should not be copied by travellers.

Table 8.1.3 Water safety and drowning prevention recommendations

1. Bring personal flotation devices (PFDs) along if you think they will not be available, especially for adult non-swimmers and children, and use them when in and around the water. Select a correctly-sized, coastguard-approved PFD by looking at the label to ensure a safe and proper fit. Use PFDs when water skiing, during towed activities, on personal watercraft, during white water boating, sail boarding, and on moving vessels of <26ft. Children under 13 years should use them at all times. Identify their location a yacht or cruise ship.

2. Learn CPR prior to departure. CPR is critical in improving the outcome should a near-drowning occur.

3. If travelling with children, enquire whether there is 4ft climb-proof isolation fencing around the pools and/or if there is a barrier between your lodging/ hotel room and any body of water in which your child may drown.

4. Limit alcoholic consumption to one beverage (preferably none) if planning to be in or around the water, or on a boat. Alcohol should be avoided when adults are supervising children around the water.

5. Swim in designated swimming areas, preferably ones that provide trained and certified lifeguards. The presence of lifeguards will improve the outcome should a near-drowning occur.

6. Learn about animal-related risks and other environmental risks in and near the water in your travel destination. Be aware of signs posting surf and weather conditions, or other environmental risks that may be present in natural bodies of water.

7. When diving or participating in more strenuous water activities than normal, a re-assessment of physical, mental, and medical fitness is recommended prior to travel, at regular intervals and following an illness or injury.

Risks at your destination

Road hazards

Bad roads with ill-maintained surfaces and local traffic laws that are not enforced or are even dangerous may compound the risks of driving abroad. Cities where traffic laws are ignored can be recognized by the constant sound of car horns—the last resort of drivers struggling to make their presence known.

Unfamiliarity with road signs, local customs, and driving habits, and especially driving on the 'wrong' side of the road (see Box 8.1.1) are a hazard to drivers and pedestrians alike, so take extra care.

Greece and countries in Southeast Asia have a particular problem with moped accidents; and such accidents are also a serious problem in many island holiday destinations, such as Bermuda, the Caribbean, and Bali. The problems are made worse because most people who rent mopeds abroad are not skilled riders, do not wear crash helmets or protective clothing, and good quality medical care is often not available in the event of injury.

Box 8.1.1 **Countries that drive on the left**

Antigua/Barbuda	Indonesia	St Vincent & Grenadines
Australia	Jamaica	Seychelles
Bahamas	Japan	Singapore
Bangladesh	Kenya	Solomon Islands
Barbados	Macau	Somalia
Bermuda	Malawi	South Africa
Bhutan	Malaysia	Sri Lanka
Botswana	Malta	Suriname
British Virgin Islands	Mauritius	Swaziland
Brunei	Montserrat	Tanzania
Cayman Islands	Mozambique	Thailand
Cyprus	Namibia	Tonga
Dominica	Nauru	Trinidad & Tobago
Eire	Nepal	Turks & Caicos Islands
Fiji	New Zealand	Uganda
Grenada	Pakistan	UK
Guyana	Papua New Guinea	US Virgin Islands
Hong Kong	St Kitts & Nevis	Zambia
India	St Lucia	Zimbabwe

One survey of motorcycle and moped accidents abroad found that 60% were simply due to loss of control and 20% involved collision with an animal. Other vehicles were involved in only 20% of incidents.

A recent analysis of injuries to cyclists has found that wearing a bicycle helmet reduces the risk of serious head injury by 63–88%.

Political and cultural risks

Insurance policies exclude war risks and riots, but unfortunately civil disturbances, bombings, or even invasion may occur virtually anywhere.

Politically unstable areas are obviously best avoided, although this may not be possible for business travellers. A more recent problem has been the specific targeting of tourists by fundamental terrorists.

Foreign ministries (such as the Foreign Office in the United Kingdom, ℜ www.fco.gov.uk/en/ and the Department of State in the United States of America, ℜ www.state.gov/travel/) publish country-by-country advice on their websites, with frequent updates, and will generally provide specific guidance for trouble spots on request. If you are unfortunate enough to be caught up in a riot, *coup d'état*, terrorist attack, or invasion, keep in contact with your own country's consular or diplomatic representatives. Prior to travelling, always register your trip details and locations with your country's embassy or consulate in the country of destination. Consider additional insurance with an assistance company (e.g. International SOS—ℜ www.internationalsos.com) that includes cover for telephone support and medical evacuation to your country of origin, usually at little additional cost.

At a more personal level, most difficulties with the local population or authorities can be avoided by finding out how you are expected to behave. Avoid political discussions of any type or making political statements, even in private. Don't use cameras or binoculars in aircraft, airports, government installations, or ports, however great the temptation. In some societies, women still have a very sheltered status; visitors to such countries are well advised to comply strictly with local customs. Such issues are considered further in the next chapter.

Theft

Be discreet with large amounts of cash, and shop only in areas that are known to be safe for visitors—this can reduce the risk of theft. If a bag, briefcase, or handbag is snatched, particularly by a motorcyclist, let it go. More people are seriously injured by being pulled over in this situation than from any other type of robbery.

Hotel safety

Fires

Hotel fires are unfortunately all too common, and smoke, reduced visibility, and panic are the most serious hazards. Basic precautions include finding out where the fire escape is as soon as you arrive at a hotel, following it down to see exactly where it emerges, and, if possible, finding out what the fire alarms actually sound like. Keep a torch or flashlight handy in your hotel room in case of an alarm, and in the event of a fire, above all try to stay calm. Remember that smoke rises and that it is safest to crawl on the floor of a smoke-filled room.

Lifts or elevators

If the lift looks unsafe, it probably is; use the stairs instead. Lift cages with only three sides (the fourth side being the wall of the lift shaft) pose a particular danger. Do not under any circumstances lean against the wall of the lift shaft as it slides by. Sadly, people have had limbs severed when their clothes became trapped between the lift cage and the shaft wall.

Balconies

Remember that hotel balconies and their balustrades are often designed to look nice, rather than as a safety feature. Make sure the balustrade is secure, and that the height is sufficient to stop you overbalancing and falling. Each year there are at least 20 deaths of UK citizens resulting from falls from hotel balconies, often related to alcohol consumption.

Campsites

Campsites in all countries pose particular risks—lack of security, leading to robbery and assault, and vulnerability to natural disasters, such as fires, floods, sandstorms, and avalanches. In some countries there is also the risk of being attacked by dangerous animals or bitten all over by insects. Tents should be in groups, with someone always on the watch. If you choose to camp alone in a remote area, then you must accept that you are taking a serious risk.

Sports, hobbies, and special pursuits

Most sporting activities involve a risk factor that is often an important component of the sport's attraction. When accidents do occur, they can usually be traced to avoidable factors, such as poorly maintained equipment, lack of training or an inadequate level of fitness, rather than to any intrinsic danger of the sport itself. Most serious skiing accidents, for example, are due either to inadequate mental and physical preparation, or to badly adjusted equipment (see Chapter 8.9).

As a traveller intent on maximizing the amount of enjoyment into the time available, you may be tempted to cut corners, but this is unwise. Always make sure that the equipment you use is maintained to the highest standards (as the experts do), and if the sport you are interested in involves a high level of exertion, avoid overdoing things until you have built up an appropriate level of fitness and stamina.

Certain pursuits—for example, scuba-diving (Chapter 8.8) and hang-gliding—can be carried out safely only after a fairly long period of graduated instruction, including training in the avoidance of the specific risks involved. While abroad you may be offered an opportunity to indulge in such pursuits with only a minimal degree of instruction: offers of this type are best declined until you have undergone proper training.

If your pursuit carries you far away from human habitation, make sure that a responsible person knows where you are going and when you expect to return to base. If possible, take a radio or satellite phone. If you are injured in a crevasse on a mountain, or marooned in a boat at sea, nobody can help you unless they know where you are.

It is not the esoteric pursuits while travelling that carry the biggest risk, but the simple ones. Those unaccustomed to exercise seem particularly prone to ligament and bone injuries, or even heart attacks, from playing sports in the heat of the day on a beach. Every year, there is a terrible toll from diving into shallow water, with serious neck and spinal injuries in young men, leading to paralysis for life. This accounts for approximately 10% of all spinal cord injuries. Do not under any circumstances dive into water of uncertain depth, or take running dives into the sea from a sloping beach.

Accidents and injuries do not need to be serious in order to be inconvenient: make sure that you are prepared for the run-of-the-mill cuts, scrapes and grazes, stubbed toes, and sprains that are a common by-product of travelling, and that you have a sensible supply of first-aid supplies, such as antiseptic, dressings, painkillers, and basic medical care essentials.

Alcohol

Travellers may use alcohol as an adjunct to enjoyment. However, it increases all other risks of injury and should be used with great care. Alcohol and swimming make a particularly bad mix—almost half of all drownings are associated with alcohol consumption (Chapter 8.8). Drinking and driving increases the risk of a RTA. The WHO recommends a blood alcohol concentration limit of 0.05g/dL for adult drivers. Less than half of countries worldwide have drink-driving laws set at this limit. Fig. 8.1.1 illustrates the proportion of alcohol-related fatal crashes for 93 countries worldwide. A recent study has shown that in road traffic accidents involving pedestrians, the pedestrian is more likely to be intoxicated with alcohol than the driver of the car that hits him.

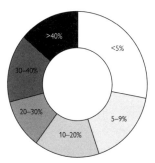

Fig. 8.1.1 The proportion of deaths related to alcohol varies from countries with strict drink/drive legislation, where this figure is less than 5 per cent, to those where alcohol contributes to 40 per cent or more of all road traffic deaths.

Reproduced and adapted from *Global Status Report on Road Safety: Time for Action*, 2009, p.25 with permission from the World Health Organization. ✑ www.who.int/violence_injury_prevention/road_safety_status/2009.

Consequences of injury abroad

The consequences of any injury abroad are often more serious than they would be at home. In many areas no emergency medical services are available to provide care at the site of an accident or even an ambulance service to take the casualty to hospital. The more remote and picturesque the location, the greater the probability that no emergency medical services (EMS) and pre-hospital transport exist.

No medical help may be available at all. Small tropical islands are always a risk. Usually, it requires a population of about a quarter of a million people to support a comprehensive medical service, and an island with fewer people may well not have one (although better facilities may be available within reasonable range). If the island is many miles from the nearest mainland, even the simplest injury can cause problems. Similar risks apply to travellers visiting small, isolated communities anywhere—desert oases, for example.

If you or any of your companions suffer an injury and you cannot speak the local language, you may not be able to summon help even when it is available. Find out how the local system works and what the emergency telephone number is. Remember that however good the local EMS, you have problems if you cannot contact them or make yourself understood.

Box 8.1.2 **Accident prevention for travellers**

- All travellers look forward to new adventures while on holiday. In a new environment, examine all the risks and decide whether they are justified
- Have a strategy for safety and avoid risks while travelling that you would never take at home
- Prior to leaving for your destination, review travel warnings and travel alerts on government websites (⅏ www.travel.state.gov)
- Also, learn about the common travel safety concerns, health risks and travel health notices related to the destination, as some locations are prone to certain natural disasters (⅏ www.cdc.gov/travel)
- Understand local laws and culture of the destination (⅏ www.who.int/countries)
- See Table 8.1.4 for general safety precautions while travelling.

Table 8.1.4 General injury prevention recommendations

1. Review travel warnings and travel alerts for your destination.

2. Learn about the common travel safety concerns, health risks, and travel health notices related to the destination, including susceptibility to natural disasters.

3. Understand local laws and culture.

4. Purchase appropriate international travel and medical evacuation insurance.

5. Register your travel itinerary with the appropriate government agency (state department or embassy) for assistance should an emergency or natural disaster occur. (Governments cannot assist their citizens if they do not know their whereabouts.)

6. Develop an emergency response plan, know the name and location of the nearest major medical centre and embassy, and whether or not it is safe to receive blood products in their country of destination.

7. Consume alcohol responsibly and in moderation when in an unfamiliar environment. Alcohol should be avoided if one is operating a vehicle, boat, machinery, or supervising children around water. Alcoholic beverages should not be consumed if planning to be in or around the water.

8.2 Personal safety and security

Charlie McGrath

The last decade has seen a continued growth in the numbers of people travelling abroad coupled with an increase in range of destinations and activities. The world is becoming less predictable for the traveller: political, religious, and civil instability is a constant risk; crime rates fluctuate in tune with the economic situation; the number of road traffic accidents continues to rise (see Chapter 8.1); and terrorism is a constant worry. Where to start, what to focus on?

For all travellers the 'Big 3' risks are: road traffic accidents, crime, and disease—most probably in that order! Whilst it may seem strange, in many cases, the further you are off 'the beaten track', the safer you will be because you are less likely to get robbed or mowed over by a truck if you are away from the crowds. If there was only one piece of advice to follow, it would be to always wear a seatbelt in a vehicle.

Research your destination

The risk posed to individuals or groups will vary according to many factors—their experience, their profile (the ability to 'blend in'), the current disease or security situation, known standard of road safety, etc. With the availability of the Internet there is no excuse for not knowing what to expect; really good starting points are government travel advice websites:

- *UK:* ✆ www.fco.gov.uk
- *USA:* ✆ www.travel.state.gov
- *Australia:* ✆ www.smarttraveller.gov.au

There are also a number of very good security and safety company websites that one can subscribe to for daily updates and in-depth country profiles. On arrival, add to your knowledge by chatting to local contacts, hotel check-in staff, airport information desks, and some taxi drivers, and access the local media.

- ✆ www.lonelyplanet.com/thorntree
- ✆ www.red24.info
- ✆ www.journeywatch.com

Crime

The recent downturn in the world economic situation has inevitably increased the chances of becoming a victim of crime whilst travelling. The risk to travellers will depend on a number of factors; where they are visiting and the known threat from crime, their profile, gender, and above all, what they do to minimize the risk and how they react if a crime is committed.

Crime avoidance

It's obvious that crime tends to flourish where there is a high concentration of tourists/travellers, one only has to consider the reputation of certain streets in Barcelona or parts of London. So to avoid becoming a crime victim, three strategies will assist:

- Be aware
- Lower your profile
- Look confident.

Be aware
- Know where the high-risk areas are; they are likely to be bus and railway stations, crowded markets, shopping centres, tourist sites
- Know where you are. Study the map before going out so you can avoid the dodgy areas
- Be extra vigilant at night; travelling in the early morning/day time is generally safer than at night
- Avoid using a mobile phone on the street; don't 'walk and talk'. If necessary, stop and put your back to a wall. Adopt the same tactic if you are getting belongings out of brief cases, rucksacks, etc.
- Walk facing the traffic: it's more difficult to pull someone into a car
- Back up your information by copying the contacts and photos on your mobile and camera, so you will not be tempted to resist a mugging
- Trust your instincts. If it feels wrong, it probably is!
- Women must be especially careful of the image and 'signals' they send out. Inappropriate dress or behaviour might encourage an aggressor
- Have any useful emergency contact or consulate telephone number stored on your mobile phone.

Lower your profile
- Don't be noticed; play the 'grey woman/man'
- Don't walk about carrying high-value goods on show. Keep cameras out of sight, don't wear rings and watches, do not store laptops in obvious laptops bags (the logo tells thieves what make you are carrying!)
- Wear appropriate clothing and avoid wearing executive suits if possible
- Consider staying in lower profile hotels, especially important for business professionals in countries where there is a significant risk of terrorism (Al Qaeda targets high-profile hotels) or kidnapping
- Keep voice lower in places where your language/dialect will mark you out as a 'foreigner'.

Look confident
- Don't look lost
- Perhaps walk slightly faster, head up; give the impression that you know what you are doing
- Look relaxed, acknowledge street traders
- If you need directions, ask in a shop and ask someone who is unlikely to have any interest in you.

Muggings

Despite one's best effort, in many places there is the threat of muggings. Two strategies will help you to stay safe—avoidance and compliance. You can reduce the chances of being mugged by adopting the tactics listed above. Before going out, consider what the chance of being mugged is and then reduce it. Avoid high-risk areas, don't wear rings, watches, or jewellery. Annoying as it may be, a mugging is an economic transaction. In the vast majority of cases, provided you give thieves what they want, be it money, your watch, or mobile phone, then you will be unharmed.

Don't resist, just comply. It's a good idea to have some 'mugging money' on you so you have something to hand over and you will be more likely to comply if you have a reserve hidden in a shoe. In certain high-risk cities, such as Johannesburg, the local advice may well be to avoid eye contact, look down, and hand over.

Money

There is often a direct link between crime and money, from business travellers becoming victims of credit card fraud to gap year students being robbed at ATM machines. In addition, in hostile environments, journalists may have to carry thousands of US dollars to buy their way out of trouble. Getting the money part right is important for one's safety. Here are a few tips:

- *Budget:* have an idea how much you will need each day, a gap year student in Latin America is likely to need about $35 per day, a journalist up to $500 per day in hostile environments
- Know which cash or travellers cheque currency is best; $, £, Euros, Rand, etc.
- If there is a significant risk of being mugged, don't have a debit card on you—you are likely to be 'marched' to an ATM machine.
- If taking travellers' cheques, keep the purchase receipt, record cheque numbers, and leave a copy of this information at home so they can be cancelled and replaced
- If using an ATM machine, be accompanied if possible and do it in daylight, preferably outside a bank so you can recover the card if it's swallowed
- Take a mixture of cash, credit/debit cards, and perhaps travellers' cheques
- *Split it up:* have some currency squirreled away—in a medical pack, bottom of a suitcase, sewn into clothing—so you have a reserve
- Be very careful if tempted to use the 'Black Market'—it will be illegal and there is a high risk of fraud. Change money in a shop or hotel, not on the street
- Money belts can reduce the chance of being pickpocketed, but they need to be concealed.

Kidnap

Whilst stories of kidnap can be found frequently in the news or on TV, it is a very rare event and low risk for the vast majority of travellers. The highest threat of kidnap is currently concentrated in parts of Central and South America—Mexico, Colombia, Venezuela, and growing in some Central American countries. Other areas include some parts of North Africa, Central Asian republics, Pakistan, some parts of Northeast India (where Maoist guerrillas are operating), the Niger Delta, piracy off East Africa, and parts of Indonesia. Those being kidnapped are generally locals, as kidnapping is done for economic reasons and it's necessary for the captors to know their targets. In recent years, especially in South America, there has been a growth of 'express kidnapping', where a person is held for a short period of time, perhaps a matter of hours, whilst small sums of money, a few hundred US dollars, are demanded and paid by the family.

Although the threat may be of concern, a few avoidance strategies will further reduce the risk to a very manageable level. If the chance is deemed significant you will need to establish where and who is being targeted, reduce your profile, and be meticulous with your security. Be careful who you trust, don't give your escort or taxi too much information. If you are somewhere for a length of time, change your routine—swap hotels, change your route and timings to work or social gatherings.

In the event of being taken there are some simple rules to follow:

- Remain calm
- Comply—do as you are told
- Try to build an informal relationship with your abductors, try to find a common theme by chatting about family, sport, etc.
- Accept food and water, and seek any special needs—medications, etc.
- Try to remain as mentally and physically active as possible. Ask for access to radios/newspapers and do some exercise—walking and stretching as the minimum
- Don't try to negotiate, let the professionals handle that. You are too emotionally involved, have nothing to negotiate with, and lack experience.
- Don't try to escape. Statistically, you have about a 95% chance of survival, so don't 'roll the dice'. Clearly, in rare circumstances, if you come to the conclusion that it's not simply an economic transaction, and you may be killed for religious or political reasons, then escape may need to be an option. 'Go early' is then generally the best advice
- If you are not alone, help others; having read this, you may be better prepared and can assist
- As part of the negotiation process you may be asked to provide a proof that you are alive
- Rescue operations pose a high risk to you—stay hidden, don't move, and wait for instructions from your rescuers.

Getting about

Although national idiosyncrasies play a part, a few ubiquitous tips can prevent the traveller getting into trouble when getting about on local transport, so let's take a journey:

The aeroplane and arrival

Whilst travel by air is the safest of all modes of mass transport, in some countries the safety record of some local carriers may be poor, so check the Internet and/or national civil aviation organizations for safety data. Getting a seat near an emergency exit is useful; besides, it will give a lot more leg room. It's worth quickly counting the seat rows to the exits and keeping your seat belt on at all times in case the aircraft encounters turbulence or, worse, an air pocket so that one doesn't have a close encounter with the cabin roof.

On arrival, stay switched on, especially around the luggage carousel. Prior to going through immigration, check that your luggage hasn't been tampered with—if it has been, don't touch the offending item and alert security. If you are being met, try to have a contact name and ask for ID.

Road traffic accidents

Before one considers tips for taxis and buses, it's worth remembering that the risk of being killed or injured in a vehicle accident is perhaps the greatest threat facing *all* travellers. According to the WHO, it is the biggest killer for the age group 18–29 years. Consider the rightful publicity when approximately 180 people were killed in the November 2009 terrorist attack in Mumbai, India. Yet how many die on average every day on India roads? Two-hundred-and-fifty. So be you a business traveller, NGO, or an expedition leader, focus on not getting squashed. Ensure your vehicle is in good condition, the driver alert, all passengers are wearing seat belts, and don't drive at night unless absolutely necessary (Chapter 8.1).

Taxis

The standard of service a traveller can experience varies dramatically from the safe and reliable to the downright corrupt and dangerous. Here are a few tips that will assist in most countries:

- Use registered taxis only. Country advice websites and guidebooks will tell you how to recognize them
- Where possible, book a taxi from a hotel, business address, etc.
- Assess the condition of driver and vehicle before getting in
- When a taxi arrives, check it's for you. Ask who it has come to collect, don't say 'Have you come for X?'
- Have an idea of the expected fare, direction, and distance to destination
- Women are advised to sit in the back. For men, if using a taxi late at night with a long journey ahead, it's perhaps best to sit in front in order to talk to the driver to ensure he/she doesn't fall asleep
- Wear a seatbelt
- If the driver is going too fast ask him/her to slow down, threatening to report the driver to the company boss or pretending you are about to vomit may do the trick
- Be careful if you have luggage in the boot. If you are travelling with other people, one should remain in the taxi, whilst the others get the luggage out, so as to prevent a corrupt driver racing off with your luggage!

Buses

Once again the statistics are depressing—up to 600 people die annually on Peru's buses; however, much can be done to reduce that risk. Again, do your research, seek out those companies with a better safety record and reputation. Wearing a seatbelt (take your own cargo strap as a precaution) is the best advice. In addition, check out the driver, and keep an eye on him/her. For long overnight journeys (saves accommodation cost), expect to pay more for a decent bus company, and choose one with minimum stops to reduce the chance of your luggage going missing. Border and/or banditry areas should be avoided at night.

Hotels

Hotel security has become a major issue for journalists, NGOs, and business professionals travelling in countries where Al Qaeda or other terrorist groups have attacked high-profile hotels. Attacks have occurred in India, Pakistan, Algeria, Indonesia, Kenya, and Lebanon to name just a few:

- For those travelling to countries where the risk from terrorism is significant, consider choosing lower profile hotels
- If staying in a hotel that is a potential target for a terrorist attack, choose a room that has no road access below (Figure 8.2.1)
- Avoid the ground or first floor, but don't go too high; no fire ladder will reach much above the seventh floor
- Check the fire escape
- Consider using a mechanical door lock or wedge to secure your room from the inside
- Consider using the manager's safe or room safe
- When leaving your room, consider leaving the TV on or put a 'Do not disturb' sign out
- Know if you are in an earthquake zone.

Fig. 8.2.1 Bomb damage at the St George Hotel, Beirut; note less damage to the side of the hotel.

Environmental risks

Finally, a few thoughts on environmental threats. Water-related accidents are common, too often people are injured or killed by drowning in rip currents, diving into shallow water, or being eaten by marine residents! So be careful, think before you swim. Don't swim alone and if there are people about, but no one in the water, it's probably for a good reason. Tsunamis (tidal waves) are linked to earthquakes; if the former occurs get away from the beach. However, if the earthquake occurs hundreds of miles away (e.g. Thailand, 26 December 2004, Japan 11 March 2011), water rapidly receding from a beach is a recognition signal of an incoming wave. Hundreds of earthquakes occur every day, most too small to be felt. Ensure you know whether you are in an active area. If a quake occurs when you are outside, stay outside and get low. If indoors, the general advice is to get under heavy furniture, hold on to it, and get out of the building once the quake has stopped. Carrying a whistle, even when in bed, could save your life if you get buried. In a lightning storm move off high points, get away from trees and metal objects, and get out of water.

8.3 Altitude illness

Buddah Basnyat

High-altitude destinations attract increasing numbers of travellers and are ever more accessible. All travellers to high places need to understand the risks of altitude illnesses and how to prevent them.

Climbers, trekkers, porters, skiers, pilgrims, military personnel deployed to high regions, diplomats posted to La Paz, and miners in South America, have something in common: they are all exposed to the effects of high altitude and may be at risk from a potentially fatal, but eminently preventable problem—acute mountain sickness (AMS).

Symptoms of AMS consist of headache plus any one of the following symptoms to different degrees—nausea, tiredness, sleeplessness, or dizziness. It occurs at altitudes of around 8000ft (2400m) or higher, where pathophysiological changes due to lack of oxygen may manifest. In keeping with the Jesuit tradition of painstaking documentation, Father Joseph de Acosta, a 16th-century Spanish Jesuit priest, is credited with having first described the effects of high altitude in humans.

Another term, 'altitude illness', is also widely used. This 'umbrella term' includes the benign AMS and its two life-threatening complications, water accumulation in the brain (high-altitude cerebral oedema or HACE) and water accumulation in the lungs (high-altitude pulmonary oedema or HAPE). These complications may follow AMS, especially when people continue to ascend in the face of increasing symptoms. Those most at danger are people who do not 'listen to their body' and do not heed the early warning signals of AMS.

Acute mountain sickness

AMS may set in within hours to days of arrival at high altitude. The onset of symptoms is usually gradual, which is why it is so vital to watch out for early warnings. Does a person feel excessively tired? Is that person the last one to return to camp?

What causes AMS?

AMS is caused by a lack of oxygen. Just what causes some people to suffer from AMS, but not others is largely unknown, but there are clear-cut and important preventive factors that are well established (see 'Preventing altitude illness', p.248).

High-altitude cerebral oedema (HACE)

The headache and fatigue of AMS may progress to lethargy and coma, or there may be confusion and disorientation. A useful test is to see if the person can walk in a straight line. If he walks like a drunk, it has to be assumed that he has life-threatening HACE and needs to descend promptly with assistance.

HACE is probably caused by shifts of fluid into the tissues of the brain. Reduced oxygen levels cause swelling within the confines of the bony skull.

High-altitude pulmonary oedema (HAPE)

This disease may follow AMS, but often it appears independently. The typical scenario would be a trekker who may have no headache or nausea, but finds he has a harder time walking uphill, or that he is out of breath on slight exertion compared with the initial days of the trek. There may be a nagging cough.

Low oxygen causes the pulmonary artery to narrow and this results in exudation of blood near the smaller branches of the lungs (the alveoli). If the exudation continues, blood may escape into the alveoli, leading to a cough with watery, blood-tinged phlegm. Such exudation or 'water-logging' of the lung tissue interferes further with oxygenation. A popular, compact device, called a pulse oximeter, can measure the oxygen level of the blood, simply and rapidly, using a sensor attached to the index finger, allowing assessment and monitoring of symptoms.

What is acclimatization?

Acclimatization is a state of physiological 'truce' between the body of a visitor and the low-oxygen environment of high altitude. This truce permits the trekker to ascend gradually. For acclimatization to take place, the single most important step is *hyperventilation*—the trekker unconsciously breathes *faster* and *more deeply* than normal, even at rest, to make up for the lack of oxygen. However, hyperventilation also leads to loss of carbon dioxide from the blood, making the blood more alkaline and, in turn, depressing ventilation. Some 48 to 72 hours after exposure to high altitude, the kidney comes to the rescue and begins to excrete alkali from the blood to restore a more balanced environment in which hyperventilation can continue unabated. Acclimatization is distinct from 'adaptation,' which suggests change at a genetic level to facilitate survival at altitude.

Preventing altitude illness

There is little doubt that altitude illness is entirely preventable: no one should die from it. There are four golden rules, plus some important general principles that should always be followed:

1. *Understand and recognize the symptoms of AMS:* recent growth in adventure travel has made trekking at high altitude more accessible, with the result that more and more people who go trekking are ignorant of the basic facts of altitude illness
2. *Never ascend with obvious symptoms:* incredibly, I have known people who have hired a horse or a yak to go up higher when they were too sick to walk
3. *Descend if symptoms increase:* it is amazing how dramatic the relief may be with even a couple of hundred feet of descent. People with signs of HAPE or HACE have to descend with a friend who speaks the same language
4. *Group members need to look out for one another* (perhaps like the buddy system in scuba-diving): this rule gets broken with unfailing regularity every trekking season in the Himalayas, because people are

just too determined to complete their trek, even if one of their party members is ill. A trekker with AMS, HAPE, or HACE will want nothing more than to be left alone, unbothered, at the same altitude—potentially a fatal option.

Following a conservative rate of ascent

Going too high, too quickly, is the single most important cause of susceptibility to AMS. Beyond about 9000ft (2750m), the sleeping altitude should be no higher than about 1500ft (450m) from the previous night's altitude. The *sleeping* altitude, not the altitude achieved during the daytime, is what is important. Altitude sickness often manifests at night because during sleep the oxygen level in the blood may dip further.

While ascending, every second or third day should be a rest day for acclimatization. The trekker should not be in a hurry in the mountains. The itinerary should have enough 'leeway days' in case more time is needed to acclimatize.

Avoiding excessive exertion in the initial days

Excessive physical exertion at high altitude makes one more susceptible to AMS.

Avoiding alcohol

Alcohol may dehydrate the trekker, but more importantly, it depresses breathing or ventilation. Sleeping pills may have a similar effect.

Maintaining adequate hydration

Adequate amounts of fluid (about 3L/day) are necessary in the mountains. On the other hand, excessive water drinking should also be avoided as this may lead to electrolyte imbalances.

Pre-acclimatization

Over 4 days exposure above 3000m in the last 2 months has a protective effect when re-ascending to high altitude.

Drug prevention (prophylaxis)

Diamox (acetazolamide), the primary drug for prevention of AMS, may be necessary for people with a prior history of AMS, people on rescue missions to high altitude, or when flying in to high-altitude cities like La Paz or Lhasa. People with sulpha allergy should avoid Diamox.

A second drug, dexamethasone (see p.250), should also be carried, particularly if the destination is remote; this can be life-saving if HACE supervenes.

Ginko biloba does not seem to prevent AMS. Some studies have recently shown that drugs like ibuprofen may also prevent AMS.

Treatment

Descent

For life-threatening HACE and HAPE, descent is usually mandatory.

Oxygen

If available it should be used, especially for HAPE and HACE.

Drugs

Acetazolamide (Diamox)

For prevention of AMS, 125mg twice daily, starting the evening before and continuing for 3 days once the highest altitude is reached, is effective.

Sojourners who are on low-dose aspirin can continue this medication in addition to taking Diamox for prevention or treatment.

Side-effects of Diamox are:

- An uncomfortable tingling of the fingers, toes, and face
- Carbonated drinks tasting flat
- Excessive urination
- Rarely, blurring of vision.

If gradual ascent is possible, prophylaxis should be discouraged.

Certainly, if trekkers develop symptoms of AMS, Diamox is useful. The treatment dosage is 250mg twice daily for about 3 days.

Dexamethasone

This steroid drug can be life-saving in people with HACE. The dosage is 4mg three times a day, and obvious improvement usually occurs within about 6hr. Like the hyperbaric bag (see below), this drug 'buys time', especially at night, when it may be problematic to descend. Descent should be carried out the next day. *It is unwise to ascend while taking dexamethasone.* Unlike Diamox, this drug only masks the symptoms. Dexamethasone needs to be used cautiously, however, because it can cause stomach irritation, euphoria, depression, or blood glucose changes.

It may be wise to pack this drug for emergency usage in the event of HACE during a high-altitude trek. In people allergic to sulpha drugs (and therefore unable to take Diamox), dexamethasone can also be used for prevention: 4mg twice daily for about 3 days may be sufficient. Dexamethasone has recently been shown to be effective in the prevention (but not treatment) of HAPE.

Nifedipine

Nifedipine can be used to treat HAPE. The dosage is 20mg of long-acting nifedipine, every 6 hours.

It can cause sudden lowering of blood pressure, so the patient must be warned to get up slowly from a sitting or reclining position. It has also been used in the same dosage to prevent HAPE in people with a history of this disease.

Asthma drugs (specifically, beta agonist inhalers, e.g. salbutamol) may also help prevent HAPE. Recently, Viagra (sildenafil) has been used successfully in the prevention of HAPE, although intense headache is an important side effect. Finally, echocardiography (a cardiac test) may be useful for people with HAPE at a relative low altitude (3000m) to rule out heart or lung problems.

The hyperbaric bag

This is a simple, portable, and effective device made of airtight nylon that helps increase oxygenation. Just like dexamethasone, this bag only helps to 'buy time': descent is still mandatory as soon as possible.

Other problems at altitude

Periodic breathing

An abnormal breathing pattern (Cheyne Stokes respiration), whilst asleep is a common occurrence at high altitude. It is a problem only if it makes the sufferer wake up repeatedly, breathless, anxious, and unable to sleep.

An effective remedy is Diamox, 125mg before dinner, which counteracts the low oxygen dips during sleep that trigger the problem. Sleeping pills should be avoided.

Cough at altitude
Many people develop a persistent, bothersome cough and cold-like symptoms in the cold, dry air at high altitude. Keeping the head and face covered, and breathing through a silk or wool scarf to humidify the air may also help. Codeine at night and a steroid inhaler has also been used with mixed results.

Peripheral oedema
There may be swelling around the eyes, fingers, and ankles at high altitude, but this may not indicate AMS *per se* unless accompanied by the symptoms of AMS.

High-altitude syncope (fainting)
This is a well-known, but harmless problem in which fainting occurs suddenly, usually shortly after arrival. Simple measures, such as keeping the individual in a reclining position and raising the legs are helpful.

Gastrointestinal problems
Because of expansion of air in the intestine, a feeling of abdominal distension is common. Haemorrhoids are also common at altitude and can be dealt with by hot soaks, steroid cream, and a high-fibre diet.

Travellers with pre-existing health problems or conditions

High blood pressure
Blood pressure initially increases at high altitude due to the initial stress of low oxygen triggering neurohumoral changes. However, people who suffer from high blood pressure can go up to high altitude as long as this is well controlled and they continue to take their medication. People with a fluctuating high blood pressure should carry a blood pressure cuff so that it can be monitored.

Coronary heart disease
People with a history of heart attack (myocardial infarction) and even those with coronary artery bypass grafts or angioplasty, but with no angina can trek up to high altitude provided they are fit and able to walk rigorously at low altitude. The high altitude does not seem to add any extra burden to the heart.

Epilepsy
Although seizures may be provoked by altitude, there is no convincing evidence that it is unsafe for well-controlled epileptics to travel to high altitude—although such people should always take their anti-seizure medications conscientiously.

Migraine
Sufferers may have more attacks in the mountains, and this may sometimes be difficult to distinguish from AMS. If in doubt, it is best to descend.

Lung disease

Bronchial asthma does not seem to be exacerbated at high altitude due to the cold and exercise. However, it is prudent for asthmatics to carry inhalers and other medications, including oral steroids. Obviously, people with chronic obstructive or restrictive lung disease may be more short of breath, and travel at high altitude would be inadvisable.

Diabetes

Diabetics on insulin should have a reliable glucometer to check their blood glucose regularly, and they need to have caring fellow travellers who understand diabetes.

Corneal surgery

People who have had non-laser surgery (radial keratotomy) to correct their short sightedness may run into problems at high altitude and they should carry corrective lenses.

Pregnancy

Pregnant women should not sleep higher than 12 000ft (3650m) as this may endanger the foetus. Additionally, high-altitude places are generally remote, making emergencies difficult to deal with.

Children

Children do not suffer any more from the effects of altitude than adults. However, it is important that a child should be able to communicate any symptoms to a responsible adult.

Contraception

Oral contraceptive pills may predispose a woman to abnormal blood clotting (thrombosis) at high altitude. It is therefore better to use other forms of contraception (Chapter 10.3).

Other disease risks

Many high-altitude destinations are in developing countries, so it is important to be up to date with vaccinations, to know about travellers' diarrhoea and its treatment, and to understand the other precautions described elsewhere in this book.

Box 8.3.1 **Summary of advice for travellers**

Most of the problems of high altitude are totally preventable. With careful precautions, your experience in the mountains should be safe and rewarding.

Further information

Recommendations of the Medical Commission UIAA (International Mountaineering and Climbing Federation). Available at: ℘ http://www.theuiaa.org/medical_advice.html#AMS,_HAPE,_HACE_-_Emergency_field_management_

The Wilderness Medical Society guidelines. Available at:
℘ http://www.wemjournal.org/article/S1080-6032(10)00114-6/abstract

International Porter Protection Group. Available at: ℘ www.ippg.net

Royal Geographic Society: Guidance for trekkers on Mt Kilimanjaro. Available at:
℘ www.rgs.org

8.4 Effects of climatic extremes

Chris Johnson

Introduction

By combining physiological acclimatization with technological adaptations, native peoples have colonized the harshest environments. Until quite recently, such remote and rugged places were visited only by determined travellers trained to cope with extreme conditions, but nowadays package tours can whisk anyone to the Greenland ice cap, the Amazon jungle, or the Mongolian desert. However, you don't need to travel to an exotic destination to encounter environmental hazards; hypothermia is quite common amongst visitors to the British mountains, while heatstroke can affect endurance athletes anywhere in the world.

General considerations

Humans are good at changing the world to suit their needs; an air-conditioned hotel provides the same environment anywhere on earth, but this chapter assumes that you want to travel beyond the limits of luxury. In extreme climates your life will then depend upon your knowledge, skills, and equipment: ensure that these are adequate. In a survey of expeditions, environmental hazards, such as cold injury and altitude sickness caused 14% of *all* medical problems, while animals and insects caused another 8%, but together, these categories accounted for nearly half the *serious* medical problems that travellers to remote areas encountered.

When arranging any adventurous trip, try to evaluate the capabilities and competence of the tour company and their local guides. Prepare carefully, using the advice offered elsewhere in this book, as well as any local resources. If travelling independently, ensure that you know how to access local rescue and medical services. Find out about specific local hazards and disease risks, and make sure that your vehicle and equipment are in good order.

Extreme environments

Extreme environments are characterized by their weather conditions (Table 8.4.1).

Temperature

If wearing light clothing, humans are most comfortable in temperatures around 28°C. Below this, you have to exercise or wear clothes to maintain body heat, above it you need to sweat to lose heat.

Wind

Still air, especially if trapped in clothing, is a good insulator and will rapidly warm to skin temperature. Wind strips away this insulation and increases the rate of heat loss from the body. In cold climates, wind speed enhances the chilling effect of the air and markedly affects perceived weather conditions, while in hot climates a breeze makes heat more bearable by aiding the evaporation of sweat. The combination of temperature with wind speed in the cold—the *wind chill index*—enables the hazard of the weather to be evaluated (p.268). High wind-chill conditions cause rapid heat loss from exposed parts of the skin, resulting in frostnip or frostbite.

Table 8.4.1 Physical characteristics of extreme environments

	Temperature	Moisture	Radiation	Wind	Pressure
Tropical	Hot	Humid	Low	Low	Normal
Desert	Hot	Dry	High	Variable	Normal
Polar	Cold	Dry	Variable	Variable	Normal
Temperate	Moderate	Wet	Variable	Variable	Normal
Mountain	Cold	Variable	High	High	Low
Caving	Cool	Humid	Nil	Locally	Normal
Marine	Variable	Wet	Variable	Variable	Normal
Sub-Aqua	Cold	Submerged	Nil	Nil	Very high
Space	Cold	Nil	Very high	Nil	Very low

Humidity

Humidity describes how much moisture is in the air. Moist air conducts heat up to 30 times faster than dry air. Humid environments are less comfortable than dry because damp clothing loses its ability to insulate. The dank conditions of a European coastal town in winter may be far more unpleasant than the drier, but colder environment of polar regions. In hot conditions, high humidity makes it more difficult to sweat, with perspiration droplets often dropping off the skin, rather than evaporating effectively on the skin surface. A chart similar to the wind-chill chart, but combining heat and humidity to produce an evaluation of 'Apparent Temperature' (AT), permits evaluation of the hazards of a hot climate (p.256).

Radiation

Sunlight directly warms the skin, leading to an obvious difference in perceived temperature between shade and sun. The effect of sunlight is obvious in a desert; less apparent is the importance of radiation as a heat source at high altitude where the atmosphere has less chance to attenuate the sun's rays, and in snowfields where much radiation is reflected off the snow. Reflected solar ultraviolet (UV) radiation in Antarctica can be four times as intense as in the Sahara desert.

Pressure

Environmental pressure is not usually a physiological challenge, but the effects of pressure are very important during diving and at high altitude.

This section will discuss the health consequences of environmental heat and cold; other extremes are covered elsewhere. (Space has yet to become a popular destination, although Virgin Galactic has, at the time of writing, signed up 430 would-be astronauts.) Even when the weather itself is not awful, extreme exertion can enhance its effects. People participating in charity challenges and endurance sports encounter the risks of extreme environments.

Human responses to extreme climates

Humans precisely regulate the temperature of their 'core' body organs, such as brain, heart, lungs, kidneys, and liver; normally, these organs are maintained within 0.5°C of 36.7°C. A rise or fall in core temperature of over 1.5°C results in measurable deterioration in thought processes, co-ordination, and physical performance. If core temperature rises above 40°C—*hyperthermia*, or falls below 35°C—*hypothermia*, rapid treatment is essential to avoid serious consequences. Surrounding this core of vital organs is a 'shell' of insulating tissues, including the skin and limbs, whose temperature can vary considerably. Complex behavioural and physiological mechanisms, regulated by the brain, are involved in keeping body temperature constant.

Heat can be gained or lost by the physical mechanisms of:

- *Conduction:* heat transmitted by direct contact between two materials of different temperature. Heat is conducted into the body from an electric blanket, warm drink or chemical heat pack, and lost by direct contact with snow or running water
- *Convection:* air currents generated because warm air rises over cold air. In cold, still air up to 30% of body heat is lost by convection from the skin of the head and neck
- *Radiation:* hot bodies such as the sun or an electric fire transmit electromagnetic radiation and can be sensed as heat on the skin. In the cold, the skin radiates heat
- *Evaporation:* heat is lost when moisture such as sweat vaporizes on the skin surface.

In addition to these physical mechanisms humans adapt to extreme conditions through behavioural changes including:

- Eating
- Altered rates of exercise
- Varying clothing
- Adapting work to the prevailing conditions
- Sheltering from sun, wind, or rain, being indoors or outside
- Lighting a fire
- Fanning themselves.

Hot climates

Describing hot climates

Humans are believed to have evolved in tropical Africa and most people cope well with temperatures up to around 30°C. Above this, thermal stress increases. Hot dry climates, such as in equatorial deserts are more comfortable than the hot, humid conditions of a tropical rain forest. A steady breeze, characteristic of many tropical islands, makes hot conditions much more bearable. Temperatures in cities are usually higher than in the surrounding countryside, especially at night, because buildings and paved areas trap heat.

Measuring heat stress

One way of measuring heat stress is the 'Heat Index', which combines humidity and temperature to give an apparent temperature (AT; see http://www.nws.noaa.gov/om/heat; see Fig. 8.4.1), from which the risk of heat illness is determined.

Figure 8.4.1 shows a useful evaluation of the hazards of daily living in a hot environment, but does not take into account the heating effect of sunlight: to evaluate the risk of strenuous activities such as running or hiking with a pack, the preferred international measure is the wet bulb globe temperature (WBGT), which uses a formula to combine measurements of shade temperature, solar radiation, and absolute humidity—see ℘ http://www.bom.gov.au/info/thermal_stress for a full explanation.

Heat Index
Temperature (°C)

	27	28	29	30	31	32	33	34	36	37	38	39	40	41	42	43
40	27	27	28	29	31	33	34	36	38	41	43	46	48	51	54	58
45	27	28	29	31	32	34	36	38	40	43	46	48	51	54	58	
50	27	28	29	31	33	35	37	39	42	45	48	51	55	58		
55	27	29	30	32	34	36	38	41	44	47	51	54	58			
60	28	29	31	33	35	38	41	43	47	51	54	58				
65	28	29	32	34	37	39	42	46	49	52	54					
70	28	30	32	35	38	41	44	48	52	57						
75	29	31	33	36	39	43	47	51	56							
80	29	32	34	38	41	45	49	54								
85	29	32	36	39	43	47	52	57								
90	30	33	37	41	45	50	55									
95	30	34	38	42	47	53										
100	31	35	39	44	49	56										

Likelihood of heat disorders with prolonged exposure or strenuous activity
☐ Caution ☐ Extreme caution ☐ Danger ☐ Extreme danger

Temperature (°F)

	80	82	84	86	88	90	92	94	96	98	100	102	104	106	108	110
40	80	81	83	85	88	91	94	97	101	105	109	114	119	124	130	136
45	80	82	84	87	89	93	96	100	104	109	114	119	124	130	137	
50	81	83	85	88	91	95	99	103	108	113	118	124	131	137		
55	81	84	86	89	93	97	101	106	112	117	124	130	137			
60	82	84	88	91	95	100	105	110	116	123	129	137				
65	82	85	89	93	98	103	108	114	121	126	130					
70	83	86	90	95	100	105	112	119	126	134						
75	84	88	92	97	103	109	116	124	132							
80	84	89	94	100	106	113	121	129								
85	85	90	96	102	110	117	126	135								
90	86	91	98	105	113	122	131									
95	86	93	100	108	117	127										
100	87	95	103	112	121	132										

Likelihood of heat disorders with prolonged exposure or strenuous activity
☐ Caution ☐ Extreme caution ☐ Danger ☐ Extreme danger

Fig. 8.4.1 NOAA Heat Index.
Reproduced with the permission of the Minister of Public Works and Government Services Canada, 2011; adapted.

Based on WBGT, please see Table 8.4.2 for the recommended exercise limits for a reasonably fit person.

Tropical forests
Characteristics of the climate
Tropical forests are hot and humid; little direct sunlight reaches the forest floor and heavy rain is common. High temperatures during both day and night create significant heat stress.

Table 8.4.2 Recommended exercise limits for a reasonably fit person

	Workload			Work–rest cycle (per hour)
	Light	Medium	Heavy	
WGBT	30.0°C	26.7°C	25.0°C	Continuous work
	30.6°C	28.0°C	25.9°C	45min work/15min rest
	31.4°C	29.4°C	27.9°C	30min work/30min rest
	32.2°C	31.1°C	30.0°C	15min work/45min rest

Source: Data from Wet Bulb Globe Temperature (WGBT) Thermal Comfort observations
ℛ http://www.bom.gov.au/info/thermal_stress

Risks

- *Animals*: the profusion of wildlife both large and small is both a delight and a hazard
- *Camps:* select campsites to avoid the risk of falling timber, and try to avoid or clear ground obstructions that could hide snakes or other animals
- *Navigation:* it is easy to become disorientated and lost. Try to stay with your group and remain on well-trodden trails. If separated from your group, consider shouting, whistling, and looking for traces of their tracks. Remember that many smartphones and cameras now include a GPS chip and compass
- *Skin:* trivial wounds, such as blisters and small abrasions can become infected and ulcerate. Prevention is better than cure
- *Travel:* in thick forest travel can be difficult away from established trails. Steep slopes may be hard to see and very slippery. Waterways are useful for getting around, but ensure that boats and their engines are well-maintained and that life jackets are worn
- *Vegetation:* take great care if clearing vegetation using axes or machetes.

Clothing

Long-sleeved shirts and light-weight full-length trousers minimize contact between your skin and irritant plants or animals. Cotton garments are usually comfortable; nylon feels sticky, while denim quickly becomes waterlogged and dries slowly. Modern cotton/synthetic combinations are easy to wash and pack. A hat protects you from falling bugs; however, up to 30% of all body heat loss occurs from the forehead and scalp; so choose hats with care: heavy or impermeable headgear will increase heat stress. In some countries the political situation is volatile, so avoid buying camouflage gear; you could be mistaken for a guerrilla!

During rough travel, you should have at least two pairs of shoes: trail shoes suitable for coping with wet, slippery conditions and camp boots suitable for work and resting. The trail shoes should be lightweight, have a protective toecap and provide good grip on mud, wet logs, or river rocks. They should dry quickly. Effective ankle protection, with high boots or gaiters, can reduce both the risk of snakebite and the number of animals getting into the footwear and settling on or in you. Properly soled, wellington boots are useful around camp to keep your feet dry. Beach shoes and sandals are unwise because parasitic insects can settle and bore into your feet.

Shelter

Shelters should keep off the rain and be designed to take advantage of any breeze. Tents should include netting and groundsheets to keep animal life out, but can be stifling hot. The classic jungle shelter is a hammock slung off the ground and roofed by a wide waterproof. Dig deep run-off drains around tents or shelters to ensure that heavy downpours do not flood the habitation. Bedding is best placed on some form of platform and surrounded by insecticide-impregnated mosquito netting.

Deserts

Characteristics of the climate

Equatorial deserts have low rainfall, low humidity, and their cloudless skies mean that there is considerable solar radiation. Daytime temperatures can be very high, but night-time temperatures are often surprisingly low and it may be frosty by morning.

Risks

- *Animals:* small creatures, such as snakes and scorpions are the greatest threat, although travellers using camels need to know their animals
- *Driving:* vehicles must be adapted to the environment with suitable ground clearance, tyres, and air filters. Know how to change a tyre and ensure that the vehicle tool kit is complete. In sandy deserts drivers must know how to drive appropriately; vehicles should travel in convoy carrying sand mats and a winch
- *Flash floods:* dry river valleys (wadis) make good campsites, but have been carved by water; thunderstorms in distant mountains may lead to flash flooding
- *Navigation:* may be very difficult. GPS helps, but only so long as the batteries last
- *Sand:* sand gets everywhere. Dunes have a windward and a slip slope, the latter being much steeper and potentially hazardous
- *Dust storms:* dust storms can be a major hazard—they can strip a campsite bare, suffocate humans and animals, and create dreadful driving conditions
- *Vegetation:* mostly tough and prickly.

Clothing

Shorts and T-shirts may be appropriate in a resort hotel, but do not protect you from sunburn and may offend local cultural norms outside the hotel. Loose fitting full-length trousers and a sleeved shirt may provide protection, but check the sun protection index of the materials you buy. Choose light materials both in colour (to reflect away radiant heat) and weight.

During the day, ensure that your skin is protected from the sun—use a broad-brimmed hat, neck protector, clothing, and sunscreen. Apart from the long-term risk of skin cancer, tropical sunburn can be extremely painful and may hinder the working of sweat glands, thus causing serious illness. The Arab head-dress, the khaffieh (a 1m square of muslin), can be wrapped around the face for protection in sandstorms or used as a neckerchief to prevent sunburn under the chin from reflected UV solar radiation (see also Chapter 8.5). Boots or trainers with thick crepe rubber soles, and suede or canvas uppers are best, and can be combined with gaiters to prevent too much sand getting into the footwear. However, if you plan to clamber around the sharp rocks found in some deserts you need much stouter boots. As in the jungle, desert footwear requires 'time off' to dry out. A shelter during the day should be designed to reflect heat; a double-layered construction with insulation between the walls minimizes the effect of solar radiation. Nights can be cold so take a pullover and an adequate sleeping bag.

Shelter

Shelter is not essential in the desert, although a sun canopy is desirable if static during the day and a fire can help to keep you warm at night. Bedding should be raised to reduce the risk of insects. Always shake out clothing and footwear before dressing to avoid scorpion bites. Small rodents and snakes are common in hot climates and will be attracted by any type of food, which should be kept away from kitbags or suitcases.

Human responses to heat

Individuals cope best with heat stress if physically fit, fully hydrated, acclimatized, well-nourished, and rested. Factors that increase the risk of heat illness include:

- Recent air travel
- Lack of sleep
- Missed meals
- Inadequate fluids
- Recent fevers
- Sunburn
- Recent gastro-intestinal upsets
- Menstruation.

Body temperature rises with vigorous exercise. Long-distance runners in humid conditions who may be unable to sweat enough to cool themselves and can collapse from overheating. Accelerated metabolism with excessive heat production is also seen as a rare, but dangerous result of sensitivity to certain drugs. Drugs increasing the risk of heat illness include:

- Alcohol
- Angiotensin-converting enzyme (ACE) inhibitors
- Amphetamines
- Anticholinergics
- Antihistamines
- Atropine
- Beta-blockers
- Cocaine
- Diuretics
- Major tranquillizers
- Phenothiazines
- Scopolamine
- Selective serotonin re-uptake inhibitors (SSRI) antidepressants
- Theophylline
- Tricyclic antidepressants.

If you take any of these medications, you might encounter problems in hot weather, or on activities such as a charity trek; discuss the implications with your doctor. A few people are genetically prone to heat illness; anyone with a history of problems should be observed carefully. In many extreme environments, alcohol may be impossible to obtain, regular drinkers should ensure that they can cope with its absence.

Body temperatures up to 40°C can occur in fever and during exercise, but judgment and physiological functions are impaired above 39°C. When air temperature exceeds body temperature, the body can no longer cool itself through radiation, convection, or conduction, and must rely *solely* on the evaporation of sweat.

Acclimatization

Transfer to a hotter climate causes changes in body function that enable a person to cope better with heat, a process termed acclimatization.

Alterations to the circulation enable water to be absorbed from the gut more quickly and improve its transfer to the skin, the sweat glands work more efficiently for longer, and salt is retained better by the body. Depending upon the severity of the heat stress and fitness level, full acclimatization takes 1–3 weeks.

Most people adapt to a hot dry desert climate faster than to a hot/wet jungle climate. This is because:

• Nights in the desert vary from cool to cold, so the body temperature can fall and the sweating mechanism has time to rest

• The high humidity of the hot/wet jungle is constant through the day and night, while the higher the humidity, the more difficult it is for sweat to evaporate and cool the body.

Acclimatization in the jungle can be transferred to the desert, but someone used to the desert may need additional time to acclimatize to a hot and humid climate.

Physical effort in the tropics is exhausting; the heart and circulation must both supply energy to the muscles, and adsorb and transport fluids around the body to allow sweating. Young, lean, and physically fit people find it easier to adapt to heat, and it is always worthwhile trying to improve fitness before an arduous trip. Thin people have a greater surface area/body weight ratio and so lose heat more easily, while fit people cope better probably because their sweat glands are used to getting rid of the heat associated with exercise. Overweight people suffer in the heat.

Some acclimatization can be induced before travel by lying for an hour or so daily in a hot bath, or by taking regular saunas—adding steam to mimic the humidity of the destination. You should however subject your body to these heat stresses only if you are physically fit with no known cardiovascular disease. Many elderly people safely globetrot to remote destinations. If, however, you are not an experienced traveller, plan a gentle trip initially. Cruise ships, international hotels and air-conditioned coaches are relatively stress-free, but sightseeing tours using local transport can be physically taxing, demanding good stamina and general health.

Air-conditioning with low humidity significantly reduces overall heat-stress, but will delay full acclimatization, and those working abroad should remember that a week in an air-conditioned office does not acclimatize you to the conditions outside.

Thirst, salt, and water
People are poor at judging how much they need to drink. Newcomers to a hot climate typically only drink three-quarters of the amount that they really need. A fit, acclimatized person can absorb and sweat up to 1L of fluid per hour, about twice the rate of an unacclimatized person. A traveller walking in a desert during the night should drink one gallon (5L) per 24 hours, while the daytime traveller needs about twice this amount. Drink water or watery drinks (beware alcohol, which dehydrates) *beyond* the point of thirst-quenching. You are drinking enough if your urine is consistently pale in colour: dark urine or low urine output are signs of developing dehydration. If you do not drink enough, you may in the short-term feel fatigued and develop a headache, while during a longer stay you may form kidney stones, which are common amongst temperate climate visitors to the tropics.

Sweating causes loss of salt from the body, and these losses must be replaced. Take salt regularly both by adding it liberally to food and also by mixing it with drinks: the required salt concentration is one-quarter of a level teaspoonful (about 1g) per pint or two level teaspoons per gallon. This concentration is below the taste threshold and must be accompanied by a mixed diet. As you become acclimatized, your need for extra salt will diminish.

Athletes planning long runs in unaccustomed heat need to learn about fluid and electrolyte replacement, and drink adequate amounts of appropriate beverages before, during, and after the event. Do not drink excessive water in the early stages of a long race, as it may result in low sodium levels and collapse. Sports drinks are a palatable way of replacing both energy and salts, but if you mix them yourself, never make the solutions too concentrated.

Children

Children are generally quite happy to travel to the tropics, but are at risk of heat illnesses, particularly if their ability to sweat is affected. Dress them in sensible clothing and use high factor sunscreens on exposed areas. They should not spend too long in the sun or exercise vigorously until they have had time to acclimatize. Left to their own devices, children may become progressively dehydrated and must be encouraged to drink regularly. Diarrhoea should be treated swiftly with oral rehydration solution (Chapters 2.1, 11.2).

Heat illnesses

Heat exhaustion, hyperpyrexia, heatstroke, and sunstroke all describe the range of symptoms associated with dangerously high body core temperature and a failure by the sweating mechanism to cool the body adequately. In its mildest form symptoms include: headache, fatigue, dizziness, nausea, vomiting and muscle cramps. In serious cases of heatstroke you may additionally notice confusion, disorientation, rapid pulse, difficulty breathing, and seizures or coma. Scientific investigations have looked at body temperature, fluid intake, and salt consumption, but the fundamental reasons why a few people cross from the common malaise of heat exhaustion to the life-threatening condition of heatstroke remain poorly understood.

Heat exhaustion

Heat exhaustion is the term used to describe the malaise related to heat exposure in people with normal or only mildly elevated core temperatures. The symptoms are usually ascribed to one of three causes: water-deficiency, salt-deficiency, or anhidrotic heat exhaustion (anhidrotic = absent sweat), although these causes form a spectrum of physiological disturbance, rather than discrete conditions.

Water-deficiency heat exhaustion occurs if you are unable to drink enough in the heat. Extreme examples occur in people stranded in a desert or adrift in tropical seas without water. The victim is thirsty and complains of vague discomforts, such as lack of appetite, giddiness, restlessness, and tingling sensations. Very little urine is passed and any is deeply coloured. Lips, mouth, and tongue become so dry that speaking is difficult. Body temperature rises steadily, the pulse rate increases, breathing becomes faster, and the lips blue. Hollow cheeks and sunken eyes complete the picture before the victim sinks into a coma and, if not treated, death.

Salt-deficiency heat exhaustion is most likely to affect an inexperienced newcomer 2 or 3 days after arrival in a hot climate. They will have been sweating a lot and may have had plenty to drink, but taken inadequate salt supplements. The condition is quite often associated with an attack of diarrhoea or vomiting. The body's salt reserves have diminished and the tissues that require it malfunction. Increasing fatigue is soon followed by lethargy, headache, giddiness and extremely severe muscle cramps. The face and lips typically look very pale as the patient collapses, still soaked with sweat.

Anhidrotic heat exhaustion is a fairly rare disorder of sweating in people who have been in a hot climate for several months. The skin of the trunk and upper arms develops a rash of little blisters (called miliaria profunda) and the affected skin is dry, while surrounding areas remain sweating profusely. It is worst in the heat of the day—symptoms include fatigue, unpleasant sensations of warmth, giddiness on standing up, frightening palpitations, and rapid, sometimes gasping, breathing. The face sweats profusely and there is a frequent and insistent urge to pass urine, sometimes in larger quantities than usual. The disorder is often preceded by an attack of prickly heat (see p.264, p.385, p.434). These seriously heat-intolerant individuals should avoid hot environments for at least a month, and then continue to exercise caution in very hot weather as another attack might progress to heatstroke.

Treatment

Fully conscious victims of heat exhaustion must be cooled and rehydrated. Get them into shade, and if near civilization get them to take a cold bath or shower. In remote areas, pour water over their clothes and fan them vigorously. Give them plenty to drink, at a rate of a pint of water every 15min. If it seems likely that the casualty is lacking salt, add salt to some of the drinks at a concentration of one level teaspoonful of salt per 0.5L fluid. Water, fruit juice, or squash are preferable to carbonated drinks as too much fizzy fluid can cause abdominal distension and slow the replacement process. Continue giving them fluid until they pass urine. Subsequently, they should not risk heat stress for the next 2 days and ensure that they continue to drink plenty. If badly affected, seek medical help and provide continuous care during transfer to hospital to ensure that they do not deteriorate.

Heatstroke

Heat exhaustion is common, but death from heatstroke is rare. Most people, if they feel very hot will stop exercising, seek a cooler environment, and drink. If, however, physical circumstances, psychological pressures, drugs, or illness prevent this normal response, then a person is at risk of developing heatstroke. Two variations of the same condition are recognized:

• Classic heatstroke affects elderly people subjected to prolonged heat stress. Continuously hot weather for several days gradually raises their body temperature until the victims lose their ability to compensate. Heat waves in large cities have claimed hundreds of lives. Babies or animals left in a sealed car on a hot day will suffer a similar fate, and the higher temperatures involved mean that death can occur in a matter of hours

- *Exertional heat stress* is more commonly seen in young fit adults who exercise vigorously in the heat. Typically psychological factors—the excitement of a marathon race or the need to reach a jungle camp—force them to continue exerting themselves beyond their normal endurance.

A key problem with heatstroke is recognizing it. Victims are often confused and refuse help. They may even complain of feeling cold and shivering. Consider the circumstances. A shivering athlete on a hot day is unlikely to be suffering from the cold. Remember that if a person has a high temperature in the tropics, they may alternatively have an unrecognized fever-producing illness such as malaria.

Heatstroke affects many body systems. The heart and lungs will be stressed with a high pulse rate and rapid breathing. The victim will be confused, irrational, suffer memory defects and their vision affected. They may develop a severe pounding headache and then lapse into coma. Unseen, their gut lining will be breaking down so that toxins from inside their intestines are released into their blood stream, and there will be numerous biochemical abnormalities, most notably their muscles begin to break down. If they have drunk plenty they may still be sweating, but their skin may be hot and dry. Usually, their core temperature, if measured by a rectal or tympanic membrane thermometer, will be above 40°C, but a lower temperature does not exclude the diagnosis. Untreated, body temperature will continue to rise and death usually occurs once core temperature reaches 44°C, although survival from higher temperatures has been reported. Untreated heatstroke kills at least half of its victims, prompt, and effective care reduces the mortality to 10%, but it remains a very dangerous condition.

Treatment

Rapid treatment is essential—heatstroke can result in death within 2–4 hours of the first symptoms. Victims require immediate cooling. The longer a person stays hot, the more damage their body suffers. As a first-aid measure, shelter the victim from the sun, remove all clothing, and cover with a wetted bed sheet, towel, or other lightweight material, and start fanning to promote cooling by evaporation. Take water to the casualty, not the casualty to water! Infection or a crocodile could both add to the victim's woes if immersed in a watercourse. Keep the coverings wet; fanning and wetting must continue all the way to hospital. In hospital, or at a base-camp or hotel, more rapid cooling can be provided by electrical fans, cold water sprays and the administration of cold intravenous (IV) fluids. Where such facilities are available, immersion of the victim of exertional heatstroke in an iced-water bath has been shown to be effective, although uncomfortable. Rehydration is also essential. Fluids can be given by mouth if the patient is conscious or by IV, although excessive IV fluid can lead to heart failure. The cooler these fluids are the better. An unconscious person must either be nursed in the three-quarter prone recovery position or, where facilities exist, have an endotracheal tube passed. Kidney failure and blood-clotting abnormalities commonly follow heatstroke and will need hospital treatment. Antipyretic drugs, such as aspirin and paracetamol (acetaminophen in the USA) are ineffective in heatstroke and should not be used.

Other conditions caused by heat

Prickly heat or miliaria rubra (literally red millet seeds) consists of a vast number of vesicles or tiny blisters set in red, mildly inflamed skin, worst around the waist, upper trunk, armpits, front of the elbows, and even on the scalp. The rash is accompanied by intensely irritating prickling sensations. The cause is unknown, but an important factor is the constant wetting of the skin by unevaporated sweat as occurs in hot/wet climates. The skin becomes unhealthy and waterlogged, sweat ducts are blocked with debris and infection starts, causing a large number of pimples. The itching prevents sleep, which is usually delayed until the coolest period of the night. Not surprisingly the victim tends to be bad tempered and inefficient. The prickling can be relieved by taking a cool shower, washing with an anti-bacterial soap, and then dab-drying the skin gently to prevent further damage. Soothing lotions such as 'cold cream', calamine or camphor-based preparations may help. Avoid oil-based preparations and steroid creams. Clothing should be starch-free and fit loosely.

Heat oedema (heat swelling) of the ankles used to be called 'deck ankles' and appeared in passengers when their ships first entered tropical waters. Nowadays. it is indistinguishable from the swollen ankles of long air journeys and lasts for a few days. The condition requires no treatment and will disappear as acclimatization progresses.

Heat cramps are common, especially amongst athletes. They are usually ascribed to sodium deficiency, although other electrolytes may be involved. They are very painful and occur at random intervals in whichever muscle group is being used most. Electrolyte replacement and rest will usually alleviate the problem.

Heat syncope (fainting) typically occurs when an unacclimatized person first arrives in a hot area. Initially, their circulation is unstable, and they may faint if they stand still for a period, or if they stand-up suddenly. Sitting with their head between their knees or lying flat will make them feel better. Rest followed by gentle exercise will prevent another faint.

Sunburn is considered in Chapter 8.5.

Cool temperate climates

Many countries lying between the tropics and the polar circles have a cool temperate climate for some of the year, with temperatures between freezing point and plus 15°C (59°F), frequent wind, rain, and low cloud. Such temperatures are not dangerous on their own, but when combined with strong winds and heavy rain it is difficult for anyone outdoors to stay warm and dry. Prolonged exposure can cause hypothermia.

Acute accidental hypothermia

Falling into water colder than 5°C (41°F) is a life-threatening emergency. Some people die immediately as a result of heart rhythm irregularities caused by the severe shock; others gasp, shiver violently, curl up, inhale water, and may be dead from drowning in 5–15min. This violent reaction to the cold is much reduced if a person is used to the stimulation, which is why experienced swimmers can brave icy water in winter. If someone is wearing reasonably protective clothing, a life-jacket that keeps the head out of the water, has protection to prevent cold water from splashing onto their face and knows to keep *perfectly still* in the water, survival rates improve. The survival times for someone with protective clothing are about 50min in freezing water; around 3 hours in water at 10°C (50°F), 6 hours at 15°C (59°F), and much longer at 20°C (70°F). Factors that accelerate the onset of hypothermia in water are increasing age, lack of fitness, liability to panic, lack of recent food intake for internal heat production, and recent ingestion of alcohol, which without food causes a severe fall in blood sugar, and immediate confusion and clumsiness.

If a casualty is rescued unconscious after 5–15min in cold water, then it is probable they have inhaled water and drowned. Vigorous CPR should begin as soon as possible. The resuscitation guidelines for drowning emphasize the urgent need to get air into the lungs. Provided the rescuer can remain safe, 'rescue breaths' (the kiss of life) should begin as soon as possible and continue for at least 1min initially. Once the victim has been removed from the water full CPR should continue until expert help arrives. A very few people have survived prolonged submersion in icy water, with good recovery after more than half an hour under water. Such survivors are nearly always young, fit, and have fallen under the ice in fresh water. Pulseless and with very low core temperatures when rescued, they have survived after rewarming on a heart by-pass machine. Always attempt resuscitation unless massive injuries, putrefaction, or rigor mortis makes the value of such attempts obviously worthless.

If the casualty is conscious, but can talk only clumsily, or is incoherent and cannot answer questions, then hypothermia is the likely diagnosis. Victims such as survivors of shipwreck who have survived for prolonged periods in water must be treated very carefully, as their circulation will have been disturbed by the hydrostatic squeeze of water on their body. Rescue from the water can cause cardiovascular collapse and there have been many instances of post-immersion sudden death. Ideally, during rescue keep the victim horizontal and try to avoid constricting their chest with any harness. Once rescued, keep the victim still, with their head slightly down, and protect them from further heat loss.

Where possible, commence rapid re-warming in a bath (showers are not of any use) in which the water is kept at 40°C. Ideally, resuscitation facilities should be available—collapse may occur at any time until the patient is rewarmed and out of danger. If rapid (bath) re-warming is not available the victim should be nursed in a warm tent or room, in a bed with duvet, 'space blanket', or light blanket insulation only. A conscious victim will rewarm as a result of metabolic heat production if given food and fluids, but an unconscious victim must be provided with external warmth. Heat packs can assist rewarming, but must be carefully wrapped and positioned to avoid burns in a person with a poor skin blood supply. The supply of external heat by forced hot-air circulation systems, electric blankets and the like requires hospital care, with intravenous fluids, oxygen, and injectable drug supplies available immediately.

Chronic accidental hypothermia

Chronic hypothermia most commonly affects elderly people in poorly heated accommodation, but outdoors affects otherwise fit adults and children exercising on a cold day that become injured, stranded, or exhausted. It usually results from the combination of soaked garments, exhaustion, or injury. It differs from acute immersion hypothermia only in its slower speed of onset and the fact that physiological derangement can be more severe.

A hypothermic person is often too exhausted to recognize that anything is wrong and may reject assistance. Key signs are the 'umbles'—the victim *stumbles, mumbles, grumbles, and fumbles*. Severe shivering is common, although not everyone shivers, even when very cold, and shivering will cease as temperature falls. Visual disturbances herald collapse and unconsciousness with dilated pupils. The victim's pulse at wrist or neck may be irregular. In the unlikely event that core temperature measurement has been possible, it will have been about 35°C (95°F) at the start of the above list of signs and symptoms, and about 32°C (90°F) by the time the shivering is diminishing. Death may occur suddenly at body core temperatures below 28°C (82°F). The sooner the following actions are taken, the better the outcome:

- Stop activity unless safe surroundings can be reached rapidly
- Protect group and casualty from prevailing conditions by rigging a tent, poncho, or other bivouac. Place the casualty in the 'head-down' position if conscious, or the 'recovery' position if not, on a groundsheet, 'space blanket', or in a large polythene bag
- Strip off wet clothing and insulate the victim with anything available. Ideally, use sleeping bags to cover the body and try to prevent further heat loss from neck, head, and face
- If unconscious, rewarm using the body heat of a companion—stripped and in bed or bag beside the casualty. If conscious, a hot sweet drink followed later by hot food will hasten recovery
- Observe for cessation of breathing or pulse in which case mouth-to-mouth resuscitation and/or external cardiac massage must start
- Send two people for help, but first give them fluid and food in case they too are affected by the cold
- Treat the patient as a stretcher case, no matter what he or she may say to the contrary. Transport facilities should include an adequate number of helpers, an effective method of keeping the victim warm and dry, and by this stage warmed IV infusions, and warm packs in the groin and armpits may improve their condition.

Value of resuscitation

It can be extremely difficult to determine whether a victim of severe hypothermia or drowning is dead or alive. They will look blue and feel rigid, pulses will be very difficult to feel and the pupils may be fixed and dilated. It is always worth attempting resuscitation unless the casualty has a catastrophic injury, is putrefying, or if freezing or rigor mortis makes resuscitation impossible. Casualties with core temperatures as low as 9°C have survived.

After effects

A person who has been even mildly hypothermic is likely to feel weak and exhausted for several days; they should rest. Profound hypothermia can result in serious damage to muscles and secondary damage to other body organs. Medical assessment with possible hospitalization is essential.

Non-freezing cold injury (trench foot, paddy foot)

Non-freezing cold injury develops when the lower limbs and feet remain cold, but not frozen for several hours or days. The term 'trench foot' was given to this condition in the First World War and is still used by military personnel who, under field conditions, are unable to dry their socks and feet regularly. Amongst civilians, white-water rafting in cold rivers is a cause. If a foot remains chilled at between 0°C and 10°C for several hours, damage to nerves and blood vessels develops. After the first sensation of cold passes off, the feet feel numb, but the victim complains that it feels like walking on cotton wool. Poor footwear, inadequate food, general chilling, lack of sleep, and exhaustion complete the typical picture. There are genetic links: Nepalese rarely develop the condition, while it is quite common in those of African ethnic origin.

On examination, the skin of the affected area is blotchy-white, while ankles are swollen and marked deeply with pressure ridges from boots, etc. As the limb warms up the foot becomes hot, red, swollen, and very painful. The victim must be taken to hospital, and if this is likely to take time, should be treated with painkillers and antibiotics as for frostbite (p.273). The legs must be dried, elevated, protected from further damage and exposed in a warm room. Blisters may form on the feet in the first 2 days or so, and must be kept scrupulously (but gently) clean. After-effects, including pain and altered sensation in the affected limb can be incapacitating and will require specialist treatment.

Chilblains (Pernio)

Chilblains are the mildest form of cold injury and are due to alternate exposure to wet/cold conditions and rapid re-warming. They occur more commonly in women and are characterized by bluish changes in the skin and the formation of blisters or nodules on the surface of chilled parts of the body especially the toes, which appear 12–14 hours after rewarming has occurred. These skin lesions may be very itchy, or feel numb and tender. Affected areas should be kept clean and dry and swollen areas elevated.

Caving

Travellers exploring large cave systems encounter a unique version of the cool temperate climates. Such systems generally have a constant, quite cold temperature, often associated with high humidity, and a lot of water. Some chambers can be windy.

Risk assessment
- *Atmosphere:* decaying organic material in caves, such as guano, can result in a build-up of toxic gases, such as methane or hydrogen sulphide
- *Disease:* cave fauna can transmit several exotic diseases, including histoplasmosis, American trypanosomiasis, rabies (from bats), leishmaniasis, and leptospirosis
- *Environment:* climbs and falls in caves have the added complication that rescue can be exceptionally difficult
- *Fauna:* beware of dangerous or venomous animals and insects
- *Military:* some cave systems, especially in Southeast Asia, have been used for military purposes and mines laid near their entrances. Take local advice
- *Water:* swimming or diving in sumps is hazardous, and there is the risk of flash flooding.

General care
Appropriate clothing is essential. Hypothermia is a significant risk. Hygiene can be difficult. Food preparation must be meticulous and appropriate sanitary arrangements essential.

Polar climates

Polar regions are characterized by snow, ice, wind and brilliant sunshine. In Antarctica and Greenland the land is perpetually covered by ice, elsewhere in the northern hemisphere ice may be extensive in winter, but summer may bring warmer temperatures, and a wealth of plants and wildlife.

Humans, very efficient at acclimatizing to heat, develop few body mechanisms to improve their chances in the cold. Those who regularly expose their hands to very cold temperatures, such as fishermen, have circulatory changes that increase average finger temperature and enable them to work more efficiently. However, survival in a cold climate more often depends upon technological adaptation involving clothing, food, shelter and fuel.

Describing the climate
In cold climates the factors that govern the weather conditions are different. Very cold air is much drier than air around and above freezing point, so the predominant factors that affect perceived conditions are temperature and wind speed. Still air is a good insulator and, on a calm day, temperatures as low as −30°C can be quite pleasant, whilst even a gentle wind makes any sub-zero day unpleasant. Wind-chill tables (Fig. 8.4.2) combine these factors to give a risk rating for the conditions and enable evaluation of the hazard for activities. High winds are particularly dangerous because they not only lead to rapid chilling of any exposed skin surface, but may also cause snow to drift, which can make navigation difficult.

In mid-winter, polar areas have short days with little or no sun. By March the days are much longer and the sun is above the horizon for lengthy periods. Sunlight warms the body and reflects off snow surfaces. On a clear day UV radiation in a snowy environment may be four times that in a desert leading to the risk of both sunburn and snowblindness.

Actual air temperature T_{air} (°C)

Wind speed V_{10m} (km/h)	5	0	-5	-10	-15	-20	-25	-30	-35	-40	-45	-50
5	4	-2	-7	-13	-19	-24	-30	-36	-41	-47	-53	-58
10	3	-3	-9	-15	-21	-27	-33	-39	-45	-51	-57	-63
15	2	-4	-11	-17	-23	-29	-35	-41	-48	-54	-60	-66
20	1	-5	-12	-18	-24	-30	-37	-43	-49	-56	-62	-68
25	1	-6	-12	-19	-25	-32	-38	-44	-51	-57	-64	-70
30	0	-6	-13	-20	-26	-33	-39	-46	-52	-59	-65	-72
35	0	-7	-14	-20	-27	-33	-40	-47	-53	-60	-66	-73
40	-1	-7	-14	-21	-27	-34	-41	-48	-54	-61	-68	-74
45	-1	-8	-15	-21	-28	-35	-42	-48	-55	-62	-69	-75
50	-1	-8	-15	-22	-29	-35	-42	-49	-56	-63	-69	-76
55	-2	-8	-15	-22	-29	-36	-43	-50	-57	-63	-70	-77
60	-2	-9	-16	-23	-30	-36	-43	-50	-57	-64	-71	-78
65	-2	-9	-16	-23	-30	-37	-44	-51	-58	-65	-72	-79
70	-2	-9	-16	-23	-30	-37	-44	-51	-58	-65	-72	-80
75	-3	-10	-17	-24	-31	-38	-45	-52	-59	-66	-73	-80
80	-3	-10	-17	-24	-31	-38	-45	-52	-60	-67	-74	-81

where

T_{air} = Actual air temperature in °C

V_{10m} = Wind speed at 10 metres in km/h (as reported in weather observations)

Notes:

1. For a given combination of temperature and wind speed, the wind chill index corresponds roughly to the temperature that one would feel in a very light wind. For example, a temperature of −25°C and a wind speed of 20km/h give a wind chill index of −37. This means that, with a wind of 20km/h and a temperature of −25°C, one would feel as if it were −37°C in a very light wind.

2. Wind chill does *not* affect objects and does *not* lower the actual temperature. It only describes how a human being would feel in the wind at the ambient temperature.

3. The wind chill index does *not* take into account the effect of sunshine. Bright sunshine may reduce the effect of wind chill (make it feel warmer) by 6 to 10 units.

Frostbite guide
Low risk of frostbite for most people
Increasing risk of frostbite for most people within 30 minutes of exposure
High risk for most people in 5 to 10 minutes of exposure
High risk for most people in 2 to 5 minutes of exposure
High risk for most people in 2 minutes of exposure or less

Fig. 8.4.2 Environmental Canadian Wind Chill Chart. ℘ http://www.ohcow.on.ca/clinics/windsor/docs/workplaceconcernsseminars/windchillchart.pdf, Environment Canada.

Reproduced with the permission from the Minister of Public Works and Government Services Canada, 2012.

The influences of sunlight and wind are such that conditions on the sunny side of a valley may allow skiing in light clothing, whilst crossing a nearby mountain pass with shadow and wind can be a test of extreme clothing.

Hazards of cold climates

- *Avalanche*: heavy snow combined with layers of slippery crystals deep under the surface can cause vast quantities of snow to move. If touring off-piste, never ignore local advice and take appropriate equipment, such as avalanche transceivers, probing poles, and snow shovels. Extreme sports enthusiasts can now buy backpacks with inflatable airbags that are supposed to enable a person to float in an avalanche, but this will not help if ice slabs are on the move, or if you crash into a tree at speed

- *Carbon monoxide:* ice can melt and block ventilation systems either in buildings or in a tent. Poorly-ventilated stoves can silently produce the toxic gas carbon monoxide. Early danger symptoms include tiredness, nausea, headaches, and dizziness
- *Ice:* compacted snow turns to very slippery ice. All outdoor footwear should have good grip
- *Lakes and rivers:* a frozen landscape offers plenty of opportunities to explore the wilderness, but streams may flow under snow and ice. Particularly thin ice is common at the point where streams enter and leave lakes so extreme care should be taken
- *Travel:* all forms of travel in cold regions are dependent upon the weather. Vehicles should be appropriately prepared with fuel, tyres, lubricants and windscreen wash suitable for the temperatures. If travelling any distance, ensure that you carry spare food and clothing in case you are stranded
- *Water:* Because of the dry air, dehydration is common in polar areas. Travellers need to drink. Freshly fallen snow is usually safe to drink, but melting it requires large amounts of fuel. Sucking small amounts of clean ice or snow if you are hot does no harm, but will chill the body, and it is impossible to survive without fuel. Stream water, where available, reduces fuel consumption, but unless the flow is close to a spring, there is a potential risk of giardiasis (Chapter 2.2)—especially in areas where beavers live. Glacier outflow streams carry fine rock particles—'rock flour'—in suspension, which is a powerful laxative: it should be filtered before drinking
- *Whiteout:* cloudy skies and deep snow can combine to create circumstances in which there is no contrast. It becomes impossible to determine what is up or down and very easy to fall over an invisible snow bank, cornice or crevasse
- *Wildlife:* in Arctic Russia, Canada, Greenland, and Spitzbergen, take precautions against falling prey to attacks by polar or grizzly bears, particularly in late spring when they emerge hungry ('Attacks by land animals', Chapter 6). More mundanely, collisions between cars and animals such as moose or elk are a common problem in Scandinavia and northern Canada.

Travelling in cold climates

Even brief exposure to the outdoor climate in polar areas, such as disembarking from aircraft, can involve exposure from extreme cold. Consider before departure what you will wear on arrival; whilst airline terminals and coaches may be heated, imagine how you will cope if a vehicle breaks down and you are forced to seek shelter.

Clothing in cold climates

Clothing should fit well and be selected on the 'layer' principle from the innermost air-trapping layers to the outermost windproof and/or waterproof coverings. Each layer must be larger than the one beneath it to prevent constrictions and to preserve the insulating air. As many layers as possible should be made from materials that retain a high level of insulation, even if they are damp. Polypropylene or merino wool undergarments are popular next to the skin. Down jackets are superbly warm in cold dry environments, but do not insulate once they become wet. A good quality outer shell garment is vital and one can nowadays select from a huge choice. In cold wet climates they should prevent rain soaking into clothes, but allow sweat to escape. Neck, wrist, and underarm openings in anoraks enable air-flow to be quickly adjusted so that water vapour from sweat can escape when one is working hard. In polar climates, aim to minimize sweating as moisture will accumulate in clothes. Rucksacks can be a particular problem as they prevent the normal transmission of sweat through clothes and can cause the underlying garments to become saturated. Damp clothing must be regularly aired and dried.

In still air at 0°C, a quarter of the body's heat production can be lost from the face and scalp, and this loss will rise substantially in colder conditions. Headgear should be able to cover the scalp and ears completely. A good scarf or thermal sleeve (Buff or equivalent) protects neck and chin. Select socks with care. Those that are worn for too long become a double hazard by becoming matted or developing holes so that they lose insulation value, and by shrinking so that the blood supply to the toes and feet is impeded. In extreme conditions, mittens are more effective than gloves at keeping fingers warm, but whichever is chosen, ensure a good overlap of sleeves with the hand wear, because a strip of chilled skin on the inner side of the wrist is extremely painful. Always carry spare gloves and a hat with you in case the originals are blown away.

In very cold conditions (below −15°C) avoid wearing metal adornments especially earrings, facial piercings, or metal-rimmed spectacles. The metal can conduct heat away from the body and cause localized cold injury. Spectacles usually frost over in driving snow or if the temperature falls below −20°C and you may do better to obtain contact lenses (Chapter 9.3). Goggles or glasses with protective side flaps are necessary to prevent painful ultraviolet damage to the cornea—snowblindness (see Chapter 8.9).

Shelter in cold climates

Most people prefer to stay in heated accommodation, but this may be impossible. Snow holes take several hours to construct, but a well-constructed snow hole is quite warm. Igloos are a great idea, but very difficult to build. A good double-skinned polar pyramid tent must be well secured by guys and a snow valance, but once erected enables survival through a storm; such tents are very heavy. Lighter nylon tents may not stop all the wind, the poles may bend or collapse in a storm and can be very cold, but may be the only option if travelling light. Digging a trench and erecting any form of shelter over it can be worthwhile in an emergency. If a person is injured it is very important to insulate them from the snow or ice surface as they will rapidly lose heat by conduction.

Great care is needed when cooking in any of these shelters, both to avoid the risk of fire and because the deadly gas carbon monoxide can accumulate in poorly ventilated shelters.

Special hazards

Cold weather presents special hazards to some people:

- *Heart disease and angina:* cardiac conditions are made worse by severe cold
- *Asthma:* may be triggered by cold, especially when associated with exercise
- *Raynaud's disease:* poor peripheral circulation may increase the risk of frostbite and chilblains. Sufferers should consider taking chemical hand warmers or battery-warmed gloves
- *Cold agglutinins:* some individuals have abnormal proteins in their blood that affects circulation in the cold.

Leisure activities

Each pastime carries its own hazards (see also Chapter 8.9):

Downhill skiing: downhill skiing has an injury rate of approximately 2 per 1000 skier days. Commonest problems include collisions on piste, twisting falls that damage knee ligaments, and difficulties getting on and off lifts. Try to ensure that you are reasonably fit before skiing, that you do not drink alcohol and ski, and that your bindings are properly set up. Consider wearing a helmet.

Snowboarding: this is the most hazardous snow sport, at around 5 injuries per 1000 days. The commonest injury is to the wrist as someone tries to avoid falling backwards.

Telemark/cross-country skiing: free-heel skiing is the safest type of the skiing, with an injury rate of about 1 per 1000 skier days. The skis are generally narrower and lighter than downhill equipment, while the loose heel binding means that forward falls injuring the upper body or shoulder are characteristic. Backcountry touring can take parties far from civilization; they should be appropriately equipped and skilled to deal with adverse conditions.

Dog sledding: some native communities still take great pride in their dog teams—typically of heavy Greenland or Malamute huskies hauling heavy sledges and loads on multi-day trips. Tourism firms, however, favour the smaller, faster Alaskan cross-bred husky, with three or four dogs hauling a light pulk. A pulk passenger is immobile and can chill rapidly if not well wrapped. Huskies are working dogs, not pets, and should not be approached—especially by young children—unless their handlers have given permission. Huskies can catch rabies from wild wolves and foxes, and in endemic areas owners should have vaccinated their dogs.

Snowmobiles: snowmobiles range from relatively slow load-carrying workhorses to lightweight racing machines. On prepared tracks they can be exhilarating to drive, but in deep snow they can easily overturn, dig themselves into holes or topple on top of their drivers. A crash helmet, appropriate driving skills, and maintaining a sensible speed especially on tracks also used by skiers are essential.

Children in the cold

Children and teenagers are not always good at dealing with the effects of cold. They don't always dress sensibly, their hands and feet can become very cold, and they may become unwilling and withdrawn if they develop early hypothermia. Infants in backpacks where circulation to legs may be restricted and small children being towed in pulks are at particular risk of cold injury. Be aware of their limits, turn back early in difficult conditions, and carry food and chemical warmers.

Frostbite

Local chilling of exposed or poorly insulated tissues such as nose, cheeks, chin, ears, hands, or feet can result in that body part freezing without the general chilling of hypothermia. The time required for the 'frost' to 'bite' depends on the degree of wind chill and the amount of tissue at risk. If the air temperature is below −30°C and there is a wind, cold injury can develop is less than a minute. Downhill skiers and snowmobile drivers are at high risk of developing cold injuries on exposed parts of the head and neck. Frostbite of the hands and feet is more likely to occur if the blood supply to the periphery has been reduced either by general body cooling, dehydration, or tight clothing. Touching bare metal or spilling volatile fluids, such as petrol or stove fuel onto bare skin can accelerate the process.

The initial stage of the process is *frostnip* and experienced cold weather travellers may notice its development by a transient burning 'ping'. More often this warning sign goes unnoticed and a companion has to draw attention to the problem. The skin looks pale and waxy, becomes freezing cold and feels hard. At this stage, rewarm facial skin by blowing exhaled air over the skin surface or placing a warm hand on top of the affected area. The skin should become painful and flush as the blood supply returns. Never rub frostbite with anything, because the delicate tissues will suffer more damage. Severe chilling of the hands or feet is a more serious problem. Hands can be rewarmed by swinging them wildly to restore circulation, by the cautious use of chemical warming pads or by persuading a companion to warm them inside their jacket. In the outdoors, feet are a greater problem, but ensure that nothing is restricting circulation to the feet and that socks are not compressing the toes. If initial rewarming is successful, head for shelter as swiftly as possible.

Established frostbite is a very serious problem; permanent and disabling damage can develop, though appropriate treatment can minimize this. A speedy, but gentle journey to hospital is essential. Once frostbitten tissue has thawed, lengthy skilled medical attention will be needed; moreover, if tissue that has thawed is even slightly chilled again, it is liable to develop much more extensive damage. In an emergency involving a frozen foot (the worst) far from any hospital, there are three options:

1. If the journey must be completed and no transport is available, it is possible to walk to safety on a frozen foot, although NEVER on one that has thawed. Give hot food and drinks to maintain core temperature, and correct any clothing defects. Give a painkiller and, if available, an antibiotic, such as a penicillin or tetracycline to prevent infection

2. If there's a stretcher with men to carry it, or sledge transport is available, treat the victim in a warm shelter. Remove the boot and sock as carefully as possible, cover the foot lightly with gauze, pad it with cotton wool, and wrap it up loosely. Make the casualty

comfortable and warm, and immobilize the foot gently before setting off. Ensure that the patient remains warm throughout the transfer

3. Once the patient is at a habitation with medical advice available and the possibility of eventual evacuation, then they should stay put. The affected part should be rewarmed in water at 40°C (104°F) to which a mild antiseptic, such as dilute chlorhexidine has been added. The rewarming process will be intensely painful and, if available, a powerful painkiller, such as morphine, nalbuphine, or tramadol will be required to control the agony. If there is no contraindication to its use, an anti-inflammatory painkiller, such as ibuprofen (400mg twice daily) may reduce tissue damage. Broad-spectrum antibiotics, painkillers, and anti-tetanus toxoid should be given as soon as possible to patients with significant tissue damage. Water bath treatments can be repeated twice daily to keep the area clean. Between treatments keep the affected area warm, dry, and elevated. If the fingers or hand are frostbitten, clean the skin regularly and dab dry very gently. Separate the fingers with cotton wool after winding a sterile bandage around each, and place a thick sterile pad in the palm of the hand so that the fingers are in a 'glass-holding' position. Bandage the whole lightly and elevate the forearm in a sling.

- After rewarming, the frostbitten part will look dreadful—a mixture of black skin, and pale or blood-filled blisters. Any blisters that have burst will leak copious amounts of fluid and dressings will need to be changed regularly. However, the end results of the injury are likely to look much less spectacular. It can be helpful to photograph the evolving injury as this may improve evaluation by an expert remotely accessed by telephone or Internet. Early surgical intervention should be discouraged
- Topical aloe vera is a popular additional treatment in the USA, while European studies suggest that the combination of aspirin and iloprost (a synthetic prostacyclin analogue) reduces the risk of amputation in severe frostbite
- Some experts now recommend early use of sophisticated scanning techniques such as magnetic resonance angiography or technetium scanning in order to define the limits of damage, followed if appropriate by thrombolysis of the affected zone. These high-tech therapies are only available at the largest hospitals, must be performed soon after the initial injury, and then only after seeking expert advice. Hyperbaric oxygen has also been used in a few centres for treatment of late frostbite with some beneficial effects, but must still be regarded as an experimental treatment.

Once a person has been frostbitten, the affected part of the body is more likely to freeze again and special care must thereafter be taken to protect it against further injury. Severe frostbite may lead to long-term disability with chronic pain and cold hypersensitivity.

Other cold-associated conditions

Lung injury: severe exercise in polar conditions (below −30°C) can result in frosting of the lungs. Chest pain develops and blood may be coughed up. Extreme exertion is required to overcome the extremely efficient heat exchange mechanisms in the upper airway and this problem is only likely to affect the very athletic.

Asthma: cold weather may precipitate asthma and athletes in cold climates have been shown to be more prone to develop a wheeze. Asthma sufferers should be wary of very cold areas.

Infection: very cold weather may worsen the effects of respiratory viruses. There is no firm evidence for this at present, but athletic exertion during a viral illness is never wise.

Cold urticaria: a widely distributed itchy pale rash covering parts of the skin that have become chilled is common as people rewarm after a day's skiing. No treatment is necessary.

Sunburn: ultraviolet (UV) radiation levels on a bright day in polar areas can be intense and in springtime in Antarctica are made worse by the ozone hole. Exposed areas of skin must be protected by an SP30+ suncream. Much UV is reflected upwards off the snow, so ensure the nostrils and underneath of the chin are protected. Effects can still occur on overcast days.

Snowblindness: snowblindness is the term given to sunburn of the conjunctiva—the clear membrane in front of the eye. Unprotected exposure to bright UV radiation leads a few hours later to reddening and watering of the eyes, swelling of the eyelids, and an intense gritty pain as though sand is in the eyes; the eyes may close completely and the casualty will have to be assisted to shelter. It can be prevented by wearing good quality sunglasses or snow goggles. If snowblindness develops, first check to ensure that no foreign body or contact lens remains in the affected eye. Give simple painkillers such as paracetamol or codeine, pad the eyes and leave the casualty to rest. Eye drops that reduce ciliary muscle spasm such as tropicamide 0.5% may reduce discomfort, but antibiotic and local anaesthetic drugs, although soothing, may lead to greater damage unless there are specific reasons to use them. Healing will usually occur uneventfully within three days; specialist help should be obtained if there is infection or persistent visual disturbance.

Other eye injuries: the cornea of the eye can freeze in those who force their eyes to remain open in high wind-chill situations. The condition produces symptoms similar to those of 'snowblindness' caused by UV light. Rewarming and rest are the only treatments. Proper snow goggles prevent the problem and it is worth putting them on as severe injury may require a corneal transplant to prevent loss of sight. Contact lenses should not be left in place for unusual lengths of time, they can adhere to the cornea, also potentially causing severe eye damage (see also Chapter 9.1).

8.5 Sun and the traveller

Anthony Young

Introduction

A tan is socially desirable in Western society, when it is, in fact, the skin's response to damage by the sun's ultraviolet radiation (UVR). Nonetheless, it is possible to tan wisely and minimize the harmful effects of solar UVR, including sunburn.

The sun emits radiation that enables life. Visible radiation (light) initiates photosynthesis, the basis of the food chain. The eye registers light with special nerve cells. Infrared radiation (heat) warms the earth, and our skin has heat sensitive nerve cells that detect temperature. However, humans have no UVR sensitive nerve cells and we only know we have had UVR exposure after sunburn. The only benefit of solar UVR is photosynthesis of vitamin D which is essential for healthy bones, although there is increasing evidence that vitamin D prevents some cancers and multiple sclerosis. Unfortunately, most of the effects of solar UVR are harmful to the skin and eyes. Apart from sunburn, UVR causes accelerated skin ageing (photo-ageing), skin cancer, and cataracts. UVR from sunbeds can also have the same effects.

Other skin reactions may occur. As many as 15% of UK inhabitants develop an irritating, spotty, but harmless rash within a few hours of sun exposure, which may last for up to a week. This is *polymorphic light eruption* (often mistakenly called 'prickly heat'). Another abnormal reaction is an excessive sunburn-like response caused by some oral medications.

The skin has evolved protective responses against some of these adverse phenomena, particularly tanning, but these occur after sun damage. Thus, a tanned skin may give modest protection against further damage, but unless already present as in naturally dark skin, its acquisition is always associated with injury. Artificial tanning lotions are the preferred safe alternative, although not very protective against later sun exposure.

The skin and solar UVR

The skin has many functions that include temperature regulation, perception, and a barrier against infection. It has two main layers; the outer epidermis and the underlying dermis. The epidermis contains different highly specialized cells. The dermis has few cells, but contains collagen and other molecules that give strength and elasticity. The dermis also contains the skin's blood supply.

The sun's UVR is sub-divided into three types:
- *UVC:* totally absorbed by the ozone layer and of no concern at the earth's surface
- *UVB:* partially absorbed by the ozone layer. Its intensity depends on the height of the sun which varies with season, latitude and time of day, and so is greatest at noon. UVB also increases with altitude. The maximal UVB content of solar UVR is never more than about 5%, but this causes most of the short-term and long-term damage to the skin and eyes

- *UVA:* 95% of solar UVR and shows much less variation with height of the sun than UVB. About 1000 times more UVA than UVB is needed to cause similar effects to the skin.

Circumstances leading to damage

The amount (dose) of UVR received by the skin depends on the factors described previously. If, in addition, if there are adjacent UVR-reflecting surfaces, such as snow, shiny metals, white materials, or clear blue sky, the exposure dose will be greater, resulting in more damage. Sunburn is therefore particularly likely on beaches, in deserts, and on ski slopes, even in winter in the last instance. A good tip is the 'shadow rule'; protection is necessary when your shadow is shorter than you.

Individual susceptibility to skin damage

The damage caused by UVR depends on skin phototype, which can be subdivided as follows:

- *Types I and II:* fair-skinned, burns easily with poor ability to tan, often with blue eyes, freckles, and fair/red hair, e.g. Celtic
- *Types III and IV:* white to olive skin that tans readily, ranging from Northern Europe to Mediterranean, also Far East types
- *Types V and VI:* brown or black skin, dark eyes, and hair, e.g. from the Indian sub-continent and Africa.

As a general rule, the lower the skin type the greater the risk for all types of UVR-induced skin damage. An important factor in minimizing your risk is to know your skin type. For example, a skin type I, has a negligible tanning response and so, with the exception of vitamin D, there is not even a cosmetic benefit. In contrast, a skin type IV tans very easily with a lower risk of sunburn. Most people know how they react in summer sunlight and should protect themselves accordingly. Particular care should be taken with children, and babies should always be kept in the shade when the sun is high.

The effects of UVR exposure

UVR readily penetrates the skin and causes cell damage. Tissue may die as a result and cell debris and chemicals produced during the process may also damage surrounding structures (e.g. blood vessels), contributing to the following short-term and long-term changes.

Early changes

1. *Sunburn:* redness, soreness, increased sensitivity to pressure and heat, and in severe cases swelling and blistering of the exposed skin; typically maximal about 24 hours after exposure
2. *Tanning:* formation of the protective brown pigment, melanin, in the skin over days to weeks following exposure
3. *Suppression of the skin's immunity:* a single exposure to UVR, even at doses that do not cause sunburn, reduces the skin's immunity. This probably plays a role in skin cancer
4. *Hyperplasia:* thickening of the epidermis, especially the dead outermost layer. This is why the skin can feel scaly after a sunny holiday.

Late changes
1. *Photo-ageing:* degenerative changes in epidermis and dermis, apparent as a loss of elasticity, along with dryness, coarseness, irregular pigmentation, yellowing, and wrinkling
2. *Skin cancer:* the most common cancer in white-skinned people and its incidence is increasing. This results from UVR-induced DNA mutations in epidermal cells. Most skin cancers respond to treatment. However, mutations to melanocytes, the specialized tan/pigment producing cells, can result in malignant melanoma which is often fatal. Malignant melanoma risk is associated with sunburn in children and adults. Skin cancer presents as persistent rough patches or irregular, steadily enlarging moles, lumps, or sores.

The only beneficial effect of UVR exposure is vitamin D synthesis in the skin. Vitamin D is also available from some foods (e.g. oily fish) and supplements; however, most people do not receive enough via these routes. Thus, solar UVB is mainly responsible for maintaining vitamin D status and this can be done with summer day-to-day exposure that does not result in sunburn.

Sunbeds
Regular sunbed use increases the risk of malignant melanoma, especially in the young, and sunbed use has recently been designated as carcinogenic by the International Agency for Research on Cancer (IARC). Sunbeds should never be used without good eye protection, and should never be used by children.

Sunbed use has ill-advisedly been advocated to give a pre-holiday tan and consequent protection against later sun exposure. Such protection is at best very modest. However, a cosmetic pre-holiday tan can be achieved with three times weekly (e.g. Mondays, Wednesdays, and Fridays) exposures for 2–3 weeks, but holiday sunscreen use is still necessary. In addition, you should not undertake such a course more than twice a year.

Sunscreens
The regular, careful use of sunscreens is a very effective way of protecting against sunburn and many other effects of UVR. There is increasing evidence that sunscreen use may protect against some types of skin cancer.

Sunscreens are labelled with their sun protection factors (SPF) which is a measure of protection against sunburn; the higher the SPF the higher the protection. Sunscreens usually have an index of UVA protection. In the UK, UVA protection is often indicated with a star system: the higher the number of stars (maximum 5), the better the UVA protection. However, this is a secondary index and a purchase should be based on SPF. This is determined, under laboratory conditions, with a thicker film of sunscreen than typical everyday use. This means that in practice, the real SPF will be approximately 1/4 to 1/3 of that on the label. To achieve a real SPF of 15 you need to apply an SPF of about 40–50, unless you apply an SPF = 15 product very liberally. All SPF values are approximate, and so a preparation of SPF 15 is not necessarily much different from one of 13 or 17. Sunscreens vary in cosmetic acceptability, and some high SPF products may leave a whitish residue. In addition, cost is no guide whatsoever, so choose the cheapest product that suits you.

As a general rule, the lower the skin type the higher the SPF you should use. It must be reiterated that sunscreens work only if applied before exposure and frequently thereafter, especially after swimming or exercise, so remember this or they will prove useless in practice. Sunscreens should be used to reduce total UVR exposure to the skin, rather than just receive the same dose over a protracted period.

If you get a spotty red, itchy rash when using your sunscreen, it is likely to be polymorphic light eruption (though allergies occur sometimes). Cover up for a few days and use a higher SPF product with good UVA protection when things have settled; if the trouble persists or recurs, you may need to see a doctor, perhaps a dermatologist, on your return.

Cold sores may also worsen on sun exposure, so use a high SPF sunscreen on any susceptible sites. Melasma—a blotchy, brown discoloration, most common on the cheeks—may occur too, particularly in women, especially if on the pill or pregnant. A very high SPF sunscreen with good UVA protection will reduce the chances of this.

On holiday

An Internet search of the UV Index at your location will provide a guide to the strength of the sun, often with advice on safe exposure times for a given skin type. If a tan is not your priority, and even if it is, aim for exposure towards the start or the end of the day, when the UVB intensity, even in hot weather, is lower. Otherwise, wear loose-fitting but tightly woven clothing and a hat. A high SPF (at least 20) sunscreen should be liberally applied every hour or so when outside, especially after swimming and other physical activity. The first application should be made before you go out in the sun.

If your goal is a tan, you should take extra care of unacclimatized skin during the first few days. You can gradually increase your exposure time and/or decrease your SPF if your skin feels comfortable. It is also worth using a moisturizing after-sun cream to help minimize any skin dryness or irritation. If you tan readily, you should be fairly brown after about a week to 10 days, although increasing tanning may gradually continue for a week or so. Since most people initially burn easily on sensitive areas of the body such as the nose, lips, and very white areas, you should take extra care at these sites. Conventional high SPF sunscreens are generally effective for these regions, but thicker, over-the-counter creams, and pastes containing zinc oxide or titanium dioxide are particularly good.

If you wear very little, you need to be especially careful with the pale, previously unexposed areas of skin, particularly when UVB intensity is high. If you start feeling uncomfortable and weather-beaten, however, cover up before it is too late. A severe burn could spoil your holiday, your tan, and your skin!

In general, you should have no major problems, especially if you expose mostly towards the ends of the day and cover up, or else carefully and regularly use a high SPF sunscreen. If you must have your tan, you should acquire it using the relatively careful approach outlined above. On the other hand, carelessness and overdoing it during the first few days will probably lead to painful burning, and may increase your chances of wrinkling and skin cancer.

Treatment

Sunburn usually resolves within hours to days unless extraordinarily severe. However, simple calamine creams or lotions may sometimes soothe burnt areas, and mild analgesics, such as aspirin, paracetamol, or ibuprofen tablets, taken as soon as possible after exposure, may further relieve pain and inflammation. Steroid creams (obtainable only on a doctor's prescription, except for the mildest types) used frequently and early after exposure may be helpful. Ibuprofen gel or mousse preparations may also be worth trying.

In addition, to minimize damage, do not sunbathe for 2 or 3 days after any burn, thereby allowing some healing to take place. If you are unfortunate enough to develop a patch of severe burning, treat it in the same way as an ordinary heat burn—keep it clean and dress it regularly to avoid infection. Widespread severe sunburn may, on the other hand, require plentiful oral fluids and bed-rest with painkillers, perhaps steroid tablets, and antibiotics. If very severe, hospital admission with IV fluids and other intensive care measures may be necessary. Some people have even died as a result of overdoing sunbathing, e.g. during a day out on a boat with a cooling breeze and soothing alcohol as distractions.

Most skin cancers can be successfully treated; the exception is melanoma, which can only be treated if detected early. Photo-ageing cannot be satisfactorily treated, except to some extent by aggressive dermatological surgery (particularly laser techniques). In addition, the long-term application of preparations such as tretinoin (Retin-A) and alphahydroxyacids improve the skin, but the effects are modest.

Box 8.5.1 **Summary of advice for travellers**

- Know your skin type; skin types I and II have the highest risk of sunburn and skin cancer
- Too much sun exposure is harmful to the skin. Check the local UV Index (TV, newspaper, Internet) to know UVR intensity, and sometimes skin type based exposure times
- In the short term, sun exposure can cause painful sunburn. Very rarely, extreme exposure can produce fever. In the long term, photo-ageing and skin cancers are possible
- The best way of minimizing such problems is to avoid or protect against excessive exposure in the first place, rather than trying to treat resultant conditions once they have developed
- UVR intensity is greatest when the sun is high. Avoid the sun at those times where possible, or wear a hat and cover up, Use loose, tightly-woven fabrics. Use waterproof high SPF sunscreens in ample quantity, frequently; wear good-quality UVR protective sunglasses
- Take particular care with babies and children.

8.6 Hay fever seasons worldwide

Roy Kennedy

Between 15 and 25% of people suffer from hay fever (an allergy to air-borne pollen and fungal spores). Pollen and fungal spore occurrence varies between countries. A trip through Europe could take in the worst times for pollen at each stopping point. However, a similar itinerary at a later time of year might be entirely problem-free.

In order to identify a suitable pollen-free or spore-free area, it is important to know which pollen or spore types give rise to allergic reactions in the individual. Pollen from plants that cause hay fever can be generally classified as being from trees, grass, or weed species. Pollen occurs when plants are flowering and this varies according to the climatic zone. It is important to be aware of when the peak seasons occur in different locations (see Appendix 6). In general, places that usually have low pollen counts throughout the summer are exposed coastal resorts. Low pollen counts are often found in cities; however interactions with urban pollutants mean that even low levels may trigger allergenic reactions.

Grass pollen

Grass pollen is the main culprit in hay fever and pollen-related asthma. As a group, grasses are closely related, so if you are allergic to one type of grass pollen, you will react to most of the others.

The seasons start and finish earlier at lower latitudes in Europe. Typically, seasons in southern Mediterranean areas (e.g. southern Spain, Italy, and Greece) start in late April or early May. Easter holidaymakers in these locations can meet with grass pollen concentrations high enough to cause problems. The peak season comes in late May and June, several weeks earlier than in the UK. By mid-July, the grass pollen counts are going down in most of these areas.

The Mediterranean islands are especially favourable because of sparse grasslands and more mixing of air from the sea. In contrast, inland areas, such as the Po Valley, including Milan (May/June) and central southern France (May/June) can have severe grass pollen seasons.

Tree and weed pollen

Tree pollen causes hay fever in about 25% of sufferers. The amounts of pollen produced vary a lot from year to year. Birch pollen is the second most important allergenic pollen type in the UK. In Scandinavia, Germany, Austria, and Switzerland, the concentrations of birch pollen can be much higher than in the UK. People who are prone to develop allergies may become sensitized to new types of pollen, such as olive tree, when abroad. Weed pollen is more prevalent later in the year in the UK.

Summary of pollen seasons in main destinations

Pollen seasons vary with climate, vegetation and topography. In addition, local weather conditions give rise to slight differences in the timing of seasons from year to year, but the main seasons are unlikely to differ much from the 'averages'. The information given in Appendix 6 is intended as a general guide.

Box 8.6.1 **Summary of advice for travellers**

- If you suffer from hay fever, choose your destination carefully, e.g. a beach where the breeze comes in from the sea. Alpine resorts (with short pollen seasons) are also suitable
- For temperate climates, avoid late spring and early summer; for the tropics, the worst time of year tends to be immediately after the rainy season
- Avoid countryside with open meadows and well-developed agriculture
- Change your clothes after going outdoors; your clothes and hair can trap pollen, which will give trouble later
- The pollen count tends to be highest late mornings and evenings.

8.7 Yachting and sailing: 'nautical tourism'

Nebojša Nikolić

Sailing is a beautiful experience, but the cost can be high—injury, illness, and loss of life. Almost always, the problems are preventable. Careful preparation, an understanding of preventive measures and basic medical skills, and an extensive knowledge of safety procedures on board are essential requirements for success.

Background

People usually sail 7–12m yachts, with up to eight people on board. Although basic manoeuvres are simple, some can be complicated, and require prompt and precise actions. Sailing also requires a good knowledge of navigation, meteorology, and safety procedures. People sailing their own boats are usually fully trained, but the majority of tourists rent boats. The only proof of competence needed when renting a boat is a licence, but to get a licence you don't even have to know how to sail! Sadly, this inexperience may lead to particular medical problems.

Environmental problems and other stress factors

Sudden temperature changes and the effects of humidity, wind, rain, fog, and strong solar radiation have a greater effect on board sea-going vessels than elsewhere. Heavy storms may endanger the whole crew.

Hot climates

Most tourists go cruising when temperatures are high. This can become a problem for those coming from cooler areas. Acclimatization to a hot climate takes time, but boats are mostly chartered for only 1 or 2 weeks. With incomplete acclimatization, physical and mental performance suffers, which can be extremely dangerous. Under conditions of heat or cold, extreme overstressing of the circulatory system can lead to heart failure. Obesity, lack of fitness, lack of sleep, psychological instability, and finally, abuse of alcohol, nicotine, or drugs may complicate the situation.

The skin problems associated with hot, moist conditions (such as 'prickly heat') are well-known to sailors (Chapter 8.8); and sea water itself can cause problems—'seawater boils' appear when permanent wetness allows bacteria that normally inhabit the skin surface to penetrate to deeper layers. 'Immersion foot' (p.265, p.312) not only results from war conditions in the trenches, but also affects unlucky sailors who are forced to spend a long time in wet shoes.

Cold climates

With modern sailing gear, heavy and cold weather conditions pose no problem—although charter tourists are not always prepared to pay the cost of such equipment.

On the water, a foolhardy approach to the cold decreases comfort and impairs performance. Although this may not directly place life in peril, it can certainly contribute to injury or the inability to perform some vital tasks on board.

At sea, one is constantly engaged in a real battle for survival. Even in waters at a pleasant temperature for recreational swimming, like 28°C, human life can be endangered by prolonged immersion. Sailors should know how to keep themselves warm and must anticipate that in cold weather their efficiency will suffer (see Chapter 8.4).

Submersion incidents

Drowning and near-drowning from falling overboard are a major risk for every sailor. It is not a simple task to stop the boat when sailing or to perform manoeuvres that will return the boat into a position from which the victim can be lifted back on board. Once overboard, if it is not possible to hold on to the boat or get back on board, sailors should keep the heat escape lessening posture (HELP) position, with legs up and arms around bent knees. This will reduce the heat loss due to direct contact with cold water. One should always remember 'The Rule of 50': The chance of swimming 50 yards (45m) in water of 50°F (11°C) is just 50%.

Single-handed sailing, helped by the automatic pilot, is a danger of its own. It has happened more than once that a boat steered by the automatic pilot was found with dinner served on the deck, but no one aboard. Single-handed sailors usually drag a long rope behind the boat, so that they can catch it and eventually climb back on board.

Workload aboard

In bad weather heavy physical work can become unavoidable. The inability to shorten the sails in a storm because of a physically-inadequate crew can be disastrous, and a pleasant vacation can turn into a tragedy in a few minutes.

The ship's movement can also cause problems. It induces motion sickness in sensitive persons and reduces the depth of sleep, because of the unavoidable muscular compensatory movements (Chapter 7.3). Probably 90% of seafarers suffer once or even several times from motion sickness. This incidence is lower on small craft, but having a member of the crew suffering from seasickness in a storm and literally not caring if the ship capsizes is just one of the horror stories that 'weekend captains' relate.

A further stress factor on long-distance sailing is the need to keep watch. Limited numbers of crew means that this problem can turn a holiday into an exhausting experience.

Nutrition aboard

Nutrition aboard cruising vessels is usually good, but if the weather is bad and distances are longer, food preparation can become impossible and the crew forced to eat only cold meals.

Hot weather creates problems for food storage. Refrigerators are small, and due to the need to save battery power, usually operate only when the motor is on (it is usually off when sailing). On a hot day food can easily spoil and become dangerous to eat.

Common problems also include abuses of alcohol, coffee, and tobacco. Excessive consumption of cold drinks can have an adverse effect on the gastrointestinal tract, too.

Sailors often combine their sport with fishing, but even fresh fish can sometimes be dangerous to eat. Although there are numerous types of marine poisonings, the sailor needs to be aware of three major types of fish poisoning (scombroid, ciguatera, and puffer-fish) and, of course, shellfish poisoning (see Chapter 2.2).

Sociopsychological factors

Sociopsychological factors can have a profound influence on the health of the crew. Everyone going to sea has his or her own set of expectations. Everybody also carries aboard their own emotional 'baggage' and their own style of interacting with others. It is difficult to predict how each of us might respond to the stressful situations at sea. Very often, the boat functions like some kind of group therapy with every conceivable problem becoming visible, but on board, this can happen fast, unexpectedly, and without any control.

Medical care at sea

The health skills required from the nautical tourist exceed the scope of simple first aid: preliminary training, a suitable handbook and medicine chest, and access to radio medical advice are necessary. The aim is to reach a level where the sailor can perform those tasks necessary to stabilize an injured or ill person until professional help can be found. In offshore sailing, the aim is higher: the sailor has to be capable of treating the injured or sick person for longer periods of time.

Medical training is not compulsory for getting a licence, but good sailing schools now offer medical courses. There are a few manuals on the market, but the most comprehensive is still the WHO/IMO/ILO manual, *International Medical Guide for Ships*, 3rd edn. (see Further Reading). It is written for merchant marine seafarers and exceeds the requirement level of a sailing tourist, but it is still the best bet for any sailor.

International standards require every vessel to be equipped with a quality radio transmitter. Under the new worldwide Global Maritime Distress and Safety System (GMDSS), the channel for automatic digitalized calls for help—Digital Selective Calling (DSC)—is 70. If medical attention or advice is needed, the sailor is connected by radio to a centre on shore with a designated doctor. After giving appropriate details and familiarizing the doctor with the contents of the medical chest on board, the sailor receives precise instructions on further treatment.

Medical chest

There are various standards for medical kits, but the principal rule should be that it has to be co-ordinated with the manual and medical training of the person giving help. Again, regarding its contents, the best advice would be to follow the recommendations given in the *International Medical Guide for Ships*, 3rd edn.

Injuries

The amount of activity that has to take place in a confined space makes injuries more likely. There are several tasks and pieces of equipment on board that can cause injuries, from rope abrasions on hands and feet to a blow to the head from the boom, which could prove fatal. Lighting below deck is often poor and stairs can cause falls. The galley is anything but safe—cooking during a sail demands the highest attention and caution. Butane gas leaks and motor exhausts are constant hazards below deck.

Injuries caused by environmental factors

One of the commonest causes of disability is sunburn (Chapter 8.5). The risk is compounded by the cool breeze on the deck removing the usual sensation of warmth—nature's warning system. Therefore, sailors should apply an SPF25 or greater sunscreen. An adult sailor in short-sleeved shirt and shorts needs approximately 2mg of sunscreen per cm² of skin exposed. This means that most sailors will need about 15–20mL per application. Before travel, one should always obtain the UV-index data at the sailing destination.

The open sea is one of the most dangerous places to be during a thunderstorm. Lightning is attracted to the highest object, and at sea this is the boat. It can seriously damage the electrical equipment, endanger navigation, and cause injury to the sailor. Lightning kills 30% of its victims and maims two-thirds of the survivors.

Piracy

This is an escalating problem and private yachts are often targeted as well as commercial shipping. A live piracy map showing actual and attempted attacks reported to the International Maritime Bureau can be found at ℘ http://www.icc-ccs.org/piracy-reporting-centre/live-piracy-report.

Injuries inflicted by dangerous sea animals

Although most marine life is harmless, some can injure or endanger life. The most threatening of these—a shark attack—is actually rare, but caution should always be taken. Fish such as barracudas, dusky serranus, cog or conger eels, stingrays, and moray eels can also cause uncomfortable injuries.

Of all the injuries caused by marine life, the most widespread are those caused by cnidarians (jellyfish and corals). Fish with their own poisonous thorns can produce serious poisoning. Some of them, such as scorpion fish, lionfish, or stonefish, can cause death. In the Mediterranean and east Atlantic the most poisonous is the Weeverfish group (see Chapter 6).

Before embarkation

The boat and the crew must be in the best possible condition. Boats and all equipment must be thoroughly checked before every trip. Aboard, the skipper is the one who is responsible for the boat and the crew, and so is the one who has to take necessary precautions:

1. *Determine the risk:* every skipper should determine the risk of the trip by taking into account the sailing competence of the crew, current health of each member, length of time before embarkation, destination, itinerary, length of stay, purpose (cruise or race), food, and water sources

2. *Record keeping:* it is important to keep records of any illness and injury aboard, especially of medicine given, in the log. Also any existing medical conditions should be noted and a general medical examination should precede all offshore voyages of long duration. The medical background of every member of the crew should be made available to the skipper. Any member of the crew who is taking medication should bring sufficient supplies aboard and the skipper should check this

3. *Immunizations and anti-malarial protection:* should be taken according to travel health advice from a skilled source, dependent on any possible ports that the boat will visit. Immunization documents should be brought aboard

4. *Medical training:* at least one member of the crew should have medical training according to Model Course 2 recommended by the WHO (for coastal sailing) or Model Course 3 (for off-shore sailing). The rest of the crew should have medical training to Model Course 1 (corresponding to a standard first-aid course)

5. *Medical manual and medical chest:* a good-quality medical manual and a proper medical chest must be kept on the boat. The chest has to be checked before sailing and its contents selected according to the number of the crew and type of voyage

6. *Physical condition and sailing competence:* the skipper has to be sure that the crew is in good health and physically competent to carry out all tasks during the voyage

7. *Proper rest:* before departure, ample rest is necessary. During the voyage, when organizing work-shifts, the skipper must ensure that each member of the crew has enough rest and sleep

8. *Food and water supply:* nutrition has to be planned, taking into account any weather delays that might make it impossible to replenish food and water supplies. Alcohol should be avoided

9. *Minimizing the effects of the environment:* sun protection of the skin is necessary, especially for the first days of the voyage, as well as eye protection with sunglasses. Clothes should be of the highest quality to protect the body from cold and water

10. *Safety gear:* a life vest and/or safety lines must be worn in every risky situation, such as during a storm or when a sailor is alone on deck. There have been many instances where boats have been found,

running on automatic pilot, but with no sailor on board. If children are on the boat, a net should be used on the railing

11. *Electronic equipment:* radio and GPS should be checked regularly; a hand-held GPS running on batteries should be carried in addition to one connected to the main electrical supply. A magnetic compass in addition to an electronic one is a must. Radar is also strongly advised

12. *Weather forecasts:* these should be monitored regularly.

Box 8.7.1 **Summary of advice to travellers**

- Be confident in your sailing skills and experience
- Be confident in the competence of your crew
- Ensure that your boat is in perfect condition
- Check that all safety equipment is on board and working
- Ensure that you are competent in procedures of medical care at sea
- Keep a medical manual and medical chest aboard
- Ensure that you have a good-quality radio aboard.

8.8 Swimming, diving, and water sports

John Kenafake

Enjoying water-related activities is not without risk; however, the level of danger is highly variable and much can be done to stack the odds in your favour. Common activities will be discussed, with safe guidelines formulated.

Swimming

The travelling public is a swimming public. Any water may be fair game, from lakes and rivers to estuaries and ocean. The key is to enjoy the activity with minimal risk. A respectful approach to the water goes a long way in mitigating risk and enhancing pleasure

A major cause for concern is mixing alcohol with any aquatic activity. This combination is more common with swimmers, although scuba divers, if dehydrated from the previous night's festivities, are also at risk. How often does the news report say 'alcohol was a factor in this tragic drowning'? Males aged 20–30 (in drowning statistics it's more often males than females) are particularly at risk. This group's behaviour not only leads to high drowning rates, but also a much higher risk of spinal injuries often leading to paralysis—the result of diving into water and hitting the bottom. Always ascertain the depth—a job better done sober.

In countries with supervised beaches, it is wise to take advantage of the lifeguard presence. Swimming outside the flags, at dawn, dusk, alone, and in unfamiliar locations is fraught with danger. If no one else is in the water it may be for a very good reason. Conditions change constantly and water that was safe mid-morning might be nightmarishly dangerous by mid-afternoon. Tides vary in direction and strength, dragging the unwary swimmer along with them, covering and uncovering hazards.

Surf beaches can develop powerful 'along the shore' water movements called sweeps. Worse still, local conditions can conspire to create out-to-sea rips. Both phenomena may be impossible to swim against and are best escaped by swimming across, rather than against the water flow. A swimmer caught in a rip who doesn't panic will find it dissipates over several hundred metres and be able to make it back to shore eventually without too much effort. DON'T PANIC—follow the aforementioned rules.

Fast-moving water of any origin is hazardous. Rivers, streams, and waterways, especially in flood, are to be approached with caution.

The extremes of the age cohort face additional hazards. Children, especially toddlers, drown quickly and silently in any body of water, including the bathtub, so constant close supervision and vigilance are the best safeguards.

Those over 65 are also at noticeable risk. Factors such as general health, fitness, and medication are of note.

People who suffer from epilepsy have a greatly increased risk of drowning. A seizure in water is likely to be fatal unless the person is removed swiftly.

People escaping cooler regions to the summer sun may find their enjoyment dampened by sunburn (Chapter 8.5). Although usually minor, severe sunburn can cause considerable pain, which is not the best way to spend a holiday. Worse still, in the long term it can lead to skin cancer. Ideally, avoid sun in the middle part of the day, use barrier method clothing, and apply sunscreens to uncovered skin. Modern sun-protective clothing is excellent for swimming, snorkelling, and surfing. There is no such thing as safe sun-tanning.

Schistosomiasis (bilharzia) is a particular hazard in any freshwater source without rapid flow (dams, lakes, rivers) in many tropical countries (Chapter 4.4). Local advice may be inaccurate and the wise action is to stick to the hotel pool. Salt water is schistosomiasis free.

Marine creatures can impact on enjoyment, sometimes dramatically. Shark attacks are rare, but lower the risk further by staying out of the water at dawn, dusk, and during the night. River mouths attract fish and, notoriously, predator sharks. Entering the ocean near seal colonies raises the risk factor, as the Great White shark may accidently supplement its diet with a human in a wetsuit. The world's hot spots for Great Whites are the east coast of South Africa, Northern California and the Great Australian Bight.

Crocodiles inhabit tropical rivers, wetlands, and oceans in Africa, Asia, Australia, and the Americas. Take extreme care before entering any water source—this one is really common sense.

Sea jellies (they are not really fish) are a diverse group inhabiting all the world's oceans. Stings range in severity from a nuisance itch to death. The box jelly and the irukanjie are the two most often associated with fatalities. The former can be large and so translucent as to be invisible and the latter is small and invisible. Swim in protective suits ('stinger suits') or in purpose-built enclosures and follow the lead of the locals. If stung, neutralizing the nematocysts with vinegar, removing the stingers (using gloves or towel), and urgent access to antivenom are needed. CPR may be required.

The commonest stings are from the Portuguese man o' war (or blue bottle), which rarely cause more than temporary tears—ice packs and simple analgesia usually suffice.

A creature that *is* a fish, although well disguised in the rocky coast environment of the Indo–Pacific, is the stonefish. Thirteen venomous spines await the unwary, and cause severe pain and sometimes death. Soaking the damaged limb, usually a foot, in hot water at 45° provides some pain relief. Additional painkillers, tetanus, and possibly antivenom injections may be required. Wear protective footwear when walking in these waters.

Similarly, stingray blend into the sandy flats. If stood on, a barb on the under surface of the tail can cause local trauma and lots of pain. Stingrays are not aggressive and are scared away by a noisy approach (see also Chapter 6).

Underwater

SCUBA diving

The rewards of descending into superb alien worlds lure us to don scuba gear and venture below. Unfortunately, it is a hostile environment that must be respected to be enjoyed safely.

For a novice, learning to dive properly either at home or at the destination is of great importance. Improperly trained divers represent a significant group in diving death figures.

Not everyone is medically fit to dive. Conditions such as epilepsy, and major lung or heart disease preclude diving absolutely. Many conditions may be a relative contraindication, such as type 2 diabetes, obesity, and post-cardiac procedures. Hence, there is a need for a health assessment prior to taking a course. Depending on where you do the course, this may be self-assessed with any problems requiring a medical review. In some diving destinations, such as Queensland, Australia, medical consultations are mandatory. Beware of choosing an operator who doesn't follow these rules.

Fortunately, there are several worldwide organizations, including the Professional Association of Dive Instructors (PADI), Scuba Schools International (SSI) and National Association of Underwater Instructors (NAUI), which can be relied on for education, training, and safety. Courses are usually structured around theory sessions, followed by pool and then open-water dives over 4 days or so. These should be under the auspices of a qualified instructor and followed by an examination. Successful divers are issued with an Open Water Certificate allowing diving (to 18 m) pretty much anywhere in the world. Follow-up courses allow for supervised experience in wrecks, deeper water, night diving, etc., and are highly recommended.

Resort or introductory dives can be a safe way to taste the diving experience with the following proviso. These dives also require a health assessment and some instruction. Safety depends on the degree of supervision of the dive, *which must be intensive and exclusive*.

There are two unique problems of compressed-gas diving.

Pressure-related effects (barotrauma)

At sea level we all have a column of air kilometres high weighing down on us so that the pressure is one atmosphere (ATM). Yet descending every 10 metres underwater adds another 1 ATM of pressure. Due to the inverse relationship between pressure and volume (Boyle's Law), any air-filled chamber is affected by depth changes. A balloon blown up by a diver to the size of a football at 10m underwater will be twice as big when carried to the surface. Humans are 90% solid, i.e. non-compressible fluid and bone, but our ears, sinuses, and lungs (and rarely, the gut) expand like the balloon.

- The commonest form of barotrauma (pressure injury) is to the middle ear. Divers are taught to 'equalize' on descent, which means, by various manoeuvres, adjusting the pressure inside the middle-ear chamber to the ambient pressure. Factors such as poor technique, respiratory infections, anatomical variations, and trauma limit this equalizing process and result in:
  - pain
  - fluid (blood, inflammatory) accumulation
  - hearing loss
  - perforation of the eardrum
  - vertigo (dizziness)
- Similarly, the sinuses, which are air filled, tissue-lined bony chambers, can obstruct with the same consequences of pain and bleeding. The use of decongestants is common, although controversial and far from perfect. Ideally, it is better to miss a dive for a week with 'congestion' than miss a month or two with a perforation. Novice divers may reduce ear equalizing problems by descending slowly, feet first, preferably down the anchor chain, 'popping' their ears regularly
- Less commonly, but much more seriously, the lungs can suffer from pressure damage. Any condition that traps gas in the alveoli (air sacs) can literally cause them to explode on ascent. NEVER ascend without exhaling ALWAYS ascend more slowly than your bubbles. Medical conditions such as uncontrolled asthma, emphysema, or previous spontaneous pneumothorax (collapsed lung) predispose to barotraumas. The results of this lung damage are air tracks to the lung cavity causing collapse of the lung or spreading out around the heart and neck (pneumomediastinum). Both conditions are very serious requiring urgent medical attention. However, the most feared complication is if air travelling via the arterial vessels reaches the brain—an arterial gas embolism (see p.291).

Bubble formation (decompression sickness)

Air is roughly 20% oxygen, 80% nitrogen. The longer and the greater the depth at which the diver breathes compressed air, the more nitrogen is dissolved in bodily tissues. On ascent bubbles may form within blood vessels and in various organs causing an array of symptoms depending on the location and size of bubble formation. This results in a spectrum of disease, but is often thought of as:

Type 1 ('mild' symptoms)

- *Joints:* pain ('the bends'), especially in the shoulder, often misattributed to an injury

- *Skin:* rash—mottling, marbling, or itching
- *Fatigue:* feeling generally unwell.

Type 2 (potentially much more serious)
- *Nervous system:* highly variable symptoms including sensory and motor changes
- Weakness
- Paralysis
- Loss of coordination
- Loss of consciousness
- Shakes
- Bladder and bowel dysfunction
- *Cardiovascular system:* collapse.

Risk reduction for decompression sickness

Diving too deep, for too long or with a too rapid an ascent, leads to bubble formation. Traditionally, divers were taught tables to plan time and depth limits to minimize nitrogen absorption. Current students use dive computers, which analyse depth and nitrogen gassing using mathematical calculations. With computers, the profile increases bottom time by adjusting depth constantly as opposed to dive tables, which calculate according only to maximum depth. Computers are helpful, especially on multi-day trips. Neither method is perfect, so prudence is required by the diver to not push the limits.

Also a safety stop at 3–5m for 3–5min allows for further degassing and is highly recommended. Unfortunately, the 'bends' may occur with no apparent error and after operating within safe procedures, the incidence being about 1 or 2 divers per 10 000 dives. The onset is usually between 30min and 24 hours, and often the affected diver delays presentation, attributing the symptoms to other causes.

Flying after diving also causes bubble formation, again thanks to the relationship between volume and pressure. Most authorities recommend waiting 12 hours, although at least 24 hours is ideal.

Bubble formation in blood vessels (arterial gas embolism)

As previously mentioned, this involves gas escaping the lung and entering the arterial system and travelling to the brain or heart. The results may be catastrophic:
- Pain
- Weakness
- Loss of consciousness
- Shortness of breath
- Death.

Onset of symptoms is usually within 10 min of surfacing.

Treatment

Emergency treatment at the site of injury involves providing:
1. Airways, breathing, and circulation support
2. Oxygen, preferably 100%
3. Fluids, preferably IV, but oral if the victim is conscious
4. Urgent transportation to emergency medical help.

The next step for the diver may be 'recompression' in a hyperbaric chamber, where oxygen, under pressure and medical supervision, reverses the previous nitrogen accumulation. This process can take many hours following predetermined tables of pressure and time application, e.g. the US Navy Table. The long-term outcome for the injured diver is proportional to the speed of onset of recompression. Portable aircraft-carried chambers can be life-saving although expensive and travel insurance is, of course, strongly advised before planning any diving trip.

Divers Alert Network (DAN; ✍ www.diversalertnetwork.org) is an excellent service designed to improve safety and help with routine and emergency medical matters. It is an invaluable resource when problems arise—the DAN Emergency Hotline (+1-919-684-9111) offers 24 hours worldwide medical assistance. Joining this is highly recommended. Happy and safe diving!

Snorkelling

Breath-hold diving/snorkelling is also a fantastic way to experience marine environments. A certain degree of instruction may be necessary for the novice snorkeller, as is a certain level of fitness. It is wise to check with your doctor prior to travelling if you are unaccustomed to vigorous exertion, or have any heart or lung problems. Choppy surface conditions, current, and anxiety are possible, and snorkelling is best avoided if not reasonably fit. Additional flotation devices are recommended for the inexperienced and those unsure of their capabilities. Although snorkellers who stay on the surface avoid the problems of pressure and bubble formation, those who descend on a single breath (breath-hold divers) have to 'equalize 'and do it quickly. This means they, like scuba divers, may suffer ear damage. The solution is to stay on the surface. More worrying is the phenomenon of shallow-water blackout. This is a loss of consciousness on breath-hold diving with the possible and frequent consequence of drowning. It is caused by over-breathing (hyperventilating) prior to the descent as the victim tries to increase their blood oxygen. This is a mistaken belief and only reduces levels of carbon dioxide in the blood—the most potent driver in our brains to breath. As the time underwater progresses, the levels in the now oxygen-starved brain get too low, and the diver passes out underwater and may drown. The solution is *not* to over-breathe prior to descent.

Surfing

Surfers can be loosely divided into two travelling groups:

1. *The novice surfer:* often pays a guide to 'learn to surf', usually in a group. This is a low-risk activity, often using special soft boards. Apart from sunburn, chest rashes, and jelly stings, the most significant problem is trauma from boards and being 'dumped'. Occasionally, an adventurous novice risks being caught in dangerous surf conditions—prevention requires a common sense approach and respecting the power of the ocean

2. *The travelling surfer:* more 'hard core', often venturing to remote and exotic locations in search of waves. These surfers need to take preventative measures against tropical illnesses, such as mosquito and water-borne diseases, mentioned elsewhere in this book, and have the risks of isolation and challenging waves added to the equation.

There are two less serious, but important common problems.

Tropical ear (otitis externa)

This is an infection with bacteria or fungus in the external ear canal. It presents as pain, swelling, tenderness, and discharge. Leaving a low-humidity country for a high humidity, hot area and spending extended time in the water means the ear canal is always moist—an ideal habitat for bugs to grow. Risk reduction involves use of water evaporating ear-drops. Methylated spirits (8 parts) and white vinegar (2 parts) was the traditional combination, although this has given way to 'over the counter' preparations (e.g. Swim Ear). While, in theory, it would be wise to use eardrops after each water exposure, a good dose at bedtime is likely to be very beneficial. Custom-made earplugs are occasionally used by surfers who have frequent problems with their ears, usually secondary narrowing from long-term cold water immersion. Once symptomatic, medication is needed, with eardrops (antibacterial, antifungal, and anti-inflammatory in nature) and maybe oral antibiotics. These should be packed in the travelling surfer's medical kit if going off the beaten track. Of course, staying out of the water is very strongly advised, but the advice is not necessarily heeded.

Coral cuts

These are a common consequence of surfing on reef or rocks. Minor wounds are best cleaned with boiled water with some added table salt. Any debris should be removed and then a disinfectant, such as 10% povi-done-iodine (Betadine), applied and covered with a non-stick air breathing cover, bathing, and changing daily. It is wise to avoid waterproof covers in hot humid environments. Oral antibiotics should be carried and commenced if the wound reddens, discharges pus, or becomes more painful. A bonus for those surfers taking doxycycline for malaria is its action on marine bacteria, although additional antibiotics may still be needed. Now comes the hard part—staying out of the surf. The likely adherence to this advice will be proportional to the extent of the wound and inversely proportional to the quality of the waves. Larger, deeper, and dirtier wounds require medical attention as soon as possible.

A special category of travelling surfer is those on boat trips, often a long way from help. Self-sufficiency in at least the basic medical supplies is recommended, as these trips tend to be remote. Malaria if endemic on land is still a risk on the boat. Dawn surfs and sunset drinks on deck are the higher risk times as mosquitoes can fly kilometres offshore, usually well past the usual anchorage.

Other water activities

This is an almost endless list, including water skiing, sail boarding, paddling, stand-up paddling, etc. The same general principles apply, including awareness of the sport and the conditions. Most importantly, it means self-awareness and understanding one's limitations.

8.9 Snow sports

Mike Langran

Like most physical activities, snow sports do carry a risk of injury. Although this risk is smaller than most people imagine, it can be minimized by adhering to accepted rules on slope etiquette and through increased awareness of correctable factors associated with injury risk.

Clothing and personal equipment

Ski and snowboard clothing: whilst often viewed purely as a fashion item, clothing must still fulfill the practical requirements of being warm, waterproof, and windproof. Ideally, items should be worn in a layered system.

Head gear: when the head is uncovered, heat loss can be high (especially in children), so a warm head covering that will also protect the ears is essential in colder conditions. If you plan to wear a helmet as well, ensure that this will still fit appropriately. In extremely cold conditions, a facemask to protect from high wind and driving snow/ice is also a valuable asset.

Goggles or sunglasses: you should either have photosensitive lenses or exchangeable lenses for varying conditions. They should protect against driving snow and high wind, and against strong sunlight. They should also provide side cover for the eyes, which is especially important for ski mountaineering.

Mittens or gloves: whilst mittens are warmer than gloves, they restrict manual dexterity. A thin pair of warm gloves, cotton or silk, worn inside mittens allows fine manual control in very low temperatures.

Socks: one pair of high quality ski/snowboard-specific socks can make a huge difference to the comfort of wearing boots.

Helmets for snow sports: wearing a modern snow sports helmet is recommended. Helmets have been shown to significantly reduce the risk of a head injury. Many ski areas and ski schools now require helmets to be worn by children as the benefits are greater in this age group. It is important to remember that wearing a helmet does not make you invincible. It is a sobering fact that more than half of those killed skiing or snowboarding in the USA in recent years were wearing a helmet at the time of death. When selecting a helmet, the most important consideration is to ensure that it meets one of the approved standards for snow sport use. These are EN1077, ASTM 2040, and Snell RS98. This will usually be indicated on the label on the inside of the helmet. For a helmet to offer optimum protection it should also fit correctly, so check carefully for fit before buying. Modern helmets offer lightweight styling, adjustable ventilation, and the ability to integrate music players and video cameras for use on the slopes. There is no convincing evidence to date that modern helmets increase the risk of injury to the neck, impair vision/hearing, or lead to an increase in risk-taking behaviour.

Helmets should be treated with care and replaced if they are involved in an accident that causes damage to the integrity of the helmet.

Wrist guards for snowboarders: the wrist is the commonest area to be injured whilst snowboarding, accounting for 25–30% of all injuries. The risk is highest in the beginner (who has yet to gain the ability to balance on a snowboard) and in advanced riders who tend to fall at higher speeds. The use of snowboard-specific wrist guards has been shown to reduce the incidence of such injuries without causing excess injury elsewhere. Recommended makes include Flexmeter and Biomex.

Knee braces for skiers: there is evidence to support the use of a hinged knee brace for individuals who have previously sustained injury to the anterior cruciate ligament. There is currently no evidence to support the use of a brace for primary prevention of knee ligament injuries.

Other knee devices: the Ski Mojo aims to relieve the muscular strain placed on the knee joint and thigh muscles when skiing. This appears to be a useful device for offloading knee strain in those with a past history of knee injuries or osteoarthritis.

Other protective equipment: a variety of other protective devices are available, including spine and coccyx protectors. As yet there is no scientific evidence to support their use.

Backpacks: a small backpack can be used to carry clothes, food, and equipment. This pack should be small and lightweight in order to avoid impeding technique and use of lifts (a large backpack may make it difficult to sit properly on a chairlift).

Sun protection: UV radiation from reflected sunlight is high in alpine conditions. Good quality sunscreen for both skin and lips is essential. Once-a-day preparations that can be applied before leaving accommodation are recommended for their ease of use.

Physical preparation for snow sports

Snow sports are energetic activities. A 70kg adult downhill skiing at average pace will burn in excess of 600 cal/hr. A cross-country skier may expend twice this. A graded exercise programme of at least 6 weeks duration prior to participation is therefore recommended. Exercises should concentrate on optimizing cardiovascular fitness and strengthening appropriate muscle groups. Skiing places strain on the lower limbs and abdominal muscles in particular. Core muscle strength aids the maintenance of balance, particularly important for snowboarding. Cycling and swimming are both excellent activities for improving general fitness and muscle strength/co-ordination without placing undue stress on the weight-bearing joints of the body.

Stretching before and after exercise is recommended as it may reduce the risk of injury to muscles, ligaments, and tendons, as well as reducing the risk of soft-tissue pain post-exercise. Stretches should include the muscles of the calf, hip, abdomen, back, and thigh.

Injuries from snow sports
Overall risk of injury and death

The risk of injury from skiing or snowboarding on piste is relatively low at 2 and 4 injuries per 1000 participants, respectively. The risk of sustaining a fatal injury on the slopes is even lower at one death per 1.85 million participants. Most fatal accidents involve collisions with a static object (tree, rocks, or another person). Non-traumatic deaths occur as a result of heart attacks and other medical conditions, including hypothermia, epilepsy, asthma, and diabetes. A specific danger to be aware of are 'tree wells'. After a heavy snowfall, deep pits or wells build up underneath trees at the side of a piste. These wells are superficially covered by snow, which hides the danger lying underneath. If a skier or snowboarder passes too close to the tree, this snow gives way and the individual falls into the well. Unless the event is witnessed and/or help arrives rapidly, escape is extremely difficult and death ensues from hypothermia and/or snow asphyxiation. The risk is highest for those skiing or boarding alone.

Patterns of injury
The commonest sites and causes of injury from alpine skiing and snowboarding are shown in Table 8.9.1, and Table 8.9.2 shows the breakdown of injuries by type.

Table 8.9.1 Commonest sites and causes of injury from alpine skiing and snowboarding

	Injury	Cause of injury
Alpine skiing	Knee sprain	Twisting injury with or without binding release
	Head injury	Impact on snow surface; collision with another object
	Shoulder dislocation	Twisting fall onto an outstretched hand whilst moving
	Thumb injury	Fall onto hand whilst holding ski pole handle
	Lower limb fracture	Bending or twisting fall without binding release
Snowboarding	Wrist fracture	Fall onto an outstretched hand
	Head injury	Impact on snow surface; collision with another object
	Shoulder dislocation	Twisting fall onto an outstretched hand whilst moving
	Knee sprain	Twisting injury with one foot out of the binding or direct impact
	Ankle sprain	Inversion injury often from a jump gone wrong

Table 8.9.2 Breakdown of injuries by type

Injury	Alpine skiing	Snowboarding
	Percentage of all injuries	
Fracture	19.0%	35.0%
Laceration	10.3%	11.4%
Sprain/strain	47.7%	25.9%
Joint disruption	6.5%	10.0%
Bruising	12.1%	12.7%
Concussion/loss of consciousness	4.4%	5.1%

Reducing the risk of injury on the slopes

Personal factors

Inexperience and lack of skill are associated with a higher risk of injury. Beginners and those aged under 16 are particularly at risk. Investing in professional instruction, coupled with gradual exposure to higher speeds and more challenging terrain are the keys to safe progression. Learning from friends and family is not recommended as poor technique can easily become ingrained and difficult to eradicate. Skiing or boarding at speeds and/or on slopes beyond one's ability level are frequent causal factors in accidents. Take care where runs intersect, when entering 'slow zones' and when visibility is reduced. Ensure that you are familiar with the 10 FIS rules (Box 8.9.1) for conduct on the slopes. If you transgress these rules and cause an accident, then you may be held liable.

It is important to recognize when your muscles are fatigued. More injuries occur at the end of a day on the slopes. Ingesting large quantities of alcohol increases reaction times and one's sense of bravado—not a good combination on the slopes.

Equipment factors

The boot-binding interface

Sports equipment should be properly maintained and, where applicable, serviced regularly by a trained technician. Of paramount importance is a well-maintained boot-binding interface, the boot and binding working together as a unit. Poorly-maintained systems are less likely to function as expected, leading to an increased risk of inadvertent or non-release; both scenarios are associated with injury. Avoid excessive walking on tarmac in ski boots. Worn boot soles do not sit optimally in the binding. The binding itself should be set correctly and serviced regularly to ensure optimal function.

Binding self-test

It is recommended that a 'self-test' be performed on ski bindings at the start of every day. The simple test has been shown to reduce the incidence of knee injuries by up to 25%.

- *To test the toe setting (Fig. 8.9.1):* angling the ski so that the front inside edge is on the ground, try to twist your boot inwards so that the toe

twists out of the front of the binding. Apply the force gradually—you should not have to use excessive force
- *To test the heel setting (Fig. 8.9.2):* with your ski flat on the ground, slide your foot back until your leg is out straight. Then try to lift the heel of your boot out of the binding. Don't use do too much force—you could strain a muscle or possibly even rupture your Achilles tendon.

Box 8.9.1 **FIS Rules for conduct on the slopes**

1. Respect for others
A skier or snowboarder must behave in such a way that he does not endanger or prejudice others.

2. Control of speed
A skier or snowboarder must move in control. He must adapt his speed and manner of skiing or snowboarding to his personal ability and to the prevailing conditions of terrain, snow, and weather, as well as to the density of traffic.

3. Choice of route
A skier or snowboarder coming from behind must choose his route in such a way that he does not endanger skiers or snowboarders ahead.

4. Overtaking
A skier or snowboarder may overtake another skier or snowboarder above or below and to the right or to the left provided that he leaves enough space for the overtaken skier or snowboarder to make any voluntary or involuntary movement.

5. Entering, starting, and moving upwards
A skier or snowboarder entering a marked run, starting again after stopping, or moving upwards on the slopes must look up and down the slopes so that he can do so without endangering himself or others.

6. Stopping on the piste
Unless absolutely necessary, a skier or snowboarder must avoid stopping on the piste in narrow places or where visibility is restricted. After a fall in such a place, a skier or snowboarder must move clear of the piste as soon as possible.

7. Climbing and descending on foot
A skier or snowboarder either climbing or descending on foot must keep to the side of the piste.

8. Respect for signs and markings
A skier or snowboarder must respect all signs and markings.

9. Assistance
At accidents, every skier or snowboarder is duty bound to assist.

10. Identification
Every skier or snowboarder and witness, whether a responsible party or not, must exchange names and addresses following an accident.

Reproduced with permission from the International Ski Federation (FIS).

Fig. 8.9.1 Toe setting.

Fig. 8.9.2 Heel setting.

If you can't release either the heel or the toe from the binding, then, using an appropriate tool, reduce the binding setting by 0.5 and try the test again. Keep reducing the binding setting like this until you can release your boot at both the heel and the toe. One might need more adjustment than the other. There is no evidence that the self-test—when applied correctly— makes your binding too slack and liable to inadvertent release. At the end of each day, if you have made an adjustment dial your binding back to its original setting ready to repeat the test the next day.

Skis, boards, and ski poles

Skis and boards should have sharp edges in order to grip the snow surface and reduce the risk of unintentional sliding. Falling with a ski pole in the palm of one's hand can lead to 'skier's thumb', a significant ligamentous injury caused by the pole handle applying force to the thumb joint. Avoid using your pole straps on-piste if possible or try to discard the pole from your hand when you fall. Alternatively, invest in a pole with a releasable system that may help avoid this injury.

Weather and snow conditions

Unfavourable and variable snow conditions (such as patches of deep snow, wet snow, or ice) may contribute to accidents. Firm, crisp, granular snow accompanied by good weather gives ideal skiing conditions. In contrast, ice or wet, sticky snow requires greater caution and slower speeds. In deep or heavy snow there is an increased tendency to 'catch an edge', leading to injury. The presence of fog, mist, hail, sleet, or falling snow, often combined with wind or low cloud, leads to poor piste conditions. At such times the light is diffuse and there are no shadows—a condition known as 'flat light'. It therefore becomes very difficult to see piste contours and features. The sensation of movement is also reduced and there is often a weird feeling that you are still moving even when you stop. In such conditions the skiing is much easier and more pleasant if there are dark objects such as trees, rocks, pylons or lift towers to break up the whiteness of the foreground and give you some idea of the whereabouts and steepness of the fall line of the slope. The fall line is the steepest and shortest line down the slope from where you are standing. Travelling in tandem behind a colleague and taking it in turns to lead down the slope also helps when visibility is poor.

Do not hesitate to leave a ski field early if the weather deteriorates—follow the advice of the ski patrol or area management. Weather can change very rapidly in the mountains and with little warning. Beware of taking high-level lift links to adjacent resorts if the forecast is doubtful.

Terrain parks

Terrain (fun) parks have become popular features at most ski areas. They offer the chance to perform tricks and jumps safely isolated from main pistes. Common features include half and quarter pipes, rails and large jumps (called kickers). Initially the domain of snowboarders, more and more skiers are attracted to the challenge of terrain parks. Inexperienced skiers and boarders should enter terrain parks with care, as injuries sustained in parks tend to be more severe in nature.

Injuries from ski-lift machinery

Approximately 10% of all snow sports injuries result from the use of ski lifts. Injuries from major access lifts, such as cable cars and gondolas, are extremely rare. The majority of lift accidents involve the use of a chairlift or a surface 'drag' lift, such as a button tow or T-bar.

Chairlift injuries

Chairlift injuries tend to occur on mounting and (especially) dismounting the chair. Edges can catch in the snow and on multi-person chairs lack of co-ordination on dismount can lead to collisions. Snowboarders, who often ride with one boot out of the bindings, are particularly susceptible to lower-limb twisting injuries in such circumstances. People have also been injured by falling out of chairs, and by having rucksacks or articles of clothing hooked or trapped by the chair as they alight.

Surface lift injuries

Surface lifts such as button 'poma' tows and T-bars are tricky to master as a beginner. Injuries usually occur when someone falls over and continues to be dragged along by the lift. It's not unusual for the person who falls off to land on someone else and injure them instead! If you do fall off, alert the tow operator if possible and move away from the line of the tow as soon as possible. On some T-bars, there is a risk of the bar recoiling and hitting you on the head in the dismount area. Follow the guidance provided by the ski area and move away from the lift quickly. Many surface lifts have red stop buttons positioned along their length for use in an emergency. Do not be afraid to activate one if you see someone being dragged along by the tow.

With all lift systems, if the lift stops resist the temptation to jump off. Wait for the lift to restart and alight at the designated station.

Conclusion

Snow sports are enjoyable and popular activities. With care and attention to simple safety precautions, the small risk of injury can be minimized. *Après* ski activity has its pleasures and its hazards as well—but that is another story!

Chapter 9

Some common problems

9.1 Skin problems

Francisco Vega-Lopez

Skin problems typically account for up to one third of all problems in travellers. This chapter explains how to recognize, treat, or prevent the most frequent problems.

Diseases of the skin are amongst the commonest causes of medical consultation. It has been estimated that more than half of the global human population suffers or will develop a skin complaint at some stage in their lives. In Britain and other European countries, up to 20% of all patients who consult a GP do so because of skin disease or symptoms. A similar picture has been recorded in many tropical developing countries. Despite their frequent presentation, fortunately most skin diseases have a very low mortality rate. However, the main problems linked to several skin conditions are the high costs in psychological and emotional terms, burden to the health care system, and variable degrees of resulting disability.

Ideally, a traveller requires a healthy skin. Itchiness, a burning sensation, oozy skin, a painful and nasty-looking spot or abscess, and the need to apply frequent medicated creams and ointments are just a few of the ways in which the ideal holiday or business trip can turn into an unforgettable nightmare.

This chapter presents a brief description of the commonest skin disorders and symptoms relevant for travellers of all ages. Particular emphasis is given to practical aspects of diagnosis, prevention, and treatment of skin problems during travel. Certain skin diseases occurring in specific areas of the world are presented by geographical region in other chapters of this book. Finally, a few simple but essential recommendations to prevent skin problems are provided.

The traveller with previous skin disease

Psoriasis

This is a very common skin disease worldwide, particularly affecting young individuals of both sexes. The main clinical signs and symptoms include the presence of raised plaques, pink or red, with white scaling. The inflammatory plaques are usually located on the extensor surfaces of the body, but the scalp and nails can also be affected. Less common clinical presentations occur in the skin folds, such as under the breasts, between the buttocks, the armpits, the groins, and external genitalia. Psoriasis commonly adopts a chronic, unpredictable course with alternating periods of activity and remission. It may cause itchiness or a burning sensation on the affected areas of the skin, but it can also be symptomless. Although there are a number of successful treatments to improve the condition, there is currently no definitive cure. In general, psoriasis tends to improve on holidays in sunny climates, but sunburn is known to trigger its development. Bathing in sea waters in sunny or tropical countries seems to have a beneficial effect in many people with psoriasis. Moisturizing of the skin is essential for the traveller with psoriasis, and fresh water showers followed by moisturizing cream after bathing in chlorinated water result in improvement of the skin symptoms. Travellers with this condition taking other medications for different medical conditions may experience a flare up shortly after the start of the treatment. Hence, caution should be taken by those requiring beta-blockers, ACE inhibitors, lithium, and anti-malarials.

Atopic eczema

This frequent skin condition tends to affect several members in the family, and can coexist with asthma and/or allergic rhinitis (hay fever). Commonly, it appears in early childhood and the inflammatory activity tends to subside after a few years. Atopic eczema manifests as patches or raised plaques of inflamed skin causing severe itchiness and irritation. These plaques may be thickened and suffer from fissuring which predisposes to bacterial infections. Atopic eczema commonly affects the face, and flexural areas of the body surface, such as the neck, forearms, and behind the knees.

Many young individuals tend to improve while on holiday, but very hot and humid environments may not be tolerated and cause a flare up. Frequent moisturizing of the skin is essential to control the itchiness, protect the barrier function of the skin, and prevent infection. Toddlers, school age-children and young individuals with atopic eczema are particularly susceptible to acquiring superficial bacterial, viral, and fungal infections. These include impetigo, molluscum contagiosum, herpes simplex, and ringworm, respectively.

Contact eczema

Irritating chemicals, water, detergents, and a vast number of allergenic substances (compounds that induce allergy) can cause this form of acute or chronic eczema. Common allergens include nickel, cobalt salts, cosmetics, perfumes, textiles, rubber, inks, hair dyes, and food proteins. Young individuals of both sexes are commonly affected, but all age groups can develop this problem when the skin surface becomes in direct contact with the offending agent. In many cases, contact eczema represents an occupational disease for persons involved in the handling of animal proteins, latex gloves, dentistry materials, nursing activities, and hairdressing— to mention but a few.

The palms of the hands and the palmar aspect of thumbs and index fingers are most usually affected as they are commonly exposed areas of the body surface. However, other anatomical regions including face and upper body can subsequently be involved. Caustic substances will cause a severe burn, but milder irritants can induce itchiness, burning sensation, redness of the skin, pain, and blistering. The best measure to prevent contact eczema is the avoidance of irritating or allergenic substances.

The traveller with contact eczema in hot and humid climates may develop symptoms on areas of skin subjected to pressure from tight clothing, shoes, money belts, and straps from backpacks causing severe friction on the skin surface. Medicated adhesive tape and bandages used to treat wounds in the traveller may also cause acute contact eczema. Hotel soaps and toiletries can sometimes cause similar problems.

Simple measures to treat most forms of mild acute contact eczema include the use of a mild antiseptic applied in soaks three times daily, moisturizing of the skin, and 1 or 2% hydrocortisone cream to provide anti-inflammatory action. Tests to accurately diagnose troublesome allergic forms of contact eczema have to be carried out in a dermatology department.

Travellers at particular risk

Individuals with previous medical conditions are at a higher risk of developing skin problems, particularly those that are infectious in origin. Most travellers at increased risk of skin infection are aware of this and already know how best to avoid trouble or, if unlucky, the best ways to deal with it.

All medical conditions that interfere with the proper functioning of our immune system or tissue repair mechanisms increase the risk for infectious skin diseases. In particular, individuals suffering from one or more of the following conditions—diabetes mellitus, chronic alcoholism, intravenous drug use, a variety of cancers, and AIDS—should take careful advice from doctors, nurses, and travel specialists before embarking on a holiday or business trip, particularly to high risk endemic regions of the world. Chronic liver and kidney diseases as well as long-term treatment with corticosteroids and immunosuppressive medication may also predispose travellers to acquiring skin infections. Patients with high blood pressure and other cardiovascular problems taking specific medication must be aware of the possibility of developing skin reactions when exposed to direct or indirect sunshine (see pp.311–2).

Skin wounds

Minor abrasions, wounds, and injuries to the skin occur commonly in travellers. Fortunately, only a few of these result in serious localized or even systemic life-threatening infections. Following an accident, the open wound should be thoroughly washed with clean water and mild soap. A sterile, non-allergenic (does not cause allergy) dressing should be used to protect the wound from dirt and prevent the entry of unwanted microbes. Resting of the affected body part should help trigger the protective mechanisms of tissue repair to complete healing successfully. Particular attention should be paid to wounds occurring on the hands and feet while scuba-diving, snorkelling, or trekking in the tropics. Harmful bacteria and fungi can be directly deposited into the skin following an injury from coral reefs, tree bark, soil, vegetation, thorns, rusty metal, or wood debris.

Voluntary service or aid workers in developing countries must be aware that personal health is a priority. Minor skin wounds have to be readily treated, and strong protective footwear as well as proper clothing should be the norm. Particular protection with mask and gloves is recommended in tree-planting projects, farming, masonry, and activities involving contact with livestock in the tropics. These measures are valuable in the prevention of fungal and bacterial infections that can be acquired through direct skin contact or by inhalation of the infective organism.

Other common minor skin wounds, such as those from stings or bites by scorpions, spiders, and snakes require immediate attention.

Specific anti-serum to inactivate a particular poison will be required as well as treatment of the skin wound with water and soap, antiseptics, topical, and in some cases systemic antibiotics. The same applies to bites inflicted by small vertebrates such as racoons, otters, rats, squirrels, armadillos, and dogs. Infected mosquito and sandfly bites require topical antibiotics such as fusidic acid in combination with a potent corticosteroid. Non-healing sandfly bites require specialist medical attention (Chapter 5.5). (See Chapter 6, 'Animal bites' for more information on snakes, scorpions, and spiders, as well as rabies.)

Skin diseases caused by pathogenic organisms

Viruses

Molluscum contagiosum infection consists of small, discrete, whitish millimetric pimples, acquired by direct contact with an infected person. The condition is common worldwide in healthy children and particularly represents a nuisance to individuals with deficient immunity such as those with organ transplants or HIV. Also, young travellers with atopic eczema can be more susceptible to acquiring this viral infection.

The lesions are usually asymptomatic but some children experience moderate itchiness. Scratching of the lesions may result in self-spreading of the infection to nearby sites on the skin. Most commonly, the disease affects the face, neck, and trunk, but any part of the skin can be affected. Superimposed secondary superficial skin infections may be the result of scratching and picking of the pimples. Avoidance of direct skin contact with infected persons is the best preventive measure. Individual pimples can be removed by a variety of topical and minor surgical procedures, but very young children are reluctant to accept this approach. Often the best strategy is to leave the lesions untreated in order to allow the normal immune system to eventually eliminate the infection; this may take 18 months or more.

Common warts are caused by a papilloma virus. Although strictly not a traveller's disease, their appearance may coincide with a journey overseas. People with deficient skin immunity show a marked predisposition to developing warts, and young individuals with atopic eczema are frequently troubled by them. A number of preparations to treat common warts can be purchased over the counter, but severe cases require the attention of a doctor or nurse. Common warts require treatment by a dermatologist only in certain individuals, such as those recovering from a transplant, under immunosuppressive therapy, or with a previous history of skin cancer.

Infections by *Herpes simplex* (cold sores, genital herpes) can be acquired through direct skin contact, kissing, and sexual contact. Most commonly, localized infection on the lips or oral mucosa manifests after febrile illness or prolonged sun exposure and intense physical exertion during a beach holiday. In the exhausted traveller, a primary infection by herpes virus inside the mouth and upper pharynx may present with fever, painful ulcers, odorous breath and lymph node enlargement on the upper neck. Severe cases make eating and drinking impossible, requiring specific intravenous medication and bed rest following the accurate diagnosis by a doctor.

Bacteria

Many travellers suffer from superficial skin infections following minor injury such as from knocks and scrapes, or during physical activity. Bacteria such as staphylococci and streptococci can penetrate the skin and cause red patches, a localized boil or even superficial ulceration. Sweating around the warmer parts of the body and skin folds subjected to friction from unusual physical activity may in some cases predispose to these infections. Clinical diseases in this group include impetigo, folliculitis, boils, abscesses, and cellulitis.

Minor injuries at home or in the garden usually heal satisfactorily within a few days. The picture can be modified, however, by deficient hygiene, change of diet, excessive drinking, and 'roughing it' whilst travelling. Washing of the skin in antiseptic soaking water, two or three times a day, will resolve most superficial skin infections. Some infections, however, will require medical attention and systemic antibiotics. This also applies to travellers developing an allergic reaction to common insect or mosquito bites and subsequently suffering a superimposed bacterial infection.

Uncommon, but more severe skin infections may result from practising sports in polluted estuaries or tropical oceans during the hot summer months. Skin infections acquired through injuries while fishing, snorkelling, and scuba-diving, or following ingestion of raw seafood (oysters in particular) usually require immediate medical attention. Serious skin infections in this group present with a high fever, painful skin, dark red/violaceous lesions, and general malaise. The skin becomes red and shiny from inflammation.

Proper menstrual hygiene, with a frequent change of tampons, is the best preventive measure for a potentially lethal bacterial condition named *toxic shock syndrome*, which requires treatment in hospital. This simple measure also prevents mild, but very uncomfortable irritation from 'nappy-type' *vulval dermatitis* caused by friction and frequently complicated by yeast or bacterial infection. If you are travelling in remote areas and medical services are not available, initial antiseptic treatment of superficial *vulvo-vaginitis* can be carried out by vulval bathing in 50–80mL of vinegar (any locally available brand) diluted in 5–8L of water, twice daily for 10–15min each time, and for 2–3 days. Improvement of symptoms such as irritation, burning sensation, and itchiness should be expected following the very first or second treatment. This mildly acidic solution changes the superficial chemical balance and most common yeasts as well as bacteria are successfully eliminated. Soothing of irritated broken skin and vestibular mucosa of external genitalia can also be achieved by using a barrier cream such as zinc oxide (Lassar paste).

Finally, travellers must be aware that tampons and sanitary towels may not be readily available in rural regions of the tropics (see Chapter 10.1). A definite diagnosis and proper treatment of most vulvar skin conditions requires a physician and often a dermatologist.

Fungi

Several common fungal infections occur worldwide, both at home and during travel. Frequent examples include superficial infections such as *ringworm*, *athlete's foot*, and *thrush*. Proper hygiene, including a daily shower and change of clothes, may prevent skin colonization by fungi. Compounds such as those contained in 'over-the-counter' creams like Canesten and Daktarin, applied for 4–6 weeks, are sufficient to cure superficial fungal infections. Pessaries for single-dose vaginal treatment are also readily available.

However, a number of other deeper fungal infections (subcutaneous and systemic) are not only more severe in clinical terms, but also more difficult to diagnose and treat, as many of them occur only in particular regions of the world. Most of these rather serious diseases are caused by direct inoculation of the fungus into the skin, but they can also be acquired through inhalation of infecting spores during normal breathing. This occurs during trekking excursions where the walker is exposed to soil, vegetation, tree bark, and decomposing organic debris, where fungi have their natural habitat. Desert regions, tropical rainforests, and jungles, in particular and also archaeological sites and caves are renowned sites for acquired respiratory and/or skin diseases by fungi. Some of these fungal infections (known as mycosis) include uncommon diseases such as *sporotrichosis*, *chromoblastomycosis*, *mycetoma*, *histoplasmosis*, and *coccidioidomycosis*. These represent only a few and there are many others posing a risk for the most adventurous traveller exploring remote regions in deserts or the tropics.

Avoidance of infection can best be achieved by wearing strong shoes and proper clothing at all times. Sandals (no matter how expensive, comfortable, or trendy) would represent a health hazard when walking in rural Africa, southern USA, Latin America, or Southeast Asia. Tourists in sandals climbing pyramids, walking in the jungle, or kicking scorpions off their path must be desperate to catch a skin infection! Walkers, archaeologists, and explorers venturing inside caves (mountainous, ground level, or underground) and grottoes must be familiar with specific environmental hazards and wear masks in order to avoid inhaling infecting spores which may result in fungal disease of the lungs. Avoid especially those areas covered in droppings from bats and a variety of birds to prevent catching *histoplasmosis*.

Safety standards established by qualified national tourist operators should be followed when planning holidays to the jungle, to caves, or, even more so, to partially unexplored remote regions of the world. The treatment of all deep fungal infections is highly specialized and can be offered only by local physicians who are familiar with particular diseases or by medical centres in capital cities in the developed world. Unfortunately, there is no simple approach to cure several of these severe fungal diseases of the skin.

Parasites

Unlike fungal diseases, infections caused by parasites are commonly seen in the returning traveller. Such parasites include simple microscopic organisms of only one cell, as well as complex worms with a very sophisticated anatomy and physiology. Some parasitic diseases are transmitted by insect bite, as in the case of *leishmaniasis* and *onchocerciasis*; others, like *schistosomiasis* (*bilharzia*), are acquired through the skin by swimming in contaminated waters; and others, as in the case of *cutaneous larva migrans*, by walking or laying down on infested beaches. Unfortunately, most travellers like to visit nature, or swim in a lake, or walk bare-footed in the sand.

The term *leishmaniases* (see also Chapter 5.5) refers to a group of skin conditions which, on rare occasions, causes a potentially lethal organic disease of the liver and spleen. These conditions represent a public health problem to local indigenous communities in certain areas of the world. Of more relevance to the traveller are those skin leishmaniases acquired through the bite of sandflies carrying particular species of the parasite *Leishmania*. Correspondingly, different skin diseases result from different species of parasites.

Cutaneous Leishmaniasis can be acquired in all the countries of the Mediterranean basin, Afghanistan, North Africa, Middle East, and Latin America. In general, skin leishmaniasis from the Old World is less severe than that originating in Central and South America.

A few weeks after the sandfly bite, a red nodule or an ulcer are the first signs of illness. The initial skin lesion appears on the site of the bite (usually face, ears, hands, forearms, ankles) but, in aggressive forms, new lesions can appear and spread to nearby sites within a few weeks. Unless infected by bacteria, the nodules and ulcers may not be symptomatic at all, and this can be a determining factor in delaying seeking medical advice. Some lesions acquired in the Middle East may heal spontaneously after a few months, without treatment, but if the diagnosis is suspected, referral to a specialized centre is compulsory. Certain forms of Central and South American leishmaniasis can produce fast disfiguring ulceration of the face, tissue destruction, and scarring. Investigations for diagnosis and treatment are available only in specialized hospitals.

Onchocerciasis (also called river blindness) is transmitted by the bite of a blackfly in specific regions of African and Latin America that are near to fast-flowing streams or rivers where the blackflies breed (see also p.136). As happens with other insect bites, these bites occur on exposed parts of the body such as the face and upper and lower limbs. Several weeks after the bite, the adult worm (*Onchocerca volvolus*) reaches maturity inside the human body and reproduces periodically to yield generations of young worms causing skin symptoms. Such periodic reproductive activity can last for many years, in spite of treatment.

The main symptoms of disease include severe itchiness and eczema-like lesions on the limbs, back, and buttocks. Firm nodules on the skin of the scalp, neck, and buttocks can also be found. In some cases, generalized itchiness all over the body can be desperate. One of the most severe complications of this disease occurs in the eye, resulting in blindness.

Tests for the diagnosis and specific treatment are available only in specialized centres. Protection from insect bites and avoidance of travelling in endemic areas of the world are the best preventive measures against onchocerciasis.

Schistosomiasis (also called swimmers' itch or bilharziasis) is acquired by swimming or bathing in contaminated waters. Young parasites penetrate the skin leaving a minute, usually unnoticeable, wound. The parasite matures within the human body and causes acute as well as chronic disease of the skin, respiratory system, liver, and bladder. Common skin symptoms are allergic reactions such as urticaria, swelling of the face (eyelids, cheeks, and lips) and severe itchiness. Specific tests for diagnosis and treatment are available only in specialized centres. Prevention includes strict avoidance of bathing or swimming in contaminated waters of Africa and the Far East.

Cutaneous larva migrans results from acquiring the dog or cat hookworm parasite which is found in beaches or soil contaminated by faecal matter passed by infested pets (see also p.86). Parasitic larvae readily penetrate the human skin on buttocks, back, abdomen, or feet. Potentially, any site of the human body resting on the infested sand or soil may become the port of entry for these parasites. Once in the skin, the parasite migrates within this tissue and does not cause symptoms in other organs. After a few days or weeks in the skin, symptoms and signs of disease manifest as an intensely itchy rash with burning sensation, spots, and the characteristic red, angry-looking larval track left by the serpiginous movements of the parasites. Scratching and breaking of the skin results very often in superimposed superficial bacterial infection. The infection by this parasite may last several months if left untreated. Specific treatment with anti-helminthic drugs has to be provided by a qualified physician. The outcome is complete cure in most cases.

Ectoparasites

This group of infestations is caused by a number of mites, lice, bugs, fleas, and ticks which induce disease not only in humans but, in some cases, in many other living animals. In most cases, disease remains confined to the skin but in others, these ectoparasites may transmit serious illness such as typhus (by ticks, body louse, and fleas) and other fevers.

Scabies is caused by a microscopic organism, *Sarcoptes scabiei*, and is usually acquired from another person by direct skin contact (see also p.163). In the right context it may be transmitted sexually. Very itchy small papules (spots, pimples) affect the trunk, upper limbs (often hands), external genitalia (particularly in males), and thighs a few days following transmission. Infants and immunosuppressed individuals may, however, present with a severely itchy disseminated or generalized rash.

Left untreated, scabies may persist for months, and regular hygienic measures that help to prevent the disease are no use as a cure. Also, it is well recognized that even very clean individuals may acquire the infestation. Diagnosis and treatment require a physician. Cure is achieved with one treatment applied topically in most cases. Few individuals may require a second course of topical treatment, but most cases still complain of itchiness for several weeks after effective treatment. Complicated cases and outbreaks of scabies in institutions require treatment with tablets.

Pediculosis (*lice*, *nits*, *crabs*, *ladillas*) of the scalp and hair, body, and pubic area are caused by organisms respectively called *Pediculus capitis*, *Pediculus corporis*, and *Phthirus pubis* (see also p.163; and Chapter 10.1). Nits and head lice are a common experience in school children all over the world, and most teachers and parents are familiar with the diagnosis and treatment. Over-the-counter anti-nit combs and preparations resolve the problem satisfactorily with one or two treatments. Re-infestations can be a problem in deprived or overcrowded communities.

In contrast, the *body louse* can be acquired during travel as these millimetric insects are transmitted by direct contact with persons or their infested hair and clothes, including bed linen. Camping sites, refugee camps, and other overcrowded environments are renowned for outbreaks involving dozens of individuals. In the past, severely affected regions of the world included those with temperate climates where the peak incidence was observed during the coldest months of the year. These small insects suck blood from the human skin and inject irritating substances that may cause not only the common symptoms of severe itchiness and burning, but less commonly, allergies and superimposed bacterial infection. They can also transmit serious fevers such as typhus.

The *pubic louse* or *crab* cements its eggs to the pubic or perineal hair, but in cases with heavy infestation, eggs can also be found on the eyebrows, eyelashes, moustache and beard, arm pits, and body hair. Again, itchiness and burning sensation are the main symptoms. Lice can be seen by the naked eye, and the search has to include all the suspected body regions. Effective treatment includes the use of one topical preparation such as malathion, carbaryl, or permethrin lotions. Twice-daily moisturizing of the skin, 24 hours after the treatment, may result in symptomatic relief. Superficial infections from scratching have to be treated accordingly.

Bed-bugs occur worldwide and bite humans, particularly at night, in order to obtain a blood meal. During the day they hide in walls or bed cracks, folds of old wallpaper, mattresses, carpets, and floor boards (see also p.160). These wingless insects measure a few millimetres and the commonest species is *Cimex lectularius*. Characteristically, the bites will be in clusters on those parts of the body that have come into contact with the mattress, such as the buttocks, back, abdominal skin, and thighs. Travellers must be particularly aware of them in 'budget' hostels with low standards of hygiene. Heavy biting causes disturbed sleep; in some uncommon chronic cases in babies it has resulted in iron deficiency.

The main symptom is severe itchiness and red, angry-looking bites measuring up to 1cm or sometimes more. Measures for control include the spraying of all suspected furniture and run-down buildings with 5% DDT. Soothing calamine cream or 1% hydrocortisone cream provide symptomatic relief. The bites will heal without treatment within a few days unless they are complicated by secondary bacterial infection.

A high number of *flea* species are found worldwide and cause skin irritation and nuisance by biting humans in order to obtain a blood meal. These small insects can also transmit severe diseases such as typhus, tularemia, and plague. The commonest flea causing bites in humans is *Pulex irritans*. However, in the tropics another species, *Tunga penetrans*, will bite humans and pigs, inducing a disease named chigoe or 'jigger'. Female fleas of this type burrow into the soft skin of toes, toe-webs, groins, or genitals causing severe itchiness, irritation, and nearly always a superimposed bacterial infection produced by scratching. Chigoe fleas may attach to the skin and increase their body size up to 1cm following a few days of blood feeding. If the engorged flea body is removed, the small head part may remain buried in the skin of the patient. Advice from a physician should be sought in these cases (see also p.158).

Strong and comfortable shoes and socks prevent the acquisition of these types of fleas that are poor jumpers. Avoidance of walking on bare feet and insecticide spraying are effective measures of control and prevention. Symptomatic relief from common flea bites can be provided by 1% hydrocortisone cream applied four times a day for a few days.

Soft and hard *ticks* belong to a subclass of arthropods and can be found worldwide in nature and also in other vertebrates acting as reservoirs.

Trekking in woodlands and areas with rough vegetation represent the main risk for tick bites. Aid workers in farms and horse-riding travellers can also acquire ticks from cattle and horses. A number of species not only cause limited skin disease following a blood-sucking bite but also act as agents of serious systemic illness such as typhus, relapsing fever (borreliosis), and Q fever (see also p.161).

Ticks are very resilient organisms and they can survive in nature for several months and even years after a single blood meal. The bite is quite painful and as the efforts to remove the tick from the skin can be unsuccessful, secondary bacterial infection represents a common problem. Careful attention must be paid to ensure that the whole body and mouth parts of the tick are removed from the skin as soon as possible. Application of Vaseline to cover the tick and surrounding skin interferes with their respiration and the organism drops off the skin after a few minutes.

Measures of prevention include strong footwear, trousers tucked into the socks, and regular examination of the skin on the lower legs, ankles, and feet in order to search for attached ectoparasites. Spraying of insecticide on suspected areas is also recommended. In unfortunate cases of Lyme disease or typhus, a reddish/brownish circular lesion can be found on the skin around the tick bite at the same time that fever and a skin rash develop. Immediate medical advice is necessary should fever and a rash on the trunk develop several days after a trekking, farming, or horse-riding holiday (Chapter 5.4).

Skin diseases from sun exposure

Acute damage

Direct irradiation of the skin from acute exposure to sunlight, even if only for a few minutes, may result in severe burns in the susceptible individual (see also Chapter 8.5). Persons with very pale skin, red hair, light-coloured eyes, and freckles represent the population at highest risk. However, most white individuals experience sunburn following sustained exposure to direct sunlight during the peak hours of sun irradiation (11:00–16:00 hours). All travellers to the tropics and to mountainous resorts are at risk of developing problems from sun exposure.

Ultra-violet irradiation is only one of the components of sunlight causing inflammation of the skin and tissue destruction. These clinically manifest as *sunburn*, with redness of the skin, pain, burning sensation, and blistering. *Prickly heat* refers to an acute condition presenting with itchiness and small blistering of the neck and trunk following sun exposure in hot and humid environments. The small vesicles/blisters appear as the result of blockage of the sweat glands. Symptomatic relief can be achieved by moisturizing the skin with 'cold cream'.

Polymorphic light eruption (PLE) is an itchy, spotty rash—often over the upper body—following exposure to very strong sunlight. It's 2–3 times more common in women, affects 10–20% of the population, and is sometimes incorrectly called 'prickly heat', though it is a completely different condition. An immune reaction in the skin, triggered by the sun's UVA rays, is to blame, so phase in sun exposure slowly, use sunscreen with high UVA protection, and avoid other creams, perfumes, cosmetics, or toiletries. Stronger steroid creams, and referral to a dermatologist, are sometimes needed (see also p.278).

Severe cases of sunburn can be complicated by dehydration with symptoms of sunstroke and by superimposed infection of the skin after rupture of the blisters. Oral rehydration with 3–4L of water for an adult is recommended once the problem has occurred. Sunburn can be prevented by the use of protective clothing (hat, T-shirt), parasols, sunblock cream or lotion, and above all, by avoidance of intense and acute exposure to direct or indirect sunlight. Persons with very pale skin, who tend to burn, are advised to use sunblock factor 25 or higher. For all white individuals, sunblock (factor 20 or above) should be applied every 3–4 hours during daylight time. Following a swim in the pool or ocean, sunblock cream or lotion needs to be re-applied.

Long-term damage

Premature ageing and *cancer of the skin* result from overexposure to sunlight, particularly in individuals with fair skin, freckles, red hair, and blue eyes. However, all white individuals are at a higher risk than those with darker skin, and we now know that cancer of the skin manifests in individuals with particular genes. It is clear, however, that not only genes play a part in the development of skin cancer. Environmental factors, such as intense and episodic exposure to sunlight, are most important for the traveller.

Malignant skin tumours include *basal cell carcinoma* (often presenting as rodent ulcer), *squamous cell carcinoma*, and *malignant melanoma*. Skin cancers are uncommon in children and young individuals (indeed, they are commonly diagnosed in persons above the age of 20); and the risk increases with age. Persons with many dark moles on the body (nevi), and particularly large nevi of 5 or more millimetres in diameter, have been found to have an increased risk for the development of malignant melanoma. Suspicious-looking nevi, skin cancers, and malignant melanoma require immediate consultation with a dermatologist.

Uncommon problems

A number of complicated sun-related conditions are familiar mainly to doctors and dermatologists practising in the tropics. However, certain travellers from temperate latitudes may develop these rarer diseases as a result of exposure during a holiday. Such diseases include solar urticaria, actinic prurigo and actinic dermatitis. Diagnosis and treatment of these conditions is highly specialized.

Sun exposure and travellers at special risk

Individuals with certain skin or general diseases may particularly suffer as a result of sun exposure. Usually, such patients are aware of the risks and successfully avoid sunny environments. Some of the commonest problems are found in persons with the following conditions: lupus erythematosus, rosacea, cutaneous or liver porphyria, seborrhoeic dermatitis, atopic eczema, herpes simplex, and dermatomyositis.

Skin diseases from cold exposure

Prolonged exposure to very cold or freezing environment results in damage to the skin and other soft tissues, particularly in those individuals who have an increased susceptibility. Cold exposure can result in *frostbite* or a condition named *trench foot*; those with increased susceptibility manifest with *chilblains* and a number of other less common conditions (see also Chapter 8.4). In all cases, the symptoms start following exposure to cold, with or without other aggravating factors such as wind and immersion in water. The main symptoms are pain or numbness, followed in severe cases by blistering and gangrene of body areas with poor circulation in the fingers, nose tip, cheeks, ears, and toes. A pale and bluish discoloration of the affected region or limb indicates such poor circulation. Protective clothing and avoidance of immersion in freezing waters are the best measures to prevent these conditions.

Once any of the aforementioned problems has developed, immediate warming of the affected region is indicated, but may not result in full recovery. Medical advice may be necessary in determining whether other forms of treatment or surgery are indicated in severe cases.

Skin diseases from drug reactions

Most medicines taken by mouth or injection can induce allergic reactions in normal individuals. Persons taking several medicines at the same time and/or those above the age of 60 represent the population at highest risk for the development of drug reactions. It is advisable for the traveller to take a medical kit with safe drugs previously known to be effective and well tolerated. This should include painkillers, anti-inflammatory drugs, anti-histamines, and in certain cases, antibiotics (Chapter 13.5).

Redness of the skin and urticaria

Allergic reactions to medicines usually appear within minutes or a few hours after taking the suspected drug. Most commonly they present with redness of the skin on the face and neck, but the upper trunk, buttocks, and rest of the body can be affected as well. Very itchy and raised urticarial wheals (hives) may also be observed on the same sites; they usually last minutes or a few hours and disappear without leaving a scar. More severe cases involve swelling of the face (particularly of the eyelids and lips) and of the upper respiratory tract, causing difficulty in breathing and requiring obvious emergency diagnosis and treatment by a hospital doctor.

Future attacks of drug allergy can be avoided by stopping the medication. In the absence of medical help, an anti-histamine tablet (chlorphenamine, diphenhydramine, or aminopiridine, three to four times daily; cetirizine, once or twice daily) may result in symptomatic improvement. Moisturizing of the skin with any available cold cream or milk cream may also soothe the itchiness and burning sensation. Although any medicine can induce an allergic reaction, most rashes result from *antibiotics* (penicillins, gentamicin, tetracyclines, sulphonamides), *anti-epileptic* drugs (carbamazepine, barbiturates, phenytoin), *beta-blockers* to treat blood hypertension (propranolol, atenolol), *anti-inflammatory drugs* (ibuprofen, naproxen) and *anti-malarials* (chloroquine).

Medicines reacting with sunlight

Travellers in the tropics or sunny skiing resorts need to be aware that certain medicines can induce very uncomfortable, and potentially very dangerous, skin conditions following sun exposure. These can manifest as acute dermatitis with redness, itchiness, stinging sensation, and blistering of the skin exposed to sunlight. The clinical range of presentation on the skin is quite variable and can be life-threatening in cases accompanied by fever, general malaise, or severe blistering with superficial ulceration and complicated by secondary infections.

If you are taking any of the treatments listed in Table 9.1.1, ask your doctor for advice before exposing your skin to strong sunlight. Remember that you *must not stop* taking your regular medication without your doctor's advice. Extra care and protection from direct or indirect sunlight represents a simple answer for most travellers. Contact with plants and plant saps can have a similar sensitivity effect (see Table 9.1.2).

Table 9.1.1 Drugs and medicines that can cause photosensitivity

Amiodarone	Coal tar
Oral contraceptives	Retinoids
Antihistamines	Frusemide
PABA	Sulphonamides
Beta-blockers	Hexachlorophene
Piroxicam	Tetracyclines (including doxycycline)
Chlorpromazine (Largactil)	Nalidixic acid (Negram)
Promethazine (Phenergan)	Thiazide diuretics (like bendrofluazide)
Ciprofloxacin (and related antibiotics)	Non-steroidal anti-inflammatory drugs
Psoralens	

Table 9.1.2 Plants that can cause photosensitivity

Agrimony	Cow parsley, wild chervil	Parsnip
Angelica	Dill	Persian lime
Bergamot	Fennel	Red quebracho
Bind weed	Figs	St John's wort
Buttercup	Giant hogweed	Wild carrot
Celery	Mangoes (sap from skin of fruit)	
Citrus plants	Milfoil	

Seek medical attention in case of tropical skin disease

If you suspect a travel-associated condition, seek skilled care as soon as possible. Whilst away, early signs and symptoms of most tropical diseases afflicting the traveller can often be easily recognized and treated by local physicians. If symptoms or signs of disease develop upon return to your home country, seek medical advice from your own doctor or specialist in travel health.

Most cities in developed regions of the world offer specialist treatment for the traveller, and many capital cities (in both the developed as well as developing world) have centres of excellence in medical care and research in the field of tropical diseases.

Once you are home, remember that a skin rash, a non-healing insect bite, a skin ulcer, a fever, general malaise, irritability, tiredness, and diarrhoea, all require skilled medical attention.

Box 9.1.1 **Summary of advice for travellers**

A few simple measures can help prevent serious skin disease:

- *Basic hygiene*: daily shower and hand washing before meals protects against bacterial skin infections and diarrhoeal diseases. This will also prevent minor skin cuts and abrasions, as well as mosquito bites, from turning into serious bacterial skin infections
- *Proper menstrual hygiene*: prevents vulval acute contact dermatitis ('napkin-like' inflammation), vulvo-vaginitis, chronic eczema, and toxic shock syndrome
- *Footwear*: strong and comfortable shoes prevent blistering from friction and superficial infections, and protect against infection. Strong, good-quality swimmers' fins protect against cuts and wounds from sea urchins, coral reefs, and poisonous marine flora and fauna. Avoid sandals during trekking and visits to archaeological sites; they expose your toes to scorpions as well as fungal and bacterial infections. Use them on the beach, however, to avoid cutaneous larva migrans
- *Clothing*: protects against sunburn and, for trekkers, against minor skin cuts and abrasions which may be the port of entry for unwanted fungi and bacteria. Beware of bed linen in budget hostels or pensiones. Avoid wearing clothes belonging to others with uncertain personal hygiene. All these measures will prevent superficial infestations by ectoparasites
- *Insect repellents*: repellents applied directly to the skin in the form of an oily lotion or spray, such as 20–50% DEET, can be very effective. Use permethrin solution to impregnate clothes while trekking, farming, or horse riding in order to avoid bites from mosquitoes, ticks, and other insect species that may transmit serious illness
- *Mosquito nets*: very useful in preventing minor skin lesions from insect bites and reducing the risk of serious illnesses like malaria and dengue fever
- *Sun protection*: light, cotton tops are the best protection in hot sunny weather. Apply sunblock (SPF 20+ and 4–5* for UVA protection) to all exposed skin, every 3 hours. This is particularly important for those with white skin. Avoidance of direct sun irradiation between 11:00 and 16:00 hours, and using parasols, hats, and sunglasses, are the most effective measures to prevent acute burns, sunstroke, and long-term effects of intense, sporadic exposure, such as skin cancers
- *Protection from cold weather*: proper winter clothing and adequate indoor heating will prevent frostbite, chilblains, and hypothermia. Persons with an exaggerated response to cold (Raynaud's phenomenon, vascular lability), may need to avoid cold environments
- *Protected sexual activity*: condoms are the main protection against most sexually transmitted infections and unwanted pregnancy. Kissing and oral sex, however, play a role in acquiring conditions such as herpes simplex and syphilis. Scabies and other ectoparasitic infestations may be acquired through sexual activities
- *Moisturizing of your skin*: restoration of the skin barrier protects against a number of minor events. After showering or swimming, moisturizing of the skin and re-application of sunblock prevent flare-ups of eczema and ensure protection against sunlight
- *First-aid and medical kit*: your medical kit should include insect repellents, skin moisturizer, painkillers, anti-histamines, and mild antiseptics, plus any regular medication (see also Chapter 13.5). Freshly brewed black tea (without milk or sugar) is a cheap and effective antiseptic to use in soaks or in bathing superficial skin infections.

9.2 Dental problems

Andrew Dawood

A relatively trivial dental problem can easily cause a disproportionate amount of pain, discomfort, and inconvenience while abroad. Most prospective travellers give dental problems little thought, but if an emergency arises, travellers may have difficulty finding expert help, and are more likely to have to pay for it out of their own pocket than if they have a medical problem.

Before departure

Travellers on short trips are unlikely to face a dental emergency (other than an accidental one) if they have had a recent careful examination by their own dentist, including radiographs, and any necessary treatment has been completed. The examination is not a guessing game, and the dentist should be told about current symptoms or problems; it should be scheduled long enough before departure to permit treatment to be completed. People with heavily restored mouths, or large, complex restorations should seek advice from their dentist on any problems likely to arise.

Travellers intending to spend a long time abroad should consider treatment for conditions likely to cause future trouble—for example, currently symptomless impacted teeth or the replacement of a just adequate but ancient denture. Dental implant restorations frequently need repair and maintenance; knowing details of the manufacturer and the system used makes remedial treatment more straightforward. Dental problems in long-term expatriates are surprisingly common. In American Peace Corps Volunteers (who each spend 2 years overseas), such problems consistently rank third or fourth in the most frequently reported health problems.

The cost of specialist dental care can vary considerably around the world and can come as a shock to people who have only ever used the NHS in the UK. In general, it is always best to have any routine dental work carried out in your home environment.

Dental problems associated with travel

Few dental problems are directly related to travelling. Seasick passengers may lose their dentures if they vomit over the side of the ship! Swimmers also may lose dentures or orthodontic plates. Changes in air pressure can produce pain in teeth with leaking restorations or inflamed dental pulps. This 'barodontalgia' is occasionally seen in scuba divers or pilots, and usually improves when pressure returns to normal. Unaccustomed alcoholic intake can precipitate 'periodic facial migraine' (Horton's syndrome)—severe throbbing pain in one cheek. People who drink more wine and spirits than usual on a flight may come to associate such attacks with flying.

Dental emergencies

Toothache

Sensitivity to hot and cold may be the first sign of trouble. If treated at this stage, the tooth may settle down. Untreated, the pain may become spontaneous and long lasting; the nerve in the tooth may die, and act as a focus for infection and abscess.

A dental abscess can cause severe persistent pain, exacerbated by pressure. A swollen face should be taken seriously; seek treatment early as there is a small, but significant risk of life-threatening spread of infection—not uncommon before the days of antibiotics! The usual treatment for an abscessed tooth in many countries would be extraction. However, if the abscess is caused by death of the nerve, root canal treatment may save the tooth—the nerve chamber is opened, the infection drained, and the chamber is filled with an inert or antiseptic material. If good dental treatment is available, baby teeth may be treated similarly; otherwise it may be more sensible to accept the loss of a milk tooth, rather than risk further infection.

If treatment is unavailable antibiotics should be taken, although every effort must be made to see a dentist swiftly. Once an abscess develops, extraction with a local anaesthetic may prove more difficult, and antibiotics may be needed until the infection subsides and the extraction may be performed.

Gum disease can also cause an abscess. Such an abscess may sometimes be treated by deep cleaning of the tooth to remove infected deposits under the gum. However, once again, the only treatment offered may be extraction.

A similar abscess may develop around a lower wisdom tooth—often in young adults, especially in smokers or if 'run down'. Extraction of the impacted tooth is often necessary, although antibiotics, antiseptic mouth wash, and good tooth brushing may help to control the infection until the traveller returns home.

Individuals who have previously suffered from a dental abscess should discuss the management of such problems with their own dentist, who may recommend travelling with appropriate antibiotics.

Occasionally, 2–3 days after a tooth has been extracted, the jaw may become extremely painful. Typically the 'clot' is lost from the socket, exposing bone, giving the appearance of a 'dry socket'. Painkillers, irrigation and a medicated dressing may be needed.

The pain associated with toothache will usually respond to analgesics such as paracetamol or ibuprofen, which may be used together if discomfort is severe.

Fillings, crowns, bridges, and dentures

Loss or breakage of a dental restoration is not a true emergency. The exposed tooth surface may be sensitive and unsightly, jagged edges may be irritating, but immediate treatment is seldom essential unless there is considerable discomfort. A tooth's survival is unlikely to be affected by a delay of even a few weeks, so it is almost always possible to wait until you can see your own dentist or find a dentist on personal recommendation.

It is often wise to seek provisional treatment only, temporarily re-cementing a crown or bridge, or providing a temporary filling, until better facilities are available.

Repair kits

Dental restorations are usually lost only as a result of underlying problems such as decay, breakage, or poor dentistry. 'Do-it-yourself' temporary repair kits are available, and these may contain a dental mirror, a mixing spatula, and tubes of a dental dressing and cement. One tube contains the paste, the other the catalyst to make it set. The cement will form a temporary filling for a tooth cavity, or can be used to provisionally re-cement a crown or bridge. Any debris inside the crown or bridge may prevent it from seating fully, and must be completely removed before the restoration is fitted. It is a good idea to check that the restoration can be properly inserted before mixing the cement. If the restoration is loose, it should be removed as there is a risk that it may be inhaled or swallowed.

Dental implants

Dental implants are titanium fixtures inserted into the jawbone to replace missing teeth. These types of restorations have become commonplace, and often represent the best approach to tooth replacement.

There are hundreds of different varieties produced by countless manufacturers, and each system has its own instrumentation and protocols. Implant crowns or bridges are usually screwed or cemented into place on to the implant. Remedial treatment may require the use of special screwdrivers, and familiarity with careful cementation techniques. (Travellers should know the system that has been used, and should discuss likely problems prior to departure.) If an implant crown or bridge comes loose or falls out, it may be better to wait until expert assistance is available, even if this takes some days or weeks. Under these circumstances be sure to keep the area clean.

More serious emergencies

Fractured jaws and spreading infections need hospital treatment by an oral or maxillofacial surgeon. If skilled treatment is not available, and if after emergency care the patient is deemed fit to travel (and not at risk from airway obstruction), it may be best to return home for further treatment.

A front tooth broken as a result of a blow—particularly in a child—may not always seem to need urgent care, however, expert treatment within a matter of hours can make all the difference between preserving a tooth or losing it.

If a permanent front tooth is knocked out, it may be possible to re-implant it as a temporary measure. The roots of re-implanted teeth tend to be subsequently eaten away, like those of baby teeth, and the tooth is lost again; but some survive and give good service if replaced within 20min, perhaps up to 2 hours if kept moist. Hold the tooth only by the crown, and do not touch, rub or scrub the root. Put the tooth in a clean container, in cold drinking water to which salt has been added (one teaspoon per glass), or some milk. If the tooth has been washed, it should be pushed back fully into its socket straight away. Be sure that the crown is the right way round! The procedure will not be too painful. Ideally, the patient should get to a dentist as soon as possible to have the tooth 'splinted' into place for a week or so. The patient should receive antibiotics, and may need a tetanus booster. Milk teeth should not be re-implanted.

Re-implanted teeth, or teeth loosened by a heavy blow, should be splinted to their neighbours for a period of about a week. A temporary splint may be improvised using softened chewing gum (preferably sugar-free), pressed around the tooth and its neighbours, and covered with aluminium foil. It is best not to re-implant a tooth that has fallen on to pasture grazed by animals, because of the increased risk of tetanus infection.

The tooth should be checked by a dentist upon returning home, and subsequently at regular intervals. Root-canal treatment is usually necessary and if the tooth fails, it may be replaced by means of a denture, bridge, or ideally a dental implant.

Choosing a dentist abroad

Non-sterile instruments and needles may be a source of hepatitis B, hepatitis C (see Chapter 2.4), and HIV infection (Chapter 10.2). You should satisfy yourself that any dentist you consult uses instruments that have been adequately cleaned and sterilized. Instruments contaminated with traces of blood or injection syringes used on more than one patient are dangerous: make it clear that you are prepared to pay for any 'disposable' items.

'Cartridge' syringes are the safest for giving local anaesthetic. These are made of metal, and a fresh glass tube, closed with a bung at each end and filled with sterile local anaesthetic solution by the manufacturer, slides into the barrel for each patient. A fresh needle from an intact plastic capsule should be used for each patient. The syringe itself should be washed and sterilized between patients. 'Push-on' needles and plastic syringes should come from intact original packages, and should be discarded after each patient.

Beware of needles re-sterilized by soaking in antiseptics or by boiling and, particularly, of plastic syringes 're-sterilized' by soaking in antiseptic. Watch out for bottles of solution from which doses for other patients have been withdrawn. If needles that have been used on other patients are used to withdraw a further dose they can easily contaminate the contents.

The dentist should wear rubber gloves—a fresh pair for each patient, though this may simply not be possible in some parts of the world. High-speed drills use water as a coolant, and this (and any other water used in your mouth) may be only as clean as the local supply.

Personal recommendation is usually the best basis for choosing a dentist.

Important points to mention

If you have had rheumatic fever, have a heart valve defect or disease, a hole in the heart, a heart murmur, or have had heart valve surgery, or an artificial joint, then you should discuss the possible need for antibiotic cover for dental procedures with your doctor, and make this plain to any dentist you see. Carry a suitable antibiotic with you if cover is needed.

Anyone taking anticoagulant drugs, or with haemophilia or other bleeding tendency, should ensure the dentist understands the situation.

Tell the dentist about any serious illnesses, routine medication, or allergies; carry a translated note if necessary.

Remember also that not all cultures attach a great deal of importance to saving teeth. You must make your own feelings on this subject quite clear.

Financial matters

Many travel insurance policies do not include specific sections on emergency dental treatment; inquire beforehand about what is covered. Travellers at special risk of accidental injury (e.g. on skiing holidays) should make certain they are fully insured—the cost of emergency treatment, and any crown, bridge or denture work, may be very high.

Looking after your teeth

When travelling in a hot country, it is sometimes tempting, and often necessary to drink large amounts of bottled soft drinks. In some countries it may also be customary to serve guests with heavily sweetened tea or coffee. Frequent consumption of sugary food or drink is especially damaging to teeth, and should be avoided. It may take only a few months for early decay to develop in a previously unaffected tooth.

Tooth cleaning becomes even more important when sugar consumption is frequent. Using floss or an interdental brush every day will help prevent decay on otherwise inaccessible surfaces. Dental floss has been found to be a versatile and indispensable travelling companion by this author, who has had cause to use it on occasion as a clothes' line, for repairing a tent and for hanging a hammock. The possibilities are limitless.

Fluoride and living abroad

A small amount of fluoride (one part per million in temperate climates) in drinking water undoubtedly reduces the likelihood of tooth decay, particularly in children; however, excessive intake (greater than two parts per million) can lead to mottling and discoloration of developing teeth. In countries with a well-developed mains drinking supply, the fluoride content is carefully controlled to the proper level—a small amount is added where required or a natural excess removed.

Unless it is known for certain that fluoride is absent from the local water supply or is present only in a very low concentration (much less than one part per million), the use of fluoride supplements for children is unwise. Supplements should be used when prescribed by a knowledgeable dentist or doctor. Where fluoride levels are high, use bottled water for babies and small children, bearing in mind that water intake and thus total fluoride intake is higher in hot countries.

Young children swallow a significant amount of toothpaste when they brush their teeth. If the toothpaste contains fluoride and fluoride levels in the drinking water are already high, this may result in an excessive intake. Only under these circumstances is it better for babies and young children to use fluoride-free toothpaste.

9.3 Eye problems

Gillian Whitby

Eye problems are common in travellers, but sight-threatening problems are very rare. Most people are unduly scared when they experience an eye problem, but should remain calm.

The effects of dust, dry or polluted atmospheres and infection are the main difficulties travellers face, compounded by limited access to professional help. Intense pain or sudden visual loss demand immediate attention.

Standards of treatment vary considerably. In many countries the number of trained ophthalmologists is tiny; in several African states there is not even one trained ophthalmologist per million people. Local doctors and pharmacists may have skill in treating eye problems, but do not rely on this, and beware of the risks of inappropriate therapy, harmful patent medicines and folk cures.

Many eye diseases occur in tropical countries, but most are unlikely to affect short-term travellers. This chapter considers the commonest troubles they may come across, which can be categorized into external and internal problems. It is only the external problems that travellers can attempt to deal with by themselves.

Dust particles under the eyelid

In dusty conditions, particles of grit may get stuck under the top eyelid. This should be suspected if nothing can be seen on the eye surface but the eye still feels as though something is inside it.

Removing a foreign body from under someone else's upper eyelid is a simple procedure (Fig. 9.3.1) and gives immediate relief. Sit in front of the affected person (who should also be seated) and ask him or her to keep looking down. Gently pull the eyelid away from the eye by holding the lashes firmly between the index finger and thumb of your left hand. Using a cotton bud, gently press the centre of the eyelid about 5mm from its margin, where you can see a shallow groove in the skin. This will flip the lid inside out; if you adjust your pull on the eyelashes slightly upwards, the

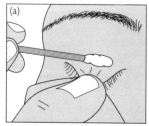
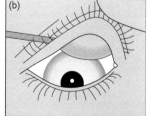

Fig. 9.3.1 Removing foreign body from under someone else's upper eyelid.

eyelid will remain everted. Now wipe the inside of the eyelid gently with the tip of a clean wet cotton bud or tissue to remove the particle of grit, which is often too small to see. Finally, return the lid to its normal position. (You can find this manoeuvre demonstrated on the Internet.) Seek help if symptoms persist. If the foreign body is stuck on the corneal surface, it is unlikely you can remove it without professional help. This involves anaesthetizing the corneal surface and examining it at 40x magnification, under sterile conditions. Don't rub your eye—that usually scratches it further and embeds the foreign body more deeply.

Corneal problems

Ultraviolet rays in strong sunlight can cause acute temporary damage to the front surface of the eye; there are also longer-term effects on the skin of the eyelids and on the internal structures of the eye, particularly the lens (leading to cataracts) and the retina (leading to retinal degeneration).

In mild cases, there is discomfort, redness, inflammation, and watering. When severe, there is more pain, extreme sensitivity to light, spasm of the lids and blurred vision. This is more common with high-altitude mountaineering or skiing (snow blindness)—Chapter 8.9. Excessive radiation causes swelling and loss of epithelial cells on the cornea, which is extremely painful. It equates to bad sunburn on the front surface of your eye! Apply eye ointment to lubricate the corneal surface. This usually provides relief within a few hours. Milder conditions can be treated with lubricant eye drops. The best approach is to avoid trouble by wearing sunglasses, ski goggles or a sun hat. Although wearing an eyepad can often ease discomfort from painful corneal conditions, it is no longer generally recommended: it can make it harder to recognize deterioration or interference with vision.

Allergies

If you have a tendency to allergies, travel with antihistamines and any other medication such as cromoglycate drops (Opticrom). The eyelids are very vascular and swell greatly in allergic situations. It takes time for swelling to reduce, so be patient.

Other eyelid problems

Lid problems may look alarming, but they do not have sight-threatening consequences.
- *Stye (hordeolum)* is an infection of the sebaceous glands of Zeis at the base of the eyelashes. Hot compresses and (under clean conditions) trying to squeeze out pus or other contents is the remedy. Antibiotics are not required unless the condition is severe
- *Chalazion* is a cyst in the eyelid, following inflammation of a blocked meibomian gland, usually on the upper lid. These are usually painless nodules; they may become acutely inflamed, but chalazia usually point inside the lid rather than on the lid margin. A chalazion or meibomian cyst could take months to heal fully
- *Blepharitis* is the medical term for inflamed eyelids. The inflammation is like eczema of the skin, with red, scaly eyelids. You may notice tired or gritty eyes, which may be uncomfortable in sunlight or a smoky

atmosphere. They may feel as though there is something in them. The eyelids have tiny surface glands, which make substances that mix with and spread tears across the eye—hence the gritty feeling.

Atmospheric irritation

Dust, pollen, smoke, chemicals, and pollutants can all cause chronic discomfort. When chemicals or sprays get into the eyes, the immediate treatment is copious irrigation with an eye bath, under a running tap or even, in extreme circumstances, by immersing the head in a bucket of water with the eyes open!

Dryness/air quality

Dryness is a major cause of ocular discomfort, from mildly uncomfortable to seriously debilitating. Factors such as air conditioning, air travel, tiredness, alcohol, some types of medication (including diuretics and hormone replacement therapy (HRT)), and wearing contact lenses have a cumulative effect. Investigate the wide range of lubricating products available before you travel.

Flying

Avoid wearing contact lenses on long flights. If unavoidable, apply lubricating eye drops liberally. Humidity aboard an aircraft can be as low as 2%. Try not to sleep in lenses. Always keep a lens case and lens solutions in your hand luggage.

Staring at a laptop screen for prolonged periods in a dry cabin when you are wearing lenses is a recipe for disaster.

In accordance with international regulations, aerosol insecticide sprays are used to clear the cabin of stray insects that might spread disease. In a confined space, these chemicals irritate the eyes, so keep your eyes closed during spraying and for a minute or so afterwards.

Sub-conjunctival haemorrhage

Commonly discovered on waking, and often following coughing or vomiting, haemorrhages can be dramatic in appearance but no treatment is required. Think of a bruise under the skin, but here the 'skin' is the transparent conjunctiva. At first the colour is red, but over time it may turn different colours, becoming yellowish before it completely clears 7–14 days later. If it recurs regularly, have your blood pressure checked.

Infection/conjunctivitis

Eye infections occur more frequently in hot climates, where a variety of germs may be present in the atmosphere, rivers, swimming pools, and the sea. They can be bacterial (most common), viral or fungal (very rare, and beyond the scope of this chapter).

Bacterial conjunctivitis

Typically, the eye is red, itchy, or gritty, producing a sticky or crusty yellowy or green discharge. It is best not to rub, as this can spread infection to the other eye. Bacterial infection usually responds quickly to treatment with antibiotics, such as azithromycin 1.5% drops twice daily for 3 days (if available) or chloramphenicol ointment or drops. Avoid using antibiotic preparations (or other eye medicines) that also contain steroids: *steroids may be widely available without a prescription in many developing countries, but may harm your eyes in the presence of a virus infection, which has similar symptoms.*

Viral conjunctivitis

The symptoms are excessive watering, redness, and pain, with no discharge or itching. Antibiotics are ineffective. Mild attacks usually clear unaided, but treatment is needed if symptoms are severe. Patients with a history of herpes virus should wear sunglasses because attacks can be triggered by exposure to strong sunlight.

During an infection, the eyes can be kept clean by frequent warm saline washes with an eye bath or by wiping the lids with moistened cotton wool.

Conjunctivitis is very infectious and is easily transmitted to others. Do not share handkerchiefs, towels, face cloths, eye baths, or eye drops, and avoid swimming until the infection has subsided.

The painful condition of keratitis is an inflammation of the cornea, caused by bacteria (usually staphylococci) and viruses (either *Herpes simplex*, which also causes herpes blisters, or *adenovirus*, responsible for the common cold). This sort of keratitis is treated with either antibiotic drops (such as gentamicin or neomycin) or anti-viral ointment (aciclovir).

Recent eye surgery

If you have recently had eye surgery, ask your ophthalmologist when it is safe travel or pursue an active sport. Anyone who has had surgery for retinal detachment should avoid all air travel for at least 3 weeks (Chapter 7.1). People who have undergone recent refractive laser surgery should take note of the problems that may occur at altitude (Chapter 8.3). You will also be at increased risk of infection in swimming pools, etc.

Contact lenses

At the first hint of irritation or discomfort, leave your lenses out as long as symptoms persist. The commonest problems for gas permeable lens wearers are over wear or dust trapped under a lens. Remind yourself to keep blinking to circulate fresh tears. Symptoms of over wear are similar to over-exposure to UV (see 'Corneal problems', p.322). A scratch on the cornea from a dust particle trapped under the lens will feel much the same. Excessive watering will usually make you keep your eyes closed. Anti-inflammatory medication may be helpful.

Internal eye problems

These problems do occur, but much less frequently. There are some serious but painless eye problems, such as retinal detachment or venous occlusion that present with visual symptoms. Uveitis and acute glaucoma are painful but are also not amenable to self-treatment. Highly skilled, specialist medical attention is necessary for diagnosis, treatment, and management. You must evaluate the suitability of dealing with such problems where you are, or trying to get yourself to somewhere with better facilities. Use everything in your power to help you make the correct decision, from information on the Internet to phoning your eye care professional at home for advice. Email and digital photography can often help in diagnosis.

Contact lenses: some travel tips

- Don't wear contact lenses on any flight longer than 4 hours
- Daily-wear lenses are preferable to extended-wear ('sleep-in') lenses as they are less likely to cause long-term physiological changes to the eye and reduce the potential for bacterial infections and ulcers
- If travelling under extreme conditions of poor hygiene, it may be better to sleep in your lenses to avoid handling them. If you need to alter your wearing pattern consult your contact lens specialist before you travel, or consider reverting to spectacles.

Eye-care items to pack

- Quality sunglasses that screen blue and ultra-violet light (UVA and UVB)
- Spare spectacles
- Extra disposable contact lenses, a copy of your prescription, and your optometrist's contact details
- Spectacle screwdriver
- Lubricating eye drops or gel
- Antibiotic eye drops or ointment (avoid types that need refrigeration)
- Plenty of any regular medication and supplies (such as contact lens solutions), as well as written details of existing eye problems and any treatment
- Keep any essential items in your hand luggage or on your person, and take more than you need to cover unforeseen delays
- Painkillers.

If you are caught up in a war zone or civil unrest, a good tip for protecting your eyes from tear gas and smoke is to put on swimming or diving goggles.

9.4 Foot care

Paula Dudley

Most people spend more time on their feet when travelling than they do at home, and foot problems are frequently encountered.

Footwear

Choose appropriate footwear for sightseeing, hiking or any other activity with great care for maximum comfort. When buying new shoes, allow enough time to obtain good advice and find something suitable.

Footwear should have soft uppers, while the sole should provide shock absorption and surface grip, especially in wet conditions—many synthetic materials have properties superior to leather. New footwear should be worn-in gradually, well prior to the trip, especially if rigid. Older footwear should be examined for worn areas on the outside and also inside where nails or rivets may be exposed. Where the lining has worn, a cork insole can cover imperfections, preventing friction over thin-skinned sites that may shear and blister. If this ruptures, the underlying skin is left raw, painful, and vulnerable to infection.

Preventing blisters

Take a spare pair of comfortable shoes to alternate with newer footwear. Activity footwear should be reasonably waterproof, with 'breathable' upper materials allowing vapour to pass through. The upper and lining material of the shoe should be quick drying.

Friction is greatest on damp skin and feet, and footwear should be ventilated as often as possible (removing insoles).

Surgical spirit, applied to the skin before and during a trek, helps toughen skin. Blister dressings (such as Compeed) are useful both for prevention and treatment. They are thin, conformable and waterproof and can be left in place until they fall off. Feet swell in hot conditions and during flights, so wear adjustable footwear.

Treatment

Shearing of skin can be reduced with petroleum jelly, or by applying surgical tape. Protect as soon as discomfort or redness appears. If a tense blister must be drained, leave the skin intact except for a small aperture made with a sterile needle, gently press out the fluid and apply a dressing firmly to prevent re-filling. If the blister has broken, use antiseptic before applying a non-adherent dressing. Switch to a softer type of footwear if possible.

Fungal infections

Preventatively, wash and dry feet carefully and dust with anti-fungal powder daily. Where infection is present, apply anti-fungal medication sparingly but regularly, using a spray or cream formulation depending on whether skin is moist or dry. Without prompt treatment, fungal infections may spread rapidly, becoming disabling beyond all proportion to the area affected.

Choose socks with a high percentage of a natural fibre: cotton, silk, or wool, though synthetic fibres are often added to make them more durable and 'wick' away moisture from skin. Footwear can be occlusive, keeping skin warm, damp, and vulnerable to fungi, so feet should be allowed a 'footwear free' period daily and shoes changed regularly.

Soft-tissue injuries

When sandals are worn, the top of the feet can become sunburned, so protect with a high SPF product.

Sprains result from stretching and/or tearing the soft tissues supporting joints, and produce swelling, bruising, and pain—most commonly of the outer ankle, from wrenching the foot when walking over uneven terrain. Apply an ice pack to reduce any swelling and use an elastic, tubular bandage (e.g. Tubigrip) for support. This should feel firm, not tight. Adjust footwear fastenings as necessary. Treat with rest and elevation, using anti-inflammatory medication to help reduce pain and swelling. More serious injury may require complete rest. When weight bearing is unavoidable, bandaging can minimize harmful movement, but is best done by a trained professional or first-aider.

The back of the heel may also be subject to constant friction from a boot or shoe, causing painful inflammation (bursitis) and/or irritation of the tendon. The treatment is the same—to reduce inflammation—and it can be helpful to cut away or cover the offending portion of the shoe with a softer material.

Severe, persistent aching or joint pain may result from unaccustomed levels of activity or faulty foot mechanics. A supportive off-the-shelf or prescribed insole can significantly reduce discomfort.

Cuts, abrasions, and insect bites

Injuries to legs and feet take longer to heal than at other sites, and become infected more easily (see Chapter 9.5): clean even small wounds thoroughly. Abrasions and wounds should be irrigated with clean, running water where possible, and then gently dried with clean tissue or gauze. Small wounds can be covered with a plaster but larger wounds may require antiseptic cream or spray and a protective, absorbent dressing, changed regularly.

Foreign bodies sometimes enter the sole, needing removal with tweezers or a sterile needle. Deeply embedded fragments may require specialist treatment: meanwhile the area should be protected with an improvised dressing to prevent further pressure. Ensure your tetanus protection is up to date.

Insect bites, usually on the thinner skin on the top of the foot or around the ankle, can be problematic. They often itch, and scratching can lead to infection. Anti-histamine tablets may help, but infected bites should be treated as any wound and observed for deterioration. Tea tree oil (*Melaleuca alternifolia*) can be dabbed on fresh bites to prevent infection and promote healing.

Parasites

Avoid going barefoot in soil or water that may carry parasites, as these can enter through the skin of the foot. Such infestations can cause local skin irritations or more serious systemic problems via the blood stream. Check for unusual marks or tracks on the sole or between the toes and seek advice.

9.5 Skin and soft tissue infections

Matthew Dryden

Infections of the skin and soft tissue are amongst the most common travel-associated infections. Common germs that cause these infections at home, also cause them when travelling, but they often do so with greater speed and severity, especially in the tropics. Attention to hygiene and good first aid is important with even the most minor breaks in the skin, including insect bites and blisters, or more serious infection may develop.

Small cuts, wounds, and insect bites easily become infected on expeditions, particularly in the tropics. Most of these infections are caused by staphylococcal or streptococcal bacteria. Any cuts, however small, should receive first aid treatment and be cleaned with an antiseptic solution and covered with a small dressing or plaster. Wounds that are infected are red, painful, inflamed, and pus may be present. Boils are abscesses of the skin and are usually caused by staphylococci. Soft tissue infections respond to antibiotics, such as flucloxacillin. Larger abscesses may require incision and drainage of the pus.

Sometimes large areas of skin on the legs develop a rapidly spreading infection, usually caused by streptococci, and cause the leg to become painful, red, and usually swollen. Sometimes blisters appear in the skin and the lymph glands above the affected area may be swollen and tender. This condition is called *cellulitis* and requires antibiotics. If not treated quickly, the infection may spread further, necessitating hospital admission with intravenous antibiotics. Initially, large oral doses of ampicillin or amoxicillin are the most effective treatment.

Animal bites similarly need urgent attention. Clean thoroughly with antiseptic solution, or if unavailable, soap and water. Treat with co-amoxiclav (Augmentin) (see also Chapter 6).

Treatment summary

Minor wounds

Prevent infection by cleaning all minor wounds with antiseptic, then keeping them covered and dry. Breaks in the skin caused by cuts, trauma, thorns, insect bites, coral injuries, and even blisters should be cleaned carefully with clean water and soap. Apply a small amount of a topical antiseptic such as chlorhexidine ointment (Savlon) and cover with a plaster or gauze dressing; use a blister dressing (e.g. Compeed) for blisters.

Animal and human bites

For animal and human bites, thorough early cleaning is essential followed by preventive antibiotic treatment, such as: co-amoxiclav (Augmentin) (375mg, three times daily for 5 days), consider the risk of rabies (p.178). For patients genuinely allergic to penicillin (total body rash or facial swelling and breathing difficulties) an alternative would be to treat with a course of clindamycin (300mg, four times daily for 5 days; plus doxycycline 100mg 12-hourly for animal bites).

Infected skin/soft tissue

Infected tissue is red, inflamed, and tender, and may discharge pus. Treat with flucloxacillin 500mg 6-hourly for 5 days.

Cellulitis

Spreading cellulitis should be treated with ampicillin or amoxicillin, 500mg–1g, three times daily for 5 days. It should be observed carefully for progression, in which case hospital treatment may be needed.

9.6 Respiratory and airborne problems in travellers

Richard Dawood

In almost every study of health problems relating to travel, respiratory problems consistently rank in the top five that travellers encounter, while away or on returning home. One fifth of all travellers may be affected, yet such problems receive scant attention. Perhaps we assume too readily that such problems are incidental to travel, rather than linked more closely.

Upper respiratory infection

Air travellers often worry that recirculation of cabin air is responsible for poor air quality on commercial jet aircraft, and helps spread disease. Expecting to confirm a possible link, researchers looked at passengers travelling between San Francisco and Denver on one of two types of aircraft: older Boeing 727s and DC10s that only delivered 100% fresh air; and newer, more economical 737s that supplied 50% re-circulated air during the 2 hour flight. Among the 1100 passengers taking part, they found *no statistical difference* in the rate of reporting a cold between those who had travelled on the older aircraft and those subjected to the re-circulated air.

However, their study also found, regardless of any exposure to re-circulated air, that as many as 21% of the air travellers taking part reported having a cold within 1 week of their flight—an intriguingly high rate that accords with the personal experience of many frequent fliers. The background rate of colds in the general, non-travelling population is around 3%.

We can only speculate on the cause: taxis, buses, trains, terminals, the inevitable stresses of a journey, meeting new people—and their germs—at your destination, may contribute to the probability of catching a cold.

In-flight, low cabin humidity may also be a contributing factor. The thin film of moisture that lines the membranes of the nose and throat is our first line of defence against airborne bacteria and viruses—and is the first casualty of a moisture-free environment. It is easily corrected with saline sprays, drops, or gel, or proprietary nasal sprays such as Vicks First Defence.

Research suggests that lack of sleep may also be a factor: one recent study found that people who slept for less than 7 hours per night were three times more susceptible to colds, under experimental conditions, than those who slept for 8 hours or more; jet lag and the inevitable sleep disturbances of travel may contribute to the problem.

Avoid flying with a heavy cold: you risk pressure damage to your ears and sinuses, and may infect those around you.

Pollutants, pollen, and other airborne particles

Regular or even occasional sufferers from sinus problems, allergies, or hay fevers should ensure that they have all they need to treat exacerbations. Atmospheric pollution in major cities across the developing world may be dramatic and unexpected, so be prepared. Hay fever is considered in

Chapter 8.6. Particulate matter in the air may cause more problems than has hitherto been recognized; facemasks may provide limited, short term protection.

Lower respiratory infection

Problems involving the lungs and lower respiratory tract are more serious. Many of the diseases referred to elsewhere in this book have airborne spread, or pneumonia as a feature—e.g. Legionnaires' disease, influenza, meningitis, TB. Viral infection may lead to secondary bacterial infection.

It makes sense for travellers who have experienced problems in the past to discuss a plan of action with their own doctor prior to travel, and to be ready to treat a suspected chest infection. Anyone with previous pneumonia should consider the pneumococcal vaccine (p.451), and should always be vaccinated against flu.

Pre-existing respiratory problems

With today's ageing populations, the number of travellers with respiratory issues is expected to rise; the longer range of new passenger jets raises concerns about more prolonged exposure to the lower oxygen conditions of the aircraft cabin. The British Thoracic Society has updated its guidelines for doctors looking after prospective travellers with lung disease (ℜ http://www.brit-thoracic.org.uk) and advises careful specialist assessment before travel (including a 'hypoxic challenge test' if appropriate—to measure tolerance of reduced oxygen).

Box 9.6.1 **Do facemasks work?**

When a person coughs or speaks, droplets of secretions containing bacteria and viruses are expelled. Larger droplets have a limited range; most fall, contaminating nearby surfaces for several hours. Fine droplets travel further, losing moisture by evaporation, leaving microscopic particles (droplet nuclei) suspended in the air.

Surgical masks protect against larger droplets, splashes, and sprays, are inexpensive and offer limited personal protection when in close proximity to others who are coughing. In some Asian countries they are just a fashion statement. They do not protect against inhalation of tiny particles, but may protect others when the wearer has a cough.

High filtration facemasks (also called 'respirators') must meet recognized national standards (e.g. FFP3, N95) and do protect the wearer from tiny airborne particles provided they fit the face well, so that air passes through the filter, not around its edges. Valved respirators are more comfortable, allowing air to be exhaled without passing through the filter. Masks and respirators should be worn once, then discarded.

Commuter masks sometimes contain activated charcoal to absorb pollutants.

I sometimes take facemasks with me when flying, just in case I'm seated next to a person who can't stop coughing, but for best protection, give your mask to the person with the cough!

Some additional things to take

- *Routine medication*, plus anything you might need to treat an exacerbation: asthma inhalers, allergy medication, steroids, and decongestants
- *Antibiotics and/or antiviral medicines*
- A note of your *medical history*, with details of any recent tests
- *Alcohol gel/hand sanitizer*: hand hygiene plays a vital role in preventing upper respiratory tract viral transmission
- *Remedies for colds and flu*: consistently the most frequently-used items in travel medical kits by visitors to any destination.

9.7 Gynaecological problems

Jerker Liljestrand

Gynaecological problems are common in women travellers. Most problems are not serious in terms of their impact on your health, but even a minor problem can ruin a trip.

Women travellers who plan a long trip abroad, or who plan to live in a country where good medical facilities may not be easily accessible, are well advised to have a gynaecological check-up and routine screening procedures before they leave home—preferably 6 weeks or so before departure; it is always a good idea to begin a trip with a clean bill of health. Those with previous gynaecological problems should have a clear understanding of their medical history, or should carry a written note of any problems.

Menstrual problems

Personal supplies

Although women throughout the world menstruate, not all of them take the same approach to feminine hygiene. So if you don't feel willing to experiment with the only facilities that might be available locally (e.g. balls of cotton wool, cloths, and towels), be certain to ensure an uninterrupted supply of your own preferred variety of tampon, sanitary napkin, or pad. The Mooncup is a reusable, eco-friendly alternative, popular with some.

Menstruation

Some women prefer, or need, not to have periods at all while travelling or working abroad; this can be accomplished by taking the Pill (the combined contraceptive pill of the type where all 21 pills in each packet are identical) continuously, without a break between packets (see Chapter 10.3).

Women who travel to game parks should consider this option or should avoid close proximity to predatory animals (bears, lions, tigers, etc.) while menstruating. There have been a number of reported attacks on menstruating women. Likewise, if they swim in shark-infested waters, they may possibly be at increased risk of attack.

In some parts of Southeast Asia, such as Indonesia, women may be asked not to enter local temples if they are menstruating.

Irregular bleeding

Periods may stop completely in travellers. Often, the cause of this proves to be pregnancy. However, an irregular cycle is usually the result of the hormonal changes that follow any disruption of normal routines, and may even be partly psychological in origin. Extra bleeding between menstrual periods should be investigated as soon as possible as it can be a symptom of genital infection (see Chapter 10.1), or other underlying disease that may require surgical treatment.

Heavy bleeding

Some types of heavy or frequent vaginal bleeding may be due to a serious underlying condition requiring expert advice and possibly surgical treatment.

In many cases, bleeding will respond to hormonal treatment. If you are bleeding heavily and are in a remote area where no medical advice can be obtained, it is worth trying the following treatment *provided that* you have had a recent check-up, you are otherwise healthy and you *are certain that you are not pregnant.*

Take one combined oral contraceptive pill (for example, Norinyl 1 or Eugynon 30) four times daily for 5 days. These pills contain standard doses of progesterone and oestrogen hormones, and are readily available worldwide. Bleeding should stop during treatment, and you should have a period by the seventh day after the last day of treatment. If bleeding does not stop during treatment, the problem will require a skilled assessment and probably surgery or curettage. If you do not have a period within 5–7 days of stopping treatment, you may be pregnant.

Remember that even if this treatment is successful, there may still be an underlying problem, so specialist advice should be obtained at the earliest opportunity.

Unintended pregnancy

Emergency contraception (the 'morning-after' Pill) is discussed on p.367.

Some women become pregnant while travelling, and others begin their trip in the earliest stages of pregnancy. Those who choose not to allow the pregnancy to continue are advised to be very careful. A termination of pregnancy in a country in which facilities and specialist skills are widely available is generally safe; a termination of pregnancy performed without these facilities and under unhygienic conditions, can cause life-threatening complications and may have serious implications for the woman's future health and fertility. This applies both to surgical abortion and medical abortion. Ensure any facilities you choose are clean and safe—even if this means returning home.

In most cases, time is on your side. Up to 6 weeks from the last menstrual period, a simple menstrual regulation procedure can be performed. In countries where it is available, misoprostol can be used up to 9 weeks from the last period (see Chapter 10.3). Up to 12 weeks from the last period, a surgical procedure is safe, although you should definitely avoid any further delay. In exceptional circumstances, action can be taken at up to 18 weeks, depending upon local laws (see p.368).

Those who are happy to continue with their pregnancy should make sure that they have access to adequate medical care (see Chapter 11.1).

Genital and urinary tract infection

Thrush, yeast infection

This is one of the commonest gynaecological problems encountered by travellers in tropical environments, and is caused by overgrowth of yeast normally found in the female genital area. Heat, humidity, the Pill, certain antibiotics, and diabetes increase the risk. Doxycycline is one of the antibiotic drugs that can trigger thrush; it is often used as an anti-malarial drug, so any woman taking it should also bring enough anti-candida medication for treatment if problems arise. Prevention includes keeping the genital area dry and cool; cotton underwear that absorbs perspiration is strongly recommended. A yeast infection is characterized by a red rash, itching, and a thick white 'cottage cheese' vaginal discharge.

Treatment

Daily vinegar douches (1–2 tablespoons/15–30mL, vinegar per L of water) may be sufficient to relieve the itching and return the vagina to its correct pH (acidity). If nothing else is available, yoghurt may also provide relief. When stronger treatment is required, clotrimazole (Canesten) 100mg intravaginally, daily for 7 days, or 500mg intravaginally as a single dose (Canesten 1, Mycelex) or nystatin (Nystan) 100 000 units intravaginally for 14 days may be used. An effective single-dose treatment is available without prescription in many countries—fluconazole 150mg (Diflucan 150) by mouth. Despite treatment, the condition may recur if the predisposing factors mentioned above have not been rectified.

Cystitis

Cystitis, also called urinary tract infection, is a common condition in women but may be particularly inconvenient in travellers. It often follows an increase in sexual activity. Symptoms usually consist of painful, frequent urination. The infection is usually due to contamination of the urinary passage with bacteria from the patient's own anal area, but may be the result of a sexually transmitted disease. If laboratory facilities are available, cultures should be performed.

Pain on urination without frequency may be due to vaginal infection or to genital herpes. A thorough examination should be obtained.

Treatment

If symptoms of cystitis appear, drink plenty of fluids, particularly cranberry juice if available, because it alters the acidity of the urine and may provide some symptomatic relief. If you are a frequent sufferer, discuss the problem with your doctor and bring antibiotics with you. Otherwise, self-treatment with antibiotics is usually inadvisable. If there is no prospect of skilled medical care, tetracycline 500mg by mouth, four times daily for 7 days (total dose 14g) or doxycycline 100mg by mouth, twice daily for 7 days, may be taken. These drugs will cover the important possible causes of urinary symptoms, but may not treat antibiotic-resistant gonorrhoea (Chapter 10.1). *These treatments are not recommended for pregnant/lactating women or those under 15 years old.* Complete the full course, and note that milk products interfere with absorption of these drugs.

Only if there is no possibility of a sexually transmitted disease would we advise using more conventional antibiotic treatment for a urinary infection—such as trimethoprim 200mg twice daily for 3–5 days, or cotrimoxazole (Septrin, Bactrim, etc.), two tablets 12–hourly for 5 days. Ampicillin or nitrofurantoin may also be used. Advice from a qualified medical practitioner should be obtained as soon as practicable.

Choosing a doctor abroad

Unfortunately, it is not safe to assume that a high standard of professional behaviour applies to all doctors everywhere. For obvious reasons, when dealing with gynaecological problems in a strange country it is important to choose your doctor with care. Embassy or consulate staff and expatriates may be able to recommend a suitable physician; often, the most reliable recommendations come from satisfied patients. If you can find a female doctor so much the better.

Always insist on a chaperone when being examined; use your common sense, but be prepared to refuse if you are asked to submit to what seems to you to be an unreasonable procedure.

A gynaecological examination on return home is a sensible precaution; be sure to tell your doctor where you have been.

9.8 Psychological disorders

Michael Phelan

We associate holidays with relaxation, excitement, and fun. We expect an enjoyable well-deserved rest. If travelling alone, we look forward to making friends; if we are with other people, we assume that relationships will flourish. Sadly, experience does not always live up to these high expectations. Travel delays, discomfort, unfamiliar climate, strange food, and language difficulties are all stressful. The end result can be misery, arguments with your companions and, occasionally, serious psychological disorders.

Sensible preparations and an awareness of the risks will help prevent serious problems. This section describes what you can do to reduce the chances of psychological problems and describes some specific conditions that can affect the traveller. Some advice is also offered to travellers who have had, or have, a psychiatric disorder.

Preventing problems

Having decided where to go, the most important decision is whether you are going to go with others, or alone. On your own you have complete freedom to decide how to get there and what to do when you arrive. Lone travellers often describe an intensity of experience which is missing when accompanied and relish meeting new people; but others return having felt lonely and with a feeling that they missed sharing experiences with companions.

Travelling with others has its difficulties. In everyday life it is unusual to spend all day, every day, with another person. The stresses of such intense closeness are compounded by the other tensions of travelling. Even the happiest relationships are put under pressure, and less secure partnerships can be destroyed. For some, the answer is to go away with a group of friends, but this can make things more difficult: there is a continual need for compromise. The larger the group, the more likely that someone will not be happy and that tension will develop.

For the more sociable, an organized group holiday can work well, but for others, the idea of being with comparative strangers all day is unbearable. Before setting off, couples need to consider that they may find themselves ostracized in a group of single people. Alternatively, there may be tension if one person fits in well and their partner is isolated.

Whether travelling alone or with others, do everything you can to reduce the inevitable stress of the trip. Money is a common source of worry and conflict. It is easy to underestimate how much you will need, and it is vital to keep some in reserve for emergencies and unforeseen expenses. Agree beforehand how much you can afford to spend, but be prepared to spend more! Check all your travel arrangements, take out insurance, and ensure that you have the right luggage and clothes. Nevertheless, even the best made plans go astray. Try to expect disruptions, delays, and changes to your arrangements. Predict that your plane will be delayed—and be delighted and surprised if it arrives on time.

The days leading up to holidays are usually particularly busy. Packing and last-minute arrangements have to be fitted around work and domestic responsibilities, and you can end up departing in an exhausted and irritable state. Jet lag can exacerbate the situation (see Chapter 7.2). The first few days of any trip are usually the most stressful—recognize this and do not plan to do too much too soon.

Box 9.8.1 **Reduce stress on holiday**

- Pick your companions carefully
- Recognize when you are tired
- Have realistic expectations
- Stay healthy
- Have enough money and insurance
- Expect delays, frustrations and changes
- Keep your sense of humour.

Trips lasting more than a month require particular strategies. After a while, the lack of structure can become unsettling, especially in unfamiliar environments. Travelling every day soon becomes exhausting, so try to stay in one place for a few days each week. If possible, establish a daily routine. It can be helpful to keep a diary—this allows a period of peaceful reflection, as well as a chance to ventilate any frustrations. The longer you are away, the more important it becomes to have contact with friends and family at home; make use of email and social network sites to stay in touch. Arrange to have post sent to you and, if possible, speak on the telephone or via the Internet. Reading newspapers from home can help to tackle any feelings of homesickness.

Travelling for work can be seen as a glamorous perk, but for those who have to do it on a regular basis it quickly loses its charm. All the stresses of travelling are compounded by having to spend time with work colleagues, with whom you may have little in common. It can also have a profound and damaging effect on family life. Think very carefully before accepting a job entailing extensive travelling. If you have to do it, negotiate time off after trips to relax at home.

Mental health disorders

Mental ill health is common: it is often said that one in four people will suffer from a specific psychiatric disorder during their lives, but it is also true that no one goes through life without some form of mental health problem. Whatever the nature of the problem, it may become apparent for the first time on holiday.

Panic attacks

These can occur spontaneously but will usually be precipitated by a feared situation, such as being in an enclosed space. The sufferer will rapidly develop a sense of extreme fear, and may believe that he or she is about to die. This fear will be accompanied by a number of physical symptoms, including dizziness, chest pain, breathlessness, and tingling in the extremities. Associated hyperventilation (over breathing) can exacerbate the physical symptoms, which in turn will convince the sufferer that he or she has a possibly fatal condition. Alarmed bystanders, who do not understand what is happening, will increase the person's anxiety through their own panic.

The immediate treatment for a panic attack is calm reassurance, and encouragement to breathe in and out of a paper bag held over the mouth and nose. After the initial attack, further episodes are likely, but they are usually less severe. In the longer term, medication and specific psychological therapies are sometimes required to reduce the frequency and severity of panic attacks.

Depression

It is not uncommon to feel rather miserable or sad, at times, on any holiday, especially if things have not worked out as hoped. Occasionally such feelings can develop into clinical depression. Serious depression can also spontaneously occur. It can be exacerbated by excessive use of alcohol or illicit drugs. The affected person will have a persistent low mood, and may appear distant or irritable. The first visible sign to others that someone might be depressed is that they struggle to complete straightforward tasks. Other characteristic features are:

• Loss of appetite
• Reduced energy and interest
• Poor concentration
• Disturbed sleep—usually early morning waking
• Frequent tearful episodes
• Preoccupation with worry and guilt
• Thoughts of suicide.

The most important thing to try to do when helping someone with depression is to encourage them to talk. Just knowing that others understand how they feel can be a great comfort to someone with depression. Severe depression must be taken seriously, especially if suicidal thoughts are present. Specialist help should be sought without delay. Anti-depressant treatment is usually effective, but will take at least 2 weeks to work; it is therefore sensible for the person to return home.

Acute psychotic states

These are rare, but extremely alarming for all concerned. Psychosis can start insidiously or suddenly. Symptoms vary, but are usually associated with a loss of reality and strange frightening thoughts. People with psychosis will often be preoccupied with persecutory ideas, feel that they cannot fully control their thoughts, and have auditory and visual hallucinations. They may be disorientated in time, place, and person. Their behaviour is often bizarre and inexplicable, and may include a change in previously regular activities such as washing or sleeping.

Such experiences may be the beginnings of a serious mental illness such as schizophrenia, but this is unlikely. It is far more likely that the cause is illicit drugs and that the effects will quickly wear off. Other causes of such states include severe heatstroke, malaria, and head injuries. In the case of head injuries, the onset maybe delayed for many hours, and should be treated as a medical emergency. Prescribed medication can also be the cause for a number of psychiatric symptoms. In particular, the anti-malarial drug mefloquine (Lariam) can cause a range of psychiatric symptoms, including psychosis, in as many as 1% of people who take it, and it should not be used by those who have a history of psychological problems.

The treatment of psychosis requires the use of antipsychotic drugs and should be undertaken by experienced medical practitioners. If this is not possible, short-term treatment with benzodiazepine drugs, such as diazepam, may bring about some relief and should, at least, not make things worse.

Post-traumatic stress disorder (PTSD)

When travelling you may experience and/or witness a traumatic incident, such as a serious road traffic accident or a personal attack. The psychological impact of such an experience can be profound, and may result in the development of PTSD, especially if the trauma is exceptionally threatening and physically close. Having an early opportunity to talk to someone about what has happened may help, but will not necessarily prevent the subsequent development of PTSD. If you feel more comfortable about trying to forget about what you have seen and do not want to talk about it, then that is right for you, and you should not be pressurized to accept counselling or any other form of talking therapy, unless and until you feel that it would be helpful.

PTSD may take weeks or months to develop. The symptoms include re-living of the experience in the form of nightmares, intrusive thoughts, and/or sudden flashbacks. These can be associated with a desire to avoid reminders of what happened, e.g. avoiding friends who were there at the time, and various emotional responses including irritability and emotional numbness. A general sense of nervousness and hyper-arousal are also common. PTSD will often improve with time, but if severe, then professional help should be obtained.

Drug and alcohol misuse

Traveling may expose you to increased temptations to use various street drugs. The obvious advice is—don't. The risks are going to be greater than if you are at home. You will be easy prey for law enforcement agencies who may be under pressure to demonstrate their effectiveness against drugs users and be keen to demonstrate that they show no favors to foreigners. The physical and medical risks are also far greater, due to uncertainty about the strength and precise nature of what you are being offered, the potential lack of sterile equipment and limited medical treatment for accidental overdoses or withdrawal symptoms.

Equally, you should avoid any temptation to drink more than a modest amount of alcohol. Getting drunk will increase your risk of an accident and make it more likely that you become the victim of crime.

Travelling with a psychiatric disorder

Having a stable, long-standing psychiatric disorder should not stop you going abroad, but there are some sensible precautions to take. Following a serious mental breakdown, which has required hospital admission, in most circumstances you should not travel abroad for at least 6 months. If in doubt, seek advice from a psychiatrist.

Certain psychiatric drugs may be affected by travel. For instance, some anti-psychotic drugs (especially chlorpromazine and trifluperazine) can increase susceptibility to sunburn (Chapter 8.5). Lithium levels can be increased by hot weather and inadequate fluid intake. Some drugs that can be bought over the counter abroad may interfere with your regular medication. If you are on any psychiatric medication it is important that you discuss your travel plans with a psychiatrist, and take adequate supplies of medication in well-labelled bottles (Chapter 13.5).

Coming home

Returning home is usually associated with a mixture of emotions—sadness that the holiday is over, but pleasure at seeing friends and family again. Your keenness to talk about your experiences is often met with a disappointing lack of enthusiasm from others. The best policy is to start thinking about your next trip!

9.9 Fever and undifferentiated febrile illnesses

Mark Bailey

Although definitions vary slightly, most doctors would consider an oral temperature of >38°C to be a significant fever. Temperatures of 37.5–38°C may be described as 'low-grade' fever and those >39°C may be described as 'very high'.

Historically, most infectious diseases were just called fevers unless they had obvious symptoms relating to a particular organ system, such as the respiratory or gastrointestinal tracts. With increasing medical knowledge, most infections can now be identified from their specific clinical features, and then confirmed with microbiology tests. However, there remains a group of diseases that cause 'undifferentiated febrile illnesses' because they produce fever with non-specific clinical features only. Unfortunately, the microbiology tests needed to confirm these infections are not widely available and this adds to the problems of diagnosing and treating them. The micro-organisms that cause undifferentiated febrile illnesses are most prevalent in the tropics, sub-tropics and developing countries and have been a problem for travellers ever since the time of the Crusades!

If an undifferentiated febrile illness continues for over 3 weeks and cannot be diagnosed after 1 week of hospital investigations then it is called a 'fever (or pyrexia) of unknown origin'. However, this is of little comfort to the unwell traveller, who would like to be treated as soon as possible.

Malaria

The most important possible cause of an undifferentiated febrile illness in travellers is malaria, which can be either falciparum (life-threatening) or benign (due to one of four other species) (Chapter 5.1). Initial symptoms include fever, hot/cold sweats with rigors (shivering and shaking), headache, and muscle pains. However, these features are not specific to malaria and can occur in more than 20 other infections that also present with an undifferentiated febrile illness. Gastrointestinal symptoms are quite common and can be misleading. Falciparum malaria may progress to septic shock (fever with low blood pressure) and life-threatening complications affecting the lungs, kidneys, brain, and blood-clotting system. Even at a late stage the diagnosis is not certain unless microbiology tests are performed and yet early treatment is needed to prevent complications.

Every person who develops a fever during or within a year of travel to an area affected by malaria should therefore have blood tests to look for this disease. The necessary tests usually consist of either blood films (widely available, but open to human error) or malaria antigen tests (less widely available, but less open to human error). If these tests are not available or if the results are uncertain, then there is still a role for empirical (presumptive) treatment of malaria as described in Section 5.4.1 of the British National Formulary (BNF) at ℘ www.bnf.org (see also Chapter 5.1). If complications have occurred, then intensive-care treatment may also be required. The prevention of malaria relies on drugs (pp.112–5) and bite-prevention measures (Chapter 5.12). Detailed and up-to-date malaria maps can be found at: ℘ www.fitfortravel.nhs.uk

Arbovirus infections and viral haemorrhagic fevers

Dengue fever is another common mosquito-transmitted disease that presents with an undifferentiated febrile illness and is one of many known arboviruses (arthropod-borne viruses) (Chapter 5.2). Dengue classically produces fever, joint pains, and a widespread rash that consists of almost-confluent, inflamed blotches in the skin. However, other non-specific features (e.g. headache) usually occur and the rash is often absent. If a person catches dengue fever on a second or subsequent occasion, then they are at risk of bleeding complications and life-threatening fluid loss. Although no anti-viral treatment is available, treatment to relieve the symptoms and correct any fluid loss is extremely valuable.

Other arboviruses can produce similar symptoms (e.g. chikungunya), haemorrhage (e.g. yellow fever) or brain infections (e.g. Japanese encephalitis). Some other haemorrhagic viruses that are not associated with arthropods (e.g. Lassa fever) can also be life-threatening and highly infectious from person to person (Chapter 4.10). These viral infections are less common than dengue fever and may be endemic in small areas or else occur as epidemics.

Very few of these diseases have specific anti-viral treatments or vaccines available, so it is essential that bite-prevention measures (Chapter 5.12) be used in areas where they occur. Travellers should always seek up-to-date pre-travel health information; an indication of the risk areas can also be found from websites such as ✆ www.nathnac.org

Other insect-borne infections

Visceral leishmaniasis (kala-azar), African trypanosomiasis (sleeping sickness) and American trypanosomiasis (Chagas disease) are caused by protozoa that are transmitted by insect bites and occur in small foci across Asia, Africa and Latin America. Visceral leishmaniasis has a gradual onset over weeks to months and eventually produces marked enlargement of the liver and spleen and low blood counts (Chapter 5.5). African trypanosomiasis also has a gradual onset over weeks to years. It may produce a local infection (chancre) and lymph node swelling at the bite site before it infects the brain and causes a gradual reduction in conscious level over months to years (Chapter 5.6). American trypanosomiasis may also cause a local infection (chagoma) and lymph node swelling at the bite site before causing heart and gastrointestinal complications over months to years (Chapter 5.7).

Since these infections are caused by protozoa, rather than bacteria or viruses, they require specialized diagnostic tests and quite toxic drug treatments that are not widely available. No preventive drugs or vaccines are available for these diseases and so bite-prevention measures are essential in affected areas (Chapter 5.12).

Tick- and louse-borne infections

Bites from ticks and lice are more easily identified because the culprit is often discovered! These bites can transmit a variety of infections, including typhus, spotted fevers, and relapsing fevers that present with undifferentiated febrile illnesses. (Lyme disease is also transmitted by ticks, but this normally produces a characteristic rash around the bite; see Chapter 5.4) Reliable microbiology tests for these infections are rarely available, but fortunately all will respond to treatment with doxycycline (or equivalent antibiotics in children). No vaccines are available, but doxycycline prophylaxis for malaria (Chapter 5.1) may be protective and bite-prevention measures are also important (Chapter 5.12).

Ingested diseases

Infections that are ingested, but then spread to other parts of the body can cause undifferentiated febrile illnesses. Examples include enteric fever (typhoid or paratyphoid) (Chapter 2.1), viral hepatitis (types A & E) (Chapter 2.4) and amoebic liver abscess. Enteric fever can be confirmed by blood cultures and is best treated with azithromycin or an intravenous cephalosporin (e.g. ceftriaxone). Viral hepatitis A and E may be severe illnesses, but are usually self-limiting and no anti-viral treatment is available. Amoebic liver abscess (Chapter 2.2) is best diagnosed with microbiology tests and an ultrasound scan and is usually treated with metronidazole and diloxanide.

Infections from bodily fluids

Infections that are transmitted in bodily fluids from contaminated injections or intimate personal contact may also produce undifferentiated febrile illnesses. Examples include viral hepatitis (types B & C), HIV (causing AIDS) and common viruses such as EBV (causing glandular fever) and CMV. Viral hepatitis B is preventable by vaccination and possible HIV exposure may justify the use of post-exposure prophylaxis with anti-viral drugs (Chapter 10.2). Chronic infection with hepatitis B or C or HIV will require anti-viral treatment in due course.

Inhaled infections

Infections that are inhaled, but then spread to other parts of the body can cause undifferentiated febrile illnesses with relatively minor respiratory features. Examples include mycoplasma, Legionnaire's disease (Chapter 4.6), Q fever and occasionally influenza (Chapter 4.12), which all cause 'atypical pneumonia'. The bacteria responsible are usually treated with clarithromycin or doxycycline, whereas the viruses are usually not treated (though flu is treatable with oseltamivir—Tamiflu). One other 'inhaled' organism is the meningococcus bacterium that causes meningitis, and also meningococcal septicaemia without meningitis. The pink/red spots that appear in the skin and are not blanched with pressure from a glass container, are the characteristic feature of this infection. Urgent treatment with an intravenous penicillin or cephalosporin is required (Chapter 4.5).

Freshwater contact

Infections that are transmitted through contact with freshwater (usually immersion) also produce undifferentiated febrile illnesses. Leptospirosis (Weil's disease) occurs worldwide and the bacteria responsible are excreted by various animals. The disease presents with fever and non-specific symptoms and may progress to liver, kidney, and multi-organ failure. However, treatment with any of several antibiotics is effective if started early enough (Chapter 4.11).

Schistosomiasis (bilharzia) occurs in the tropics and the worms (flukes) responsible are excreted by humans. The disease presents with 'swimmer's itch' initially, and then several weeks later as acute schistosomiasis (Katayama fever), which causes fever and allergic symptoms affecting the skin and lungs. Treatment with praziquantel and steroids may be given at this stage, but praziquantel needs to be given again 4 weeks later to ensure a complete cure (Chapter 4.4).

Sex and contraception abroad

10.1 Sexually-transmitted infections

Jerker Liljestrand and Ping Chutema

Travellers are at increased risk of acquiring sexually-transmitted infections (STIs). They should know how to reduce the risks if they do not intend to avoid them.

When Christopher Columbus returned from his voyage of discovery to the New World, an epidemic of syphilis swept Europe. Ever since, historians have debated whether or not Columbus and his sailors were to blame. One thing that *is* certain, however, is that today's traveller is at as great a risk as ever of acquiring a sexually-transmitted infection.

STI has reached epidemic proportions in many countries and is a major problem worldwide, encompassing a wide range of infections. STIs are nearly as common as malaria: there are more than 250 million new cases each year. Chlamydia has become twice as common as gonorrhoea and syphilis, but is often harder to detect. Antibiotic resistance is a major problem. Herpes, once the subject of much public interest, has been eclipsed by the risk of human immunodeficiency virus (HIV). Although HIV infection may be transmitted in other ways (discussed in the next chapter), it is still above all else an STI.

As far as the traveller is concerned, however, the public health aspects of STIs are less important than their immediate implications.

Risk factors

All STI risk factors depend on individual behaviour. The only absolute ways of avoiding STI are abstinence, or sexual intercourse with a partner who is known to be disease-free and is completely faithful. Any other type of behaviour places you at risk of infection.

Travel

People behave differently when they travel. In one study, 1 in 10 British travellers reported having sex with a new partner whilst abroad; only 75% used condoms on all occasions. Sex is sometimes the sole purpose of travel, as evidenced by the continuing growth of the 'sex tourism' industry. The usual norms of the home environment no longer control behaviour.

Number of partners

The more sexual partners a person has, the greater the risk of acquiring an STI. Prostitutes in some Asian and African cities have infection rates reaching 100%. Even with only one single contact there is a high risk of contracting an STI.

Frequency of sexual contact
The greater the frequency of sexual contact, the greater the risk of acquiring an STI. For example, men have a 20–35% chance of acquiring gonorrhoea from each contact with an infected partner. Two exposures would obviously increase the risk.

Age
The highest incidence of STI is found in the 15–30-year-old age group. The incidence declines as age increases.

Choice of partner
Certain groups are at higher risk, including intravenous drug users, homo-sexuals, prostitutes, young people with multiple sex partners, people who work at entertainment places (bars, karaoke bars, massage par-lours), and bisexual men; special categories of high-risk groups for HIV infection include people who have received multiple blood transfusions, or anyone who has had regular sexual intercourse with individuals in the above categories.

Blood products
Blood transfusion carries a risk of HIV, hepatitis B and C, syphilis, and malaria. Developed countries have instituted screening measures to reduce the risk, but developing countries lag behind. Avoid unnecessary blood transfusions and injections, unless the blood has been adequately screened and the equipment is known to be sterile (see Chapter 13.6).

Tattoos
Unsterile tattooing instruments can put travellers at risk of HIV and other STIs.

Medical care
In addition to an increased risk of acquiring an STI, travellers face difficul-ties on seeking medical care. They may be going to an area with unso-phisticated facilities. The medical professionals may not be well trained, the laboratory back-up services may be non-existent and the instruments may not be properly sterilized. Language barriers may pose an obstacle to communication.

Diseases
Some of the most important STIs are considered in Table 10.1.1.

Bacteria, viruses, protozoa, and arthropods may all be transmitted sex-ually. Sexual intercourse is the usual mode, but any close contact that allows transfer of infected materials or secretions may transmit disease. The disease can establish itself wherever it finds a suitable environment—warm, moist, dark areas, lined with a mucous membrane, such as the geni-talia, the mouth, and rectum.

The spectrum of STI infection is immense and there is no limit to the number with which one may be afflicted at any one time. For most dis-eases, immunity is not possible, so re-infection is likely unless continuing precautions are taken.

The impact of infection is wide ranging. Crab lice are merely a nui-sance. Herpes may recur and be particularly troublesome. Human papil-loma virus (HPV) infection, however, is linked to cancer of the cervix, and of the head and neck (a vaccine is available—p.451). Gonorrhoea and chlamydia can cause infertility and painful, incapacitating pelvic infection. Syphilis can lead to insanity and damage to the nervous system, heart, and major blood vessels. Infected women can pass this infection on to their babies, causing congenital disease. HIV kills or becomes a chronic, debilitating disease, and is a hazard that every sexually active male or female traveller must take seriously.

Geographical distribution

While some places have a higher incidence of STI than others, risk depends primarily on *behaviour*, not *geography*.

STIs are a major public health problem everywhere, but rates are higher where treatment is less accessible. In developing countries, rates of syphilis may be 10–100 times higher, gonorrhoea 10–15 times higher. In large African cities, gonorrhoea may infect as many as 1 in 10 people. Whereas, in the USA, about 3 in 1000 are infected. STIs appear to be more common in Eastern, Central, and Southern Africa than in Asia or Latin America. It is recognized that the practice of parallel ('concomitant') sexual contacts contributes to these high frequencies in parts of Africa.

HIV infection has been reported from almost every country, with the highest incidence in Southern and Central Africa. In the UK and USA, it has been mainly a disease of homosexual and bisexual men, but the rate of heterosexual transmission is rising. In 2009, in the UK, 54% of all new cases were acquired heterosexually, with 68% of these acquired from sexual contact abroad, mostly in southern Africa.

Hepatitis B is spread by the same route, occurs all over the world, and is more easily transmitted. Hepatitis C is also transmissible by intimate contact.

Lymphogranuloma venereum (LGV) and granuloma inguinale (GI) are mainly diseases of the tropics and subtropics.

Most other STIs occur worldwide. Gonorrhoea and syphilis in particular are found more often in urban settings, seaports and trading centres; the young (15–35 years) are most often infected; males outnumber females.

Prevention

Public health measures

STD prevention/control relies on:
• *Education* about risk reduction
• *Detection* of people with no symptoms, or those who would not otherwise seek treatment
• Effective diagnosis and *treatment* of infected people
• Evaluation, treatment, and *counselling of sex partners*.

Personal protection

The only sure way to avoid STI is to avoid sexual contact altogether, or have a mutually faithful relationship with one partner known to be disease-free. Anyone not willing or able to do either, should minimize the risks and maximize protection.

Understand the risk factors, and avoid sexual contact with individuals at highest risk. If a partner is infected or their infection status is unknown, use a new latex condom with each act of intercourse. When a male condom cannot be used, consider using a female condom.

Table 10.1.1 Sexually-transmitted diseases

Disease	Causal agent	Occurrence	Incubation	Likely symptoms	Complications
Gonorrhoea	Neisseria gonorrhoeae	Worldwide (250 million people affected at any one time)	2–7 days	Male: burning on urination, penile discharge Female: vaginal discharge, burning on urination, abnormal bleeding	Male: prostatitis, urethral stricture, arthritis, infertility Female: Infertility, arthritis, pelvic abscess Newborn: conjunctivitis
Chlamydia	Chlamydia trachomatis	Worldwide	5–7 days	Same as gonorrhea, but for females, only 30% have symptoms	Same as for gonorrhoea
Syphilis	Treponema pallidum	Worldwide (50 million cases each year)	10 days–10 weeks	Early stage: painless ulcer Early latency: no symptom Late stage: rash, cardiovascular or neurological symptoms	Occur late: cardiovascular problems or mental charges Pregnancy: spontaneous abortion, intrauterine death, premature delivery Newborn: congenital syphilis
Chancroid	Haemophilus ducreyi	Subtropical and tropical	3–14 days	Painful necrotizing ulcers, painful swelling of lymph nodes	Localized
Lymphogranuloma venereum	Chlamydia trachomatis	Subtropical and tropical	3–30 days	Small painless ulcer	Stricture of rectum, genital elephantiasis

Table 10.1.1 (Contd.)

Disease	Causal agent	Occurrence	Incubation	Likely symptoms	Complications
Herpes	Herpes simplex virus	Worldwide	2–12 days	Painful multiple shallow ulcers	Recurrence
Trichomoniasis	Trichomonas vaginalis (a protozoan)	Worldwide	4–20 days	Vaginal discharge and irritation	Local only
Non-specific vaginitis	Gardnerella vaginalis	Worldwide	7 days	Odoriferous vaginal discharge	Local only
Anogenital warts	Human papilloma virus (HPV)	Worldwide	1–20 months	Cauliflower-like growths	Localized; HPV also causes cancer of the cervix
Scabies	Sarcoptes scabiei (a mite)	Worldwide	2–6 weeks	Itching; skin eruptions	Local infection
Pubic lice	Phthirus pubis (the crab louse)	Worldwide	1–2 weeks	Itching	Local infection
Intestinal infections	Campylobacter jejuni, Shigella spp. non-typhoidal salmonella, Entamoeba histolytica (amoebic dysentery), Giardia lamblia (giardiasis)	Worldwide in those who practice anal-oral sex, as well as by non-venereal transmission	Varies	Diarrhoea, jaundice, etc.	Depend on disease
AIDS	HIV	Worldwide	2 weeks–12 years (or more)	Fever, weight loss, etc.	Opportunistic infection, death
Hepatitis B	Hepatitis B virus	Worldwide	2–6 months	Jaundice	Carrier state: chronic liver disease

The ABC of safe sex

"'A' is for abstinence. If you can't abstain, 'B' faithful. If you can't be faithful, use 'C' for condoms."

Juan Flavier, former Health Secretary, Philippines

When choosing a partner, bear in mind that many people are prepared to lie in order to have sex; one survey of young, sexually-active Californians showed that 47% of the men and 60% of the women claimed that they had been lied to for the purposes of sex; 34% of the men and 10% of the women admitted that they themselves would also lie; 20% of the men said that they would lie about having a negative HIV-antibody test; and nearly half of both men and women said that they would understate their number of previous partners. Patients with a wide variety of infections, including HIV infection, often look and feel healthy. It is important, therefore, to try to find out about their sexual history.

Safer sex

STIs are transmitted by body fluids, such as blood, semen, vaginal secretions, urine, breastmilk, and saliva. Examples of safer sex are mutual or simultaneous masturbation, and consistent and correct condom use from start to finish of sexual contact (vaginal, anal, or oral). This approach should be the rule in all casual encounters.

Contraceptive measures

Male condom

When used correctly, condoms are the only contraceptive method that is effective in preventing HIV and pregnancy, but they are not 100% effective in preventing certain STIs. Condom failure usually results from incorrect use rather than breakage. It is important for condoms to be used correctly:

- Examine the condom to make sure it is in good condition (leakage, dryness, expired)
- Use a new condom with each act of intercourse
- Carefully handle the condom to avoid damaging it with fingernails, teeth or other sharp objects
- Put the condom on after the penis is erect and before any genital contact with the partner
- Ensure that no air is trapped in the tip of the condom
- Ensure that there is adequate lubrication during intercourse
- Use only water-based lubricants (e.g. K-Y Jelly or glycerine) with latex condoms. Oil-based lubricants (e.g. petroleum jelly, mineral oil, massage oils, body lotions) that can weaken latex should never be used
- Hold the condom firmly against the base of the penis during withdrawal, and withdraw while the penis is still erect to prevent slippage
- Spermicides do not prevent HIV transmission. However, good lubrication can help avoid micro-erosions during intercourse. Therefore, latex condoms with or without spermicides are recommended.

Female condoms
Laboratory studies indicate the female condom to be an effective mechanical barrier to viruses, including HIV.

Vaginal spermicides, sponges, and diaphragms
Vaginal spermicides used without condoms may reduce the risk for cervical gonorrhoea and chlamydia, but give no protection against HIV. The vaginal contraceptive sponge protects against cervical gonorrhoea and chlamydia, but increases the risk of candidiasis. Diaphragm use protects against cervical gonorrhoea, chlamydia, and trichomoniasis.

Non-barrier contraception, surgical sterilization, hysterectomy
Women using oral Pills, Norplant, Depo Provera, other hormonal injections, or who have had hysterectomies are not protected from STI/HIV infection.

Intrauterine contraceptive device (IUCD)
The IUCD does not protect against STI/HIV. *Vasectomy* does *not* protect against STI/HIV.

Other time-honoured methods of STI prevention include washing the genital area and urinating immediately after intercourse. These may appear to be sensible measures, but they have no scientific basis. Avoiding transfer of body fluids is safer.

In case of infection

If you think you might have caught an STI, seek examination by a fully qualified medical practitioner. Early prompt treatment is essential to avoid complications. Incorrect treatment may mask symptoms and allow infection to advance. Some diseases, such as syphilis, disappear for long periods after the initial symptoms, as if cured, only to reappear again in a more serious form at a later date. There is no effective cure for HIV infection, but rapid 'post exposure' treatment is effective (p.360).

Obtaining correct diagnosis and treatment is more difficult during travel. Some STIs take weeks to appear, by which time the traveller may be in a new country where the disease is unfamiliar. Always tell the physician exactly when and where exposure took place. To prevent possible complications due to delay, many physicians now manage STI cases with 'syndromic treatment', as recommended by the WHO. This means that treatment is based on symptoms and history, and therefore on probability, rather than on laboratory tests.

Try to locate the best possible medical facilities. In areas where STIs are common, STI clinics can be found. You should not be reluctant to attend a clinic: we all think it will never happen to us, but it can. Remember—many STI cases are asymptomatic. Your suspicion is sufficient reason to attend a clinic.

Diagnosis

Some diagnoses can be made on simple inspection, some require microscopes and cultures, and some a serological examination (blood test). The more reliably a diagnosis can be documented, the greater the likelihood that treatment will be effective. It is very important to give complete information. Keep detailed records of any symptoms you have had, any diagnoses that have been made, any laboratory examinations done, and all treatment. This may be valuable to your physician upon your return home, should you fail to get better. We also recommend taking an HIV test if you are diagnosed as having an STI.

Dangers of self-diagnosis and treatment

We would discourage you from attempting either self-diagnosis or self-treatment. Some sort of medical advice should always be possible. Drugs are available in some countries without prescription, but you may do yourself much harm because:

- No one drug will treat all sexually-transmitted infections, and using the wrong drug may not cure the infection or may *incompletely* cure it
- You may expose yourself to undesirable side effects without obtaining any benefits
- There is an on-going problem of *resistance* to antibiotics and other drugs
- You may give yourself a false sense of security that your disease has been cured when, in fact, it has subsided, only to reappear at a future time
- STI needs to be treated in both partners. If only you are treated, and your partner is infected, infection can be transmitted back and forth.

Prophylactic treatment

For similar reasons, you should avoid using antibiotics or other drugs to prevent infection. Prophylactic treatment should only be given to a traveller who has been raped (p.356).

Correct treatment

When prescribed a treatment, always complete the course, taking the correct amount for the correct time—incomplete treatment may not effect a cure and encourages drug resistance. Symptoms often subside 24–48 hours after starting treatment: resist the temptation to stop the treatment early, even if the medicine is making you feel lousy.

A summary of recommended treatment schedules is listed in Table 10.1.2. Space does not permit a listing of all effective treatment schedules. We have provided these *not* so that you can treat yourself, but rather to enable you to compare them with any treatment you are offered. If you are offered treatment that appears to be substantially different, request an explanation. HIV-infected individuals may require a different treatment schedule and should automatically seek expert medical advice.

Anyone given treatment for an STI should always return to a clinic for a follow-up examination, to confirm that treatment has been successful.

Sexual activity should be avoided during treatment, both to prevent further spread of disease and to avoid confusion: it is easier to distinguish recurrence from re-infection if one remains celibate during treatment.

Contacts

In some countries, it is a legal requirement for sexual contacts of individuals who have contracted an STI to be identified, traced and treated. This is the only way to stop the spread of disease. Even where it is not the law, mere concern for others should prompt anyone who is being treated for an STI to tell their contacts so that they, in turn, can seek medical advice. This may be embarrassing, but it is essential.

End of journey

We strongly advise travellers with any possibility of exposure to STI to take the precaution of seeking a physical and laboratory examination on their return home.

Travel, sex, and cancer

A British study has shown that wives of frequent travellers are at higher risk of contracting cervical cancer than any other women. A sexually-transmitted virus, HPV, is responsible, and having multiple partners is a major risk factor. The study did not show, however, if the high rate was caused by husbands who passed the virus to their wives on return home, or by the wives themselves taking advantage of their husbands' absence to find other partners.

What to do in an emergency

In the unusual situation of a traveller developing symptoms of STI in a remote place, where no medical advice can be obtained, but there is access to a supply of medicines, we advise the following approach—bearing in mind the warnings given in the text regarding self-treatment:

Penile discharge in males

The most likely causes of this are gonorrhoea and chlamydia. Previously, one drug could have treated both. Antibiotic resistance now makes this impossible. Some strains of gonorrhoea are resistant to tetracycline. If you can find cefixime you can take 400mg orally, in a single dose; or ceftriaxone, 125mg (IM) in a single dose; or ofloxacin, 400mg orally, in a single dose. To treat chlamydia, you should take doxycycline 100mg orally twice a day for 7 days, or erythromycin 500mg orally four times a day for 7 days, or azithromycin 1g orally once in addition to one of these drugs. Where available, a one-dose treatment with cefixime 400mg by mouth and azithromycin 1g by mouth would be optimal.

Even if treatment succeeds, we strongly recommend a check-up after your travels. You might have contracted syphilis at the same time and this treatment may not have eradicated it.

Vaginal discharge in (non-pregnant) females

Anything that changes a woman's hormonal balance, vaginal flora, or cervical secretions can change the ecology of the vagina, facilitating overgrowth by groups of microbes. Such imbalance can thus happen without sexual intercourse or STI, and if characterized by grey-white, bad-smelling (smell of fish) discharge is often called 'vaginosis'. For such a condition we would advise to treat with 2g metronidazole (Flagyl), orally, in a single dose to treat vaginal bacteria, and 500mg of clotrimazole or miconazole, inserted once into the vagina to treat mycosis. If this treatment fails, we would then give the same oral treatment to the male partner, for the same reason. If this also fails, then specialist medical advice must be sought, even if this means changing your travel plans.

Table 10.1.2 Recommended treatment schedules for various STIs

Disease	Recommended treatment	Dose/route (Tablets/capsules unless stated otherwise)	Alternative
Urethral/cervical infection			
Gonococcal infections	Cefixime (Suprax)	400mg, single dose	Azithromycin 1g, single dose
	OR		Spectinomycin 2g, single dose by i.m. injection
	Ciprofloxacin	500mg single dose	
	OR		
	Ofloxacin	400mg, single dose	
	OR		
	Ceftriaxone (Rocephin)	125mg, single dose by IM injection	
Chlamydial infections	Azithromycin (Zithromax)	1g, single dose	Erythromycin base 500mg, 4 times daily for 7 days
	OR		Erythromycin ethylsuccinate 500mg, 4 times daily for 7 days
	Doxycycline	100mg, twice daily for 7 days	(Erythromycin is 80% effective, but may need to be repeated)
			Ofloxacin 400mg, 2 times daily for 7 days
Epididymitis	Ceftriaxone (Rocephin)	250mg, single dose by IM injection	Ofloxacin 400mg, for 10 days
	+ Doxycycline	100mg, twice daily for 10 days	
Pelvic inflammatory disease	Ceftriaxone (Rocephin)	250mg, single dose by IM injection	
	+ Doxycycline	100mg, twice daily for 14 days	
	+ Metronidazole	500mg, twice daily for 14 days	
	OR		

Pelvic inflammatory disease (Contd.)	Cefoxitin	2mg, single dose by IM injection	
	+ Probenecid	1g, single dose	
	+ Doxycycline	100mg, twice daily for 14 days	Doxycycline 100mg, twice daily for 14 days
	OR		
	Ofloxacin	400mg, twice daily for 14 days	
	+ Doxycycline	100mg, twice daily for 14 days	
	+ Metronidazole (Flagyl)	500mg, twice daily for 14 days	
Infections with ulceration			
Syphilis	Benzathine penicillin G (Bicillin)	2.4 million units, single dose by IM injection	
Early disease			
Chancroid	Azithromycin (Zithromax)	1g, single dose	
	OR		
	Ceftriaxone	250mg, single dose by IM injection	
	OR		
	Ciprofloxacin	500mg, twice daily for 3 days	
Genital herpes simplex (HSV)	Acyclovir (Zovirax)	400mg, 3 times daily for 7–10 days	
First clinical episode of genital, anal, or oral HSV		200mg, 5 times daily for 5 days	
	OR		
	Famciclovir (Famvir)	250mg, 3 times daily for 7 days	
	OR		
	Valacyclovir (Valtrex)	1g, twice daily for 7–10 days	

(Continued)

Table 10.1.2 (Contd.)

Disease	Recommended treatment	Dose/route (Tablets/capsules unless stated otherwise)	Alternative
Genital herpes simplex (HSV) (Contd.)	Acyclovir	400mg, 3 times daily for 5 days OR 200mg, 5 times daily for 5 days OR 800mg, twice daily for 5 days	
Episodic recurrent infection			
	OR Famciclovir	125mg, twice daily for 5 days	
	OR Valacyclovir	500mg, twice daily for 5 days	
Vaginal infection			
Trichomoniasis	Metronidazole (Flagyl)	2g, single dose	Metronidazole 500mg, twice daily for 7 days
Bacterial vaginosis	Metronidazole (Flagyl)	500mg, twice daily for 7 days	Metronidazole 250mg, 3 times daily for 7 days
	OR Clindamycin cream 20%	One 5g application intravaginally, four times daily for 7 days	Metronidazole 2g, single dose
	OR Metronidazole gel 0.75%	One 5g application intravaginally, twice daily for 5 days	Clindamycin 300mg, twice daily for 7 days
Candidiasis	Fluconazole (Diflucan)	150mg, single dose	
	OR Butoconazole	2% cream, 5g intravaginally for 3 days	
	OR Clotrimazole	1% cream, 5g intravaginally for 7–14 days OR 100mg vaginal tablet, daily for 7 days	

Candidiasis (Contd.)	OR Miconazole (Monistat)	2% cream, 5g intravaginally for 7 days	
	OR Nystatin	500mg vaginal suppository, single dose 200mg vaginal suppository, daily for 3 days 100mg vaginal suppository, daily for 7 days 100 000 unit vaginal tablet, daily for 14 days	
Miscellaneous			
Human papilloma virus (HPV) *External genital warts and perianal warts*	Podophyllin resin 10–25%	Apply small amount, dry. Wash off in 1–4 hours. Repeat weekly as required.	Intralesional interferon Laser surgery
	OR Trichloracetic acid (TCA) OR Bichloracetic acid 80–90%	Apply to area, wash off after 10min.	
Pediculosis pubis *Pubic lice*	Permethrin 1% cream rinse	Apply to area, wash off after 10min.	
	OR Lindane 1% shampoo	Apply to area, wash off after 4min.	
	OR Pyrethrins with piperonyl butoxide	Apply to area, wash off after 10min.	
Scabies	Permethrin 5% cream (Elimite)	Apply to all areas of body from neck down. Wash off after 8–14 hours.	Lindane 1%, 1 oz of lotion or 30g of cream Apply thinly to body from the neck down. Wash off after 8 hours

Genital ulcers

Genital ulceration is another major manifestation of an STI. There are several diseases that can produce genital ulcers. A good treatment to start with would be tetracycline hydrochloride, 500mg orally, four times a day for 15 days or doxycycline 100mg twice daily for 14–21 days. This would treat syphilis and lymphogranuloma venereum. To treat chancroid, you should take erythromycin 500mg, orally, four times a day for 7 days or ciprofloxacin 500mg twice a day for 3 days. These treatment schedules should give you enough time to find medical assistance.

Finally, we would caution you once again to seek medical assistance if at all possible, and not to attempt treat yourself unless there is no alternative. These treatments may not be suitable in your particular case, and tetracycline is unsuitable for use in pregnant women.

Sexual assault

The most commonly diagnosed STIs following sexual assault on women are trichomoniasis, chlamydia, gonorrhoea, and bacterial vaginosis.

If possible, a physical examination, gonorrhoea/chlamydia cultures, microscopic examination of vaginal discharge and blood samples should be obtained. A follow-up examination for STIs should be repeated after 2 weeks, and serological tests for syphilis and HIV infection should be performed after 12 weeks.

Most victims will benefit from prophylaxis because follow-up may be difficult and treatment provides reassurance. Prophylactic measures should include:

- Hepatitis B vaccination (if the woman is Hepatitis B antigen negative and not vaccinated)
- Antibiotics, including ceftriaxone, 125mg IM, in a single dose; metronidazole, 2g orally, in a single dose; and doxycycline, 100mg orally, two times a day for 14 days. This treatment should deal with chlamydia, gonorrhoea, trichomoniasis, and syphilis
- HIV post-exposure prophylaxis (PEP) may need to be considered (see Chapter 10.2), though the risk in most instances is minimal. The overall rate of HIV transmission from an HIV-infected person during a single act of heterosexual intercourse is considered to be low (less than 1%), but the risk depends on many factors, such as the degree of HIV spread in the country where the assault took place.

Conclusion

Scare tactics have never yet been successful in campaigns to stop any epidemic. The best protection against STIs is education and a common-sense approach to prevention, combined with prompt treatment of both partners if treatable disease occurs.

Risks for STI and HIV infection are determined by what you do. If you are not monogamous or abstinent, you must use condoms regardless of your sexual orientation. Both male and female travellers should carry condoms with them and use them every time they have sex.

10.2 Human immunodeficiency virus

Andrew Freedman and Owen Seddon

This chapter aims to explain some of the biology behind HIV, give a global picture of HIV infection worldwide, and provide specific advice for travellers seeking to minimize their risk of contracting the virus.

The immune system is the body's defence mechanism against disease and infection. Key to this are the body's white blood cells, of which one type, the CD4+ T Helper Cell (abbreviated to CD4) is responsible for recognizing foreign microbes when infection occurs. Infection with the HIV virus results in destruction of these cells. Although initially the body is able to counterbalance this destruction by producing replacement cells, over several years the level of CD4 cells in the blood (CD4 count) progressively falls in untreated HIV, until the pool of cells is too small to fight new infections. This resulting state is termed immunodeficiency, and leaves the body vulnerable to infections that healthy (immunocompetent) individuals would normally eradicate. As they take advantage of this weakened state, such infections are termed 'opportunistic'.

There are many strains of HIV, all are transmitted in the same way and cause the same clinical syndrome. HIV currently has no cure, although many effective drugs are used in its treatment, which can lead to longer, healthier lives in infected individuals. Extensive research is ongoing into novel treatments, as well as effective vaccines and other ways of preventing infection.

HIV worldwide

Some 30 years on from its initial recognition, over 25 million deaths have been attributed to HIV, more than 33 million people are estimated by the WHO to be living with HIV infection, and 2.6 million new infections occur every year.

HIV is present on every continent, but the 19 countries with the highest rates of the disease are all in sub-Saharan Africa, making up 60% of the worldwide numbers infected. South Africa has the largest population of HIV positive individuals, with over 5 million. HIV has undergone a rapid increase in Eastern Europe and Asia, particularly southern Asia, where case reports show transmission both from prostitution and drug abuse. HIV is also spreading in India and China, with India having the second largest HIV positive population in the world. The problem in South America is also growing, with Brazil second only to the USA in the number of reported cases in the Americas (see Map 10.1).

Avoiding HIV entirely is therefore impossible in any travel, but avoiding high-risk behaviour has more impact on the risk of infection than geographical location.

How HIV is spread

HIV is present in infectious quantities in blood, breastmilk, and genital fluids, including ejaculate and pre-ejaculate. HIV infection is known to have occurred in people who:
- Have had heterosexual intercourse with an infected man or woman
- Have had homosexual intercourse with infected gay or bisexual men

GLOBAL REPORT
Adults and children estimated to be living with HIV | 2009

Total: 33.3 million [31.4 million–35.3 million]

Map 10.2.1 Global distribution of HIV (2009).

Redrawn with permission from UNAIDS/ONUSIDA 2009.

- Have used injectable or intravenous (IV) drugs and have shared needles, syringes, or injecting paraphernalia with an infected individual
- Have been treated for haemophilia (or certain other severe bleeding disorders) with contaminated blood products
- Have received transfusions of whole blood or its components (in countries where donations are not adequately screened)
- Are children born to, or breastfed by, mothers infected with HIV.

The most important behavioural risk factors for contracting HIV infection include having multiple sexual partners and needle sharing among drug abusers. In poor countries, re-use of needles, syringes or other blood-contaminated items presents a potential route of transmission; and safe alternatives to breast-feeding may not be available, contributing further to the local problem.

HIV levels in saliva are too low for transmission to occur unless wounds, e.g. mouth ulcers, mean that there is contamination with blood.

HIV is not transmitted via casual contact. Several studies of the families and communities of HIV patients, and of medical personnel involved in HIV patient care, show no virus transmission via household contact (including sharing kitchens, utensils, toilets, and baths), or other means, such as mosquito bites. Animals, food, water, air, the environment, schools, the workplace, public areas, or use of public transportation, coughing and sneezing, and swimming pools have not been associated with HIV transmission.

Natural history and symptoms

A person newly infected with HIV may suffer from a 'flu-like' illness that resolves without any treatment. The symptoms are non-specific and can include fevers, a rash, swollen lymph glands, sore throat, and mouth ulcers. Typically these symptoms arise 2–4 weeks following infection. This is termed a 'seroconversion' illness and represents the transient rise in viral levels in the blood, before infection is suppressed by the immune system. This results in the production of antibodies/antigens, molecules used by the immune system to recognize and defend against the HIV virus, which can then be detected in a HIV test. A window period exists between initial infection, and the test becoming positive, and may lead to negative test results in people newly infected with the virus, who will still be infectious.

Most patients are asymptomatic in the early years after acquiring HIV infection, but they remain highly infectious in the absence of treatment. Typically, this period lasts 8–10 years, but can be as short as a few months and rarely lasts 20 years or more. The term 'Acquired Immunodeficiency Syndrome' (AIDS) was first used to describe the clinical syndrome of opportunistic infection in severely immunosuppressed individuals, prior to detailed knowledge of its underlying cause (HIV). The terminology now more commonly used is advanced or late-stage HIV infection (see Figure 10.2.1).

Diagnosis

The HIV test is used to screen donors of organs, blood, plasma and other tissues for transfusion, transplantation or manufacture of clotting-factor concentrates for people with haemophilia, and for other blood products. It is used to diagnose HIV infection and to assist in prevention-oriented counselling of sexually active men and women at risk of HIV infection, women who are pregnant or contemplating pregnancy, IV drug abusers, and groups with other associated infections, including tuberculosis or viral hepatitis, who may have concurrent infection.

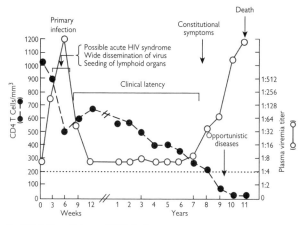

Fig. 10.2.1 Natural history of HIV infection.

Used with permission from G. Pantaleo, et al., Mechanisms of Disease: The Immunopathogenesis of Human Immunodeficiency Virus Infection, *The New England Journal of Medicine*, Volume 328, Number 5, p. 329, 2003, © New England Journal of Medicine.

Some countries require HIV antibody testing before granting certain classes of visas (usually longer-term immigrant, resident, work or student visas). The WHO does not endorse or approve of this practice, and travellers should check testing requirements of nations on their itinerary with appropriate consular authorities.

Treatment

As HIV belongs to a class of virus known as retroviruses, treatments are known as anti-retroviral drugs (ART). There are multiple different classes of drugs that can be used, and normally a combination of three or four different medications are prescribed together, which increases effectiveness and reduces the risk of HIV drug resistance.

Although trials to establish the optimal time to begin treatment in someone infected with HIV are continuing, consensus is that once started, anti-retroviral treatment should continue for the patient's lifetime, placing a heavy burden both on the patient and on healthcare services. Considerable effort has been made by the pharmaceutical industry to simplify drugs regimens into combination tablets, and many patients are able to take a single pill, once daily.

Post-exposure prophylaxis

This refers to treatment with anti-retroviral drugs immediately after actual or suspected exposure to HIV, and aims to prevent transmission of the virus. It can be of considerable practical importance for anyone exposed during travel.

PEP was first used in health care workers exposed to HIV in the course of their work, usually by 'needlestick' injury. The treatment involves taking a course of anti-retroviral drugs for 4 weeks, beginning within hours of sustaining a needlestick injury or other documented exposure to HIV. PEP is now also recommended for potential non-occupational (i.e. sexual or drug-injecting) HIV exposure.

The UK Department of Health offers specific PEP guidelines for occupational HIV exposure. The guidance covers healthcare workers on overseas secondment including medical students on electives. The detailed advice can be found at: http://www.dh.gov.uk/en/Publicationsandstatistics/Publications/PublicationsPolicyAndGuidance/DH_088185

Key points in the healthcare setting

The risk of acquiring HIV infection following occupational exposure to HIV-infected blood is low. The average risk for HIV transmission after exposure to HIV-infected blood, penetrating the skin, in healthcare settings is about 3 per 1000 injuries. Risk following exposure to mucous membranes, such as the mouth is less, and there is no risk of HIV transmission where intact skin is exposed to HIV-infected blood. Consideration must be given to other blood-borne infections that could be transmitted at the same time, particularly hepatitis B and C. The importance of infection control precautions in exposure-prone procedures is reinforced. These risks may be higher abroad.

PEP should be offered where significant exposure to blood or high-risk bodily fluid has occurred, and the patient is either known to be HIV positive or at high risk of being so. Testing of the source patient requires their consent and should be done promptly. Studies in animals show that PEP is most effective when given within an hour of exposure, before test results are available if necessary. It should be continued for four weeks, and expert advice should have been sought by this time for follow-up counselling, post-exposure testing and monitoring. PEP is normally not recommended if exposure has occurred more than 72 hr previously.

UK guidelines recommend a triple combination anti-retroviral approach. The same regimen is advised for use in 7-day PEP 'starter packs'—a short-term supply of anti-retroviral drugs suitable for use as PEP when access to other sources is not available, and dosage/details are available at the link on p.360.

In recent years, access to PEP abroad has improved considerably. When planning to work in a healthcare setting abroad or undertaking medical 'elective' placements in the developing world, most hospitals are likely to have PEP policies and access. Taking a starter pack of PEP is likely to be required only where this is not the case, or it has been impossible to determine prior to travel.

Box 10.2.1 **Travel advice for avoiding HIV infection**

- A mutually monogamous sexual relationship with a non-infected person is a safe way to avoid HIV infection
- Use of condoms is recommended for all other sexual relationships. Condoms reduce, but do not eliminate, risk of HIV transmission
- HIV infection is commoner in high-risk groups such as IV drug abusers, prostitutes, or sex-workers. Avoid sexual intercourse with them
- IV drug abuse carries a high risk of HIV infection as well as other health problems
- Having multiple sexual partners increases the risk of contracting HIV
- Travellers are normally at no special risk for HIV infection unless their sexual or drug-taking behaviour puts them in contact with people who might be infected with HIV
- When living or travelling in countries where re-use of medical equipment is common, ensure medical staff looking after you observe good infection control techniques, such as sterilizing needles, syringes and surgical equipment before re-use. Blood transfusion abroad is discussed in Chapter 13.6
- Unless you are certain that new or sterile equipment is being used, skin piercing, such as tattooing, ear piercing, acupuncture or electrolysis, should always be avoided
- Even in the developed world up to a quarter of HIV positive patients are unaware of their diagnosis; this group will be larger elsewhere
- PEP should be considered following potential exposure to HIV in healthcare settings
- Any returning traveller who thinks they may have been at risk of HIV exposure should request HIV testing, either through their GP or their local sexual health clinic.

It is important to consider HIV when planning an elective. It may be inadvisable to participate in high-risk activity, e.g. surgery or obstetrics, in high-prevalence areas. Electives should be avoided in areas where the risks to which you may be exposed—e.g. by poor facilities for protection against blood-borne viruses—outweigh the possible educational benefits. HIV infection rates will be much higher in hospitalized patients than in the general population, and in sub-Saharan Africa may approach 100%.

When starting PEP in areas where specialist advice is not available, telephone advice should be sought, and should include assessing the need for continuing PEP and possible repatriation for continuing medical care. Insurance to cover such costs should be considered before you go.

PEP following non-occupational exposure will only be available from a specialist centre. Factors affecting the use of non-occupational PEP include the probability of HIV infection in the source, the likelihood of transmission by the particular exposure and the interval between the exposure and presentation for PEP. It is most often used in the context of possible sexual exposure. Any concerns about the possibility of exposure to HIV whilst travelling abroad should prompt presentation to a local centre for advice.

10.3 Contraception and travel: be safe, be prepared

Elphis Christopher

Contraception is a neglected aspect of healthcare for travellers. Not all methods of contraception are equally problem-free in travellers: choose a suitable method carefully before departure.

Away from everyday stresses and routines, vacations and travel bring relaxation of inhibitions and are undoubtedly a time of increased sexual activity both for couples and for people travelling on their own.

Too many travellers leave home unprepared. Single women may be unwilling to anticipate a sexual adventure on the grounds that 'I am not that kind of girl'; they may find it difficult to believe that contraceptive precautions may be necessary in advance of a romantic attachment. Others, men and women, simply don't bother.

Avoiding an unwanted pregnancy is not merely a question of chance; travelling prepared must not be confused with promiscuity, and it is always better to be safe than sorry.

If you are sexually active and settled on a particular contraceptive method, all you may need to do is visit your own doctor or clinic for a check-up and obtain any contraceptive supplies you will need while away—and also to confirm that the method you are using is appropriate for the length and nature of your trip. For prolonged periods abroad, it is worth finding out what is available in the country or countries you intend to visit before you leave. Further information may be obtained from International Planned Parenthood Federation [IPPF], 4, Newhams Row London SE13UZ UK. Tel: +44 (0) 2079398200; info@ippf.org; ॐ http://www.ippf.org.

Travelling may reduce the effectiveness of contraceptive precautions that are otherwise perfectly adequate at home, and specific problems that arise for each method are discussed below. These may not warrant changing from your established method, but you should perhaps be prepared to switch to another method if necessary.

Get used to any new method well in advance of your trip, to enable any problems to reveal themselves in time to be sorted out. This is a particularly important consideration with the Pill—nausea and tiredness and slight spotting (breakthrough bleeding) are common when taking it for the first time, but usually settle by the third packet—and with the intrauterine device (IUD).

It may be advisable to travel with two methods to ensure against failure of one of them. Remember to use a condom with a new sexual relationship, regardless of what method is chosen, to prevent transmission of sexual infection.

The combined oral contraceptive: 'the Pill'

The Pill is convenient to use; with correct use its reliability is 99–100%. It works mainly by suppressing egg release (ovulation). If you are on the Pill be sure to travel with an adequate supply. Allow for delays and unexpected extensions of your trip—further supplies of your particular brand may not be easy to obtain.

If you run out, keep an empty pack so that a doctor or a pharmacist can identify your Pill—brand names for the same variety of Pill differ from country to country. If exactly the same Pill cannot be obtained and a different one is prescribed, do not leave a 7-day gap between packets, but go straight on to the new Pill regardless of any bleeding. Other contraceptive precautions will not then be necessary.

Stomach problems and diarrhoea affect most travellers at some time or another. Stomach problems and severe diarrhoea reduce absorption of the Pill and may leave the traveller without protection. All travellers on the Pill should be prepared to use an alternative method when necessary.

A barrier method (p.366) should be used to protect intercourse over the duration of the stomach problem and for 7 days after it has ended. If vomiting occurs within 3 hours of taking a pill, an additional pill should be taken. If vomiting continues, another method of contraception will have to be used.

Forgotten pills

The possibility of pregnancy when pills are missed depends on how many and where in the packet. Effectiveness is reduced if pills are missed at the beginning or end of the packet. If at the beginning or middle of the packet, you may need to consider emergency contraception if there has been unprotected sexual intercourse. Take the pill as soon as remembered and use a condom for seven days. If the pill is forgotten at the end of the packet go straight to the next packet. Do not leave a 7-day break.

Using the Pill with antibiotics, anti-malarials, and other medicines

Antibiotics such as tetracycline or ampicillin also reduce the absorption and effectiveness of the Pill, and another method of contraception should be used during a course of antibiotics and for seven days afterwards. Doxycycline, widely used as an anti-malarial, is a tetracycline and has the same effect. Anti-fungal medication, such as griseofulvin, and anti-epilepsy drugs may also reduce the effectiveness of the Pill. Additional precautions are needed when these are being taken.

In both instances, if the 7 days coincide with the seven pill-free days, do not take a break of 7 days, but carry straight on with another packet of pills. Do not worry if there is no withdrawal bleeding.

Using the Pill across time zones

Time zones cause another potential hazard to Pill users. When time zones are crossed, make sure that you take a pill every 24 hours, and continue to do so every day at the same time. If that means having to wake up in the middle of the night to take a pill, take it *earlier* before going to sleep, rather than later; no more than 24 hours should elapse between doses—particularly with newer varieties of the low-dose Pill—both for protection against pregnancy and to prevent breakthrough bleeding or spotting.

Flight attendants and others who are continually travelling may find it useful to have two wristwatches, and to keep one of them on 'home time' for this purpose.

Altitude

High altitude, dehydration, and extreme cold stress are all associated with changes in blood viscosity. Although, as yet, there is no clear evidence of an increased thrombosis risk among women taking the Pill at high altitude, it would seem wise not to do so (Chapter 8.3).

Long-haul air travel

Immobility increases the risk of thrombosis with or without the Pill. Wear compression stockings (Chapter 7.1), drink water not alcohol, and take exercise during the flight.

Using the Pill to avoid menstruation

Travel can interfere with periods even when a woman is on the Pill; so a missed period does not necessarily mean that she is pregnant (Chapter 9.7)—provided of course that the daily doses have been taken regularly. Women who prefer not to have periods at all while travelling can take the Pill continuously, without a seven-day break in between packets; but remember to take extra packets to allow for this. This is not advisable with biphasic or triphasic Pills because the dose in the first seven pills is too low to prevent possible breakthrough bleeding; triphasic brands are probably best avoided for long journeys that cross time zones, since the margin of error is less and the risk of pregnancy increases if they are not taken regularly.

The progestogen-only pill

The progestogen-only Pill (POP), is sometimes used by women who cannot take the combined pill. It is taken every day continuously without a 7-day break. It is not 100% effective (about 96–98%).

There are two main types. The older ones have to be taken at a fixed time each day in order to remain effective. The newer POP containing the hormone desogestrel is more effective and does not have to be taken at a fixed time each day. If a pill is forgotten, take one as soon as it is remembered, but use a condom for 2 days. Antibiotics do not affect the POP.

The patch

Hormonal contraception is also available in the form of a patch. Each patch is worn for 7 days for 3 weeks consecutively followed by a patch-free week. It offers many advantages for travel such as usability by women taking doxycycline for malaria protection and those with travellers' diarrhoea. It has similar side effects to the combined oral contraceptive pill and is 98–100% effective. More information can be found at ℘ www.orthoevra.com

Vaginal ring

The hormonal vaginal ring is similar to the combined oral contraceptive pill. It is retained in the vagina for 3 weeks, removed for 1 week for a withdrawal bleed, and then a new one inserted. As with the patch, it could be used continuously, avoiding the 7-day break. It is not affected by antibiotics. However, its effectiveness is reduced by anti-epileptic drugs so additional precautions are needed.

Long-acting reversible contraception: LARC methods

The intrauterine device

Women who already have an IUD should have it checked before going abroad—make sure that it is not due for a change. Most devices are copper bearing T-shaped and last five to eight years. (The older all-plastic devices, rarely used now, can remain in the womb for many years provided that there are no problems.)

The IUD is about 97–99% effective. It has the advantage that it is not affected by stomach upsets or time zones. It can, however, be expelled by the uterus, so it is a sensible precaution to check after each period that the threads can still be felt. If a 'hard bit' (part of the IUD itself) can be felt, as well as the threads, the IUD may be coming out and will need to be checked by a doctor or nurse. An examination is not necessary once the IUD has come out; obviously protection ceases immediately and another method must be used.

The IUD is not suitable for women with heavy or prolonged periods—it may make these worse. A newly fitted IUD may also cause irregular and sometimes heavy bleeding in the first couple of months—hardly ideal if you are just off on holiday. It is therefore a good idea to have the IUD fitted well in advance, so that any problems can be sorted out before you travel.

Mirena—the levonorgestrel-releasing system (IUS)

This is a T-shaped IUD that releases levonorgestrel, a progestogen hormone, at a rate of 20µg/24 hours. It works locally, suppressing the womb's lining, changing the mucus of the neck of the womb, and impairing sperm migration. It is effective for five years, is 99% reliable, and is convenient with few side effects.

It is different from other IUDs in that it reduces the amount and duration of the periods. Its main side effect is frequent though light bleeding during the first few months of use, so it is best fitted several months before travelling. Eventually, the periods may cease; this is not harmful—fertility returns rapidly after the IUS is removed. It appears to reduce the frequency of clinical pelvic inflammatory disease. Fitting may be slightly more difficult than other types of IUD, and a local anaesthetic may be needed.

Injectable contraceptives

Injectable contraceptives (Depo-Provera and Noristerat) are virtually 100% effective and work by suppressing ovulation, although they only contain one hormone, progestogen.

Depo-Provera remains effective for 3 months. It is useful for women going on long trips and crossing time zones frequently. Stomach upsets or antibiotics do not affect it. Side effects often occur, such as irregular bleeding, especially with the first injection. With subsequent injections, the periods may stop altogether. This is how the injection should work, which makes it an ideal method for the woman who does not want regular periods. If Depo-Provera is chosen, the woman needs to be settled on it before she travels.

A second injectable contraceptive, Noristerat, has similar properties (and side effects) to Depo-Provera and is equally effective. Noristerat is also available in many countries, including some where Depo-Provera is unavailable. This is effective for eight weeks.

The contraceptive implant: Nexplanon

This is a long-acting (up to 3 years) hormonal method containing one hormone, etonogestrel, similar to the newer progestogen only pill. It works rather like the combined pill and is similarly effective. A single rod 40mm long and 2mm in diameter is inserted just under the skin in the upper arm under local anaesthetic. The procedure takes around five minutes. It provides a high level of protection against pregnancy (99–100%). Its main side effect is irregular vaginal bleeding, which is occasionally prolonged. Stomach upsets or antibiotics do not affect it. Certain anti-convulsants may reduce its effectiveness.

Barrier methods

The condom

The condom is 85–98% effective when used correctly. It provides some protection against sexually-transmitted disease including HIV (see Chapter 10.2), and is particularly useful for the man or woman travelling alone. It is also valuable in case of problems with the Pill, or in case the IUD is expelled. The condom is a good method for the chance sexual encounter and travels well.

Female condom

This is a condom that is put inside the vagina and the area just outside the vagina. There are two soft plastic rings, an inner one to help put the condom in the vagina, the outer one to help the condom to stay in place outside the vagina. Reliability is probably the same as for the male condom. It protects both partners against sexually-transmitted disease, including HIV. It is used once only and is sold under the brand name *Reality*.

The diaphragm and cervical cap

The diaphragm, covering the cervix and front wall of the vagina, and the cervical cap, covering the cervix, are useful methods with about the same effectiveness as the condom. They need to be fitted by a doctor or family planning nurse, and the woman must be taught how to use them correctly. A diaphragm or cap lasts for about 1 year, so on a long trip it may be advisable to take along a spare.

They must be used with a spermicide. These come in the form of creams, gels, foams, vaginal suppositories, or film. Creams may become more messy in hot climates, but do not lose their effectiveness. Foams in aerosol containers can be a useful alternative. In addition, vaginal suppositories should be inserted if a second act of intercourse takes place soon after the first. They are designed to melt at body temperature, and this can be an obvious problem in hot countries; brands wrapped individually with silver foil travel best, and should be kept in a cool place.

Foaming tablets also travel well, although if conditions are humid the lid of their container should always be firmly closed: moisture will make the tablets dissolve. The diaphragm and cap provide some protection from sexually-transmitted diseases (see Chapter 10.1).

Using contraception for the first time

The Pill is probably the most sensible method for a couple going on honeymoon, who have not had sex before and who do not want a pregnancy straight away. Although honeymoons are often pictured to be idyllic and carefree, in reality they can be a time of anxiety and stress, with both partners worrying whether sex will be all right.

Sexual adjustment to each other may take time, and methods that directly interfere with intercourse—such as the condom or diaphragm—may interrupt love play and can make that adjustment more complicated. If you choose the Pill, begin taking it a few months in advance, so that any problems can be dealt with before you leave.

Emergency or post-coital contraception: PCC (the 'morning after' pill)

This method of birth control may be used in an emergency. It works mainly by inhibiting ovulation. It is preferable to abortion, but should not be used on a regular basis. It is useful on those occasions when a contraceptive method fails (e.g. a condom splitting, forgotten pill) and the woman has had unprotected intercourse.

One tablet of the progestogen-only pill Levonelle (levonorgestrel 1.5mg) is taken as a single dose. It is more effective if taken in the first 24 hours but it can be taken up to 72 hours of unprotected act of sexual intercourse. Nausea and vomiting are rare. The next period may arrive slightly earlier or later than expected but usually within 3 weeks of prescribing PCC.

PCC can be obtained from pharmacies in the UK without a prescription, or from contraception/sexual health clinic or your own doctor or gynaecologist. Ideally, a follow-up visit should be arranged after taking PCC.

A new emergency pill—ulipristal acetate—has recently been approved to be taken within 120 hours of unprotected intercourse. A failure rate of 2% has been observed in clinical trials. It is expensive and not currently available in contraceptive clinics in the UK. The copper intrauterine device can be inserted up to 5 days after unprotected intercourse. It prevents fertilization and implantation. It is the most effective emergency contraception.

Abortion

Travellers who want an abortion while abroad may find this difficult to arrange. At the last count 50 out of 128 countries listed by the IPPF prohibit abortion except in extreme circumstances (e.g. rape or life-threatening illness). Skilled medical care may be very expensive, or almost impossible to obtain (see Chapter 9.7).

Medical termination of pregnancy (MTOP)

Mifepristone is a synthetic steroid that counteracts the hormone progesterone. Progesterone is produced naturally in the body and is essential to maintain a pregnancy. By blocking the action of progesterone, mifepristone induces a miscarriage. It is more effective when used with another drug, prostaglandin. Mifepristone is given as a single dose (200mg × 3 tablets) by mouth, and a suppository of prostaglandin is inserted into the vagina 48 hours later. The abortion or miscarriage happens spontaneously about 6 hours later. This treatment can be given to women who are up to 9 weeks pregnant and is effective in 95% of cases. Side effects include period pains and prolonged bleeding. Less than 10% of women have severe pain lasting about an hour. This responds to a strong painkiller. It has no adverse effects on future fertility. It is licensed for use under medical supervision in France and Britain; it has been approved although not as yet introduced for use in China. A few countries ban abortion entirely—Chile, El Salvador, Malta, and Nicaragua.

In some countries abortion is illegal, but is permitted to save the woman's life (see Table 10.3.1). Most Islamic countries require that the woman's husband consent to the abortion.

Table 10.3.1 Legal status of abortion

Countries where abortion is only permitted to save a woman's life

Afghanistan	Iran	Palestinian Territory
Angola	Ireland	Paraguay
Andorra	Ivory Coast	Philippines
Antiqua	Laos	San Marino
Brunei	Lebanon	Senegal
Central African Republic	Lesotho	Somalia
Congo	Libya	Sri Lanka
Cote D'Ivoire	Madagascar	Sudan
Dominica	Mali	Syria
Dominican Republic	Mauritania	Tonga
Egypt	Mauritius	Tuvalu
El Salvador	Mexico	Surinam
Gabon	Myanmar	United Arab Emirates
Guatemala	Malawi	Venezuela
Guinea–Bissau	Micronesia	Yemen
Haiti	Oman	
Honduras	Palau	

Countries where abortion is illegal but is permitted both to save a mother's life and to protect her physical health

Argentina	Eritrea	Saudi Arabia
Bolivia	Indonesia	Zimbabwe
Burkina Faso	Kuwait	
Burundi	Morocco	
Cameroon	Mozambique	
Costa Rica	Niger	
Ecuador	Pakistan	
Ethiopia	Rwanda	

Source: Data from Pregnant Pause ⅋ http://www.pregnantpause.org/lex/world02.jsp

Chapter 11

Travellers with special health needs

11.1 Travel in pregnancy

Jerker Liljestrand

There is absolutely no way of knowing in advance that a pregnancy will be trouble-free, and for travel, some extra precautions are necessary.

Increasingly, we take travel for granted, but its implications for women who are or may become pregnant while travelling are worth a little thought. Large numbers of women do travel in pregnancy, and they sometimes travel long distances; most have no real problems, but an unlucky few regret having ventured forth. The widely varying standard of medical care and its availability in different countries is more important than the direct effects of travel on pregnancy. But at least being aware of the problems may help you to minimize their effects.

Possible problems

The likelihood of a problem needing medical attention arising is greater during pregnancy than at other times. Women should hesitate before travelling to any area where medical services will be of doubtful quality or where misunderstandings due to language or cultural problems are going to make diagnosis and treatment more difficult.

No woman can be realistically assured that she will have a trouble-free pregnancy. The World Health Organization (WHO) estimates that while 85% of pregnancies are 'uneventful', the remaining 15% have a potentially serious complication. So it is worth remembering that pregnancy is normal only *after* no problems have occurred.

Antenatal care and routine tests in early pregnancy

Don't miss out on antenatal care and important tests that need to be completed in the first half of pregnancy—postpone your trip, if necessary. Routine screening includes blood tests for infections, and to detect blood group incompatibility problems. Serious blood conditions of the foetus such as thalassaemia (in those of Mediterranean or Asian origin) or sickle cell anaemia (in those of African origin) can be detected early in pregnancy—in time for a pregnancy to be terminated if the foetus is affected. The screening tests for malformations and chromosomal abnormalities are carried out at 12–14 weeks. In some clinical situations, earlier tests can be done. A routine ultrasound examination is usually carried out at some time in the first 18 weeks (usually at 12–18 weeks) to confirm the age of the foetus in case of problems later in pregnancy, to detect twins and to detect abnormalities in the foetal organs. Folic acid can help prevent malformations (see Box 11.1.1).

Box 11.1.1 **Folic acid**

Between 50 and 70% of neural tube defects (such as spina bifida and anencephaly) could be prevented by taking sufficient folic acid in the diet—at least 400mcg/day—before conception and during early pregnancy. Folic acid is present in green leafy vegetables, beans, and legumes, and also in specially fortified foods such as breakfast cereals, but these can be an unreliable source, especially when travelling. So all women who might conceive while travelling—and arguably all women of childbearing age, anywhere—should take a daily supplement of at least 400mcg of folic acid. (Take a higher dose when using proguanil (Paludrine) for malaria prevention—see Chapter 5.1.)

Miscarriage

Spontaneous abortion (miscarriage) is the commonest problem of early pregnancy. It usually occurs within the first 3 months. If it merely threatens, as evidenced by vaginal bleeding, the eventual outcome will *not* be altered because the woman travels.

Miscarriages in the early months are due to the inevitable errors of a biological system—errors in cell division of the foetus or the placenta, and errors concerned with the attachment of the placenta to the wall of the uterus (womb). Travel won't cause miscarriage other than *indirectly*, through the effect of, say, high fever associated with infection or severe dehydration associated with diarrhoea.

Of more pressing concern are the complications of miscarriage, which occasionally include life-threatening haemorrhages and serious infections, or the problems of inept medical treatment employed to cope with them.

Miscarriage, although uncommon at a later stage of pregnancy, can occur, though once the foetus is able to survive, it is termed premature labour; the above complications are more common with later miscarriages. Any woman who has had a previous late miscarriage, or has any condition predisposing to miscarriage, is ill-advised to travel in mid-pregnancy.

Ectopic pregnancy

This may be a problem in the first few months, and affects one pregnancy in 200. The foetus grows in the fallopian tube instead of in the uterus, and this can lead to life-threatening haemorrhage. If abdominal pain occurs in pregnancy, always consult a doctor.

Premature labour

If labour starts early but at a time when the resulting baby could live (any time after 24 weeks), then the whole future of the baby can depend on the availability of expert care. Without this, the baby risks being seriously mentally or physically handicapped for life. If expert care is available it can be extremely expensive. Where good obstetric care is available, treatment can sometimes be given to stop or delay premature labour, and through steroid medication of the pregnant woman, accelerate pulmonary maturation of the baby.

Other complications

In late pregnancy, other possible problems include haemorrhage from the placenta, pregnancy-induced hypertension, and premature rupture of the membranes. Such complications threaten both mother and foetus, and ready availability of expert care reduces the risks.

Many of the complications that occur in pregnancy may result in haemorrhage and the need for a blood transfusion; some of the risks associated with this are discussed in Chapter 13.6.

Birth

If contemplating giving birth in another country, the quality of the available care should be carefully assessed. Over-medicalization, inappropriate treatment, restrictions of humane birthing care and the risk of acquiring a serious infection from the hospital care all need to be considered.

Before you go

If you are planning to live overseas, you should ensure that you will have access to good quality maternal and newborn health care and advice, and also that you will have all the social and emotional support you may need.

Insurance

Be sure to check that any travel or medical insurance covers medical care for the consequences of pregnancy; many policies specifically exclude this, and additional cover often needs to be arranged separately (Chapter 13.3). If you are British and travelling to an EU country, you should obtain an EHIC card.

Immunization

Vaccinations that involve a live virus or are likely to lead to a high temperature should be avoided during pregnancy (see p.451). A medical certificate can circumvent the vaccination requirements for travel.

Anti-malarial medication

If you are pregnant and are travelling to an area where there is a risk of contracting malaria, it is vital to be adequately protected (see p.108)—malaria is far more common and more serious in pregnancy. The drug-resistance patterns change fast in many regions; so get advice from a travel medicine specialist in your own country, *and* combine this with information from local specialists. Chloroquine (Avloclor, Nivaquine) and proguanil (Paludrine) are generally agreed not to cause harm in pregnancy, but resistance to these drugs means that in many regions they provide insufficient protection. A larger than usual daily dose of folic acid supplementation (5mg) is advised when taking proguanil (Box 11.1.1).

Of the other, more effective options, mefloquine (Lariam) can be used in pregnancy but is not usually recommended during the first 12 weeks; it is not believed to harm the foetus after this time. Doxycycline is unsuitable for use in pregnancy, and as yet there is insufficient experience with Malarone for this to be an option.

The best preventive action against malaria is to avoid mosquito bites through discipline (long sleeves, no bare legs/ankles during critical parts of the day, especially at dusk and dawn), and strategic use of bed nets and repellents.

Expert help in balancing the risks and benefits is often needed, but, in general, travel to high-risk malarial regions is best avoided during pregnancy.

Travel

Air

Provided that the cabin is pressurized, reduced pressure on board an airliner (Chapter 7.1) should have no adverse effect upon healthy pregnant women. If a problem with the function of the placenta is suspected, however, air travel should be avoided because the slightly reduced oxygen level may harm the foetus.

Most airlines will not accept you for travel after 32 weeks of pregnancy, but will sometimes stretch this to 36 weeks if you have a medical certificate stating that all is well. Policy varies between airlines and also depends on the length of the flight.

Pregnant women and those in the first month after delivery have a small but definitely increased risk of developing a blood clot in the deep veins of the legs (deep-vein thrombosis). When travelling by air do not sit in a cramped position for a long period, because pressure from the seat and from the foetus slows the circulation in the legs. Tense up the legs and wriggle the toes from time to time; stand up and walk about at least every hour. Also consider wearing compression stockings during the flight.

Other forms of travel

Sitting in a cramped position in a car, bus, or train has the same effect of impairing blood circulation in the legs. Do what it takes, stopping the car if necessary, to walk about every hour or so.

During pregnancy, women should drive with more care and more slowly, as pregnancy sometimes affects concentration and reaction time in an emergency.

Nausea and vomiting

The tendency to nausea and vomiting in early pregnancy is likely to be aggravated by travel. All travel sickness tablets cause some unwanted effects, such as drowsiness, altered reaction time, dry mouth and blurred vision, and so should be used only when symptoms warrant (and not at all when driving). Drugs based on hyoscine (e.g. Kwells) and anti-histamine preparations such as promethazine (Phenergan, Avomine) are safe for use in pregnancy.

At your destination

Food and drink

- *Dehydration:* try to avoid dehydration during air travel or in a hot climate—this aggravates the tendency to thrombosis and also the problem of constipation, which is common in pregnancy. Drink plenty of fluids, preferably plain water—bottled or boiled if the local supply isn't safe (Chapter 3.1). Take a supply of natural bran and increase your intake of fruit and vegetables to counteract the constipation that often goes with changed daily routines. Avoid alcohol, not only because of its dehydrating properties but also for its possible harmful effects on the foetus. *Severe* dehydration—such as may follow prolonged diarrhoea—increases the risk of miscarriage

- *Toxoplasmosis:* do not eat undercooked meat; the condition toxoplasmosis may result. It causes only mild illness in adults but occasionally has serious effects on the foetus. You could be checked to see whether you are immune, but it is a difficult test, not generally available
- *Listeriosis:* this infection is acquired from contaminated food, particularly poultry that is either fresh or frozen, and then *incompletely* cooked. It also occurs in cows' and goats' milk and is not always eliminated by pasteurization. Soft, ripened cheeses often contain the bacteria in high numbers and pre-prepared salads are not safe, as the bacteria can survive refrigeration. All these points should be borne in mind, as the infection can cause serious effects in the foetus. If a 'flu-like illness' develops in pregnancy, then it is probably wise to have antibiotic treatment (such as amoxicillin), just in case.

Drug treatment abroad

There is widespread tendency to over-medicalization of pregnancy in many countries. This may lead to incorrect information, anxiety, and incorrect prescriptions. It is safest to avoid medicines altogether if you can, other than iron supplements and vitamins. One group of drugs that may be prescribed for you, but which should be avoided, are the tetracycline group of antibiotics. Other drugs to avoid include bismuth subsalicylate (Pepto–Bismol); metronidazole (Flagyl), which should not be taken during the first trimester unless absolutely necessary; and the fluoroquinolone antibiotics (e.g. ciprofloxacin and norfloxacin). Amoxicillin and ampicillin are safe. Recreational drugs may endanger the foetus, 'crack' cocaine, in particular, causes serious brain abnormalities.

See Box 11.1.2 for a summary of advice.

Box 11.1.2 **Summary of advice for travellers**

You will probably have gathered that we are rather against travelling to remote spots at any time in pregnancy, but if a time for a break has to be selected, between 18 and 24 weeks is probably the best. This is after the risk of nausea and miscarriage—and after the necessary tests should have been completed—but before the problems of premature labour loom. You should be back at base for late pregnancy, just in case!

Box 11.1.3 **Radiation and flying**

Exposure to cosmic radiation at normal flying altitudes (35,000 feet) is more than 100 times greater than at ground level. There has been increasing concern about the effects of low-dose radiation, and it is certainly possible for frequent fliers to build up a significant radiation exposure. Solar flares—bursts of energy on the surface of the sun—account for periodic increases in such exposure, and occur in unpredictable patterns. The radiation exposure for a return trip between London and New York is roughly equivalent to the exposure from a single chest X-ray (0.1mSv); a return flight between London and Los Angeles would clock up 0.16mSv.

Calculations on the extent of harm associated with radiation exposure are generally based on the effects of much larger doses—such as at Hiroshima. It is difficult to know how such data extrapolate to lower doses, and it is conceivable that low doses may be relatively more harmful. It is also difficult to document the effects, and to know whether subtle changes such as differences in intelligence or minor defects can be attributed to such exposure rather than nature. For this reason, it has been suggested that pregnant women should avoid unnecessary long-distance flights during the early, most vulnerable stages of pregnancy, and most airlines now have a policy of 'grounding' any flight crew who become pregnant.

11.2 Children abroad

Tony Waterston

Problems of travelling with children vary according to where you intend to go, how you will be getting there, and how long you will be away. Whether you are moving abroad to live or are merely off on a short trip, careful preparation will be amply rewarded.

Parents travelling abroad often anticipate all sorts of problems with their children, some concerned with the journey itself, others with what will happen at the destination. Will the food be suitable? What dreadful diseases might they get? How will the baby take the heat?

Fortunately, the reality of travelling with children is generally a formative and valuable experience for the whole family.

In this chapter, I hope to answer some of the most common questions about children's health abroad and help you prepare for your trip. I will discuss three aspects of the trip with respect to children. First, what preparations to make, and the journey itself; second, health hazards encountered while living abroad; and third, some points about children's diet and baby care.

Before you go

Plenty of time spent finding out as much as you can about the country you plan to visit will be amply repaid. Try to find out all you can about the following:

The local health system

Make sure that you have adequate insurance for the whole family, and find out if the cost of return travel home will be paid in case of major illness.

What are the facilities available for treating sick children? Wherever you are, a child may get appendicitis, a fracture or a severe infection and need specialized care. This might be available only at a major centre and could be a factor in deciding where you live.

Can medicines be obtained easily? You will quite likely need anti-malarials if visiting a tropical zone and may need antibiotics. A small supply of over-the-counter remedies will come in useful for minor illnesses and should be bought in advance.

If you have a baby and are going for more than a few weeks, find out where and how routine immunizations can be carried out (see p.378 for schedule). There should not be any difficulty in obtaining immunization in any country you visit, although there may be a queue.

In many developing countries, the emphasis in the medical system will be on *primary health care*. This means basic care, concentrating on common ailments and on prevention, delivered by workers with a short training. Do not therefore be surprised if you do not see a doctor at a clinic—the health worker you see should be trained to recognize and treat the common childhood complaints.

Be sure to avoid all treatment by injection unless it is absolutely essential, and unless you are certain that the needle has been sterilized (see p.468).

Dental care

Dental care abroad is often expensive or non-existent. The whole family should have a dental check and receive essential treatment before going. Fluoride drops or tablets, for the prevention of dental caries, are recommended for infants and young children (see Chapter 9.2).

The main diseases

In Europe, North America, and Australia, the diseases are very similar to those encountered in the UK, whereas the developing countries of Africa, Asia, and South America share a wide spectrum of infectious diseases, which are discussed elsewhere in this book.

Find out what the main problems are in the country you intend to visit (e.g. whether drug-resistant malaria is present and the prevalence of HIV infection) and what specific precautions you should take. Do not feel that it would be unsafe to take children to a country where tropical diseases are common: simple precautions will protect against these diseases, and it is often more trivial complaints such as cuts, bites, diarrhoea, and respiratory infections that become important when you are there. These problems are dealt with below, but you would be wise also to take with you one of the many childcare books that deal with the management of minor illnesses at home.

Water and food

Find out whether the local water supply is drinkable—if not, you should pay careful attention to the information in this book about water purification (Chapter 3.2). Clean water is essential for young children, as stomach upsets are the commonest disorders encountered. It always pays to be careful about water quality when travelling—even bottled carbonated drinks are not necessarily always safe. It may be wise to stick to tea when in doubt.

What are the major local foods? If they are not of a kind you feel up to preparing (such as maize meal, plantain, yam) you will need to depend on imported foods. Is there always a constant supply of these? Foreign exchange is scarce in many countries, and Weetabix or even wheat may not be at the top of the list of priorities. Can you bake bread? Sacks of flour can sometimes be obtained and will allow you to live through temporary bread shortages. You could arrange to have limited stocks of food sent out, but it is sensible to try to 'live off the land'.

Is the milk drinkable and, if not, is powdered milk available? This is something you could quite easily take and may need to if you have a formula-fed baby (see notes on p.387).

In most cases, it is quite easy to provide a balanced diet for children, but it will pay if you learn something about the nutritional content of the foods you will encounter abroad.

Immunization

Children should have had the normal schedule of immunization set out in Table 11.2.1, before travelling abroad—and the same schedule or a recognized schedule of your country of origin should be used for babies living abroad. Any omissions should be updated before departure. Additional vaccines, not currently part of the UK schedule, could also be considered, e.g. rotavirus (2 doses, one month apart, given between the age 6 weeks and 24 weeks) and varicella (chickenpox) for children over 1 year. See also Chapter 13.2, pp.67–8, p.450.

BCG is not routinely given in the UK, but may need to be considered if going to live abroad, and should be given at birth to babies born in countries where tuberculosis is common. (Children over 6 years may need a TB test first.)

In addition, yellow fever immunization may be mandatory for the country you are to visit. Protection can optionally be obtained against typhoid, hepatitis A and B (see Chapter 2.4), and rabies. Malaria prevention is dealt with separately on p.380.

Table 11.2.1 UK immunization schedule for children

When to immunize	What is given	Vaccine and how it is given
2 months old	Diphtheria, tetanus, pertussis, polio and *Haemophilus influenzae* type b (DTaP/IPV/Hib)	One injection (Pediacel)
	Pneumococcal (PCV)	One injection (Prevenar)
3 months old	Diphtheria, tetanus, pertussis, polio and *Haemophilus influenzae* type b (DTaP/IPV/Hib)	One injection (Pediacel)
	Meningitis C (MenC)	One injection (Neisvac C or Meningitec or Menjugate)
4 months old	Diphtheria, tetanus, pertussis, polio and *Haemophilus influenzae* type b (DTaP/IPV/Hib)	One injection (Pediacel)
	PCV	One injection (Prevenar)
	MenC	One injection (Neisvac C or Meningitec or Menjugate)
Between 12 and 13 months old— within a month of the first birthday	Haemophilus influenzae type b, Meningitis C (Hib/MenC)	One injection (Menitorix)
	Measles, mumps and rubella (MMR)	One injection (Priorix or MMRvaxPro)
	Pneumococcal (PCV)	One injection (Prevenar)
3 years 4 months to 5 years old	Diphtheria, tetanus, pertussis and polio (dTaP/IPV or DTaP/IPV)	One injection (Repevax or Infanrix-IPV)
	Measles, mumps and rubella (MMR)	One injection (Priorix or MMRvaxPro)
Girls aged 12–13 years	Human Papillomavirus Vaccine (HPV)	3 injections given at 0,1–2 month and 6 month intervals.
13 to 18 years old	Tetanus, diphtheria and polio (Td/IPV)	One injection (Revaxis)

Reproduced from: ☞ http://www.hpa.org.uk/web/HPAweb&Page&HPAwebAutoListDate/Page/1204031508623 with permission from the Health Protection Agency.

The journey

Here are some tips on how to reduce the stress of travelling with children:

- *If you have a baby:* breast-feeding on the move is far easier than formula feeding. If you bottle-feed, prepacked milk is very useful for the journey. If you are flying, ask for a 'sky cot' well in advance (and check again before travelling), otherwise you will be balancing the baby on your knee all the way. Disposable nappies are a boon for the journey, even if you normally despise them, and often some airlines may have emergency supplies.
- *Suitable books and toys or games:* these should be kept handy, as bored children sitting in an enclosed space for a long period will not stay happy.
- *A small supply of food and drink* should be taken (e.g. sandwiches, biscuits, and a bottle of water), as the meals available *en route* may be neither palatable nor healthy. Allow extra for delays.
- *Travel sickness* should be prevented in advance if your children are prone to it. Kwells (containing hyoscine hydrobromide) is a suitable medication. Avoid over dosage, which leads to sleepiness, dry mouth, and irritability.
- *A light sedative* may help children get through an especially long journey, though most medication tends to have side effects.
  A suitable choice is promethazine (Phenergan), in a dose of 15mg for 1–5-year-olds, and 10–25mg for over-fives. It is available as tablets or elixir (prescription not required in the UK).

Health hazards at your destination

Short visits (under 1 month)

For short periods abroad, you do not need to be too concerned about exotic diseases—the most likely infections to crop up are the everyday ones. Make sure that you are prepared to deal with problems like diarrhoea or respiratory infections (sore throat or ears). The contents of a simple first-aid kit for young children on a beach holiday are shown in Box 11.2.1.

You should *always* be aware of the risk of malaria if you are going to a part of the world where it is endemic: babies and young children must be protected even on a short visit (see p.380). Check what immunizations are needed, and make sure that children are up to date.

Box 11.2.1 **First-aid kit for short holiday trips**

- Rehydration solutions (Dioralyte, Electrolade)
- Paracetamol tablets or elixir (Calpol, Disprol)—for fever
- Antiseptic solution (TCP, Dettol)
- Elastoplast, band-aids
- Sunscreen—high factor
- Calamine lotion—for sunburn
- Mosquito repellent
- Simple eye ointment.

Longer visits (over 1 month)

For longer visits, more careful preparation will be needed, as well as an awareness of the endemic diseases in the country concerned. Consider taking suitable antibiotics.

Malaria

Malaria is fully considered in Chapter 5.1, and the manifestations, treatment, and choice of anti-malarial tablets will not be discussed again here, although you should note these points:

- A baby is at risk of malaria from birth, so in a malarial area, protective measures should be taken from then on
- The main anti-malarial drugs are safe for children, in reduced dosages (not doxycycline for under 12s, mefloquine not for babies under 5kg)
- In malarial areas, taking the tablets or medicine should become a routine, like brushing your teeth
- As with adults, children should commence taking anti-malarials one week before departure and continue for at least 4 weeks after returning (1 day before, and 7 days afterwards, if using Malarone)
- Keep the tablets or syrups in a safe, secure place—even the most trustworthy toddler may swallow a bottleful.

As well as the use of anti-malarial tablets or syrups, control measures should be used to reduce the likelihood of mosquitoes biting (see Chapter 5.12). Netting is valuable, though hot to sleep under. You may obtain insecticide impregnated netting, which is more effective in protecting against mosquitoes. If the windows are screened, an individual cover will not be necessary—but check for holes in old window netting. Infants should always be covered with a separate net. It may be wise to take nets with you for use when travelling outside urban areas.

Mosquito control consists of ensuring that there is no standing water near the house to act as a breeding ground, and spraying the bedroom at night.

HIV and AIDS

The risk to children is mainly from contaminated injections or blood transfusions. Check needle sterility before allowing your child to receive an injection; if necessary take a small supply of needles and syringes with you when travelling to a high-risk country (see p.468). It is worth knowing your child's blood group, and your own; if they are compatible, you may be able to act as a donor in an emergency.

Fever

Fever is a much more worrying complaint in children overseas than at home, because of the fear of tropical infections. Although malaria is an ever-present worry (even in the child on anti-malarial tablets or syrup), the vast majority of fevers in children have the same causes anywhere—namely, viral nose and throat infections (coughs, colds, tonsillitis, and the like). The symptoms of these will usually include cough and a runny nose, with perhaps a sore throat, or earache, and general malaise with loss of appetite, and sometimes vomiting due to swallowed phlegm. Warning signs of another cause would be these:

- A very high fever (40°C, 104°F) with headache (? malaria)
- A severe headache and vomiting with neck stiffness and possibly a non-blanching rash (? meningitis)
- The presence of jaundice, with yellow eyes (? hepatitis or malaria)
- Blood in stools or severe diarrhoea (? dysentery)
- A feeling of burning on passing urine or needing to visit the toilet frequently (? urinary infection)
- Refusal to feed in a baby (? blood infection)
- Severe cough with breathing difficulty (? pneumonia)
- Persistent abdominal pain (? appendicitis).

Box 11.2.2 **Some safety tips**

- Children should know how to use child seats and safety belts
- They should be taught not to go anywhere with a stranger
- They should know the name of their hotel, and should always know what to do if they get lost (if necessary, they should carry a written note of their name, address, and other appropriate information)
- Parents should always carry at least one full-face photograph of all children they are travelling with
- Never leave children alone to watch luggage or to keep a place in a queue
- Never leave children alone in a car in the sun.

If these signs are not present but cold symptoms are, then it is quite reasonable to give the child paracetamol and extra fluids, keep him or her cool, and carry on as normally as possible (an antibiotic does not help most throat and nose infections, which are usually caused by a virus, but may be needed for severe sore throats or earache). If one of the above features is present, if the fever is in a baby under a year, or if it lasts over 2 days without improvement and fever is the only symptom, then medical help should be sought.

Should a fever in a malarial area be routinely treated with anti-malarial drugs, just in case it is malaria? This is difficult to answer (see Chapter 5.1). Certainly a supply of suitable treatment medication (such as Malarone) should be kept in the house and you should know how much to give. If medical aid is not readily available, the child has been exposed to mosquitoes, and the features are not typical of a cold, then a course should be given.

However, a *blood test should, if practicable, always be taken for malaria* before giving the treatment—only a few drops of blood on a slide are needed for this. Otherwise it will be hard to decide later whether it was malaria or not. The local hospital or clinic may show you how to take the test yourself.

Respiratory infections

These seem to be worse in children living in the tropics, perhaps because of more frequent swimming leading to ear infections, or perhaps because of exposure to a new set of infective agents. The commonest serious infections are *tonsillitis* and *otitis media* (middle-ear infection), both of which may need antibiotic treatment, though it is commonly advised to treat ear infections symptomatically (i.e. with paracetamol) as most are due to viruses. Penicillin, amoxicillin, or cefuroxime are the most effective antibiotics used for these conditions and they are available worldwide. If your child is allergic to penicillin make sure that this is clear to anyone giving treatment.

Diarrhoea

Diarrhoea is extremely common in children during travel (see Chapter 2.1). 'Gastroenteritis' is simply the technical name for a stomach or intestinal infection leading to diarrhoea and is not necessarily severe or life threatening. The seriousness of diarrhoea depends on how much fluid is lost from the body: because a child's total fluid volume is greater in proportion to body weight than an adult's, the effect is greater the younger the child. A baby can become dehydrated (dried out) within a few hours of the onset of severe diarrhoea.

Diarrhoeal disease is usually contracted by contact with infected food or fluid, but also from hands that have touched infected material. Faeces of an infected person are highly contagious, and therefore very careful handwashing is essential after using the toilet. These diseases spread more easily in the tropics and also certain causative agents are commoner—the features of some of these are given in Table 11.2.2.

Suspect one of the causes in Table 11.2.2 if the diarrhoea is bloody, very profuse and watery, or associated with a high fever. If one of these symptoms is present, or if the diarrhoea goes on for longer than 3 days (one day in a baby), medical help should be sought. However, in most cases a rotavirus or similar infection will be the cause, and the natural course is only 2 or 3 days.

Replacement of fluid loss is the most important part of treatment. Drugs are ineffective in the vast majority of cases. A suitable fluid-replacement solution may be made with a finger pinch of salt and a teaspoon of sugar added to 250mL (about one mugful) of boiled water, with a squeeze of orange or lemon juice to provide flavour (and a token amount of potassium). The concentration is very important as the sugar helps aid the absorption of the salt, but too much of either is harmful. Taste the solution before giving it to your child, and if it tastes saltier than tears, discard it and start again (see also Chapter 2.1).

Special packets of powder (e.g. Dioralyte, Electrolade) for adding to water may be obtained from your doctor or at a pharmacy before you go and are valuable for journeys. Give one cupful of mixture for each loose stool. Seek medical help if the child vomits or appears drowsy, has fast breathing, or is dehydrated (eyes become sunken, tongue is dry, skin loses elasticity). Profuse diarrhoea in a baby is also a reason for seeking assistance early.

Whilst awaiting assistance or on the way to a doctor, you should give oral rehydration solution in small amounts frequently. A baby may take fluids better by cup and spoon than from a bottle and there is less likelihood of vomiting.

- *Diet:* feeding should be continued during diarrhoea if the child feels like eating—especially high-calorie, low-residue foods. Bananas, cereals, bread and margarine or butter, biscuits, eggs, and milk are all suitable—concentrate on the foods the child likes most. It is undesirable to starve a child with diarrhoea, though often the child will not be keen to eat

- *Drug treatment* is necessary only for some of the specific types of diarrhoea mentioned in Table 11.2.2, such as severe dysentery, typhoid, cholera, and giardiasis—all of which are much less likely than a viral cause. Anti-diarrhoeal agents such as kaolin, codeine, diphenoxylate (Lomotil), and over-the-counter mixtures should be avoided in children under 5 years. Lomotil, in particular, has toxic side effects (depression of the respiratory system) and should not be used in young children, nor should preventive drugs such as clioquinol (Entero–Vioform). For the older child (over 5 years), loperamide (Imodium) is the most acceptable drug if parents feel that symptomatic treatment is absolutely necessary.

Prevention

The likelihood of diarrhoea can be minimized by observing these tips:

- *Pay close attention to household hygiene*: particularly hand-washing before meals and after using the toilet
- *Maintain good hygiene in the kitchen* by washing hands before food preparation; keeping stored food in the fridge (especially meat); covering all food left out in the open, even for short periods; cooking meat thoroughly, boiling water if there is any doubt about its purity

Table 11.2.2 Some causes of children's diarrhoea in the tropics

Cause	Symptoms
Rotavirus (commonest cause)	Mild fever, watery diarrhoea, vomiting
Salmonella (food poisoning)	Diarrhoea and vomiting, abdominal pain, fever, malaise
Shigellosis (bacillary dysentery)	Bloody diarrhoea, high fever
Cholera	Profuse watery diarrhoea, leading rapidly to dehydration
Typhoid	Diarrhoea or constipation, fever, headache, rash, persistent weakness
Giardiasis	Offensive stools, recurrent diarrhoea, malaise, abdominal pains (this is a more chronic or longer-lasting condition)

(then keeping it in the fridge—it will taste better); washing fresh fruit and vegetables thoroughly before eating; and not permitting flies in the kitchen

- *Avoid* pre-cooked foods bought in the streets; milk and milk products (especially ice cream) unless you are quite sure they are manufactured hygienically; salads and other uncooked foods; and cold meat eaten in hotels and restaurants.

Viral hepatitis

- Hepatitis comes in two main forms—A and B. Of these, hepatitis A or 'infectious hepatitis' is more common in children; it is usually spread by the faecal–oral route and resembles diarrhoea in its origins. It is not usually a serious disease in children, and indeed may sometimes not be noticed ('subclinical') but is nevertheless best avoided. The features of the illness and how to deal with it are covered in Chapter 2.1
- Prevention depends mainly on food hygiene and avoiding dubious foods, as discussed under diarrhoea. Hepatitis A vaccines are available in children's formulations and provide long-lasting protection. A vaccine is also available against hepatitis B.

Swimming hazards

Schistosomiasis (Bilharzia) is present in most rivers and lakes in Africa, the Middle East, Asia, and some parts of South and Central America. Its presence prohibits swimming with only a few exceptions (see Chapter 4.4). Be sure you have a reliable local source of information on this. The infective risk of a single, brief exposure is not great and may be reduced by showering in clean water immediately afterwards, but it is better to be safe than sorry.

Before swimming in pools, check that the chlorine supply has not run out—a common problem in developing countries.

Babies may be encouraged to swim from a very early age quite safely as long as the water is safe and you are careful to avoid sunburn.

Ear infections occur quite frequently in hot countries and swimming should be avoided until well after recovery from an episode.

Drowning is sadly still an important cause of accidental death in children. The first rule is to teach your children to swim at the earliest opportunity. The second is to fence off any swimming pool to which your (or visitors') children might have access. Thirdly, always to keep a watchful eye on any young child (below five) or a non-swimmer of any age when there is water about. Toddlers have been known to drown in quite shallow pools. See also pp.234–5.

Other hazards

Sunburn is an obvious environmental hazard, particularly in high or mountainous countries where the tropical sun burns very quickly (see Chapter 8.5). Also, beware of burning even when it is cloudy. The usual advice of big hats and covering the arms and legs should be followed rigorously until all the children are mahogany-coloured. High-factor sunscreens, preferably water-resistant, are advisable when at the swimming pool or seaside. Sunburn should be treated by puncturing blisters and draining the fluid. Clean the burned area and paint with calamine lotion. Protect against contact and further exposure to the sun.

Prickly heat is common in hot climates and particularly in humid countries, and can be very troublesome. It is caused by sweating, with blockage of the sweat ducts leading to itching red spots and tiny blisters, usually on the neck, back, and chest. Treat by washing the area with an antiseptic soap, then dry and powder with talc. Calamine lotion may also be used.

Prevent prickly heat by avoiding sweating if possible, by frequent bathing, by wearing loose clothing (Chapter 8.5), and by drying the skin whenever it becomes wet.

Walking barefoot should be avoided even in your garden or land you know well. Snakes are more afraid of people than we of them, but if stood on will bite defensively (Chapter 6). A more common hazard for the bare foot is *hookworm*, acquired from soil contaminated with human faeces (Chapter 4.7). The worm passes through the skin of the feet and circulates through the lymphatics and lungs before eventually settling in the small intestine, where chronic bleeding leads to severe anaemia.

Tumbu fly (also known as 'Putsi' in some areas) is another infestation commonly picked up from soil in which eggs of the fly have been laid (see p.157). It does not depend on faecal spread and may occur even where sanitation is perfect (e.g. your garden). Larvae may enter the skin directly from the soil or from eggs laid in clothes left to dry outside. Lesions resembling boils develop under the skin and may be very painful. The main preventive measure is to iron all clothes and sheets which have been left out to dry, so as to kill the eggs.

Cuts, sores, and insect bites are common in hot countries but heal more slowly than at home, probably because of greater sweating. Treat them meticulously in the early stages by cleaning, disinfecting, and covering. Gentian violet is a good standby for skin disinfection despite its messiness—the tropical bathroom should preferably be painted purple so that the stains don't show up. Gentian violet is no longer licensed for use in the mouth as it may be an irritant; it should only be used on the skin. For itchy skin lesions and bites, calamine lotion is effective.

Cycling: safety helmets may not be available overseas and should be brought from home (see Chapter 8.1).

Roads: traffic accidents are a serious hazard in tropical countries, with fewer options for good emergency care. Don't let young children out on the road on their own, and ensure that child seats and seat-belts are *always* used.

Poison prevention: syrup of ipecac to induce vomiting after the ingestion of a poison is a must for families with young children, and may not be available locally. The dosage is:

- *infants, 6 months to 1 year*—5mL
- *children, 1–12 years*—15mL
- *over 12 years*—30mL.

The syrup should be followed by one or two glasses of water; repeat the dose if vomiting does not occur within 20–30min. Gastric lavage will be necessary if no vomiting occurs within a further 20min.

Pets: if you keep a dog ensure that rabies vaccine is given at the right time and that the dog is dewormed. Also be on the lookout for ticks and remove them immediately (drop into methylated spirits or paraffin). They can cause *tickbite fever* in animals and humans (Chapters 5.9, 5.11). Cats (as well as undercooked meat) may be a source of toxoplasmosis, which causes a glandular fever-type illness. An infected pregnant woman may transmit the disease to the foetus causing congenital deformities, although this condition is rare (Chapter 11.1).

- Cats and dogs may both spread toxocariasis, another parasitic infection which is a rare cause of blindness in children. Infection may occur through contamination of food by cat and dog faeces, so scrupulous hygiene is necessary when handling food if there is a pet around—and be sure to keep animals away from food dishes and to dispose of their litter effectively
- Remember that if you bring a pet back to the UK, quarantine rules still apply unless you are returning from a country that participates in the Pet Transport Scheme (PETS) and your pet has an official PETS certificate. Details are available from vets (try ✆ http://findavet.rcvs. org.uk/home/). (In the UK, more information is available from the PETS helpline: 0870 241 1710, email: helpline@defra.gsi.gov.uk; ✆ http://www.defra.gov.uk/wildlife-pets/pets/travel/pets/

Stray animals should be avoided and children warned carefully of their risks. Animals in the street should never be petted because of the risk of rabies and other diseases.

Children's diet abroad

Children tend to eat less in a hot climate, so it is all the more important to ensure a balanced intake of nutrients. Foods obtainable will generally be healthier (few junk foods and sweets) and vegetables and fruit will be abundant and fresh (but always wash them thoroughly if eaten raw). Remember that too many mangoes/guavas/pawpaws may cause intestinal upsets. Here are some tips:

Meat should be thoroughly cooked, particularly beef which may carry tapeworms.

Eggs are likely to be readily available.

Milk and milk products (particularly cream and ice cream) should be viewed with caution, and milk boiled unless you are sure it has been hygienically prepared.

A reasonable *salt* intake is necessary but usually this may be obtained by adding extra to food, without the need for salt tablets.

Vitamins should be readily available from the following sources:

- *Vitamin A*—carrots, highly coloured or dark green vegetables/fruit (e.g. mango, guava, pawpaw, spinach)
- *Vitamin B*—nuts, cereals, milk, eggs, meat
- *Vitamin C*—oranges, lemons, guavas, potatoes
- *Vitamin D*—margarine, eggs, fish, sunlight
- *Folic acid*—green leafy vegetables.

Fluoride is valuable in preventing dental caries but water supplies overseas are rarely fluoridated. Fluoride supplements are quite safe but best obtained before departure; they are recommended from infancy to

12 years of age *if the local water supply is deficient*. Drops are available for babies. A prescription is not needed in the UK but is necessary in the USA (see also Chapter 9.2).

Baby care abroad

In general, the care of babies in hot countries does not differ from anywhere else, but a few tips may be helpful.

Breastfeeding

Breastfeeding should be carried out if possible in preference to bottle-feeding, not just because it is better for the baby, but because of the example the expatriate mother sets to the local community. Bottle-feeding is a major cause of death among babies in poor countries because of the difficulty mother's face in boiling water, keeping bottles clean, and just buying milk powder. One reason why the local mother may turn to bottle-feeding is because it carries prestige—since expatriate mothers do it.

Extra water is not needed routinely by the breastfed baby, even in hot climates, unless he or she is feverish or suffering from diarrhoea. However, the mother must be sure to maintain a high fluid intake herself.

Infant foods

For the same reason, it is preferable to use natural foods rather than commercial tins or jars for weaning the baby—it is also cheaper and probably healthier, as some proprietary foods have a high concentration of salt and other additives. The first food will probably still remain a proprietary cereal but when mixed feeding is commenced, liquidized vegetables, fruit, meat, cheese, and eggs may all be used quite safely (this will usually be over the age of 6 months). The WHO recommends exclusive breast feeding until 6 months in all countries (this means that if you breast feed, solids should if possible not be started before that age, to reduce infection and allergy risk).

Nappies and nappy rash

Disposable nappies may be unobtainable or in short supply, so it is wise to take terry nappies and nappy liners for long-term stays. Use cotton pants, because plastic pants predispose to nappy rash, and leave the baby without a nappy for some of the time. A nappy rash will clear up well if the baby is allowed to play out in the sun without anything on the bottom. Remember to press terry nappies on both sides with a hot iron, in tropical countries, to kill the eggs of the tumbu fly.

Sunshine

Babies have a sensitive skin and burn easily. Always protect them from direct sunlight by using a sunhat or sunshade. Cars left in the sun become very hot inside—never leave children unattended in a parked car, and ensure that there is always sufficient ventilation.

Malaria prevention in babies

Malaria prophylaxis in babies should be started immediately after birth. Even if you are breast-feeding and taking a drug yourself, an insufficient amount will reach the baby to be effective. Use nets carefully to avoid mosquito bites.

Cots

A basket is a better place for a baby to sleep than a carry-cot, as it will be cooler. If using a straw basket, line the inside with netting to prevent mosquitoes and ticks from getting in. After dark, always put a net over the basket, even in a room with screened windows—mosquitoes are expert hole-finders.

Summary

Be sure to take with you items you will need as the baby grows, such as a potty, toilet seat, baby chair, travelling cot, car seat, and toddler toys. Clothes should usually be obtainable locally. Mail order may be possible, but in some countries there may be long delays at customs.

Children with special problems

If you have a child with diabetes (see Chapter 11.4), cystic fibrosis, coeliac disease, or another chronic disorder or a disability, you will need special advice before travelling abroad. Obtain this early from your usual specialist or one of the support organizations, as a lot more advance planning will be required.

Conclusion

Do not let the list of exotic diseases and problems overwhelm you with horror. Most can be prevented by simple precautions and, on the positive side; there will be the outdoor life, the absence of junk foods and TV, and the exposure to quite different cultures and traditions. You and your children should come back with a much deeper understanding of people of other cultures and of the problems facing developing countries. It will be worth it.

11.3 Elderly travellers

Iain McIntosh

People often face a long retirement, with the opportunity to travel extensively. Relatively affluent and with time to spare, they may undertake prolonged, adventurous journeys. Most travel safely and successfully. The vital prerequisites are preparation, a sensible itinerary, and awareness of health concerns associated with advancing age.

The dictionary definition of elderly is 'quite old' or 'very old', but age alone does not determine health risk in post-retirement global wanderers. Most people can anticipate a decade of sound health after retirement and can pursue far distant journeys. They account for an increasing share of the foreign travel market and a preponderance of travellers on cruises.

One in five people in the UK is over 65, and 7% of the population is aged over 75 years. A third of these will have travelled abroad during the previous 3 years. Popular destinations are Borneo, Thailand, China, South Africa, Nepal, and India. Antarctica and the Arctic attract many senior citizens. More prosaic destinations in or near Europe attract those following the sun on extended vacations. These venues offer a variable quality of health care to visitors if illness or trauma intervenes. Most people return home in good health, but all need to be aware of the effects of ageing, travel-associated health risks and preventive measures needed to maintain well-being. Planning a pragmatic itinerary, taking suitable precautions both en route and on arrival, can ensure safe, healthy travel and minimize illness, accidents, and the need for medical aid.

Common health problems affecting older travellers

Up to 40% of travellers abroad can suffer from diarrhoea and vomiting. Elderly people are more susceptible to gut infection than the young. They are also more vulnerable to complications such as fluid loss and dehydration.

In many holiday destinations, roads, pavements, stairs, and lighting may be poorly maintained. Falls with fractures are more likely and potentially much more serious in older people.

With advancing years, pre-existing health problems become more likely. People suffering from heart and lung problems, diabetes, arthritis, and urinary problems may be less able to cope with a hostile environment.

Illness and accident may be more likely to result in complications if the individual becomes dependent upon health care in the developing world.

These factors are a challenge to the health of elderly travellers and the downfall of the chronically ill, but they should not deter older people from globetrotting. They will meet contemporaries on cruises to distant waters, on the approach to Everest, in Antarctica or up the Amazon. A pre-travel health consultation, preparatory homework, and sensible precautions can ensure safe and healthy travel.

Fitness and planning

Sound professional advice on health risks can contribute much to maintenance of good health while away. Ideally, some weeks before departure, a health consultation at a travel clinic or GP surgery should consider itinerary, current health status, and environmental threats in the foreign location.

Age-related impairments to travel

Physical and physiological changes that occur with advanced years and can restrict and inhibit distant travel include:

- *Loss in lung function*: a 90-year-old has half of the lung capacity of a 30-year-old
- *Poorer tolerance to low-oxygen pressures*: e.g. in air travel or high altitude
- *Impaired heart activity*: the heart is not as effective a blood pump as in youth
- *Kidney function* is poorer
- *Water and salt regulation* are less effective
- *Decrease acid in stomach juices* make intestinal infection more likely
- *Decreased immunity to infection*, e.g. influenza
- *Acquisition and retention of new information* is more difficult
- *Memory* is poorer.
- *Poorer coping ability* with travel stressors and information overload.

Travel-related hazards to which the elderly may be more vulnerable:
- Motion sickness and jet lag
- *High temperatures:* causing heat-related illnesses and dehydration
- *Low temperatures:* leading to hypothermia
- *Excessive humidity:* can upset body temperature balance
- *Air travel and high altitude:* resulting in reduced oxygen levels, especially in those with chronic lung problems and anaemia
- *Enforced immobility in coaches, trains, and aeroplanes:* leading to deep vein thrombosis
- *Fatigue and exhaustion:* from long journeys and travel delays
- *Physical stress* from walking long distances and carrying heavy luggage
- *Risk from infections* uncommon in the home environment
- *High risk and worse consequences* of road traffic accidents and other sources of injury.

Issues to consider at an early stage include:
- Appropriate routing and travel arrangements
- Appropriate choice of final destination
- Added health risks, from infection, trauma, and the environment
- The risk that illness abroad might exacerbate the effects of ageing and vice versa
- The risks of poor/delayed emergency medical care, in the event of illness or accident
- Purchase of adequate travel health insurance and need for EHIC protection in Europe
- Is medical evacuation and repatriation available and practical?
- Sensible planning of the trip as a whole.

Travel health insurance considerations
- Foreign emergency health care can be expensive
- GPs, ship's doctors, and hospital services may all be chargeable
- Travel health insurance is a priority for older travellers
- Premiums are loaded for those aged over 65 years and cover is sometimes unobtainable or unaffordable
- Exclusions of pre-existing illness may remove cover for the conditions most likely to occur
- Cover must be adequate and provide home repatriation.

Elderly travellers and risk
Elderly travellers do not all face the same degree of risk:-
- *Low risk:* the 'young' old. Those journeying to low-risk destinations e.g. Western Europe; those taking short-haul air journeys; and those with no pre-existing illness
- *Medium risk:* as above, but where travel involves environmental extremes or tropical countries; and medium- to long-haul air travel. The frail old and those with pre-existing chronic illness
- *High risk:* those who are medically unfit or terminally ill. Those with pre-existing illness going to high-risk areas, such as developing countries; and where there will be prolonged travel under cramped conditions. Travel to North America is a high financial risk if insurance cover is absent.

A health assessment at a specialist travel health clinic or by a doctor or nurse with appropriate expertise is advisable for medium- or high-risk travellers.

The pre-travel consultation

Make sure that the following are carefully discussed at your pre-travel consultation:

- Past and current physical status, current medication, transport mode, destination, itinerary, nature of trip, and environmental hazards en route and at the destination, plus advice on:
- Appropriate vaccinations, including pneumonia and influenza protection. Consider vaccination against shingles (Zostavax)
- Malaria prevention and personal repellent protection from mosquito bites
- Medication for motion sickness
- Changes to medication that may be needed because of time zone changes with travel
- Hazards of air travel, jet lag, and avoidance of deep vein thrombosis
- Effects of high altitude and prophylaxis
- Management of travellers' diarrhoea and dehydration
- Chronic and pre-existing illness, functional disability and its effects on travel.

Problems with medication are common—pitfalls include:

- Quality and availability of medical and emergency resources
- Omitting routine medication on day of travel
- Failure to carry routine medication/prescriptions in hand luggage
- Failing to take sufficient medication to cover duration of trip
- Forgetting that pharmacies and ship dispensaries may not carry required medicine, and
- Not recognizing that pharmacies may be far distant, absent, or closed when required. A pre-travel consultation provides a good opportunity to forestall such problems
- Not carrying a personal clinical history summary, to facilitate care in emergency.

Effects of pre-existing health problems (see Table 11.3.1)

Air travel

There are few absolute contraindications to flying—examples include a stroke, coronary or cerebral infarction within 2–3 weeks of intended travel; severe anaemia; and angina or breathlessness while at rest, abdominal surgery, stomach or intestinal bleeding within the previous 3 weeks (see Chapter 7.1).

Anyone with pre-existing health problems should complete an airline form (MEDIF), advising the airline of their condition. Ability to walk about 80m and climb 10–12 steps without symptoms should allow access to the aircraft.

Deep vein thrombosis (DVT) and lung effects

Sitting for prolonged periods can cause leg clots (DVT) and lethal pulmonary embolism (see Chapter 13.6). Aspirin may cause gastric bleeding, and does not protect against DVT. Wear compression stockings. They should be put on before leaving home at the start of the journey, preferably with legs elevated before application. If there is a history of previous DVT or anticoagulant medication, the risk should be discussed with your GP beforehand. Exercise legs regularly on long journeys.

Table 11.3.1 Effects of pre-existing health problems

Problem		Precaution
Heart and circulatory problems	Unaccustomed physical stress and increased activity may cause angina and heart disturbance	Anticipate physical and mental stress and take anti-angina medication
		Use compression stockings for long-haul flight or coach journeys
		Use (and when possible, book) porters for luggage, wheelchairs and buggies for transit, at stations and airports
Lung problems	People with breathlessness at rest should not fly	Those with considerable breathing difficulties can arrange supplemental oxygen during flights
Arthritic disability	Restricted mobility may create problems in cramped airline seating and difficulties in toilets	Book wider seating near entrance doors and the toilet
		Purchase entry to executive lounges
		Consider travelling in business class
Diabetics	Travel across time zones, long journeys, delays, unfamiliar foods, and disruption of the home routine, can lead to problems with blood sugar control	Carry adequate insulin and medication on the person
		Avoid 'diabetic' meals on aeroplanes but have the ordinary meal and count calories instead. See also p.377.

Advice for the fit older traveller

- Ageing skin is more fragile and vulnerable to the effects of strong sunlight—apply high-factor sun block and wear sun-protective spectacles
- Dehydration and extreme heat can increase the risk of a stroke—drink 4L of water per day
- Extremely cold or hot environments are better avoided
- Enter high altitudes above 4000m with forethought and consider anti-acute mountain sickness medication
- Carefully consider availability and quality of medical resources, evacuation, and repatriation facilities at destination.

Advice for older travellers with pre-existing illness

- Check before departure that alteration in drug dose is not required en route or at destination
- Take medications as usual on day of departure
- On flights crossing many time zones adhere to home time until arrival at destination for taking medication
- Carry adequate medication in hand luggage and never stow it in hold baggage
- Carry enough medication for duration of trip and allow 10% extra for delays
- Carry a list of medications routinely taken and a synopsis of past medical history
- Take precautions against DVT (see pp.207–9).

Summary

- Old and very old people travel extensively across the world
- Most can do so safely and will return in good health
- Some are in a higher health-risk group and need to take extra care
- Pre-travel health advice should be considered and is a must for those at higher risk
- All should plan their itinerary carefully, adapting it to needs and limitations
- Take sensible precautions to minimize health risks
- Obtain adequate health insurance, including repatriation cover
- UK travellers should carry the EHIC care when visiting countries with reciprocal medical care.

11.4 The traveller with diabetes

David Matthews

Diabetes is a common health problem that should not cause too much trouble for the well-prepared traveller.

In the UK about 5% of the population have diabetes, in the USA this is nearer to 8% and in the developing world the problem is far greater. In urban Sri Lanka, over 18% of the adult population have diabetes.

Types of diabetes

There are two main types. Type 1 diabetes is generally diagnosed in younger people and always needs insulin therapy. Type 2 diabetes is much more common, usually begins in middle age or above and can often be controlled by diet and tablets. Later in the disease process, many people with type 2 also need insulin.

Travel

With travel, diet is likely to change, the day-to-day routine may be disrupted, the usual supply of tablets or insulin may be more challenging to find, gastro-intestinal upsets are more likely and moving across time zones can raise concerns. Carrying syringes and needles can be a problem at security checks, so proper documentation of diabetes is always necessary.

Before you go

Immunization and malaria protection

Those with diabetes should be immunized in exactly the same way as others. Malaria medication does not interact with medication commonly used in diabetes.

Supplies

Ensure that ample supplies of tablets or insulin, syringes, needles, and blood-testing equipment are carried. All medical supplies should be taken as hand-luggage and kept in a plastic bag for separate security screening. Ensure that all medications are in their original packaging. It is essential that you carry clear identification that you have diabetes, and a list of what items are needed. Insulin is very stable, so storage is generally not a problem.

Do not discontinue any medications without careful medical consultation. If you run out of supplies, some are more critical than others. Insulin must NEVER be discontinued, and doing so can lead to serious problems.

Insurance

Adequate insurance cover (Chapter 13.3) is always essential, and travellers to EU countries should always obtain the EHIC card. It is important to declare any pre-existing conditions to avoid loss of cover.

Thinking about your general health before departure

Particular problems associated with diabetes should be considered. Unstable retinopathy (problems at the back of the eye) can worsen with reduced air-pressure, so ensure your eye review is up-to-date. Some swelling of the legs is normal, but this may exacerbate leg ulcers or foot problems. Deep vein thrombosis (DVT) is more common in those with pre-existing leg and foot ailments—discuss prevention with your doctor (pp.207–9).

Documentation

Some form of documentation of your medical history and current therapy is essential. The documentation should preferably be on a doctor's headed paper. The Medic Alert (✆ www.medicalert.org.uk) bracelet is widely known. Identification will also help if there are any problems with regard to customs officials and security. You should not surrender your equipment to anyone.

The journey

Flying west—on insulin

The time between injections can be lengthened by 2–3 hours twice daily. Regular tests should be performed and if the blood glucose is high a little extra insulin can be given—a fair rule of thumb would be to adjust upwards by 10%. If you have the choice between long-acting and short-acting, then use the short-acting. For those on insulin pumps the basal rate should stay the same and bolus injections given at mealtimes.

Flying east—on insulin

The time between injections will need to be shortened by 2–3 hours each time, which could result in low blood-glucose readings. Careful testing should be performed, and if required each dose can be reduced by 10%. Meals should be taken as normal. Airlines will normally make special provision for those with diabetes if they are notified in advance. For overnight flights, it is sometimes worth eating and taking insulin *before* embarkation.

Hypoglycaemia—relating to travel

One should be especially wary of hypoglycaemia (an abnormally low blood glucose), which may occur in those taking insulin or sulphonylurea tablets. Those on insulin should always have some rapidly absorbable carbohydrate snacks available.

Delays happen frequently, so always carry spare food in case of hypoglycaemia. Fruit, vegetables, nuts, and meat can sometimes be problematic with regards to customs, so check the regulations for the country that you are entering. Cereal bars, biscuits, and sweets or Dextrosol are generally suitable.

Abroad

Whilst away, the chief problems are:
- Vomiting, either from motion sickness or stomach upsets
- Other illnesses affecting diabetic control, e.g. infections
- Hypoglycaemia (a low blood-glucose level)
- Alterations of diabetic control due to changes in diet or activity
- Minor injuries or burning feet on hot sand or stones—so foot protection with sandals or trainers is important, as well as careful attention to injuries and insect bites. If infection develops, take medical advice at once.

Motion sickness

Those with diabetes can use the same anti-motion-sickness tablets as others (Chapter 7.3). If vomiting should occur, the method of managing diabetes is described below.

Vomiting and other illness

The blood-glucose level tends to increase during any illness, even if little food is being taken, and quite often the insulin dose needs to be increased. *Insulin should never be stopped*, otherwise deterioration of diabetes is inevitable, leading to diabetic ketoacidosis (pre-coma) and hospital admission.

Take the following steps:
- Monitor blood-glucose levels carefully at least four times daily. If the results are high (blood-glucose readings greater than 15 mmol/L), then extra insulin is needed. This can be done at the normal times by increasing insulin by about 10%
- Carbohydrate should be maintained if possible by taking the normal quantity in fluid form
- If vomiting persists, or if the general condition deteriorates, you should seek medical help.

Hypoglycaemia—for those on insulin and abroad

Low blood glucose develops if too much insulin is taken; too little food is eaten, if there is a marked increase in activity, and just from lying in the sun. Split insulin doses if you are sunbathing. Take half the usual dose in the morning and the remainder mid-morning.

Alteration of diabetic control

A change in lifestyle may alter diabetic control. If physical activity is much greater than at home, hypoglycaemia is more likely to occur. With unusual exercise the insulin dose (short-acting component) at the time before exercise may need to be reduced by about 50%. Carbohydrate following vigorous exercise is important—this is the time of the greatest danger of hypoglycaemia; extra carbohydrate is also needed *before* prolonged physical exertion.

Alcohol has paradoxical effects on glucose control: beer and lager contain sugar and might cause the blood glucose to rise; on the other hand alcohol can induce hypoglycaemia. So treat alcohol with caution.

Type 2 (non-insulin-dependent) diabetes

There are few problems for those not taking insulin but tests should be conducted as if at home. Above all, those with diabetes should not overeat—actually no one should! If any illness occurs, control must be monitored with care, and attention from a doctor may be necessary

Travelling should not present problems for those with diabetes. Generally, common sense will get one through.

11.5 The immunocompromised traveller

Camille Kotton

International travel exposes travellers to a variety of pathogens that are absent or uncommon in their country of residence. The level of risk depends on the location of travel, types of food, activities pursued, and length of stay. In general, travel within developed countries poses a minimally increased risk for travellers. Visits to developing countries expose travellers to greater risks. Areas in the yellow fever zones are of special concern to immunocompromised travellers.

Definitions of the immunocompromised traveller

Many people have immune systems that are suppressed either because of medications they are taking and/or because of certain diseases they may have, such as cancer, HIV, or other conditions. The risk of infection is directly related to how immunocompromised they are.

People with chronic conditions associated with limited immune deficits, e.g. asplenia, renal disease, chronic liver disease including hepatitis C, diabetes mellitus, those on low-dose corticosteroids, and various complement deficiencies, do not have normal immune systems in general, thus tend to be at lower risk for acquiring infection while travelling. There is very limited information on possible decreased vaccine efficacy or increased adverse events with administration of live vaccines for this group.

Similarly, those with asymptomatic HIV infection are also at only moderately elevated risk of infection, whereas those who are severely immunocompromised due to symptomatic HIV/AIDS or non-HIV, as outlined in Box 11.5.1, are at significantly greater risk.

Timing of travel

Appropriate timing of travel may help decrease the risk of infection and subsequent complications. Waiting until one's health issues are stable is paramount. In general, it would be prudent to wait 1 year after solid organ transplant and 2 years after bone-marrow transplant before travelling to the developing world. Optimal timing should be discussed on an individual basis with one's medical team.

Travel destinations including yellow fever zones

Destinations in the developing world are variable regarding risk of infection. For example, some areas may have higher rates of diarrhoeal disease and typhoid fever or transiently elevated risks of infections such

---

Box 11.5.1 **Significantly immunocompromised hosts**

- HIV+ with CD4 <200/mm^3
- Active leukemia or lymphoma
- Other active cancers
- Aplastic anaemia
- Congenital immunodeficiency
- Persons who have received current or recent radiation therapy
- Solid organ transplant within first year
- Bone marrow transplant recipients within 2 years of transplantation (or >2 years ago, but who are still taking immunosuppressive drugs)
- Graft-versus-host disease after bone marrow transplant
- High-dose corticosteroids. Most clinicians consider a dose of either >2mg/kg of body weight or ≥20mg/day of prednisone or equivalent, when administered for ≥2 weeks, as sufficiently immunosuppressive to raise concern about the safety of vaccination with live-virus vaccines.

Patients taking any of the following:
- Cancer chemotherapy (excluding tamoxifen) including methotrexate within the past 3 months
- Transplant-related immunosuppressive drugs (e.g. cyclosporine, tacrolimus, sirolimus, and mycophenolate mofetil)
- Tumour necrosis factor (TNF) blocking agents such as etanercept, adalimumab, and infliximab
- Alkylating agents (e.g. cyclophosphamide)
- Antimetabolites (e.g. azathioprine, 6-mercaptopurine)
- Mitoxantrone (used in multiple sclerosis).

Source: Data from Elaine C. Jong and David O. Freedman, Advising Travelers With Specific Needs: Immunocompromised Travelers in CDC and edited by Gary W. Brunette, CDC Health Information for International Travel 2012, 2012,© Oxford University Press Inc.

as dengue fever. Since it is not safe for severely immunocompromised hosts to be given yellow fever vaccination, they may wish to skip travel to such regions (see Chapter 5.2). Also, the quality of healthcare available in certain areas is better than in others. For example, those wishing to go on an African safari may find better healthcare in southern Africa.

Discussions with your healthcare team

Before making any significant plans, it would be prudent to discuss your proposed travel agenda with your healthcare team. They may have further input regarding optimal timing of travel, specific risks, and decisions about specific destinations, and they may request a referral to a travel medicine specialist. In addition, they may have local contacts in your destination that could be helpful if illness arose.

Vaccinations

Immunocompromised travellers need many of the same vaccines as other travellers. Certain live vaccines, however, should not be given to the most vulnerable people, including vaccines against yellow fever, *Salmonella typhi* (as oral Ty21a), polio (oral vaccine only), measles, varicella, mumps, rubella, and tuberculosis. Additionally, vaccines may not give as much protection due to the attenuated immune system. Sometimes gamma globulin is given in lieu of hepatitis A vaccine; it may provide protection against other types of infection as well. For more information, see Table 11.5.1.

Yellow fever vaccine should not be given to persons who are significantly immunocompromised. Travellers who are mildly immunocompromised should be offered the choice of being vaccinated. If immunization is not performed, the traveller should be advised of the risks, instructed in methods to avoid mosquito bites and provided with a vaccination waiver letter. Those whose destinations or transit stops include countries requiring yellow fever vaccination (see Map 5.2.2) should also carry a vaccination waiver letter, which is available through a yellow fever vaccination centre and must be signed by a physician.

Medications and drug interactions

Immunocompromised people should be aware of the risk of drug interactions as well as side effects from new medications, both with those they are given for malaria prophylaxis and treatment of diarrhoea and other infections, as well as for other medical problems they may develop while travelling. For example, many liver transplant recipients are told to not take acetaminophen; in many countries, this is called paracetamol and the transplant patient may not realize that it is the same drug. Given the complexity of individual medical regimens, it is recommended that computer-based drug interaction calculators be used. It is prudent to check with your usual healthcare team in order to make sure new medications are safe. Additionally, it is important to ask whether new medications should be dosed based on reduced renal or liver function. All medication should be appropriately labelled and in original packaging to prevent confiscation at a port of entry.

Food and water precautions

Food and water present the highest risk of infection for travellers. Food-borne illness can be more severe and even fatal for the immunocompromised traveller. For example, *Salmonella* bacteria, which may be present in unpasteurized dairy products, or raw or undercooked eggs, poultry or meat, causing diarrhoeal illness in the healthy traveller, may cause a life-threatening bloodstream infection (septicaemia) in immunocompromised people. Similarly, infections caused by *Shigella* and *Campylobacter* can be more severe.

It is strongly recommended travellers be extremely careful with what they eat and drink. All water should be bottled, boiled, or chemically treated before consumption. Ice should not be used unless one is sure that it is made with treated water. Pasteurized beverages and dairy products may be safely consumed. Fresh fruits and vegetables should be washed and peeled before consumption. Salad, tomatoes, grapes, raspberries, and other produce that cannot be peeled should not be consumed. Meat and fish should be cooked thoroughly. Risky foods, such as sushi and steak tartar, or any type of food served from street vendors should not be eaten. Before eating, travellers should wash their hands or use hand sanitizer. It is important to be as careful about eating in friends' homes as in commercial establishments. Eating in the homes of friends and relatives has been shown to convey a slightly higher risk of food-borne illness, perhaps due to a false sense of safety.

All travellers should carry antibiotics for self-treatment in the event that they develop significant diarrhoea, especially if they have fever or blood in their stool. Immunocompromised people should have a lower threshold to take such antibiotics for self-treatment of diarrhoea. Appropriate antibiotics include fluoroquinolones (such as ciprofloxacin or levofloxacin) or azithromycin. Rifaximin has a narrower spectrum of coverage and has not been tested in immunocompromised hosts.

Water-borne infections may also result from swallowing water during recreational activities. Therefore, travellers should avoid swallowing water while swimming and should not swim in water that may be contaminated. In general, clean chlorinated swimming pools should be fine for swimming.

Avoiding insect-borne disease and sun exposure

Numerous diseases can be transmitted by insects. Travellers should be vigilant, and use insect repellent containing DEET, which is the most effective repellent available. They should also use clothing to protect against bites. At night, they should sleep in a well-screened room or use mosquito netting, as well as mosquito coils. In areas endemic for ticks, they should be careful to do skin checks and remove ticks properly. In certain regions, travellers should be aware of the risk of leishmaniasis, a parasitic infection transmitted by the sandfly (Chapter 5.5).

In malarial zones, prophylaxis against malaria should be used. All of the anti-malarial preventative medications can be used, although the providing clinician should look carefully for potential drug interactions. (See Kotton and Hibberd (2009), on p.506, for specific guidance.)

Table 11.5.1 Significantly immunocompromised hosts

Vaccine	Recommendations for adults	Recommendations for children
Routine		
Influenza—parenteral	Yearly	Yearly
Influenza—intranasal*	Contraindicated	Contraindicated
Pneumococcal polysaccharide	Recommended: booster after 5 years	Administration at age 2 years
Tetanus/diphtheria	Recommended: booster after 10 years	Recommended per CDC guidelines
Pertussis	Recommended in combination with Tetanus and Diphtheria once	Recommended per CDC guidelines
Human papilloma virus	Recommended when indicated	Recommended per CDC guidelines
MMR*	Contraindicated	Contraindicated
Varicella*	Contraindicated	Contraindicated
Varicella zoster*	Contraindicated	Not applicable
Travel-related		
Hepatitis A	Recommended when indicated	Recommended per CDC guidelines, minimum age for first dose age 12 months
Hepatitis B	Recommended when indicated	Recommended per CDC guidelines, at birth
Meningococcal conjugate	Recommended when indicated	Recommended per CDC guidelines, minimum age for first dose age 2 months
Typhim Vi	Recommended when indicated	Recommended when indicated for >6 years old
Polio-inactivated (IPV)	Recommended when indicated	Recommended when indicated, minimum age 2 months
Polio-oral (OPV)*	Contraindicated in patients/family members	Contraindicated in patients/family members
Rabies	Recommended when indicated	Recommended when indicated, any age
Japanese encephalitis	Recommended when indicated	Recommended when indicated, minimum for first dose age 12 months

(Continued)

Table 11.5.1 (Contd.)

Vaccine	Recommendations for adults	Recommendations for children
S. typhi Ty21a*	Contraindicated	Contraindicated
Bacille Calmette Guerin*	Contraindicated	Contraindicated
Yellow fever*	Contraindicated	Contraindicated

* Live, attenuated.

For quality of evidence, please see Kotton CN, Hibberd PL (2009). Travel medicine and the solid organ transplant recipient. Am J Transplant **9**: S273–81.

Adapted from the Centres of Disease Control 'Recommended Adult Immunization Schedule-United States 2007-2008' (7) 'Advising Travelers with Specific Needs: The Immunocompromised Traveler' in Centers of Disease Control's Health Information for International Travel' (50), and 'Guidelines for Vaccination of Solid Organ Transplant Candidates and Recipients' (9).

Reproduced from Kotton CN, Hibberd PL, and the AST Infectious Diseases Community of Practice (2009). Travel medicine and the solid organ transplant recipient. Am J Transplant **9**: S273–81, with permission of Wiley Blackwell.

Many immunocompromised people are at higher risk of developing skin cancer. In addition, their medications may make them more photosensitive, thus at higher risk for developing rashes after sun exposure. Travellers should use sun lotion with a high protection factor (SPF). They should also use appropriate clothing to avoid exposure to direct sunlight, in particular between 10am and 2pm.

Tuberculosis

TB poses a significant risk in some regions. All immunocompromised persons should receive a skin or blood test for TB as part of routine care. Since this test becomes less reliable as immunodeficiency advances, any symptoms suggestive of TB (prolonged cough, fever, weight loss, night sweats) should prompt evaluation by a physician even if the skin or blood test is negative. Travellers should consult with their physician regarding appropriate testing for TB before and after travel.

Insurance and medical care abroad

Travellers should make sure their insurance will cover them for medical expenses (Chapter 13.3). In addition, they should develop a plan for obtaining excellent healthcare as well as medications while travelling. Their embassies or consulates in the destination country should be able to provide guidance. Certain websites can also help provide such information (for example, see individual country information at ℘ www.mdtravel-health.com). They should ask their usual medical team for recommended healthcare institutions in the destination countries.

HIV-infected travellers should be aware that some countries may inquire about HIV status, some may require HIV testing as a condition of travel, and some may even deny entry to HIV-infected persons. Information on regulations and requirements maybe obtained from appropriate consular authorities.

Returning home

Anyone who returns home unwell, or who becomes ill shortly after travel, should highlight the recent travel to the treating healthcare team, as certain regions carry higher risks for specific infections. If necessary, care from a clinician trained in travel medicine should be sought.

Box 11.5.2 **Summary of advice for immunocompromised travellers**

• Review your itinerary with your healthcare team well in advance of travel to developing countries
• Obtain appropriate vaccinations before travel. Live vaccines should generally be avoided
• Follow the advice in this book about avoiding food- and water-borne diseases, since some can be particularly dangerous for immunocompromised travellers
• Carry a supply of antibiotics to take in the event of diarrhoea, but consult a physician if they don't work or if you develop shaking chills, bloody diarrhoea, or dehydration
• Be aware of and know how to avoid health risks in the regions in your itinerary
• Be prepared to seek healthcare during travel and understand what your insurance benefits are prior to travel.

11.6 The disabled traveller

Agnes Fletcher

These days, taking a holiday is no frivolous luxury. It can make a huge difference to your health and how you cope with life. Increasingly, holiday accommodation in the UK and abroad has accessible features, such as ramps, handrails, and raised toilets. Facilities for people with visual and hearing impairments and long-term health conditions are also improving. There are more insurance companies offering affordable travel insurance, too.

These changes are partly due to legislation and partly to businesses recognizing the case for making their services accessible. Disabled people number up to 20% of the population in most countries. Along with friends and families travelling with them, that's a huge potential volume of business.

While many disabled people are seasoned travellers, experienced in the art of getting from A to B in difficult circumstances, others need the reassurance of knowing exactly what the journey and destination will bring. For some, comfort and safety demand precision planning and support from staff.

Planning and booking a holiday

Before you book, be clear about what type of trip you are making. Will you travel on your own, with family and friends, as part of an organized group? Do you want to stay somewhere where all the meals are provided or would you prefer self-catering accommodation? What part of the world do you fancy?

Local tourist office publications should give some information on accommodation and attractions suitable for people with mobility difficulties and possibly hearing and visual impairments. Think about what is essential and what is desirable to meet your needs.

Next, make arrangements for getting to and from your holiday destination and make sure you have adequate insurance cover—particularly for healthcare if you are going abroad. A lot of insurers exclude pre-existing conditions, but some don't. Shop around to get adequate coverage—it could be important (Chapter 13.3).

If you take medication, make sure you have adequate supplies. You could also take relevant written prescriptions for use in an emergency (see Chapter 13.5).

Disabled travellers should follow the same general guidance on health found elsewhere in this book, and should carry the European Health Insurance Card to make use of reciprocal health agreements with a number of other countries, particularly in the European Union (Chapter 13.3).

Details of specialist immunization clinics can be found in Appendix 1.

When booking travel and accommodation, ask questions that are sufficiently detailed and consider what arrangements will suit you best:

Aeroplanes: Is there a ramp or mobile corridor for boarding? A wheelchair-accessible lavatory? An aisle chair for moving disabled passengers to their seats? What are the oxygen regulations? Is a companion necessary? Can you have a bulkhead seat that allows more room for manoeuvre? Can you take your own wheelchair to the aircraft door? If you use a pressure-relieving cushion, place it on the airline seat. Take advantage of early boarding even if you are not visibly disabled—it is there for your convenience and may mean you don't have to stand for long periods in a queue. Business-class lavatories are likely to be bigger and the seats and aisles wider—upgrade if possible.

Buses: Is there a mechanical wheelchair lift? Are employees permitted to lift passengers manually? On group tours, are buses available in which passengers can remain in their wheelchairs, and can these be safely secured to the floor? Do rest stops have accessible lavatories and restaurants?

Car travel: Many European countries operate national schemes of parking concessions similar to the UK's blue badge scheme. Often these concessions apply to visitors who are blue badge holders but make sure you understand the local rules. Details are available from the Department for Transport.

Ships: How wide are the cabin, bathroom, and lift doors? Is there enough turning space to allow a wheelchair user to get into the bathroom? Is there room for a wheelchair user at restaurant tables? Are there ramps over doorsills? If not, are portable ramps available? Is there accessible transport for sightseeing in port?

Trains: Are there accessible lavatories? Where are they located? Can food be brought to the passenger? Is there a difference in height between the platform and the train? Do the stations have accessible lavatories? Are porters and ramps available?

Hotels, hostels, and campsites: What is the physical access like? Are there rooms on the ground floor? Are the doors wide enough? What are the measurements of the bathroom? Is there a bath or shower with pull-down seat? What support can they offer someone with a hearing or sight impairment or a learning disability, in terms of orientation, refreshments, and fire safety?

Particular conditions and travel

Blindness

Staff should be able to read information to a visitor with a visual impairment. If flight attendants do not volunteer the information, they should be asked the number of rows to the nearest exit. Passengers should check whether assistance dogs are permitted in cabins and what quarantine restrictions apply. Some countries require medical certificates for dogs (see also p.386). Check with the embassy or consulate of the destination country and don't rely on airlines for complete information.

Deafness

Transport and hotel staff should be informed about a hearing impairment and asked to make sure that announcements are delivered visually or in person. Many hotels have installed fire and smoke detectors with flashing lights as well as sirens. Hearing-assistance dogs, trained to alert their owners to specific situations, are becoming more common. The same precautions apply as for other assistance dogs.

In some countries, text telephone (minicom) reservation systems for those with hearing or speech impairments are widely available. In the UK, Text Relay is a national service that allows people who are deaf to use a text phone to speak to hearing people.

Diabetes

Major requirements for people with diabetes are refrigeration facilities for insulin and 24 hour access to food. It is best to carry small snacks at all times, since meals in transit may be delayed or even skipped.

Diabetes UK offers information to people with diabetes, including a travel guide leaflet and specific guides for popular holiday destinations (see also Chapter 11.4).

Heart disease

Heart conditions should not preclude travelling, unless constant medical supervision is necessary, but it is important to take sensible precautions. Avoid high altitudes and extremely cold weather, keep schedules flexible enough to avoid stress, and use luggage with wheels or a collapsible luggage carrier. If you prefer the convenience of an organized tour but want to avoid the often frenetic pace, consider going on a tour specifically for disabled people. This can be an excellent choice for people with heart conditions or anyone who simply requires a slower pace. Cruises, too, provide an especially low-key mode of travel, but be sure that all decks of the ship are accessible by lift.

Kidney disease

With their doctor's approval, people with kidney problems can travel abroad and maintain their dialysis routine at hospitals and renal centres that give treatment to visitors. A doctor's summary and recommendations for treatment will be required. If travel plans are delayed or cancelled, the host unit should be notified immediately because failure to appear could disrupt scheduling and inconvenience regular patients.

Mental health conditions

If you experience anxiety, it is particularly important to feel confident that you have planned all aspects of a trip carefully. Knowing what to expect and making contact with relevant staff can make a big difference to how smoothly things go. There should be no stigma about discussing your condition—if people know what support you need, they should be keen to make your travel experience as easy as possible.

Respiratory problems

If you have a respiratory condition and use an oxygen-powered respirator, you must make special arrangements with airlines and shipping companies. Most ships, but not all, permit passengers to bring their own oxygen aboard. Airlines require 24 to 48 hr notice and must abide by strict safety regulations, so it is best to consult as far in advance of travel as possible. Often, only airline-supplied oxygen may be used, for which there may or may not be an additional charge. Dry-cell battery respirators are allowed on aircrafts. If your respirator needs a domestic electrical supply, you must be able to manage without it for the length of your air journey, plus a couple of hours' leeway (in case of delay in take-off or landing).

While the USA and Canada use a 110-volt electrical system, most other countries operate on a 220-volt electric current. A converter is necessary to use a respirator on an incompatible current, plus adaptors for differently shaped plugs even with similar current.

11.7 Expedition medicine

Jon Dallimore

Expedition team members represent a unique group of travellers. Preparing them for their trip involves a thorough understanding of the problems they may encounter. They may operate in remote, even hostile, environments with unreliable or non-existent communications, limited medical supplies and little or no medical back-up. In all cases, careful preparation avoids many problems.

Expedition teams and organization

An expedition can be defined as a journey with a purpose. Expeditions vary in terms of numbers of team members, planned activities, and duration. Some consist of solo adventurers; others join together in large numbers to undertake multiple projects.

Team members need to be motivated, suitable for the task and thoroughly briefed and trained. They need to understand the risks and to undertake expedition-specific training, such as crevasse rescue, or medical training.

When contemplating taking part in an expedition important factors to consider include:

- Duration of the planned expedition
- Personal reasons to participate
- Activities to be undertaken
- Costs—what is included, and are there any hidden costs?
- Personal skills and experience required
- Who are the other participants?
- Who is leading and organizing the expedition? Are they suitably experienced?
- Will there be any pre-expedition training?
- Are there robust medical back-up and rescue plans in place?

Expedition risks

The health and safety risks should be identified so that individuals become aware of the dangers they may face. The risks to health will vary depending on the location, the activities and the participants themselves. In general, expeditions do not result in many serious injuries. The common risks are the same as for other travellers: diarrhoea; coughs, colds and sore throats; skin problems; strains, sprains, and minor injuries. Depending on the activities there may be risks of altitude sickness, heat illnesses, or tropical diseases (particularly malaria). Psychological or behavioural problems may also occur. Serious illnesses and injuries might include drowning, falls, traffic accidents, altitude illness, and heatstroke, infections (malaria, hepatitis, and HIV) and very rarely homicide or kidnapping.

Incidence of expedition medical problems

A few studies have been undertaken to look at the incidence of health problems on expeditions. There was a large study of youth expeditions in 2001. In this study, 2915 teenagers aged 15–18 years visited 34 different countries on 250 expeditions. Illness or injury was reported in 64%, of these 6% required hospital treatment or local medical treatment, seven of them were repatriated to the UK and there was one fatality, following a fall while trekking in Vietnam. Five youngsters were involved in a single road accident and there were two snakebites, one from an anaconda, the other a king brown. In this study population there were 13 psychological issues, including para-suicide, deliberate self harm and panic attacks. The most prevalent problems were diarrhoea (22%), nausea/vomiting (20%), respiratory infections (13%), headache (11%). Injuries accounted for 10% of the reported problems.

The Royal Geographical Society examined data from 246 expeditions with 2381 participants. In this study there were nine repatriations and two deaths (from kidnapping). There was a calculated incidence of 6.4 incidents per 1000 man days. Again, gastrointestinal upsets were common (33%), 17% were related to injuries, and environmental problems accounted for 14%.

See Box 11.7.1 for a summary of risks and hazards.

Managing the risks—health advice for team members

The success of the expedition is likely to depend on the health of its members. All team members should be given clear advice:

Before departure everyone should be physically fit for the planned activities, have had all the necessary immunizations (see Chapter 13.2) and have a supply of anti-malarial medication (see Chapter 5.1). Pre-expedition briefings should cover methods of insect bite avoidance (Chapter 5.12).

Box 11.7.1 **Expedition risks and hazards**

General risks
- *Effects of the sun*: sunburn and dehydration
- *Thermal injuries* (hot and cold)
- *Poor water quality*: risks of diarrhoeal illnesses
- *Food hygiene*: gastroenteritis
- *Isolation or overcrowding*: psychological issues and increased risks of infection
- *Human behaviour*: attitudes, and behaviour.

Expedition risks and hazards
- *Wildlife*: animal bites or attacks, insect bites
- *Local conditions*: lack of shelter, dangerous roads, open fires, endemic diseases
- *Human factors*: assault, kidnapping, political unrest, and other conflict.

Specific expedition risks and hazards
- *High altitude*: acute mountain sickness (AMS), falls, hypothermia, frostbite, snow blindness, carbon monoxide poisoning
- *Desert*: sunburn, dehydration, heat-related illnesses, snakes, scorpions
- *Jungle*: wound infections, injuries, river crossing, danger of deadfall
- *Maritime*: hand injuries, blisters, motion sickness, psychological reactions, eye damage
- *Diving*: decompression sickness, marine envenomation, ear infections, drowning.

Blisters are common on trekking trips and are best avoided by wearing worn-in, comfortable boots or trekking shoes. A 'hot spot' on the feet should be treated with a plaster or specialized blister dressing before it worsens. Athlete's foot can be a problem in jungle areas. The feet must be dried at the end of the day and treated with anti-fungal creams as necessary. See foot care, Chapter 9.4.

Sore knees and twisted ankles may be avoided by an already high level of fitness and by warming up and stretching. Using trekking poles, knee or ankle supports and anti-inflammatories can also help.

- *Dental problems:* everyone on the trip should have a check-up 3 months before departure. See Chapter 9.2
- *Traveller's diarrhoea:* though common, it is usually short-lived and clears up with rest and fluids. Antibiotics such as ciprofloxacin or azithromycin are sometimes needed to treat more persistent diarrhoea or if blood is present in the stools. See Chapter 2.1
- *Dry skin:* this can be troublesome—particularly at high altitude in cold climates. All team members should carry lip balm and hydrating cream. See Chapter 9.1 for dermatological problems

- *Female health:* menstrual periods are often missed while travelling, especially at high altitude. Some women choose to delay their period by taking norethisterone or running packets of the combined oral contraceptive pill together without having a pill-free break. Sanitary towels or tampons may be difficult to obtain and this should be considered. Hygienic ways of sanitary product disposal will vary depending on the environment. Some women develop vaginal thrush in hot, humid climates. Anti-fungal cream or fluconazole tablets can be used to treat this irritating condition. See gynaecological issues, Chapter 9.7
- *Human behaviour:* this can affect the wellbeing of any expedition team. In particular, drug and alcohol use make accidents more likely. Sometimes, particularly on diving trips, there may need to be very clear rules about the use of alcohol. Unprotected sexual intercourse can spread sexually transmitted infections and result in unplanned pregnancies. These issues must be discussed openly beforehand.

Environmental conditions

Participants should be aware of the signs and symptoms of hypothermia and local cold injuries. Wet and windy conditions make hypothermia most likely and temperatures below minus 32°C are very dangerous. If a party member starts shivering, stumbling or becomes very cold the activity must be stopped and shelter sought rapidly. The victim must be placed in a warm sleeping bag with dry clothes.

In frostbite, parts of the body become frozen and ice crystals form in the cells. Hands, feet, and face are the most likely sites. Frostbite should be suspected if there is a loss of feeling in the extremities. Treatment of frostbite includes re-warming, elevation, strong painkillers, and evacuation for specialist assessment. Frostbite and hypothermia are best prevented by using the correct clothing and judging weather conditions carefully (Chapter 8.4).

Ultraviolet rays can burn the eyes and skin and participants should all wear sunglasses in snow. Snow blindness produces bad headaches and gritty eyes and is treated with rest, painkillers, and eye patching. See Chapter 8.5.

Sunburn is common. At high altitude there is less protection from the sun's rays so hats, long-sleeved shirts, and trousers should be worn. High-factor sun creams help to prevent sun damage. Remember reflected light from snow or water may burn nostrils and under the chin.

Desert and jungle areas can lead to heat illnesses. Over-exertion and inadequate fluid intake in hot environments are usually the causes. See Chapter 8.4. AMS occurs above 2500m. It is potentially deadly but can be prevented by taking note of warning signs and taking necessary precautions. Awareness of the dangers is essential. See altitude-related illnesses, Chapter 8.3.

Fleas and bed-bugs can be avoided by keeping clean and not sharing bedding. Leeches lie in wait in jungle areas and can work themselves into boots and socks. They can be removed with salt, alcohol, or lighters. Leech bites cause bleeding and bruising and rarely become infected, but leeches do not spread diseases. Ticks can spread diseases, so they should be removed on discovery and the skin cleaned. It is important to watch the bite site to make sure it has not become infected as this may be a sign of typhus or other diseases (see Chapter 5.11).

Scorpion stings are very painful, but rarely lethal. Treatment is with pain-killers. Snake bites are very rare as most snakes move away when anyone comes near. Team members need to know about the risks from snakes and be advised to wear boots and be careful when collecting firewood. Torches should be used at night. Treatment of snakebite involves rest, cleaning with antiseptic, a compression bandage, and evacuation. In some circumstances, it may be appropriate to have anti-venom available (Chapter 6).

All water supplies should be treated with suspicion and part of the pre-expedition briefing should include methods for purifying water. Bottled water is usually safe but creates a large amount of unsightly plastic waste. Other methods to purify water include boiling, halogens, filtration, and UV sterilization. See Chapter 3.2.

Everyone should wash his or her hands carefully before eating or handling food. Alcohol hand gels are very convenient for expedition use. When eating out, ice cubes, ice cream, and unboiled milk should be avoided. Salads are only safe if they have been washed in purified water.

Careful food handling is key to the success of an expedition. All team members are likely to be involved with preparing food and it is essential that food is carefully stored, prepared, and cooked. Waste food must be carefully disposed of to avoid attracting animals into camping areas.

Where to seek help

Medical support and evacuation plans should be researched before the expedition starts. A list of questions to ask are given in Box 11.7.2.

Box 11.7.2 **Questions to ask**

- Is there medical support in country—clinics, hospitals, and dispensaries?
- What are the methods of communication—radio, satellite phones, email, cell phone?
- Are there local rescue services—military, national parks, mountain rescue teams, flying doctors (e.g. Himalayan Rescue Association, Medical Air Rescue Service, Zimbabwe or AMREF, Kenya)?

Written risk assessment

A formal assessment should identify all the hazards and potential risks. If risks are identified then the risk level should be estimated and measures to control them clearly documented. The process should be regularly reviewed as risks change with time and as the expedition undertakes different activities in new environments.

Pre-existing health problems

Some expedition team members will have ongoing health problems and these must be considered during the planning stage. Most will be able to travel safely, provided any risks are addressed beforehand. Often the main concern is that adequate medical facilities to deal with potential problems may be remote. There is always a balance to strike between risks and benefits of expedition travel.

To minimize the risks all participants should complete a carefully worded health questionnaire. In some cases, it will be essential to obtain more information from the patient, the GP, or specialist. Important questions to consider include:

- Has the individual been able to travel safely in similar circumstances?
- How stable is the condition?
- When severe, how bad can the medical problem become?
- Is there a treatment plan for managing exacerbations?
- In all cases, the environment, duration of the expedition, medical back-up, communications, and evacuation logistics will help to stratify the risks
- Full details of the medical condition should be available
- The group medical kit may require extra items
- Where is the nearest *suitable* medical facility and how would the patient get there quickly?
- If there are outstanding risks, is the individual prepared to accept them?
- Has the insurance company agreed to cover the pre-existing conditions?

In a very few cases individuals may be deemed to be travelling at *unacceptable* risk and they should not join the expedition. Where uncertainty remains, performance during training courses or an independent medical examination may help determine fitness to partake.

Box 11.7.3 **Suggested screening questions**

Is there a history of:
- Asthma, epilepsy or diabetes?
- Allergies?
- Are medications taken on a regular or occasional basis?
- Heart problems?
- Recurring back or joint problems?
- Psychological or psychiatric disorders, including eating disorders, deliberate self-harm, overdoses, depression, or anxiety?
- Objections to any form of treatment including blood transfusions, immunizations, or conventional medication?

Legal issues for expeditions

Moral and ethical duties may exist to rescue another person, but must be distinguished from legal duties. Most people are willing to help sick or injured people in their own party or strangers whom they encounter, however, in some countries, e.g. France, it a legal offence not to provide assistance.

Each person has a duty of care to not injure others. Leaders or members of a group have a clear duty of care to each other should they become ill or injured. Once a person undertakes a rescue, there is a legal duty to complete the rescue without causing personal injury, but the law does not expect anyone to lose his or her own life. Physicians are under a legal duty to render emergency care to their own patient, and the General Medical Council expects doctors to provide emergency assistance. British Standard 8848 makes clear the requirements and responsibilities for those who organize expedition and adventure travel.

Many expedition teams consider providing medical help to local people and this also raises important ethical and legal concerns:

1. Local health problems may be unfamiliar and there is a risk that these will be diagnosed incorrectly
2. The main purpose of the expedition medical officer is to provide healthcare for the team, not for others who may be encountered during the trip
3. Local healthcare professionals and healers may be offended by the actions of well-intentioned expedition medics
4. There may be no opportunities for medical supervision and follow-up as the expedition moves on
5. Expectations among local people may be raised that the local medical services cannot meet.

For most expedition groups it is sensible to treat serious illness or injury conditions in local people, and it is important to remember that cook boys, porters, muleteers, and other local staff who are part of the 'extended expedition team' should be cared for by the group.

Confidentiality

Sensitive, private medical information should be kept confidential from non-caring staff during and after any expedition. Communications with the home country organizers, employers, and via radio links, websites, blogs, and expedition reports may unwittingly breach an individual's rights to confidentiality. Medical records must be stored securely and health issues should not be discussed 'around the campfire' without a patient's express consent.

Medical negligence

There have been no cases, to date, of an expedition doctor being sued in the United Kingdom but this does not mean that one can be complacent. Negligence is difficult to prove and the 'Bolam test' examines whether a practitioner owed a duty of care, if there was an accepted standard of care, whether this duty was breached and if this breach caused or materially contributed to an injury. For doctors, 'the test is the standard of the ordinary skilled man exercising and professing to have that special skill. A man need not possess the highest expert skill at the risk of being found negligent. It is sufficient if he exercises the skill of an ordinary man exercising that particular art'. (Bolam v Friern Hospital Management Committee 1957). This means that if a practitioner holds himself out to be an expedition doctor his actions are judged against what might reasonably be expected of a competent expedition doctor, even if this is the first time he has ever taken on such a role.

Avoiding litigation

Brief, accurate, and contemporaneous medical records should be made for all clinical encounters. Whenever a patient is evacuated or referred to a formal medical facility, they should be accompanied by clear notes outlining the history and treatment to date. The law courts will take into consideration the difficulties of operating in challenging environments but it is essential to ensure that all potential patients are aware of the medical skills of the medical officer, the limitations of possible treatments, the medical equipment carried, and evacuation times for each stage of the expedition.

Doctors must contact their professional indemnity insurance providers before each trip. Some doctors may provide advice to expeditions, or prescribe medication for use by expeditions departing without a medically qualified team member. In these cases, there must be clear, written guidelines for the use of medication or how to manage medical conditions. Medication guidelines should include drug indications, doses, and common side effects.

Expedition insurance

Specialized insurance companies are often needed for expeditions to remote places. The insurers require full disclosure or they may decline to meet the cost of a claim—this is very important for those with pre-existing medical conditions, e.g. diabetes. Any expedition travel policy must cover search and rescue costs, medical repatriation, and evacuation and may need to cover specialized medical or other equipment.

Research on expeditions

Some expeditions involve research on the participants or local populations. For example, important work on high-altitude physiology has been conducted during expeditions and this has contributed to scientific understanding of altitude-related illnesses. All research must be ethically approved and each participant must give his or her informed consent. Participants have the right to withdraw from a study at any point and their rights to confidentiality must be respected. All data should be collected and stored securely.

Qualities of the expedition medical officer

The appointed medical officer must be a member of the team and be happy to join in—including preparing food, contributing to the project work, and helping with the day-to-day running of the expedition. Most medical problems on expeditions are minor and the medical officer should encourage the team members to manage these themselves, with guidance if required. It is never possible to cater for every possible eventuality and so the ability to improvise is desirable. The medical officer should have an easy-going nature but maintain a professional relationship with everyone—all are potential patients, so one cannot fall out with team members (or fall in love with them either!).

Whoever takes on the role of medical officer should be suitably experienced and comfortable operating in difficult terrain. Sometimes it may be possible to get a more senior medical opinion via satellite phone, radio or even email, but communications are not always available. It helps to be comfortable with the management of uncertainty as many illnesses present gradually without any clear features to indicate the need for more advanced medical help. Tests and investigations may have to wait until a patient can be evacuated to a clinic or hospital and this might take a long time.

The expedition medical officer must be prepared to share a tent with patients and to be permanently 'on call' as emergencies can arise at any time.

Medical kits

A general medical kit may be used for most expeditions but will need to be tailored to a trip according to the local medical facilities, the number in the team and the potential need to treat local people. Members of the team with special medical needs may require particular medications and the medical experience of the medical officer will also influence the choice of items in the group kit. The weight and bulk of the medical kit need to be considered.

It is never possible to have medical supplies for every eventuality. For most expeditions few serious medical problems are anticipated but it is important to have adequate supplies to treat minor ailments—blisters, headaches, cuts, sprains, diarrhoea, sunburn, bites, and stings. Serious illnesses and injuries can occur and there should be some provision for these but the risks and hazards vary enormously depending on the activities and the environment.

Each team member should carry their own first-aid kit and this should contain a simple painkiller, antihistamine tablets, a blister kit, oral rehydration salts in sachets, adhesive plasters and dressings, hydrocortisone and Eurax cream for bites and stings together with a generous supply of any regular medication with some spare. Depending on the destination, insect repellents and sunblock cream may be required. Sometimes altitude drugs and drugs for the treatment of malaria and tropical disease will be needed.

See Chapter 13.5; see also Box 11.7.4.

Box 11.7.4 **Important points about medical kits**

- Every team member should know where the medical kit is kept
- Items should be packed in waterproof and dustproof containers
- Some liquids may need to be protected from extremes of heat
- Liquid medicines are best avoided because of weight and bulk
- Pills and capsules should be packed as complete courses, preferably in blister packs
- Pack related items together and clearly mark the contents and dosages
- Depending on the type of expedition, consider smaller kits for outlying camps.

Box 11.7.5 **Expedition medication checklist**

Antimicrobials
- Ceftriaxone 1g ampoules
- Chloramphenicol ointment
- Ciprofloxacin 250mg tabs
- Clarithromycin 250mg tabs
- Co-amoxiclav (Augmentin) 375mg tabs
- Doxycycline 50mg caps
- Metronidazole 200mg tabs
- Quinine sulphate 300mg tabs.

Painkillers and local anaesthetics
- Aspirin 300mg tabs
- Co-codamol (30/500) tabs
- Ibuprofen 400mg tabs
- Lidocaine 1% 5mL ampoules
- Paracetamol 500mg tabs
- Tetracaine (amethocaine) eye drops
- Tramadol 50mg caps
- Tramadol for injection 100mg ampoules.

Other medication
- Acetazolamide 250mg (Diamox) tabs
- BiSoDol antacid tabs
- Chlorphenamine 4mg (Piriton) tabs
- Chlorphenamine 10mg for injection
- Dexamethasone 2mg tabs
- Dioralyte sachets
- Epinephrine (adrenaline) 1mg ampoules
- Hydrocortisone for injection 100mg ampoules
- Loperamide capsules
- Movicol sachets
- Nifedipine MR 10mg tabs
- Prochlorperazine 5mg (Stemetil) tabs
- Prochlorperazine 12.5mg for injection
- Prochlorperazine (Buccastem) 3mg sublingual tabs
- Ranitidine 150mg tabs
- Salbutamol inhaler (Ventolin) inhaler.

Creams and ointments
- Anusol cream
- Aqueous cream
- Bactroban cream
- Betadine
- Betnesol-N ear drops
- Canesten cream
- Hydrocortisone cream 1%.

Dressings
- Adhesive plasters
- Antiseptic wipes
- Crepe bandages 7.5cm
- Eye dressing No. 16
- Fluorescein eye test strips
- Gauze swabs 5 × 5cm^2
- HSE large dressing
- Micropore tape 2.5cm
- Non-adherent dressings 5 & 10cm^2
- Steri-strips, assorted
- Triangular bandages
- Vaseline gauze 10cm^2
- Zinc oxide roll plaster.

Hardware
- Anaeroid sphygmomanometer
- Dental first aid kit
- Disposable scalpels
- Economy stethoscope
- SAM splint
- Gloves sterile (medium)
- Isolaide resuscitation aid
- Latex gloves (non sterile)
- Otoscope
- Pen torch
- Safety pins
- Sterile supplies kit
- Stifnek select neck immobiliser
- Thermometer (digital)
- Tuff Cut scissors.

Medical supplies

A large amount of the expedition medical officer's time can be taken up devising and procuring a suitable expedition kit. Buying a medical kit may be very expensive and it can be tempting to buy items in the developing world, but there are many counterfeit drugs on the market and purchasing in some countries is not recommended. Occasionally, pharmaceutical companies may donate drugs to expedition groups and pharmacists may help to provide drugs at cost price.

Medical supplies for specific environments

Mountaineering expeditions above 3000m should have supplies of aceta-zolamide, dexamethasone, and nifedipine for the treatment of altitude-related illness. Emergency oxygen is available using sachets of peroxide (Emox®) and this may represent a cost-effective way of providing chemical oxygen for short periods of time. Larger expedition groups should consider buying or renting a portable altitude chamber such as Certec, Gamow or PAC. Lightweight pulse oximeters can be helpful.

Expeditions to the tropics should have extra supplies of antibiotics, as wounds tend to become infected, and standby drugs to treat malaria are recommended. Snakebite serum should be considered, too.

Sailing trips can provoke incapacitating seasickness and a selection of anti-sickness drugs should be carried—Stemetil or Cyclizine for injection, Buccastem for use inside the cheek as well as oral anti-emetics. Wrist bands help some people with seasickness.

Trips that include SCUBA diving should have supplies of oxygen and plans to evacuate a diver to a recompression chamber should be drawn up beforehand. Diver's ear is a common problem and may be treated with eardrops; marine envenomation might also be a problem. See Box 11.7.5 for a medical checklist.

Medical training for expeditions

It is preferable for each member of an expedition team to have basic first-aid training. This should include cardiopulmonary resuscitation and the management of choking. Other topics should include:

- Safe approach to an accident scene
- Simple management of dislocations and fractures
- Care of the unconscious casualty
- Shock and bleeding control
- Moving the injured casualty, including log-rolling
- Improvised splints and stretchers
- Use of the expedition medical kit contents
- Specific training for environment—heat stroke, Gamow bag, snake bite, use of Epi-pen …

Summary

Thorough preparation before an expedition will prevent many problems. All participants should be aware of the risks they may face. Those who take on the role of the medical officer should be well informed about the illnesses or injuries they may encounter and be trained to deal with potentially life-threatening medical situations.

11.8 Medical tourism

Richard Dawood

Travel for the purpose of obtaining medical treatment is a major industry, often driven by a quest for lower cost or higher quality care. There are many pitfalls, and the best option—for travellers from every country—is to be looked after at home whenever possible.

People travel for all kinds of reasons. Travel for the purpose of obtaining treatment is usually called 'medical tourism'. It most often involves treatments for non-urgent, elective conditions: one-off treatments such as surgical procedures, or perhaps an expert opinion, rather than for emergency care or the ongoing management of chronic disease. It now occurs on a substantial scale—according to some estimates, up to 1% of all travel to or from the USA is for medical treatment.

Travellers affected by illness or injury in the course of their travels, are clearly excluded from this definition: they are not health tourists, though they do face similar issues. But they may become unintentional health tourists when they buy local medicines, or try out local therapies and treatments, even if this is not the main purpose of their trip.

Background

Medical tourism is not new. People have travelled great distances in search of cures from the earliest times, a notion that was commonplace to the ancient Greeks and Romans, and a recurring biblical theme. (Even today, holy places attract pilgrims by the thousand, seeking hope and health where other avenues have failed.)

Spas and places linked with healing can be found across Europe, attracting health seekers and therapists in equal measure. In England, the discovery of the rejuvenating properties of the Chalybeate Spring in 1606 by a young nobleman, Lord North, led to the creation of the spa town of Royal Tunbridge Wells, which became a place of fashion during the 18th century. Its reddish waters offered the prospect of cures from 'obstructions, especially of the spleen and liver; dropsy, jaundice, scurvy, the green sickness, defect and excess of female courses, inward inflammations and hot distempers …' At the time, medicine had had little else to offer, and any health benefits probably came from the water's high iron content. Around the same time, the purgative effects of the waters of Epsom led to the creation of another popular spa. The waters were rich in magnesium sulphate, a laxative still referred to as 'Epsom salts'.

In France, Italy, and Germany, spas remain part of daily life, with health insurance schemes often covering costs of treatment. In eastern European countries, some spas are even State-owned.

During the latter part of the twentieth century, the developed countries of Europe and North America saw a massive influx of 'health tourists' from the oil-rich countries of the Middle East, seeking high quality care that was unobtainable in their own countries. Some Middle Eastern governments view such options as an extension of their countries' own health services. Today, there is an established, two-way flow of health tourists between developed and developing countries.

Current situation

Globally, medical tourism is believed to be a $40 billion industry. There has been a rapid growth in health tourism from developed to developing countries, most marked in regions such as Southeast Asia. More than 1.28 million foreigners underwent treatment in Thai hospitals in 2005. In Malaysia, 300 000 foreign patients were treated in 2006, a figure said to be growing at an annual rate of 30%. In 2006, 410 000 foreigners visited Singapore in order to obtain healthcare. India is also a popular destination, as are Hong Kong, South Africa, Israel, Jordan, Cuba, Costa Rica, Greece, and Croatia.

The impact of the changing economic climate is not yet fully known. According to the organization 'Treatment Abroad', about 60 000 British patients travelled abroad for treatment in 2009, including over 25 000 dental patients, 17 000 cosmetic surgery patients, and 16 000 seeking fertility treatment, orthopaedic, and other surgery.

Why go?

- *Cost:* by far the most powerful driver for this recent trend. The high cost of healthcare in the USA leads many uninsured Americans to feel they have no alternative but to look overseas. Long waiting times in a country such as the UK, where care is publicly funded, and private medical costs are also high, has a similar effect. In the UK, public funding does not cover cosmetic surgery, for which there is eager demand, or provide adequately for specialized psychiatric services, including rehabilitation for alcoholism or drug addiction. Many organizations have sprung up to offer overseas care as part of a travel package that can seem highly attractive
- *Skilled care:* resource availability is the main factor attracting medical tourists in the reverse direction, when this can be afforded: reliable facilities may simply be unavailable locally, at any price
- *Legal and social issues:* there are legal and social factors that drive people to seek medical care elsewhere. Examples include: women seeking termination of pregnancy where it is not legal or accessible in their own country; fertility treatment outside locally acceptable social criteria (such as age limits); sex change procedures; organ transplantation; people seeking access to unlicensed or experimental treatments; and people seeking assisted suicide.

Benefits and pitfalls

The idea of low-cost healthcare, in an exotic and alluring environment, with the added prospect of being able to enjoy a leisurely recuperation far from the routine stresses of one's home surroundings, is an attractive prospect (see Box 11.8.1).

Unfortunately, for many people, the reality can be very different. Many prospective 'medical tourists' don't know how important the professional indemnity cover of the doctors looking after them can be. Long term, follow-up care is of immense practical importance, and so is easy access to a doctor who can take full responsibility when things go wrong, or when healing takes much longer than expected. Procedures are seldom as simple as we hope them to be, and any economic advantages may quickly be destroyed by the need to travel long distances repeatedly for management of complications.

Language and cultural differences are important, too. The words we use to describe our symptoms, wellbeing, health, and level of pain are subtle and nuanced, and not always easily translatable into other languages and cultures. Unpleasant decisions—about complications, surgical options, and end-of-life care—are also culturally loaded, and are fertile territory for miscommunication.

As you may have gathered, I believe there is a strong argument for obtaining care in one's own, familiar environment!

Before you go

If you are determined to go, do your homework well, and pick a facility on the basis of personal recommendation if at all possible. If cost is the major factor for being treated abroad, make sure your calculations allow for any extra costs of travel, or additional private care if things go wrong. Will you be insured, and what will your insurance cover? The anticipated savings can turn out to be illusory.

In developing countries, there is an increased risk of blood-borne viruses such as hepatitis B, C, and HIV, and blood transfusion, if needed, may carry increased risk. At a minimum, it makes sense to be vaccinated against hepatitis B (see also Chapters 2.4, 10.2).

Take careful advice regarding fitness for air travel, the timing of flights, and any associated risks such as DVT, in relation to surgery (see Chapter 7.1) and any measures needed to reduce them.

Box 11.8.1 **Dangers of traditional therapies**

Specialist tour operators now offer the opportunity to combine travel with traditional health practices—such as Ayurvedic medicine in the Indian subcontinent. Ayurvedic medicine purports to be based on a 3000-year-old tradition; treatments consist of varying combinations of oil application, yoga, special diets, steam baths or purgatives. The potential for harm arises when Western medicine really can help, but is shunned in favour of therapies that offer no possibility of benefit. Examples include the problem of snakebite in Sri Lanka, and other types of poisoning. Ayurvedic medicine has nothing to offer, but denies many victims the option of effective treatment. Ayurvedic medicines have been linked to heavy metal toxicity. Even within India, the Ayurvedic system has come under attack for irrational and outdated practices. A news report in the Lancet quoted Vaidya Balendu Prakash, chair of the Health Ministry's Central Ayurvedic, Siddha and Unani Drugs Technical Advisory Board: 'The majority of Ayurvedic formulations available on the market are either spurious, adulterated, or misbranded.' In 2008, a study of Ayurvedic medicines purchased over the Internet found 20% to contain lead, mercury or arsenic.

11.9 Health protection of Armed Forces personnel

Steve Schofield, Martin Tepper, and James Campbell*

If expeditions are 'organized journeys with a purpose', then armed forces must be considered adept at undertaking them. Accordingly, the chapter on Expedition Medicine (Chapter 11.7) is appropriate for soldiers who travel, as is advice provided throughout this book. However, soldiers are also different from most other travellers in that, from an occupational perspective, they have limited choice in when and where they are going, and can be put into harm's way. Thus, health protection for this population needs to be different, not only because of potentially different risks, but critically in that organizations deploying military personnel have a duty

---

*The views expressed in this chapter are those of the authors and do not necessarily reflect the views or policies of the Department of National Defence (Canada).

to reduce health threats. A complicating factor is that operational realities and standard public health practices do not always coincide. For example, a forward deployed infantryman might not use a bed net to protect against insect bites—perhaps because it did not fit into a rucksack, or because the tactical situation precludes use. Fortunately, health protection and operational needs align more often than not, not least because healthy soldiers are deployable soldiers.

A 'typical' military traveller

There is no typical military traveller. While the stereotype of young and fit soldiers deployed to a foreign country rings true, it is not the whole story. First, because military personnel can also be typical travellers in their leisure time at home or while on deployment (see p.425, 'Travel while travelling'). Secondly, even if the focus is on occupational travel, a 'one size fits all' rule does not apply. Sometimes very large groups (10 000 plus) deploy, often with significant health infrastructure. Thus, some deployment areas offer standards of health protection that exceed home country levels. The critical difference being that, if a soldier steps away from the installation, the protective envelope is shed and locally prevalent threats become more manifest. Other deployments consist of small groups (10 or fewer) for whom infrastructure is limited, and increased self-sufficiency is required. Thirdly, while soldiers are, on average, fitter and younger, this is not universal and health protection needs to be nuanced accordingly.

N.B. We use the terms 'soldier' and 'military' for convenience, but in so doing are actually referring to personnel from all armed forces components.

Just follow the orders

"Good doctors are no use without good discipline. More than half the battle against disease is fought not by the doctors, but by the regimental officers."

Viscount Field Marshal Slim. 1956. Defeat into Victory

It is often assumed that militaries have it easier because they can order soldiers to do things. If only it were so simple. The reality is that, while the military structure can offer an advantage, the eyes of commanders and soldiers tend to focus on non-health matters. Further, Command direction regarding health protection, no matter how reasonable, is not always followed and adherence is a significant challenge. Command emphasis likely improves intervention uptake. Similarly, health protection advocacy among soldiers is presumed important—reminding your buddy to use his bed net, and conversely him reminding you to watch what you eat/drink just might protect the health of both of you.

What we will (and will not) discuss in this chapter

The point has already been made that military personnel can be exposed to grave security-based threats. We will not, however, discuss these, nor will we consider associated problems, for example, post-traumatic stress disorder (this does receive attention in Chapter 9.8) or battle injuries. Instead, the focus will be on pre-, intra- and post-deployment health protection, with an emphasis on prevention of diseases caused by naturally occurring infectious agents. We emphasize deployment from lower to higher risk areas, though the opposite is also possible.

Preparation for deployment/travel

A significant advantage for military travellers is the presence of 'in-house' expertise in risk assessment and travel medicine, and complementary processes to maximize the likelihood that a thorough pre-deployment health-risk assessment takes place. Further, many militaries provide all materials and medicines that are needed for health protection. Even so, it is incumbent on the soldier to actively participate in preparation—while systems are often good, individuals can 'slip through the cracks'.

Though the list is not exhaustive, the deploying soldier should take account of the following:

- *For a deployment, there must be a plan, and this plan should include an appraisal of destination health risks and recommendations for prevention.* Ensure that you are familiar with this information. If it is not obviously available, request a preventive medicine briefing. For leisure travellers, there often will not be destination-specific information *per se*. However, many militaries provide support for this type of travel. Taking advantage of it can be as simple as contacting your medical unit
- *Work with your health advisers to ensure that you have been medically prepared.* Recommendations are developed with an 'average' healthy soldier in mind. They might not be perfect for everyone. Be sure to tell a health care adviser factors that might affect approaches to *your* health protection (e.g. previous negative experience with anti-malarials or allergic reactions to vaccines, G6PD deficiency, other medications being taken, pregnancy, immunosuppression and/or other serious conditions/diseases). Preparation involves more than just taking medications: you should attend briefings and other training relevant to health protection; and verify that you have up-to-date equipment and supplies. This latter could include making sure bed nets are in good repair, that clothing and bed nets have received insecticide treatments, that water purification tablets are available and that issued personal protective equipment (e.g. respirators, ear defenders, ballistic eyewear) is in good order
- *Do some research in preparation for travel.* The active involvement of the military traveller is a key to preparedness. This is especially important for small groups who will deploy to remote locations. Ask questions, look after your physical conditioning, speak to peers who have been deployed to the destination and prepare yourself and your family for your absence
- *Before departure, review information and self-test to verify recollection of major health-based issues and appropriate use of countermeasures.* Be sure that you understand the process to follow should you become ill and/or if you have other health concerns.

During deployment

> "A soldier can't fire a gun while sitting on the crapper."
>
> *Anon*

Whether travel is for deployment or leisure, there are 'four infectious horsemen of the apocalyptic journey'. All affect individual health, and the first three can present a serious operational threat (see Box 11.9.1). They are:

- *Faecal-oral diseases* (Chapter 2.1). These are associated with faeces, e.g. salmonellosis, norovirus, typhoid, hepatitis A. Transmission may be through ingestion of contaminated food or water, or by contact with dirty body parts, e.g. hands
- *Respiratory diseases* (see Chapter 9.6). These are associated with respiratory secretions from the nose and mouth, e.g. influenza, tuberculosis, measles. Transmission can be through inhalation of microbes sneezed or coughed out by someone else or less directly from contaminated objects such as telephones
- *Vector-associated diseases* (see Chapter 5). Usually transmitted through the bite of an insect or other arthropod that is infected with the microbe, e.g. malaria, Lyme disease, dengue
- *Sexually transmitted diseases* (see Chapter 10.1). Transmission occurs through direct sexual contact, e.g. gonorrhea, chlamydia, AIDS. Transmission from inanimate objects, e.g. toilet seats, probably doesn't occur.

Box 11.9.1 **Examples of infectious diseases affecting deployed military personnel**

- A malaria attack rate of up to 40% was observed among certain military units deployed to Liberia in 2003. Many individuals were evacuated with severe malaria. Compliance among cases was poor, e.g. only about half used insect repellent or malaria pills and none used bed netting
- A sizeable outbreak of cutaneous leishmaniasis (almost 20% of personnel) occurred among a group of NATO soldiers deployed to Mazar-i-Sharif (Afghanistan) in 2004/2005. The outbreak was attributed to insufficient availability of preventive measures and poor adherence to those measures
- In 2003/2004, diarrhoea was reported by about three quarters of a western nation's soldiers deployed to Iraq and over half deployed to Afghanistan. Severe diarrhoea was reported in a fifth of those in Iraq and a sixth of those in Afghanistan. Diarrhoea was associated with time spent off military camps and eating local food
- An outbreak of 29 cases of viral gastroenteritis occurred among soldiers and staff at a field hospital in Afghanistan in 2002; eleven patients were evacuated out of the war zone. To control the outbreak, the field hospital was temporarily closed.

Prevention of infectious diseases is possible with techniques that are well described throughout this book. Militaries often describe these approaches as the 'disciplines':

Personal hygiene discipline: wash your hands, keep skin clean and dry and don't share personal items. Operational imperatives can limit what is possible. If there is one thing to do, it is to keep your hands as clean as possible, whether by washing with soap and water and/or by using hand sanitizer.

Food/water discipline: militaries often inspect/test water and food, restaurants, food handling practices, etc. Where possible, limit your food and drink to items and/or establishments that are approved. Otherwise, the adage 'boil it, cook it, peel it, or forget it (for food), or purify it (for water)' applies. Heat kills most microbes and can be used to treat food and water (care must be taken to avoid recontamination). Small and large water purification units can remove many materials, including microbes, but are not a guarantee of potable water as they (or the container you are using) can become contaminated. Hence, some militaries insist that potentially contaminated water first be purified and then treated with a disinfectant.

N.B.: If you must 'eat on the economy', evaluate establishments critically: Do they seem clean, including the lavatories? Are plates and utensils washed? Do staff seem to have good personal hygiene? Is prepared food left out at room temperature?

Insect discipline: the rule is simple—'if you don't get bit, you don't get sick.' However, achieving this can be tricky. Insects differ and multiple insect-bite precautions (IBP) are needed to reduce the threat they present. Some mosquitoes that transmit malaria usually bite indoors and in the middle of the night, and for these use of bed nets is crucial. Other types of mosquito attack outdoors and earlier in the evening, which makes treated clothing and repellents relatively more important:

- Do not trust your instincts as to when to use IBP! This is because many soldiers have experienced savage attacks by mosquitoes or other biting insects in their home countries, but without the disease risk. The result is that they can be quite tolerant of bites. This tendency does not work for insect vectors of disease because their populations are often low and they can be such gentle biters you might not even notice them. Use of interventions should therefore *not* be based on perceived presence or annoyance by insects but rather on knowledge of the disease threat. In large installations engineering solutions (screening and air conditioning, pest management) might substantially reduce the threat of bites and disease. Options might be very limited in tactical engagements, which is why treatment of uniforms with insecticide is strongly endorsed—your uniform will provide some protection even if other interventions are not easily employed
- Remember to reapply repellents as needed, such as if you happen to notice bites or at specific times of day (in late afternoon or when getting up from under a bed net). Remember that protection time estimates on product labels can be optimistic. In our opinion, there are no currently available insect repellents that, under extreme operational conditions, will provide high levels of protection for more than 4 or 5 hours.

Malaria discipline: malaria has been covered in many other sections of this book (see Chapter 5.1), but nevertheless merits mention here. It is the travel-associated disease for which militaries have a particular fear—this is warranted, as malaria continues to kill soldiers and affect operations.

> "This will be a long war if, for every division I have facing the enemy, I must count on a second division in hospital with malaria and a third division convalescing from this debilitating disease."
>
> *General MacArthur, 1943*

The usefulness of IBP has already been discussed. Antimalarial medication (chemoprophylaxis), which is the most critical specific intervention for malaria, has not. This approach has in the past made the difference between operational success and failure. When malaria does strike, it is usually because soldiers have not taken their malaria pills regularly and/or not used their IBP. Medication is often taken for a few days to weeks before departure to evaluate tolerability (it can be changed if required), during travel, and then for some time after coming home to treat malaria parasites that emerge. Some militaries also use a second medication, called primaquine, to deal with the types of malaria parasites that can lie dormant for extended periods in the liver (see also p.110).

Experience has shown that soldiers of different nationalities like to compare notes about malaria pills. Often, opinions about medication differ—do not allow this to affect what type of pill you take. Always consult an appropriate medical authority, if possible from your home country, before stopping or changing your malaria pills.

Malaria is a medical emergency: if you are in or have been in an area of risk and develop a fever, seek medical attention immediately. Some militaries have found that malaria is over-diagnosed in personnel assessed 'in country'. This means that treatment is sometimes given when it is not needed. While not ideal, this is preferable to developing severe malaria because it is left untreated. Hence, accepting treatment even where there is uncertainty about the diagnosis is prudent—but do not allow this to change your approach to use of chemoprophylaxis without medical advice.

Sexual discipline: sexually transmitted infections (e.g. gonorrhea, chlamydia, syphilis, AIDS virus) are some of the most commonly reported diseases in soldiers (and civilians), sometimes as a result of activities undertaken while travelling. The latter is concerning. First, because it can present an operational issue when, for example, symptoms (pain, lethargy, fever) present in a forward operating area where support is limited and the performance of a single soldier can affect mission parameters. Secondly, exposure is sometimes associated with travel to exotic locales where sexual relations can be based on some kind of payment, and therefore might be ethically inappropriate. Finally, what you get on deployment can have serious repercussions for relations at home. Ideally, soldiers will avoid risky sexual relations all together. If not, using suitable protection, such as condoms, provides some protection. Many militaries encourage soldiers who have had a high-risk sexual encounter to seek a medical consultation post-encounter to determine whether disease screening and/or treatment is warranted.

Box 11.9.2 **Case history**

A soldier deploys to central Asia and operates out of a fairly large installation. He is prescribed malaria pills, but does not take them. Risk of
malaria is pretty low in the area, so there are no problems. 3 months
into his tour, he receives 2 weeks' leave, and travels to sub-Saharan
Africa for a safari. He does not seek pre-travel advice, nor does he take
malaria pills. 1 week after returning, he finds himself back in remote
central Asia and, over a two-day period, becomes extremely ill. Malaria
is not initially suspected but, after a potentially catastrophic delay, the
soldier is diagnosed with severe malaria. He must be evacuated out of
country to receive aggressive anti-malarial treatment.

Travel while travelling

The case history in Box 11.9.2 is not an isolated incident. Risk can be significantly higher when soldiers travel from their deployment location to
another locale while on leave (or because they are redeployed). This 'travel
while travelling' presents some unique challenges, not least because the
specifics of the secondary travel are not always known pre-deployment.
However, some militaries offer soldiers a pre-leave preventive medicine
briefing. In effect, this is the same process as for pre-deployment preparations, though in this case 'slipping through the cracks' is more likely. For
this reason, it is even more critical that the soldier takes an active role
in his/her preparations by seeking out advice. Ideally, soldiers will make
travel leave plans before deployment. This would enable both a proper
assessment of risk and provision of countermeasures. The latter is particularly important as appropriate preventive interventions (e.g. immunization
agents) are not always readily available 'in country'.

Occupational and environmental health

While acute infectious disease can affect an operation (or ruin a vacation),
occupational diseases such as hearing loss can last a lifetime. While not
the specific focus of this chapter, occupational and environmental hazards
can and do impact soldiers. Many concerns are not military-specific and
are covered elsewhere in this book (e.g. heat and cold, see Chapter 8.4;
altitude, see Chapter 8.3). As with infectious diseases, occupational and
environmental risk factors will have been taken into account for large
deployments. Management approaches might involve shifting training to
cooler times of the day, or locating activities that generate air particulates
as far away as possible from military quarters. Soldiers should, however,
be proactive when it comes to protecting themselves, whether by using
ear defenders for noise, sunscreen for sun exposure, work-rest cycles for
heat, or respiratory protection for specific tasks (e.g. pesticide application). As for any traveller, taking measures to reduce the probability of
accidents is critical to health protection (see Chapter 8.1).

Military-specific threats

Threats to soldiers can include biological, chemical or other warfare
agents. While these are not covered here, they deserve mention as they
are associated with countermeasures, including vaccines, medications

or devices. Typically, these military-specific countermeasures have been subject to external review for safety and efficacy. Any concerns regarding these products should be discussed with appropriate military medical advisers.

After deployment (or leisure travel)

You are almost there—you have made it back and, so far as you know, you are not carrying any unwanted guests. This is not the time to let your guard down, as things can happen after returning home. The classic situation is the development of malaria, sometimes months after getting back. This is why it is crucial to continue taking prescribed medications so that they can continue to protect you.

The returning soldier should also take account of the following:

- If any concerning illness develops, even many months later, be sure to seek medical advice and let them know that you have been abroad
- Follow through on post-deployment questionnaires and medical processes, such as testing for tuberculosis (if it has been recommended). While bothersome, it is these processes that allow medical practitioners to identify potentially worrisome conditions
- Take care not to give anything you bring back with you to others. For many microbes, following standard hygiene practices (washing hands, sneeze etiquette) will provide significant protection. For certain things, such as STIs (e.g. if you had unprotected sex while abroad), a medical follow-up and perhaps testing and treatment could be necessary.

Living and working abroad

12.1 Becoming an expatriate

David Snashall

Expatriates—people who live outside their native country—are in a better position than visitors or travellers to avoid diseases and accidents: they have time on their side and a degree of stability, but psychological and cultural pressures take their toll. A degree of 'culture shock' is inevitable, but good preparation, careful briefing, and an understanding of some of the factors involved in adjusting to a new environment, can contribute much to the success of an overseas posting.

Spending a period of time in a foreign country is a quite different matter from being a short-term visitor. Living in a less developed country inevitably confronts an expatriate with hazards to health and safety, but there may also be cross-cultural and psychosocial difficulties. Going in the other direction—to a more sophisticated country—can provoke psychological problems too and may require just as much adjustment. This chapter deals mainly with the more common situation, where an individual, with or without spouse and family, leaves home to take up residence in a developing country.

Who goes to live abroad?

The number of long-term expatriates in developing countries has diminished considerably since colonial and post-colonial times. Administrators in khaki shorts, bellicose rubber planters, and shipping agents gone to seed in tropical climes are no more. These men, with or without their families, would prepare themselves for many years overseas with no ticket home, and devised for themselves a particular expatriate lifestyle. The main tenet seemed to be that 'abroad' was different and difficult, and that you had to adapt yourself forcefully to it or else it would get the better of you.

That is probably the main difference in approach between those hardy individuals and today's expatriates, who often regard themselves as essentially home-based. However extensive, their foreign tour almost always falls far short of a lifelong commitment. Today's expatriates are diplomats with their families, aid workers, businessmen employed by multinational corporations, healthcare staff, construction workers, students, and a diminishing number of academics, journalists, teachers, and missionaries.

There is inevitably a difference in attitude, and in the resulting experience, between those who go abroad motivated purely by financial and career rewards, and those whose aims are actually to live abroad and achieve an understanding of the country and its culture. The rest of the family may not always share the desire or necessity to accomplish any of these objectives. In health terms—physically and psychologically—they may be the ones who suffer most.

A shock to the system

What is different about living abroad? How can it cause ill health and how can this be prevented, or at least coped with, should it occur?

Adjustments

Moving to a new country demands a number of adjustments. The following categorization is based on a study done some years ago by Craig Storti, of problems in Peace Corps Volunteers—mainly young, healthy Americans going abroad for a 2-year tour of duty.

1. *Adjustment to the new country:* the climate may be very different. In the tropics, some people find the uniform limitation of daylight to about 12 hr and the lack of marked seasons, unsettling. There is different food, a different language, and different people. Many people start expatriate life exhausted from the move itself
2. *Adjustments to a new working environment:* a new job, new skills and responsibilities, and new colleagues. Even worse is learning to live without a job—the unenviable position occupied by spouses—the 'trailing partners'
3. *Adjustments to the local community:* a different transportation system, perhaps an erratic post and telephone system, different shops and services
4. *Cultural adjustment:* I once worked in a community where 268 saints' days were celebrated. Quite a nice custom, you might think, but it led to very few full working weeks. People's behaviour may appear quite alien—habits like spitting in public and refusing to form queues. Coming to terms with different sets of values and attitudes can be most difficult. In some countries there might, on the face of it, seem to be a lesser value placed on human life, as evidenced by crazy driving and a lack of urgency in dealing with emergencies. Attitudes to time may be different: to the expatriate for whom time management has been an essential part of an efficient working life, coming to a country where punctuality is a rarity can be seriously destabilizing. If this extends to the full-blown *mañana* culture, goal-orientated sticklers must adjust—or go under
5. *Life in developing countries tends to be more 'raw':* expatriates may find the experience of being non-aggressively jostled in crowds to be an invasion of personal space—the loss of privacy can feel very threatening. Witnessing cruelty to animals, being expected to give bribes, or abet minor forms of corruption are facts of life that may have to be faced. Curiously, one's own appearance and cultural reputation may rebound in wounding ways. '*We*' are the foreigners and are liable to be judged, fairly or unfairly, by a population who, because they have seen it on TV, believe that extravagant lifestyles, naked pursuit of money, drug dependence, and loose morals are the norm in '*our*' countries.

The expression 'culture shock' describes the impact that all these simultaneously occurring differences can have, and the attempts to adjust. Whatever the cause of the shock, it can and frequently does cause real psychological problems that range from insomnia and irritability to profound home sickness, depression, drug dependence, and general inability to cope to the extent of packing up and going home.

Prevention in practice

How can you prevent these problems from becoming overwhelming?

1. *Recognize that everyone suffers from a degree of culture shock,* even the most seasoned of travellers, and this is normal
2. *Limit your expectations:* do not expect to be able to achieve on a daily basis what you do at home. Most developing countries are simply not set up to nurture the achievement ambitions of foreigners. Indeed, some expatriates feel that the thwarting is almost deliberate. This can be the first step towards paranoia
3. *Be satisfied with small tasks:* especially at the beginning when five telephone calls and a meeting take all day, and leave you feeling as if you have done a week's work
4. *Remember you have successfully survived what once seemed like tough transitions before*: from junior to high school, from school to work. Recognize that you really will survive *this* transition
5. *Take care of your physical health in a positive way:* as well as taking the advice in the rest of this book, get adequate sleep and take regular exercise
6. *Don't abuse drugs like alcohol:* they make things worse and make you look foolish
7. *Find a mentor:* someone with experience to whom you can tell your troubles and with whom to share your successes
8. *Don't withdraw:* even if you feel like it, even if some of the people with whom you have to mix are not entirely to your liking
9. *Keep in touch with home to a reasonable degree by cultivating the disappearing art of letter writing:* hopefully, your mobile phone will have reception and your computer will connect reliably to the Internet, and give you the benefits of e-mail and Skype.
10. *Learn the local language:* however fruitless you think it might prove in the future
11. *Reach beyond your own expatriate community and make friends with other expatriates and local people:* avoid excessive gossip that can have a tendency to be harmful in small communities. Don't try to create a little England, a little America, or a little anywhere in the middle of a foreign country. Of course, you can keep elements of your national identity, some national foods and celebrations of national events. This kind of patriotism is fine and healthy. When it mutates into nationalism and the development of a collective concept by an expatriate community that they represent a superior cadre in the midst of a backward populace, it becomes very ugly
12. *Most important of all cultivate a positive attitude:* actively seek out the good things and the interesting people, and deal with the bad things with a measure of humour.

Stages of adjustment

However well or badly you cope overseas, the following states are usually experienced. Enthusiasm and excitement that can last from a few hours to a few months—rather like a honeymoon. This is usually succeeded by a negative phase—rejection of the new country and everyone who lives in it, withdrawal into your own little world of expatriate clubs or coffee mornings, and even into yourself, with consequent loneliness. This does not look or feel good, but it is normal. By familiarizing yourself with a few new places or practices, sometimes helped by a friend, it is succeeded by re-emergence and adjustment, paving the way to achievement and a return of enthusiasm.

Throughout the process it helps to try to understand the cultural elements of the new country as different from your own—not necessarily better or worse, but just different for reasons that are interesting and possibly worth studying. Then, look at yourself and your own expatriate group. Go through the same process and try to appreciate the impact *you* have on your host country.

After some years in the developing world many people are worn down by the effort needed to survive, and become jaded and unproductive. Then is the time to move on.

Spouses

Someone who goes abroad to work is not likely to find much time to be bored, but this can easily be the fate of their spouse, partner, or family members, and is a significant health hazard. In some countries, partners are not allowed to work, but it may be possible to find voluntary work, or to enrol in an academic course. If there really is much spare time, make use of it to learn about the country, to travel, to learn to play a musical instrument, to cook better—maybe even to think about starting or extending a family!

Physical health

This should be no worse than at home; given a pleasant climate and an interesting life, it should be better. 'Tropical' diseases, many of which are diseases of poverty and under-development, still occur, but as an overseas resident you are in an excellent position to protect yourself against them—especially in comparison with tourists. After all, you have better control of your immediate environment—you can ensure that your food is hygienically prepared, that your water supply is pure, that your home is protected from mosquitoes and other pests, and that vehicles are properly maintained. No longer do doctors see expatriates who are chronically debilitated by amoebic dysentery, recurrent malaria, or tropical sprue. This is because of a better understanding of health precautions and better provision for medical treatment. Expatriates who 'don't believe in' or 'forget' to take malaria prophylaxis still contract and sometimes die from malaria, and diarrhoeal illness is also still common, especially if meals are eaten away from home (immunity is slow to build up and is unreliable.).

Unfortunately, the quality of available medical care in many developing countries is still unsatisfactory. Previously improving general health is being reversed by the HIV epidemic. Serious illnesses do occur amongst expatriates, but because of their lifestyle and the length of time they are abroad, these are more likely to be the same kinds of illnesses they would get at home such as heart disease, high blood pressure, diabetes, cancer and mental health problems. Some of these are simply routine disorders of affluence (which also affect well-off locals and emigrants from poor to wealthy countries). The seeds of these kinds of diseases are often sown many years before, sometimes in childhood, and the fact of residence in a developing country does not have much to do with their appearance. What is important, however, is that there should always be adequate arrangements for ensuring access to good care should a medical emergency arise, with evacuation to another country if necessary.

Local diseases vary from region to region. Sub-Saharan Africa provides employing organizations with the biggest headaches, followed by South and Southeast Asia, and then by the Far East, South America and the Caribbean, and the Middle East.

US Peace Corps volunteers are the subject of regular medical surveillance, and are a well-studied group of mainly young medically fit individuals (Table 12.1.1).

Table 12.1.1 Illness rates in US Peace Corps volunteers, 1989

	No. of cases per 100 volunteers per year
Non-specific diarrhoea	45.3
Amoebiasis	18.4
Problems requiring counselling	18.2
Dental problems	17.2
Bacterial dermatitis	15.8
Injuries	15.3
Malaria	13.9
In-country hospitalization	9.6

Reproduced from Bernard KW, Graitcer PL, van der Vlugt TB, Moran JS, Pulley KM. (1989). Epidemiologic surveillance in Peace Corps Volunteers: a model for monitoring health in temporary residents of developing countries. *Int J Epidemiol* **18**: 220–6, with permission of Oxford University Press.

British VSO volunteers, studied in 2009, suffered more from diarrhoea and skin problems than their Peace Corps equivalents, but the same rate of dental problems.

Over one-third of Red Cross employees living abroad across the world, working in demanding healthcare-related jobs reported worse health on return from the mission (Table 12.1.2; Box 12.1.1). An even greater percentage engaged in risky behaviour likely to have health consequences.

Certain infectious diseases increase in incidence with increased length of stay—hepatitis and worm infestations, for example, and malaria, if prophylaxis is not maintained.

Expatriates have a higher chance of dying early than if they had stayed at home—mostly due to trauma (70%, US Peace Corps), although this incidence rate has declined over the years)—and then mainly on the road.

Table 12.1.2 Medical problems experienced by expatriates on mission—Red Cross 2003/4

Medical problem*	Total n = 1190	
Diarrhoea	523	(44.0%)
Fever	308	(25.9%)
Headache	135	(11.3%)
Fatigue	237	(19.9%)
Dermatological	194	(16.3%)
Respiratory	90	(7.6%)
Dental	150	(12.6%)
Urological	45	(3.8%)
Sexually transmitted diseases	4	(0.3%)
Allergies	115	(9.7%)
Neuropsychological	174	(14.6%)
Cardiovascular	20	(1.7%)
Gastrointestinal (not diarrhoea)	186	(15.6%)
Musculoskeletal and joint	126	(10.6%)
Gynaecological-obstetric	46	(8.5%)
Other	105	(8.8%)

*More than one answer possible; percentages do not add to 100.

Adapted from Dahlgren AL, Deroo L, Avril J, Bise G, Loutan L. (2009). Health risks and risk-taking behaviours among International Committee of the Red Cross (ICRC) expatriates returning from humanitarian missions. *J Travel Med* **16:** 382–90, with permission of Wiley Blackwell.

Risky behaviour

People enjoy taking risks, but in their home environment have a much fuller appreciation of the pitfalls and consequences. Freedom from the constraints and conventions of home can make some of the risks more tempting.

Drugs

In some countries the penalties for buying, selling, or using drugs or even alcohol can be severe, despite the fact that in the same countries they are often easy to get hold of, more widely used, and very much cheaper than at home.

Alcohol is a major problem, and every expatriate group has its core of abusers. Many become problem drinkers as a result of prolonged consumption of cheap or subsidized alcohol, especially if their job involves

> Box 12.1.1 **A 2006 study of 2020 British expatriates over 1 year**
>
> - New event reported to a doctor: 21%
> - Major event needing secondary care: 14%
> - New events requiring hospital admission: 4%
> - New events requiring evacuation to home country: 2%.
>
> *Causes*
> - Injury: 29%
> - Musculoskeletal: 19%
> - Infectious disease: 13%
> - Psychological: 5%
> - Trauma (50% sports injury; 32% slip, trip, fall; 11% road traffic accident)
> - Psychological problems were the most common cause of a terminated posting.
>
> Source: Data from Dahlgren AL, Deroo L, Avril J, Bise G, Loutan L. (2009). Health risks and risk-taking behaviours among International Committee of the Red Cross (ICRC) expatriates returning from humanitarian missions. *J Travel Med* **16**: 382–90.

selling goods or services, and entertaining or being entertained. Yet others, unable to work, drink to relieve boredom or anxiety. Above about 20 drinks per week, the incidence of medical problems including frank dependency increases dramatically. The sensible expatriate will try to keep below this number, if necessary by keeping to rules like not drinking until the sun goes down, never drinking spirits, having 2 days a week off drinking, or switching to low-alcohol or alcohol-free drinks. Alcoholics Anonymous has branches in most countries and is often the only available resource for those affected.

Addiction to tobacco constitutes a major health hazard, but giving up in a developing country can be more difficult, particularly for people who smoke to relieve stress. Cigarette smoking is more common and well accepted in developing countries. Well-known brands often have a higher carcinogen content than they do at home, and may be much cheaper.

Sex

People tend to become more promiscuous when they are away from home. One study from the Netherlands showed that 23% admitted to unprotected sex with partners from HIV-endemic areas whilst overseas. Particularly prone were young single men who were lonely. This means that the incidence of sexually-transmitted diseases in expatriates is relatively high (see Chapter 10.1). HIV infection and hepatitis B are spread mainly heterosexually in developing countries, and anybody who has sex with more than one partner or with prostitutes without using a condom is simply crazy. The same applies to homosexual promiscuity.

Driving

Driving overseas can be a hair-raising experience, and not only on unmade roads. Road accidents are all too common, and frequently have a fatal outcome because of poor rescue and medical facilities. Road traffic accidents are the major cause of death in expatriates—particularly in the age group 20–29. Not all countries have seat-belt rules, but not to install and wear front and rear seat belts, in a dangerous driving environment, is asking for trouble. If you are going to have to drive an off-road vehicle, it is worthwhile getting some practice in your home country first—manufacturers of such vehicles often run training courses.

Swimming

Swimming is another risky activity. Amongst the many additional hazards of swimming in developing countries is the fact that beaches and swimming pools are rarely patrolled. Children should be particularly closely watched.

More people die in Britain from swimming accidents than in any other sport. Amongst US Peace Corps staff 18% of injury deaths were due to drowning—the second most common cause of accidental death. Abroad, seas and rivers may well be polluted with sewage. It may be safer to stick to swimming pools and bilharzia-free lakes.

Home life abroad

Clothing

It should not be necessary to give advice on what to wear, but expatriates living in the tropics still present with prickly heat and peeling scalps, caused by wearing tight denim jeans and no hat. Long-term exposure to the sun ages skin and causes cancer. Protect yourself and your children with sunblock and suitable clothing, or stay in the shade. Pure cotton clothing (the looser the better) is still the most comfortable in hot humid conditions because of its absorbent qualities, but modern synthetics are catching up.

Servants

For most expatriates, having servants is a new experience. They may themselves constitute a health hazard, and it makes sense to arrange for them to have a medical check-up by a known and trusted medical practitioner before they start work. Transmissible diseases are common in many developing countries—pulmonary tuberculosis, for example, for anyone handling food, intestinal infections such as amoebiasis or typhoid. HIV positive servants are not an infection risk, but may well become ill and need medical care.

Oddly, the hazards are more often psychological, with servant and employer annoying each other. There is nothing wrong with having servants as long as you employ them honestly. Stick to local laws on employment (for example, you may find yourself responsible for medical care), pay them local rates, show them clearly and repeatedly what you want them to do. If they can't or won't do it, terminate their service according to the proper process. Never get into the dreadful habit of complaining about your servants to colleagues.

Violence

Criminal attacks, robberies, and muggings are all too frequent in developing countries, especially in cities. Even where personal crime is uncommon, such as in many Muslim countries, there may be terrorism or violent fanaticism. Rape is also common in some places. Make personal protection and security a part of your everyday life, and follow local safety advice carefully. This may involve dressing inconspicuously, not driving at night, securing the sleeping quarters of your house, or any number of other strategies, depending on the actual security situation. See also Chapter 8.2.

Naturally, many expatriates find a partner. Mixed-race marriages are increasingly common, and probably more readily accepted, but there may still be problems of adjustment in couples who return together to the expatriate's home country.

Before you go

Not everybody is fit to go overseas for a prolonged period. A medical check may be required before going, and other family members may also need to be examined (see Chapter 12.2).

Find out as much as possible about your *exact* destination before you go. 'Latin America' or 'Asia' may sound exotic, but in reality you may be living in a city with worse traffic and air pollution problems than the one you have left. Remember, not all places in the tropics are hot, especially those at higher altitudes.

If you are being sent by an institution or company, it is very important to find out exactly what your contractual rights are as far as healthcare is concerned, and what facilities will be provided for medical support, including evacuation and general welfare. Some organizations use professional relocation services that deal with many of these time-consuming practicalities. If you are not being supported in this way, check the terms of your medical insurance (not the same as travel medical insurance) and try to find in advance something about the medical system in the country—do you have to register with a general practitioner? Where is the recommended hospital? Try to meet others who have recently returned from a posting in the same country, and attend any briefing courses that may be available. Many of the problems referred to in this chapter could be avoided if intending expatriates did some research on these matters and employers took more care in choosing their staff and provided sensitive, accurate information in advance and, of course, good working conditions.

Returning home

For many expatriates, living abroad is a wonderful experience: the problems start when they come home. Much has been written about 'reverse culture shock'—known in French as '*la réinsertion en metropole des cadres expatriés*'. The return to horrible weather and life in the fast lane, with no home help, can be a shock indeed. Friends seem depressingly parochial and secretly jealous. Getting back to work, commuting, and the old routine can be almost as difficult as becoming an expatriate in the first place. Employers can help, by arranging educational and other programmes to enable returning expatriates to settle in. Medical staff should be alert to more serious mental health problems in returnees such as depression and substance misuse.

Depending on where you have been, it may also be worth a simple medical check on a blood and stool sample to detect any parasites you may have acquired during your sojourn overseas (Appendix 5).

12.2 Fitness for working abroad

Will Cave

Think carefully about your current and future health needs if you plan to work abroad. Do you have any past or active health issues that need to be reviewed? Are there any special risks attached to your employment? A general health screen is a sensible precaution for anyone going to work in an environment where medical care might be harder to access and the medical system unfamiliar.

There are risks associated with any travel and these are usually modifiable through a timely pre-travel health assessment that educates, informs and delivers whatever preventive measures may be required. This assessment should also examine the various aspects of your fitness to undertake work abroad and is an invaluable part of a pre-deployment consultation.

Pre-existing health problems

Established medical conditions do not automatically preclude working abroad, but the initial consideration is your safety in travelling to and living at your intended destination. Long-haul flights, for instance, are a necessity for which there are multiple cautions. You should also consider the effects of the destination environment on any medical problems you have, such as the effect of air pollution on respiratory conditions or any practical issues when using mobility aids. Make sure you travel with all your relevant medical details, including your own doctor's contact details and any recent test results. The importance of high-quality health insurance can never be overstated.

Vaccinations

Pre-travel vaccinations should be performed after a careful risk versus benefit assessment by an experienced adviser. Most vaccines have an excellent safety profile, but particular care must be taken with certain conditions, such as poor immune function and pregnancy, as well as with those at extremes of age.

Medication

If you have a chronic disease, such as hypertension or diabetes, you will need to consider your access to quality medication, particularly in countries where counterfeit medicines circulate or drug stability is affected by extreme climates. There may be local regulations surrounding importing medication. Monitoring of some drug effects, such as international normalized ratio (INR) testing if you use warfarin, will require a high quality laboratory. Diabetics using insulin will need uninterrupted power for refrigeration.

Preventive health care and screening

This is often neglected in resource-poor countries so the availability of routine tests may be limited. Do not underestimate the importance of health screening before you depart. If your family will be going with you, their routine care (e.g. cervical smears, childhood immunization) will need to be considered, too.

Managing unforeseen health risks

Along with known disease risks, preparing for work abroad means considering unforeseen events. For instance, an unplanned leisure trip may take you away from your 'safe' air-conditioned environment and into a higher risk area for insect-borne diseases, such as malaria. Social pressures may lead you into high-risk sexual encounters. Injuries increase your risk of acquiring viral infections such as hepatitis B and C, or HIV, through exposure to blood products or improperly sterilized medical equipment. Travel into insecure destinations with very poor health infrastructure, such as disaster areas or war zones, requires a higher degree of self-sufficiency. You should consider taking a comprehensive medical kit and possibly training in such things as first aid, wound care, hostile environment survival and self-diagnosis.

Psychological health

Psychological stress at unfamiliar destinations originates from a variety of sources. Nocturnal noise is common in tropical cities and the resulting sleeplessness may lead to psychological decompensation. Isolation and loneliness in unaccompanied deployments is likely to be transient if you can establish a socially supportive network. Those with a history of depression may find working abroad particularly challenging and care should be taken with some anti-malarials that should not be used by those with mental health disorders.

Drug and alcohol abuse

Different countries have different attitudes to recreational drugs, and you may find that they are more widely available and culturally acceptable than at home. Additionally, there may be over-the-counter access to drugs that are usually strictly controlled. Alcohol use may be more prevalent in overseas residents due to altered social norms within expatriate communities. You should be aware of the increased risks of drink and drug abuse, so use your fitness assessment to address any concerns you may have.

The success of your time spent working abroad will hinge on your ability to provide for your needs and those of your family. It is not just about physical and mental health, but also social and spiritual wellbeing. If you remain curious, open-minded, and prepared to embrace the inevitable difficulties, the experience should be positive.

Chapter 13

Preparing for travel

13.1 Risk and risk assessment for travellers

Ron Behrens

When travellers seek professional pre-travel health advice, they are seeking information about risk. As in many healthcare settings, the purpose of this information is to help evaluate risks or threats, and to help the individual decide upon the best course of action that may be taken to reduce them.

For travellers to make the best use of the advice they receive, they also need to understand how the advice has been formulated, the factual basis of any data provided, and how to apply the information to their own circumstances.

Much of the advice on health risks given by travel health advisers is not scientifically-confirmed fact, but is often derived from a consensus, an agreement by experts as to what they believe the likely situation to be. Recommendations based on this projected risk are decided in a similar manner.

Examining the risks: two examples

Malaria in Cambodia

Consider the risk of a traveller intending to visit Cambodia for 2 weeks, with a trip to Angkor Wat: British experts and UK guidelines would designate this to be a journey carrying a risk of malaria, and malaria tablets would be recommended for *prevention*. However, travel medicine experts in Germany consider that the malaria risk is not high enough to need preventative tablets, and instead advise travellers to carry malaria *treatment*, to be used in case they develop malaria.

Scientific evidence from the World Health Organization is that malaria is present and transmitted in some regions of Cambodia, and affects the local population. What has not been scientifically defined is the likelihood of the average traveller to Angkor Wat becoming infected with malaria.

The 'malaria risk' is therefore an 'opinion' of experts, not an epidemiological measurement, and is in effect a 'guestimate' (guessed estimate).

One recent epidemiological measurement in a research study calculated the malaria risk in visitors to Cambodia as one malaria case in every 100 000 visitors.

Why not therefore give *everyone* malaria tablets where there is any malaria? Unfortunately, malaria tablets are not totally without risk, and have a measurable rate of side effects. We are more certain of the likelihood of side effects than we are of the risk of getting malaria, since drug reactions are well researched. Between one in three to one in five users of malaria tablets (depending on the type) will have some sort of side effect.

The majority are not serious, but are unpleasant and may interfere with the traveller's plans and their enjoyment of their trip. More serious side effects are infrequent, developing in around one person in 10 000 users, but might require hospital treatment and might be long lasting.

So how do we decide whether it is better to use tablets to avoid a serious illness such as malaria but risk a drug reaction, or to use no tablets? We need to understand whether the 'guestimate' of malaria is higher or lower than the risk of a serious reaction to the malaria tablets.

Such information should be available, and should be provided to travellers to help them decide what is the greater threat to their health. Along with appropriate recommendations and an understanding of the consequences of developing malaria, the traveller can then make an informed choice about malaria prevention for their trip. This process works well when there is enough epidemiological data to help us determine the risk. However, many health risks are very rare or random so that the process is no longer helpful.

Rabies in India

Understanding the risk of rabies exposure during travel would be useful when deciding whether a course of expensive vaccinations makes sense. Very few travellers have died from rabies, so the risk cannot be determined using this data. However in India, 17 000 inhabitants die every year from rabies. What is the risk for a traveller on a 2-week holiday, or a 1-year journey; does the risk warrant vaccination? If the purpose of the journey is to study dogs, then obviously this is a risky activity and vaccination is appropriate. If it involves 14 days of sightseeing, or a beach trip, the chance of a dog bite is small and the chance of a rabid dog bite is even smaller. For a 1-year journey the risk is 351 times higher, but it is still very low.

The next consideration is that *rabies immunoglobulin*, which is critical in the treatment of an animal bite, should be administered within 24 hours of a rabid bite to prevent the disease from becoming established; however, it is only available within large capital cities, where it is very expensive, difficult to find, and may be of doubtful quality. Over 98% of animal bites are not treated with immunoglobulin because most health facilities don't have it. To be absolutely certain of not developing and dying from rabies, a traveller needs to be immunized before travel (pre-exposure).

Pre-exposure rabies vaccination is an insurance against an unknowable rabies risk; the decision to have the 3-dose course of rabies vaccines is personal to the individual's own risk threshold and finances: cost and personal risk assessment guides the decision.

Risk assessment

The above examples focus on the concept of risk/benefit—avoiding risk (and therefore obtaining benefit) with a vaccine or drug.

However, at a travel health consultation—when obtaining vaccines, drugs or advice—the most important process is *risk assessment*, with careful consideration of the health risks associated with a journey. Once identified, these can be ordered either by likelihood, or seriousness; the traveller can then decide, with the help of a health professional, which risks are important and how they should be dealt with.

The simplest method of deciding importance is to consider whether the risk is common, fatal or can be avoided by drugs, vaccines, or advice.

Epidemiological evidence of health problems faced by travellers provides the most accurate method of estimating the risk or threat faced during travel.

Unfortunately such data can be difficult to use, because they are diverse, collected in many different ways, in different types of travellers and are often selective to countries and groups of travellers. Another option is to look at what causes deaths in people who travel. In some countries, such as the USA and Scotland, a central register of deaths overseas and their causes is maintained and so can be examined. Death clearly is not an accurate indicator of common health problems but it is the tip of a much larger iceberg of ill health and a reasonable indicator of serious health problems that would require medical attention; it can therefore give a very useful insight into the life-threatening problems that occur during travel.

In young travellers, road traffic accidents, drowning, and criminal events are the most important causes of death during travel. In older adult travellers, heart attacks, strokes, and complications of existing medical problems are the commonest causes of death, while road traffic accidents and trauma are the next most common. Infections such as malaria, typhoid fever and other tropical diseases make up less than 5% of all deaths.

The key message from this data is that if you are young, the greatest threat to your health is travelling on the roads, and that this is still a major threat to older travellers. For travellers with significant health problems, their underlying medical problems could lead to major ill health during the journey. Notable highlights of the fatality data are that drowning and motorbike accidents are near the top of the list.

Travellers need additional information in order to make informed decisions—such as what interventions are available, and their 'cost'. How should a 20-week pregnant woman decide whether to travel to Kenya for a beach holiday? A risk assessment would consider her risk of acquiring malaria in her resort (low, but present), the risk she faces to her pregnancy by taking the malaria tablets (very low) and the consequences to her and the pregnancy if she should catch malaria (very serious and life-threatening). There are, in fact, other risks, too, such as possible problems with the pregnancy, access to appropriate medical care, and one that is relevant for all travellers, the risk of injury and accidents whilst travelling on the roads. The decision to travel in such a circumstance is a very personal one, based on the individual traveller's risk threshold and the level of risk they are prepared take.

Conclusion

Risk assessment is therefore about deciding which of the risks that will be faced when travelling are important, and what can be done to reduce them—taking account also of any risks associated with preventive measures.

Enough information needs to be available for the risks to be understood; and travellers need to be clear about the level of risk they personally are comfortable with.

Some travellers may simply rely on the opinion or recommendations of their travel health adviser. However, where there is a significant cost for drugs and vaccines that that might be unnecessary or more likely to cause side effects than to yield benefit, I would strongly advise the traveller to get involved with the decision-making process.

13.2 Immunization

Richard Dawood

Remote places have become increasingly accessible, fewer countries require vaccination certificates as a condition of entry, and most travellers now book their own travel arrangements: it is easier than ever before—though not less hazardous—for travellers to visit risk areas without first obtaining specialist professional advice.

Immunization offers safe, reliable protection against a limited number of important diseases. It is easy to make this the focus of your preparations for travel, but remember that staying healthy abroad is not just about vaccines. Use every attendance for vaccination to update your knowledge about other protective measures as well, including the latest advice on malaria protection and other key precautions.

Mandatory and non-mandatory immunization

The only *mandatory* immunization requirements for travel (i.e. officially sanctioned by the WHO) relate to yellow fever, for travel in or through certain parts of Africa and South America. Most vaccines are *non-mandatory*, but may still be strongly advised for most destinations outside northern Europe, the USA, Canada, Australia, and New Zealand. In terms of protecting your health, these non-mandatory vaccinations are often far more important than mandatory ones.

Health information from travel agents, tour operators, and embassies often relates purely to mandatory requirements, sometimes giving the misleading impression that no other precautions are necessary: such sources cannot be expected to provide detailed information about optional vaccinations, and should not try to; but they should certainly inform travellers of any mandatory requirements and remind them to consult a doctor or a travel clinic for individual advice.

About vaccines

Most people use the words 'vaccination' and 'immunization' interchangeably (though strictly the word 'vaccination' refers to the original vaccines against smallpox, produced in cows).

Vaccination stimulates the body's defence mechanism by exposing immune cells to a small amount of bacteria, virus, or material derived from them, or synthetic 'look-alike' material. Some vaccines contain the killed or inactivated organism or its toxin; others contain a related live organism known to be safe for inoculation. Some vaccines also include additives that attract immune cells to the injection site, enhancing the immune effects, but sometimes also causing soreness and inflammation. The vaccine stimulates the production of antibodies, which are then ready for combat when the real infection is later encountered.

The number of doses required and the spacing between them varies between vaccines and depends on past vaccine history. Once initial courses of some vaccines have been completed, single 'booster' doses every few years may be all that is needed to maintain protection. The period of protection conferred by a vaccine varies (see Table 13.2.1).

It is important to realize that few vaccines provide 100% protection, and other precautions such as care with food, drink, and personal hygiene are still necessary. Not every vaccine is suitable for every person, for reasons such as allergy, pregnancy, age, or because of certain medical conditions.

Immunity can also be provided 'passively' by giving an injection of immunoglobulin—purified antibodies extracted from a donor who is already immune. Such injections are sometimes used to protect against diseases such as rabies or hepatitis B, in people exposed to infection who haven't been vaccinated.

Obtaining immunization

Where?

Specialist travel clinics provide up-to-date advice and a full vaccine service. GP practices and non-specialist clinics can also give vaccines—although not all are licensed to give yellow fever, or are experienced with less frequently used vaccines or complex destinations and situations. Ideally, pick a clinic that has:

• *The full range of travel vaccines:* going to different clinics for different vaccines results in poor, fragmented care
• *Evidence of specialist involvement in Travel Medicine:* e.g. a clinic run by practitioners belonging to professional bodies such as the International Society of Travel Medicine
• *Enough time allocated for each appointment:* at least 30 min for an initial visit
• *A large throughput of other travellers* with similar travel plans to your own
• *An ability to advise you if you become ill abroad* or need help on your return
• *A good reputation.*

When?

Ideally, at least 4–6 weeks before your trip: courses might take a month or more to complete, and most vaccines have a lead time for full protection (Table 13.2.1); for travel to Africa or South America, remember that the *vaccination certificate does not become valid until 10 days after vaccination.* Because of the way vaccines are manufactured, supply problems occasionally occur, which is another good reason for planning ahead.

Last-minute travel

Common reasons for last-minute vaccination requests include:

- Unexpected business trips
- News of outbreaks
- The discovery that 'no vaccinations are necessary for your trip' actually means that there may still be optional immunizations that are advised
- Late bookings and last-minute deals—increasingly common, and for some popular destinations (e.g. West Africa), not without risk.

People who need to travel at short notice should plan to keep protection continuously up-to-date. At the Fleet Street Clinic, where we look after large numbers of news reporters, this is our routine approach. Even when ideal vaccine schedules cannot be followed, worthwhile protection can still be gained at the last minute; incomplete courses should be completed on return, to reduce the risk of the problem recurring on a future trip.

Immunization schedules

For simple trips to common destinations, a single clinic visit may be all that is necessary—there is no problem with having several different vaccines on the same day.

For some vaccines—notably rabies and hepatitis B—the initial course requires three visits, usually over 3–4 weeks. Other vaccine doses can sensibly be divided between the visits, more for comfort than any proven medical advantage.

The intervals quoted for initial vaccine courses (e.g. 'day 0, day 7, day 21') refer to minimum recommended dose intervals. They can be extended without detriment: it is better to follow an imperfect schedule than to omit doses or forego protection.

Your past vaccine history should not be a guessing game, and there's no point repeating protection that is still in date: bring vaccination records, certificates, and details with you, every visit.

The injections

A surprising number of people are frightened by the thought of an injection. However, modern disposable needles are fine, sharp, and frictionless, and in practised hands, almost painless. For true needle-phobes, various techniques are available to numb the skin, such as by cooling. Smaller doses and purer vaccines make adverse reactions now less common.

Most travel vaccines are given into different layers of the skin, or into the muscle, and the outer part of the upper arm is a convenient site.

Eat normally beforehand; it may be sensible to avoid strenuous exercise or excessive alcohol for several hours afterwards. Anyone with a tendency to faint should ask to have the shots lying down, and should lie down or stay sitting for 15min afterwards.

Needle-free vaccines

Needle-free vaccines are available against typhoid and cholera—see p.448. There is also a skin-patch vaccine against travellers' diarrhoea caused by enterotoxigenic *E. coli* at an advanced stage of development: the toxin

Table 13.2.1 Dose intervals for travel vaccines

| Vaccine | Initial Course | | | Duration of protection (years) | Lead time for protection (single dose vaccines) | Minimum age |
	No. of doses	Interval between 1st & 2nd doses	Interval between 2nd & 3rd doses			
Killed vaccines						
Cholera (Dukoral)	2	1 week	Children 2–6 need a 3rd dose	2	2 weeks from start	2 years
Diphtheria/tetanus/polio	Initial course usually completed in childhood. Unvaccinated adults: 3 doses one month apart			10		n/a
Hepatitis A	2	6–12 months		> 20	2 weeks	1 year
Hepatitis B—rapid schedule	4	7 days	14 days	1, then 5		birth
Hepatitis B—standard schedule	3	1 month	5 months	5 +		birth
Hepatitis A/Hepatitis B combined	3	1 month	5 months	25+/5		1 year
Influenza	1	(children may need a 2nd dose 4 weeks later)		1	1–2 weeks	6 months
Japanese encephalitis (Ixiaro)	2	4 weeks		1+ (not yet known)		17 years
Meningitis ACYW (conjugate vaccine)	1			5	2 weeks	2 years

Pneumonia (Prevenar, Pneumovax)	1		5 +		birth
Rabies (intramuscular or intradermal)	3	7 days		14–21 days	birth
Tickborne encephalitis	2–3	28–42 days	3 +		1 year
Typhoid/Hepatitis A (combined)	2	6–12 months	Typhoid: 3 years; Hep A: 1 yr, then >20 years	2 weeks	16 years
Typhoid injected (Typhim Vi)	1		3	10 days	2 years
Live vaccines					
MMR (Mumps/measles/rubella) —adults	2	4–6 weeks			
TB: BCG (must have TB test first if aged 6+)	1				birth
Typhoid oral (Vivotif)	3	2 days	1 +	10 days	6 years
Varicella (chickenpox)	2	4 weeks	(children 2–12 need 1 dose only)		1 year
Yellow fever	1		10	10 days	1 year

Live vaccines: usually given on the same day as each other or 3–4 weeks apart; NOT if pregnant or immunosuppressed is harmful when injected, but capable of stimulating immunity without causing harm when placed in contact with slightly abraded skin.

Any doctor or nurse administering vaccines should always advise about malaria and other appropriate protection without being asked, but it is sensible for travellers to check on this if it is not mentioned. Similarly, this is a good time to ask about other potential problems, such as travellers' diarrhoea, or what medication to include in a medical kit.

Individual vaccinations

Travel is a good opportunity to check that routine immunization is complete, and to review and update it where needed.

Yellow fever (see Chapter 5.2)

Yellow fever is the only disease for which a certificate can be required as a condition of entry under the International Health Regulations of the WHO; this is to reduce the risk of importing yellow fever, rather than to protect incoming travellers. Asia, for example, is yellow fever free, but there are plenty of mosquitoes capable of spreading it: introduction by an infected traveller could result in a catastrophic outbreak.

Yellow fever exists in two zones, one across tropical Africa and the other in the northern part of South America. The disease pattern fluctuates—outbreaks can flare up after decades without a single case. Some countries require a certificate from all travellers; the rest may not require a certificate from those on direct flights from North America or Europe, but may do so for travel from one country to another within the zone. In addition, it may be worth taking the vaccine for personal protection even if a certificate is not required (Appendix 1).

There are many misconceptions about yellow fever regulations: many travellers ask for it when it is not needed, or don't realize that it may be an absolute requirement for onward destinations on their itinerary. Much effort has recently been devoted to producing updated yellow fever vaccination maps (see Maps A1.1 and A1.2), showing destinations for which yellow fever vaccination should normally be given.

Defining the areas of exact risk has partly been motivated by an increasing understanding that yellow fever vaccine carries a small risk of serious complications (notably 'yellow fever vaccine associated viscerotropic disease')—the risk is between 0.13 and 0.4 per 100 000 vaccine doses. The risk is age-related, and rises to 2.5 cases per 100 000 vaccine doses in people aged over 60 years. (This risk only applies to people who have never previously received the vaccine.) It is therefore important to ensure, especially with older travellers, that the vaccine is used only when the likely benefit outweighs this small risk.

The vaccine should *not* be used, or should be used with caution, in:
- Infants aged less than 9 months
- Anyone with a previous severe allergic reaction to a vaccine, including anaphylaxis to egg protein (egg anaphylaxis is very rare)
- People with reduced immunity (including HIV infection—see Chapter 11.5)
- Diseases involving the thymus gland
- Pregnancy/breastfeeding.

Vaccination is normally given at designated official yellow fever vaccination centres that have to comply with formal standards. The vaccine provides virtually 100% protection, and the vaccination certificate lasts 10 years.

All of the vaccines mentioned below are optional, except that meningitis vaccination is required for the pilgrimage to Mecca.

Tetanus, diphtheria, polio, pertussis

Tetanus can follow an injury (Chapter 4.2), so everyone should be protected whether travelling or not. Certain kinds of travel activities—hiking, sports holidays, camping trips—carry an increased risk of injury. An outbreak of diphtheria in the former USSR during the mid-nineties followed a lapse in the routine immunization programme, and showed that childhood immunization does not always produce lifelong protection. Polio has been the subject of a concerted eradication campaign (see Chapter 2.3) but is still present in parts of Africa and Asia; the oral ('sugar lump') vaccine is no longer used in the UK.

A combined vaccine against tetanus, diphtheria and polio is normally given every 10 years. Increasingly, whooping cough (pertussis) vaccine is added to the combination, because of concerns that the protection from childhood pertussis vaccination is not lifelong, and that pertussis can produce unpleasant infections in adults and spreads easily to babies too young to be vaccinated. There has been a recent, serious increase in the number of pertussis cases in the UK, the USA, and several other countries.

Mumps, measles, and rubella (MMR)

All children going overseas who have not completed their routine childhood immunization course, including two doses of measles vaccine, should do so (see Chapter 11.2); in 2011, many children in the UK who had missed out on protection succumbed to travel-related measles, and in 2009, travellers returning from the UK to the USA caused a major mumps outbreak. Some adults may also need to have their protection topped up—it is possible to check immunity with a blood test if in doubt.

Hepatitis A (see Chapter 2.4)

Hepatitis A is an unpleasant virus infection that causes a long and potentially serious illness. The vaccine offers reliable protection and should be considered by every traveller to hot countries and places where hygiene is poor. An initial dose protects within a few days. A second dose, 6–12 months later, protects for 25 years or longer. The course does *not* need to be restarted if the second dose is delayed. The vaccine is sometimes combined either with typhoid or with hepatitis B.

An attack of hepatitis A gives lifelong immunity to the disease. Some people who have spent time in the tropics may therefore already be protected; a blood test is available to confirm immunity.

Other forms of hepatitis can also be transmitted by food and water, so careful hygiene precautions are advised even for people who are immunized.

Typhoid (see Chapter 2.1)

Typhoid is spread by contaminated food and drink, so the risk is greatest where hygiene conditions are poor. Vaccination is certainly justified for rural travel through developing countries, especially to the Indian subcontinent, where the risk is highest.

The current injected vaccine protects for approximately 3 years. It causes less soreness at the injection site than previous typhoid/paratyphoid vaccines.

There is an oral vaccine in the form of three capsules, swallowed on alternate days, with protection lasting 1 year. (In some countries, notably the USA, this is given in a four-capsule regime, with longer-lasting protection—5 years.) The oral vaccine is 'live', and therefore has some additional contraindications.

Vaccines against typhoid typically provide 70 to 80% protection: care with food hygiene is still important even if vaccine is taken.

Cholera

Cholera causes catastrophic, watery diarrhoea. It is a disease of poor hygiene, transmitted via the faecal/oral route, usually by water, and can therefore also be prevented by water purification, hygiene, food, and water precautions.

There is no effective injectable vaccine. The Dukoral vaccine is a drinkable vaccine that uses killed cholera bacteria and a modified form of the cholera toxin to generate localized immunity on the surface lining of intestinal cells. It is taken as two doses, 1 week apart, completed ideally at least 1 week prior to travel (children aged 2 to 6 receive three doses), and protection lasts 2 years. There is debate as to whether this vaccine also protects against other causes of diarrhoea as well, since the cholera toxin is similar to the toxin produced by enterotoxigenic *E. coli*.

Cholera remains a problem in Africa, Asia, and elsewhere, though outbreaks tend to be limited to settings with severe overcrowding or extreme poverty. Improved ability to treat cholera with simple fluid replacement has made the consequences of infection less severe, but they can still be devastating—as in the ongoing outbreak in Haiti.

The average traveller is unlikely to be at risk, but taking the vaccine may be a sensible precaution for situations involving close contact with local communities, work in refugee camps or travel under conditions of poor hygiene in many parts of the world.

Hepatitis B

Hepatitis B is a serious viral infection spread by sexual exposure, contact with body fluids, blood and blood products, non-sterile needles, medical or dental instruments acupuncture, or tattooing (see Chapter 2.4); it is a hazard in all developing countries.

Vaccination is recommended for long-term or frequent travellers, particularly if they are sexually active, in close contact with local people, or more likely to need medical or dental treatment where sterile instruments and screened blood transfusions might not be available; and for anyone contemplating sexual contact with new partners abroad—see Chapter 10.1.

(Healthcare professionals should be vaccinated whether at home or abroad.)

Traditional vaccine schedules take 6 months but accelerated schedules are a more practical option (for example, doses on days 0, 7, 21–28 with a booster dose at 1 year).

Hepatitis B vaccination has already become part of the standard childhood vaccination schedule in many countries, and should be added to the UK schedule.

Rabies (see also Chapter 6)

Modern rabies vaccines are effective and safe, and important for every serious traveller, because animal bites, licks, and scratches are not always easy to avoid. Good quality vaccines and treatment are often unavailable where rabies poses the greatest problem.

Post-exposure treatment can be (extremely) expensive, excruciatingly painful, and often requires a trip to be cut short or abandoned.

Vaccination before you go vastly simplifies the treatment needed after a bite—fewer vaccine doses and no need for immune globulin injections—and is strongly recommended, especially for longer trips to the Indian subcontinent and Southeast Asia, Bali, and parts of Africa and South America. It is also important for small children, who may be strongly attracted to animals, and may not easily be able to report bites and saliva exposures.

Three doses of the vaccine are needed (on days 0, 7, and 21–28), so plan ahead. The vaccine can either be given by intramuscular injection, or at a reduced dose, and therefore lower cost, intradermally (with a tiny needle into the topmost layer of the skin). (Intradermal vaccination is not given to animal handlers, or to travellers who have already started taking chloroquine or mefloquine for malaria prevention.)

Rabies vaccine protection lasts at least 3 years. High antibody levels can be maintained by booster doses every 3 years, though some experts believe that a single vaccine course is all that is necessary to assure a good immune response to future booster doses following a bite.

Meningococcal meningitis

Meningitis causes serious outbreaks in many parts of the world, most notably in the 'meningitis belt' from Senegal, to Sudan and Ethiopia (see Chapter 4.5). Cases have been linked to the Hajj and Umra pilgrimages, where spread of infection is a serious risk; since 1988, Saudi Arabian health authorities have required pilgrims to show proof of vaccination.

There are new, conjugated vaccines against the A/C/Y/W135 strains that are more effective (and more expensive) than their predecessors. Protection lasts approximately 5 years. (There are also vaccines at advanced stages of development against the important B strain.)

Vaccination is advisable for travellers to places with outbreaks in progress, anyone visiting or working in refugee camps, or people travelling to the meningitis belt at times of peak transmission. (See also the note on p.83 regarding protection of travellers who have had their spleens removed.)

Children and young adults who have received the meningitis C vaccine should additionally receive the A/C/Y/W135 vaccine if they need protection for travel.

Influenza (see Chapter 4.12)
Seasonal flu is the world's most highly prevalent vaccine-preventable disease. It occurs during the winter months in the northern and southern hemispheres, but many people from temperate climates don't realize that it occurs year-round in the tropics.

People in risk groups should be vaccinated every year, especially if they plan to travel during the flu season. There is also a strong case for healthy adults and children to do the same. A vaccine against H5N1 bird flu, called Vepacel, has now been licensed.

Japanese encephalitis (see Chapter 5.2)
This disease is endemic across Asia. It is seasonal in the temperate zones affected, but may be all-year-round in the tropics.

The virus is transmitted to humans by mosquitoes that have bitten farm animals or birds, so rural travel poses the highest risk. The disease can be serious or fatal, but it has fortunately been reported in only a tiny number of Western travellers.

A new cell-culture vaccine (Ixiaro) is replacing the older, mouse brain derived vaccine. Ixiaro requires two doses, given 1 month apart. A third dose is recommended 12–24 months later, but beyond this, the duration of protection is still being studied.

It is not yet licensed for use in children.

Tick-borne encephalitis
Tick-borne encephalitis (TBE) is an arbovirus infection that occurs especially in late spring and summer in the forests of eastern and central (mainly Austria, Germany, and Switzerland) Europe, including parts of the states of the former USSR and Scandinavia. It is a risk to anyone using paths not only in the wooded areas but also through shrubbery on forest fringes, where undergrowth can brush against their legs or arms, allowing the ticks to attach themselves (see p.131). The virus can also be transmitted by drinking unpasteurized milk.

Infection carries a small risk of serious disability. A safe vaccine is available, and medical experts in the affected regions strongly advise visitors to be vaccinated. In Austria, the entire population is vaccinated routinely.

The vaccine requires two, or preferably three, doses for protection, starting at least 3 weeks prior to travel. A common approach is to give two doses 28 days apart or three doses at days 0, 7, and 21. Tick avoidance measure should be followed regardless, because of the growing additional risk of Lyme disease.

Tuberculosis
BCG vaccination (against tuberculosis—see Chapter 4.1) is no longer routinely used in the UK. However, it can be given to children and adults going to live or work in high risk countries, or if special occupational risks apply (e.g. healthcare workers).

Smallpox, plague and anthrax

Smallpox was eradicated worldwide in 1978—though the vaccine made a brief comeback following concerns about biological weapons in 2003. Military vaccines are still made against anthrax and plague. None of these vaccines is currently available for general use.

Other vaccines to consider

Although vaccines against human papilloma virus (HPV) and shingles (the new Zostavax vaccine) are not 'travel vaccines', they may be worth considering for some travel situations—such as relocating abroad, or spending much time in a setting where access to medical care might be difficult. The pneumococcal vaccine (against pneumonia) should be considered by travellers with a history of lung problems or other risk factors, and by older travellers. Two vaccines are available—Pneumovax, and the conjugated vaccine Prevenar, which offers enhanced protection, though against fewer strains.

Vaccines for the future

Vaccines against dengue fever are at an advanced stage of development, though it is likely that they will first be aimed at protecting local people in high risk parts of the world, rather than short term travellers. Lyme disease is also an active target. Various research vaccines have been tested against malaria and show promise for the distant future.

When not to be vaccinated

Each case will always be considered individually, but here are some general guidelines.

Vaccines to which the recipient has a known allergy are not normally given, and vaccines should not be given during acute illness or infection, especially if a fever is present, or in cases of some serious chronic diseases. Otherwise, there are no particular circumstances when *killed* vaccines (see Table 13.2.1) should be avoided. *Live* vaccines are generally contraindicated in disorders of immunity or pregnancy (see below).

Gastrointestinal infections at the time of vaccination may inhibit oral typhoid and cholera vaccines from becoming effective. Antibiotics and mefloquine (anti-malarial tablets) may also inhibit oral typhoid vaccine.

Other specific cautions are allergy to eggs for yellow fever, tick-borne encephalitis, flu, and measles vaccines; and to several rare antibiotics for flu and diphtheria/tetanus/polio.

Immune disorders

People with an impaired immune system, whether due to serious disease, or cancer chemotherapy or radiotherapy, should not usually take live vaccines (see Table 13.2.1) and may have a poor immune response to other vaccines (see Chapter 11.5).

Pregnancy

In pregnancy (see Chapter 11.1) live vaccines are generally avoided, but may sometimes still be advisable when there is a *real* threat from the disease (not just a certificate requirement). Despite theoretical concerns, there is no evidence that yellow fever vaccine in pregnancy has ever caused harm to the fetus. Oral typhoid vaccine is not used in pregnancy.

In theory, killed vaccines are safe, but since no manufacturer tests vaccines during pregnancy, it may take years to build confidence that each new vaccine is safe to use. The generally accepted approach is to evaluate each case and to give vaccines where benefits clearly outweigh the dangers. Seasonal flu vaccine is recommended during pregnancy.

Small children
Routine childhood vaccinations are very important and should be updated where necessary (Table 11.2.1, p.378). Minimum recommended ages for travel vaccines are shown in Table 13.2.1.

Exemptions and waivers
Where a certificate would normally be required, a letter or medical certificate of exemption signed by a doctor is usually acceptable to the authorities. People who cannot be vaccinated on medical grounds have to consider the risks of travel without protection.

Reaction to vaccines—what to expect
Yellow fever usually produces virtually no local reaction, though occasionally flu–like aches are reported several days later. Other injected vaccines tend to produce a slightly sore area at the injection site, but are not likely to make you feel unwell. Oral typhoid can produce nausea and other gastric upset. BCG (TB vaccine) can produce an open ulcer, which can take several weeks to heal, and is the only vaccine that leaves a scar.

Side effects
Isolated cases of more serious side effects have been recorded following several vaccines *but are extremely rare.*

Box 13.2.1 **Vaccines abroad**

Dangers from injections abroad under unhygienic conditions are considered further on pp.468–9, but counterfeit or ineffective vaccines can be a serious problem. Vaccines need careful manufacture, storage, handling, and preparation. There are well-documented cases of people dying from rabies in Pakistan, or acquiring hepatitis A in the countries of the former Soviet Union despite 'vaccination'. Have all vaccines *before* you leave home; or if that's not possible, go only to a reputable clinic that can satisfy you that all vaccines come from a safe and reliable source.

Box 13.2.2 **Summary of advice for travellers**

- If you are travelling through Africa or South America, check whether you need an international certificate of vaccination against yellow fever
- Obtain up-to-date advice on the best protection for your trip
- Don't forget to find out about the other measures you can take to protect yourself, such as food and water precautions, and malaria protection.

13.3 Travel insurance: the whys, whats, and hows

Rochelle Turner

The vast majority of our holidays and trips overseas pass off without any trouble. A small number will not turn out as planned; however, around one in 10 travellers will have a need to claim on their travel insurance for lost or stolen bags, cancelled flights, or medical emergencies. 2010 was a particularly shocking year for travellers. Nearly five million people were caught up in disruptions caused by snow, volcanic ash, or industrial action, costing each of them, according to lastminute.com, an average of £151 just in financial terms, not to mention any compensation for emotional stress or time.

Why do I need travel insurance?

In April 2010, research from the consumer group *Which?* found that the average cost of a claim among people who had called on their travel insurance over the past 2 years was £956, however 5% of all claims were for more than £3000. Given that most travel insurance claims arise out of a need to have emergency medical treatment abroad, many end up costing considerable sums of money. Medical repatriation from the USA or Caribbean could easily cost around £25,000, for example, especially if a traveller suffered from an injury or condition that required immobilization or an air ambulance. Hospital bills of more than £1 million are, unfortunately, not uncommon, especially in the USA.

Many countries have a reciprocal relationship for health care costs with the UK (see ✍ www.dh.gov.uk/travellers). As trips to European destinations represent nearly eight in 10 of all trips abroad, the European Health Insurance Card (EHIC) is the scheme most relied upon by UK travellers. The EHIC entitles UK residents to emergency medical care at reduced rates and at times free of charge, in state-funded hospitals across Europe. It covers emergency treatment for pre-existing medical conditions or chronic medical conditions such as asthma or diabetes—something that many standard travel insurance policies exclude. It's an important card to get, and to renew every 5 years, as some insurance policies state that they will not pay out for expenses that would have been free with an EHIC and many insurers will waive the excess on claims for medical treatment if the card is used. It is important to be aware that state-run medical facilities in Europe may not be as comprehensive as the NHS provides.

Reimbursement after needing to cancel a holiday is another main reason people make a claim on travel insurance. This could be due to your own ill health before the holiday takes place, or the illness or death of a non-travelling relative. In the past few years, events such as weather or natural disasters have also given rise to thousands of holiday cancellations. With people spending £656 per person on average for their holidays, according to *Which?* magazine, and £1250 and upwards for a cruise, it is imperative that a prime consideration when taking out travel insurance is that any cancellation limit will cover the full cost of the holiday.

Lost or damaged bags and personal belongings and travel delay are also common reasons given for claiming on insurance and elements of these policies will vary considerably from policy to policy.

When to buy insurance?

Travel insurance companies work on a number of assumptions, one of the first being that when a policy is taken out, the traveller has no reason why they might not be able to go on the holiday they have just booked. The insurer will assume that before booking, travellers will have considered their own health and the health of people close to them who are not travelling but who could impact their travel decisions. Other issues such as planned strikes, scheduled redundancies at work, uprisings or known disasters in the destination at the time of booking the holiday would nearly always result in an insurance claim for those particular reasons being rejected.

Having booked a holiday in good faith, it is best to get insurance at the same time in case there are any reasons that subsequently crop up that would prevent you from travelling or requiring you to change your trip.

How to buy travel insurance

When buying travel insurance, it is essential to get a policy that suits travellers' own personal circumstances as well as the circumstances of the holiday. Research from *Which? Travel* shows that, in 2010, 10% of people were disappointed to find that they couldn't make a claim against the policy they had purchased.

Typical policies will provide cover for trips abroad lasting around 30 days and for the types of activities that are common on holidays. If travelling abroad for longer, or if you plan to be doing activities that are deemed to be more risky (winter sports or white water rafting, for example), then you'll need to get a policy to cover this. If you plan to travel more than a couple of times in the year, an annual policy may work out better in terms of value and convenience.

Both age and medical condition will have an impact on the cost of insurance and should be borne in mind in terms of your entire holiday budget. One 80-year old *Which?* member was recently quoted nearly £900 for a 3-week trip to New Zealand before finding insurance elsewhere for less than half that price. Analysis of travel insurance claims shows that the likelihood of making a claim does increase with age and insurance prices are set by actuaries to reflect that risk.

You should always tell the insurer if you are taking regular medication and declare any medical condition past and present, even if you are no longer receiving medical treatment. No matter how insignificant you may feel the condition is, failing to declare it could invalidate your policy if you need to make a claim when you are overseas. Let the insurance company or broker decide if your condition has any bearing on your policy. Inform them, too, if you have experienced any changes in your health, for example, a change to medication, a diagnosis of a new ailment or a referral for tests or to see a consultant.

It is important to be aware that pregnancy is not always covered in travel insurance policies, particularly any costs arising from the baby's birth.

Transport operators will try to limit their risks of an early birth by setting limits on when pregnant women can travel; however, many women have been forced to cancel pre-booked holidays without reimbursement because of the small print in their policy.

Your travel insurance policy should meet these minimum criteria:

- At least £2 million of medical cover. This should include an air ambulance to get you home or to a nearby centre of medical excellence
- At least £1500 baggage and belongings cover. Policies often have a single item limit so be careful what you take away with you
- At least a cancellation or curtailment limit that will cover all costs of your holiday including any excursions that you would want to pre-pay and the costs of getting you home (for example, if a close relative falls ill)
- Personal liability cover of at least £1 million. This covers any costs as a result of you injuring someone, or damaging their property
- A 24 hour emergency line and cover for legal expenses
- Membership of the Financial Ombudsman Service (FOS). If you have a dispute that you can't settle with the insurer, you can complain to the ombudsman free of charge. They can force the insurer to settle claims and pay compensation.

What to watch out for?

The small print on travel insurance policies can be a huge stumbling block when making claims. Strike, terrorism, personal car breakdown, and disruption caused by poor weather are not covered in all standard travel insurance policies. Other common areas where people get caught out include:

Visas and passports: If the destination requires a visa to be arranged in advance, it is up to the traveller to get it. The airline or port authorities should check passports at check in, but the responsibility for any omission on arrival in the country belongs to the traveller. Some countries also require 6 months left on a passport before it expires. The Foreign and Commonwealth Office regularly updates the requirements for individual countries on its website (see p.456).

Inoculations: Getting ill from a disease that travellers should have been inoculated against, or taking medicines to prevent (i.e. malaria) but had not done so, is unlikely to be covered by insurance. Seek skilled advice before you go

Medical cover: travellers will have to adhere to the insurer's policy on pre-existing medical conditions (and have a duty to disclose any important information before purchase), but should you fall ill abroad, the assistance company must approve any treatment before you have it. Some insurers insist on you having an EHIC card for European travel, and nearly all will require you to register with Medicare if admitted to hospital in Australia. Coverage for any treatment required as a result of you being under the influence of alcohol (or drugs) is likely to be rejected

Cancellation cover: holidaymakers needing to cancel their holidays can be caught out if the cost of their holiday is more than the level of cover provided. Insurers also place other conditions when deciding whether to pay out. If your car has broken down on the way to the airport or seaport, causing you to miss your transportation, you may need to be able to prove the car was roadworthy and fully serviced; you are only likely to be covered if travelling directly from home to the place of departure. Any accidents or breakdowns caused after taking major detours along the way to the port may negate your policy

Lost or stolen items: insurers are strict in ensuring that you take reasonable care of your possessions. 'Valuables' tend not to be covered unless they have been kept in a room safe or locked in a car's glove box or boot (although not overnight) and a police report within 24 hours of any incident will always be required. Some items, such as electronic goods and contact lenses or things confiscated by customs, are rarely covered on a standard policy and all policies will have a maximum payout value for any one or pair of items—often much lower than the replacement value. Original receipts or valuations are also required.

Further information

Association of British Insurers. Available at: ℘ www.abi.org.uk
British Insurance Brokers Association. Available at: ℘ www.biba.org.uk
European Health Insurance Card (EHIC). Available at: ℘ www.ehic.org.uk
The Foreign and Commonwealth Office. Available at: ℘ www.fco.gov.uk
National Travel Health Network and Centre. Available at: ℘ www.nathnac.org
Which? Available at: ℘ www.which.co.uk

13.4 Travel law

Simon Butler

When an injury or illness is contracted abroad, it is important for travellers to understand how laws relating to travel and tourism apply, In 1992, the Package Travel, Package Holidays, and Package Tours Regulations (SI 1992/3288) came into force in the UK, and imposed a regulatory framework to govern the relationship between consumers and the suppliers of travel services where a holiday is booked in advance and is sold at an inclusive price, meaning that you pay for everything all together.

As a consumer, you are protected by the travel regulations if you are injured or contract an illness (e.g. salmonella infection) during your stay, as long as the injury or illness has been caused by the person(s) providing the services as part of the package. The operator is liable to you for any damage caused by its failure to perform the contract or the improper performance of the contract. It may also be liable for negligence. Be aware that many holiday arrangements are not covered by the travel regulations. For example, if you arrange your own holiday on the Internet and book your own hotel and excursions, then you will need to pursue a claim against the supplier of the service abroad. This will require a clear understanding of the law on contract and tort in the jurisdiction in which the accident occurred.

If you pay for the holiday on a credit card, then you may be entitled to pursue a claim against the credit card company. In the UK, consumers are protected by the Consumer Credit Act 1974, which entitles a consumer to bring a claim against the credit card company for any negligence and/or breach of contract on the part of a supplier of services.

Travel claims also require evidence. It is therefore important that you take photographs of the location and cause of the accident, and retain all relevant documents, names of witnesses etc. If you contract an illness, then keeping a note of the symptoms, location, what you had to eat and drink etc. is of critical importance, not only for the medical team treating you, but also for any future claim against the supplier. Receipts should also be retained to establish that payment was made (contract entered into) for the service. I appreciate that the last thing on your mind when travelling is to think about the legal consequences of sustaining an injury or illness abroad. However, accidents do happen.

Before concluding contracts for a package holiday, please remember to check that the contract contains the following information: the travel destination, accommodation, characteristics, and categories of transport to be used, the itinerary, the name, and address of the organizer, the retailer and, where appropriate, the insurer.

If you do sustain significant injury or illness abroad, consider seeking legal advice as soon as possible following your return so that the evidence and person at fault can be ascertained swiftly. You should also report the matter to the operator, if purchased as a package, the credit card company, and your insurance company.

13.5 Medicines and medical kits

Richard Dawood and Larry Goodyer

Creating the perfect travel medical kit is a matter of striking the right balance between size, weight, cost, and practicality, and thinking clearly about what you are most likely to need. This chapter reviews the commonest likely problems and their remedies. A concise checklist is given in Appendix 4. Expedition kits are considered in Chapter 11.7.

Some general points about medicines

Safety

All drugs with useful effects can also be harmful, especially if taken inappropriately. No drug suits everyone: begin by seeking advice from your doctor about any medication you intend to use abroad. Ask for the manufacturer's data sheet, and follow instructions carefully:

- Keep all drugs and medicines out of reach of children
- Check 'expiry' dates: out-of-date medicines can be harmful or ineffective
- Ensure that pharmacists or doctors appreciate any drug allergies you may have—carry a translation, if necessary; and ensure *you* fully understand instructions you are given.

Box 13.5.1 **Counterfeit drugs**

Counterfeit drugs and medicines are a major problem worldwide; some cause harm because they are ineffective, while others are actually toxic. It is a multi-billion pound industry reported to cause up to half a million fatalities every year. Fake medicines are far more common in developing countries with poor regulatory processes. They can also be found on the Internet and travellers should obtain medicines via this route only from properly registered and regulated 'e-pharmacies', if at all.

There have been many cases involving well-known brand names where counterfeiting occurs on a massive scale. The first known case of such drugs penetrating the British market occurred in 1989, when a large quantity of fake Zantac tablets (the anti-ulcer treatment) had been illegally imported, probably from Greece. There have been several cases since. In Nigeria, industrial solvent in paracetamol syrup killed 109 children and maimed 600. In China, two people died and nine were hospitalized by taking tablets for diabetes containing six times the intended amount of drug. According to the WHO, 30–60% of medicines in Russia and some countries in Africa, Asia, and Latin America may be counterfeit.

In some countries, manufacturing is poorly controlled. In Africa, quality studies found many anti-malarials contained the wrong dose of drug: too much, too little, or none. Similar problems have been found in South America and Asia.

It can be tempting to buy medicines in places where 'copies' of well-known brands are sold at a fraction of the cost, but it is always much safer to take along anything you know you will need, particularly anti-malarials and antibiotics. Inspect all packaging, though fakes can be concealed in authentic packaging. And be alert to this risk if locally purchased medication fails to produce the desired effect.

Dosage
- Keep strictly to recommended doses—twice as much is not necessarily twice as effective!
- Always complete a full course of treatment if you are taking antibiotics (usually 5–7 days), but discontinue any drug you suspect of causing adverse effects.

Drug names

Most drugs have two names—a *generic*, or scientific name, which is usually the same in most countries, and a *trade* or *brand* name that may vary from one country to another. Beware—completely different medicines can have confusingly similar names. To complicate matters further, tablets containing combinations of drugs are given *special* generic names: paracetamol plus codeine is called co-codamol, for example, and the antibiotic amoxicillin/clavulanic acid is called co-amoxiclav. Make sure that you get what you *want*.

Current and existing medical problems

Take an adequate supply of all routine medication, as well as a prescription or written record giving *generic* names in case more is needed. It is also sensible to travel with medication to cover any condition that might recur, e.g. cystitis, asthma, back pain. For hay fever (Chapter 8.6) and asthma in particular, unusual environments may readily precipitate an attack. If you need to take psychoactive drugs, see Chapter 9.8. Always mention any medication you are currently taking when buying medicines or seeking treatment, at home or abroad.

In the UK, only 3 months' supply of medicines intended for use abroad is obtainable via the National Health Service.

Box 13.5.2 **Never be separated from important medical supplies when you travel**

Deaths have occurred when travellers have been separated from essential supplies, such as asthma medication. As a rule of thumb, always take more than you need, ensure medicines are labelled, and divide them between carry-on and checked baggage or between yourself and a companion. You may not be able to recover the cost of replacement medication from travel insurance if your baggage is *delayed*, rather than *lost*; and if you need a prescription to get a fresh supply, you will have the added cost and hassle of trying to find a doctor.

Prescriptions

Medicines marked * are available in the UK only on a prescription. Some doctors may be unwilling to prescribe medicines on a 'just in case' basis. These drugs do warrant medical supervision, but are carried only because of the potential for unreliable quality or non-availability.

You may find that you can buy 'prescription only' medicines at any pharmacy without restriction; you should treat all such medicines with respect and note the points made earlier regarding potential problems. Avoid 'herbal' remedies (below).

Box 13.5.3 **Herbal remedies**

Don't try herbal cures and medicines when you travel, however harmless they may seem. Such products are sometimes found to contain toxic adulterants, such as lead, or are sometimes 'spiked' with conventional medicines, such as powerful steroids. Herbal teas marketed for weight loss in the UK and Europe were found to contain the powerful diet drug sibutramine, which has been banned due to sometimes fatal side effects. Popular herbal remedies such as St John's Wort, Ginko, Ephedra, and Kava can have serious side effects or interact with other medicines.

You can reduce the risk of customs difficulties by ensuring all medicines are in their original containers, and carried with a prescription or doctor's letter. Unidentified loose pills invite unwanted interest. Strong painkillers, such as codeine, sleeping tablets, or any medicine acting on the central nervous system need extra care: most countries permit a few weeks' supply for personal use if you have a copy of the prescription. Others, such as the United Arab Emirates (UAE), have a complete ban. Similar problems have occurred in Mexico and Japan (see below).

'Controlled drugs' include strong prescription painkillers. Carrying more than 3 months' supply into or out of the UK requires a license (🐾 http://www.homeoffice.gov.uk/drugs/licensing/personal/).

Box 13.5.4 **Case study**

A court in Dubai acquitted Tracy Wilkinson, an osteopath, 2 months after she was found to have traces of the painkiller codeine and the sleeping medicine temazepam in her urine when she was detained at the airport. Mrs Wilkinson, 44, spent 8 weeks in prison on remand. Codeine is illegal in the UAE, where it is considered to be a mind-altering drug, without proof it was obtained on prescription. A Foreign Office spokesman said advice to travellers had been changed since Mrs Wilkinson's arrest. It now reads: 'If you are taking medication prescribed or obtained in the UK for use in the UAE, and you have any doubts as to whether it is approved for use, you should consult the UAE authorities.'

Packaging for travel

Carry tablets in blister packs in re-sealable plastic bags, with manufacturers' instructions, rather than loose or in a bottle. A plastic zip wallet or waterproof pouch can be used to store medicines and first-aid equipment. Protect creams from contamination during use; protect pessaries and suppositories from heat—they are designed to melt at body temperature.

Box 13.5.5 **Treating local people**

It can be an act of kindness to help local people in cases of emergency, but travellers need to be extremely cautious about giving medicines or any form of treatment to others. They may cause harm and can undermine confidence in the local health system. Travellers—even doctors—may not understand locally prevalent diseases or problems such as drug resistance. If you have spare supplies, give them to a local doctor, nurse, or health worker (see also p.410).

Athletes abroad

Athletes packing a travel kit should know that some of the medicines listed here may be banned from use in competitive sport, and they should be wary of remedies purchased abroad. There may be important differences in formulation between the same brand of product sold in different countries: a British skier in the 2002 Winter Olympics was stripped of a bronze medal after using a USA version of Vicks Sinex nasal inhaler. Unlike the UK product, the USA formulation contains amphetamine derivatives, banned from sports. In the UK, further information can be obtained from UK Anti-Doping (🖰 http://www.ukad.org.uk). Elsewhere, athletes should contact national sporting bodies.

Diarrhoea

Anti-diarrhoeal agents for symptomatic treatment are discussed on p.25. One of the following should suffice:
- Loperamide hydrochloride (e.g. Imodium)
- Codeine phosphate.*

Loperamide is preferable—it is the fastest acting and has fewest side effects. Anti-diarrhoeals should *not* be used in children, or in dysentery (with fever, or blood in the stools) (see p.382).
   There is also a drug called Hidrasec (racecadotril) that dramatically reduces secretion of fluid into the gut; it appears to be safe and highly effective. It is available in France and many other countries, though not in the UK.
   See below for antibiotic treatment/prevention, and treatment of dehydration.

Intestinal infections

Treatment

Treatment of diarrhoea with antibiotics is discussed on pp.21–5. The following may be useful for possible self-treatment:
- Ciprofloxacin (e.g. Ciproxin)*
- Azithromycin (e.g. Zithromax)*
- Metronidazole (e.g. Flagyl)*
- Rifaximin* (a new antibiotic in the UK, but available for some time in other countries)
- Tinidazole (e.g. Fasigyn).*

A single dose of ciprofloxacin is sufficient to treat 80% of cases of travellers' diarrhoea—if symptoms persist, a 3–5-day course should be completed (it should not be used in pregnancy or in children).
   Azithromycin is a possible alternative. It is suitable for travellers to parts of Southeast Asia where ciprofloxacin resistance is more common, and is suitable for children.
   A relatively large quantity of metronidazole would be needed to treat a bout of amoebic dysentery, so tinidazole can be a more practical alternative—just 4 tablets a day for 2 or 3 days would be required for a complete course.
   All of the above may be used safely in people who are allergic to penicillin.

Mebendazole (Vermox)* can be used for the treatment of some worm infestations mentioned in Chapter 4.7. For the treatment of threadworm, a single tablet of mebendazole 100mg (e.g. Ovex) can be purchased in the UK without a prescription.

Prevention

Prevention of travellers' diarrhoea with antibiotics is discussed in Chapter 2.1.

Dehydration

Severe diarrhoea causes rapid loss of fluid and salts: potentially dangerous in small children, but also affecting adults. Glucose promotes intestinal absorption of salts and water, and an understanding of this mechanism led to the formulation of oral rehydration solutions. These are effective and easy to prepare—see p.21, p.382. A double-ended plastic spoon for measuring the correct amounts of sugar and salt can be obtained from suppliers such as Nomad (see Appendix 4).

Oral rehydration powders such as Electrolade and Dioralyte provide all the necessary ingredients in sachets that can simply be added to water, and should be carried in high-risk zones, especially by the elderly and children. Similar products are readily available worldwide.

Salt losses increase through sweating and salt replacement may be necessary. Consider travelling with a small supply of table salt sachets. Salt *tablets* should not be used.

Constipation

Travel can tip the balance even for those who normally have no problem. A high fluid intake and a high-fibre diet are preferable to medication; it may be worth travelling with a small supply of natural bran (also available in tablet form). Senokot tablets are an effective laxative.

Heartburn and indigestion

Unfamiliar foods and too much alcohol easily exacerbate this complaint. The various antacid preparations are equally effective; select one that is to your taste.

Gastric acid has a slight protective effect against several intestinal infections, so drugs that reduce acid secretion, such as the 'H$_2$ antagonist' ranitidine (Zantac), should be avoided unless symptoms warrant. 'Proton pump inhibitors' (PPIs) such as omeprazole (Losec)* stop acid secretion almost completely—when taking them regularly, preventive antibiotics may need to be considered (p.26).

Vomiting

Specific treatment of vomiting in food poisoning is not advised unless severe enough to require skilled medical treatment. Once vomiting has begun, tablets are unlikely to afford relief and prochlorperazine suppositories 25mg (Stemetil)* would be an alternative to injections, although they could melt in very hot climates. Prochlorperazine (Buccastem)* can be placed between the upper lip and gum; it is absorbed through the lining of the mouth: the dosage is one or two 3mg tablets twice daily.

Metoclopramide tablets (Maxolon)* 10mg or domperidone (Motilium)* are occasionally useful to treat nausea unrelated to motion sickness. Ondansetron (Zofran)* is powerful, fast acting, and absorbed through the mouth, but more expensive.

Motion sickness

Motion sickness is discussed in greater detail in Chapter 7.3. Susceptible individuals may need to try different medicines to find the best option. Both hyoscine-containing pills such as Kwells and anti-histamine-containing remedies such as promethazine (Phenergan) can have side effects, such as drowsiness (see also Chapter 7.3). Cinnarizine (Stugeron) is also very effective and will take effect more quickly if the tablet is sucked.

Hyoscine (called scopolamine in the USA) is also available in the form of an adhesive patch (Scopoderm TTS)* that allows absorption of the drug through the skin; it remains effective for up to 3 days (see p.219). These should not be used in children or the elderly, and may also cause drowsiness. Some preparations (e.g. Kwells) contain instructions to dissolve the tablets in the mouth, for rapid absorption. Anti-motion-sickness pills are of little use once vomiting has started, so take any pills some hours before your journey begins.

Urinary tract infections

Symptoms of 'cystitis' are common in women and troublesome during travel: discuss treatment with your doctor before leaving home. Not drinking enough during long journeys is a common precipitating cause.

Trimethoprim* in a dose of 200mg, twice daily, is effective for most urinary tract infections, but will not treat gonorrhoea, a possible cause of urinary symptoms in travellers (see p.333). Other options: nitrofurantoin *50mg four times a day, or ciprofloxacin (Cipro) *250–500mg twice daily. Three days' treatment is usually sufficient.

Vaginal infection (candidiasis, thrush, yeast)

Like cystitis, this can be very annoying: travel with a suitable remedy if you are prone. Fluconazole (Diflucan 150) is an effective single-dose oral treatment. Alternatively, one clotrimazole 500mg vaginal suppository (Canesten 1, Mycelex) will clear up an infection. See also p.333.

Other infections

Causes of fever in travellers are discussed in Chapter 9.9. Do not rely on antibiotics to treat a fever without seeking medical advice unless the cause is obvious. It is sometimes worth packing a course of antibiotics in case of throat, chest, or middle-ear infections. Amoxicillin (Amoxil)* is probably a good choice. Clarithromycin* is an alternative for those allergic to penicillin and is suitable for respiratory infections. For skin infections and animal bites, consider taking co-amoxiclav (e.g. Augmentin)*.

Generally, the first sign of allergy is a rash and any antibiotic should be discontinued if this develops. Consider travelling with antiviral medicines such as Tamiflu, for treatment/prevention of influenza (p.98). (Tamiflu can be taken at a dose of 75mg once daily for prevention, or twice daily for 5 days, for treatment.)

Pain

Mild to moderate pain responds well to aspirin, paracetamol, or ibuprofen. If you anticipate severe pain (e.g. from backache or arthritis), consider taking a more powerful painkiller.

- *Aspirin:* water-soluble preparations produce fewer gastric side effects (pain, bleeding) than tablets, and are absorbed sooner. Aspirin reduces temperature in a fever. It should not be given to children. The dosage for pain relief is 300–900mg (usually 1–3 tablets) 4–6 hourly
- *Paracetamol* (Panadol, Tylenol): has comparable pain-relieving and temperature-reducing effects and causes no gastric symptoms. Available for children as Calpol, in bottles or sachets
- *Codeine phosphate:** sometimes used to relieve diarrhoea; in a dose of 30–60mg, 4-hourly, it is also a valuable remedy for moderate pain. Smaller doses can be purchased without a prescription in the UK when combined with paracetamol or aspirin (e.g. Codis). *Ibuprofen* (e.g. Nurofen) has anti-inflammatory properties that make it useful for treating muscle and joint aches and pains. It can be taken together with paracetamol for an additive effect, and a combined preparation is available in the UK (Nuromol)
- *Diclofenac (Voltarol):** like ibuprofen, this is a 'non-steroidal anti-inflammatory drug' (NSAID), although more suitable for moderate to severe pain; also available in soluble, slow-release and suppository formulations. It can be purchased over the counter in the UK.

Aspirin, ibuprofen, diclofenac, and naproxen should be avoided by people with a history of stomach ulcers.

- *Tramadol (Zydol, Ultram):** the most potent painkiller that is not a controlled drug. Side effects can be unpredictable and sometimes severe
- *Dihydrocodeine (DF118):** an alternative (30mg every eight hours) although not as useful for very severe pain; there is a combined preparation with paracetamol, called co-dydramol (Paramol)*, and a non-prescription formulation containing less dihydrocodeine. Codeine, dihydrocodeine and hydrocodone are all related to morphine and highly regulated in some countries (see warnings above).

Children

Anyone travelling with small children should also take along a suitable children's analgesic such as Calpol (available in sachets) or ibuprofen syrup (e.g. Junifen).

Jet lag

Melatonin is discussed in Chapter 7.2. It is widely available in the USA and several other countries. In the UK, a slow-release 2mg preparation (Circadin)* is available.

Studies have shown modafinil (Provigil*) and related drugs to aid alertness, and short-acting hypnotics such as zolpidem* or zopiclone* may help to readjust sleep patterns.

Sleep

Sleeping medicines may seem an attractive option on overnight journeys but may be harmful: immobility increases the risk of deep vein thrombosis. Sleeping medication should be used in the lowest possible dosage and only when you can stretch out fully in a horizontal position.

Adults

- *Zopiclone (Zimovane):** (3.75–7.5mg) has a metallic taste, which some people don't like but which helps you tell when it has been absorbed and when it is out of your system. It provides 6–8 hr of sleep
- *Zolpidem (Stilnoct, Ambien):** 5–10mg; is shorter-acting. It can be used at bedtime, or during the night if you awake and cannot get back to sleep.

A longer acting drug such as Temazepam* 10mg may help prevent early morning waking. (It is a controlled drug in the UK.)

Children

Promethazine (Phenergan) in a dose of 5–10mg for children aged 6–12 months, 15–20mg for children aged 1–5 years and 20–25mg for children aged 6–10 may be useful occasionally (see p.379).

Malaria prophylaxis and treatment

A detailed discussion of the choice and dosage of anti-malarial drugs can be found in Chapter 5.1.

Insect bites

Treatment

- *Crotamiton (Eurax) cream or lotion:* often sufficient to relieve local irritation. Other options: tea tree oil, and the Chinese remedy, White flower lotion
- *Antihistamines:* may be required to relieve itching. Anti-histamine creams and ointments should be avoided—sensitivity is common. Chlorpheniramine maleate (e.g. Piriton) tablets in a dose of 4–16mg daily are helpful, but cause drowsiness. Loratadine (Clarityn) 10mg or desloratadine (Neoclarityn) 5mg once daily is an effective anti-histamine that does not do this and could be taken continuously if needed
- *Steroid creams:* such as betamethasone (e.g. Betnovate, Diprosone)* are advised for more severe reactions to bites—provided there is no infection and the skin is unbroken. Hydrocortisone cream (HC45, Lanacort) is a milder steroid cream that may be purchased without a prescription
- *Antibiotic treatment:* occasionally necessary when bites are scratched and become infected. Such bites also need careful local treatment to prevent long-lasting infection. See also Chapter 9.5.

Prevention

Insect repellents are essential for travel to a hot country—see Chapter 5.12.

DEET is the best choice, it has been in use since the 1950s and is the most widely tested. Its main drawback being the need to reapply it frequently; more concentrated products last longer. Products containing 30–50% DEET are optimal for skin application. It is very safe, with remarkably few reports of problems in normal use. Use in children is sometimes questioned because of a tiny number of reports of seizures over the years. Even in these cases it is difficult to confirm a definite link to use of DEET.

Outside malaria-endemic areas, products containing an extract of lemon eucalyptus (Mosiguard) or icaridin (Autan range) can be useful alternatives; they are present in other brands, too. For instance, icaridin might be labelled as Picaridin, Bayrepel, or even its full chemical name (2-hydroxyethyl)-piperidinecarboxylic acid 1-methyl ester, while lemon eucalyptus extract is often labelled as PMD. There is little evidence that plant extracts (e.g. citronella) are any safer than DEET or effective enough to give worthwhile protection.

Allergies

Treatment of bee-sting allergy is discussed in Chapter 6. Travellers who have had a serious allergic reaction should travel with their emergency medicines, including adrenaline syringes (e.g. EpiPen, AnaPen)* (when travelling with these it is important to take more than one).

Antihistamine tablets (or syrup for children), steroid creams, eyedrops and inhalers may also be useful.

If you suffer from hay fever, take along any medication you may need. Hay fever seasons vary considerably between countries (see Chapter 8.6).

Sunburn

Prevention

Use high SPF sunscreens (Chapter 8.5) liberally. Water-resistant sunscreens are recommended for children. Stated protection factors usually refer to protection from UVB; check for UVA protection. Discard sunscreens after a year—they lose potency.

Treatment

In addition to after-sun products, ibuprofen may be of value if used soon after exposure to strong sunlight (tablets, gel or mousse—p.280). Calamine lotion may be helpful for treatment of mild cases; calamine-containing creams (e.g. Lacto calamine) are less drying on the skin.

Eyes

Irritation following exposure to sun and dust, and minor eye infections, are common problems (Chapter 9.3).

Lubricating drops are invaluable for flying and dry/dusty environments.

Antibiotics can be used to treat conjunctivitis: azithromycin* (Azyter, Azasite) is simple, effective, and convenient for travel. Chloramphenicol drops are more commonly prescribed but require refrigeration.

Colds/sinusitis

Air travellers liable to colds or sinusitis should travel with a decongestant spray (e.g. Sinex, Otrivine). Oral decongestant tablets containing pseudoephedrine (Sudafed) are also useful.

Nasal saline drops, spray, (e.g. Sterimar) or oil (Nozoil) may aid comfort and possibly reduce the risk of airborne infection.

Cold sores, herpes blisters

Strong sunlight, cold and wind can trigger cold sores (Chapter 8.5). Anyone prone to them should use a high SPF sunscreen on the lips. Aciclovir cream (Zovirax) at an early stage can help reduce the duration and severity of attacks.

Ear problems

External ear infections can be a problem for swimmers and divers. The problem is just as likely to be due to fungal infection as bacterial; see advice on p.293 for suitable drops.

First-aid—cuts, grazes, and animal bites

Prompt cleansing of any wound—with running water, or better still, an antiseptic solution—is the most important step in treatment. Subsequently, keeping a wound clean is essential. See also Chapter 9.1.

Treatment

- *Iodine* is a valuable antiseptic agent, and povidone iodine (e.g. Videne Antiseptic Paint—Nomad) is a good option. A dry powder povidone iodine spray is available in a small container (Savlon Dry) that does not sting. Other useful options for cleaning minor wounds: *Cetrimide and chlorhexidine cream* (e.g. Savlon); chlorhexidine spray (e.g. Savlon First Aid Wash); and antiseptic wipes
- *Steristrips* and similar adhesive tapes, and possibly (with training) tissue glue, are useful for holding together the edges of a clean, gaping wound if medical care cannot be obtained
- *Wound dressings:* Band-Aids or other sticking plasters are essential for minor. Also useful: non-adherent dressings (e.g. Melolin) plus tape (e.g. Micropore or zinc oxide); or non-adherent dressings with surrounding adhesive pads (Melolin adhesive, Primapore). A standard wound dressing (BPC No. 14) might be useful for larger wounds. Keep wounds clean and dry; if fluid is seeping through, change dressings frequently
- *Bandages:* a crepe (ace) bandage may provide relief following a joint injury, but anything smaller than 7.5cm would be of little use on a large joint. Cohesive bandages are easier to apply. Other bandages and slings can usually be improvised. Larger expeditions may need more extensive first-aid supplies, including inflatable or malleable aluminium (SAM) splints. For walkers and trekkers the hydrogel-containing blister plasters (Compeed) are essential
- *Antibiotic treatment* may be necessary. Animal bites warrant preventive antibiotic treatment (see Chapter 6), e.g. with flucloxacillin, clarithromycin, cefuroxime axetil, or co-amoxiclav.

Fungal skin infections

Anti-fungal cream and dusting powder is useful for treatment of athlete's foot and other fungal skin infections. See also Chapter 9.1.

Some other things to take

1. *Water purification supplies* are discussed in detail in Chapter 3.2
2. *Contact lens solutions.* Take ample supplies. Bottles of sterile intravenous saline can usually be obtained from pharmacies in most countries if supplies run out
3. *Contraceptive needs* are discussed in Chapter 10.3. The 'morning after' pill may also need to be considered
4. *Feminine hygiene.* Take all your likely needs with you, unless you know that acceptable supplies will be available locally (Chapter 9.7)
5. Male travellers over the age of 65, or who have a history of prostatic symptoms (such as hesitancy or difficulty passing urine, or a poor urinary stream) should consider travelling with a sterile *urinary catheter* that could be used by a local doctor in an emergency. Such items may not be easily available
6. *Thermometer.* Digital thermometers are excellent. Ordinary clinical thermometers are unsuitable for detecting or monitoring hypothermia (Chapter 8.4); a special, low-reading thermometer should also be taken if likely to be needed. Disposable liquid crystal thermometers are cheap, lightweight and accurate
7. *Toilet paper.* Away from the beaten track, it is advisable to take your own supply
8. *Alcohol hand gel or sanitizers* are essential for cleaning hands before touching food. Wet wipes are also useful, and at a pinch can be used on plates and cutlery
9. *Altitude.* Diamox, dexamethasone and other medication for altitude are discussed in Chapters 8.3 and 11.7. Also consider taking a pulse oximeter to measure blood oxygen and monitor response to treatment
10. *Rubs.* If there is much walking to be done, a rub for muscle aches or sprains can provide relief. Options range from anti-inflammatory preparations such as ibuprofen or diclofenac cream, gel, or mousse, to traditional remedies like Tiger Balm
11. *Malaria diagnosis.* Self-testing kits can help guide treatment of malaria—a small finger prick of blood gives a rapid result (Chapter 5.1). Their main drawbacks are cost, limited shelf life, and the need for careful instruction
12. *Tick tweezers.* Available from pet shops and veterinary suppliers
13. *Blood group record* (see Chapter 13.6)
14. *Toiletries.* If you have sensitive skin, consider travelling with your usual brands.

Injections abroad: needle kits

According to the WHO, about 12 billion injections are given each year—5% are immunizations, the rest for medication. Non-sterile injections cause 21 million cases of hepatitis B every year, 2 million cases of hepatitis C, and 260,000 cases of HIV/AIDS (see opposite). *Always satisfy yourself that there is a genuine need for an injection before accepting one.* Further information can be found at: ✑ www.injectionsafety.org

---

Box 13.5.6 **Case study**

In China 60% of the population is hepatitis B positive—largely as a result of unsafe injections. A UNICEF study in 2000 found that up to 65% of children in rural areas had received injections as a treatment for their most recent cold; many children receive more than six injections a year (other than immunizations) and in one rural county, 88% of the injections given were found to be unsafe. Many patients are culturally attuned to expecting an injection, just as poorly trained doctors and medical people may be culturally and perhaps financially attuned to providing them.

Disposable pre-sterilized needles and syringes are not widely available in poor countries, so consider taking your own. In the UK, needles and syringes are available at the discretion of a pharmacist, or in kits. They are also available in kits that include other medical items, from suppliers listed in Appendix 2. In the USA and most other countries, a prescription is necessary, and a prescription should always be carried when travelling.

13.6 Blood transfusion, blood products, and the traveller

Michael Thomas

In the event of injury or illness abroad, a blood transfusion may be life-saving, but may bring dangers of its own. Would you know whether the blood provided in that particular country met the standards of your national transfusion service? And what would you do if you were bitten by a stray dog and needed rabies immunoglobulin? It is important to be aware of the risks, and to consider whether 'blood and rabies cover' through an organization such as the Blood Care Foundation may be appropriate for your needs.

Blood transfusion

The problems with having a transfusion overseas fall into three groups: availability, transfusion-transmitted diseases (TTDs), and testing of blood donations.

Availability

In many countries there is a constant shortage of blood. This may be due to financial constraints, local custom, or the genetic make-up of the population.

Transfusion-transmitted diseases

In many parts of the world, the incidence of TTDs, such as HIV and hepatitis, is as much as 10000 times higher than in the UK. This means that a donated unit of blood is much more likely to be infected. Additionally, in some countries diseases are prevalent that do not occur in Europe, but that can be transmitted by blood transfusion—such as malaria, leishmaniasis, Chagas disease, and filariasis.

Testing

In many countries, the health budget is insufficient to allow units of donated blood to be fully tested. If they are tested, frequently the test kits used are of a lesser quality.

Basic points

Avoidance

There is much truth in the old saying that 'the best blood transfusion is no blood transfusion'—so travellers should do everything possible to avoid needing one.

Medical

Don't travel to countries where the transfusion facilities may be inadequate if:

- You suffer from a coagulation disorder, or you are not properly stabilized on anticoagulant medication
- You have a medical condition that commonly requires transfusion
- You are pregnant.

Behaviour

Being involved in an accident is the commonest reason for a traveller to require a blood transfusion. Avoiding accidents is, therefore, the most effective way of avoiding a transfusion.

- *Driving on the road:* if you are driving in a foreign country, take extra precautions, always remembering that you may have to drive on the opposite side of the road from that in your own country. Always wear seatbelts; don't drive in the dark; don't drive too fast; and never drink and drive no matter how great the temptation. In many countries, holidaymakers are encouraged to hire mopeds. If you do, always wear a crash helmet and protective clothing
- *Exploring on foot:* one of the commonest causes of road accidents amongst travellers is looking the wrong way when crossing the road. If the traffic drives on the opposite side of the road to that to which you are accustomed, take great care, as your natural instinct is to look in the wrong direction and then step off in front of oncoming traffic. As you will be unfamiliar with the surrounding area, keep to well-lit streets where there are plenty of other people. Do not venture into areas where you are likely to be attacked
- *Hazardous sports:* avoid hazardous sports, especially if you are not being properly supervised. Take care when going off on mountain walks or hill climbing

- *Disease:* ensure that you avoid catching any disease that might require a blood transfusion as part of the treatment. The most common such disease is malaria; so when you are in an area where malaria is endemic, take adequate malarial prophylaxis, wear long-sleeved shirts or blouses and long trousers after dark, and always sleep under a properly impregnated mosquito net.

Be prepared

Before leaving home, there are a number of things that you can do to minimize any risks whilst you are abroad:

- *Blood group:* have your blood grouped before departure and make sure you take a copy of the laboratory report with you. Knowing your blood group in advance will make it easier to find a blood donor in an emergency
- *Sterile needles and syringes:* take a supply with you, as these may not be readily available in the countries to which you are going
- *Intravenous fluids:* it is possible to take plasma substitutes and/or crystalloid solutions for use in an emergency, though such products require skill to use, and an adequate supply is bulky and heavy. Sterile transfusion equipment (giving sets and cannulae) may be difficult to obtain. Large expeditions with trained medical officers may find it valuable to travel with such resources, but these are impractical for the majority of travellers. If you do take such supplies with you, do not attempt to insert an intravenous line unless you are skilled in transfusion techniques. Failed attempts may ruin the only good venous access available and make it much more difficult for a doctor to eventually set up a transfusion
- *Medical assistance:* it is vital that you take out adequate health insurance, which includes telephone support as well as emergency evacuation by air ambulance if indicated
- *Blood cover:* it is also advisable to obtain cover from an institution that can provide properly screened blood (see p.472).

Solutions

Walking blood banks

These are composed of a group of people who would be prepared to donate blood to meet a particular emergency. However, there are numerous problems associated with such a venture including:

- Numbers are usually so small that there is a significant chance that sufficient blood of the required group will not be available
- As the members of the blood bank live locally, they will be liable to carry the diseases endemic to that area
- As all the members probably know each other, it is much more difficult for someone to opt out of donation if their social behaviour has put them at risk of transmitting infection
- Adequate quality control of such a small venture is very difficult, and the problems of product liability now make such blood banks non-viable.

For these reasons, walking blood banks are now no longer clinically acceptable within the international medical community. Blood, whenever practically possible, should be provided from a major licensed blood bank, to ensure high quality and to increase the likelihood that the requested number of units of suitable blood will be available rapidly.

Artificial blood

These solutions carry oxygen but do not perform any of the other functions of the blood. They fall into two groups, haemoglobin solutions and perflourochemicals. None of these products are currently available for human use.

The Blood Care Foundation

In response to the difficulties in locating reliable sources of blood a charitable organization, the Blood Care Foundation (BCF), was established in 1991 and now provides, in emergencies, blood screened to the highest international standards, resuscitation fluids, and sterile equipment when these are not readily available.

BCF operates a global network of blood banks, enabling it to provide whole blood, by courier service, to almost any location in the world within 12 hr (subject to the availability of scheduled air services).

Response

Should an emergency occur, one of the Foundation's alarm centres is contacted. The Duty Medical Officer (DMO) in the alarm centre will contact the doctor in charge of the case to identify the transfusion requirements. If required, the DMO will arrange for a courier to take blood to the patient. The couriers are doctors or paramedics, trained in cardiopulmonary resuscitation, and capable of putting up a transfusion, even in the shocked patient.

Rabies immunoglobulin

Rabies is a viral infection of the central nervous system which, if not treated, is invariably fatal. It is usually caused by a rabid animal biting you and injecting infected saliva (Chapter 6). However, cases have occurred when an infected animal has licked an area of broken skin. Rabies causes about 80 000 deaths a year and more than 4 million people requiring treatment. For those who have been previously immunized against rabies, a booster dose of vaccine is adequate, but both immunoglobulin and vaccine is required for the unimmunized. BCF can supply both.

The Blood Care Foundation and BCF Travel Club

Details of the services, including transfusion cover, sterile syringe kits, and blood grouping kits, provided to individual travellers, families and small groups by the BCF Travel Club can be found on ✆ www.bcftravelclub.com by telephoning +44(0)1403 262652 or writing to the BCF Travel Club, PO Box 588, HORSHAM, West Sussex, RH12 5WJ, UK.

Details of the services provided to corporate bodies, including transfusion cover, rabies cover, and sterile transfusion/resuscitation kits, by the Blood Care Foundation can be found on ✆ www.bloodcare.org.uk, by telephoning +44(0)1403 262652 or writing to the Blood Care Foundation, PO Box 588, HORSHAM, West Sussex, RH12 5WJ, UK.

Can I give blood to a friend?

In situations where no blood is readily available, members of the party may be called upon to donate (see Table 13.6.1). This table shows which blood from the healthy members of the party (Donor's Group) can be safely transfused to the person requiring a transfusion (Recipient's Blood Group). The format in which the blood groups are shown indicate the ABO group (O, A, B, or AB) followed by whether the person is rhesus Positive or Negative (+, or −). For example O+ = Group O rhesus Positive and B− = Group B rhesus Negative.

Table 13.6.1 Safe transfusion

Donor Group	Recipient's blood group							
	O+	A+	B+	AB+	O−	A−	B−	AB−
O+	✓	✓	✓	✓	✗	✗	✗	✗
A+	✗	✓	✗	✓	✗	✗	✗	✗
B+	✗	✗	✓	✓	✗	✗	✗	✗
AB+	✗	✗	✗	✓	✗	✗	✗	✗
O−	✓	✓	✓	✓	✓	✓	✓	✓
A−	✗	✓	✗	✓	✗	✓	✗	✓
B−	✗	✗	✓	✓	✗	✗	✓	✓
AB−	✗	✗	✗	✓	✗	✗	✗	✓

Further information

Cell-free oxygen-carrying resuscitation fluids (CFOCRFs)
- Hemopure: ℘ www.hemopure.co.za
- Oxyglobin: ℘ www.oxyglobin.com
- Oxygent: ℘ www.allp.com

Rabies
- PubMed Health: ℘ www.ncbi.nlm.nih.gov/pubmedhealth/ PMH0002310/
- CDC Atlanta: ℘ www.cdc.gov/rabies/
- NHS: ℘ www.nhs.uk/Conditions/Rabies/Pages/Introduction.aspx

Chapter 14

Emerging infections: the future

David Heymann

Far from diminishing, many disease hazards are on the increase. They sometimes have exotic names, such as Ebola, Lassa, or severe acute respiratory infection (SARS), while at other times their names reflect their source, as in avian or swine influenza. Travellers need to inform themselves about the likely infectious disease risks in their destinations and take appropriate steps to protect themselves.

The problem

During the past 30 years, more than 35 new infection-causing organisms have been identified, ranging from new strains of influenza and hepatitis to haemorrhagic fevers and AIDS. Many, if not most of these emerging infectious agents are thought to have been transmitted to humans by animals, as in the case of bovine spongiform encephalopathy (BSE) in the UK, where infectious material in beef and other cattle products led to a fatal neurological disease in humans; or SARS in China, where a virus spread from live market animals to humans and caused a fatal lung disease.

Other agents that infect animals can breach the species barrier between animal and humans to infect humans who are in close contact with the animal during slaughtering, or by some other means, a more recent example being avian influenza, which continues to infect humans from infected chickens since it was first identified in 1997.

Finally, emerging infectious disease agents can infect humans from the excretions of animals, such as the Ebola or Marburg virus, thought to infect humans who are in contact with the guano of bats in caves or other partially enclosed areas. Emerging infections are a risk to the traveller from contact with infected humans or infected animals and their excretions, or as a result of eating contaminated food, drinking contaminated water, being hospitalized in an environment where infections are present, or receiving an unsafe injection or blood transfusion.

While new infections are emerging, known infections such as tuberculosis, cholera, and dengue fever have re-emerged, sometimes with a vengeance. Outbreaks of dengue have occurred when travellers enter areas where mosquitoes that transmit infection from person to person are present; while tuberculosis, legionnaires' disease and sexually-transmitted infections have also been clearly linked with travel. The development of drug resistance to infections such as tuberculosis, gonorrhoea, and other common infections has further added to the problem, leading to the conclusion that an infectious disease in one country is the concern of all, including travellers to areas where they are present.

Each year there are countless travellers who cross international borders by land, air, and sea. They travel in small groups for pleasure, business, humanitarian work, or personal reasons, such as religious pilgrimage. They may travel in larger groups as refugees for reasons of security, to seek safety from wars or natural disasters. With increases in travel, and a decrease in the time required to arrive at the final destination, humans have become vectors of infection, carrying new and old infectious diseases from place to place within and between countries and continents. Recently, seriously ill travellers who were medically evacuated to hospitals in Switzerland and South Africa were later found to have Ebola infection, and in South Africa fatal infection was spread to a health worker.

In 2000, a sports event in the jungle and rivers of Malaysia (*Eco Challenge*)—in which athletes from around the world participated—led to the importation of leptospirosis on four continents. Athletes returned home while the infection was silent in its incubation period, and became seriously ill or died after arrival (see Map 14.1 and Chapter 4.11).

In 1997, an outbreak of influenza among passengers and crew on a cruise ship travelling from New York to Montreal also clearly demonstrated the ease with which infectious diseases can be transferred across international borders. In this outbreak, 3% of passengers and many crew presented with acute febrile respiratory illness caused by a variant of a common influenza virus, and introduced this variant into both Canada and the USA.

In 2003, a new and emerging infection that caused an atypical pneumonia-like illness in China, spread from Guangdong Province to a hotel in Hong Kong via an infected health worker, and then spread around the world in travellers who stayed overnight in the same hotel. During this one overnight stay, these travellers became infected with what we now know as the SARS coronavirus, and spread the infection first to their families and health workers who cared for them, then to their communities, causing outbreaks in major cities in Asia, Europe, and North America (see Map 14.2).

Each year more than 10 000 cases of malaria are reported among travellers returning to countries of the European Union. Such cases are often misdiagnosed by healthcare staff, with potentially fatal consequences, if no information is provided about recent travel to a risk area for the disease.

The solution

The role of travel in the spread of infectious diseases has been known for centuries, and controlling this has long been a concern. Countries have attempted to limit the spread of disease since at least the fourteenth century when the city-state of Venice introduced quarantine legislation aimed at keeping shipboard rats from introducing plague.

Infected humans travelling prior to the advent of air travel often developed illness, and then either recovered or died before they arrived at their destination. With air travel today, when a traveller can be in a European or Latin American capital one day and in the centre of Africa or Asia the next, an infectious disease can remain silent in the incubation period, and not appear until several days or weeks after travel has been completed.

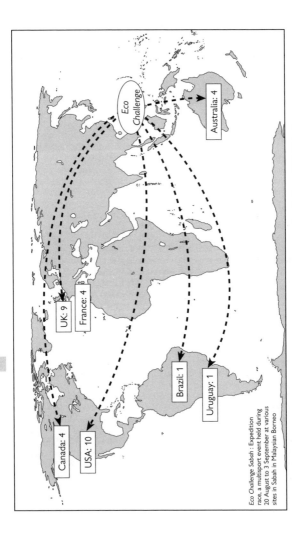

Map 14.1 Outbreak of leptospirosis (confirmed and suspected cases) among 312 participants, Eco Challenge 2000, Malaysia.

Eco Challenge Sabah : Expedition race, a multisport event held during 20 August to 3 September at various sites in Sabah in Malaysian Borneo

Source: Data from World Health Organization.

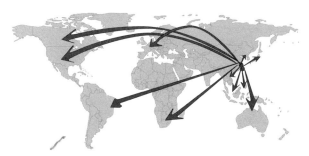

Map 14.2 The international spread of SARS, 2003.

International co-operation to control infectious diseases among travellers has been documented since 1851, with the first International Sanitary Conference in Paris. Many different treaties followed between countries, but they were often contradictory and remained non-standardized until 1951, when the World Health Organization (WHO) adopted the International Sanitary Regulations. These regulations were amended and renamed the International Health Regulations (IHR) in 1969. In 2005, the IHR were updated to better meet their objective to provide maximum protection against the spread of infectious disease, with minimum interference with world travel and trade. The IHR of 2005 are now much better adapted to prevent and control infections in today's globalized world, where emerging infections appear to be increasing, and more and more people travel internationally each year.

Although regulations such as the IHR provide an important structure for co-operation and dialogue about infectious diseases among countries, and set out standards and norms for preventing and controlling infectious diseases, they are not a replacement for vigilance and response through strong national disease detection and control systems. None of these are a replacement for the international traveller's personal responsibility and protection.

There have been several recent cases of travellers returning to the USA, Switzerland, and Germany who had contracted yellow fever infection while on safari in jungle areas of Latin America and Africa. They had not been vaccinated prior to travel, thereby endangering not only their lives (they later died), but also those of their communities' after their return home—where mosquitoes could have transmitted the disease to others. Had these travellers been vaccinated prior to travel, the risk of a yellow fever infection would have been minimal. Personal responsibility requires that knowledge obtained in guides such as this, and available from other sources in hard copy or on the Internet, be read, assimilated, and applied.

International organizations such as the World Health Organization (WHO), and national health services, such as the UK's Health Protection Agency and Department of Health, are good sources of additional information. The responsible traveller should become informed and take the necessary precautions prior to and during travel, and remain aware of the possibility of the onset of travel-related infection after return.

Further information

The WHO issues an annually updated publication containing recommendations for travellers, *International Travel and Health*, which can also be consulted at ℗ www.who.int/ith

WHO information about outbreaks and disease surveillance can be found at ℗ www.who.int and other sources listed in Appendix 2.

Vaccination requirements and recommendations

Richard Dawood

Requirements

The only formal international vaccination certificate requirements relate to yellow fever vaccination. (Outside the International Health Regulations, Saudi Arabia may require proof of vaccination against meningococcal meningitis for those undertaking the Hajj and Umrah pilgrimages.)

If you are travelling in or through any country in South America or Africa, you should research the certificate requirements carefully, and allow for any possible changes of plan. Vaccination against yellow fever is an important public health measure that countries take seriously: many countries require proof of vaccination from travellers who may not necessarily have been at high enough personal risk to otherwise consider being vaccinated. Requirements change, so it is vital to seek up-to-date advice, even for itineraries you may be familiar with. Check the minimum age requirements for children (usually 9 months or 1 year); a medical waiver may be needed if you cannot be vaccinated for valid health reasons.

The following countries require a yellow fever vaccination certificate from ALL arriving travellers:

• Angola	• Gabon
• Benin	• Ghana
• Burkina Faso	• Guinea-Bissau
• Burundi	• Liberia
• Cameroon	• Mali
• Central African Republic	• Niger
• Congo	• Rwanda
• Côte d'Ivoire	• São Tomé and Principe
• Democratic Republic of Congo	• Sierra Leone
• French Guiana	• Togo

The following countries require a yellow fever vaccination certificate *only* from travellers arriving from African or South American countries they consider at risk for yellow fever, usually in the yellow fever endemic zone, but it is *essential to check individual country requirements*, since these are subject to change. These requirements do not apply to direct travel from the UK, USA, or Australasia:

- Afghanistan
- Albania
- Algeria
- Anguilla
- Antigua and Barbuda
- Australia
- Bahamas
- Bahrain
- Bangladesh
- Barbados
- Belize
- Bhutan
- Bolivia
- Botswana
- Brunei
- Cambodia
- Cape Verde
- Chad
- Christmas Island
- Costa Rica
- Djibouti
- Dominica
- Ecuador
- Egypt
- El Salvador
- Equatorial Guinea
- Eritrea
- Ethiopian
- Fiji
- Gambia
- Grenada
- Guadeloupe
- Guatemala
- Guinea
- Guyana
- Haiti
- Honduras
- India
- Indonesia
- Iran
- Iraq
- Jamaica
- Jordan
- Kazakhstan
- Kenya
- Kiribati
- Korea Democratic People's Republic
- Lao People's Democratic Republic
- Lebanon
- Lesotho
- Libya
- Madagascar
- Malawi
- Malaysia
- Maldives
- Malta
- Martinique
- Mauritania
- Mauritius
- Montserrat
- Mozambique
- Myanmar
- Namibia
- Nauru
- Nepal
- Netherlands Antilles
- New Caledonia
- Nicaragua
- Nigeria
- Niue
- Oman
- Pakistan
- Panama
- Papua New Guinea
- Paraguay
- Philippines
- Pitcairn
- Reunion
- Russia
- Saint Helena
- Saint Kitts and Nevis
- St Lucia
- St Vincent and the Grenadines
- Samoa
- Saudi Arabia
- Senegal
- Seychelles
- Singapore
- Solomon Islands
- Somalia
- South Africa
- Sri Lanka
- Sudan
- South Sudan
- Suriname
- Swaziland
- Syria
- Tanzania
- Thailand
- Timor Leste
- Trinidad and Tobago
- Tunisia
- Uganda
- Uruguay
- Vietnam
- Zimbabwe

Maps A1.1 and A1.2 shows the countries for which yellow fever vaccination is normally recommended. Updated information from the WHO can be found at: ✎www.who.int/ith.

Recommended vaccines

Recommendations vary from source to source; for example, WHO and national health departments in different countries often give slightly differing recommendations. Your own special risk factors and circumstances will also need to be taken into account.

Travellers should therefore seek skilled professional advice from a knowledgeable source, to help make the best choices—not only about vaccines, but about other key health precautions as well. The summary below is a quick guide to current recommendations for routine travel according to their national schedule.

All travellers should keep up-to-date with routine immunizations, including MMR, if they might be non-immune, and tetanus/diphtheria/ polio. Flu vaccination is also recommended for travellers.

Region 1: North America, Western and Southern Europe, Australia, New Zealand, Japan

No additional travel vaccinations are likely to be recommended. In some parts of Europe, tick-borne encephalitis can be a risk for people taking part in outdoor activities (see Chapter 8).

Region 2: Eastern (Asian) Mediterranean and North Africa

Hepatitis A and typhoid protection are recommended.

Region 3: Tropical Africa

Hepatitis A, and typhoid: in addition, yellow fever is recommended for travel to many parts of Central, West, and East Africa. Travellers should also consider vaccination against hepatitis B, rabies, and possibly cholera. In some areas protection against meningococcal disease may be advisable for long-stay travellers, as well as for short-stay visitors during an outbreak.

Region 4: Middle East

Hepatitis A, and typhoid: in addition, travellers on prolonged visits should be vaccinated against hepatitis B and possibly rabies. Meningitis vaccine is required for the pilgrimage to Mecca and is recommended if there are any current outbreaks in the region.

Region 5: Asia

Hepatitis A, and typhoid: those staying for prolonged visits should be vaccinated against hepatitis B. In addition, rabies, cholera, and Japanese encephalitis should be considered.

Region 6: Mexico, Central and South America

Hepatitis A, and typhoid: in addition, travellers staying for prolonged visits should be vaccinated against hepatitis B and rabies. Yellow fever vaccination is advised for travel to Panama and the Amazon basin area.

Region 7: Caribbean and Pacific Islands

Travellers to places other than the usual tourist destinations should be immunized against typhoid and hepatitis A, and possibly cholera—especially important for travel to Haiti and the Dominican Republic; those staying for prolonged visits should be vaccinated against hepatitis B and, for certain Caribbean islands, rabies.

For websites listing country-by-country advice, see Appendix 2.

Map A1.1 Yellow Fever—South America (2010).

Reproduced from CDC and edited by Gary W. Burnette, *CDC Health Information for International Travel 2012*, 2012, pp.343–344 with permission from Oxford University Press Inc.

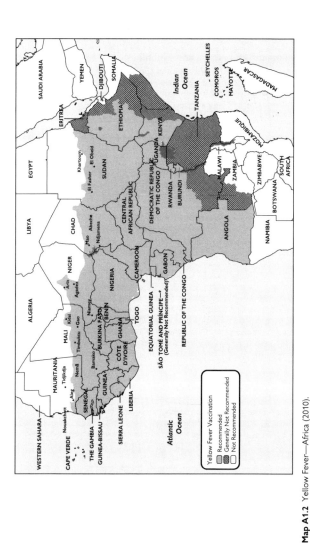

Map A1.2 Yellow Fever—Africa (2010).

Reproduced from CDC and edited by Gary W. Burnette, *CDC Health Information for International Travel 2012*, 2012, pp.343–344 with permission from Oxford University Press Inc.

Appendix 2

Resource guide

Richard Dawood

Finding and choosing a travel clinic

Most people think of travel clinics as places to go for vaccines before a trip, but a good travel clinic is much more than a 'vaccine shop'. It should offer a complete review of the health issues that relate to your trip and where relevant, any future travel plans, taking into account numerous personal factors, including whether you are young or old, male or female, pregnant, diabetic, immunosuppressed, or have pre-existing health conditions. Don't be swayed by minor differences between vaccine costs, and do your research carefully. Medical personnel at a good travel clinic should provide detailed information about likely health risks at your destination, as well as advice on the prevention and treatment of common problems such as intestinal infections, what medicines and supplies to travel with, and guidance on how and when to seek further help.

How do you choose a travel clinic or travel medicine specialist? Experience counts, so pick one that treats a large number of patients and that has staff who are familiar with issues around the globe and with treating travellers after they return from a trip—*travel medicine is not just about pre-travel care*. Although it's not a complete guarantee of excellence, look for evidence that the clinic or practice is run by a medical person with longstanding membership in and certification by a professional or academic organization, such as the International Society of Travel Medicine (ISTM); and/or other national, regional, or international institutions or associations such as the Faculty of Travel Medicine of the Royal College of Physicians & Surgeons of Glasgow and the British Travel Health Association (in the UK); the American Society of Tropical Medicine and Hygiene (in the USA); the South African Society of Travel Medicine (SASTM); or the Asia Pacific Travel Health Society. You can find a full listing of professional organizations devoted to Travel Medicine in our web guide (p.487). Membership and involvement in one or more of these is a good indication of a commitment to travellers' health. Other signs of accomplishment in travel medicine are authorship of books or journal articles on the subject; involvement in teaching, research, or international public health or professional associations; and a history of practising medicine overseas. Travel vaccines are available in a wide range of commercial settings; avoid those where vaccine sales take precedence over professional consultation and risk assessment.

A good place to begin your search is the online travel clinic directory of the ISTM (⅋ www.istm.org), but many other sources are listed in our web guide (p.487). Clearly, some cities have a wide selection of specialist clinics to choose from, while in others the options are more limited. Your own doctor, and other travellers who have found a clinic or a doctor who provides excellent care, may be able to point you in the right direction.

For students travelling abroad, the most suitable source of advice will almost always be a university or college health centre. Some companies have their own occupational health arrangements for business travellers.

Whichever type of clinic you attend, bring with you any records of past vaccines you have received, and pick a quiet time where possible, so that staff can give you their full attention.

Country basics

Some key resources are summarized, but since so many resources are now online, much more information can be found via our web guide (see p.487).

It is usually sensible to follow national guidelines that relate to your country of origin or permanent residence. Wherever in the world you come from, however, it is always worth considering current advice from other sources too, since there may not always be a single 'right' answer to every question.

United Kingdom

In England, Wales and Northern Ireland, yellow fever vaccine centres are regulated by the National Travel Health Network & Centre (NaTHNaC), and in Scotland, by Health Protection Scotland. A complete list of yellow fever centres can be found online at ℘ www.nathnac.org/yellowfever-centres.aspx or ℘ www.hps.scot.nhs.uk/yellowfever/. Not all clinics or medical practices offer yellow fever vaccines, but it makes sense to pick one that does. Malaria medication and most travel vaccines are not normally available on the NHS. NaTHNaC and Health Protection Scotland publish specific country-by-country health information and advice on their websites.

Travel clinics
- *Hospital for Tropical Diseases*, Mortimer Market, Capper St, London WC1E 6JA. Tel: 020 3456 7891; ℘ www.thehtd.org
- *Fleet Street Travel Clinic*, 29 Fleet Street, London EC4Y 1AA; also custom medical kits and supplies. Tel: 020 7353 5678; ℘ www.fleetstreetclinic.com
- *Trailfinders Ltd*, 194 Kensington High Street, London W8 7RG. Tel: 020 7938 3999; ℘ www.trailfinders.com
- *Royal Free Travel Health Centre*, Pond Street, Hampstead, London NW3 2QG. Tel: 020 7830 2885; ℘ www.travelclinicroyalfree.com
- *Liverpool School of Tropical Medicine*, Pembroke Place, Liverpool, Merseyside L3 5QA. Tel: 0151 708 9393; ℘ www.welltravelledclinics. co.uk (satellite clinics also in Manchester and Chester)
- *MASTA* operate several clinics around the UK (they also provide many health-related supplies and services)—for more information see ℘ www.masta.org
- *Nomad Travellers Store and Medical Centre*, 40 Bernard St, London WC1N 1LE, Tel: 020 7833 4114, 3 Turnpike Lane, London N8 0PX, and elsewhere. Tel: 020 8889 7014. Travel pharmacy plus vaccines, medical kits, and supplies. ℘ www.nomadtravel.co.uk

Major UK centres specializing in tropical diseases
- *The Hospital for Tropical Diseases*, Mortimer Market, Capper Street, Tottenham Court Road, London WC1E 6AU. Tel: 020 7387 9300 or 020 3456 7891; ℘ www.thehtd.org
- *Liverpool School of Tropical Medicine*, Pembroke Place, Liverpool L3 5QA. Tel: 0151 708 9393; ℘ www.lstmliverpool.ac.uk
- *The Centre for Tropical Medicine*, Nuffield Department of Clinical Medicine, John Radcliffe Hospital, Oxford OX3 9DU. Tel: 01865 222316; ℘ www.tropicalmedicine.ox.ac.uk

Other key UK resources
- *The HPA (Health Protection Agency) Malaria Reference Laboratory.* ℘ www.malaria-reference.co.uk/ provides downloadable leaflets about malaria, for the public, and specialist advice for healthcare professionals
- *Official UK guidelines on malaria* prevention are published on the HPA website ℘ www.hpa.org.uk and are updated from time to time
- *The Foreign and Commonwealth Office*, King Charles Street, London SW1, provides information about political risks abroad, and should be consulted if you intend to visit a part of the world where there is currently unrest or instability, via its website: ℘ www.fco.gov.uk/en/ travel-and-living-abroad. You can also subscribe to e-mail notifications and alerts.

Ireland

Basic, official information can be found online at ℘ www.citizensinformation.ie. Vaccines are available privately.
The main specialist travel clinics/tropical medicine centres are:
- *Tropical Medical Bureau* (℘ www.tmb.ie), which has a network of clinics around the country, and the *Royal College of Surgeons in Ireland Travel Health Clinic*, Mercers Health Centre, Lower Stephens Street, Dublin 2, Ireland. Tel: 01–497 6379 ℘ www.travelvaccinations. goldenpages.ie
- *The Department of Foreign Affairs* website is ℘ www.foreignaffairs.gov.ie

United States of America

The major source of health information for international travel is the federally funded *Centers for Disease Control and Prevention* (CDC), 1600 Clifton Road, Atlanta, GA 30333. A vast range of information is available online at ℘ www.cdc.gov. This is an essential resource for travellers and healthcare professionals from all over the world, not just the United States. The *Travelers' Health* section of the website lists state-licensed yellow fever vaccinating centres, and links to the ISTM (℘ www.istm.org) and ASTMH (℘ www.astmh.org) private travel clinic directories.

The *State Department* website (℘ www.travel.state.gov/) carries the latest information on US government travel warnings, consular information sheets, and public alerts and announcements, and provides access to a host of other important information services. It also provides emergency consular assistance on +1 (202) 501-4444 (24 hour).

Canada

Health Canada provides current information on international disease outbreaks, immunization, general health advice for travellers, and disease-specific treatment and prevention guidelines, as well as more detailed advice for healthcare professionals. Information is accessible online from ℘ www.phac-aspc.gc.ca/tmp-pmv/index-eng.php. This website also contains a directory of travel clinics throughout Canada, plus links to other key resources and downloadable leaflets and guides.

Information about safety and security is provided by the *Department of Foreign Affairs and International Travel* (℘ www.voyage.gc.ca).

Australia

The Australian Department of Health and Ageing publishes guidance for travellers and healthcare professionals, online at ℘ www.health.gov.au. Information about approved yellow fever vaccination centres are maintained by State and Territory departments of communicable diseases, which are listed on the same website. Information is also available from GPs and university health centres.

The *Travel Doctor Group/TMVC* (℘ www.tmvc.com.au); *The Travel Medicine Alliance* (℘ www.travelmedicine.com.au/); and *Travel Clinics Australia* (℘ www.travelclinic.com.au) are three of the best known travel clinic networks.

The *Australian Department of Foreign Affairs & Trade* provides advice on safety and political risks via its website at ℘ www.smartraveller.gov.au.

New Zealand

The Ministry of Health publishes information online at ℘ http://www.health.govt.nz/yourhealth-topics/travelling. Information and advice are available from private clinics, such as the Worldwise (℘ www.worldwise.co.nz) and TMVC (℘ www.traveldoctor.co.nz) groups.

The New Zealand Ministry of Foreign Affairs & Trade provides advice on travel security and safety, ℘ www.safetravel.govt.nz

South Africa

Up-to-date advice on requirements and recommendations, and information about yellow fever vaccination centres are available from GPs. There is a high degree of awareness generally on travel and tropical health issues.

- The South African Society of Travel Medicine provides a list of travel clinics on its website (℘ www.sastm.org.za)
- The Department of Health website is at ℘ www.doh.gov.za
- Travel advice from the Department of Foreign Affairs can be found at ℘ www.dfa.gov.za

Web guide

Our web guide provides links to a wide range of additional Travel Medicine resources. Some are aimed at travellers, while others are primarily for health professionals. You can find this at:
℘ www.travellershealth.com/webguide

Appendix 3

Some hints on eating abroad under extreme conditions of bad hygiene

Richard Dawood

Choice of food

Diarrhoea is preventable, not inevitable, but precautions often run counter to instinct. At home, we think of a salad as being healthier than a plate of chips, and fresh juice as healthier than sugary soda; in hot, poor countries, they are not. At home, we use 'appetite appeal', not safety, to choose from a menu; they don't always go together. When travelling, it is hard to accept that we can't always eat what we want or what we have already paid for, especially when we feel tired and hungry. These are the times to be most careful. Cultivate the art of defensive eating—especially if gastronomy is not the major purpose of your trip.

Here are some general principles to follow when you know or suspect that hygiene conditions are very poor:

- When possible, choose food that *must* have been freshly cooked e.g. omelette, chips; try and think of items that are not on the menu or on display, that therefore have to be cooked specially for you
- Freshly boiled food, served piping hot, is always safe, e.g. rice, sweetcorn
- Eat fruit or vegetables that are easily peeled or sliced open without contamination e.g. bananas, citrus fruits, melon, papaya, avocado
- Eat food from sealed packs or cans (take emergency supplies!)
- Look for freshly baked bread (find the bakery)
- Choose acceptably prepared local dishes, rather than incompetently prepared imitation western-style food
- Regard all cooked food as safe only when *freshly* prepared and served hot (not stored and then reheated)
- Be prepared to send food back and to complain when appropriate
- Where necessary, or possible, prepare your food yourself, or watch it being cooked.

Don't eat

- Salads
- Food that you do not *know* to have been freshly cooked, including hotel buffet food left out in warm temperatures
- Food on which flies have settled or may have settled
- Shellfish, crab, prawns, etc. (which need 8 min vigorous boiling as an absolute minimum)
- Intricate dishes that have required much handling in preparation
- Unwashed (in *clean* water), or unpeelable fruit or vegetables
- Ice cream and ices

- Dairy products made from unpasteurized milk. In some countries, not all 'pasteurized' milk has really been pasteurized
- Rare meat, steak tartare, raw fish
- Unpeelable fruit (berries, grapes) or fruit peeled by others (fruit buffets)
- Fruit, butter, or other foods chilled by adding ice
- Food handled with dirty fingers; avoid foods that necessarily require much handling during preparation, such as canapés
- Spicy sauces, salsa, relishes, mayonnaise left out on the table (hot sauces, however spicy, are not self-sterilizing!).

On a 2-week trip, you will probably be eating 42 meals prepared by others: the only way to protect yourself is to be selective about what you eat.

Beware of hospitality—if the food is not safe, refuse it, and plead an upset stomach—local people will usually understand. Where there is no alternative to unsafe food, smaller quantities on an empty stomach are safer. Consider missing a meal; many Western travellers can afford to lose a little weight, and it is safer to do so by choice than from illness.

Plates and cutlery

These need to be washed with detergent, rinsed with clean water, and protected from flies. When this has not or cannot be done, and you suspect that they are contaminated, the risk can be reduced by rinsing with hot weak tea, a small amount of whisky or other duty free spirit, or by cleaning with an alcohol swab or wet wipes. Use wipes on cutlery, or flame them with a candle or a cigarette lighter.

Otherwise, don't eat the bottom layer of food on the plate—easy when food is served on a bed of rice. Alternatively, use paper plates and your own cutlery. (Plastic airline cutlery is great for emergency use; in Asia, packs of disposable chopsticks are cheap and widely available.)

Hands and fingers

Should be washed at every opportunity. Always try to keep one hand clean for touching food. Avoid shaking hands with others when handling food. Travel with alcohol hand sanitizer, and/or wet wipes, and use immediately before eating. Only eat food that you have handled if your hands are scrupulously clean; otherwise, use a clean tissue, the inside of a clean plastic bag, or a piece of bread to handle food; or use your fingers, but discard any part of the food that you have handled.

Drinks

Drinking water should be sterilized with chlorine (or iodine if you can find any) or boiled. Hot tea is often easily available. Bottled drinks should be opened in your presence—safest if carbonated. In the tropics, also try coconut water (bring your own straws). Don't drink fruit juices from street vendors. Get into the habit of never using ice. Don't use tap water—even for brushing teeth; if you really must, water from the hot tap is likely to be safer.

Cups and glasses

Those that may be contaminated can be swilled out with hot tea or boiling water before use. Flies often settle on rims—pour away a little tea to rinse the rim of a teacup. Otherwise, use your own cup or water bottle, or drink bottled drinks directly from their bottle.

Appendix 4

Medical kit checklist

Richard Dawood

Here is a checklist of things to consider when putting together a medical kit for travel. It is unlikely that all of these would be needed—the exact choice will depend on where you are going, how long you will be away, and what you will be doing. Read Chapter 13.5 and the other relevant sections of this book before drawing up your own final list. See also p.415.

Basic medical kit

Sterile supplies

Syringes/needles to reduce risk of HIV or hepatitis B from medical treatment.

Wound dressings

- Assorted plasters
- Bandages
- Micropore tape, Coban.

Antiseptic

- Cream (e.g. Savlon) and/or
- Spray (e.g. Betadine) and/or
- Solution (e.g. Chlorhexidine) and/or
- Antiseptic wipes, alcohol swabs.

Medication

- Pain relief (e.g. paracetamol, ibuprofen)
- Antihistamine (e.g. Piriton, Neoclarityn)
- Antidiarrhoeal (e.g. Imodium)
- Rehydration sachets (e.g. Electrolade, Dioralyte)
- Antibiotics (e.g. ciprofloxacin*, azithromycin*)
- Steroid cream (e.g. 1% hydrocortisone).

Other useful products

- Scissors
- Tweezers
- Non-sterile gloves
- Anti-insect supplies—repellent, nets, etc.
- Water purification supplies.

Additional supplies for frequent, extended, or high-risk travel

Sterile supplies

- Sterile gloves
- Steristrips (for wound closure)
- Sutures and/or tissue glue (e.g. Liquiband)
- Lancets (for popping blisters)

- Sterile non-adherent dressing (melolin)
- Gauze pads, more specialized dressings
- Dental repair kit.

Creams and lotions
- For itching and insect bites: steroid cream
- For fungal infections: miconazole or clotrimazole cream
- For pain and stiffness: Ibuprofen gel
- For lips and cold sores:
  - acyclovir
  - lipsalve with UV protection
- For vaginal infections:
  - fluconazole tablet
  - canesten pessary
  - miconazole cream.

Additional medication

- Pain relief: diclofenac* (stronger pain killer with anti-inflammatory properties)
- Antibiotics:
  - ciprofloxacin*
  - co-amoxiclav*
  - metronidazole*
  - doxycycline*
  - amoxicillin*
- Motion sickness/nausea:
  - promethazine
  - cyclizine
  - dimenhydrinate
  - buclizine
  - scopolamine patches*
- Eye drops: azithromycin* or other antibiotic drops*.

Additional items to consider
- Sleeping tablets
- Vitamins
- Antacids
- Laxatives
- Cold/sinus medicines
- Anti-worm medication (mebendazole)
- Anti-insect supplies—insect repellent etc
- Water purification tablets/iodine
- More serious trauma supplies, on medical advice.

In-flight kit

- Saline nasal spray, or First Defence
- Graduated compression stockings—for prevention of deep vein thrombosis.

---

* Prescription required for these drugs.

Appendix 5

Post-travel health screening

Richard Dawood

Some people find health screening beneficial after prolonged travels abroad, especially to remote, tropical places. If you have been ill while away, have any persisting symptoms, or feel you have been exposed to any particular risks, a medical examination and laboratory testing can help identify any problems. Negative tests can be worthwhile also, often providing valuable reassurance. A post-travel check provides a useful opportunity to review psychological wellbeing, not just physical health, and this can be especially important for people who have been working or travelling under arduous or hostile conditions.

If you have no symptoms or signs of illness

Opinions vary on the value of a check-up in people without symptoms or signs of illness. There is no particular reason for a check-up following a short trip, unless you have been ill, or there has been a particular risk or problem. If you have been living or working in a developing country, a check-up may be more relevant.

In the absence of symptoms, it may be appropriate to check for sexually-transmitted infections (STIs), and possible exposure to schistosomiasis (bilharzia). A stool examination to rule out parasitic infestation and a blood count may be worthwhile (see Chapter 4.4). Specific hazards linked to your precise itinerary may also need to be considered, possibly with specialist advice. Following the nuclear reactor disaster in Fukishima in 2011, many journalists and some expatriates who had spent time in the affected areas, required extensive, specialist follow-up in order to rule out significant radiation exposure, and to restore peace of mind.

For those with symptoms

If you actually have symptoms, you do not need post-travel *screening*, you need examination, investigation, and treatment! Your doctor may well need to seek advice from a tropical disease unit, which will probably offer a gentle reminder that any delay in looking for malaria can be extremely dangerous. It is not good enough simply to send a blood sample off to the local laboratory, expecting the result back after a weekend: you can die from malaria within 24 hours of the first symptom. Common symptoms following travel abroad include:

- *Fever:* this generally indicates infection, and when linked to travel, needs careful urgent investigation—specifically to rule out malaria, but also to establish the exact cause if malaria has been ruled out. Do not assume that it could simply be flu! (See also Chapter 9.9.)
- *Diarrhoea:* if this has lasted longer than 48 hours and persists beyond your return home, it needs investigation and treatment. If you have

been given antibiotics for self-treatment while away (i.e. where medical care and laboratory tests may be difficult to find), try to obtain medical advice before using them

- *Jaundice:* may be due to infection with a hepatitis virus, leptospirosis, or malaria, and therefore always warrants investigation
- *Respiratory symptoms:* such as sore throat or productive cough are common in travellers and need investigation and treatment
- *Malaria:* a killer, the symptoms are often vague and non-specific. Fever, chills, and headache are the most likely symptoms, but others include diarrhoea, vomiting, cough, abdominal pain, and jaundice
- *Rash:* caused by a wide range of possible tropical infections or diseases—should always be reported and investigated
- *Other infections:* can cause vague symptoms initially, including tiredness and loss of appetite, night sweats, swollen glands, or weight loss. Such symptoms should always be reported and followed up.

Examination:

- A tropical or travel medicine specialist may be more familiar with many of the health conditions likely to be acquired abroad, than doctors with a more general background working in temperate climates
- Quite often, the abnormalities detected by examination turn out to be incidental to travel, rather than caused by it: high blood pressure, obesity, and diabetes (on dipstick urine testing), rather than exotic or tropical diseases.

Tests:

- A full blood count can be very useful, with a white cell differential examination to detect a rise in eosinophils—a general indicator of infection with certain parasites (see Box A5.1). Producing a stool sample for lab testing is a rite of passage for every serious tropical traveller: microscopy can detect cysts, ova, and parasites, and may need to be repeated (up to three samples) in order to rule out infection if this is suspected. More specific stool antigen tests are available in some countries, for organisms such as giardia. A dipstick urine test will detect sugar, blood, or protein in the urine—all of which warrant further investigation
- For anyone exposed to fresh water in schistosomal areas, a blood test for schistosomiasis should be performed—at least 6 weeks after the last possible exposure, so as to avoid false negatives
- High-risk sexual exposure (or exposure to non-sterile needles or medical treatment) might warrant screening for antibodies to HIV, hepatitis B, syphilis and other STIs.

And finally

Travel-related symptoms can sometimes take a very long time to appear—remember to tell your doctor about any travels for at least a year after your return. Any visit to a doctor on returning home should be used as a reminder to carry on taking malaria medication for the appropriate period. The visit should also be used as an opportunity to update any vaccine courses that might not have been completed prior to travel.

Box A5.1 **Tests for travellers with eosinophila**

In patients who have lived in or visited the tropics:
- *All areas:* stool microscopy for cysts, ova and parasites, plus strongyloides serology
- *All Africa:* additional schistosoma serology and microscopy of terminal urine for schistosomes
- *West Africa:* additional filaria serology.

Source: Data from Checkley et al., Clinical Guidelines of the British Infection Society, Eosinophilia in returning travellers and migrants from the tropics: UK recommendations for investigation and initial management, *Journal of Infection*, Volume **60**, Issue 1, pp.1–20, 2010.

Hay fever seasons worldwide

Roy Kennedy

The seasonal variation in pollen type in the UK can be accessed through the following link: ✍ http://www.worcester.ac.uk/discover/pollen-calendar. html. The variation in tree, grass and weed pollen for different regions of the world is as designated herein:

Europe

Austria
Seasons vary between the mountains and the plain.

Mountains
- Peak grass pollen season is June–August, otherwise counts are low
- Main tree pollen season is March–May (hazel and alder in March, then birch in April and May—note, these cross-react and can cause a long period of symptoms), otherwise counts are mainly low
- Weed pollen counts can be high May–September, otherwise generally low.

Lowlands
- The grass pollen season is May–September, otherwise counts are low
- Tree pollen counts are low generally, apart from February–July
- Weed pollen counts are low generally, apart from May–September.

Note: ragweed blows into Austria if the wind is from Hungary, where ragweed is prolific. It causes problems for sensitive people. Concentrations peak at night and are lower in the daytime.

France
Corsica
- Counts low near coasts
- Generally good after the end of June
- Weed pollen season over by end of October.

West coast
- Pollen counts are generally low near west coasts, but can be high inland
- Tree pollen season is over at the end of June
- Grass pollen season is usually over by August
- Weed pollen season lasts until the end of October.

Northwest
- Counts low on Brittany and Normandy coasts, but can be high inland in rural areas
- Grass season over by end of July
- Tree pollen season over by end of June
- Weed pollen season goes on until September.

South coast

- The mild climate allows plants to flower all year; vegetation is diverse and some grass pollen may be in the air all year, but the peak time is April–July
- High counts of tree pollen can occur January–July (abundant cypress trees planted in some areas as wind breaks can produce very high concentrations)
- The peak weed pollen season is March–October.

Paris basin

- Grass pollen counts are low apart from in the peak season (May–August)
- Peak season for tree pollen is February through to July, when chestnut pollen is abundant in Paris
- Weed pollen is abundant May–September.

Greece

- Drought in late summer (from July onwards) tends to reduce grass pollen counts to low in all areas, but some weeds, e.g. *Pareitaria* (pellitory) may be prolific locally
- Counts are lowest on the islands, especially the smaller ones
- Grass season over by the end of June
- Tree pollen season over by the end of June
- Weed pollen season over by the end of September.

Italy

Considerable regional differences in Italy arise from the geography of the country.

Po Valley including Milan

- Grass season is April–August; very high count in May and June
- Tree pollen season is February–June
- Weed pollen season is May–October.

North-west/Tuscany/Pisa

- Grass season is March–June
- Tree pollen season is February–June
- Weed pollen season is April–October.

Adriatic

- Grass season is April–August. (*Note:* coastal resorts do not always have low counts because land/sea breezes carry pollen and spores out to sea and back again)
- Tree pollen season is February–June
- Weed pollen season is May–September.

Central areas, Florence, and Rome

- Grass season is April–July
- Tree pollen season is January–June
- Weed pollen season is March–September.

Portugal
Algarve
- Pollen counts are low near coasts, especially from June onwards
- Grass season is usually over by end of June
- Tree pollen season is over by end of May
- Weed pollen season is over by end of September.

Madeira
- Counts generally low
- Grass season is usually over by end of June
- Tree pollen season is over by end of May
- Weed pollen season is over by end of August.

Spain
Northern areas
- Places near coasts have low pollen counts, but counts may be high inland
- Grass pollen may continue into early August
- Tree pollen season over by end of June
- Weeds may flower until November.

Costa del Sol, Costa Almeria, Costa Dorada
- Moderate counts for grass, May and June; low grass pollen counts after June
- Trees flower January–June and October and November
- Weed pollen season is over by end of September.

Balearic Islands
- Counts are generally low
- Very low grass counts after June
- Tree counts are low, especially after July
- Weed pollen season over by end of September.

Canary Islands
- Generally low counts, even during pollen seasons
- Grass season is over by the end of June
- Tree pollen season is over by the end of May
- Weed pollen season is over by the end of June.

Central areas including Andalucia
- Olive pollen counts can be very high in May and June, especially near Cordoba
- Grass season is April–July
- Tree pollen season is February–June
- Weed pollen season is April–September.

Switzerland
Mountain areas
- Grass season is May–August
- Tree pollen season is March–August
- Weed pollen season is May–September.

Lowlands
- Grass season is April–August
- Tree pollen season is February–August
- Weed pollen season is May–September.

Turkey
Coastal areas in West
- Grass season is May–September
- Tree pollen seasons are February–June, and September and October
- Weed pollen season is June–September.

North America

Ragweeds are present throughout the whole USA and Southern Canada, but are most prolific in Central and Eastern USA. These flower mainly in July–September causing great problems to sensitive people. In the USA, estimates suggest that over half of the cases of hay fever are caused by ragweeds.

USA

I have included here some of the most popular destinations, noting the low seasons, rather than pointing out low-pollen venues, many of which are not typical holiday destinations.

Florida
- Lowest counts on coasts; some pollen is in the air all year round
- Low season for grass pollen is November–April; for tree pollen, June–December; and for weed pollen, December–April.

California
- Lowest counts near coasts, but there will be some pollen in the air all year in the south; long seasons elsewhere
- Grass pollen low season, November–April
- Tree pollen low season, June–January
- Weed pollen low season, January–April.

North-east seaboard (e.g. New York, Washington DC) Low counts on coasts
- Grass low season, August–April
- Tree low season, June–January
- Weed pollen low season, October–April.

South Central (e.g. Mississippi, Alabama)
- Grass low season, December–April
- Trees flower all year, but lowest pollen times are June–August and October–March
- Weed pollen low season, November–June.

Hawaii
- Some differences between islands and locations
- Lowest counts are on coasts with onshore winds
- Grass pollen all year, but lowest December and January
- Tree pollen low season, May–December
- Weed pollen low season, December–mid-May.

Canada

British Columbia
- Grass pollen seasons tend to be mild, especially near coasts
- Grass low season, September–May
- Tree pollen low season, June–March
- Weed pollen low season, October–June.

Great Lakes area
- Counts are high during main flowering times for allergenic plants
- Grass low season, August–May
- Tree pollen low season, July–March
- Weed pollen low season, October–June.

Prairies
- Again, counts are high during the main flowering times
- Grass low season, September–May
- Tree pollen low season, July–March
- Weed pollen low season, October–July.

Caribbean

The tropical climate allows plants to flower all year, but there are peak times. Pollen counts are lowest on coasts with onshore winds. Local topography and climates differ greatly over short distances. Avoid main pollen seasons which are:
- Grass, October–March, June and July
- Trees, February–May and June–October
- Weeds, December–August.

Africa

Egypt
- Grass pollen season, February–November
- Tree pollen season, all year
- Weed pollen season, March–November.

South Africa
- Grass pollen season, November–January
- Tree pollen season, September–December
- Weed pollen season, November–February.

Gambia
- Grass pollen season, all year
- Tree pollen season, all year
- Weed pollen season, all year.

Kenya
- Grass pollen seasons, September and October, December and January
- Tree pollen season, July–December
- Weed pollen season, June–January.

Zimbabwe
- Grass pollen seasons, July and August, October and November
- Tree pollen seasons, July and October
- Weed pollen seasons, July and August, October and November.

Australasia

Australia

South coast of southern Australia
- Grass pollen season, July–March
- Tree pollen seasons, August–November and March–July
- Weed pollen season, August–April.

South-west of western Australia
- Grass pollen season, September–March
- Tree pollen season, July–November
- Weed pollen season, July–February.

Southeast Australia
- Grass pollen season, August–May
- Tree pollen season, June–December
- Weed pollen season, August–March.

New Zealand
Seasons start earlier in the north e.g. in most years there is about 1 month difference in the grass seasons between the north and the south:
- Grass pollen season, October–February
- Tree pollen season, August–October
- Weed pollen season, January–March.

Asia

India
- Grass pollen season, September–January
- Tree pollen season, October–January
- Weed pollen season, September–February.

Northern Thailand
- Grass pollen seasons, June and July, October and November
- Tree pollen season, March–December
- Weed pollen season, May–July.

Southern Thailand and western Malaysia
- Grass pollen season, all year
- Tree pollen season, all year
- Weed pollen season, all year.

Treatment scheme for adults with a severe allergic reaction (anaphylaxis)

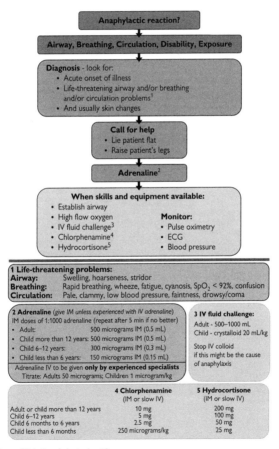

Figure A7.1 Anaphylaxis algorithm.

Further reading

Air travel, jet lag

Aerospace Medical Association; Alexandria, VA. Useful tips for airline travel; Available at: ℘ http://www.asma.org/publications/tips.php

Aerospace Medical Association (2003). *Medical Guidelines for Air Travel*, 2nd edn. Alexandria: Medical Guidelines Task Force. Available at: ℘ http://www.asma.org/pdf/publications/medguid.pdf

*Bor R. (2003). *Passenger Behaviour*. London: Ashgate Publishing.

Bor R, Eriksen C, Oakes M. (2009). *Overcome Your Fear of Flying*. London: Sheldon Press.

Bor R, Josse J, Palmer, S. (2000). *Stress-Free Flying*. London: Quay Books.

British Thoracic Society Air Travel Working Group (2011). Managing passengers with stable respiratory disease planning air travel: British Thoracic Society recommendations. *Thorax*, **66**(Suppl 1).

*Davis JR, Johnson R, Stepanek J, Fogarty JA. (2008). *Fundamentals of Aerospace Medicine*, 4th edn. Philadelphia: Lippincott Williams and Wilkins.

Dowdell N. et al (2001). *British Airways Manual of Inflight Medical Care*. Harlow: Dorling Kindersley.

Ehret C, Scanlon L. (1988). *Overcoming Jet Lag*. New York: Berkley Publishing Group. The jetlag diet: now a classic, but does it work?

Hunter J. (2001). *Anger in the Air*. London: Ashgate Publishing.

*Rainford DJ, Gradwell DP. (2006). *Ernsting's Aviation Medicine*, 4th edn. London: Hodder Arnold.

*World Health Organization (2006). *Tuberculosis and Air Travel: Guidelines for Prevention and Control*. Geneva: WHO.

World Health Organization. (2010). *International Travel and Health*; Chapter 2, Mode of travel: health considerations (2.1) Available at: ℘ http://www.who.int/ith/chapters/en/index.html

Children

Barta B. (2009). *Travel with Children*, 5th edn. Melbourne: Lonely Planet.

Beckerman D, Morgan P. (2006). *Children's Medical Guide: The Essential Guide from Birth to 11 Years*, Harlow: Dorling Kindersley/Great Ormond Street.

de Francisco, FR. (2008). *The Rough Guide to Travel with Babies & Young Children*. London: Rough Guides.

Spector, JM, Gibson, TE. (2009). *Atlas of Pediatrics in the Tropics and Resource-limited Settings*. Elk Grove Village: American Academy of Pediatrics.

Wilson-Howarth J, Ellis M. (2004). *Your Child's Health Abroad*. Chalfont St Peter: Bradt.

Diabetes/Disabled/Elderly/Higher risk traveller

Automobile Association, UK. (2004). *Disabled Traveller's Guide*, Basingstoke: AA Available at: ℘ www.theaa.com/staticdocs/pdf/services/disabled_travellers_guide.pdf

Fiennes R, Liston R. (2007). *Travels with My Heart: The Essential Guide for Travellers with Heart Conditions*. Leicester: Matador.

Kruger DF. (2006). *The Diabetes Travel Guide: how to travel with diabetes anywhere in the world*, 2nd edn. Alexandria: American Diabetes Association.

Matthews D, Meston N, Dyson P, Shaw J. (2008). *Diabetes (The Facts)*. Oxford: Oxford University Press.

*McIntosh I. (1993). *Health Hazards & the Higher Risk Traveller*. London: Quay Books.

Rattray G. (2009). *Access Africa: Safaris for People with Limited Mobility*. Chalfont St Peter: Bradt Travel Guides.

Ronald, R. (2001). *Air Travel Guide for Seniors and Disabled Passengers*. Chicago: Independent Publishers Group.

---

* Mainly for a medical readership

Diving and marine hazards

*Bove AA, Davis JC. (2003). *Diving Medicine*, 4th edn. Philadelphia: W.B. Saunders.
*Brubakk A, Neuman T. (2002). *Bennett and Elliotts' Physiology and Medicine of Diving*. Philadelphia: WB Saunders.
*Edmonds C. (1978). *Dangerous Marine Animals of the Indo-Pacific Region*. Newport: Wedneil Publications. Classic guide to identification and treatment. Out of print, but occasionally available via Amazon.
Graver D. (2003). *Aquatic Rescue and Safety*. Pudsey: Human Kinetics Publishers.
Williamson J, Fenner P, Burnett J, Rifkin J. (1997). *Venomous and poisonous marine animals*. Oxford: Blackwell Science.

Drugs and medicines

British Medical Association. (2011). *Guide to Medicines and Drugs*, 8th edn. Harlow: Dorling Kindersley.
British National Formulary. London: Pharmaceutical Press. Updated frequently. Useful technical reference on medicines or drugs; paediatric edition also available. More information:
  📖 www.bnf.org.

Expeditions, outdoors, survival

Auerbach PS. (2005). *Medicine for the Outdoors*, 5th edn. Maryland Heights: Mosby.
Auerbach PS. (2008). *Field Guide to Wilderness Medicine*. New York: Mosby-Elsevier.
*Auerbach PS. (2011). *Wilderness Medicine*, 6th edn. Maryland Heights: Mosby. Superlative study of everything from plant and wildlife hazards to lightning, forest fires, and drowning.
Bezruchka S. (2011). *Trekking in Nepal*, 8th edn. Seattle: Mountaineers Books. How to do it safely.
Davies B. (2011). *SAS Desert Survival*. London: Virgin Press.
Duff J, Gormly P. (2007). *Pocket First Aid and Wilderness Medicine*. Milnthorpe: Cicerone.
Forgey W. (2006). *Wilderness Medical Society: Practice Guidelines for Wilderness Emergency Care*, 5th edn. Northampton: Falcon Press.
Forgey W. (2008) *Basic Illustrated Wilderness First Aid*. Northampton: Falcon Press.
Giesbrecht G, Wilkerson JA, Gravatt A. (2006). *Hypothermia, Frostbite and Other Cold Injuries*, 2nd edn. Seattle: Mountaineers Books.
Johnson C, Anderson S, Dallimore J, Winser S. (2008). *Oxford Handbook of Expedition and Wilderness Medicine*. Oxford: Oxford University Press.
Kamler K. (2002). *Doctor on Everest*. London: Robinson.
Tilton B. (2007). *Backcountry First Aid and Extended Care*, 5th edn. Guilford: Globe Pequot Press.
Tilton B. (2009). *How to Die in the Outdoors: From Bad Bears to Toxic Toads, 110 Grisly Ways to Croak*, 2nd edn. Northampton: Falcon Press.
Wilkerson JA. (2010). *Medicine for Mountaineering and Other Wilderness Activities*, 6th edn. Seattle: Mountaineers Books.

General first aid

British Red Cross Society. (2011). *First Aid Manual*. Harlow: Dorling Kindersley.
Lynch C. (2010). *American Red Cross Abridged Textbook On First Aid: A Manual of Instruction*. Charleston: BiblioBazaar.

General travel medicine

Chiodini J, Boyne L. (2011). *Atlas of Travel Medicine & Health*. Basingstoke: McGraw-Hill Medical.
*Jong EC, Sanford C. (2008). *Travel and Tropical Medicine Manual*, Philadelphia: W. B. Saunders.
*Keystone JS, Kozarsky PE, Freedman DO, Northdurft HD. (2008). *Travel Medicine*. Maryland Heights: Mosby.
Mills D. (2010). *Travelling Well: The 'Must Have' Guide to a Safe and Healthy Journey*. Albion: Author.
*Schwartz E. (ed.). (2009). *Tropical Diseases in Travelers*. Oxford: Blackwell.
*Steffen R, DuPont H, Wilder-Smith A. (2003). *Manual of Travel Medicine and Health*. Hamilton: BC Decker Inc.
Wilson-Howarth J. (2009). *The Essential Guide To Travel Health*. Enfield: Cadogan Guides.
*Zuckerman J. (ed.) (2011). *Principles and Practice of Travel Medicine*. Hoboken: Wiley-Blackwell.

Government and WHO publications and advice

*Brunette G, Centers for Disease Control, Atlanta, (2012). *CDC Health Information for International Travel 2012—'The Yellow Book'*. Oxford: Oxford University Press. Available at: ℘ http://wwwnc.cdc.gov/travel/page/yellowbook-2012-home.htm. Updated every 1–2 years.

Foreign and Commonwealth Office, UK. Country by country advice. Available at: ℘ www.fco.gov.uk/en/travel-and-living-abroad/travel-advice-by-country

*Field VK, Ford L, Hill DR. (eds). (2012). *Health Information for Overseas Travel*. London: Nathnac. The UK's 'Yellow Book'.

National Health & Medical Research Council (Australia). (2008). *The Australian Immunisation Handbook*, 9th edn. Melbourne; NHMRC. Available at: ℘ www.health.gov.au/internet/immunise/publishing.nsf/Content/Handbook-home

US Dept. of State, Bureau of Consular Affairs. Publications for travelers, available at: ℘ www.travel.state.gov.

*World Health Organization (2012). *International Travel and Health*. Geneva: WHO. Official WHO summary of information and recommendations for travel. Also available electronically and online at: ℘ www.who.int/ith/en (WHO also produces many other useful publications, including: *World Health Statistical Quarterly*; *WHO Weekly Epidemiological Record*; *Atlas of the Global Distribution of Schistosomiasis* (1987); Yellow fever vaccinating centres for international travel; International medical guide for ships; The rational use of drugs in the management of acute diarrhoea in children; Prevention of sexual transmission of HIV; Plague manual.

High altitude

*Heath D, Williams DR, Williams I. (1995). *High Altitude Medicine and Pathology*, 4th edn. Oxford: Oxford University Press.

*Milledge JS, West JB, Schoene R. (2007). *High Altitude Medicine and Physiology*, 4th edn. London: Hodder Arnold.

Pollard A, Murdoch D. (2003). *High Altitude Medicine Handbook*, 3rd edn. Abingdon: Radcliffe.

Immunization

*Department of Health (UK) (2006). *Immunization Against Infectious Disease*. London: DoH. Downloadable, with updates, at: ℘ www.dh.gov.uk/en/Publichealth/Immunisation/Greenbook/index.htm

Influenza A and B

Adisasmito W, Chan PJS, Lee N, et al. (2010). Effectiveness of antiviral treatment in human influenza A (H5N1) infections: analysis of a global patient registry. *J Infect Dis* **202**(8):1154–60.

Aoki FY, Macleod MD, Paggiaro P, et al. (2003). Early administration of oral oseltamivir increases the benefits of influenza treatment. *J Antimicrob Chemother* **51**:123–9.

Cauchemer S, Vallerton A, Boëlle R, Flahault A, Feguson N. (2008). Estimating the impact of school closure on influenza transmission from Sentinel data. *Nature* **452**:749–54.

Coleman CH, Reis A. (2008). Potential penalties for health care professionals who refuse to work during a pandemic. *J Am Med Ass* **299**:1471.

Collier L, Kellam, P, Oxford JS. (2010). *Human Virology: A Text for Students of Medicine*, 4th edn. Oxford: Oxford University Press.

Council of Canadian Academies. (2008). *Report in Focus. Influenza Transmission and the Role of Personal Protective Respiratory Equipment: An Assessment of the Evidence*. Ottawa: CCA.

Gubareva LV, Laiser L, Hayden FG. (2000). Influenza virus neuraminidase inhibitors. *Lancet* **355**:827–35.

Hayden FG, Osterhaus AD, Treanor JJ, et al. (1997). Efficacy and safety of the neuraminidase inhibitor zanamivir in the treatment of influenza virus infections. GG167 Influenza Study Group. *N Engl J Med* **337**:874–80.

Monto AS, Pichichero ME, Blanckenberg SJ, et al. (2002). Zanamivir prophylaxis: an effective strategy for the prevention of influenza type A and B within households. *J Infect Dis* **186**:1582–8.

Oxford JS. (2003). Influenza A pandemics of the 20th century with special reference to 1918: virology, pathology and epidemiology. *Rev Med Virol* **10**:119–33.

Oxford JS, Aoki FY. (2009). *The Practical Use of the Anti Influenza Drug Oseltamivir to Combat Influenza*. Oxford: Atlas Medical Publishing.

Phillips, H, Killingray D. (2002). *The Spanish Influenza Pandemic of 1918-1919: new perspectives,* Routledge Social History of Medicine Series. London: Routledge.

Rambaut A, Pybus OG, Nelson MI. *et al.* (2008). The genomic and epidemiological dynamics of human influenza A virus. *Nature,* **453**:615–19.

Rappuoli R, Del Giudice, G. (2010). *Influenza Vaccines of the Future.* Berlin: Birkauser.

Simmerman JM, Suntarattiwong P, Levy J, *et al.* (2010). Influenza virus contamination of common household surfaces during the 2009 influenza A (H1N1) pandemic in Bangkok, Thailand: implications for contact transmission. *Clin Infect Dis* **51**:1053–61.

Stohr K. (2005). Avian influenza and pandemics—research needs and opportunities. *N Engl J Med* **352**:405–7.

Stuart-Harris CH, Schild GC, Oxford JS. (1985). *Influenza, the Viruses and the Disease.* London: Edward-Arnold.

Tran TH, Nguyen TL, Nguyen TD, *et al.* (2004). Avian influenza A (H5N1) in 10 patients in Vietnam. *N Engl J Med* **350**:1179–88.

Webster RG, Govorkova E. (2006). Influenza virus evolution and spread. *N Engl J Med* **355**:2174–7.

Webster RG, Peiris M, Chen H, Guan Y. (2006). H5N1 outbreaks and enzootic influenza. *Emerging Infect Dis* **12**:3–8.

Welliver R, Monto AS, Carewicz O, *et al.* (2001). Effectiveness of oseltamivir in preventing influenza in household contacts: a randomised controlled trial. *J Am Med Ass* **285**:748–54.

Yu H, Liao Q, Yuan Y, *et al.* (2010). Effectiveness of oseltamivir on disease progression and viral RNA shedding in patients with mild pandemic 2009 influenza A H1N1: opportunistic retrospective study of medical charts in China. *Br Med J* **341**:c4779.

Yuen, KY, Chan PK, Peiris M, *et al.* (1998). Clinical features and rapid viral diagnosis of human disease associated with avian influenza A H5N1 virus. *Lancet* **351**:467–71.

Living abroad

Hansen LK. (2007). *Destination Integration: A Guide to Living Abroad, Long-term Travelling and Successful Immigration.* Leicester: Matador.

Pascoe, R. (2006). *Raising Global Nomads: Parenting Abroad in an On-Demand World.* Expatriate Press.

Pascoe R, Martins A, Hepworth V. (2011). *Expat Women: Confessions—50 Answers to Your Real-Life Questions About Living Abroad.* Cotton Tree: Expat Women.

Living and working abroad

Bernard KW, Graitcer PL, van der Vlugt TB, Moran JS, Pulley KM. (1989). Epidemiologic surveillance in Peace Corps Volunteers: a model for monitoring health in temporary residents of developing countries. *Int J Epidemiol* **18**: 220–6.

Bhatta P, Simkhada P, van Teijlingen ER, Maybin S. (2009). A questionnaire study of Voluntary Service Overseas (VSO) volunteers: health risk and problems encountered. *J Travel Med* **16**: 332–7.

Dahlgren AL, Deroo L, Avril J, Bise G, Loutan L. (2009). Health risks and risk-taking behaviours among International Committee of the Red Cross (ICRC) expatriates returning from humanitarian missions. *J Travel Med* **16**: 382–90.

Patel D, Easmon C, Seed P, Dow C, Snashall D, (2006). Morbidity in expatriates – a prospective cohort study. *Occup Med (Lond)* **56**: 345–52.

Lyme disease

British Infection Association (2011). The epidemiology, prevention, investigation and treatment of Lyme borreliosis in the United Kingdom. A position statement of the British Infection Association. *J Infect* **62**: 329–38.

Edlow JA. (2002). *Bull's eye. Unraveling the Mystery of Lyme Disease.* Yale: Yale University Press, p. 304.

Infectious Disease Society of America. (2010). *Final Report of the Lyme Disease Review Panel of the Infectious Diseases Society of America.* ℘ http://www.idsociety.org/uploaded Files/IDSA/Resources/Lyme Disease/.DSA-Lyme-Disease-Final Report:pdf.

Johnson L, Strickler RB. (2010). *The Infectious Disease Society of America Lyme Guidelines: a cautionary tale about the development of clinical practice. Guidelines.* ℘ http://www.peh-med.com/content/5/1/9

Rahn DW, Evans J. (ed.) (1998). *Lyme Disease.* Philadelphia: American College of Physicians.

Schuist IJ, Hovius JW, van der Poll T, van Dam AP, Fikrig E. (2011). Lyme borreliosis, vaccination, the facts. Challenge for the future. *Trends Parasitol.* **27**: 40–7.

Malaria

Chiodini P, Hill D, Lalloo D, Lea G, Walker E, Whitty C, et al. (2007). *Guidelines for malaria prevention in travellers from the United Kingdom*. London: Health Protection Agency. Available at: ℅ http://www.hpa.org.uk/Publications/InfectiousDiseases/TravelHealth/0701MalariapreventionfortravellersfromtheUK/

Dondorp AM, Fairhurst RM, Slutsker L, Macarthur JR, Breman JG, Guerin PJ, et al. (2011). The threat of artemisinin-resistant malaria. *N Engl J Med* **365**(12): 1073–5.

Lalloo DG, Shingadia D, Pasvol G, et al. (2006). UK malaria treatment guidelines. *J Infect* **54**: 111–21. Available at: ℅ http://www.hpa.org.uk/web/HPAweb&HPAwebStandard/HPAweb_C/1195733815652

Mali S, Steele S, Slutsker L, Arguin PM. (2010). Malaria Surveillance --- United States, 2008. *MMWR* **59**(SS07):1–15. Available at: ℅ http://www.cdc.gov/mmwr/preview/mmwrhtml/ss5907a1.htm?s_cid=ss5907a1_e

Schlagenhauf P, Petersen E. (2008). Malaria chemoprophylaxis: strategies for risk groups. *Clin Microbiol Rev* **21**(3): 466–72.

Warrell DA, Gilles HM. (ed.) (2001). *Bruce Chwatt's Essential malariology*, 4th edn. London: Edward Arnold.

Warrell DA, Hemingway J, Marsh K, Sinden RE, Butcher GA, Snow RW. (2010). Malaria, in DA Warrell, TM Cox, JD Firth (eds) *Oxford Textbook of Medicine*, 5th edn. Oxford: Oxford University Press, 1045–88.

World Health Organization (2000). Severe falciparum malaria. *Trans Roy Soc Trop Med Hyg* **94**(Suppl. 1) L 51/1–51/90.

World Health Organization (2010). *Guidelines for the Management of Malaria*, 2nd edn. Geneva: WHO.
Available at: ℅ http://www.who.int/malaria/publications/atoz/9789241547925/en/index.html

Sea travel and sailing

MacFarlane B. (2011). *Cruise Ship SOS: The Life-saving Adventures of a Doctor at Sea*. Harlow: Wiley Nautical. Anecdotes and cautionary tales.

Maritime and Coastguard Agency (1999). *The Ship Captain's Medical Guide*. London: Stationery Office Books.

Roberts, S. (2010). *First Aid Afloat*. Harlow: Wiley Nautical.

World Health Organization (2007). *International Medical Guide for Ships: Including the Ships Medicine Chest*, 3rd edn. Geneva: WHO. Also, the Quantification Addendum, which gives recommended quantities of medicines to be carried.

Security and personal safety, hostile environments

Bolz F. (2001). *The Counter-Terrorism Handbook*. Abingdon: CRC Press.

Buma AH, Burris D, Hawley A, Ryan J. (2009). *Conflict and Catastrophe Medicine: A Practical Guide*. Berlin: Springer.

Feinstein A. (2006). *Journalists under Fire: the Psychological Hazards of Covering War*. Baltimore: Johns Hopkins University Press.

Garthwaite R. (2011). *How to Avoid Being Killed in a War Zone*. London: Bloomsbury.

Rail R. (2010). *Surviving the International War Zone: Security Lessons Learned and Stories from Police and Military Peace-Keeping Forces*. Abingdon: CRC Press.

Wiseman J. (2009). *The SAS Survival Handbook*. Hammersmith: Collins.

Self-help

British Medical Association (2008). *Complete Family Health Encyclopaedia*, 5th edn. Harlow: Dorling Kindersley. Excellent, comprehensive home medical encyclopaedia.

Dickson M. (1999). *Where There Is No Dentist*. Palo Alto: Hesperian Foundation.

Halestrap DJ. (1981). *Simple Dental Care for Rural Hospitals*, 4th edn. London: Medical Missionary Association.

*McLatchie GR, Borley N, Chikwe J. (eds) (2007). *Oxford Handbook of Clinical Surgery*. Oxford: Oxford University Press.

Milne AH, Siderfin CD. (1995). *Kurafid: The British Antarctic Survey Medical Handbook*. London: British Antarctic Survey.

Patel V. (2003). *Where There Is No Psychiatrist: A Mental Health Care Manual*. Bidford: Gaskell.

Werner D, Maxwell J, Thuman C, *et al*. (1993). *Where There Is No Doctor: a Village Health Care Handbook*. London: Macmillan Press.

Werner D. (2009). *Where There Is No Doctor: a Village Health Care Handbook for Africa*. London: Macmillan Press.

Sex and contraception

Guillebaud J. (2008). *Contraception: Your Questions Answered*, 5th edn. Philadelphia: Churchill Livingstone.

Guillebaud J, MacGregor A. (2009). *The Pill and Other Forms of Hormonal Contraception (The Facts)*, 7th edn. Oxford: Oxford University Press.

Skiing and sports

BMA (2010). *The BMA Guide to Sport Injuries*. Harlow: Dorling Kindersley.

*Brukner P, Khan K. (2011). *Brukner & Khan's Clinical Sports Medicine*. Oxford: McGraw-Hill Medical.

*MacAuley D. (2006). *Oxford Handbook of Sport and Exercise Medicine*. Oxford: Oxford University Press.

Snake bite

*Chippaux JP, Goyfon M. (1983). Producers of antivenomous sera. *Toxicon*, **6**: 739–52.

Nichol J. (1989). *Bites and Stings: the World of Venomous Animals*. London: David & Charles. Includes listing of anti-venom suppliers, world-wide.

O'Shea M. (2011). *Venomous Snakes of the World*. London: New Holland Publishers Ltd.

*Sutherland SK, Tibballs J. (2001). *Australian Animal Toxins: the Creatures, Their Toxins, and Care of the Poisoned Patient*. Melbourne: Oxford University Press.

*Warrell DA. (1990). Venomous and poisonous animals, in: KS Warren, AAF Mahmood (eds) *Tropical and Geographical Medicine*. New York: McGraw-Hill.

Special health needs

Kotton CN, Hibberd PL (2009). Travel medicine and the solid organ transplant recipient. *Am J Transplant* **9**: S273–81.

Murray CK, Horvath LL. (2007). An approach to prevention of infectious disease during military deployments. CID. **44**: 424–30. ℘ http://cid.oxfordjournals.org/content/44/3/424.full.pdf

℘ http://wwwnc.cdc.gov/travel/yellowbook/2012/chapter-8-advising-travelers-with-specific-needs/special-considerations-for-us-military-deployments.htm

Sunlight

Hawk J, McGregor J. (2005). *British Medical Association Family Doctor Series: Skin, Sunlight and Skin Cancer*. London: BMA.

National Cancer Institute (USA). (2011). *What You Need To Know About Melanoma and Other Skin Cancers*. Washington DC: US Government. Also Kindle edition.

Newcombe R. (2010). *Skin Cancer and Sun Safety: The Essential Guide*. Peterborough: Need2Know.

Travel tips

Collis R. (2002). *The Survivor's Guide to Business Travel*. London: Kogan Page.

Hall T. (2010). *Lonely Planet's Best Ever Travel Tips*, 2nd edn. Melbourne: Lonely Planet.

Tropical and infectious diseases, international health

*Ciottone, G, Anderson PD, Auf Der Heide E, Darling RG. (2006). *Disaster Medicine*. Maryland Heights: Mosby.

*Cochi D. (2011). *Disease Eradication in the 21st Century: Implications for Global Health*. Cambridge: MIT Press.

*Cook G. (2008). *Manson's Tropical Diseases*, 22nd edn. Philadelphia: WB Saunders.

*Eddleston M., Davidson R, Brent A, Wilkinson R. (2008). *Oxford Handbook of Tropical Medicine*. Oxford: Oxford University Press.

*Gill G, Beeching N. (2009). *Lecture Notes on Tropical Medicine*, 6th edn. Hoboken: Wiley-Blackwell. A much-respected introduction to the subject. Highly recommended.

*Hawker J, Begg N, Blair I, Reintjes R. (2012). *Communicable Disease Control and Health Protection Handbook*, 3rd edn. Hoboken: Wiley-Blackwell.

*Heymann DL. (2008). *Control of Communicable Diseases Manual*, 19th edn. Washington DC: American Public Health Association.

Honigsbaum M. (2001). *The Fever Trail: Malaria, the Mosquito and the Quest for Quinine*. London: Macmillan.

Jamieson A, Toovey S. (2006). *Malaria: A Traveller's Guide*. Cape Town: Struik Publishers.

*Lucas AO, Gilles HM. (2004). *A Short Textbook of Public Health Medicine for the Tropics*, 4th edn. London: Hodder Arnold.

*Magill A, Ryan E, Hill D, Solomon T. (2012). *Hunters Tropical Medicine & Emerging Infectious Diseases*. Amsterdam: Elsevier.

McCormick JB, Fisher-Hoch S. (1996). *The Virus Hunters: Dispatches from the Frontline*. London: Bloomsbury.

*Peters W, Pasvol G. (2006). *Colour Atlas of Tropical Medicine & Parasitology*, 6th edn. Maryland Heights: Mosby. The ultimate picture guide.

*Petersen E, Chen L, Schlagenhauf P. (2011). *Infectious Diseases: A Geographic Guide*. Hoboken: Wiley-Blackwell.

Rocco F. (2010). *The Miraculous Fever-Tree: Malaria, Medicine and the Cure that Changed the World*. Hammersmith: HarperCollins.

Schull CR. (2009). *Common Medical Problems in the Tropics*, 3rd edn. London: Macmillan. Guide for health workers in developing countries.

*Service M. (2001). *Encyclopedia of Arthropod-transmitted Infections*. Wallingford: CABI Publishing.

*Service M. (2001). *Medical Entomology for Students*. Cambridge: Cambridge University Press.

Spielman A, D'Antonio M. (2002). *Mosquito: The Story of Man's Deadliest Foe*. London: Faber and Faber.

Wilschut J, McElhaney J, Palache A. (2006). *Influenza, Rapid Reference*, 2nd edn. Maryland Heights: Mosby.

Magazines and journals

The following regularly publish articles relevant to travel medicine and health:

Aviation, Space and Environmental Medicine, Journal of the Aerospace Medical Association. Available at: 🖰 www.asma.org.

*British Medical Journal, British Medical Association, London. Available at: 🖰 www.bmj.com.

Condé Nast Traveler, Condé Nast Publications, New York. Available at: 🖰 www.cntraveler.com, Carries travel health news items, and a good read for anyone interested in travel

*Emerging Infectious Diseases, Online journal from the CDC. Available at: 🖰 http://wwwnc.cdc.gov/eid.

Flight International, Reed Business Press, UK. Available at: 🖰 www.flightglobal.com. Air transport industry information, statistics and news.

Geographical, Royal Geographical Society, News, features, geographical and environmental issues. Available at: 🖰 www.geographical.co.uk.

*Journal of Travel Medicine, Wiley, Journal of the International Society of Travel Medicine. Available at: 🖰 www.istm.org.

*Medical Letter, Medical Letter Inc., New Rochelle, NY. Available at: 🖰 www.medicalletter.com.

New Scientist, Reed Business Information, UK. Available at: 🖰 www.newscientist.com

The Lancet, the Lancet, London. Available at: 🖰 www.thelancet.com.

*Travel Medicine & Infectious Disease, Elsevier. Journal of the Faculty of Travel Medicine, Royal College of Physicians & Surgeons of Glasgow, Available at: 🖰 www.travelmedicinejournal.com.

*Tropical Doctor, Royal Society of Medicine Press. Aimed at doctors working in the tropics. Available at: 🖰 www.td.rsmjournals.com.

*Tropical Medicine and International Health, Wiley-Blackwell, Hoboken. Available at: 🖰 www.onlinelibrary.wiley.com/journal/10.1111/(ISSN)1365-3156.

Which holiday?, Consumers' Association, 2 Marylebone Road, London NW1 4DX. Available at: 🖰 www.which.co.uk/magazine/holiday, Covers consumer issues relating to travel.

*Wilderness and Environmental Medicine, Elsevier, Journal of the Wilderness Medical Society. Available at: 🖰 www.wms.org.

Glossary

We've done our best to avoid unnecessary technical medical terminology, but it is not possible to avoid it altogether. Here is a brief explanation of some of the terms in the main text.

Acute: An acute illness is one that is sudden in onset, regardless of severity.

Anaphylaxis: Severe, generalized allergic state.

Antibody: A protein made by the body in response to anything that it recognizes as 'foreign'—such as components of bacteria and viruses called antigens. Antibodies bind to antigens and inactivate them, and are 'tailor-made' for each antigen. The principle of 'active' immunization is based on the fact that exposure to a small amount of harmless antigen—present in a vaccine—stimulates the production of antibodies that remain ready for action when infection threatens. (See also immunoglobulin.)

Antigen: Any substance capable of triggering an immune response. They include components of bacteria, viruses, toxins, and vaccines. Hepatitis B surface antigen (HBsAg) is an antigen present in the blood of people who have had hepatitis B, and can be detected by laboratory tests.

Ascites: Fluid in the abdomen.

Attenuated: Live bacteria or viruses that have been modified to render them harmless.

Bacillus: 'Rod-shaped' bacteria. Anthrax, leprosy, and tuberculosis are examples of diseases caused by bacilli.

Bacteria: Tiny organisms that consist of a single cell and have a cell wall, but no nucleus. There are a great many types, not all of which cause disease.

Chemoprophylaxis: The use of drugs to *prevent* disease.

Chronic: A chronic disease process is one that develops gradually or lasts a long time.

Contra-indication: Any disease or condition that renders a proposed form of treatment or course of action undesirable.

Culture: Growth of micro-organisms in the laboratory for testing and identification.

Cutaneous: Of the skin.

Diuretic: A drug that increases urine production.

Dysentery: Severe diarrhoea with blood, fever, mucus, and abdominal cramps.

ELISA test: Enzyme-linked immunoabsorbent assay—a general test for detecting antibodies.

Embolism: The sudden blockage of an artery, usually by a blood clot that has travelled in the bloodstream from elsewhere in the body. A clot (or 'thrombus') sometimes forms in the veins of the legs; 'pulmonary embolism' occurs when it travels to, and blocks, the arteries of the lungs. Gas entering the bloodstream can have a similar effect—'gas embolism'.

Endemic: A disease that is constantly present in the human population, to a greater or lesser degree, in a particular region.

Enzootic: A disease that is constantly present in the animal population, to a greater or lesser degree, in a particular region.

Eosinophilia: An increase in the number of eosinophils, a type of white blood cell, in the blood. This can be a general indicator of infection with certain types of parasite.

Erythrocyte: Red blood cell.

Eschar: A dark scab or slough, often at the site of an insect bite or skin infection.

Gram negative/positive: A way of classifying bacteria according to their staining properties under the microscope; sometimes helpful in choosing the right antibiotic.

Haematocrit: Relative volume of the blood occupied by erythrocytes, usually around 45%. Easy test to perform with limited laboratory facilities, so commonly used in the tropics.

Hepatocyte: Liver cell.

Host: Man or any animal that harbours a parasite.

Immunity: A state in which the individual is resistant to specific infections.

Immunoglobulin: A protein possessing antibody activity. Most immunoglobulins circulate in the bloodstream, and 'gamma-globulin' is a preparation of 'ready-made' antibodies from donated blood. 'Passive' immunization consists simply of injecting such ready-made antibody into someone who does not have it.

Incidence: The number of new cases of a disease in a given period.

Incubation period: The time between exposure to an infection and the first symptoms.

Intradermal; intramuscular; intravenous: These terms refer to the position of the tip of the needle during an injection. An intradermal injection is given as close to the skin surface as possible; an intramuscular injection is given deep into a muscle—often in the buttock; an intravenous injection is given into a vein, directly into the bloodstream.

Jaundice: Yellow discoloration of the skin and whites of the eyes, due to the presence in the blood of excess amounts of a substance called bilirubin, which is normally excreted by the liver into the bile. It occurs in hepatitis, other liver diseases, and sometimes malaria, and is a sign of reduced liver function. Lay people sometimes use this term to mean hepatitis.

Ketoacidosis: Acidosis (excessive blood acidity) arising from accumulation of ketones (acetone-like substances) in body tissues and fluids; this can be a complication of uncontrolled diabetes.

Lesion: Sore, wound, ulcer, or area of tissue damage.

Leukopenia: Reduction in the number of white blood cells.

Lymphocyte: A type of white blood cell.

Lumen: The cavity or channel within a tubular organ such as the intestine.

Lymph nodes (glands): Part of the immune system. Some can normally be felt as small lumps close to the skin in the neck, groin, and armpit. They may enlarge or become inflamed during an infection.

Maculopapular: Term used to describe a spotty rash consisting of tiny circumscribed elevations of the skin.

Meningo-encephalitis: Inflammation of both the brain and meninges (its surrounding membranes).

Micro-organism: Any microscopic organism, including viruses, bacteria, funguses and yeasts, protozoa, and rickettsiae.

Mucocutaneous: Affecting the mucous membranes and skin, commonly refers to a particular type of leishmaniasis common in Central and South America.

Myelitis: An inflammation of the spinal cord, often resulting in paralysis.

Narcosis: Depression of the nervous system—by a drug or other agent such as an excess of dissolved nitrogen in the blood. (The latter is called nitrogen narcosis, which may occur in divers.)

Oedema: Fluid in the tissues, causing swelling. Also spelled *edema* (US).

Oesophagus: The gullet or food passage from mouth to stomach. Also spelled *esophagus* (US).

Papule: A small, circumscribed, solid elevation of the skin.

Parasite: An animal that lives within or upon man or any other animal (its host), and upon which it depends for nutrition and shelter—sometimes to the detriment of the host.

Pathogen; enteropathogen: Any disease-producing micro-organism. Enteropathogens produce intestinal disease.

PCR test (polymerase chain reaction): A very sensitive method for detecting tiny amounts of DNA.

Petechiae: Tiny, multiple haemorrhages, sometimes most easily seen in the skin, for example in the non-blanching rash of meningococcal meningitis.

Pharynx: Back of the throat.

Photophobia: Discomfort or pain from bright light.

Physiological: Normal or related to the way the body functions in health rather than in disease. Physiology is the science of the mechanisms of normal body function.

Pleural effusion: Fluid around the lung.

Prevalence: The total number of cases of a disease at a certain time in a given area.

Prophylaxis: A word that doctors use when they mean prevention!

Protozoa: The simplest organisms in the animal kingdom, consisting each of a single nucleated cell. Some of them cause disease. Malaria, amoebic dysentery, sleeping sickness, trichomoniasis, and giardiasis are all caused by protozoa.

Purpura: Gross bleeding into the skin, resulting in large purple patches.

Retro-orbital: Behind the eye.

Rickettsiae: A group of micro-organisms that have many similarities to bacteria. They include the micro-organisms that cause typhus.

Rigor: Shiver accompanying fever; may signify severe infection or malaria.

Serology: A blood test that detects the presence of antibodies to a particular antigen (e.g. HIV test).

Serotype: The particular sub-type of bacteria or virus, as determined by antibody testing.

Sputum: Phlegm; mucus secretions from lung and respiratory passages.

Subcutaneous: Under all layers of the skin. Many immunizations are injected subcutaneously.

Systemic: Affecting the body as a whole. Systemic treatment is the opposite of local or topical treatment.

Thrombosis: Clotting of blood within a vein.

Thrombocytopenia: Reduction in the number of platelets in the blood; may lead to bleeding.

Toxin: A specific chemical product produced by a living organism that damages or poisons another organism (e.g. man).

Trophozoite: The active, feeding, growing, disease-producing form of a protozoan parasite.

Ulcer: An inflamed defect following damage at the surface of the skin, the stomach lining, or any other tissue surface.

Vector: A carrier of infection or of a parasite from one host to the next.

Viruses: Tiny, particulate micro-organisms; much smaller than bacteria and too small to be seen without the aid of the electron microscope. They live inside our cells, multiplying within them, and it is this characteristic which protects them from antibodies and drugs, and makes viral infections so difficult to treat.

Visceral: Internal.

Abbreviations

ACE	angiotensin-converting enzyme
ACEP	American College of Emergency Physicians
ACT	artemisinin combination therapy
AED	automated electrical defibrillators
AIDS	acquired immunodeficiency syndrome
AKI	acute kidney injury
AMS	acute mountain sickness
ART	anti-retroviral drugs
AT	apparent temperature
ATM	atmosphere
BCF	Blood Care Foundation
BCG	bacillus Calmette-Guérin
BGA	blue-green algae
BNF	British National Formulary
bpm	beats per minute
BSE	bovine spongiform encephalopathy
CCHF	Crimean-Congo haemorrhagic fever
CDC	Centers for Disease Control and Prevention
CLIA	Cruise Lines International Association
CPAP	continuous positive airway pressure
CPR	cardiopulmonary resuscitation
CRP	C-reactive protein
CT	computed tomography
DEET	n,n-diethylmetatoluamide
DMO	Duty Medical Officer
DSC	digital selective calling
DSP	diarrhoeic shellfish poisoning
DVT	deep venous thrombosis
ECC	European Cruise Council
ECG	electrocardiogram
EHIC	European Health Insurance Card
ELISA	enzyme-linked immunoabsorbent assay
EMS	emergency medical services
ERIG	rabies immune globulin raised in horses
ESR	erythrocyte sedimentation rate
ETEC	enterotoxigenic *Escherichia coli*

FEE	The Foundation for Environmental Education in Europe
FOS	Financial Ombudsman Service
GI	granuloma inguinale
GMDSS	Global Maritime Distress and Safety System
HACCP	Hazard Analysis Critical Control Point
HACE	high-altitude cerebral oedema
HAPE	high-altitude pulmonary oedema
HELP	heat escape lessening posture
HEPA	high efficiency particulate air
HIV	human immunodeficiency virus
HPA	Health Protection Agency
HPV	human papillomary virus
hr	hour(s)
HRIG	rabies immune globulin raised in humans
HRT	hormone replacement therapy
HTIG	human tetanus immunoglobulin
IARC	International Agency for Research on Cancer
IBP	insect-bite precautions
IBS	irritable bowel syndrome
ID	intradermal
IFA	immunofluorescence assay
IGRA	interform gamma release assay
IHR	International Health Regulations
IM	intramuscular
INR	international normalized ratio
ITN	insecticide-treated mosquito nets
IUCD	intrauterine contraceptive device
IUD	intrauterine device
IV	intravenous
LBRF	louse-borne relapsing fever
LGV	lymphogranuloma venereum
LLIN	longer-lasting insecticide nets
MDRTB	multidrug-resistant tuberculosis
min	minute(s)
MMR	mumps, measles and rubella
MRI	magnetic resonance imaging
mSv	milliSievert
MTOP	medical termination of pregnancy
NI	neuraminidase inhibitors
NSAID	non-steroidal anti-inflammatory drug

NSP	neurotoxic shellfish poisoning
PCC	post-coital contraception
PCR	polymerase chain reaction
PEP	post-exposure prophylaxis
PETS	Pet Transport Scheme
PFD	personal flotation device
PLE	Polymorphic light eruption
POP	progestogen-only pill
PPI	proton pump inhibitors
Pro-MED	programme for monitoring emerging diseases
PSP	paralytic shellfish poisoning
PTSD	post-traumatic stress disorder
RIG	rabies immune globulin
RTA	road traffic accident
RVF	Rift Valley fever
SAM	inflatable or malleable aluminium splints
SARS	severe acute respiratory infection
SBET	standby emergency treatment
SC	subcutaneously
SPF	sun protection factors
SSRI	selective serotonin re-uptake inhibitors
STI	sexually-transmitted infection
TB	tuberculosis
TBE	tick-borne encephalitis
Td/IPV	tetanus, diphtheria, and polio combination vaccine
TNF	tumor necrosis factor
TTDs	transfusion-transmitted diseases
UAE	United Arab Emirates
UV	ultraviolet
UVR	ultraviolet radiation
VHF	viral hemorrhagic fevers
VSP	Vessel Sanitation Program
WBGT	wet bulb globe temperature
WHO	World Health Organization

Index